GOVERNMENT AUDITING

STANDARDS AND PRACTICES

FIFTH EDITION

Cornelius E. Tierney

CCH INCORPORATED
Chicago

EDITORIAL STAFF

Coordinating Editor: Lisa Mahoney

Production: Carolyn Doughty, Julius Lowe, Andrew Thew

This publication is designed to provide accurate and authoritative information in regard to the subject matter covered. It is sold with the understanding that the publisher is not engaged in rendering legal, accounting or other professional service. If legal advice or other expert assistance is required, the services of a competent professional person should be sought.

ISBN: 0-8080-0436-0

©2000, **CCH** INCORPORATED

4025 W. Peterson Ave.
Chicago, IL 60646-6085
1-800-449-6435
http://business.cch.com

No claim is made to original government works; however, the gathering, compilation, magnetic translation, digital conversion, and arrangement of such materials, the historical, statutory and other notes and references, as well as commentary and materials in this Product or Publication, are subject to CCH's copyright.

All Rights Reserved
Printed in the United States of America

About the Author

Cornelius E. Tierney is a certified public accountant, a professor of accountancy at The George Washington University in Washington, D.C., a retired general partner of Ernst & Young LLP and the past National Director of Ernst & Young's public sector practice. Throughout a career spanning four decades, Mr. Tierney's specialty has been exclusively government auditing, accounting and financial management. He served for 10 years, before entering private practice, as a federal financial executive and then for over 20 years as an auditor and consultant to entities at all levels of government.

Professor Tierney has been an active participant in the major initiatives to improve public sector auditing and accounting for over 35 years. Representatives of the U.S. General Accounting Office have consulted him on every edition of the government auditing standards since their conceptualization in the late 1960s. He has repeatedly appeared before congressional committees, worked with their staffs and met with senior executives at all levels of government on issues of importance in public sector financial management. Over the years, he has chaired national committees on governmental finance issues for both the American Institute of Certified Public Accountants and the Association of Government Accountants, heading task forces and being a principal author of reports issued by these organizations that preceded and helped form the Single Audit Act of 1984 and the Chief Financial Officers Act of 1990. Later, he chaired the AICPA's task force for and was one of the principal authors of the profession's audit guide to implement the single audit concept nationwide. Nominated by the Comptroller General of the United States, the Secretary of the Treasury and the Director of the Office of Management and Budget, and then reappointed, Mr. Tierney was a member of the Federal Accounting Standards Advisory Board since its inception in 1990 through 1996. The Board recommends accounting standards to assist in implementing the CFO Act of 1990. Since 1993, he has been a member of the federal government's Advisory Council on Government Auditing Standards.

Cornelius E. Tierney, as one of the profession's leading authors and spokespersons on governmental financial management subjects, authored or co-authored eleven earlier books and many articles on governmental auditing and accounting.

Preface

Since the 1950s, a revolution occurred in auditing, generally, and particularly audits conducted of governmental entities. Fifty years have witnessed increased demands on the auditing profession; many laws were passed, much litigation initiated, public expectation raised, and distinct government standards emerged. Government now has its own accounting standards board and separate government accounting standards exist. Problems of decades necessitated normalization of separate government auditing standards to parallel the accountancy changes.

This book is devoted entirely to government auditing with the express objectives of assisting practitioners to address the uniqueness of auditing public sector entities and to provide a single reference for academicians and their students not having the resources or knowledge to compile an individual reference library of government auditing requirements.

Auditing, as portrayed in the texts of the times, is primarily the auditing as defined in the general accepted auditing standards published by the American Institute of Certified Public Accountants. These are the auditing standards for conducting financial statement audits of non-governmental entities. First published in 1972 and most recently revised in 1994, government auditing standards were intended to provide guidance for audits of governmental programs, activities, and functions. Federal laws and regulations have extended the application of government auditing standards to over 80,000 federal, state and local governmental units and over 100,000 nonprofit and institutions of higher education.

Government auditing continues to evolve; some issues have been settled over the years; others have arisen. To the extent that it exists, authoritative guidance, even if tentative or preliminary, has been provided in this edition to assist practitioners and students.

Over the years, consultations with practitioners, professional organizations and governments and nonprofit organizations affected by government auditing standards have been many and reliance has necessarily been placed on bodies of knowledge created by Congress, the General Accounting Office, Office of Management and Budget, American Institute of Certified Public Accountants, Governmental Accounting Standards Board, Financial Accounting Standards Board, the many federal inspectors general, the Federal Advisory Council on Government Auditing, and more recently on the Federal Accounting Standards Advisory Board.

These views, conclusions and recommendations are mine and not necessarily the views of the firm of Ernst & Young LLP or The George

Washington University. A considerable effort was made to ensure accuracy. But, if errors exist, these, too, are mine. I made every one, for which I apologize in advance.

Cornelius E. Tierney
The George Washington University
Washington, D.C.

Table of Contents

Chapter		Page

Part I—A Demanding Specialty

1	Overview: Government Audits	11
2	Accounting Principles and Auditing Standards	33

Part II—Broader, Different Audits for Governments

3	Government Auditing Standards—General Standards	59
4	Government Auditing Standards—Field Standards	79
5	Reporting Standards—Financial Statements	99
6	Audit Standards—Financial Related and Performance Audits	119
7	Reporting—Pursuant to the Single Audit Act of 1996	147

Part III—Concerns/Issues of Governmental Auditing

8	Review of Internal Controls—Generally Accepted Standards, Government Standards, Single Audit Requirements	189
9	Compliance Auditing—Generally Accepted Standards, Government Standards, Single Audit Requirements	223
10	Auditing for Allowable, Unallowable, Indirect Costs	251
11	Working Papers and Audit Evidence	279
12	Quality Control and Audit Oversight	309

Part IV—Illustrative Audit Approaches and Methodologies

13	Auditor Relationships, Responsibilities and Reliance	329
14	Audit Methodology—Financial Statement Audits	345
15	Audit Methodology—Single Audits	369
16	Audit Methodology—Financial Related Audits	399
17	Audit Methodology—Performance Audits	423
18	Audit Methodology—Contracts and Grants	451

Chapter		Page
19	Audit Methodology—Special Focus Government Audits	479

Appendices

A	Single Audit Act Amendments of 1996	509
B	Chief Financial Officers Act of 1990	519
C	OMB Circular A-133, Audits of States, Local Governments, and Non-Profit Organizations	543

PART I
A DEMANDING SPECIALTY

Foreword—

Government Auditing Standards,

June 1994

"To meet demands for more responsive and cost-effective governments, policymakers and managers need reliable financial and performance information. The assurance auditors provide about that information as well as about systems producing that information, may be more important now than ever before. This reliance on auditors enhances the need for standards to guide auditors and allow others to rely on auditors work."

Charles A. Bowsher
Comptroller General of the
United States

Since the 1950s major changes occurred in auditing, particularly the audits conducted of public sector entities.

Increasingly many want to know "what happened to my tax money?" "what was accomplished with the public funds?" "how accountable are governments?" "are the stewards meeting their stewardship responsibilities?" "whose watching those doing the business of governments?" "who's watching the books?" and inevitably "where were the auditors?"

These questions are not answerable solely by voucher examinations, tests of fiscal practices or financial statement audits, or by the application of auditing procedures carried over from the private sector. While all of these are valuable, each has been found to be inadequate at times or at least not responsive to the questions asked of and answers required by public officials, legislatures, government managers, regulators and even private citizens.

An audit in accordance with generally accepted auditing standards, while possibly acceptable for exercising corporate oversight, often will not produce the necessary insights into government organizations, programs or operations. To be meaningful and useful, government audits must additionally report on accountability of governments—the economy, efficiency, and effectiveness of organizations, programs, activities, and functions.

10

Fifty years have witnessed increased demands on the auditing profession, generally. New standards boards were needed for government accounting. By the 1990s, there was a new specialty in the field of accountancy—governmental accounting and auditing.

Chapter 1

Overview: Government Audits

Foreword—

Government Auditing Standards,

February 1981

"In the past few years, we have seen an unprecedented interest in government auditing. Public officials, legislators, and private citizens want and need to know not only whether government funds are handled properly and in compliance with laws and regulations, but also whether government organizations are achieving the purpose for which programs were authorized and funded and are doing so economically and efficiently.

Forty years ago auditors concentrated most of their efforts on auditing the vouchers which supported expenditures. But today, auditors are also concerned with the economy, efficiency, and effectiveness of government operations."

Elmer B. Staats
Comptroller General of the
United States

A PERSPECTIVE

Auditing has been defined, in the country's first book on auditing by Robert H. Montgomery, CPA, as one of the two branches of accountancy:

> *"Auditing is the analytical, as practical accounting is the constructive, branch of accountancy."* [1]

A more complete definition would be:

---

[1] Robert H. Montgomery, *Auditing—Theory and Practice,* Ronald Press Company, New York, 1912.

Auditing, i.e., widely accepted to be reviews to determine the accuracy and validity of financial records and reports, especially the examination of financial statements of an organization by an independent certified public accountant to determine whether, in the accountant's opinion, the statements fairly present the organizations financial position, results of operations, and changes in cash flow, performed pursuant to generally accepted auditing standards.[2]

These views of *auditing* evoke an image of examinations of financial statements, financial performance, profits and losses, and statements of cash flows. That is, audits performed of financial positions and activities of non-governmental organizations. These are views of auditing governed by rules of the Securities and Exchange Commission, the Financial Accounting Standards Board (setting generally accepted accounting principles for non-government organizations), the American Institute of Certified Public Accountants (prescribing the generally accepted auditing standards for audits of corporate financial statements). And, this has been so since the 1930s.

ANOTHER PERSPECTIVE

Interestingly, financial statement audits have not always been society's perspective of auditing. As a profession—i.e., specialists practicing their specialty—the history of auditing extends backwards millenniums, with its roots more in the public sector and governments than in the audits of commerce. The earliest recordings of audits were examinations of accountability and stewardship of the public's or sovereign's assets and valuables entrusted to or managed by or for government.[3]

Over the past 50 years the public sector has witnessed a steady, perceptible shift from exclusively financial statement audits of governments to the audits of governmental activities and operations, with objectives broader than the examination of only historical financial data. The objectives of these audits differ from audits primarily concerned with balance sheets and profits and losses. Once again, there is an increasing demand for reports of government stewardship, accountability, and more importantly government performance.

Thus, this book is dedicated to *government auditing:*

i.e., the validation, evaluation or assessment of compliance with laws and regulations and of what has been achieved for the

---

[2] Estes, Ralph, *Dictionary of Accounting*, The MIT Press, Cambridge, Massachusetts, 1981.
[3] Chatfield, Michael, *A History of Accounting Thought*, Robert E. Kreiger Publishing Company, Huntington, New York, 1977.

expenditure or consumption of a government's resources; not merely the audit of financial statements, but audits of compliance, relative economy and efficiency, and results."

Government auditing in this context, and in practice, is distinctive from corporate auditing. This distinction is apparent in the scope, approach, tests, and reports of audits of governments. Since the early 1970s, government auditing has been evolving into a specialty, every bit as technical and complex as financial statement auditing. Now, in the 1990s, corporate and government auditing have distinctive auditing standards; both have accepted auditing practices; both need specialized practitioners, but with different skills. And, users of these two different audit services—non-government versus government—must have a clear understanding of the differences. Mistaken reliance on one type of audit when another audit was intended could as a minimum lead to wrong conclusions or, more injurious, result in unintended and wrong decisions.

Like the accounting of private sector entities, government accounting must also conform to specific criteria, but there is a difference. To be generally accepted, the accounting of governments must conform to the prescriptions of the Government Accounting Standards Board (if state or local governments) as well as the Financial Accounting Standards Board (if a government has business-type operation). To be generally accepted, the audits of governments must conform to prescriptions of the American Institute of Certified Public Accountants, particularly those refinements and revisions applicable to public sector entities and to government auditing standards.

GOVERNMENT AUDITING STANDARDS

Initially issued in 1972, government audit standards declared that audits may include not only work typically done by CPA's in auditing financial statements, but must include audits that assess compliance with laws and regulations, audits of efficiency and economy of operations, and audits of effectiveness in achieving program objectives and results.

Some government officials, and certified public accountants, equated these early government audit standards with the level of work required to support the typical auditor's management letter commonly given to corporate audit clients. This comparison was in error and the AICPA quickly pointed out that management letters were almost exclusively a by-product of a financial audit and that the U.S. General Accounting Office had clearly stated that the government auditing standards did not refer to a by-product but instead to separate audits that required separate audit programs. [4]

Government auditing standards were refined and reissued in 1981, 1988, 1994 and most recently in 1999. For the first time, auditors of government financial statements were required to report on tests made for compliance with laws and regulations and tests of internal controls. Heretofore, tests of controls and compliance that could materially affect balances on financial statements were expected of auditors—by the AICPA—but no written reports were required. Additionally, the 1988 edition introduced a mandate that auditors practicing in the public sector were required to have specialized training in government accounting and auditing. Further, organizations auditing governments were required to have extensive systems of quality controls for audits made by their organizations.

Federal and state laws, local government statutes, even laws of foreign countries, over the years have accorded the government auditing standards formal standing by codifying application of the government auditing standards. In the United States, government auditing standards are the professional audit criteria for the reviews being made of more than 80,000 governmental units and more than 100,000 non-profit contractor and grantees and hundreds of colleges and universities receiving federal financial assistance.

The AICPA has informed the public accounting profession, in its Ethical Interpretation, 501-3, that the failure to follow standards and procedures or other requirements in governmental audits would be an act discreditable to the profession and subject to review by its Ethics Division and possible referral to the Trial Board for disciplinary action.

AUDITING IN AMERICA

Since the late 1800s, audits by accounting firms seemed to have two characteristics: the audits were directed towards examining the financial statements and the audited statements seemed to be predominantly those of corporations. While CPA firms were involved with audits of various levels of government from the early 1900s, their involvement seemed more directed toward assisting with or evaluating government accounting rather than auditing governments. [5]

While some governments had independent audits earlier, governmental audits became a concern to the profession and public sector executives in the early 1900s and, again, in the 1940s, but still the

---

[4] AICPA, Report by Management Advisory Services Committee, New York, N. Y., 1973.

[5] Carey, John L., *The Rise of the Accounting Profession—From Technician to Professional*, AICPA, New York, N. Y., 1969.

emphasis was on financial statement audits. The 1950s saw changes in the purposes for which governments retained accounting firms and the nature of the audit services rendered by CPA's to government. By the 1960s, 30 federal agencies had published 80 different audit programs that resulted in 51,000 annual audit engagements, many requiring more than just the audit of financial statements. It was clear, as reported by the AICPA, that "Washington officials learned that practicing certified public accountants could do other things than audit balance sheets and income statements, important and pervasive as this function was." [6]

CHANGING EMPHASIS

Auditing, with the emphasis on attestation of amounts on financial statements as of a specific point in time, shed no information on whether the entity's operations were economical or efficient. And, even less insight was provided on whether the entity achieved its objectives or if it could have done even better. Financial statement audits do not address the points of whether the entity should have been in the business at all or whether there were alternative and better or cheaper methods of achieving goals. Compliance with laws and regulations are important and the presence or continuing soundness of a governmental entity's systems of accounting, internal, and administrative controls are vital, but minimal audit testimony is provided on these matters in the audit reports for financial statement audits. Throughout the 1960s and continuing into the 1970s, these and even more penetrating issues were regularly being addressed by governments and those that audited governments.

More than any other organization, the U.S. General Accounting Office must be credited with shifting the focus of auditing, from only rendering opinions on financial statements to attesting on performance, management, compliance, controls, and operations. This change was formalized by GAO in 1972, after several years of research, with the publication of the initial edition of the government auditing standards, popularly referred to as the "yellow book." The forewords to subsequent editions of the "yellow book" pointed out that the numbers, dollars and growth of government programs was enormous and that the country had:

"... seen an unprecedented interest in government auditing. Public officials, legislators, and private citizens want and need to know not only whether government funds are handled properly and in compliance with laws and regula-

---

[6] Carey, John L., *The Rise of the Accounting Profession—To Responsibility and Authority*, AICPA, New York, N. Y., 1970.

tions, but also whether government organizations are achieving the purposes for which programs were authorized and are doing so economically and efficiently." [7]

The 1970s, 1980s and the 1990s witnessed enormous and continued growth in governmental spending and the problems of government caused by that spending. The continuous urging of citizens that elected representatives curtail, cap and control public expenditures and the need to increase taxes were accompanied by demands to know: "What are we getting for our tax dollars? "What happened that resulted in year after year of unfilled promise?" and sooner or later, the ultimate question for the profession, "Where were the auditors?" Audits of only the financial statements of government did not answer to these questions.

Commenting on the three decades of increasing concern about governments, GAO, in the 1988 edition of the government auditing standards, points out that there arose " ... a demand for full accountability by those entrusted with public funds and the responsibility for properly managing government programs and services." GAO's government auditing standards, the "yellow book," were intended to be the auditing standards that ensured "full accountability" of governments and their management.

These auditing standards apply to all recipients of federal financial assistance. Laws defined federal recipients as including: state and counties and cities and other local governmental units, public authorities and commissions, school districts, Indian tribes, trust territories, contractors, nonprofit organizations, educational institutions, health organizations and many other entities receiving federal financial assistance. Government auditing standards are intended to be followed by all auditors and audit organizations when auditing financial statements, conducting financial related audits, and in conducting performance audits required by federal or other laws, regulations, agreements, contracts or policies.

EARLY CONCEPTS

While auditors have had a standing in government since the beginning of the country, what the auditors of governments do and the breadth of their responsibilities varied significantly and changed extensively over the years.

Generally, there has been a formal interest in verifying the treasurer's accounts of government, dating to the Plymouth Colony. In fact these early audits—of conformance with budgets and appropriateness

---

[7] U. S. General Accounting Office, *Government Auditing Standards*, Washington, D. C., 1981.

of expenditures—were seen as the genesis of present day municipal accounting and public sector auditing. Again, while not professional auditors, as we know the term today, these appointed auditors placed a high value on independence. The reports of many auditors of the times seemed to form the basis for the court records and case settlements, reporting on a broad range of subjects such as economic development, fiscal stewardship, changes in financial position and other subjects beyond the mere rendering an opinion on financial statements. Annual audits of the accounts of the Boston Town records date to the 1590s. [8]

The auditing of public accounts seemed to be an English tradition and a responsibility of the Auditor of the Exchequer, first established in 1314 and was medieval in its origins. Early on, though, legislatures have decided that the right to vote for revenues and expenditures was not sufficient control. What was needed was a check on how the monarch raised, allocated and applied the funds of the kingdom. [9]

At the time of the Constitution, founders of the country were concerned about several matters: compliance with laws, purpose of government expenditures, conformance to Congressionally imposed limits, authority to tax, collection of funds, borrowing and credit of the country, to mention a few. This concern about control over government spending was expressed by Congress in Article 1 of the Constitution:

"No money shall be drawn from the Treasury, but in consequence of appropriations made by law; and a regular statement and account of receipts and expenditures of all public money shall be published from time to time."

Writing at the time Alexander Hamilton, as Secretary of the Treasury, stated that this provision of the Constitution was to:

"... secure these important ends,—that the purpose, the limit, and the fund of every expenditure should be ascertained by a previous law. The public security is complete in this particular, if no money can be expended, but for an object, to an extent, and out of a fund, which the laws have prescribed."

The Treasury Act of 1789 provided for an auditor, and later several auditors, in the Department, to audit compliance with this condition. But, a disinterested Congress and executive branch had minimal interest in audits of performance. One hundred years later, by the Dockery Act of 1894, Congress established a chief comptroller as well as the 6 auditors of the Treasury Department, designated according to the governmental agencies whose accounts they serviced. But,

---

[8] William Holmes, Linda H. Kistler, Louis S. Corsini, *Three Hundred Years of Accounting in Massachusetts*, Arno Press, New York, N.Y., 1978.

[9] Chatfield, Michael, *A History of Accounting Thought*, Robert E. Kreiger Publishing Company, Huntington, N. Y., 1977.

the audits of the day were of limited utility, still primarily post-audit in nature, considerably after the incurrence of the expenditures and disbursement of cash. This lack of Congressional and Presidential concern set the stage for a federal government that operated for 200 years without uniform accounting practices. It condoned inconsistent financial reporting, required no department wide or government wide financial statements and had minimal interest in independent audits of its performance. [10]

Still dissatisfied in 1921, Congress passed the Budget and Accounting Act creating the U.S. General Accounting Office to be headed by the comptroller general with the mandate to ensure that incumbents could not see their position as purely administrative or ministerial in nature. The 1921 Act required the Comptroller General to investigate, at the seat of government or elsewhere, all matters relating to the receipt, disbursement, and application of public funds. However, until the passage of another law, the Budget and Accounting Procedures Act of 1950, the quality and nature of auditing in government did not appreciably improve. With the 1950 Act, GAO instituted a more detailed and selective audit approach that placed increased emphasis on sound systems of both accounting and internal controls. At the same time, GAO moved away from the early, post-audit, fiscal type voucher examinations that had consumed thousands of GAO fiscal clerks. For the first time, the U.S. government aggressively recruited, in large numbers, high quality college graduates and experienced accountants from major CPA firms to serve as auditors for the government.

Prior to 1948, GAO discharged its audit responsibilities through after-the-fact "desk audits" of expenditure documents shipped to it by all federal departments and agencies; an approach that was not conducive to assessing the "application" of federal revenues and expenditures. Nor did the approach permit analyses assessing the effectiveness and economy of government operations. GAO saw the 1950 Act as a mandate to increasingly focus on audits of efficiency and economy of federal agency activities. This Act changed the focus of government audits to more management reviews, evaluations, and assessments—i.e., performance audits—of federal activities. This expanded view included audits of systems of accounting and control, property management (whether in the hands of federal representatives, contractors, universities or grantees), computers, budget execution, defense and civil agency personnel and procurement practices, industrial and working capital funds, waste, fraud and abuse, in general. [11]

---

[10] U. S. Senate, Committee on Government Operations, *Financial Management in the Federal Government—a Comprehensive Analysis of Existing and Proposed Legislation Including Financial Management Improvements Made on a Government-wide Basis*, U.S. Government Printing Office, Washington, D. C., 1961.

[11] *Id.*

Later in the 1960s and 1970s, the GAO expanded its staff of evaluators, recruiting as many non-accountants as accountants in some years, and moved aggressively into performance audits—e.g., audits of results, assessing whether governmental activities achieved the goals or results contemplated by Congress when it appropriated funds. GAO had taken the lead role in advocating performance audits and widely distributed guidelines on performing program results audits. [12] By the 1980s, the GAO was regularly performing "3 E"—efficiency, economy, and effectiveness—audits.

ABSENCE OF FINANCIAL AUDITS

For a variety of reasons, few with merit, independent financial statement audits were not favored by either federal government or local governmental public sector entities. Governmental auditors were often not trained in procedures for completing such audits. Governmental entities that volunteered for such audits were few in number, thus providing auditors of government with a limited experience base for increasing their competence in performing financial statement audits. Moreover, legislators and governmental managers did not demand such reviews of their activities, either. However, during the three decades preceding the 1990s, several factors caused many—in Congress, state and local governments, plus professionals, security analysts and even the relatively unsophisticated taxpayers—to question the accounting and reporting practices of governments.

At all levels of government, maybe more so at the federal level, citizens learned that financial statements of governments may not have been consistent with those published for prior years. Governments moved rather casually from a cash basis to an accrual basis of accounting. Governments at times excluded from their reports the effects of uncollected receivables, unpaid vouchers and stockpiles of materials and supplies purchased in one year to support operations of future years. Many revenues and expenditures were historically excluded from a governmental unit's statements. Other revenues and expenditures were accounted for as "off budget," which generally meant "off the books."

From late 1970s, into the 1980s and 1990s, concern over the incomplete, inaccurate, and inconsistent governmental financial statements grew. The news media widely reported that governments deferred payments beyond year-ends, held back cash overdue to others; failed to recognize the total liabilities for pensions, uncompensated overtime, vacation and sick leave, to mention just a few of the prevalent accounting "sleights of hand." Unfortunately, the practices were

---

[12] General Accounting Office, *Comprehensive Approach for Planning and Conducting a Program Results Review* (Exposure Draft, June 1978), Washington, D.C.

lauded by some as "creative" and "innovative" accounting and budgeting practices.

Generally accepted accounting principles of government, when closely examined, were found to not be the same accounting rules used by corporations. The government accounting rules were different: the accounts of government did not reflect costs, but rather expenditures—a basis of accounting that was close to but not always synonymous to cash. Further, governmental financial statements looked strange. The balance sheet did not contain only one column of financial data. It had as many as 12 columns described variously as fund types, account groups, component units, memo totals—terms not used at all in the private sector. And, many governments, including the federal government, did not prepare, publish, or have the financial records and statements independently audited.

Each generation of students is surprised to learn anew that none of the publicly traded securities of any government are subject to oversight by the Securities and Exchange Commission. They were specifically exempted by Congress, with the passage of initial securities legislation in the 1930s.

The fiscal disciplines, imposed by governments on all that they do business with, were not imposed by governments on themselves. This fact was learned by the general public as all governments, in the 1980s, were faced with falling revenues, expenditures that kept rising, record deficits and an almost universal reluctance of elected officials to make the collective decisions to address the fiscal and managerial problems. Relatively few governments truly fixed their problems. The preferred political solution was to defer or pass pressing maintenance, capital equipment needs, provisions for pension commitments, and the need for more cash resources to future generations of taxpayers. Many governments hoped for economic recovery to cure all the ills. Ever-increasing and record levels of new government debt securities were sold in the public markets. [13]

DIFFERENT AUDITS

At all levels, the executive branch of governments had grown progressively larger, more complex, and increasingly distant from citizens and even the elected legislative bodies having the legal oversight responsibility. New legislation, the Single Audit Act of 1984, required that an annual comprehensive audit be made of governmental and other entities. This includes an audit of their financial statements, a review of an entity's compliance with laws and regulations, and an

---

[13] Cornelius E. Tierney, *Governmental Auditing—pursuant to the Single Audit Act of 1984*, Commerce Clearing House, Chicago, Illinois, 1989.

assessment of internal accounting and administrative controls. By the law and federal regulations, the single audit concept was imposed on state and local governments, colleges and universities, contractors, grantees, nonprofit organizations, Indian tribes, and others in receipt of federal financial assistance.

The need for these types of audits, as pointed out in the AICPA's 1986 audit guide, arose after World War II when the federal government became increasingly involved in providing financial assistance to state and local governments, and more recently as federal and state governments mandated that local governments perform or operate programs to serve particular constituencies or achieve certain mandated objectives.[14] Before the Single Audit Act, the federal government performed thousands of limited scope audits of grants and contracts and other forms of financial assistance awarded or legislated to state and local governments. These audits provided no perspective about the overall financial management by a federal recipient.

State and local governments may or may not have had annual audits of their governmentwide financial statements. At the federal level, no agency was responsible for monitoring all of the federal funds and assistance provided to a recipient. The Single Audit Act and in 1990 the Chief Financial Officers Act required audits, performed by a single auditor, every single year. These audits placed substantial emphasis on an entity-wide financial statement audit, but new focus was given to the fact that financial statement audits were not totally adequate for providers needs. Under the Act, far greater emphasis was given to the study and evaluation of internal controls and to the mandated testing of compliance with laws and regulations and requiring that written audit reports be submitted on the audit work performed in these areas, as well.

As more governments prepared financial statements and had independent audits, it was clear that these audits presented only a partial picture of what was happening to the money citizens paid to governments via their taxes. These types of audits were viewed as either not asking the right questions or not providing the answers to many questions raised by others. Enter the "3E" audits, with the purpose of assessing the relative economy, efficiency, and effectiveness of governmental activities. These "3E" audits are known by various titles, but generically have been referred to as "performance" audits. They were more directed to what ails governments, what is important to those with oversight responsibilities, and to the citizens. The "3E" audits had been evolving for years.

---

[14] American Institute of CPAs, *Audit and Accounting Guide—Audits of State and Local Governmental Units*, New York, N. Y., 1986.

It is important to make a distinction: performance auditing is not program evaluation. By one definition, program evaluation " ... seems to be used primarily by academics in education and psychology to describe an activity more related to scholarly research rather than to legislative oversight. On the other hand, 'audit,' denotes an independent third-party report of a non-sympathetic nature." [15]

One explanation, ventured in the early 1980s, discussed this distinction between evaluations and audits in the following way:

"Significantly, the technique and personnel needed to adequately evaluate the effectiveness of increasingly widespread and complex public services have normally been available neither to bureaucrats nor to elected officials. Formerly, academic specialists attempted to analyze public programs from their own limited perspectives. No comprehensive, interdisciplinary approach was available. Once a science was developed, its techniques normally could not be applied by officials with limited training and little background in management. Furthermore, it became apparent that the absorption of adequately trained program evaluators into the government subjected these individuals to the ingrained influence of routine, program identification and self-preservation, thus potentially compromising the independence necessary for valid assessment." [16]

This assessment is unusually harsh. The mentioned science was still evolving and was yet to fully arrive. But, there had been a recognition that financial statement audits must be supplemented by other evaluations of managerial and operational performance. Further, program evaluations often suffered more from the lack of professional evaluators and resources than the inability or unwillingness of these professionals to conduct reviews. Typically, auditors of government seemed to be, organizationally, the most independent and best positioned to perform these performance examinations that seemed to respond to the need for greater accountability.

While neither formally planned nor centrally mandated, a broadly accepted program of auditing for governments evolved that requires a blend of financial, functional, and performance audits to comprehensively examine and then to continuously monitor a department, agency, program, function or activity. Each audit has its own objectives and requires auditors and reviewers with differing skills, directed towards

---

[15] Frank L. Greathouse and Mark Funkhouser, "Audit Standards and Performance Auditing in State Government," *Government Accountants Journal* (Winter Edition 1987-88), Association of Government Accountants, Alexandria, Va.

[16] Roland M. Malan, James R. Fountain, Donald S. Arrowsmith, Robert L. Lockridge, *Performance Auditing—in local government*, Government Finance Officers Association, Chicago, Illinois, 1984.

answering different questions about the relative financial position, economy, efficiency and effectiveness.

TYPES OF GOVERNMENT AUDITS

Governmental auditing encompasses a spectrum of audits in addition to audits now generally made by all levels of government of their annual financial statements. Each grouping of audits has a different focus, at times requiring different skills, and often each having a different reporting focus. Several examples are highlighted in this section and are discussed in greater detail in separate chapters.

Systems Audits

An audit performed pursuant to generally accepted auditing standards, at the conclusion of which the auditor renders an opinion that the financial statements "present fairly," is not an audit of the entity's system of accounting or internal controls. Audits of financial statements and audit opinion relates only to the data appearing on the reported financial statements for the date or specific moment in time identified in the auditor's report.

To contrast, **systems audits** are made pursuant to specially prepared audit plans and programs, and include many specific audit procedures that are tailored to the specific system to be examined. These audits, while varying in scope, could include an examination of: the structure of the accounting system, control accounts hierarchy; structure and adequacy of subordinate subsidiary accounts; and procedures for accurate cost accounting of activities or functions. Alternatively, or in addition, systems audits could involve a study of the efficacy of the transaction coding structure or the account classification and summarization hierarchy. Or, the systems audit could include a determination of the degree to which the appropriate data is being recorded, aggregated, and reported to support management needs, i.e., is the system producing information that directly relates to the critical activities, functions and entities that must be managed. And, none of the audited operations or data may be the same information required to produce financial statements in accordance with generally accepted accounting principles.

System audits may require that the auditor conclude on the adequacy of matters such as the transaction and account recordation and aggregation processes, standard or automated, and special journal entries, expense allocation procedures, and a host of other system characteristics or limitations, many of which may not be of primary concern when auditing financial statements.

Functional Audits

Often because of statute, agency regulations, or accepted practices, limited scope audits must be performed, possibly annually or on some frequent cycle. Sometimes referred to as *functional* or *cross cutting audits*, these audits may be department or agency wide. When performed by a central audit agency (e.g., the General Accounting Office at the federal level or a state auditor), these audits may encompass more than one department or organization and, in smaller governments, could be government-wide. Generally the overall objective of such audits is to ensure that the activities and operations related to a functional area are being conducted in a manner that complies with applicable laws and regulations.

Personnel and Payroll audits. At all levels of government expenditures, personnel and related fringe benefit costs are the largest expenditures in budgets (approaching 90 percent of total expenditures in some instances). The laws, rules and regulations governing the hiring, promoting, retiring, terminating, vacationing, and paying of personnel are voluminous and detailed. The objective of such audits are generally to assess compliance with legal proscriptions, civil service regulations, labor union agreements and other rules affecting conditions of employment, compensation, and related benefits.

Travel and Transportation audits. Budgets for travel and transportation and the actual costs for these activities are monitored, by all governments, almost as closely as payrolls. Governmental statutes, regulations and rules relating to the travel of personnel or the transportation of goods and property are detailed and, from an internal control standpoint, contain many checks and balances. More often, the concerns and cost of auditing these activities far outweigh any financial benefits or opportunities to initiate financial recoveries. But, the objectives of officials is not usually with the individual dollar amount of these types of transactions, but rather the opportunity that such activities present for abuse or personal gain.

Property audits. Governments own much property and, in many instances have supplied more property to their contractors and grantees or have permitted these organizations to procure property with government funds. The objectives of a property audit is to determine the adequacy of the government's policies, procedures, and practices relating to the full life-cycle (purchase, receipt, accounting, storage, usage, maintenance, disposal and reporting for all phases of the life-cycle) of buildings, equipment, furniture and fixtures.

Contract and Grant audits. These audits are often made from a variety of perspectives. For example, audits of government contracting and grants management personnel could assess the extent to which practices comply with the government's and their department's policies and procedures. Audits of contractors and grantees might evaluate the extent to which these organizations expend government funds and perform the desired services in a manner consistent with the contract or grant terms and conditions. Some audits of these agreements might assess the extent to which the contract or grant expenditures achieved or did not achieve predetermined program goals and objectives.

Petty Cash and Imprest Funds audits. As in the private sector, use of petty cash funds and imprest funds minimize administrative costs and simplify cash disbursement procedures, particularly for minor disbursements. But, the existence of such funds present an opportunity for misuse or abuse. Such cash funds are subjected to periodic, often unannounced audits that have the objectives of validating cash balances, examining the nature of transactions flowing through the fund, examining the support documents and timeliness of accounting, and, at times, assessing the volume of disbursements and frequency of the fund balance turnover. In certain instances, because the fund cashiers are bonded, these audits are an essential aspect of control and fiscal prudence on the part of the government.

Obligations or Encumbrances audits. Audits of obligations and encumbrances are uniquely governmental audits performed to determine compliance between the amounts, rates and purposes for which public monies have been obligated or encumbered—i.e., committed—in relation to the financial appropriations passed by legislative branches. Additionally, these audits have the objective of confirming the appropriateness of the end-of-period balances for the unliquidated obligations and encumbrances and the amounts of appropriations and spending authority that will be carried over to meet expenditures in the following fiscal year. Incurrence of obligations or encumbrances in excess of a legislature's appropriations of funds is generally a violation of law—i.e., the government's budget law or statutes. At the federal level, persons found guilty of willful or negligent violations of appropriations could be subject to imprisonment and financial penalties, or both.

Settlement audits. Within government, there exist certain key executives whose responsibilities place them in fiduciary positions. These officers are "accountable" or charged with the collection of monies or the approval of anticipated commitments, and the disbursement of government funds. The federal government and some states requires that the "account" (i.e., the fund balance, receipts, obligations or encumbrances, and disbursements of government monies) of these accountable officers be periodically audited or "settled," particularly when these executives are relieved of their fiduciary-type responsibilities. The objective of such audits is to provide a financial accounting of the stewardship of these officers. These "settlement" audits seem to be among the first types of audits desired by the colonies of their governmental servants and executives

Performance Audits

The descriptor "performance audits" has evolved since the 1960s. Most recently, the term according to the U.S. General Accounting Office is inclusive of audits to assess a government's economy of operations (Can it be done cheaper?), efficiency of operations (Can it be done faster?) and effectiveness of operations (Can it be done smarter?) or program results (Were planned or desired purposes achieved?). Each of these audits have different objectives, requiring different approaches and evaluation skills, and will, thus, result in different reporting.

The GAO, in its government auditing standards, defined these audits in the following manner.

Economy and efficiency audits—These are evaluations to determine:

a.) Whether the entity is acquiring, protecting, and using its resources (people, property, space) economically and efficiently;

b.) The causes of inefficiencies or uneconomical practices; and

c.) Whether the entity has complied with laws and regulations concerning matters of economy and efficiency.

Program results and effectiveness audits—These are evaluations to determine:

a.) The extent to which the desired results or benefits established by the legislature or other authoring body are being achieved;

b.) The effectiveness of organizations, programs, activities, or functions; and

c.) Whether the entity is complying with requirements of laws and regulations applicable to the program.

Generally, an auditor is not required, and may not be able to, express an overall or all-encompassing audit opinion on the relative economy, efficiency or effectiveness of an entity subjected to a performance audit. Alternatively, though, the auditor is expected to report, in narrative form, findings, conclusions and recommendations arising from the performance audit.

Single Audits of Governments

The Single Audit Act of 1984, amended in 1996, imposed a new audit concept that all state, county, city, Indian tribal governments, and other governmental recipients of federal financial assistance in the amount of $300,000 or more annually, are required to have a three-part, comprehensive, independent audit each year.

Those subject to the Act were required to have (1) an annual financial statement audit, (2) a review of their compliance with federal laws and regulations, and (3) a test of their internal controls, both organization-wide and with respect to the individual federal assistance programs. The single audit concept was, by federal regulation, later extended to nonprofit organizations and educational institutions.

The single audit was mandated by the federal government, but is paid for by the individual recipient governments, although there might be some partial compensation by the federal government through federal programs that permitted the recovery of audit costs as part of the programs indirect costs.

TYPES OF AUDITORS

Audits of governments are performed by many auditors. Tens of thousands of auditors are employed by the governments. Others, most often independent certified public accountants, are retained under contract to the governments. Of those employed by government, many are career civil service executives, others are appointed, and still others are elected to their office. And, the nature of the audits they perform may differ considerably.

Federal Auditors

At the federal level, a distinction exists between types of audit organizations: the General Accounting Office and other auditors employed by the many federal departments and agencies.

U.S. General Accounting Office. GAO, established by the Budget and Accounting Act of 1921, is an audit and investigative organization in the legislative branch of the federal government and is headed by the Comptroller General of the United States. The Comptroller General, directly responsible to only Congress, is nominated for the office by the President, must then be confirmed by the Senate, and may serve for one 15-year term. The Comptroller General is subject to removal from office only by a joint resolution of Congress for specified causes or impeachment. This executive is not eligible for reappointment.

By law GAO is required to investigate " ... at the seat of government or elsewhere, all matters relating to the receipt, disbursement and application of public funds .... [17] With few exceptions, the authority of GAO extends to all organizations, programs, activities, and functions, contracts and grants that, directly or indirectly, spend federal monies or have received or use federal resources. For example, GAO has access to and conducts audits and investigations of federal agencies, entities of

---

[17] Budget and Accounting Act of 1921, Washington, D.C.

other governments and private contractors and grantees and others who received financing or financial assistance in any form from the federal government.

Offices of Inspectors General. Since October 1978, with the passage of Public Law 95-452, federal agencies have been required to have or have appointed an inspector general. By the law and related legislative history, these officers were to:

- Conduct and supervise audits and investigations of programs and operations of their departments and agencies;

- Provide leadership and coordination of recommend policies for activities designed to promote economy and efficiency in administration of, and to prevent and detect fraud and abuse in, such programs and operations;

- Provide a means for keeping agency heads and Congress fully and currently informed of problems and deficiencies relating to administration and the necessity for, or progress of, corrective actions.

All federal inspectors general are appointed to their position, but those of the larger departments and agencies are also confirmed by Congress.

Interestingly, inspectors general must concurrently report both to the head of their department or agency and to Congress. Congress has imposed a semi-annual and annual reporting requirement on these executives and, additionally, requires that all serious and flagrant problems, abuses or deficiencies be reported immediately (1) to the head of the department or agency and (2) then to Congress within 7 calendar days.

By the Inspectors General Act, these reports shall be transmitted to the head of the federal entity and to Congress without further clearance and without approval by the entity head, except that the prescribed reports must be delivered to the entity head sufficiently in advance of the due date to permit the inclusion of federal entity comments prior to delivery to Congress.

State and Local Government Auditors

Different authorizing legislation and local statutes makes categorization of auditors of state and local governments difficult. Nor, are the titles or responsibilities of these governmental auditors consistent or, at times, indicative of the audit responsibilities they possess. For example, a survey of characteristics of state auditing offices disclosed, among many facts, that: [18]

- Auditors exercising statewide auditing responsibilities could have the title of chief, auditor, examiner of public accounts, legislative auditor, auditor general, legislative budget assistant, executive director, comptroller, or director.

- The method of selection of these audit executives included: general election by voters, appointment or vote by legislatures, appointment by the governor or secretary of state, appointment by legislative committee, and appointment by state budget and control board.

- Many, but not all states had certain prerequisite conditions to holding the auditor position that mainly related to age, years of U.S. citizenship, residency in the state, and experience. A few required that the state auditor be a certified public accountant.

As is evident, the state auditor could be in either the legislative or executive branch. Also, depending upon the method under which the auditor assumed office (i.e., elected or appointed), the auditor will be more or less independent, possess varying scopes of audit responsibility and may or may not be an accountant.

Similarly, at city, municipal, and other governmental units, auditors hold their positions by appointment, election, or under a civil service merit appointment. Also, these auditors could report to either the legislative or executive governing body, the chief elected official, or others.

Quite often, auditors of state and local governments will not perform financial statement audits, but may concentrate more on conducting internal-type audits of these entities, typically voucher audits, procedural or compliance reviews, fiscal post audits, functional and performance audits, and other evaluations of importance to their governments. The financial statement audit are generally done under a government contract by independent CPAs.

Independent Public Accountants

The 1980s saw increased retention of certified public accounting firms by all levels of government to perform a wide variety of audits of public sector entities, including audits, reviews or evaluations of financial statements, compliance with laws and regulations, adequacy of controls, systems reviews, and, to a lesser degree, the three "E" (economy, efficiency, effectiveness) type performance audits.

---

[18] National State Auditors Association, "Auditing in the States—A Summary," Lexington, Kentucky, 1992.

The method of retaining independent CPAs differs. At times and for specific audits, government entities retain the CPA firm under contract directly. In these instances the contract will outline a specific scope of audit. In these circumstances, the contracting agency is most often the audit client, and under the contract the contracting government makes payment directly to the audit firm. At other times, the CPA firm will be retained by one level of government and be expected to serve multiple "clients." This is particularly true with respect to audits made pursuant to the Single Audit Act of 1984. Under this act and implementing federal regulations, the CPA firm is retained by the state or local government to conduct audits that meet both the requirements of the state or local government as well as those imposed by the sponsoring federal grantor and other federal agencies (such as the Office of Management and Budget and GAO).

COORDINATION OF AUDITS

Cross Servicing Audits

This extensive network of auditors and varieties of audits that might be performed on governmental units necessarily raised concerns about audits that might be duplicative, overlapping, and maybe even unnecessary. For this reason, Congress, through implementing regulations of OMB, directed every federal agency to give full consideration to establishing cross-servicing audit agreements between two or more federal agencies to minimize the impact of duplicate audits on a single auditee. This program, outlined in OMB's Circular A-73, has been rather extensively implemented in the federal government with respect to audits of federal contract and grant programs and operations. Under this regulation, a single cognizant or lead federal audit agency is appointed, often based on which federal agency has the most funds involved to monitor and the number of federal audits being made of nonfederal organizations. [19]

Coordination with Other Governments

OMB Circular A-73 directs federal departments to consider audit partnerships with audit offices of state and local governments and to coordinate audits of these organizations to the maximum extent possible. This reliance is also required of those federal agencies whose contract and grant programs are subject to the regulations in OMB Circular A-102, the administrative, management and financial guidelines for contracts and grants to state and local governments. [20] Pursu-

---

[19] OMB, Circular A-73, *Audit of Federal Operations and Programs*, Washington, D. C.

[20] OMB, Circular A-102, *Grant and Cooperative Agreements with State and Local Governments*, Washington, D.C.

ant to Circular A-73, federal audits must give full consideration to nonfederal audits and, if the following conditions exist, the report of nonfederal auditors will be used in lieu of federal audits:

1. If the reports and supporting workpapers are available for review by the federal agencies.

2. If tests by federal agencies indicate that the audits were performed in accordance with generally accepted auditing standards, including the government auditing standards.

3. If the audits otherwise meet the requirements of the federal agencies.

Since 1984, Congress, by the Single Audit Act, requires that all federal agencies support a single, organization-wide, comprehensive audit of governmental and other entities receiving federal financial assistance. Under the Act, audits made pursuant to the Act shall be in lieu of any financial audit that a recipient of federal assistance is required to undergo under any other federal law or regulation.

GOVERNMENTAL AUDITING

Objectives of governmental auditing have evolved over some 50 years to the present condition where governmental executives and legislators expect a rather comprehensive audit report including not only an expression of an opinion on the fairness of the government's financial statements, but also a reporting on the adequacy of controls and the extent of compliance with laws and regulations.

Today, therefore, a *governmental audit* can be defined as:

an examination or review of transactions, accounts, systems and controls of a public organization in accordance with generally accepted auditing standards and government auditing standards to provide assurance that the results of financial and economic activities are presented fairly and that controls and financial practices are adequate to assure compliance with laws, statutes, regulations, and other criteria related to the expenditure and application of government resources.

Auditors of public sector entities are acutely aware that application of the AICPA's generally accepted auditing standards to governments provide only a partial response to concerns that many have with respect to governmental operations. To perform qualifying audits of governments, certain prerequisites must be met by an auditor of government:

● An auditor must have an understanding of the generally accepted accounting principles applicable to governmental organizations, the importance and legal significance of public sector budgets, and the accounting and reporting processes of the government being audited.

- An auditor must be knowledgeable of and possess sound understanding of the accounting and reporting systems, systems of controls, and general operations of the governmental entity to be audited.
- An auditor must be an expert in the application of government auditing standards that require an assessment and reporting on internal controls and compliance with laws and regulations, in addition to a government's cost-based financial statements.

To address the scope of governmental auditing with comprehension, the book is divided into several parts:

Part I describes the public sector audit evolution and unique accounting principles and standards which auditors of public sector entities must apply.

Part II examines general government field work and reporting auditing standards, with emphasis on financial statement audits, financial related audits, performance audits, and single audits.

Part III is directed to several specific concerns or areas of particular importance to auditors of public sector entities, such as (1) reviews of controls, (2) testing compliance with laws and regulations, (3) examining allowable, unallowable and indirect costs charged to federal programs, (4) criteria for evidence and working papers of government audits, (5) auditor relationships, responsibilities and reliance and (6) external quality control reviews by the federal government of government audits.

Part IV contains several chapters each illustrating the more common types of governmental audits and describes specific planning considerations and methodologies for: (1) financial statement audits, (2) single audits, (3) financial related audits, (4) performance audits and (5) other special focus audits.

The appendices to the book includes the Single Audit Act of 1996 which re-defined the nature and depth of audits made of recipients of federal financial assistance, and OMB Circular A-133 which provides detailed procedural guidance for conducting single audits.

Chapter 2

Accounting Principles and Auditing Standards

All types of auditing have an accounting or financial basis or consequence. In the end all economic activity comes down to dollars and cents—What did one get for what was paid? What is the financial position? What resources are needed for the next fiscal period? Were the funds adequate to meet objectives?

Implicit for all types of audits is the prerequisite that there is a basis of accounting, uniformly used by all entities within generally homogenous groupings, and consistently applied from one fiscal period to another. Stated in another manner, there must be accounting rules or "principles" that must be used and persons relying on the accounting rules should be informed when the rules are no longer being used or have been violated.

The relationship between accounting and auditing is a close one, but there is an important distinction: accounting principles define what should be done with respect to financial stewardship and disclosure; auditing standards define processes to assess whether the accounting and disclosures were done. Or, as more as eloquently noted in *The Philosophy of Auditing*:

> *"Accounting includes the collection, classification, summarization, and communication of financial data; it involves the measurement and communications of business events and conditions as they affect and represent a given enterprise or other entity. ... Auditing does none of these things. ... Its task is to review the measurements and communications of accounting for propriety. Auditing is analytical, not constructive; it is critical, investigative, concerned with the basis for accounting measurements and assertions."* [1]

---

[1] R. K. Mautz and Hussein A. Sharaf, *The Philosophy of Auditing* (monograph No. 6), American Accounting Association, Sarasota, Florida, 1985.

STATE AND LOCAL GOVERNMENTAL ACCOUNTING

Until 1984 various organizations had an interest in and influenced the accounting and financial reporting of state and local government units. These included the National Council on Governmental Accounting (NCGA), American Institute of Certified Public Accountants, state and local governments and to some extent Congress and federal departments through their rules and regulations. For the most part, though, the NCGA and the AICPA were the primary setters of governmental accounting standards. Since 1984, though, the Governmental Accounting Standards Board (GASB) has been recognized as the source of generally accepted accounting principles for governments.

The AICPA had assumed a dual role issuing pronouncements that affected governmental accounting and reporting as well as setting the standards by which the accounting and reporting would be audited. (The AICPA, until 1973, also defined the accounting and reporting standards for the corporate sector.) In 1973, the Financial Accounting Standards Board (FASB) was organized to establish and monitor the accounting practices of the private sector, although its promulgations apply to business-type governmental operations, unless such standards are exempted by GASB.

National Council on Governmental Accounting

NCGA, a part-time, voluntary organization, had for years done much to establish uniform and consistent accounting principles for government. NCGA's Statement No. 1, "Governmental Accounting and Financial Reporting Principles," issued in 1979, continues to be the most succinct summary of accounting and financial reporting practiced by state and local governments.

In the 1970s, there was no national requirement to insure uniformity of accounting and reporting among the 50 states. But, NCGA's Statement No. 1 and its other promulgation's did enjoy widespread application and, until the establishment of the more formal Government Accounting Standards Board, were the accounting and reporting basis on which independent audits were performed and audit opinions rendered. GASB Statement No. 1 defined and outlined 12 principles of accounting of NCGA—i.e., fund accounting—that distinguished the accounting of public sector operations from accounting in the private sector.

Government accounting is predicated on an overriding concern with legal compliance and almost equal concern with stringent fiscal controls, both of which are related to the legality of expenditure of public resources. For this reason, a state or local government's accounting and reporting systems may appear somewhat fragmented in relation to the single accounting system and the more simplified financial statements of a corporation. The foundation of governmental accounting, reporting, stewardship, and performance is the *fund,* i.e., fund accounting. A fund is defined by NCGA in Statement No. 1 as:

> *" ... a fiscal and accounting entity with a self-balancing set of accounts recording cash and other financial resources, together with all related liabilities and residual equities or balances, and changes therein, which are segregated for the purpose of carrying on specific activities or attaining certain objectives in accordance with special regulations, restrictions, or limitations."*

The 12 accounting principles that apply this concept of fund accounting, enunciated by NCGA in Statement No. 1, and adopted by the successor GASB, include:

1. **Accounting and Reporting Capabilities.** A governmental accounting systems must make it possible both: (a) to present fairly and with full disclosure the financial position and results of financial operations of the funds and account groups of the governmental unit in conformity with generally accepted accounting principles; and (b) to determine and demonstrate compliance with finance-related legal and contractual provisions.

2. **Fund Accounting Systems.** Governmental accounting systems should be organized and operated on a fund basis. Three categories of funds are employed in governmental accounting: (1) governmental funds, (2) proprietary funds, and (3) fiduciary funds. Accountability for a government's general fixed assets and general long-term debt is accomplished through a fourth category or accounting entity known as the account groups.

3. **Types of Funds.** Within these 3 categories of funds, several types of funds were to be used by state and local governments:

Governmental funds that include the government's (1) general fund, (2) special revenue funds, (3) capital project funds, (4) debt service funds and (5) special assessment funds. (Special assessment type funds were later discontinued by the GASB and the accounting for these governmental activities are now performed in the other funds.)

Proprietary funds that include the government's:

(1) enterprise funds to account for operations financed and operated in a manner similar to private business enterprises where the intent is to measure cost of providing goods to the general public on some reimbursable basis or where the governing body decides that periodic determination of revenues earned and expenses incurred and/or net income is appropriated for capital maintenance, public policy, management control, or other purposes; and

(2) internal service funds to account for financing of goods and services provided by one department, primarily, to other departments, agencies, or units of the government on a cost-reimbursement basis.

Fiduciary funds that include the trust and agency funds to account for assets held by the government in a trustee capacity or as an agency for others (individuals, private organizations, other governments or other funds) and are typically categorized into: expendable trust funds, non-expendable trust funds, pension trust funds, and agency funds.

4. **Number of Funds.** Governmental units should establish and maintain those funds required by law and sound financial administration. Only the minimum number of funds consistent with legal and operating requirements should be established.

5. **Accounting for Fixed Assets and Long-Term Debt.** A clear distinction should be made between the fund fixed assets, the general fixed assets, the fund general long-term liabilities general long-term debt. Fixed assets related to specific proprietary funds or trust funds should be accounted for through those funds. All other fixed assets should be accounted for through the general fixed asset account group. Long-term liabilities of proprietary funds, special assessment funds (subsequently deleted) and trust funds should be accounted for through those funds. All other general long-term liabilities should be accounted for through the general long-term debt account group.

6. **Valuation of Fixed Assets.** Fixed assets should be accounted for at cost or, if cost is not practicably determinable, at estimated cost; donated fixed assets should be recorded at estimated fair value at the time received.

7. **Depreciation of Fixed Assets.** Depreciation policies must be determined for the two types of fixed assets: (a) depreciation of general fixed assets should not be recorded in the accounts of governmental funds, accumulated depreciation may be recorded in the general fixed asset account group; (b) depreciation of fixed assets accounted for in a proprietary fund should be recorded in the accounts of that fund and also recognized in those trust funds where expenses, net income and/or capital maintenance are measured.

8. **Accrual Basis of Accounting.** Governmental fund revenues and expenditures should be recognized on the *modified accrual basis*; proprietary fund revenues and expenses should be recognized on the *accrual basis*. Fiduciary fund revenues and expenses or expenditures should be recognized on the basis consistent with the fund's accounting measurement objective. Interfund transfers should be recognized in the accounting period in which the interfund receivable and payable arise.

9. **Budgeting, Budgetary Control and Budgetary Reporting.** Budgeting is essential to government accounting. The principles re-

Accounting Principles and Auditing Standards 37

quire that: (a) an annual budget(s) be adopted by every governmental unit; (b) the accounting system provide the basis for appropriate budgetary control; and (c) budgetary comparisons be included in the appropriate financial statements and schedules for governmental funds for which an annual budget has been adopted.

10. *Transfer, Revenue, Expenditure and Account Classification.* Consistent adherence to terminology and appropriate classification is required for governmental accounting:

(a) *interfund transfers and proceeds of general long-term debt* issues should be classified separately from fund revenues and expenditures or expenses;

(b) *government fund revenues* should be classified by fund and source and *government fund expenditures* should be classified by fund, function (or program), organization, activity, character and principal object classes;

(c) *proprietary fund revenues and expenses* should be classified in essentially the same manner as those of similar business organizations, functions or activities.

11. *Common Terminology and Classification.* Common terminology should be used consistently throughout the budget, the accounts, and the financial reports of each fund.

12. *Interim and Annual Financial Reports.* Generally, financial reporting for government requires three types of data: financial statements, supporting schedules, and statistical tables. The financial statements may be of three types:

(a) *interim financial statements and reports* of financial position, operating results and other pertinent information to facilitate management control, legislative oversight and, where necessary or desired, external reporting;

(b) a *comprehensive annual financial report* (the CAFR) covering all funds and account groups, including appropriate combined, combining, individual fund statements as well as notes to the financial statements, schedules, narrative explanations, and statistical tables—all of which should be prepared and published;

(c) *general purpose financial statements* may be issued separately from the CAFR, but should include the financial statements essential to fair presentation of financial position and operating results and changes in financial position of the proprietary funds and similar trust funds.

Governmental Accounting Standards Board

The Governmental Accounting Standards Board, established in 1984 as a formal organization with a full-time staff and compensated board members, is a subordinate organization within the Financial Accounting Foundation, of which the Financial Accounting Standards Board is the other component. GASB superseded the earlier NCGA and has responsibility for governmental accounting and reporting practices. By agreement, GASB establishes accounting and reporting standards for state and local governmental units; FASB establishes standards for financial activities and transactions of all other entities. This same agreement also provided that the NCGA statements and interpretations were to be recognized by GASB as being in force until modified by GASB.

Generally Accepted Accounting Principles. In May 1986, the AICPA revised its Ethics Rule 203—the AICPA code of professional conduct—and recognized GASB as the body to establish financial accounting principles for state and local governments. Thereafter, the relative hierarchical responsibility for establishing **generally accepted accounting principles** for government has been grouped by the following 5 categories:

1. *GASB Statements and Interpretations*, and AICPA and FASB pronouncements specifically made applicable to state and local governmental entities by GASB Statements or Interpretations;

2. *GASB Technical Bulletins*, and, if specifically made applicable to state and local governmental entities by the AICPA and cleared by the GASB, which have included the AICPA Industry Audit and Accounting Guides and AICPA Statements of Position;

3. *AICPA AcSEC Practice Bulletins* if specifically made applicable to state and local governmental entities and cleared by the GASB, and consensus positions of a GASB-organized accounting group reaching agreement on accounting issues applicable to state and local government entities;

4. *Implementation Guides (Q&As)*, published by GASB staff; and practices widely recognized and prevalent in state and local government; and

5. *Other accounting literature*, including GASB Concepts Statements and AICPA and FASB pronouncements when not specifically made applicable to state and local governmental entities. [2]

The objective of this hierarchy, as set forth in a Jurisdiction Determination by the Financial Accounting Foundation, is that FASB

---

[2] Governmental Accounting Standards Board, *Codification of Governmental Accounting and Financial Reporting Standards*, Chicago, Illinois, as of June 30, 1992.

Accounting Principles and Auditing Standards 39

and GASB will have the primary responsibility for setting accounting and reporting standards for the entities within their respective jurisdictions. Pursuant to this Determination, pronouncements of the other board are not mandatory unless so designated by the board with primary responsibility.

GASB Statements on Accounting Standards. Since its inception, GASB has directed its attention to refining or revising earlier NCGA Statements and positions, concentrating on identifying and implementing uniform accounting principles in three general areas:

(1) the measurement focus and basis of accounting that should be used by state and local government in accounting for and reporting their financial positions and results of financial operations;

(2) the nature of the governmental entity that is to be accounted for and reported upon in the financial statements, including definitions of the component units that should be encompassed; and

(3) the form and content, and possibly simplified financial statement for governmental units.

Through June 1999, GASB issued 34 governmental accounting financial and reporting standards.

Probably the two most significant were GASB Statement Nos. 11 and 34. GASB Statement No. 11 was an unsuccessful attempt to change the financial measurement focus and basis of accounting for governmental fund operations to an accrual basis of measurement and reporting.[3] In June 1999, GASB issued GASB Statement No. 34—*Basic Financial Statements—and Management's Discussion and Analysis—for state and local governments.*

Statement No. 34, in addition to refining certain reporting and formatting of financial data, changed the above financial reports and statements requirement by superimposing two additional financial statements: a statement of net assets and a statement of activities. These financial statements are to be government-wide (but excluding fiduciary activities), all-inclusive, accrual-based, consolidated-type financial statements. Implementation of Statement No. 34, if not rescinded or amended, is to be phased by size of government, beginning for fiscal periods after 2002.

---

[3] The effective date of GASB Statement No. 11 was amended by GASB Statement No. 17 which postponed implementation of Statement No. 11 in a manner that ensured Statement 11 would never be implemented.

FEDERAL GOVERNMENT ACCOUNTING

Before the Chief Financial Officer Act

Prior to 1990 and passage of the Chief Financial Officer Act, the responsibility for accounting and reporting by federal departments and agencies was split between the General Accounting Office (in the legislative branch) and the Office of Management and Budget, Department of Treasury, and the individual federal departments and agencies (in the executive branch).

GAO, under several laws (but, particularly the Budget and Accounting Act of 1921 and the Accounting and Procedures Act of 1950), was required to prescribe the forms, systems, procedures, and principles and standards of accounting to be observed by federal departments and agencies. At the same time, though, some of these same laws gave OMB responsibilities for systems and internal and external reporting of federal departments and agencies. Also, the head of each department or agency was required, by these same and other laws, to develop and maintain their own system of accounts and internal controls.

The medium for promulgating the accounting principles, standards, and related accounting and reporting requirements was the *GAO Manual Guidance of Federal Agencies*, specifically Title 2, *Accounting*, of the GAO Manual. Published initially in 1957, this Manual was comprised of several titles or sections and, when supplemented or revised by various laws and requirements of OMB and the Treasury Department, served as the accounting principles for the federal government. During the 30 years it was effective, neither Congress, GAO, OMB nor the Treasury Department ever made reference to the principles and standards of Title 2 as being "generally accepted accounting principles" for the federal government.

The split responsibilities for accounting and financial reporting, plus systems design and maintenance, among several federal agencies caused confusion and resulted in rather widespread noncompliance with the GAO standards over the years. Additionally, departments and agencies often commented that the accounting standards promulgated by the GAO resulted from an inadequate due process and that some standards were irrelevant to federal operations. Further, independent audits were not required of department and agency financial statements.

For these and other reasons the AICPA, concluded in a widely distributed 1989 report that an improved accounting standard-setting and reporting process was urgently needed for the federal govern-

Accounting Principles and Auditing Standards   41

ment.[4] The AICPA stated that the federal government had a fiscal and financial credibility crisis, related, in part, to several major financial management inadequacies. The AICPA drew many conclusions on the state of the federal government's financial management and recommended:

(1) that a Controller of the United States and a chief financial officer for every department and agency be appointed;

(2) that current accounting and reporting practices and procedures may not be appropriate to meet the unique needs of the federal government;

(3) that annual financial statements be required for all federal departments and government wide agencies; and

(4) that annual independent audits be made of department and agency financial statements.

After holding hearings, Congress, in November 1990, passed the Chief Financial Officer Act that addressed practically all of the AICPA concerns by requiring, among several other financial improvements:

(1) A Controller of the United States within the OMB, and a chief financial officer and deputy chief financial officer in 23 federal departments and agencies;

(2) Certain designated executive departments and agencies prepare financial statements (beginning not later than March 31, 1992, for the preceding fiscal year) for each revolving fund, trust fund, substantial commercial function, and the accounts of offices, bureaus, and activities;

(3) The form and content of these financial statements must be consistent with *applicable accounting principles, standards, and requirements*; and

(4) The required financial statements shall be audited in accordance with applicable generally acceptable government auditing standards.[5]

The CFO Act is silent on who or which agency is to set the cited *applicable accounting principles, standards, and requirements*. But, just prior to the Act, the Federal Accounting Standards Advisory Board was created by agreement between the Comptroller General of the U.S., the Secretary of Treasury, and the Director of OMB.

The agreement that resulted in the formation of FASAB is not based on any law or executive order but is essentially a "good faith"

---

[4] American Institute of Certified Public Accountants, "Federal Financial Management—Issues and Solutions," New York, N. Y., 1989.

[5] U. S. Congress, Public Law 101-576, 101st Congress, Chief Financial Officer Act of 1990, Washington, D. C., November 1990.

arrangement among these three central agencies to develop, issue, implement, and enforce government wide uniform accounting and reporting standards. The purpose of the FASAB is to recommend to these three federal executives accounting and financial reporting standards after considering the financial and budgetary needs of Congressional oversight groups and executive agencies, plus the needs of other users of federal financial information.[6] The federal accounting and reporting standards resulting from this process will replace those contained in the earlier GAO Manual.

After the Chief Financial Officers Act

The fiscal and financial management crisis that, in part, caused Congress to once again try to institutionalize sound financial management practices in the federal government was summarized by the Committee on Government Operations of the U.S. House of Representatives in its report that accompanied the bill, H.R. 5687, that preceded passage of the CFO Act of 1990. In this report, the Congress found:

● Billions of dollars are lost each year through fraud, waste, abuse, and mismanagement among the hundreds of programs in the Federal Government.

● These losses could be significantly decreased by improved financial management, including central coordination of internal controls and financial accounting.

● The Federal Government is in great need of fundamental reform in financial management requirements and practices because current financial management systems are obsolete and inefficient, and do not provide complete, consistent, reliable, and timely information.

● Present financial reporting practices of the Federal Government do not accurately disclose the current and probable future cost of operating and investment decisions, including the future need for cash or other resources, do not permit adequate comparison of actual costs among executive agencies, and do not provide timely information required for efficient management of programs.[7]

FEDERAL AUDIT RESPONSIBILITIES

The CFO Act dispersed the responsibilities for activities to improve financial management, particularly the accounting and auditing, in the federal government to OMB, GAO, Treasury Department, and the several departmental and agency inspectors general.

---

[6] Mission Statement—Federal Accounting Standards Advisory Board, 1991.

[7] U.S. House of Representatives, Committee on Government Operations, Title I of the report to accompany bill H.R. 5687, October 6, 1990.

Accounting Principles and Auditing Standards

Office of Management and Budget

Under the CFO Act (Section 303), OMB was made responsible for prescribing the form and content of the financial statements of executive agencies consistent with applicable accounting principles, standards, and requirements.[8] As noted, the Act is silent about who is to define or prescribe these standards and requirements. OMB outlined a process by which the requirements of the CFO Act would be implemented in a series of regulations, known generally as the OMB Circular and OMB Bulletin series.

OMB Circulars and Bulletins are the way governmentwide fiscal or financial or administrative requirements are promulgated by OMB. A Circular is a regulation on a specific subject that would be applicable to federal department and agency actions until rescinded or superseded (e.g., OMB Circular A-11 on budget preparation, Circular A-21 on allowable and unallowable costs of grants to educational institutions, etc.). Shorter term policy—a year or less—would be published in the form of an OMB Bulletin, having the number of the fiscal year in which issued (i.e., 97-01 on the form and content of federal financial statements).

OMB recognized the role of FASAB to deliberate and make recommendations on accounting standards for the federal government and its department and agencies. By a Circular (A-134), OMB declared that OMB's *statements of federal financial accounting standards* shall be considered generally accepted accounting principles for federal departments and agencies.

Federal departments and agencies must comply with the OMB SFFASs in preparing their financial statements in accordance with the requirements of the CFO Act of 1990. And, auditors of federal financial statements must consider OMB SFFASs as the authoritative accounting and financial reporting references—i.e., the generally accepted accounting principles for federal departments and agencies—when auditing federal financial statements. Other OMB regulations relate to the form and content of federal financial statements and implementation requirements to audit these agency financial statements.

With respect to auditing policies, the OMB is responsible for promulgation of the implementing regulations for the Single Audit Act. These audit regulations, modified and revised since 1984, are currently embodied in its OMB Circular A-133, discussed in detail in a later chapter.

---

[8] CFO Act of 1990.

Offices of Federal Inspectors General

The Inspectors General Act of 1978 (Public Law 95-452) established independent inspectors general in all major departments and agencies of the federal government and subsequently the inspectors general concept has been extended to many other federal organizations. These executives are responsible for conducting and supervising audits and investigations of programs and operations of their own departments as well as of organizations to whom their departments provide financial assistance. The various offices of inspectors general also perform the desk reviews and conduct the on-site quality control reviews of thousands of audits made by non-federal auditors of federal assistance programs.

The CFO Act (Section 305) states that federal financial statements shall be audited by the department or agency Inspector General or by an independent external auditor, as determined by the Inspector General or the head of the agency in the absence of an Inspector General. These audits are to be made in accordance with applicable generally accepted government auditing standards. These "applicable" auditing standards are promulgated by the General Accounting Office, popularly known as the "yellow book."

General Accounting Office

Section 305(4) of the CFO Act gave significant responsibilities to the Comptroller General (i.e., the executive that heads the General Accounting Office). For example, the Comptroller General:

● May review any audit of a financial statement conducted by an Inspector General or an external auditor and report the results of this review to Congress, the Director of OMB and the head of the government agency that prepared the statement;

● May audit a financial statement of a government entity at the discretion of the Comptroller General or at the request of a committee of Congress and any audit the Comptroller general performs should be in lieu of audits otherwise required by the CFO Act;

● Is to be provided all books, accounts, financial records, reports, files, work papers, and property belonging to or in use by the government entity and its auditor that the Comptroller General considers necessary to the performance of any audit or review under the Act.

These responsibilities are similar, in similar respects, to those appearing in earlier laws such as the Budget and Accounting Acts of 1921 and 1950.

AUDITING STANDARDS
AICPA's Generally Accepted Auditing Standards
Ten Standards

Prefacing comments by the AICPA to its generally accepted auditing statements distinguish between audit procedures and standards.

Audit procedures are related to the acts to be performed by auditors. *Audit standards* deal with measure of the quality of performance of those acts, the judgments exercised by an auditor, and the objectives to be attained by using the audit procedures. This distinction is somewhat blurred in practice. Auditors of government must have a command of many criteria, procedures, and standards, including: the ten basic auditing standards, the many Statements on Auditing Standards, the AICPA's state and local government auditing guide, the AICPA's attestation standards, etc.

The AICPA is responsible for issuing generally accepted auditing standards and has done so since the early 1900s. Over the years there has been general acceptance of the 10 auditing standards—3 general, 3 field work, 4 reporting—of the AICPA, which have been refined, revised, or made more responsive to changing needs and perceptions of the auditor role (see *Exhibit 2-1)*.

EXHIBIT 2-1

Generally Accepted Auditing Standards

General Standards

1. The audit is to be performed by a person or persons having adequate technical training and proficiency as an auditor.

2. In all matters relating to the assignment, an independence in mental attitude is to be maintained by the auditor or auditors.

3. Due professional care is to be exercised in the performance of the audit and the preparation of the report.

Standards of Field Work

1. The work is to be adequately planned and assistants, if any, are to be properly supervised.

2. A sufficient understanding of the internal control structure is to be obtained to plan the audit and to determine the nature, timing, and extent of tests to be performed.

3. Sufficient competent evidential matter is to be obtained through inspection, observation, inquiries, and conformations to afford a reasonable basis for an opinion regarding the financial statements under audit.

Standards of Reporting

1. The report shall state whether the financial statements are presented in accordance with generally accepted accounting principles.

2. The report shall identify those circumstances in which such principles have not been consistently observed in the current period in relation to the preceding period.

3. Informative disclosures in the financial statements are to be regarded as reasonably adequate unless otherwise stated in the report.

4. The report shall either contain an expression of an opinion regarding the financial statements, taken as a whole, or an assertion to the effect that an opinion cannot be expressed. When an overall opinion cannot be expressed, the reasons there-

Accounting Principles and Auditing Standards 47

fore should be stated. In all cases where an auditor's name is associated with financial statements, the report should contain a clear-cut indication of the character of the auditor's work, if any, and the degree of responsibility the auditor is taking.

As defined by the AICPA, these generally accepted auditing standards are primarily directed toward dictating the necessary minimum performance by an auditor to support an opinion on financial statements. Currently, refinements of these generally accepted auditing standards are promulgated by the AICPA in the form of Statements on Auditing Standards.

Generally accepted auditing standards are applicable primarily to audits of financial statements prepared in accordance with the generally accepted accounting principles applicable to nongovernmental units. Governments and others have caused the auditing profession concern, and even problems, when attempting to use these standards as criteria for other than the audit of financial statements.

Nonetheless, the AICPA's generally accepted auditing standards are important to auditors of governmental entities. The 1994 revision of the government auditing standards continues a policy of GAO, beginning with the first "yellow book" issued in 1972, that the government auditing standards incorporate existing and any new AICPA standards relevant to financial statement audits unless GAO specifically excludes standards by formal announcement. To date, GAO has not excluded any AICPA auditing standard.

AICPA's Government Audit Guide

Periodically the AICPA releases revised editions of its audit and accounting guide for audits of state and local governmental units. This Guide presents recommendations of the AICPA government and auditing committees on the (1) application of generally accepted auditing standards to the audits of financial statements of state and local governmental units, (2) descriptions of financial accounting and reporting principles and practices of state and local governmental units, and (3) audit guidance necessary to permit audits pursuant to the Single Audit Act. This Guide concentrates primarily on audit procedures unique to audits of governmental units, assuming readers are experienced in auditing generally, but not in the specialized practices applicable to state and local governments.

The Audit Guide identifies several of the unique aspects of governmental accounting and auditing and the nature of audits performed under three levels of auditing standards or requirements: (1) generally accepted auditing standards (those published by the AICPA for audits of financial statements); (2) government auditing standards (those published by the GAO for audits of entities receiving federal financing); and (3) requirements to conduct audits pursuant to the Single Audit Act.

Attestation Standards

The AICPA's generally accepted auditing standards apply to the audit's financial statements. Additionally, though, the AICPA in recent years emphasized standards that address other types of financial related audits. The GAO's government auditing standards incorporated these standards as well, which are more popularly referred to as the "attestation standards."

The attestation standards relate to those engagements where an auditor would apply *agreed-upon* procedures to an entity's assertions about internal controls over financial reporting and/or safeguarding assets, or to financial related matters not specifically addressed in other AICPA standards. In connection with these "attestation standards," the term *agreed-upon* procedures has not been defined by the AICPA, but generally relates to engagements where the practitioner performs procedures that were earlier agreed to in writing with the attestor entity.

The AICPA has identified two groups of attestation engagements, depending on the levels of assurance to be provided by the practitioner:

(1) examinations, i.e., engagements that reduce the attestation risk to an appropriately low level with the conclusion expressed in the form of a positive assurance; and

(2) reviews, i.e., engagements that reduce the attestation risk to only a moderate level.

The attestation standards are an extension, not a replacement, of the AICPA's 10 generally accepted auditing standards. Like the auditing standards, the attestation standards presume that the professional conducting these financial related audits will possess technical competence and independence in mental attitude, exercise due professional care with adequate planning and supervision, accumulate adequate evidence, and make the appropriate reporting.

As was the case with the AICPA's generally accepted auditing standards, the government auditing standards incorporate all existing and any new AICPA "attestation standards" relevant to financial related audits unless GAO specifically excludes standards by formal announcement. To date, GAO has not excluded any AICPA attestation standard.

The AICPA's Auditing Standards Board (ASB) stated (in the April 1994 *Journal of Accountancy*) that the prescribed attestation requirements for examination of compliance with laws, regulations and internal controls do not apply to engagements for which the objective is to report in accordance with (1) *Government Auditing Standards*, (2) the Single Audit Act, (3) OMB Circular A-133, and (4) program specific audits. Also, while explicit in an accompanying article, the *Meaning of Compliance Attestation*, but not explicit in the accompanying SSAE, auditors are precluded by the ASB from providing negative assurances.

STANDARDS FOR AUDITS OF GOVERNMENTS

In the late 1960s, the General Accounting Office perceived a need for information concerning governmental operations considerably broader than was being met by the public accounting profession's auditing standards related to financial statement reporting. GAO believed that responsible governmental auditing must also consider whether publicly funded programs achieved the purposes for which the programs were established, whether the operations of the programs were economical and efficient and if program operations and expenditures complied with laws and regulations.

The governmental auditing standards were founded on the premise that governmental accountability required the identification not only of what public funds were spent, but also of the manner and effectiveness of those expenditures. For this reason, the government auditing standards provided for a comprehensive scope of audit that included: financial statement auditing, financial related auditing, compliance auditing and performance auditing. But, the standards specifically state that the full scopes of these audits are not intended to apply to every or even any audit of a government. This enlarged audit scope (i.e., enlarged beyond the scope of the financial statement audits to which the AICPA's generally accepted auditing standards apply) is not desirable in all circumstances.

The legal basis for applying the federal government's auditing standards to non-federal entities was viewed as an extension of GAO's legal authority (in the Budget and Accounting Acts of 1921 and 1950) to investigate " ... at the seat of government *or elsewhere*, all matters relating to the receipt, disbursement, and *application* of public funds...," GAO's audit and investigatory authority was unrelated to whether expenditures of federal monies were made by a federal governmental department or agency, or state or local governmental entity, or federal contractor, grantee, university or nonprofit or other organization who received federal financial assistance.

That auditing authority was defined by Congress in several sections of the Budget and Accounting Procedures Act of 1950, but two sections specifically provide that:

Section 111. *(d) The auditing for the Government, conducted by the Comptroller General of the United States as an agent of Congress be directed at determining the extent to which accounting and related financial reporting fulfill the purposes specified, financial transactions have been consummated in ac-*

Accounting Principles and Auditing Standards

cordance with laws, regulations or other legal requirements, and adequate internal financial control over operations is exercised, and afford an effective basis for the settlement of accounts of accountable officers.

Section 117(a) ... *the financial transactions of each executive, legislative, and judicial agency, including but not limited to the accounts of accountable officers, shall be audited by the General Accounting Office in accordance with such principles and procedures and under such rules and regulations as may be prescribed by the Comptroller General of the United States.*

Other acts of Congress—Inspectors General Act of 1978, Single Audit Act of 1984, Chief Financial Officer Act of 1990, to cite a few—also required that the auditing activities required by federal law be conducted in conformance with the *government* auditing standards promulgated by the General Accounting Office.

Under the leadership of two Comptroller Generals, GAO established the auditing criteria for public sector entities, initially in 1972 and revised and refined in subsequent editions in 1981, 1988 and most recently, in 1994. The current edition of the government auditing standards is effective for financial audits performed of covered organizations for periods ending on or after January 1, 1995 and for performance audits beginning on or after January 1995.

The objective of this book is to review and illustrate government auditing standards and selected practices peculiar or unique to governments. No attempt has been made to duplicate the information published by the AICPA in its annual *Codification of Statement of Auditing Standards* and information in individual AICPA SASs or SSAEs, although this information is incorporated in the government auditing by reference. Knowledge of these generally accepted auditing standards of the AICPA is a prerequisite to conducting audits of governmental units. The government auditing standards must be applied to the more than 80,000 units of state and local governments that are recipients of federal financial assistance. The U.S. Bureau of Census reports the population including, in addition to states, counties, cities, towns and villages, plus hundreds and, in some instances, thousands of:

- School districts
- Municipal utility districts
- Public benefit corporations and authorities
- Public employee benefit retirement systems
- Governmental colleges and universities
- Governmental hospitals and other providers of health care

● Other special districts, authorities (e.g., school, sanitation, and other districts; toll road, airport and other authorities, etc.).

Of the governmental units, more than 30,000 are recipients of federal financial assistance and subject to the requirements of the Single Audit Act of 1984. In January 1990, by regulations (OMB Circular A-133), the federal government expanded the single audit concept to some 100,000 nonprofit organizations receiving federal financing.

Auditing regulations imposed by other governments do not supersede either the generally accepted or the government auditing standards. It is the responsibility of the auditor to comply with all appropriate and applicable audit requirements, e.g., the AICPA's, GAO's, the federal OMB, federal inspectors general, and state and local government auditing criteria. In fact, the AICPA in its Audit Guide for state and local governmental units, states that if an auditor becomes aware that the entity is subject to an audit requirement that may not be encompassed in the terms of audit engagement, the auditor should communicate to management and the audit committee or to others with equivalent authority and responsibility, that an audit in accordance with generally accepted auditing standards may not satisfy the relevant legal, regulatory, or contractual requirements.

Compliance with government auditing standards is a legal mandate for auditors. But, for certified public accountants, compliance with government auditing standards is also an ethical mandate. In literature relating to audits of public sector entity, the AICPA repeatedly notes that by Ethics Interpretation (501-3), when a member undertakes the obligation to follow government audit standards, guides, procedures, statues, rules and regulations, in addition to generally accepted auditing standards, he or she is obligated to follow such requirements. The failure to do so is "an act discreditable to the profession."

Exhibit 2-2 lists the generally accepted ***government auditing standards***—4 general, 5 field work (revised from 3 to 5 in 1999), and 5 reporting auditing standards:

EXHIBIT 2-2

Generally Accepted Government Auditing Standards
(1994 Revision, unless noted)

General Auditing Standards

1. The staff assigned to conduct the audit should collectively possess adequate professional proficiency for the tasks required.

2. In all matters relating to the audit work, the audit organization and the individual auditors, whether government or public, should be free from personal and external impairments to independence, should be organizationally independent, and should maintain an independent attitude and appearance.

3. Due professional care should be used in conducting the audit and in preparing related reports.

4. Each audit organization conducting audits in accordance with these standards should have an appropriate internal quality control system in place and undergo an external quality control review.

Field Work Auditing Standards

1. Auditors should communicate information to the auditee, the individuals contracting for or requesting the audit services, and the audit committee regarding the nature and extent of planned testing and reporting on compliance with laws and regulations and internal control over financial reporting. [Government Auditing Standards, 1994 revision, Amendment No. 2, July 1999.]

2. Auditors should follow up on known material findings and recommendations from previous audits.

3. Auditors should design the audit to provide reasonable assurance of detecting material misstatements resulting from noncompliance with provisions of contracts or grant agreements that have a direct and material effect on the determination of financial statement amounts. If specific information comes to the auditor's attention that provides evidence concerning the existence of possible noncompliance that could have a material indirect effect on the financial statement, auditors should apply audit procedures specifically directed to ascertaining whether that noncompliance has occurred.

4. In planning the audit, auditors should document in the working papers (1) the basis for assessing control risk at the maximum level for assertions related to material account bal-

ances, transaction classes, and disclosure components of financial statements when such assertions are significantly dependent upon computerized information systems, and (2) consideration that the planned audit procedures are designed to achieve audit objectives and to reduce audit risk to an acceptable level. [Government Auditing Standards, 1994 revision, Amendment No. 1, dated May 1999.]

5. Working papers should contain sufficient information to enable an experienced auditor having no previous connection with the audit to ascertain from them the evidence that supports the auditors' significant conclusions and judgments.

Reporting Auditing Standards

1. Auditors should communicate certain information related to the conduct and reporting of the audit to the audit committee or to the individual with whom they have contracted for the audit.

2. Audit reports should state that the audit was made in accordance with generally accepted government auditing standards.

3. The report on the financial statements should either (1) describe the scope of the auditors' testing of compliance with laws and regulations and internal controls and present the results of those tests or (2) refer to separate reports containing that information. In presenting the results of those tests, auditors should report irregularities, illegal acts, other material noncompliance, and reportable conditions in internal controls. In some circumstances, auditors should report irregularities and illegal acts directly to parties external to the audited entity.

4. If certain information is prohibited from general disclosure, the audit report should state the nature of the information omitted and the requirement that makes the omission necessary.

5. Written audit reports are to be submitted by the audit organization to the appropriate officials of the auditee and to the appropriate officials of the organization requiring or arranging for the audits, including external funding organizations, unless legal restrictions prevent it. Copies of the reports should also be sent to other officials who have legal oversight authority or who may be responsible for acting on audit findings and recommendations and to others authorized to receive such reports. Unless restricted by law or regulation, copies should be made available for public inspection.

Accounting Principles and Auditing Standards

Unless excluded by formal announcement, the government auditing standards for conducting financial audits incorporate all of the AICPA's standards and related Statements on Auditing Standards. As drafted by the General Accounting Office, the government auditing standards do not restate the AICPA's generally accepted auditing standards. In practice, the government auditing standards are to be applied as additional standards. In this regard, the government auditing standards are not "stand-alone" auditing criteria. On the other hand, the application of only generally accepted auditing standards to audits of governments would not be acceptable.

PART II
BROADER, DIFFERENT AUDITS FOR GOVERNMENTS

Foreword—

Government Auditing Standards,

February 27, 1981

"In the past few years, we have seen an unprecedented interest in government auditing. Public officials, legislators, and private citizens want and need to know not only whether government funds are handled properly and in compliance with laws and regulations, but also whether government organizations are achieving the purposes for which programs were authorized and funded and are doing so economically and efficiently.

Forty years ago auditors concentrated most of their efforts on auditing the vouchers which supported expenditures. But today, auditors are also concerned with the economy, efficiency, and effectiveness of government operations."

Elmer B. Staats
Comptroller General of the
United States

The generally accepted auditing standards of the American Institute of Certified Public Accountants have as objectives, the conduct of a financial statement audit and the reporting of the results of that audit in a uniform manner.

All of the AICPA's generally accepted auditing standards apply to audits of governmental entities, but the nature of audit testing and reporting on the results of audits of public sector entities varies since governmental executives, public sector recipients of financial assistance and users of government audit reports have interests and responsibilities different from those of private sector management. Most of the audit reports and certain audit procedures required by government auditing standards are not mentioned by the AICPA in its generally accepted auditing standards.

First published in 1972, the government auditing standards were intended to provide guidance for both financial audits and performance audits of governmental programs, activities, and functions. Federal laws have extended the scope of the governmental auditing standards to audits of almost any entity receiving federal financial assistance.

Like the AICPA's auditing standards, the government auditing standards include general auditing standards, standards for field work and standards for reporting. But, auditors conducting audits pursuant to the government standards must meet different proficiency standards, special continuing educational requirements, and broader criteria related to auditor independence. Plus, the government auditing standards provide for several reports of audit results that differ from those required by the AICPA's generally accepted auditing standards.

This part of the book describes these government auditing standards, several of which have little or no parallel in private sector auditing and require a performance of auditing that is beyond the generally accepted auditing standards criteria.

Chapter 3

Government Auditing Standards—General Standards

The government auditing standards apply to both financial audits and performance audits of governmental organizations, programs, activities and functions. By federal law, the government auditing standards have been extended to audits performed by almost all non-federal entities, government and non-government, that are recipients of federal financial assistance. Laws of several states and local government statutes have mandated compliance with these standards for audits of their governmental units. Additionally, several countries have adopted the U.S. government's auditing standards as the auditing criteria for their public sector activities. (The government auditing standards, as revised through 1999, are listed on *Exhibit 2-1*.)

The four general government auditing standards for conducting financial *and* performance audits are:

GOVERNMENT AUDITING STANDARDS

General Standards

1. The staff assigned to conduct the audit should collectively possess adequate professional proficiency for the tasks required.

2. In all matters relating to the audit work, the audit organization and the individual auditors, whether government or public, should be free from personal and external impairments to independence, should be organizationally independent, and should maintain an independent attitude and appearance.

3. Due professional care should be used in conducting the audit and in preparing related reports.

4. Each audit organization conducting audits in accordance with these standards should have an appropriate internal quality control system in place and undergo an external quality control review.

EXPANDED AUDITING STANDARDS

In 1973, the American Institute of Certified Public Accountants, in its publication titled *Auditing Standards Established by GAO— Their Meaning and Significance for CPAs*, cautioned the profession that the governmental auditing standards were different, going beyond the audit of only financial statements. The AICPA committee on relations with the federal government made several observations about the government auditing standards, stating at the time that:

> *"A simple comparison of the GAO Standards with the ten generally accepted auditing standards adopted by the membership of the AICPA and set forth in Section 150 of the Statement on Auditing Standards No. 1 does not disclose the impact of the GAO Standards on Auditing. Such a comparison shows a marked similarity, but the GAO Standards go further. The primary impact of the GAO Standards is in the way the scope of auditing is expanded beyond examinations leading to the expression of opinions on the fairness of financial presentation to include audits for compliance, efficiency, economy, and effectiveness.*
>
> *While the GAO Standards are intended to be identical to the profession's for financial audits, the Standards may also be concerned with efficiency and economy of operations, compliance with financial and non-financial laws and regulations and program effectiveness.*
>
> *Independent accountants must define carefully, in the engagement agreement, the scope of each engagement and the method of reporting."*

Over the years, the GAO's auditing standards have evolved, becoming more prescriptive in one sense, and broader in other ways. Nonetheless, these precautions are as appropriate today as when enunciated by GAO almost 30 years ago.

The AICPA continues to have an interest in the scope of the government auditing standards and their application since its generally accepted auditing standards have been incorporated by reference into the GAO generally accepted government auditing standards. The 1994 edition of the GAO auditing standards stated that:

> *"For financial statement audits, generally accepted government auditing standards incorporate the American Institute of Certified Public Accountants generally accepted*

auditing standards. As additional statements on auditing standards are issued by the AICPA, they will be adopted and incorporated into these standards unless GAO excludes them by formal announcement."

GAO has never excluded any AICPA auditing standard from the government auditing standards. Thus, the GAO standards of field work and reporting for *financial* audits incorporate the AICPA standards for field work and reporting. The GAO also prescribes additional supplemental field work and reporting standards needed to satisfy the unique needs of government audits.

When revised in 1994, GAO described the relationship of its standards to those of the AICPA, stating that the AICPA's auditing standards are applicable to audits conducted to express opinions on the fairness of financial statements (i.e., the financial position, statement of operations, and cash flows).

At that time GAO, also stated that the government auditing standards incorporated the AICPA's three generally accepted standards of field work and the four standards of reporting. While the general government auditing standards are similar to those of the AICPA, GAO makes no such reference to incorporating the general audit standards of the AICPA.

GOVERNMENT AUDITING STANDARDS

Application of Government Auditing Standards

The government auditing standards are to be applied to:

(1) Audits of government organizations, programs, activities, and functions, and

(2) Audits of government assistance received by contractors, nonprofit organizations and other nongovernment organizations.

By federal law, the application of the government auditing standards have been expanded to apply to almost any recipient of federal assistance.

Government auditing standards are to be applied by all auditors—governmental and nongovernmental, independent external and internal, elected and appointed, whether employees of government or contractors to governments and other organizations—when required by federal law, regulations, or rules, and contract or grant conditions. Adherence to the GAO standards is required by laws, statutes, and regulations of many state, and some local governmental units.

The GAO Standards are in two parts: (1) those relating to financial audits, and (2) those for performance audits. However, from their initial issuance, GAO never intended that adherence to both sets of standards was intended, feasible or desirable for every audit. There have been few audits performed, in or out of government, that have been sufficiently comprehensive in scope to require the application of both the financial audit and the performance audit standards.

Scope of Government Audits

The definitions of the scope of audits to which the government auditing standards relate have varied slightly over the years, but the 1994 revision of the government auditing standards still contain the following generic definitions for two types of audits: (1) financial audits and (2) performance audits.

Financial Audits

These audits are of two types: financial statement audits and financial related audits. These audits are defined in the government standards as follows:

Financial statement audits. The objective of these audits are to determine whether the financial statements of an audited entity present fairly the financial position, results of operations, and cash flows in accordance with generally accepted accounting principles or other bases of accounting as discussed in the auditing literature of the AICPA.

GAO has recognized three bodies as having the authority to set these generally acceptable accounting principles:

● Governmental Accounting Standards Board (to set accounting standards for state and local governmental units),

● Financial Accounting Standards Board (to set accounting standards for the private sector), and

● The Federal Accounting Standards Advisory Board (to set accounting standards for the federal government).

Financial related audits. The objectives of these audits include determining whether:

(1) Financial information is presented in accordance with established or stated criteria;

(2) The entity has adhered to specific financial compliance requirements; and

(3) The entity's internal control structure or specific areas of risk over financial reporting are suitably designed and implemented to achieve the control objectives.

Financial related audits may include any audit of less than the total entity. For example, the government auditing standards specifically include within the definition of financial related audits, portions of audits of entities and systems such as:

- *Segments of financial statements,* financial information (statements of revenues and expenses, cash receipts and disbursements, fixed assets); budget requests; and variances between estimated and actual financial performance.

- *Internal controls, over compliance with laws and regulations,* such as those related to bidding, accounting for and reporting on contracts and grants proposals, billings, termination claims, etc.

- *Internal controls, over financial reporting and/or safeguarding assets,* including controls using computer-based systems.

- *Compliance with laws and regulations* and allegations of fraud.

Government auditing standards recognize that in some instances other standards would be more appropriate. For example, for non-financial statement audits, it would be more appropriate to apply the AICPA's *Statement on Standards for Attestation Engagements* rather than its generally accepted auditing standards.

The attestation standards of the AICPA provide guidance for a variety of attest engagements where the CPA has been requested to provide assurances or representations on other than historical financial statements or in forms other than the traditional audit opinion. For this reason, the AICPA's attestation standards specifically omit references to audits of financial statements and the application of generally accepted accounting principles. Also, the attestation standards, particularly No. 1, do not apply to engagements whose objectives are to report in accordance with the government auditing standards, the Single Audit Act of 1984, and other engagements falling within the purview of the AICPA's standards for compliance auditing for governmental programs.

Performance Audits

Performance audits are the second group of audits covered in the government auditing standards. The GAO government auditing standards define a performance audit as:

> *" ... an objective and systematic examination of evidence for the purpose of providing an independent assessment of the performance of an existing or proposed government organization, program, or activity in order to provide useful information to improve public accountability and decision-making."*

As was the case with financial audits, the GAO's government auditing standards must be applied to performance audits of federal organizations, programs, activities, and functions. These audits include two types: (1) economy and efficiency audits and (2) program audits. Each is described more fully along with the related auditing standards in a later Chapter.

GENERAL AUDIT STANDARD FOR FINANCIAL AND PERFORMANCE AUDITS

The *general* government auditing standards apply to *both* financial and performance audits and relate to the (1) collective professional proficiency of audit staff, (2) individual and organizational audit independence, (3) the exercise of due care in conducting and reporting on the audit, and (4) adherence by the audit organization to specific internal and external quality controls.

The AICPA's general auditing standards have been included here for ease of reference and comparison. The GAO has *not* incorporated the AICPA's general auditing standards into the government's general auditing standards, but rather has specified altered or additional general auditing standards for financial statement and performance audits of public sector entities.

EXHIBIT 3-1

AICPA's General Auditing Standards

1. The audit is to be performed by a person or persons having adequate technical training and proficiency as an auditor.

2. In all matters relating to the assignment, an independence in mental attitude is to be maintained by the auditor or auditors.

3. Due professional care is to be exercised in the performance of the audit and the preparation of the report.

The AICPA utilizes only the three above standards for the financial statement audits of non-governmental entities. The government auditing standards impose the four general auditing standards highlighted earlier and described in detail in the following sections.

COLLECTIVE PROFESSIONAL PROFICIENCY

The first additional or supplemental general government auditing standard for financial and performance audits is:

1. The staff assigned to conduct the audit should collectively possess adequate professional proficiency for the tasks required.

Specific or different criteria or requirements apply to the understanding of professional proficiency in the context of government auditing standards. In particular, government auditing standards emphasizes subjects as: (1) collective competence, (2) special, unique continuing educational requirements, and (3) professional qualifications of practitioners.

Adequate Collective Professional Proficiency

The first government general auditing standard is concerned with the collective proficiency of both (1) the individual staff member and (2) to the audit team collectively. The essential issue is the fact that a governmental audit may require expertise beyond that possessed by even experienced auditors. The expertise required to complete a governmental audit may not be possessed by professionals skilled as accountants or auditors. If this is the case, the auditor has the responsibility for determining and obtaining the necessary collective professional expertise to complete the terms of the audit contract or engagement.

Note that this general standard is considerably different for generally accepted auditing standards. The general standard of the AICPA places emphasis on persons having adequate technical training and proficiency as an auditor. In its general standard, the AICPA recognizes that however capable a person may be in other fields, the person cannot meet the requirements of the generally accepted auditing standards without proper education and experience in the field of auditing.

For many audits of governmental entities—financial statement audits as well as financial related audits—the skills possessed by the most experienced auditor may be inadequate to meet the governmental audit standard. This is particularly true when the audit objective includes an assessment of compliance of a recipient of federal funds with the laws, regulations, rules and other guidance applicable to the receipt, accounting, control, use, and program accomplishment as well as financial reporting of performance or accomplishment. If these broader scope audits require backgrounds in accounting, statistics, law, engineering, or computer sciences, each individual member of the audit team need not possess all of these requisites. But, the audit organization must employ, hire, retain or otherwise avail itself of such competence to insure that the "collective" knowledge and skills are available to perform the audit.

Historically, the GAO and federal inspectors general have disclosed that public accountants have ignored these cautions for obtaining additional non-audit expertise, typically concentrating on only the financial and fiscal aspects of reporting and performance, which were aspects of an audit within the *proficiency* of an auditor. Significant parts of the contracted audit scope may not have been performed or possibly performed inadequately by the failure of the auditor to acquire or retain non-auditing skills and expertise. This could be true for those requirements that relate to compliance with governmental laws and regulations and the specific conditions and limitation appearing in the contract and grant agreements executed by the auditee with the sponsoring governmental agency.

Independent accountants have no legal obligation to perform government audit engagements, but once accepted, the AICPA believes that the accountant has the obligation to fully comply with the terms of the audit engagement contract, a large part of which is compliance with the government auditing standards. Under these conditions, compliance by the accountant with only generally accepted auditing standards is not sufficient performance if the scope of work requires compliance with governmental auditing standards.

Educational Education Requirements

General Standard No. 1 is referred to as the "qualifications" standard since to meet the standard the auditor of governments and others involved with these audits must maintain their professional proficiency through a program of continuing professional education and training.

GAO has determined that the practice of government auditing requires special expertise and training and, therefore, has imposed special continuing professional educational conditions upon these practitioners. This standard places responsibility on the audit organization to ensure that the audit is conducted by staff who *collectively* have the knowledge and skills necessary for the audit to be conducted. The knowledge and skills criteria apply to the audit organization or team as a whole and not to each individual auditor. The related AICPA's general auditing standard requires proficiency as an auditor; GAO auditing standard clearly establishes that proficiency as an individual auditor may not be adequate for the "tasks required."

To meet this requirement for continuing professional education, auditors responsible for planning, directing, conducting, or reporting on government audits should complete, every 2 years, at least 80 hours of continuing professional education. At least 20 hours should be completed in any one year of the 2 year period.

In addition, auditors responsible for planning, directing, conducting *substantial portions* of the field work, or reporting on government audits should complete at least 24 of the 80 hours of continuing professional education in subjects *directly related* to the government environment and to government auditing. If the audited entity operates in a specific or unique environment, auditors should receive training that is related to that environment.

While GAO did not formalize an earlier working definition of **substantial portion**, the guideline is still appropriate to ensure compliance with government auditing standards. That guidance suggested that *substantial* would include personnel who incurred 20 percent or more of the total hours for a particular audit or spent more than 20 percent of their work year on audits subject to the "yellow book" audit requirements. [1]

Continuing professional education ***directly related*** requires auditors to obtain the 24 hours of continuing professional education in subjects and topics directly related (1) to the government environment and (2) to government auditing, or (3) the specific or unique environment in which the audited entity operates.

"Directly Related Subjects." [2]

Subjects and topics considered to be directly **related to the government environment** could include government accounting principles; government budgeting, procurement, and contracting; legislative policies and procedures; effects of current economic conditions on governments, relevant laws, and regulations; and government program and service performance measurement and reporting.

Other subjects and topics considered to be ***directly related to government auditing*** include: government auditing standards; AICPA's SAS (since they are incorporated in the government standards); other special government audit requirements as those related to Single Audits or the Chief Finance Officers Act.

Additional subjects and topics considered to be ***directly related to specific or unique environment*** may include relevant accounting principles; economic, operating or regulatory developments in the specialized area in which the auditee operates; and relevant laws and regulations.

When accepting an audit engagement, auditors must determine if the audit is to be conducted in accordance with the government auditing standards as a result of the auditee having either accepted federal financial assistance or if the auditee has agreed to submit to audits that meet the government auditing standards. If so, these special or additional continuing education requirements are the minimum proficiency requirements that professionals must meet if assigned to audits conducted in accordance with government auditing standards.

Government auditing standards may not automatically apply to a particular industry. Rather the need to comply with the government

---

[1] U.S. General Accounting Office, "Interpretations of Continuing Education and Training Requirements, Washington, D.C., April 1991.

[2] *Id.*

auditing standards could be tied to specific contract or grant terms and conditions under which an auditee may have accepted federal financial assistance. At this time, definition of federal financial assistance does not include production contracts for design and manufacture of aircraft in the case of a defense contractor or federal deposit insurance in the case of a bank.

Non-qualifying Activities

While extremely beneficial to the auditor of government and contributing significantly to the auditor's expertise, there are many activities that do not meet the educational criteria imposed by the government auditing standards. Several examples of non-qualifying professional activities and involvement, highlighted in past years by GAO, would include:

- Service on professional committees of the AICPA or state CPA societies or the national or state boards of accountancy.

- Drafting auditing standards, even governmental, as a member of an AICPA task force.

- Membership and active involvement as a member of the federal government's Advisory Council for Governmental Accounting.

- Authorship of articles and books, if claimed educational credits exceed limits imposed by state boards of accountancy. (For example, limits might preclude claiming more than 30 hours for any type of authorship within a 3-year period.)

- Teaching, including subjects of accounting, auditing, governmental accounting, governmental auditing, if claimed educational credits exceed limits imposed by state boards of accountancy.

- Delivering of speeches and technical lectures to professionals involved in public sector audits, if claimed educational credits exceed limits imposed by state boards of accountancy.

- Testifying before committees of Congress and other legislative bodies considering legal and statutory issues relating to audits of public sector entities.

Professional Qualifications

To ensure that government audits are conducted by auditors who are competent and possess the necessary professional training and knowledge, GAO determined that accountants should possess other necessary qualifications.

Thus, to meet the general government audit Standard No. 1, a public accountant engaged to conduct audits of government pursuant to these standards must be proficient in the accounting principles and standards and in governmental auditing, *plus* must be:

(a) A licensed certified public accountant or person working for a licensed certified public accounting firm, or

(b) A public accountant licensed on or before December 31, 1970, or a person working for a public accounting firm licensed on or before December 31, 1970.

This standard requires accountants and accounting firms to meet the above licensing requirements and must comply with the provisions of the public accountancy laws and rules for the jurisdiction(s) where the audit is being conducted *and* the jurisdiction(s) in which the accountants and their firm are licensed. [3]

For example, if an independent accountant who is a resident in Washington, D. C., under a contract issued by the U.S. Department of Labor, conducts audits of grantees located in several states pursuant to the government auditing standards, the independent accountant must comply with the public accountancy laws and rules of the jurisdictions where the work is performed, as well as the accountancy laws of the District of Columbia.

This requirement has been challenged by some accountants over the years as being too restrictive and costly, but GAO has repeatedly reviewed and reiterated its position on this subject and restated that the limitation apply to all audits conducted pursuant to government auditing standards performed at all levels of government.

In a separate decision, the Comptroller General concluded that governmental entities provide some of the most diverse and challenging work in accounting and auditing. Accordingly, governments need the best audit skills obtainable. GAO concluded that authorizing auditors without the skills of rendering opinions on financial statements or conducting other types of governmental audits would not provide the public with the protection it needs.

INDEPENDENCE

The second additional or supplemental general government auditing standard for financial and performance audits is:

2. In all matters relating to the audit work, the audit organization and the individual auditors, whether government or public, should be free from personal and external impairments to independence, should be organizationally independent, and should maintain an independent attitude and appearance.

To be recognized as independent, auditors must be free of any obligation or interest in the audited organization.

---

[3] Letter (B-148144, May 28, 1975) by the Comptroller General to Senator Abraham A. Ribicoff and letter (B-148144, June 30, 1976) from the Comptroller General to the heads of all federal agencies, Washington, D. C.

To comply with this standard, *government* auditors, including their hired consultants and internal experts and specialists, must consider the three cited classes of impairments to their independence: (1) personal, (2) external and (3) organizational. Where an auditor's independence is impaired, the auditor should decline to perform the audit. Where declination is not possible, the impairment should be reported in the scope section of the audit report. Auditors employed by the audited entity must reflect that fact prominently in the audit report.

Non-governmental auditors, such as CPAs, must also consider personal and external impairments to independence that could affect their ability to do an impartial audit and report. Public accountants should follow (1) the AICPA code of ethics, (2) the code of professional conduct of the state board with jurisdiction over the accountant and the accounting firm, and (3) comply with the independence criteria in the government auditing standards.

Personal Impairments

The AICPA, in its Codification, states that independence requires the auditor to also be without bias with respect to the auditee, since the auditor would otherwise lack impartiality necessary for acceptance of any audit findings, however excellent the auditor's technical proficiency. In public accounting, apparent independence has been interpreted as being free of familial, organization, and financial conflicts of interest. For purposes of governmental audits, public accountants will be viewed as independent if they are independent under the AICPA's Code of Professional Conduct. The AICPA also points out that independence does not imply the attitude of a prosecutor, but rather a judicial impartiality that recognizes an obligation for fairness to management, owners, creditors and others who may rely upon the auditor's report.

This government standard requires that auditors consider not only whether they are independent and their attitudes and beliefs permit them to be independent, but also whether the circumstances of the audit might lead others to question their independence. Thus, the auditor must be independent in fact as well as appearance.

If auditors are employed by the governments that they audit, the issue of real as well as apparent conflicts requires impartial scrutiny. Independence, in fact and appearance, is necessary to permit the auditor's opinions, conclusions, judgments and recommendations to be impartial and to be viewed as impartial by knowledgeable third parties. Real and apparent independence is necessary to ensure that the work of the auditor is not later compromised or viewed as less than impartial.

GAO, in its government auditing standard, states that personal impairments to independence may include but are not limited to the following examples:

- Official, professional, personal, or financial relationships that might cause an auditor to limit the extent of inquiry, limit disclosure, or weaken or slant audit findings in any way.

- Preconceived ideas toward individuals, groups, organizations, or objectives of a particular program that could bias the audit.

- Previous responsibility for decision-making or managing an entity that would affect current operations of the entity or program being audited.

- Biases, including those induced by political or social convictions, that result from employment in, or loyalty to, a particular group, organization, or level of government.

- Subsequent performance of an audit by the same individual who, for example, had previously approved invoices, payrolls, claims, and other proposed payments of the entity or program being audited.

- Concurrent or subsequent performance of an audit by the same individual who maintained the official accounting records.

- Financial interest that is direct, or is substantial though indirect, in the audited entity or program.

Examples relating to personal impairments to auditor's independence were provided by GAO in its Exposure Draft of the 1994 government auditing standards and included:

- An audit organization that audits the effectiveness of internal controls after having done consulting services involving the design and implementation of those controls should have policies in place to reasonably ensure the independence of its auditors. It should also ensure that the audited entity has assumed full responsibility for activities affected by the consulting work.

- When auditing state and local governments, public accountants must be familiar with the AICPA professional ethics interpretation that establishes specific rules restricting financial relationships that impair the public accountant's independence. The AICPA's Ethics Interpretation 101-10 has several requirements related to independence with respect to governmental units, including:

1. The auditor issuing an audit report on the combined financial statements of a governmental entity must be independent of the oversight entity as well as each of the component units included in the combined report.

2. The auditor for a component unit that is material to the governmental entity must be independent of the oversight entity and each of the other component units.

3. Auditors of a nonmaterial component unit must be independent of that component unit. However, the AICPA considers all component units included in a governmental entity's financial statements to be material unless the auditor can demonstrate otherwise.

• Auditors who are required by law to exercise responsibilities should establish organizational and other policies to reasonably ensure the independence of the audit function.

• In instances where the audit organization acts as the main processor for transactions initiated by the audited entity, the audit organizations must establish policies to reasonably ensure the independence of its auditors and to ensure that the audited entity has acknowledged and has assumed full responsibility for the processed transactions and for the financial records and statements.

External Impairments

For auditors employed by governments or non-government audit organizations, GAO noted several examples of external impairments to independence in its auditing standards, including:

• External interference or influences that improperly or imprudently limits or modifies the scope of an audit.

• External interference with the selection of application of audit procedures or in the selection of transactions to be examined.

• Unreasonable restrictions on the time allowed to complete an audit.

• Interference external to the audit origination in the assignment, appointment, and promotion of audit personnel.

• Restrictions on funds or other resources provided to the audit organization that would adversely affect the audit organization's ability to carry out its responsibilities.

• Authority to overrule or to influence the auditor's judgment as to the appropriate content of an audit report.

• Influences that jeopardize the auditor's continued employment for reasons other than competency or the need for audit services.

Organizational Impairments

In the case of *governmental internal auditors*, their independence can be affected by their place in the governmental structure to which assigned and by whether they are auditing internally or auditing entities external to their organization. Organizational independence is possible, as described in the GAO Standards, by having the audit organization report and be accountable to the head or deputy of the governmental entity and organizationally be located outside of staff or line management of the unit under audit.

Governmental auditors would be free of organizational impairments to their independence if:

● The audited entity is a level of government other than the assigned entity; or

● The audited entity is a different branch within that level of government to which the auditors are assigned; or

● The head of the audit organization is elected by the citizens, or elected or appointed by a legislative body that the audit organization reports to; or

● The head of the audit organization is appointed by the chief executive but is confirmed by, reports to, and is accountable to a legislative body of the level to which they are assigned.

Early in the application of government auditing standards, one federal agency, the Office of Revenue Sharing, had issued criteria relating to independence of auditors employed by governments that the AICPA, in 1978, said were sufficiently explicit for achieving independence in fact and appearance. The ORS guidance considered two groups of governmental auditors to be independent:

(1) *State auditors* when (a) auditing local governments or (b) auditing state accounts if the auditor was elected or appointed by and reporting to the state legislature or a committee thereof, or appointed by the governor and confirmed by and reporting to the state legislature.

(2) *Local government auditors* when auditing their government's accounts if the auditor is (a) elected by the citizens of the local government or (b) elected or appointed by and reporting to the governing body of the local government or a committee thereof, or appointed by the chief executive officer and confirmed by and reporting to the governing body.

As noted earlier in this section, where an auditor's independence is impaired, the auditor should decline to perform the audit or where declination is not possible, the impairment should be clearly reported in the scope section of the audit report. Auditors employed by the audited entity must reflect their lack of independence prominently in the audit report.

DUE PROFESSIONAL CARE

The third additional or supplemental general government auditing standard for financial and performance audits is:

3. Due professional care should be used in conducting the audit and in preparing related reports.

This "due professional care" standard extends to the use of sound judgment in (1) establishing the scope of the audit, (2) selecting the audit methodology, and (3) choosing audit tests and procedures. Additionally, the exercise of "due professional care" requires that all levels of supervision critically review the audit work performed and the judgments of those participating in the audit.

The 1988 edition of government auditing standards were more explicit than the 1994 edition. In 1988, GAO stated that materiality and/or significance must be considered in planning the audit, selecting the methodology, and designing the audit tests and procedures. Factors, in addition to monetary value, have to be considered in determining materiality or significance, including:

● Amounts of revenues and expenditures;

● Newness of the activity or changes in its conditions;

● Adequacy of both accounting internal controls and controls for ensuring compliance with laws and regulations;

● Results of prior audits;

● Level and extent of review or other form of independent oversight;

● Management's adherence to applicable laws and regulations;

● Audit report user's expectations;

● Public perceptions and political sensitivity of the areas under audit; and

● Audit requirements.

The AICPA, in its Risk Alerts (an overview of current business developments that may affect audits of governments) has highlighted that the politically sensitive environment with respect to audits of governments and the potential for publicized claims of mismanagement, defalcation, or non-compliance with laws and regulations is much greater than in other audit environments. [4] There is often legislation on financial accountability and controls because of the increased public focus on fiscal accountability. The AICPA pointed out several examples that such laws and regulations often include:

---

[4] *Audit Risk Alert—State and Local Governmental Developments*—1994, AICPA, New York, NY.

● Financial management conduct and integrity, which covers topics such as internal controls, conflicts of interest, and general government ethics.

● Restrictions, particularly where federal funding is in place, on political activities and lobbying.

● Restrictions on out-of-state travel and use of publicly owned property for personal travel.

● Restrictions on acceptance of gifts, meals, and entertainment.

● Additional guidelines on investment practices and cash management, including banking relationships.

● Policies governing the recovery of indirect costs.

● Balanced-budget proposals, including restrictions on amendments to budgets.

● Requirements for additional documentation of the bidding process related to the purchase of goods or services.

● Restrictions on political contributions from investment bankers and others.

● Restrictions on negotiated bond sales.

● Potential new regulations, disclosures, and filing requirements for municipal security offerings.

This "due care" standard is different from the emphasis of the AICPA's. The AICPA's standard of "due care" imposes a responsibility on each person within an independent audit organization to observe and comply with the audit standards of field work and reporting. In this connection, the AICPA has for years quoted *Cooley on Torts* to the audit profession as defining "due care:"

> *"Every man who offers his services to another and is employed assumes the duty to exercise in the employment such skill as he possesses with reasonable care and diligence. ... But no man, whether skilled or unskilled, undertakes that the task he assumes shall be performed successfully, and without fault or error; he undertakes for good faith and integrity, but not for infallibility, and he is liable to his employer for negligence, bad faith, or dishonesty, but not for losses consequent upon pure errors of judgment."*

The "due care" standard extends to establishing the scope, selecting the audit methodology, designing the testing and other audit procedures, the execution of the audit, and the ultimate reporting on the results of the audit. But, the GAO auditing standards concur with the AICPA and notes that the "due care" standard does not imply unlimited responsibility nor does "due care" imply infallibility on the part of the auditor or the audit organization.

GAO recognizes, in its auditing standards, that situations could occur in which a governmental employee, employed as an auditor by the governmental auditee, is not able to follow an applicable standard. Unlike an independent accountant, the governmental employee may not be able to withdraw from the audit. In these situations, GAO requires that the auditor disclose the fact that an applicable standard was not followed in the scope section of the report, the reasons therefore, and the known effect of not following the standard had on the audit.

GAO, in its Exposure Draft to the 1994 auditing standards revision suggested as an additional "due care" requirement that there be a process to track and report the status of management's actions on the significant or material audit findings and recommendation of prior audits. This requirement did not survive in the final version as a 1994 formal auditing standard. But, other requirements relating to audits of federal programs make this a mandatory requirement for a governmental audit function.

QUALITY CONTROL

The fourth additional or supplemental general government auditing standard for financial and performance audits is:

4. Each audit organization conducting audits in accordance with these standards should have an appropriate internal quality control system in place and undergo an external quality control review.

By this standard, all audit organizations—government and nongovernment—must have two quality control systems in place: (1) an internal quality control system and (2) undergo, periodically, an external quality control review.

Internal Quality System

The internal quality control system must provide reasonable assurance that (1) applicable auditing *standards* have been adopted and are being followed (2) adequate audit *policies and procedures* have been established, and (3) that the policies and procedures are being followed. In 1979, the AICPA formally required CPA firms to have an installed system of quality control, including written quality control policies and procedures and a system for monitoring auditing practices to ensure adherence to the written requirements. The nature, formality, extent, and implementation practices related to an auditing organization's internal control system will vary depending on a number of factors, such as:

(1) organization's size;

(2) operating autonomy allowed to audit professionals;

(3) the number of offices;

(4) organization structure;

(5) the nature of the audits performed; and

(6) whether the audit organization is employed by a governmental unit or an independent accountant.

Essential to a sound internal quality control system is an audit organization and all of its senior management dedicated to the delivery of quality, professional audit services. Member firms of the AICPA's Division of CPA Firms (i.e., CPA firms with clients subject to SEC oversight) have also to submit to external peer reviews of the firm's accounting and audit practice, at a minimum, every 3 years. Since the 1988 edition, the government auditing standards have required similar controls relating to audits performed pursuant to government auditing standards.

External Quality System

The external quality control system part of this standard requires that there be an external quality control review made at least once every three years and the audit organization should examine and confirm that the internal quality control system is being followed. To comply with this government audit requirement, GAO requires that the external quality control review meet the following requirements:

a. Reviewers should be qualified and have current knowledge of the type of work to be reviewed and the applicable auditing standards. The individual reviewers should have a thorough knowledge of the government environment and government auditing relative to the work being reviewed.

b. Reviewers should be independent of the audit organization being reviewed, its staff, and its auditees whose audits are selected for review. An audit organization is not permitted to review the organization that conducted its most recent external quality control review. Governmental audit organizations should have reviews performed by teams that are not part of their government. Independent accounting firms should have these reviews performed by other accounting firms.

c. Reviewers should use sound professional judgment in conducting and reporting the results of the external quality control review.

d. Reviewers should use one of the following approaches to selecting audits for review: (1) select audits that provide a reasonable cross section of the audits conducted in accordance with these standards or (2) select audits that provide a reasonable cross section of the organization's audits, including one or more audits conducted in accordance with these standards.

e. This review should include a review of the audit reports, working papers, and other necessary documents (e.g., correspondence and continuing education documentation) as well as interviews with the reviewed organization's professional staff.

f. A written report should be prepared communicating the results of the external quality control review.

To comply with the 1994 edition of the government auditing standards, *nongovernment* audit organizations are also required to provide quality control reports containing significant deficiencies to those officials authorizing or arranging for the audit before an audit is commenced under the GAO standards.

GAO believes that information about deficient audit quality controls would be relevant to decisions about procuring audit services. It added this new requirement to its government audit standards for audits conducted under the revised standards.

The quality controls required of auditors conducting government audits are discussed in greater detail in a later chapter. Other reviews related to audit quality made by federal inspectors generals or their representatives, such as desk reviews and on-site quality control reviews will also be discussed.

Chapter 4

Government Auditing Standards—Field Standards

The government auditing standards for audit field work represent the audit guidance related to the actual performance of governmental financial audits.

For financial statement and financial related audits, the government auditing standards incorporate by reference, these three generally accepted audit field work standards of the AICPA:

EXHIBIT 4-1

AICPA's Standards of Field Work

1. The work is to be adequately planned and assistants, if any, are to be properly supervised.

2. A sufficient understanding of the internal control structure is to be obtained to plan the audit and to determine the nature, timing, and extent of tests to be performed.

3. Sufficient competent evidential matter is to be obtained through inspection, observation, inquiries, and confirmations to afford a reasonable basis for an opinion regarding the financial statements under audit.

The government auditing field work standards for conducting financial audits incorporate all of these AICPA standards and related SAS's for audit field work. However, GAO prescribes five additional or supplemental audit field work standards.[1] The government supplemen-

---

[1] In 1999, the General Accounting Office issued Amendment Nos. 1 and 2 to the 1994 government auditing standards.

tal or additional auditing standards, as revised through 1999, are listed in *Exhibit 2-2*.

Subjects considered by the AICPA within the areas of its field work standards for audits that apply equally to audits of governmentally-financed activities include: (1) auditors appointment, (2) planning and supervision, (3) required substantive audit tests, (4) the control structure, (5) gathering of evidential matter, (6) necessity for adequate working papers, (7) auditee and legal representations, and (8) irregular and illegal acts by auditee personnel, among others.

The AICPA has also issued Statements on Auditing Standards that interpret the above three field work standards. As noted, the government auditing standards incorporate, by reference, guidance on several subjects. Thus, all of the field work guidance appearing in the AICPA's Codification of Statements on Auditing Standards apply equally to financial audits made pursuant to government auditing standards.

The government auditing standards now include five additional or supplemental field work audit standards. These supplemental government auditing standards relate to: (1) audit follow-up, (2) noncompliance other than illegal acts, (3) assessing and documenting internal control risks, (4) working papers, and (5) field work standards that apply to all financial audits—audits of financial statements and financial-related audits—that require the auditor to express an opinion on financial presentations.

The five supplemental or additional government field work auditing standards, as revised through 1999, are as follows in *Exhibit 4-2*:

EXHIBIT 4-2

Government Auditing Standards

Field Audit Work Standards

1. Auditors should communicate information to the auditee, the individuals contracting for or requesting the audit services, and the audit committee regarding the nature and extent of planned testing and reporting on compliance with laws and regulations and internal control over financial reporting. [Government Auditing Standards, 1994 revision, Amendment No. 2, July 1999.]

2. Auditors should follow up on known material findings and recommendations from previous audits.

3. Auditors should design the audit to provide reasonable assurance of detecting material misstatements resulting from noncompliance with provisions of contracts or grant agreements that have a direct and material effect on the determination of financial statement amounts. If

specific information comes to the auditor's attention that provides evidence concerning the existence of possible noncompliance that could have a material indirect effect on the financial statement, auditors should apply audit procedures specifically directed to ascertaining whether that noncompliance has occurred.

4. In planning the audit, auditors should document in the working papers: (1) the basis for assessing control risk at the maximum level for assertions related to material account balances, transaction classes, and disclosure components of financial statements when such assertions are significantly dependent upon computerized information systems, and (2) consideration that the planned audit procedures are designed to achieve audit objectives and to reduce audit risk to an acceptable level. [Government Auditing Standards, 1994 revision, Amendment No. 1, May 1999.]

5. Working papers should contain sufficient information to enable an experienced auditor having no previous connection with the audit to ascertain from them the evidence that supports the auditors' significant conclusions and judgments.

The following sections provide an overview of these four supplemental field work audit standards.

AUDITOR COMMUNICATION

The first, and newest, additional supplemental government auditing field work standard for financial statement audits is:

1. Auditors should communicate information to the auditee, the individuals contracting for or requesting the audit services, and the audit committee regarding the nature and extent of planned testing and reporting on compliance with laws and regulations and internal control over financial reporting.

This standard is a 1999 amendment, No. 2, to the 1994 edition of the government auditing standards. The objective of this standard is to require that auditors establish a clear understanding about the audit services to be provided with the auditee and, where one exists, the audit committee.

Specifically, the auditor must communicate the nature and extent of testing and reporting that will be made of compliance with laws and regulations and of internal controls over financial reporting. The purpose of this communication is to reduce the risk that the needs or expectations of involved parties may be misinterpreted. In instances where auditors are performing the audit under a contract for a party other than the auditee, this standard requires the auditor to communicate with those who contracted for the audit or legislative officials or staff. This communication would also be required for audits made pursuant to a law or regulation. In this event, the communication would be to legislative members or staff who have oversight of the auditee.

This communication must include: (1) the nature of any additional testing of compliance and controls required by laws and regulations, and (2) whether the auditor will provide opinions on compliance and internal controls over financial reporting. While government standards leave the form and content to the judgment of the performing auditor, the standards state that written communication is preferred.

Generally, tests of compliance and internal controls in a financial statement audit do not provide a basis for opining on compliance or controls. Should opinions be required of the auditor or to meet specific user needs, these tests have to be supplemented or expanded upon. Even then, the additional tests may not meet the needs of report users, in which case supplemental or agreed-upon procedures or a special examination, resulting in an audit opinion, may be indicated.

FOLLOW UP ON PRIOR AUDITS

The second additional supplemental government auditing field work standard for financial statement audits is:

2. Auditors should follow up on known material findings and recommendations from previous audits.

This auditing standard is in addition to the AICPA's that require all audit work to (1) be properly planned and (2) all assistants to be properly supervised.

By this standard, an auditor of governments must follow-up on past audit issues. The purpose of this requirement is to have the current auditor determine and report whether the auditee has taken timely and appropriate correction actions resulting from earlier audits. Uncorrected material findings and recommendations from prior audits that affect the financial statement audit must be reported.

Compliance with this standard precludes the current auditor from ignoring problems of the past and possibly overlooking areas, subjects, accounts, policies or procedures, and practices that might continue to place government resources and assets at risk.

GAO emphasizes the benefit from audit work is not in the findings reported or the recommendations made, but in their effective resolution. An important measure of an audit organization's effectiveness is the types of issues it tackles and the changes/improvements the auditor is able to effect.

DESIGN AUDIT TO DETECT NONCOMPLIANCE

The third additional supplemental government auditing field work standard for financial statement audits is:

3. Auditors should design the audit to provide reasonable assurance of detecting material misstatements resulting from noncompliance with provisions of contracts or grant agreements that have a direct and material effect on the determination of financial statement amounts. If specific information comes to the auditor's attention that provides evidence concerning the existence of possible noncompliance that could have a material indirect effect on the financial statement, auditors should apply audit procedures specifically directed to ascertaining whether that noncompliance has occurred.

Auditing for Material Non-Compliance

Laws and Regulations

Governmental and public nonprofit entities are established by laws, are managed to comply with laws, and are subject to many more legal constraints than private sector organizations. For this reason, both the standards and SASs of the AICPA impose a greater burden on those performing these financial statement audits to design audits to provide reasonable assurance of detecting irregularities having a direct and material effect on the financial statements. Plus, the AICPA's standards require audits be designed to provide reasonable assurance of detecting material misstatements resulting from direct and indirect illegal acts.

When engaged to perform an audit in accordance with government auditing standards, an auditor has responsibilities beyond those required by generally accepted auditing standards. The government auditing standards also require that auditors report on tests made for assessing compliance with laws and regulations and terms and conditions as specified in a contract or grant governing the audit. This additional or supplemental standard requires that auditors should perform:

(1) Audit procedures to obtain knowledge about the design of internal controls structure policies and procedures to ensure compliance with laws, regulations, and any material legal provisions that could have a direct and material effect on the determination of financial statement amounts; and

(2) Conduct audit tests to determine whether these controls, policies, and procedures have been placed in operation and are, in fact, being adhered to by auditee personnel.

The AICPA's SAS No. 68 (titled "Compliance Auditing Applicable to Governmental Entities and Other Recipients of Governmental Financial Assistance) and its superseding SAS, directed primarily to entities receiving federal financial assistance, requires auditors to test for compliance with laws and regulations that could have a direct and material effect on financial statement amounts. These legal or regulatory criteria that must be tested relate to *general* and *specific* compliance requirements.

• *Examples of general* compliance requirements are federal policy, national in application, that apply to all federal assistance programs. The OMB has outlined the general requirements that must be tested and suggested audit procedures in its *Compliance Supplement* (See Chapter 10 for a detailed discussion.).

• *Examples of specific* compliance requirements are laws and regulations that apply to the specific federal assistance program undergoing audit. The specific compliance requirements include: (a) types of service allowed or unallowed, (b) eligibility of those receiving federal assistance under the program, (c) matching or level of effort or earmarking requirements, (d) special reporting requirements, and (e) special tests and provisions. The OMB has defined the specific compliance requirements for many federal programs that must be tested and suggested audit procedures in its *Compliance Supplement* (See Chapter 10 for a detailed discussion.).

By the 1994 revision, the government auditor or independent CPA who conducts an audit of financial statements assumes the responsibility to audit pursuant to government auditing standards, which mandates that tests be made for compliance with specific laws and regulations and terms and conditions of contracts and grants, as well. Under the Single Audit concept, applied to governmental and nonprofit entities, auditors must test every "major" federal program for compliance with laws and regulations that affect that specific program. Federal regulations define what constitutes a "major" federal assistance program.

Irregularities and Illegal Acts

This supplemental audit standard also directs the auditor's attention to some issues that require more auditing emphasis than might be given to the same matters in a corporate-type financial statement audit being conducted in accordance with generally accepted auditing standards.

• *Noncompliance*—a failure to follow requirements or a violation of prohibitions continued in laws, regulations, contracts, grants, or agency policies and procedures.

Field Standards

● ***Illegal acts***—a type of noncompliance; specifically an illegal act is a violation of a law or regulation.

● ***Fraud***—obtaining something of value unlawfully, through willful misrepresentation. Fraud is a type of illegal act.

The AICPA's definitions of related-type transactions are:

● ***Errors***—unintentional misstatements or omissions in financial statements involving mistakes in gathering or processing accounting data; incorrect accounting estimates arising from oversight or misinterpretation of facts; and mistakes in applying accounting principles.

● ***Irregular Acts***—intentional misstatements or omissions in financial statements, including fraudulent financial reporting undertaken to render misleading financial statements and often involving manipulation, falsification or alteration of accounting records; misrepresentation or intentional omission of events and transactions; intentional misapplication of accounting principles.

Auditors are not expected to be fraud investigators or law enforcement officials. Nor, are auditors expected to expand the audit to conduct such detailed examinations. But, auditors must be aware of the characteristics and types of vulnerabilities and possible illegal acts associated with the areas under audit and recognize indications that such acts might have been committed.

Due care is required by auditors when any of the above conditions are indicated to preclude jeopardizing or interfering with any future investigation or legal proceeding. The AICPA, GAO, and even the Office of Management and Budget have provided guidance to auditors on the nature of reporting to be made if an indication of fraud, abuse, irregular or illegal acts are uncovered. Further, requirements of specific audit engagements might override both generally accepted auditing standards and the government auditing standards.

Unfortunately, this guidance is neither identical nor consistent. As a result, if the auditor is confronted with an irregularity or illegal act, the profession and government does not have comforting directions, for example:

● The AICPA, in its SAS No. 53, requires that the auditor, after determining that an audit difference is or may be an irregularity, discuss the matter with the appropriate level of management and suggests that the auditor apply additional audit procedures if necessary to obtain an understanding of the nature of the facts.

● The GAO, in various sections of the government auditing standards, directs the auditor to report irregularities and illegal acts that have occurred or are likely to occur. This reporting should include information such as prevalence, instances identified, cases examined, dollar value involved and should be made directly to parties outside the auditee when required by law or regulation. When the auditee does not make a timely report, GAO requires the auditor to make these external reports.

While a governmental auditor may have no difficulty extending auditing procedures as indicated by the AICPA and GAO, such advice may not always be appropriate for the independent accountant. The unilateral expansion of audit steps by an auditor could unknowingly damage a later judicial action. The same government auditing standards that direct the auditor to expand the audit also cautions the auditor about reporting on any matter that will compromise investigative or legal proceedings.

On the other hand, OMB, in past years, had stated that auditors should not routinely extend audit steps and procedures if there is an indication of errors, irregularities, or illegal acts. OMB specifically addressed the extent of authority of an auditor to unilaterally expand the scope of audit to include additional procedures in the event of irregularities or fraud. In the *Federal Register*, OMB stated that the auditor has no authority to unilaterally expand the scope of a single audit to include an audit of irregularities, or illegal acts. Consistent with the OMB position, the AICPA has informed auditors retained to make a single audit of governments that it is in their best interest to insist that the basic audit contract and any extensions be in writing.

A refusal of a government to amend the audit contract to provide mutually acceptable terms (performance and fee-wise) for the expanded work should be treated as a restriction on the scope of the audit, possibly affecting the nature of the audit opinion that might be rendered by the auditor.

The unilateral action to expand the audit scope upon disclosure of an indication or actual irregularities or fraud could cause the auditor to breach a contract scope for a financial statement audit, if expanded work was undertaken without permission of the entity arranging for the audit. There is the likelihood that the auditor could be informed that the extended procedures were not authorized and therefore the work related to the extended procedures will not be paid. More importantly, there is the risk that the expanded procedures, without guidance from the auditee or entity arranging for the audit, could jeopardize subsequent legal action or do irreparable harm to implicated parties.

Most government audit contracts are for a fixed scope, i.e., conduct a financial statement audit pursuant to generally accepted government auditing standards; conduct a single audit; conduct an audit of cost incurred under a contract, etc.—for a fixed fee. Thus the unilateral expansion of a financial audit to include additional procedures to make a fraud audit will almost invariably be outside the scope of a financial audit. The contracting government would be within its rights to not pay the auditor for the additional audit work, regardless of the value of the litigation to the legal case.

The government audit standards for **performance** audits probably provides safer guidance and an important caveat for an auditor who discloses material irregularities or illegal acts. The government auditing standards for performance audits state:

"When auditors conclude that this type of illegal act has occurred, or is likely to have occurred, they should ask those authorities and/or legal counsel if reporting certain information about the illegal act would compromise investigative or legal proceedings. Auditors should limit their reporting to matters that would not compromise those proceedings, such as information that is already a part of the public record."

In 1988, GAO in Section 7.42 of that revision of its government auditing standards stated:

"Auditors generally should not release information or reports containing information on potential illegal acts ... without consulting appropriate legal counsel, since this could interfere with legal processes or subject the implicated individuals to undue publicity, or might subject the auditor to potential legal action [emphasis by author]"

This warning or caveat to independent auditors is absent from the 1994 edition of the government standards. But, the increased litigious environment in which auditors must practice continues to give that warning considerable relevance.

Given the somewhat differing guidance from the AICPA, GAO, and OMB with respect to the expansion of an audit scope or the manner of reporting disclosed irregularities and indications of fraudulent conditions, the following procedures might be beneficially used by an independent auditor:

● Bring the observed condition or indicated circumstances to the attention of the appropriate level of management within the entity arranging for the audit and inform management of other parties at interest who should be notified of the conditions.

● Request guidance from or recommend guidance to the entity arranging for the audit on (1) how the audit should proceed, including approval of all desired extended audit procedures that might be necessary, and (2) whether the remainder of the audit should or can be continued.

- Obtain written waivers, changes, or modifications to the audit engagement contract to (1) change the engagement scope to permit conduct of the suggested extended procedures and (2) provide for alternative fee and expenses to compensate for changes from the original scope of work or level of effort that are due to the disclosures.

- Document all of the above actions and separately reflect the evidence obtained to support the extended procedures in the audit working papers.

- Before releasing any information or issuing any report containing information about the condition or a statement that pertinent information is omitted from the report, the auditor should consult with knowledgeable legal counsel.

Reporting on Fraud and Illegalities

OMB, in Circular A-133, requires that the auditor shall report, as an audit finding known or likely questioned costs greater than $10,000 specifically identified by the auditor. This reporting must include known fraud affecting federal awards.

But, while the government auditing standards (§ 5.18) require that auditors report relevant information, i.e., " ... the auditor need not report information about an irregularity or illegal act that is clearly inconsequential." Also, in this connection, GAO provides the following caution:

> "Whether a particular act is, in fact, illegal may have to await final determination by a court of law. Thus, when auditors disclose matters that have led them to conclude that an illegal act is likely to have occurred, they should take care not to imply that they have made a determination of illegality."

Non-Compliance Other than Illegal

In addition to planning to detect instances of irregular and illegal activities, the 1994 edition of the government auditing standards now imposes additional requirements related to noncompliance with terms and conditions that have a direct and material effect on government contracts and grants, particularly the major federal assistance programs. Thus, auditors by the government auditing standards, now must design the audit to provide reasonable assurance of detecting such instances of material misstatements resulting from such noncompliance.

This government audit standard relating to testing for compliance clarifies that other audit criteria could declare that specific laws and regulations are relevant to a financial statement audit. When a law, regulation, grant agreement or contract, or grant governing the audit establishes the requirement that the auditor must test for compliance with these criteria, such test must be conducted. It doesn't matter whether the auditor views the specified laws as having a direct and material effect on the financial statement.

INTERNAL CONTROL AND RISK

The newer fourth additional supplemental government auditing field work standard for financial statement audits is:

4. In planning the audit, auditors should document in the working papers (1) the basis for assessing control risk at the maximum level for assertions related to material account balances, transaction classes, and disclosure components of financial statements when such assertions are significantly dependent upon computerized information systems, and (2) consideration that the planned audit procedures are designed to achieve audit objectives and to reduce audit risk to an acceptable level. [2]

The AICPA has for years considered the understanding and testing of controls to be an integral aspect of an audit made pursuant to generally accepted auditing standards. GAO, too, considers controls to be a priority and as important as the auditing of historical financial information.

The AICPA's generally accepted auditing field work standard No. 2, relating to internal control, is:

"A sufficient understanding of the internal control structure is to be obtained to plan the audit and to determine the nature, timing, and extent of tests to be performed."

Until 1999, the government auditing standards did not prescribe internal control audit standards for financial statement audits that were in addition to the AICPA's. Through the 1994 edition of government standards, auditors were required to make judgments about audit risk and the evidence needed to support their audit opinion on the financial statements. The 1994 guidance related to 4 specific areas:

(1) Control environment,

(2) Safeguarding controls,

(3) Controls over compliance with laws and regulations, and

(4) Control risk assessments.

The AICPA's auditing standards do not require that the auditor separately assess each individual element of the internal control struc-

---

[2] Amendment No. 1, to Government Auditing Standards, 1994 edition, titled, *Documentation Requirements When Assessing Control Risk at Maximum for Controls Significantly Dependent Upon Computerized Information Systems*, dated May 1999, amends earlier Section 4.21 through 4.33.

ture. But, generally accepted auditing standards do require that the auditor:

1. Obtain a sufficient understanding of each of the elements of the control structure;

2. Conduct tests to determine that control policies and procedures have been placed in operation;

3. Assess control risks for assertions implicit in account balances, transaction classes, and disclosure components of the financial statements; and

4. Make additional tests of controls to acquire evidence relating to or supportive of the financial statement assertions to permit the auditor to reduce doubts—or risks—about the audibility of the financial statements.

Evidence indicating that the control environment is ineffective could cause the auditor to question control procedures related to financial statement assertions. Such an observation could, in turn, cause the auditor to reassess earlier conclusions relating to the elements of the control structure, to modify the earlier audit plan and programs, or to increase or modify the nature, extent, or timing of detailed tests made of controls, transactions, or account balances.

Without a sound internal control structure, neither management nor the auditor have any assurance that financial and operational activities are being performed and properly recorded and reported. For smaller entities, auditors might consider changing the nature of control testing and expanding the extent of tests of transactions and account balances. But with larger entities, like governments, this may not be a realistic alternative. When an auditee's system processes upwards of a half million transactions in a year, the expansion by magnitudes of substantive audit samples to compensate for poor controls is prohibitive from both a cost and time viewpoint.

Both the AICPA's generally accepted auditing standards and the government auditing standards require auditors to document their "understanding" of the components of an auditee's internal control related to computer applications that process information used in preparing the auditee's financial statements and to develop a planned audit approach in detail to demonstrate the control systems effectiveness in reducing audit risk. This new government auditing standard does not increase the auditor's responsibility for testing controls. But the new standard does require the auditor, upon concluding that the control design or operations is ineffective, to document the reasons in the working papers.

RISK AND MATERIALITY

When planning, the AICPA standards require that audit risk and materiality, among other matters, need to be considered together in determining the nature, timing, and extent of auditing procedures to be applied and in evaluating the results of those audit procedures.

Both the AICPA and GAO recognize that materiality is a professional judgment and is influenced by the auditor's perception of the needs of a reasonable person who will rely on the financial statements. GAO, in the government auditing standards, cautions that for audits of governmental entities receiving federal financial assistance, auditors may have to set lower or even different materiality levels than for audits of private sector organizations. For public sector audits, materiality is, at times, also dictated by legal and regulatory requirements and visibility and sensitivity of the government programs and activities undergoing audit

This is an important distinction between the AICPA's guidance for private versus public sector audits. The AICPA's auditing standards for reporting on corporate financial statements, for example, make reference to the audit report containing an expression of an audit opinion regarding the financial statements, *taken as a whole*, or an assertion to the effect that an audit opinion cannot be expressed on the entire financial statement.

In the case of government audits, a different criteria or basis applies. For audits of government financial statements, the auditor's opinion is *NOT* applied to the governmental entity undergoing audit or the "whole" financial statement. The AICPA's industry audit guide for state and local governmental units states that for governments:

> "*... audit scope should be set and materiality evaluations should be applied at the fund type, account group, and discretely presented component unit column(s) when reporting on the GPFS [general purpose financial statements], or at the individual fund statement level l....*"[3]

An example of an even lower threshold of materiality with respect to government audits relates to audits made pursuant to the Single Audit Act of 1984. Under the 1984 Act (and as amended in 1996), Congress stated that tests of compliance with laws and regulations must be made for *each* major federal assistance programs. Thus, for audits made pursuant to the Single Audit Act, the auditor's opinion on compliance with laws and regulations is rendered in relation to *each* federal assistance program. The major federal program is a level of

---

[3] AICPA, *Audit and Accounting Guide—Audits of State and Local Governmental Units*, Section 18.34 New York, N.Y., 1994.

materiality considerably less than government-wide financial statements or even the fund types level set by the AICPA.

Safeguarding Controls

Safeguarding controls are defined by GAO as those controls designed to provide reasonable assurance regarding prevention or timely detection of unauthorized acquisition, use or disposition of material assets. Understanding these safeguarding controls, as described in the government standards, can help an auditor to recognize risk factors such as:

● Failure to adequately monitor decentralized operations;

● Lack of controls over activities, such as the lack of documentation for major transactions;

● Lack of control over computer processing, such as a lack of control over access to application that initiate or control the movement of assets;

● Failure to develop or communicate adequate policies and procedures for security of data or assets, such as allowing unauthorized personnel to have ready access to data or assets; and

● Failure to investigate significant unreconciled differences between reconciliations or to control account and subsidiary records.

Weak or nonexistent safeguarding controls for material assets could lead to or at least not prevent significant losses that would cause data reported in an entity's systems, accounts, and financial statements to be suspect.

Safeguarding controls are those controls directed towards the prevention or detection of unauthorized transactions, unauthorized access, unauthorized use, and unauthorized disposition or misappropriation of significant or high dollar value property whose acquisition may have occurred in another—generally past—fiscal period. Thus, sampling transactions of the current period may not have the triggering effect of causing the auditor to examine these controls.

Controls over Compliance with Laws and Regulations

Audits, pursuant to government auditing standards, must be designed to provide reasonable assurance that the financial statements are free of material misstatements that could result from violations or noncompliance with laws and regulations that directly and materially affect amounts in the statements. The 1994 edition of the government auditing standards expands the definition of "compliance" to include detection of noncompliance with or violations of term, conditions, or provisions of contracts and grants. In its standards, GAO lists several control environment factors that may influence the auditor's assessment of control risk:

- Management awareness or lack of awareness of applicable laws and regulations;

- Auditee policy regarding such matters as acceptable operating practices and codes of conduct; and

- Assignment of responsibility and delegation of authority to deal with such matters as organizational goals and objectives, operating functions, and regulatory requirements.

GAO's concerns are not unlike those of the AICPA with respect to controls. The lead issue the AICPA suggests auditors consider when acquiring an understanding of or later testing and assessing controls is "management's philosophy and operating style." So it is with public auditees, the auditor must consider the "tone at the top" of a governmental entity. If management refuses to prescribe, implement, and require adherence to sound controls, subordinate levels will not give controls a priority either.

All governments and public sector auditees are subject to a variety of laws and regulations that affect organization, operations and reporting. In fact, nothing can or should happen in a governmental unit unless the event and its financing has been previously authorized in a law or regulation. Without a precedent law or regulation, the event or expenditure of funds is an act of noncompliance or worse, an illegal act. Thus controls over compliance with laws, regulations, and where significant, the terms, conditions or provisions of contracts and grants can cause direct and material irregular or illegal acts to exist. With respect to controls, the tone of legal compliance can only be set at the top.

Control Risk Assessments

When conducting audits pursuant to generally accepted auditing standards, as well as audits under the government auditing standards, assessments of control risk is made at (1) the maximum risk (i.e., assume nonexistent or extremely poor controls), or (2) some level below the maximum risk.

When control risks are assessed at the maximum, the auditor of public sector auditees is now required to acquire an understanding and to document the control environment. Historically, the auditor might conclude that further testing of inadequate controls would not be cost beneficial. Faced with controls assessed at the maximum risk, an auditor might opt to conduct extensive detailed tests of transactions and account balances to reach a conclusion on the financial statements. The reason for the greater testing is that minimal or no reliance can be placed by the auditor on the control structure. The new standard requires that this decision to not rely on controls must be clearly and convincingly documented to meet the government auditing standards.

When control risks are assessed at below the maximum risk level, the auditor will rely on the tested controls to determine the nature, extent, and timing of detailed tests of transactions and account balances that will be made. In these circumstances, the auditor should:

a. Identify internal controls that are relevant to specific financial statement assertions.

b. Perform tests that provide sufficient evidence that those controls are effective.

c. Document the testing of the controls.

These audit procedures are not different from those required by the AICPA's pronouncements. But, GAO provides the following guidance for auditors when planning and performing tests of controls:

● The lower the auditor's assessment of control risk, the more evidence they need to support that assessment.

This is because the lower the assessment, the greater the reliance the auditor intends to place on the controls. Therefore, more testing must be done of the control structure.

● Auditors may have to use a combination of different tests of controls to get sufficient evidence on a control's effectiveness.

This guidance should read the auditor *must* use a combination of tests for controls as well as for detailed examinations. In no instance will one audit procedure (e.g., inquiry, observation, confirmation, verification, inspection, reconciliation, etc.) ever suffice to produce sufficient evidence.

● Inquiries alone generally will not support an assessment that control risk is below the maximum.

This guidance should read that inquiries alone will *never* be sufficient to support a conclusion of control risk at less than the maximum. Other procedures must always be used.

● Observations provide evidence about a control's effectiveness only at the time observed; they do not provide evidence about its effectiveness during the rest of the period under audit.

This is a comment that is apropos to every audit procedure. Each audit procedure is but a "snapshot" in time of a condition and for this reason audit conclusions must be based on the results of more than one audit procedure or "snapshot."

● Auditors can use evidence from tests of controls done in prior audits (or at an interim date), but they have to obtain evidence about the nature and extent of significant changes in policies, procedures, and personnel since they last performed those tests.

An auditor, regardless of any earlier audit procedures, must update all audit work to permit conclusions relating to the audit opinion as of the date of the audit report.

There are instances when an auditor would be correct in concluding that there should not be a study and evaluation of controls. Several reasons for not testing controls were cited in earlier editions of the government auditing standards. [While not included in the 1994 edition of the government auditing standards, the points remain valid.] Some accepted reasons why an auditor might conclude that resources should not be committed to a study and evaluation of internal controls, include:

● An adequate internal control structure does not exist to permit reliance thereon because of the small size of the audited entity.

● Personnel and management turnover, changed systems, conflicting policies and procedures of recently merged or acquired firms have caused controls and practices of the past to be dated and in a state of non-use.

● The existing internal control structure may contain so many weaknesses that the auditor can only conclude to ignore the control structure and rely on greater substantive tests of transactions and account balances.

● The auditor concludes that it would be inefficient to evaluate the control structure and related policies and procedures because the audit can be conducted more efficiently by expanding the substantive audit tests, thus placing little reliance on the control structure.

● The objective of the financial related audit did not require that the auditor acquire an understanding or make an assessment of the control structure.

EVIDENCE AND WORKING PAPERS

The fifth additional supplemental government auditing field work standard for financial statement audits is:

5. Working papers should contain sufficient information to enable an experienced auditor having no previous connection with the audit to ascertain from them the evidence that supports the auditors' significant conclusions and judgments.

The generally accepted auditing standards of the profession permit auditors to support their work by other means in addition to working papers. That is *not* the case with government auditing standards.

Under the AICPA's standards, working papers serve two main purposes: (1) support the audit report, and (2) aid in the conduct and supervision of the audit. The government standards have a *third* purpose: working papers must contain sufficient evidence to allow for the review of the audit and include a written explanation of the basis for auditor conclusions and judgments.

To comply with this supplemental standard, GAO requires that working papers contain:

● The objectives, scope, and methodology, including any sampling criteria used;

● Documentation of the work performed to support significant conclusions and judgments, including descriptions of transactions and records examined that would enable an experienced auditor to examine the same transactions and records; and

● Evidence of supervisory reviews of the work performed.

These criteria are in addition to those required by the AICPA that state working papers should be sufficient to show that the accounting records agree or reconcile with the financial statements or other information reported on and that applicable standards of field work have been observed.

AICPA standards require that working papers should include documentation to show:

a. The work has been adequately planned and supervised;

b. A sufficient understanding of the internal control structure has been obtained to plan the audit and to determine the nature, timing, and extent of audit tests to be performed; and

c. The audit evidence obtained, the auditing procedures applied, and the testing performed have provided sufficient competent evidential matter to afford a reasonable basis for an opinion.

Additionally, working papers should also provide a record of how exceptions and unusual matters were disclosed, considered, resolved if not reported, with appropriate comments relating to conclusions and recommendations for significant aspects of the audit. Well-designed working papers can provide information for many purposes and aid considerably in eliminating a need to repeatedly examine the same controls, transactions or accounts in order to obtain the information needed to meet a variety of reporting purposes.

An important reason for the GAO supplemental auditing standard is that governmental audits are subjected to review by other auditors and oversight entities more frequently than is the case with audits made pursuant to the AICPA's generally accepted auditing standards.

Federal regulations require governmental audit organizations and other audit organizations to cooperate in auditing government activities, and place a premium on using the work of other auditors to avoid duplicating audit efforts.

Working papers consisting solely of an audit plan, work programs, and checklists on which the auditor has merely indicated the steps performed do not meet the above criteria. Essentially, working papers should be sufficiently complete to permit a knowledgeable independent reviewer to "audit" the auditor with minimal supplementary explanations.

While plans, programs, and checklists are valuable tools for conducting quality audits, these tools must be annotated or cross referenced to supporting working papers containing recordings of the actual evidence examined, tests performed, analyses made, memoranda prepared or obtained, letters of confirmation and representations and any abstracts of relevant data made by the auditor.

FINANCIAL RELATED AUDITS

The 1994 revision to the government auditing standards contained a new section of field audit standards for financial related audits. The objectives of financial related audits include that these audits determine whether:

(1) Financial information is presented in accordance with established or stated criteria;

(2) The entity has adhered to specific financial compliance requirements; and

(3) The entity's internal control structure or specific areas of risk over financial reporting are suitably designed and implemented to achieve the control objectives.

Financial related audits would typically be audits of less than the total entity or the entity-wide financial statements. For example, the government auditing standards specifically include within the definition of financial related audits, audits of portions of entities and systems as: segments of financial statements; budget requests; and variances between estimated and actual financial performance; internal controls over compliance with laws and regulations; internal controls over financial reporting and/or safeguarding assets, and compliance with laws and regulations and examinations of allegations of fraud.

GAO standards for field audit work recognize that for financial related type audits it may be more appropriate to apply the AICPA's *Statement on Standards for Attestation Engagements* rather than the AICPA's generally accepted auditing standards.

The attestation standards of the AICPA provide guidance for a variety of attest—or other than financial statement audit—engagements where the CPA has been requested to provide assurances or representations on other than historical financial statements or in forms other than the traditional audit opinion. For this reason, the AICPA's attestation standards specifically omit references to audits of financial statements and the application of generally accepted accounting principles.

Chapter 5

Reporting Standards— Financial Statements

The government auditing standards define financial audits as being comprised of two types of audits: (1) financial statement audits and (2) financial related audits. This chapter discusses several aspects of reporting required to comply with government auditing standards when financial statement audits are performed.

APPLICABLE AUDITING STANDARDS

Generally Acceptable Auditing Reporting Standards

Because of the reliance that government auditing standards place on the generally accepted auditing standards of the AICPA, the AICPA reporting standards are highlighted, with the discussions of the additional governmental reporting standards appearing in following sections.

The AICPA's generally accepted auditing standards require that an auditor, at the conclusion of a financial statement audit, issue an audit report that meets the criteria of four reporting standards (see *Exhibit 5-1* at the end of this chapter.)

Generally Accepted Government Auditing Report Standards

The 1994 edition of the government auditing standards continue the policy that began in 1972, of incorporating all existing and any new AICPA standards unless a standard is excluded in a formal announcement by the U.S. General Accounting Office. To date, GAO has not excluded any AICPA auditing standards. And, as listed in *Exhibit 5-2*, the government auditing standards impose four additional reporting standards for financial statement audits.

DIFFERENCES PUBLIC VERSUS PRIVATE SECTOR AUDITING AND REPORTING

An audit and reporting made pursuant to only generally accepted auditing standards does not comply with the government's standards.

Of course, if the audit report on financial statements is required for purposes other than to comply with the government auditing standards, auditors may issue a separate report that conforms to only generally accepted auditing standards.

The standard unqualified audit report issued for a public entity's financial statements is similar, but varies somewhat from the standard three-paragraph audit report issued for corporate financial statements. These paragraphs being: the introductory paragraph, scope paragraph, and opinion paragraph.

Different Reporting Responsibilities

In the opinion paragraph of a governmental audit report, the auditor concludes (if appropriate) that the general purpose financial statements present fairly, in all material respects the financial position and results of operations and cash flows, of the audited government. The words are identical to those of an audit opinion for an audit of a corporation's financial statements. But, with respect to the actual audit performed and evaluation of audit findings, materiality decisions for governments must be made in relation to the balances of the individual fund types and not on the basis of the government as a whole.

Other audits of public sector entities have different reporting requirements. For example, the auditor's report for financial related audits might more closely parallel the AICPA's attestation standards and utilize the "positive assurance" type reporting. Performance audits of governments might employ a narrative report that includes a discussion of each material or significant finding, but provide no audit opinion or audit assurances as defined in AICPA guidance.

Different Financial Statements

The auditor's report for a private sector entity relates to the three standard financial statements e.g., the balance sheet, income and expense statement and a statement of cash flow. Until June 1999, a governmental entity's report included five financial statements. In June 1999, by the Governmental Accounting Standards Board Statement No. 34, *Basic Financial Statements—and Management's Discussion and Analysis—for State and Local Governments,* the number of governmental statements and financial reports were increased to at least nine (see **Exhibit 5-4** for these reports.).

Until governments implement GASB Statement No. 34, the introductory paragraph of the auditor's report for a governmental entity will make reference to the 5 general purpose financial statements listed in **Exhibit 5-3**. These 5 statements, plus the notes to these statements constitute the general purpose financial statements (GPFS) of a primary governmental unit.

Reporting Standards—Financial Statements 101

The GPFS are the "liftable" or summarized portion of a comprehensive annual financial report (the CAFR) which GASB requires that each primary government prepare and publish annually. The CAFR, also contains an audit opinion and, in addition to the GPFS, has the combining statements and individual fund statements of the primary government.

GASB Statement No. 34 changes significantly the financial reporting model of state and local governments and is to become effective on a phased basis, depending on a government's total revenues for the first fiscal year ending after June 15, 1999. For the larger governments, with total annual revenues in excess of $100 million, the implementation date is for periods beginning after June 15, 2001. Under this phasing, the initial financial reports to comply with GASB No. 34, would be submitted for the fiscal periods ending in the year 2002.

These newly imposed government-wide financial statements will report on the government as a whole and include the primary government and its component units except for fiduciary funds of the government and component units, that are fiduciary in nature. These fiduciary type funds and units are to be reported in separate statements of fiduciary net assets and changes in fiduciary net assets.

Different Materiality Thresholds

To comply with generally accepted auditing standards, auditors must make reference to whether the audited financial statements present fairly in all material respects the financial position and results of operations of the audited organization. Thus, for generally accepted auditing standards, the auditor's opinion addresses the financial statements of the audited organization taken as a whole.

For audits of governmental public sector entities, a considerably lower threshold applies, which affects the depth of audit performed and nature of the report required. For governmental financial statements, the auditor's opinion is not applied in reference to the financial statements of the government organization taken as a whole, but rather the fund type. The AICPA's guidance for audits of state and local governmental units requires that the:

> *"...audit scope should be set and materiality evaluations should be applied at the fund type, account group, and discretely presented component unit columns when reporting on the GPFS or at the individual fund statement level when reporting on the GPFS, combining and individual fund financial statements in a CAFR or as may be required for*

other purposes, such as the requirements for an audit to be performed in accordance with single audit requirements..." [1]

The implication of this requirement is that the threshold or level of materiality relating to: (1) the nature, timing and extent of auditing of governments will be more detailed, and (2) reporting for government audits will be at a considerably lower level than for a corporate audit of comparable revenues or expenditures.

Thus, in concluding on what is material for testing and reporting purposes, a governmental audit exception is not to be compared to the government's entity wide financial statement. Instead the comparison must be made to the general fund, special revenue, or other fund types to determine whether the exception is reportable. With this lowered level of materiality, an audit exception that is not material or significant to a corporate entity could be material in the case of the governmental unit.

Different Balance Sheets

Another difference between private sector and the public sector is apparent in scanning the balance sheet of a government unit. The balance sheet looks considerably different from a corporate balance sheet. Instead of the single column of financial data typically found in a corporate balance sheet, the balance sheet of a governmental unit will contain 10 or more columns. Most of the government balance sheets show dollar amounts for the several fund types mandated by GASB as part of the generally accepted accounting principles for government. And, as noted, when auditing governments, materiality levels must be established for each of the columns in the balance sheet.

Different Financial Information

An auditor's report for a governmental unit might make reference to "combining," and "individual funds" data. This data is neither referenced nor relevant to an audit report pursuant to generally accepted auditing standards for a private sector entity.

With respect to information accompanying the financial statement, the auditor's responsibility is the same as for audits of private sector organizations. The auditor must describe clearly the character of the auditor's work, the degree of responsibility taken for the statements, and for information that accompanies the report. The auditor may choose to perform additional audit procedures in order to express an opinion on the accompanying information. When this is done, the

---

[1] AICPA Statements of Position 98-3, *Audits of States, Local Governments and Not-For-Profit Organizations Receiving Federal Awards.*

materiality threshold would consist of the fund types, account groups, individual fund statements, etc., of the governmental unit.

Different Accompanying Information

If the accompanying information in a government's financial statements is required by GASB or FASB to conform to the public sector's generally accepted accounting principles, an explanatory paragraph will appear in the audit report. With respect to accompanying information, the auditor's responsibility is the same as for the audit. The auditor must clearly describe this fact, identify if specific audit procedures were applied to the information, indicate whether the information was audited, and if an opinion is being expressed on the accompanying information.

Detailed reporting guidance applicable to audits of both private and public sector entities appears in the AICPA's SAS No. 29, *Reporting on Information Accompanying the Basic Financial Statements in Auditor-Submitted Documents* and SAS No. 52, *Required Supplementary Information.* [2]

GOVERNMENT AUDITING STANDARDS FOR REPORTING

As mentioned earlier, the government auditing standards incorporate or include the generally accepted standards unless specifically excluded for formal announcement. None have ever been excluded. However, the government auditing standards include four additional audit reporting standards relating to (1) requiring reference to government auditing standards, (2) special reporting of examinations of compliance and internal controls, (3) treatments of sensitive information, and (4) the more extensive community to whom governmental audit results may have to be transmitted.

Application of these reporting standards alter considerably the auditor's report required for public sector entities in comparison to the auditor's report typically issued for an audit of a private sector entity.

Reference to Government Auditing Standards

The first additional government auditing standard for reporting requires that:

> *"Audit reports should state that the audit was made in accordance with generally accepted government auditing standards."* [GAGAS, § 5.11]

If an audit report is submitted to comply with a legal, regulatory, or contractual requirement for an audit made in accordance with

---

[2] AICPA, *Audit and Accounting Guide—Audits of State and Local Governmental Units*, Section 3.11 New York, N.Y., 1994.

government auditing standards, the audit report must cite the government auditing standards. The government auditing standards recognize that the auditee may need a financial statement audit for purposes other than to comply with requirements of the government auditing standards.

This standard is a change from the 1988 edition of the government auditing standards, strengthening a government position that was somewhat controversial. The AICPA Statement of Position 92-7, noted that certain governments preferred that the auditor's report on the financial statements not make reference to conformance to two sets of auditing standards because such statements were also used for securities issued to the public and the financial statements were the basis of reports to citizens.

The exposure draft (July 26, 1993) that preceded the formal issuance of the 1994 revised government auditing standards, recognized that audit reports for public sector entities routinely cited compliance with only the AICPA's generally accepted auditing standards. The Exposure Draft stated that this limited reporting was no longer acceptable because of the difference between the two sets of auditing standards. The government auditing standards [§ 5.13] now mandate that the scope paragraph for relevant public sector audits cite the government auditing standards as the criteria for the audit.

Exhibit 5-5 illustrates the reporting suggested by the AICPA, after consultation with practitioners and the government, of an auditor's report on the general purpose financial statement for a governmental unit relating to an audit made pursuant to government auditing standards.[3] The second or scope paragraph in this illustration describes the audit criteria used to conduct the audit.

To comply with government auditing standards these standards must be cited. Reference may be made to the AICPA's generally accepted auditing standards, although this citation is not necessary. An audit pursuant to the government auditing standards exceeds the requirements of the AICPA.

Government auditing standards do not apply only to audits of governments. These auditing standards apply also, when required by law, regulation, agreement, contract, grant or federal policy, to the audits of nonprofit organizations, educational institutions, contractors, grantees and other recipients of federal financial assistance.

---

[3] See also the AICPAs Codification of Statements on Auditing Standards, AU sec. 551, *Reporting on Information Accompanying the Basic Financial State-* *ments in Auditor-Submitted Documents.* New York, N.Y.

Reporting on Test of Compliance, Controls

Government auditing standards require governmental units to submit reports on the auditor's test of compliance with laws and regulations and internal controls. These reports are required by the second additional government auditing standard:

"The report on the financial statements should either (1) describe the scope of the auditors' testing of compliance with laws and regulations and internal controls over financial reporting and present the results of those tests or (2) refer to the separate reports containing that information. In presenting the results of those tests, auditors should report fraud, illegal acts, other material noncompliance, and reportable conditions in internal controls over financial reporting. In some circumstances, auditors should report fraud and illegal acts directly to parties external to the audited entity." [GAGAS, § 5.15]

The government auditing standards do not require that additional audit procedures be applied, other than those required as part of generally accepted auditing standards. However, for generally accepted auditing standards, no *reports* are routinely required for these tests. Government auditing standards do require written reports for both compliance and internal controls, which may be made in either the audit report on the financial statements or in a separate report.

If the tests performed did not exceed those the auditors considered necessary for a financial statement audit then a statement is required that the auditor (1) tested compliance with certain laws and regulations, (2) obtained an understanding of internal controls, and (3) assessed control risk. Auditors must also report, under government standards, whether or not the tests performed provided sufficient evidence to support an opinion on compliance and on internal controls.

Reporting on Tests of Compliance and Controls

Exhibit 5-6 illustrates the reporting suggested by the AICPA, after consultation with practitioners and the government, of an auditor's report on compliance and internal controls over financial reporting based on an audit of financial statements made pursuant to government auditing standards.

● The first section of this illustrative report is required and must (1) state whether an audit was made of the entity's financial statements (2) if an audit report was issued and (3) cite the auditing standards employed.

● The second section of this illustrative report must contain several statements by the auditor relating to tests for compliance with laws and regulations, specifically: (1) the nature of compliance tests made, (2) whether or not the tests performed provided sufficient evidence to support an opinion on compliance; (3) whether an audit opinion is rendered on compliance or disclaimed, and (4) the results of the performed compliance tests.

The government standards state that clearly inconsequential instances of noncompliance, fraud and illegal acts need not be reported and that when reporting on noncompliance the findings must be in proper perspective.

Particular care is required when the compliance tests disclose indications of fraud and illegal acts. In these instances, auditors should consider seeking assistance from knowledgeable counsel and discussing the issues with the audit entity management and representatives of federal funding sources.

● The third paragraph of this illustrative report contains several required statements by the auditor: (1) whether or not the tests performed provided sufficient evidence to support an opinion on internal controls; (2) whether the auditor is providing an opinion on controls; and (3) whether any instances of material weaknesses in controls were noted.

Auditors are required to report deficiencies in internal controls that are considered to be "reportable conditions." And, in reporting reportable conditions, government standards state auditors should identify those reportable conditions that are individually or cumulatively material weaknesses.

The AICPA provides the following definitions of a *reportable condition* and a *material weakness*:

Reportable condition— These are significant deficiencies in the design or operation of the internal controls structure, which could adversely affect the entity's ability to record, process, summarize, and report financial data consistent with the assertion of management in the financial statements.

This reporting, if not of material conditions, would be in a separate communication and not as a part of the auditor's report on the financial statements.

The government auditing standards (GAGAS, § 5.26), contain several examples of matters considered to be "reportable conditions" in a governmental setting, including:

1. Absence of appropriate segregation of duties consistent with appropriate control objectives;

2. Absence of appropriate reviews and approvals of transactions, accounting entries, or systems output;

Reporting Standards—Financial Statements 107

3. Inadequate provisions for the safeguarding of assets;

4. Evidence of failure to safeguard assets from loss, damage, or misappropriation;

5. Evidence that a system fails to provide complete and accurate output consistent with the auditee's control objectives because of the misapplication of control procedures;

6. Evidence of intentional override of internal controls by those in authority to the detriment of the overall objectives of the system;

7. Evidence of failure to perform tasks that are part of internal controls, such as reconciliations not prepared or not timely prepared;

8. Absence of a sufficient level of control consciousness within the organization;

9. Significant deficiencies in the design or operation of internal controls that could result in violations of laws and regulations having a direct and material effect on the financial statements; and

10. Failure to follow up and correct previously identified deficiencies in internal controls.

Material weaknesses—These are reportable conditions where the design or operation of the specific internal control structure elements do not reduce to a relatively low level the risk that errors or irregularities in amounts that would be material in relation to the financial statements being audited may occur and not be detected within a timely period by employees in the normal course of performing their functions.

There is no standard or "boiler-plate" report format should tests of compliance and of internal controls disclose material instances of noncompliance, reportable conditions or material weaknesses with respect to controls. This auditor's report, generally in narrative form, must place findings in perspective, giving the reader information to determine prevalence and consequences of the disclosed conditions. This requires that the report containing material findings identify the review objectives, scope and methodology, audit results, and even views of the responsible management.

The AICPA, in its literature (AU § 325.15) requires that reportable conditions be reported to the client, but the reporting may be done orally or in writing. To comply with government auditing standards, the report must be in writing.

Conditions Limiting Tests of Controls

Historically, government auditing standards listed several reasons when the tests of controls might not be practical, including when:

• The size of the entity is too small to permit a control structure with sufficient segregation of duties; or

• The audit might be done more efficiently by expanding the substantive audit test, placing little reliance on the control structure; or

• The existing control system is so weak that it must be ignored and reliance placed on expanded substantive tests; or

• The objectives of the financial related audit did not require that the auditor acquire an understanding or make an assessment of the internal control structure.

Reporting Sensitive Data

The third additional government auditing standard on reporting relates to the communication of sensitive information disclosed during an audit. This government reporting standard requires that:

"If certain information is prohibited from general disclosure, the audit report should state the nature of the information omitted and the requirement that makes the omission necessary." [GAGAS, § 5.29]

GAO, in various sections of the government auditing standards, directs auditors to report on observed or indications of irregularities, fraud and illegal acts that have occurred or are likely to occur. This reporting should include information such as prevalence, instances identified, cases examined, dollar value involved, and should be made directly to parties outside the auditee when required by law, regulation, or when the auditee does not make a timely reporting, itself.

But some of the government auditing standards concerning this reporting conflicts with other guidance by GAO that the auditor should do nothing nor report anything that will compromise investigative or legal proceedings.

Laws, statutes, or regulations may preclude the release of certain information except on a designated "need to know" basis. Where such a requirement exists and pertinent data must be omitted from the audit report, the auditor is directed (§ 5.31) to state the nature of the information omitted and the requirement that makes the omission necessary. But then the auditor is cautioned by GAO to consult with legal counsel. In this area, as well as with respect to disclosed instances of illegal acts or fraud, the auditor will find various sections of the GAO standards somewhat in conflict.

Literal compliance to this reporting standard places the auditor somewhat at odds with warnings that appeared in the exposure draft leading to the 1994 revised government auditing standards. While this warning is not in 1994 standards, the advice would appear to still be relevant and invaluable to auditors of governments:

"Auditors should be aware that ... reports containing information on fraud or other illegal acts that could result in criminal prosecution, or reports with references that such acts were omitted could interfere with legal processes or subject the implicated individuals to undue publicity. They also might subject auditors to potential legal action."

The government's performance auditing standards probably provide safer guidance and an important caveat for an auditor who discloses material irregularities, fraud or illegal acts. The performance auditing standards (§ 7.33) state:

"When auditors concluded that this type of illegal act has occurred or is likely to have occurred, they should ask those authorized and/or legal counsel if reporting certain information about the illegal act would compromise investigative or legal proceedings. Auditors should limit their reporting to matters that would not compromise those proceedings, such as information that is already a part of the public record."

Distribution of Audit Reports

The fourth additional government auditing standard on financial reporting requires government audit reports to be in writing and to be distributed to other than the auditee.

"Written audit reports are to be submitted by the audit organization to the appropriate officials of the auditee and to the appropriate officials of the organizations requiring or arranging for the audits, including external funding organizations, unless legal restrictions prevent it. Copies of the reports should also be sent to other officials who have legal oversight authority or who may be responsible for acting on audit findings and recommendations and to others authorized to receive such reports. Unless restricted by law or regulation, copies should be made available for public inspection." [GAGAS, § 5.32]

Auditors new to audits of public sector entities are cautioned that, unlike the private sector, the auditee and the arranger of a public sector audit may not be the same party. And, under certain conditions, the arranger may prohibit distribution of the audit report to the auditee. Also, in some instances, a third party that is neither the auditee nor the arranger of the audit may dictate who is to get a copy of the audit report.

110   Government Auditing: Standards and Practices

This reporting standard is essentially unchanged from the 1988 edition of the government standards. In the case of public accountants, the engaging organization is responsible for ensuring that the appropriate report distribution is made.

If the public accountant is to make the distribution, the engagement agreement must indicate what officials or organizations should receive the audit report. Internal auditors should follow their entity's own arrangements and statutory requirements for distribution.

Exhibits 5-1, 5-2, 5-3, 5-4, 5-5, and 5-6 follow this page.

EXHIBIT 5-1

Generally Accepted Auditing Report Standards

1. The report shall state whether the financial statements are presented in accordance with generally accepted accounting principles.

2. The report shall identify those circumstances in which such principles have not been consistently observed in the current period in relation to the preceding period.

3. Informative disclosures in the financial statements are to be regarded as reasonably adequate unless otherwise stated in the report.

4. The report shall either contain an expression of an opinion regarding the financial statements, taken as a whole, or an assertion to the effect that an opinion cannot be expressed. When an overall opinion cannot be expressed, the reasons therefore should be stated. In all cases where an auditor's name is associated with financial statements, the report should contain a clear-cut indication of the character of the auditor's work, if any, and the degree of responsibility the auditor is taking.

EXHIBIT 5-2

Government Auditing Standards of Reporting [4]

1. Audit reports should state that the audit was made in accordance with generally accepted government auditing standards.

2. The report on the financial statements should either (1) describe the scope of the auditors' testing of compliance with laws and regulations and internal controls over financial reporting and present the results of those tests or (2) refer to the separate reports containing that information. In presenting the results of those tests, auditors should report fraud, illegal acts, other material noncompliance, and reportable conditions in internal controls over financial reporting. In some circumstances, auditors should report fraud and illegal acts directly to parties external to the audited entity.

3. If certain information is prohibited from general disclosure, the audit report should state the nature of the information omitted and the requirement that makes the omission necessary.

4. Written audit reports are to be submitted by the audit organization to the appropriate officials of the auditee and to the appropriate officials of the organizations requiring or arranging for the audits, including external funding organizations, unless legal restrictions prevent it. Copies of the reports should also be sent to other officials who have legal oversight authority or who may be responsible for acting on audit findings and recommendations and to others authorized to receive such reports. Unless restricted by law or regulation, copies should be made available for public inspection.

---

[4] Revised to reflect new governmental reporting standards in Amendment Nos. 1 and 2, of May and July 1999.

EXHIBIT 5-3

Contents of Government Statements—General Purpose Financial Statements

The GASB requires that the general purpose financial statements of a primary governmental unit include the following statements:

1. Combined Balance Sheet—All Fund Types, Account Groups

2. Combined Statement of Revenues, Expenditures, and Changes in Fund Balances—All Governmental Fund Types

3. Combined Statement of Revenues, Expenditures, and Changes in Fund Balances—Budget and Actual—General and Special Revenues Fund Types

4. Combined Statement of Revenues, Expenses, and Changes in Retained Earnings—All Proprietary Fund Types

5. Combined Statement of Cash Flows—All Proprietary Fund Types

Plus:

A. Notes to the financial statements

B. Required supplementary information

EXHIBIT 5-4

Required Government Financial Reports
GASB Statement No. 34
[Effective June 15, 1999]

- Management Discussion and Analysis

- Government-wide Financial Statements
  Statement of New Assets
  Statement of Activities

- Fund Financial Statements—Governmental Funds
  Balance Sheet
  Statement of Revenues, Expenditures, and Changes in Fund Balances

- Fund Financial Statements—Proprietary Funds
  Statement of Net Assets
  Statement of Revenues, Expenses, and Changes in Net Assets
  Statement of Cash Flows

- Fund Financial Statements—Fiduciary Funds
  Statement of Fiduciary Net Assets
  Statement of Changes in Fiduciary Net Assets

- Notes to Financial Statements

- Required Supplementary Information

EXHIBIT 5-5 *

Example 1. Unqualified Opinion on General-Purpose Financial Statements and Supplementary Schedule of Expenditures of Federal Awards—Governmental Entity [1]

Independent Auditor's Report

[*Addressee*]

We have audited the accompanying general-purpose financial statements of the City of Example, Any State, as of and for the year ended June 30, 19X1, as listed in the table of contents. These general-purpose financial statements are the responsibility of the City of Example's management. Our responsibility is to express an opinion on these general-purpose financial statements based on our audit.

We conducted our audit in accordance with generally accepted auditing standards and the standards applicable to financial audits contained in *Government Auditing Standards*, [2] issued by the Comptroller General of the United States. Those standards require that we plan and perform the audit to obtain reasonable assurance about whether the financial statements are free of material misstatement. An audit includes examining, on a test basis, evidence supporting the amounts and disclosures in the financial statements. An audit also includes assessing the accounting principles used and the significant estimates made by management, as well as evaluating the overall financial statement presentation. We believe that our audit provides a reasonable basis for our opinion.

In our opinion, the general-purpose financial statements referred to above present fairly, in all material respects, the financial position of the City of Example, Any State, as of June 30, 19X1, and the results of its operations and the cash flows of its proprietary fund types and nonexpendable trust funds for the year then ended in conformity with generally accepted accounting principles.

In accordance with *Government Auditing Standards*, we have also issued our report dated [*date of report*] on our consideration of the City of Example's internal control over financial reporting and on our tests of its compliance with certain provisions of laws, regulations, contracts, and grants. [3]

---

* Reprinted with permission from SOP 98-3, *Audits of States, Local Governments, and Not-for-Profit Organizations Receiving Federal Awards*, Copyright ©1998 by the American Institute of Certified Public Accountants, Inc.

[1] Auditors may also refer to the AICPA Audit and Accounting Guide *Audits of State and Local Governmental Units* for additional guidance on reporting on the general-purpose financial statements of a government.

[2] The standards applicable to financial audits include the general, fieldwork, and reporting standards described in chapters 3, 4, and 5 of *Government Auditing Standards*.

[3] The following paragraph should be deleted if the schedule of expenditures of federal awards is not

The accompanying schedule of expenditures of federal awards [4] is presented for purposes of additional analysis as required by U.S. Office of Management and Budget Circular A-133, *Audits of States, Local Governments, and Non-Profit Organizations*, and is not a required part of the general-purpose financial statements. Such information has been subjected to the auditing procedures applied in the audit of the general-purpose financial statements and, in our opinion, is fairly stated, in all material respects, in relation to the general-purpose financial statements taken as a whole. [5]

[*Signature*]

[*Date*]

(Footnote Continued)

presented with the general-purpose financial statements (that is, a separate single audit package is issued). In such a circumstance, the required reporting on the schedule may be incorporated in the report issued to meet the requirements of Circular A-133. See notes 34 and 40 for additional guidance.

[4] If the auditor is reporting on additional supplementary information (for example, combining and individual fund and account group financial statements and schedules), this paragraph should be modified to describe the additional supplementary information. The example reports in appendix A of the AICPA Audit and Accounting Guide *Audits of State and Local Governmental Units* and SAS No. 29, *Reporting on Information Accompanying the Basic Financial Statements in Auditor-Submitted Documents* (AICPA, *Professional Standards*, Vol. 1, AU see. 551) provide useful guidance.

[5] When reporting on the supplementary information, the auditor should consider the effect of any modifications to the report on the general-purpose financial statements. Furthermore, if the report on supplementary information is other than unqualified, this paragraph should be modified. Guidance for reporting in these circumstances is described in paragraphs 9 through 11 and 13 through 14 of SAS No. 29 (AICPA, *Professional Standards*, vol. 1, AU sees. 551.09-.11 and 551.13-.14).

EXHIBIT 5-6 *

Example 2. Report on Compliance and on Internal Control Over Financial Reporting [12] Based on an Audit of Financial Statements Performed in Accordance With *Government Auditing Standards* (*No Reportable Instances of Noncompliance and No Material Weaknesses* [*No Reportable Conditions Identified*]) [13]

[*Addressee*]

We have audited the financial statements of Example Entity as of and for the year ended June 30, 19X1, and have issued our report thereon dated August 15, 19X1. [14] We conducted our audit in accordance with generally accepted auditing standards and the standards applicable to financial audits contained in *Government Auditing Standards*, [15] issued by the Comptroller General of the United States.

Compliance

As part of obtaining reasonable assurance about whether Example Entity's financial statements are free of material misstatement, we performed tests of its compliance with certain provisions of laws, regulations, contracts, and grants, noncompliance with which could have a direct and material effect on the determination of financial statement amounts. However, providing an opinion on compliance with those provisions was not an objective of our audit, and accordingly, we do not express such an opinion. The results of our tests disclosed no instances of noncompliance that are required to be reported under *Government Auditing Standards*. [16], [17]

Internal Control Over Financial Reporting

In planning and performing our audit, we considered Example Entity's internal control over financial reporting in order to determine

---

* Reprinted with permission from SOP 98-3, *Audits of States, Local Governments, and Not-for-Profit Organizations Receiving Federal Awards*, Copyright ©1998 by the American Institute of Certified Public Accountants, Inc.

[12] See paragraph 4.12 for a description of internal control over financial reporting.

[13] The auditor should use the portions of examples 2 and 2a that apply to a specific auditee situation. For example, if the auditor will be giving an unqualified opinion on compliance but has identified reportable conditions, the compliance section of this report would be used along with the internal control section of example 2a. Alternatively, if the auditor will be giving a qualified opinion on compliance but has not identified reportable conditions, the internal control section of this report would be used along with the compliance section of example 2a.

[14] Describe any departure from the standard report (for example, a qualified opinion, a modification as to consistency because of a change in accounting principle, or a reference to the report of other auditors).

[15] See note 2.

[16] See paragraphs 5.18 and 5.19 of *Government Auditing Standards* for the criteria for reporting.

[17] If the auditor has issued a separate letter to management to communicate matters that do not meet the criteria for reporting in paragraph 5.18 of *Government Auditing Standards*, this paragraph should be modified to include a statement such as the following: "However, we noted certain immaterial instances of noncompliance, which we have reported to management of Example Entity in a separate letter dated August 15, 19X1." This reference to management is intended to be consistent with paragraph 5.20 of *Government Auditing Standards* which indicates that communications to "top" management should be referred to.

our auditing procedures for the purpose of expressing our opinion on the financial statements and not to provide assurance on the internal control over financial reporting. Our consideration of the internal control over financial reporting would not necessarily disclose all matters in the internal control over financial reporting that might be material weaknesses. A material weakness is a condition in which the design or operation of one or more of the internal control components does not reduce to a relatively low level the risk that misstatements in amounts that would be material in relation to the financial statements being audited may occur and not be detected within a timely period by employees in the normal course of performing their assigned functions. We noted no matters involving the internal control over financial reporting and its operation that we consider to be material weaknesses. [18]

This report is intended for the information of the audit committee, management, [specify legislative or regulatory body], and federal awarding agencies and pass-through entities. [19] However, this report is a matter of public record and its distribution is not limited. [20]

[Signature]

[Date]

---

[18] If the auditor has issued a separate letter to management to communicate other matters involving the design and operation of the internal control over financial reporting, this paragraph should be modified to include a statement such as the following: "However, we noted other matters involving the internal control over financial reporting, which we have reported to management of Example Entity in a separate letter dated August 15, 19X1." This reference is not intended to preclude the auditor from including other matters in the separate letter to management. Furthermore, the reference to management is intended to be consistent with paragraph 5.28 of *Government Auditing Standards* which indicates that communications to "top" management should be referred to.

[19] If this report is issued for an audit that is not subject to Circular A-133, this sentence should be modified as follows. "This report is intended for the information of the audit committee, management, and [specify legislative or regulatory body]."

[20] If the report is not a matter of public record, this sentence should be deleted.

Chapter 6

Audit Standards—Financial Related and Performance Audits

The reporting for non-opinion type financial related audit reports and reports pertaining to performance audits are similar in many respects. This chapter describes the nature of the government's performance audit standards which apply to both types of audits.

FINANCIAL RELATED AUDITS DEFINED

Financial related audits are special purpose or limited scope audits that may include all aspects or parts of a financial statement audit. Government auditing standards define *financial related* audits as including audits to determine whether:

1. Financial information is presented in accordance with established or stated criteria; or

2. The entity had adhered to specific financial compliance requirements; or

3. The entity's internal control structure over financial reporting and/or safeguarding assets is suitably designed and implemented to achieve the control objectives.

Financial related audits may include audits of less than the total entity. For example, the government auditing standards specifically include within the definition of financial related audits, audits of portions of entities and systems or selected aspects of the control structure.

The government auditing standards state that the AICPA attestation standards are incorporated as part of the audit reporting standards for financial related reports. GAO requires that if a financial related audit does not fall within the earlier definitions or examples of a financial related audit, auditors must then follow the field work and reporting standards for performance audits.

PERFORMANCE AUDITS DEFINED

Most will concede the leadership to GAO in the practice of performance auditing, dating back to the 1950s. First published by the U.S. General Accounting Office in 1972, the government auditing standards were reissued in 1972, 1974, 1979, 1981, 1988, and again in 1994. The standards were intended to provide guidance for financial audits *and* performance audits of governmental organizations, programs, activities and functions.

GAO, in its standards, define a performance audit as:

> *"... an objective and systematic examination of evidence for the purpose of providing an independent assessment of the performance of an existing or proposed government organization, program, or activity in order to provide useful information to improve public accountability and decision-making."*

Discussions in earlier chapters concerning the government auditing standards made repeated references that the GAO's government auditing standards were *in addition* to or *supplemental* to the generally accepted auditing standards, promulgated for decades by the AICPA and its predecessor organizations.

With respect to the performance audit standards, though, there are *no* generally accepted auditing standards. In 1973 in its publication titled *Auditing Standards Established by GAO—Their Meaning and Significance for CPAs*, the AICPA cautioned the profession that the governmental auditing standards were different, going beyond the audit of only financial statements. The AICPA committee on relations with the federal government made several observations about the government auditing standards, stating at the time that:

> *"The primary impact of the GAO Standards is in the way the scope of auditing is expanded beyond examinations leading to the expression of opinions on the fairness of financial presentation to include audits for compliance, efficiency, economy, and effectiveness. ...*
>
> *Independent accountants must define carefully, in the engagement agreement, the scope of each engagement and the method of reporting."*

Later the AICPA, in a 1982 publication titled *Operational Audit Engagements*, describes performance audits as a distinct form of management advisory service that may also have some of the characteristics of a financial audit. The AICPA viewed the purpose of performance or operational audits as assessing performance, identifying

Financial Related and Performance Audits

opportunities for improvement, and developing recommendations for improvement.

Generally, performance audits are commissioned separate from financial audits, often because of funding limitations. Performance audits are expensive. Since the initial edition in 1972, the GAO government auditing standards provided standards or guidance for two categories of audits: (1) financial statement audits and financial related audits and (2) performance audits. From the initial issuance of the standards, GAO never intended that adherence to both financial and performance auditing standards were intended, feasible or desirable for every audit.

The GAO's performance auditing standards apply to audits of federal organizations, programs, activities, and functions. These performance auditing standards are to be applied by all auditors conducting performance audits—governmental and nongovernmental auditors, independent external and internal auditors, whether employees of or contractors to governments—if required by federal law, regulations, or rules.

The GAO definition of performance audits encompasses two general types: (1) economy and efficiency audits, and (2) program audits.

Economy and Efficiency Audits

The performance audits are directed towards assessing whether an organization might operate less expensively (i.e., economical) and better or smarter (i.e., efficient). The performance standards describe audits of economy and efficiency as including determinations or assessments of:

1. Whether the entity is acquiring, protecting, and using its resources (such as personnel, property, and space) economically and efficiently;

2. The causes of inefficiencies and uneconomical practices; and

3. Whether the entity has complied with laws and regulations on matters of economy and efficiency.

Examples of Economy and Efficiency Audits

While not intended to be an exhaustive or all-inclusive listing of examples, GAO, in its 1994 edition (paragraph 2.8) states that efficiency and economy audits may consider whether the entity:

● Is following sound procurement practices;

● Is acquiring the appropriate type, quality, and amount of resources at an appropriate cost;

● Is properly protecting and maintaining its resources;

- Is avoiding duplication of effort by employees and work that serves little or no purpose;

- Is avoiding idleness or overstaffing;

- Is using efficient operating procedures;

- Is using the optimum amount of resources (staff, equipment, facilities) in producing or delivering the appropriate quantity and quality of goods or services in a timely manner;

- Is complying with requirements of laws and regulations that could significantly affect the acquisition, protection, and use of the entity's resources;

- Has an adequate management control system for measuring, reporting, and monitoring a program's economy and efficiency; and

- Has reported measures of economy and efficiency that are valid and reliable.

These audits are made pursuant to specially developed audit guides directed towards selected areas that have been identified for review. In some instances, the audit areas are determined after performance of a preliminary survey and review. In other instances, the areas may be determined by legislative emphasis, executive branch concerns, or identified, in part, by the management of the entity to be audited. As early as 1978, GAO published an exposure draft titled, *Guidelines for Economy and Efficiency Audits of Federally Assisted Programs*, outlining a uniform approach and documentation procedures for audits with a concentration in areas such as: procurement, property management, personnel administration, fiscal management and controls, and management information systems.

Program Audits

These audits are directed towards assessing whether an entity is achieving or performing in the manner intended when the legislator provided funding for operations. The performance standards describe program audits as including determinations or assessments of:

1. The extent to which the desired results or benefits established by the legislature or other authorizing body are being achieved;

2. The effectiveness of organizations, programs, activities, or functions; and

3. Whether the entity has complied with significant laws and regulations applicable to the program.

Examples of Program Audits

While not intended to be an exhaustive or all-inclusive listing of examples, GAO in its 1994 edition (§ 2.9) states that program audits may, for example:

● Assess whether the objectives of a new, or ongoing program are proper, suitable, or relevant;

● Determine the extent to which a program achieves a desired level of program results;

● Assess the effectiveness of the program and/or of individual program components;

● Identify factors inhibiting satisfactory performance;

● Determine whether management has considered alternatives for carrying out the program that might yield desired results more effectively or at a lower cost;

● Determine whether the program complements, duplicates, overlaps, or conflicts with other related programs;

● Identify ways of making programs work better;

● Assess compliance with laws and regulations applicable to the program;

● Assess the adequacy of the management control system for measuring, reporting, and monitoring a program's effectiveness; and

● Determined whether management has reported measures of program effectiveness that are valid and reliable.

In practice, other auditors would place many of these "program" audit examples within the scope of economy and efficiency audits.

A pure performance or "program" results audit is more directed towards assessing the relative attainment of program objectives or goals and the effectiveness with which management attempts to reach these objectives or goals.

In the ideal performance audit, legislation or program rules and regulations have established objectives, goals and specific operating procedures that can be used by the auditor to develop criteria for measuring or assessing program performance. The reality is different, though. Frequently, legislation is silent as to what was desired of the program. Policies and procedures may not be directly related to specific programs. Program, historical, and performance information may not be accumulated or reported.

In all circumstances, auditors should exercise caution in developing the audit criteria for assessing or measuring program results by testing the general acceptance of the developed audit criteria. This is necessary to avoid the auditee from later rebutting the audit report findings with the retort that the performance criteria are only an opinion of the auditor and not relevant to or based on laws, regulations, or management policies or procedures.

Performance Audits—By Other Names

While some may prefer one descriptor over another, in practice most would agree with the AICPA's Special Committee on Operational and Management Auditing that found:

> *"Internal auditors, governmental auditors, and independent accountants are frequently asked to evaluate the economy, efficiency, and effectiveness of an organization's operations. These services are known by a variety of terms, such as operational reviews, performance audits, management audits, and comprehensive audits. Distinctions can be drawn between some of these terms, but the most commonly used is operational audits."*

The completion of such audits or evaluations require the application of skills, disciplines, ethical restraints, independence, and competence in the same manner as financial audits. But, performance audits require that particular attention be devoted to describing the scope of the performance audit, determining and establishing acceptance of quantifiable performance criteria, developing an audit guide and program unique to the audit, and identifying the nature of skills needed to conduct the performance audit.

In contrast to financial audits, where the AICPA has for years published standards, interpretations, and practice guidance, performance auditing has been distinguished by the relative dearth of written materials and the somewhat lack of consensus among professional organizations over exactly what is the scope or requirements for conducting "generally accepted" performance audits. In 1982, the AICPA publication *Operational Audit Engagements* distinguished an operational audit from management advisory services engagements, i.e., management consulting, that may also have some characteristics of a financial audit. At that time the AICPA defined an "operational audit" as a systematic review of an organization's activities, or a stipulated segment of them, in relation to specified objectives. The identified objectives or purposes of a performance audit were stated to be: assessing, performance, identifying opportunities for improvement, and developing recommendations for improvement.

REPORT CONTENT

Criteria for Financial Related and Performance Audit Reports

Reports for financial related and performance audits will vary and will meet different objectives. These reports will utilize agreed-to procedures that will vary by engagement. For these reasons, GAO requires that this information be provided to readers in each report for a financial related audit.

The guidance in the government auditing standards, for reporting on these type audits is general, stating that auditors should follow (1) the AICPA's standards; (2) the governmental financial reporting standards, applying or adapting as appropriate; and (3) the government reporting standards for performance audits.

Financial related and performance audit reports must be responsive to the objectives of the engagement. Regardless of format, a financial related audit report must meet several criteria. The report must contain:

- The information to satisfy the audit objectives;

- The evidence presented must be true and findings correctly portrayed;

- The report should be balanced in content and tone; and

- The information should be sufficient to enable readers to assess the validity of the findings, reasonableness of conclusions, and desirability of implementing the recommendations.

To meet these criteria, the government standards state that readers of these reports should be given a basis for judging the prevalence and consequence of the reported conditions. Thus, the standards require that reported instances or conditions be related to a universe and the number of cases examined be identified and quantified in terms of dollar value, if appropriate.

Findings Definition

The above considerations apply to auditors communicating instances of material noncompliance. reportable conditions and material weaknesses in internal controls or the results of both financial related as well as performance audits. In each type of reporting, the auditor must report on audit "*findings.*"

Though not defined in the 1994 edition of the standards, a working definition of the term *finding* (in the 1988 edition) has been generally accepted to mean:

> *"The result of information development—a logical pulling together of information to arrive at conclusions (or a*

response to an audit objective on the basis of the sum of the information) about an organization, program, activity, function, condition, or other matter that was analyzed or evaluated."

Despite a general perception or foreboding, audit findings need not be critical, negative, or be concerned only with deficiencies or weaknesses. Generally, though, a finding will be the basis for an auditor's conclusions and recommendations for change, improvement, or some corrective or protective action.

A finding is not necessarily an observation the auditor literally "finds" or that it is an observation known only to the auditor. Often, the information on which the finding is general knowledge and may have been known to others for some time.

Structure of Financial Related and Performance Audit Reports

No structured format exists for communicating *findings* of the results of financial related and performance-type audits. Generally, though, these audit reports will consist of a general section and a findings section.

The **general** section of the report would identify the scope and objectives of the audit, plus the agreed-upon or applied methodologies. The general section of a financial related report should contain background and other information to permit the reader to assess whether the auditor methodologies and audit procedures addressed the described objectives and scope. The audit objectives and scope could be established or set by those arranging for the financial related audit. Regardless of what or who caused the audit to be performed, the financial related audit report must provide sufficient information on what was to be done, why the audit was to be done, and how the audit was done.

The **findings** section of the report would separately discuss each material observation, with the discussion of each observation addressing the several standards elements of a finding.

Absence of a standard format for financial related and performance-type audits, does not imply that the content of such reports must not meet certain minimal standards. A general guide might be that a financial related report should be sufficiently complete to permit a reader to "audit" the auditor and after reviewing the reported facts and other data arrive at the same conclusions and recommendations that the auditor did. Several aspects of a financial related audit report are discussed in the following sections.

REPORTING ON FINANCIAL RELATED AND PERFORMANCE AUDITS

Audit Objectives

Audits of financial statements are made pursuant to well established standards and the results are reported in almost a "boiler plate" conclusion or opinion since the objectives are well-known. This is not the case with financial related audits of governments.

The objectives of financial related and performance audits vary in direct proportion to the number of such audits made. Each audit is unique and dependent upon criteria established for that specific audit. In the case of governmental auditors, these audit organizations may determine the audit objectives for financial related audits. With respect to CPAs, seldom will the CPA determine the objectives; the objectives of the audit will most often be set forth in the audit engagement agreement.

Communicating the purpose, need or reason—i.e., the objectives—for these audits in the audit report is essential to explain why the audit was authorized or undertaken. Without a clear statement of the audit objectives, readers are not able to assess the merits of the reported audit findings or observations. The statement of objectives sets the boundaries of the audit. To preclude misunderstanding, particularly when the audit objectives were extremely limited, the objectives or boundaries of the audit must be clearly delineated. If broader audit objectives might reasonably be inferred, the auditor should clearly state the objectives that were not pursued.

Audit Scope

In its reporting standard for financial related and performance audits, GAO states that auditors should follow the reporting standards for performance auditing. A scope description of a financial report made pursuant to GAO's guidance, appearing in the performance audit reporting standards, would encompass practically all pertinent information that a reader could or might expect. GAO requires that the statement of the scope for performance audits (and financial related audits) should:

• Describe the depth and coverage of audit work conducted to accomplish the audit's objectives;

• Explain the relationship between the universe and what was audited from that universe;

• Identify organizations and geographic locations at which audit work was conducted and the time period covered;

● Cite the kinds and sources of evidence used and the techniques used to verify the evidence;

● Explain any quality or other problems with the evidence;

● Clearly state if unverified data is referred to in the report; and

● Describe any constraints on the audit approach caused by data limitations or scope impairments.

Audit Methodologies

Government standards for performance audits, the reporting guidance of which is appropriate for financial related audits, require that the statement on audit methodology should clearly explain the evidence gathering and analysis techniques used to accomplish the audit's objectives.

The methodology section should:

● Identify any assumptions made in conducting the audit;

● Describe any comparative techniques applied and measures and criteria used to assess performance;

● If sampling is involved the sample design and why chosen; and

● Clearly describe the work done and not done, particularly if the work was limited by relying on controls or because of restraints on time, resources, or other reasons.

Findings Section of Financial Related and Performance Audit Reports

This section of financial related and performance audit reports will include audit observations or findings resulting from the audit procedures performed. The government auditing standards for reporting results of performance audits apply equally here, too. The government performance auditing standards require that each reported observation or finding should be presented in a manner that, to the extent possible, describes or discusses the several standard elements of a finding: condition, criteria, cause, effect, conclusion and recommendations.

Elements of a Finding

The elements of an audit observation or finding are generally defined in the following ways:

1. Condition—the situation, circumstance or practice which has been identified as contributing to the observed results;

2. Criteria—the goal, objective, standard, rule, regulations, or other guideline that was observed or examined by the audit;

3. Cause—the contributory circumstances or practices that have resulted in the reported observation or finding;

4. *Effect*—the dollar or other descriptor of materiality, damage or cost, loss or impairment, or benefit resulting from the existence or termination of the reported observation.;

5. *Conclusion*—the auditor's opinion or assessment of the condition, situation, circumstance, or practice observed; and

6. *Recommendation*—the suggested course of action or preferred alternatives to promote more effective or efficient operations or program performance or the desired conduct or behavior.

Condition. The reporting implicit in this element involves the determination and description—isolated or widespread—of the conditions or circumstances existing at the time the transaction or event took place not when the auditor made the examination. Fairness, objectivity, accuracy all require the auditor to be continually sensitive to the fact that "hindsight" is perfect vision—foresight never is. The auditor must repeatedly check findings against the reasonable person rule: i.e., What would have been the action of the reasonably prudent person in the circumstance that existed at the time of action?

Criteria. In governmental auditing, all programs, activities, transactions, exchange of funds, etc., are the result of some criteria, i.e., there must be an authorizing law, regulation, rule, term or condition that permits a certain action. In absence of such "criteria," there exists an indication of noncompliance, irregularity, or illegality. An important fact relating to doing the business of government is that there is no implicit or apparent authority permitting an executive to act on behalf of their government. Every action must have the prior sanction of law or the equivalent guideline.

Cause. The disclosed cause should be reported when the audit objectives require development of the reasons that contributed to the reported finding or observation. On the other hand, the objectives may be limited to having the auditor identifying only whether a problem exist, with no requirement for identifying the cause.

Identifying the underlying cause is helpful in making constructive audit recommendations. But, rooting out the cause, because of limited personnel and financial restraints, may not be possible within the period designated for the audit. Cause can be difficult to ascertain: the cause of one problem could be the effect of another problem, and vice versa. Further, the reported condition could be the result of a number of factors or causes; maybe even too many causes to individually address or explain in a written audit report.

Effect. Materiality or relative significance is a guiding criteria with respect to what should be reported in a financial related audit. But, the audit objectives will also dictate the definition of materiality or significance. Effect might be positive or beneficial happenings, or could be the financial loss, damage, or impairment suffered. Proper assessment of "effect" will require the auditor to assess immediate effects as well as collateral, intangible, long-range effects, real or potential. This is a difficult step that must be done correctly and fairly reported by the auditor.

Conclusion. Financial related and performance audit reports should contain conclusions when required by the audit objectives. Conclusions should be specific and not be left to inference by readers of the report. Conclusions can only follow from the facts appearing in the audit report. GAO, in addressing the reporting to be made on this element, states that the report should not be written on the basis that a bare recital of the facts makes the conclusion inescapable, but rather should be based on the persuasiveness of the evidence supporting the findings and the convincingness of the logic used to formulate the conclusions.

Recommendations. Financial related and performance audit reports should contain recommendations where there exists the potential for significant improvement and the case for improvement is substantiated in the audit report. In connection with recommendations, auditors should inquire about the status of any earlier recommendations made by others. Uncorrected earlier recommendations should be evaluated to determine what affect the earlier conditions may have on the current audit.

Not all of these elements of a finding will be present or necessary or required for all reported audit observations or findings. The elements needed to fully report on an observation or finding depend directly on the objective of the financial related audit. The reporting of an observation or finding is complete to the extent that the discussed elements satisfy the stated audit objectives and the report clearly relates the stated objectives to the reported observations or findings.

Further, all elements may not be reported, since what is reported depends on the objectives of the financial related audit. Also, it is quite possible that the confidential nature of audited data and other limitations may preclude the auditor from fully developing information to support reporting on each element.

Distribution of Financial Related and Performance Audit Reports

The 1994 edition of government auditing standards requires that written audit reports be submitted by the audit organization to the appropriate officials of the auditee and to the appropriate officials of the organizations requiring or arranging for the audit. These latter officials would include external funding organizations, unless legal restrictions prevent it. Copies of the reports should also be sent to other officials who have legal oversight authority or who may be responsible for acting on auditing findings and recommendations and to others authorized to receive such reports. Unless restricted by law or regulation, copies should be made available for public inspection.

Distribution or dissemination of an audit report for a governmental financial statement audit is practically routine and seldom causes problems, regardless of who make the distribution. Still, auditors should refer all requests, even for financial statement audit reports, to their clients. However, there is minimal guidance with respect to report distribution of these audits. The release of a financial related audit report must be done with more care and necessary precautions must be taken to insure that any distribution of the audit report is in strict accord with the objectives and reporting responsibilities defined by those arranging for the financial related audit.

There could be considerable risk to an auditor who assumes that the entity that arranged for the audit has also empowered the auditor to distribute the report for a financial related audit pursuant the process just described. Caution must also be exercised when the audit has been commissioned or arranged by an organization other than the auditee. The organization arranging for the audit may not desire the auditee to receive a copy of the audit report, as might be the case if an auditor were providing assistance to legal authorities that have reason to believe auditee management committed possible fraudulent acts.

This standard requires a careful reading by all auditors. Unless specifically agreed upon in the audit engagement contract, the only responsible compliance by an auditor is to refer all requests for copies of these audit reports to the officials requiring or arranging for the audit.

PERFORMANCE AUDIT STANDARDS

General Standards—Performance Audits

The government's auditing standards for many financial related and all performance audits include: (1) general, (2) field work, and (3) reporting standards.

The government's **general** audit standards for performance audits are the same as the government's general standards for financial statement and financial related audits. But, GAO has prescribed additional performance auditing standards with respect to the field work and for reporting on performance audits.

As in an earlier chapter, for GAO did *not* incorporate the AICPA's general standards, but rather specified altered or additional general auditing standards for financial and performance audits of public sector entities. standards for financial statement audits of nongovernmental and governmental entities.

132   Government Auditing: Standards and Practices

The government auditing standards include four additional or supplemental general standards. These general government audit standards are directed towards: (1) qualifications of staff, (2) auditor independence, (3) due care in performing audits, and (4) quality control required of the audit organizations.

The government's general audit standards apply to all auditing organizations—government and nongovernment, accounting and consulting firms—conducting audits of government organizations, programs, activities, and functions and of government assistance received by other organizations, including nonprofit, educational and contractor type entities.

Thus, government auditing standards impose these general standards with respect to the audits of public sector entities.

EXHIBIT 6-1

General Audit Standards For Performance Type Audits

1. The staff assigned to conduct the audit should collectively possess adequate professional proficiency for the tasks required.

2. In all matters relating to the audit work, the audit organization and the individual auditors, whether government or public, should be free from personal and external impairments to independence, should be organizationally independent, and should maintain an independent attitude and appearance.

3. Due professional care should be used in conducting the audit and in preparing related reports.

4. Each audit organization conducting audits in accordance with these standards should have an appropriate internal quality control system in place and undergo an external quality control review.

The discussion in the earlier chapter concerning the general auditing standards, should be consulted. Again, GAO intends that auditors of government apply the same general auditing standards to both financial and performance type audits.

Field Work Standards—Performance Audits

There are 5 government auditing field work standards for conducting performance audits, but which are also applicable to many financial related audits:

EXHIBIT 6-2

Government Auditing Standards for Performance Audits

1. Work is to be adequately planned.

2. Staff are to be properly supervised.

3. When laws, regulations, and other compliance requirements are significant to audit objectives, auditors should design the audit to provide reasonable assurance about compliance with them. In all performance audits, auditors should be alert to situations or transactions that could be indicative of illegal acts or abuse.

4. Auditors should obtain an understanding of management controls that are relevant to the audit. When management controls are significant to audit objectives, auditors should obtain sufficient evidence to support their judgments about these controls.

5. Sufficient, competent, and relevant evidence is to be obtained to afford a reasonable basis for the auditors' findings and conclusions. A record of the auditors' work should be retained in the form of working papers. Working papers should contain sufficient information to enable an experienced auditor having no previous connection with the audit to ascertain from them the evidence that supports the auditors' significant conclusions and judgments.

Each of these standards is separately described in the following sections.

Planning Performance Audits

Standard No. 1. Work is to be adequately planned.

With respect to many financial related and all performance audits, the objectives, scope and specific audit methodologies must be defined and described by either those arranging for the performance audit or the auditor and these must be consistent with the terms of the audit engagement:

Audit Objectives describe what the performance audit is to accomplish.

Audit Scope is the boundary of the performance audit.

Audit Methodology is the process of providing sufficient, competent, and relevant evidence to achieve the objectives of the performance audit.

The Audit Plan

Planning is distinct for these audits: no two performance audits are the same. The plan for every financial related and performance audit is to be unique, developed for that specific organization, activity, or function that is to undergo audit. With respect to financial statement audits, considerable planning has been done and is amply documented in many promulgation's of the AICPA. No such guidance exists for performance audits.

An audit plan must be prepared and reduced to writing. Because audit plans for these audits must be unique, all financial related and performance audit plans should contain or have several components. For example, the audit plan should address the:

1. Legislative and other history and legal background relevant to the audit;

2. Legal or other authority for the audit;

3. Proposed audit objectives, scope and methodologies;

4. Staff responsibilities, assignments, and work locations;

5. Budgets of time, expenses; equipment; and

6. Detailed audit programs for each area to be audited.

Planning Considerations

GAO lists, in its auditing standards, several factors that should be performed in planning these audits. An auditor must:

● Consider significance and needs of potential users of the audit report;

● Obtain an understanding of the programs to be audited;

● Consider legal and regulatory requirements;

● Consider management controls;

● Identify criteria needed to evaluate matters subject to audit;

● Identify significant findings and recommendations from previous audits that could affect the current audit objectives and if corrective action has been taken;

● Identify potential sources of data that could be used as audit evidence and consider the validity and reliability of these data;

● Consider whether the work of other auditors and experts may be used to satisfy some of the audit objectives;

● Provide sufficiency staff and other resources to do the audit; and

● Prepare a written audit plan.

Considerable literature has been published by GAO over the years on all of the above and auditors will find that each factor is discussed in detail in the GAO's performance auditing standards. As noted, these standards are equally appropriate for financial related type audits.

Staffing Performance Audits

Standard No. 2. Staff are to be properly supervised.

With performance audits, the likelihood is greater than with financial audits, that personnel with several skills in addition to accounting and auditing will be part of the performance audit team. This standard emphasizes the responsibility that all personnel—auditors and accountants, staff with expertise in other disciplines, and external consultants and specialists—must be supervised.

Supervision in the context of performance audits, defined by GAO, includes: (1) directing the efforts of auditors and all other personnel, (2) instructing staff members, (3) keeping informed of problems encountered during the audit, and (4) reviewing all work performed.

While the AICPA does not have fieldwork standards for performance audits, auditors can not ignore the AICPA's literature in conducting a performance audit. Much of the that guidance has relevance to these audits.

Testing for Non-compliance, Illegal Acts or Abuses

Standard No. 3.—When laws, regulations, and other compliance requirements are significant to audit objectives, auditors should design the audit to provide reasonable assurance about compliance with them. In all performance audits, auditors should be alert to situations or transactions that could be indicative of illegal acts or abuse.

The preface to this standard—"When ..."—is probably ill chosen. Laws, regulations, and other compliance requirements are *always* significant to the audit objectives of all governments, their activities, functions and programs.

Nothing can or should happen unless an activity, expenditure of funds, use of government property or other allocation or consumption of a government resource has been authorized by a law or regulation. No government program should exist unless there is an earlier legislative authorization. Noncompliance with authorizing legislation or operations conducted without prior legislation is significant to the objective of any audit of government and is a reportable finding in itself.

In practice, defining a general, all-encompassing, standard for determining which laws and regulations are significant and must be tested is not practicable. Many legislative mandates might apply to a single program. Thus, GAO suggests the following approach for determining laws that might be of more consequence or greater significance and therefore should be tested for compliance:

"a. Reduce each audit objective to questions about specific aspects of the program being audited—the purpose, goal, efforts, program operations, outputs, and outcomes;

b. Identify laws and regulations that directly address specific aspects of the program included in the audit objectives questions; and

c. Determine if violations of those laws and regulations could significantly affect the auditors' answers to the questions encompassed in the audit objectives. If they could, then those laws and regulations are likely to be significant to the audit objectives."

The performance auditing standards require that for audits of economy and efficiency that tests be made of laws and regulations that could significantly affect acquisition, protection, and use of government resources and the quantity, timeliness, and cost of products and services produced or delivered. Performance audits of program results require that laws and regulations pertaining to the purpose of the program, the manner of program delivery of services or operations, and the population or need to be served must also be examined.

The term "noncompliance," with respect to performance type audits, is broader than applied to financial audits. Here, noncompliance includes violations of conditions, terms, or provisions of contracts, grant and cooperative agreements as well as other agreements. Noncompliance with these instruments can be significant to the audit objectives, and particularly to nonprofit and educational type institutions, and testing for compliance must be planned, performed, and reported upon.

Noncompliance with contracts, grants, cooperative and other agreements will almost always be significant and material for programs operated by subordinate governmental units and non-profit entities, including many subrecipient organizations subject to audits under the Single Audit Act of 1984. For several of these organizations, the contract or grant agreement is the authorizing instrument that details the required performance and financial objectives and criteria that must be met by the audited organization.

In addition to noncompliance with laws and regulations and requiring the auditor to be alert to indication of illegal acts, this standard requires the auditor to also be alert to indications of abuse.

Abuse is different from illegality and other instances of noncompliance and can exist even if no law, regulations or agreement is violated. Abuse is described in the government performance audit standards, by GAO, as the conduct of a government program that falls far short of societal expectations for prudent behavior. But GAO in explaining this standard, states that " ... because the determination of *abuse* is so subjective, auditors are not expected to provide reasonable assurance of detecting it." Performance audits can only provide reasonable assurance of compliance. No audit guarantees that all indications of noncompliance, illegal acts or abuse will be discovered during the course of an audit. This recognition exists in the GAO's performance auditing standards, plus GAO provides the following caveat relating to performance audits:

> *"Nor does the subsequent discovery of illegal acts or abuse committed during the audit period necessarily mean that the auditors' performance was inadequate, provided the audit was made in accordance with these standards."*

Understand Management Controls

Standard No.4.—Auditors should obtain an understanding of management controls that are relevant to the audit. When management controls are significant to audit objectives, auditors should obtain sufficient evidence to support their judgments about these controls.

Management has the responsibility for establishing, operating, and ensuring compliance with controls. The absence of controls, regardless of conformance to legislation or regulations, is a reportable finding. Effective controls have a greater significance in governmental operations than a private corporation due to the lack of continuity among legislators, elected executives, and appointed administrative officials. No corporation could be subjected to a complete turnover of all decision-making executives and long survive. In a way neither can a government.

Turnover of government executives is excessive and an important reason for requiring installation and compliance with sound controls. Studies for decades have repeatedly showed that the senior appointed executives—generally the assistant, associate, and undersecretary of federal departments and agencies—average a term of office of less than 18 months. There is no reason to believe that this short-term occupancy is a phenomenon of just the federal government.

Without a sound system of controls, there is no assurance that programs are being effectively managed from one administration to another or within an administration and that data about these programs is accurate and properly reported. Further, all governmental entities are spending public monies for which there are long-standing and legally-based stewardship expectations and requirements.

In connection with performance audits, *Management Controls*, as defined by GAO are clearly broader than what financial auditors consider to be the internal control structure. In the performance audit standards management controls are defined as including:

- The plan of organization, methods, and procedures adopted by management to ensure that its goals are met;

- The processes for planning, organizing, directing, and controlling program operations; and

- The systems for measuring, reporting, and monitoring program performance.

As used by GAO, in its performance auditing standards, management controls are not generic, but relate specifically to what should be objectives of any government audit. For example, management controls that should exist within each of the following categories or responsibility areas or functions include:

- Controls over program operations that include policies and procedures to ensure program objectives are met;

- Controls that include policies and procedures management implemented to ensure data is valid, reliable, maintained, and fairly disclosed;

- Controls management implemented to ensure resource use is consistent with laws and regulations; and

- Controls management implemented to ensure resources are safeguarded against waste, loss, and misuse.

To acquire the understanding of management controls, the auditor must make inquiries, observations, and inspections and conduct tests of systems, transactions, support documents, records, and examine reports that relate to specific aspects of the program. These data must be considered in setting the audit objectives, the audit scope and when designing the audit methodologies for each specific performance audit.

Evidence

Standard No. 5.—Sufficient, competent, and relevant evidence is to be obtained to afford a reasonable basis for the auditors' findings and conclusions. A record of the auditors' work should be retained in the form of working papers. Working papers should contain sufficient information to enable an experienced auditor having no previous connection with the audit to ascer-

tain from them the evidence that supports the auditors' significant conclusions and judgments.

Evidence in support of a performance audit will consist of physical evidence, documentary evidence, testimonial evidence, and analytical evidence. And, seldom is one form of evidence sufficient to support an opinion or, in the case of a performance audit, the audit conclusions or recommendations. Further, evidence must be sufficient, competent, and reliable.

In explaining its performance audit standards, GAO outlines several presumptions relative to assessing the competence of evidence, i.e., validity of evidence.

● Evidence obtained from a credible third party is more competent than that secured from the auditee. Implicit in this presumption is that the auditor has other evidence to indicate that the third party providing information is in fact *credible*.

The auditor must always "consider the source" of the evidence provided, including the level of responsibility and authority of the source.

● Evidence developed under an effective system of management controls is more competent than that obtained where such controls are weak or nonexistent.

Before a judgment is reached on the competence of the evidence provided, the auditor must have earlier conducted tests and reached conclusions on the effectiveness of the controls and systems from which the data was obtained. With computer-based systems, data bases, and paperless accounting and reporting processes, auditor must more seriously evaluate the effect of weak, poor, or nonexistent controls and whether any amount of tests of transactions can provide enough confidence to "certify."

● Evidence obtained through the auditor's direct physical examination, observation, computation, and inspection is more competent than evidence obtained indirectly.

Auditors, particularly those of governments and large systems, are increasingly recognizing that these audit procedures are the only effective procedures in environments where documents, reconciliations of paper trails, and segregation of accounting and processing tasks are not practical and no longer exist.

● Original documents provide more competent evidence than do copies.

This is a caution that is especially relevant to the 1990s and the age of computers and "E-mail." Care must be taken to ensure that the auditor has examined the official record; accepting copies of records has an inherent risk. Increasingly, in paperless world, auditors will have to devote more effort to authenticating the quality of evidence and determining what constitutes "original" documents in a world where documents do not exist.

● Testimonial evidence obtained under conditions where persons may speak freely is more competent than testimonial evidence obtained under compromising or intimidating conditions.

Inquiry has been an important, if not the most important audit procedure, but one that must be used with caution and corroboration. Testimony must always be independently verified to ensure that those providing the testimony are fully knowledgeable of circumstance and conditions and have provided accurate evidence.

● Testimonial evidence obtained from individuals not biased or who have direct knowledge about the area is more competent than testimonial evidence obtained from an individual who is biased or has only partial knowledge about the area or aware of hearsay. But, the burden is on the auditor to determine the extent of bias, knowledgeability, and direct involvement of sources.

Competent evidence is not limited only to that evidence gathered directly by the auditor. Sufficient, relevant, competent evidence can be gathered by the auditee or even by third parties. In these instances, though, the auditor must independently determine the validity and reliability of the data by conducting direct tests of the data or by assessing the systems of controls from which the data originated. Obtaining written representations from officials of the auditee addressing the competence of the evidence obtained by the auditor and, possibly, the interpretations placed on the information by the auditor or the manner in which the information is being relayed all constitute invaluable audit evidence. Written representations also reduce the possibility of misunderstandings.

Working Papers

Working papers for performance audits serve three purposes: (1) working papers are the principal support for the auditor's report; (2) working papers aid the auditors in conducting and supervising the audit, and (3) working papers allow others to review the audit's quality.

In all governmental audits, the last purpose is important because audits made pursuant to government auditing standards are frequently subject to review by other auditors and oversight officials. It is also a fact that audit working papers for government audits will be reviewed, if for no other reason, to avoid duplicate audits of an auditee. To facilitate this "sharing" of working papers, contractual arrangements for audits pursuant to government auditing standards have provisions relating to working paper access.

Reporting Standards—Performance Audits

There are five government auditing reporting standards for conducting performance audits:

EXHIBIT 6-3

Government Reporting Standards for Performance Audits

1. Auditors should prepare written audit reports communicating the results of each audit.

2. Auditors should appropriately issue the reports to make the information available for timely use by management, legislative officials, and other interested parties.

3. Auditors should report the audit objectives and the audit scope and methodology.

4. The report should be complete, accurate, objective, and convincing, and as clear and concise as the subject matter permits.

5. Written reports are to be submitted by the audit organization to appropriate officials of the auditee and to the appropriate officials of the organizations requiring or arranging for the audits, including external funding organizations, unless legal restrictions prevent it. Copies of the reports should also be sent to other officials who have legal oversight authority or who may be responsible for acting on audit findings and recommendations and to others authorized to receive such reports. Unless restricted by law or regulation, copies should be made available for public inspection.

Written Reports

Standard No. 1. Auditors should prepare written audit reports communicating the results of each audit.

This standard, without exception, requires that the report be in writing. The word "should" is almost inappropriate and not intended to be generally, but only seldom, applied. Public officials are entrusted with public resources and are accountable to the public and to other levels and branches of government to carry out the programs and deliver the services authorized in legislation or required by implementing regulations. It is important to remember, when conducting a performance audit, that these are not private monies nor are the programs private enterprises, and, therefore, accountability can not be private. Implicit in accountability is that there be a reporting. This standard means that reporting of performance audits must be in writing.

Discussions of findings, judgments, conclusions and recommendations with responsible government executives must take place and are encouraged, but even these communications should be reduced to writing and compiled in the audit working papers. There may be instances when the engagement contract requires alternative reporting or briefings or oral presentation. The auditor is cautioned that a written memorandum of all communications is the only defense from possible future allegations of concealment of facts or less than full disclosure on the part of the auditor.

Issuing Performance Audit Reports

Standard No. 2. Auditors should appropriately issue the reports to make the information available for timely use by management, legislative officials, and other interested parties.

Independent auditors generally are constrained, with respect to timeliness of reporting by the engagement contract. The contract will almost always specify a report delivery date. Auditors employed by governments, however, may have some discretion on what to audit and when to make a reporting. These auditors must be particularly cognizant of the timeliness of their reporting. Reports issued too late for action—by legislators, elected officials, administrative managers—are not timely and of limited utility.

The audit reporting need not always be at the conclusion of the report. Interim reports of audit findings have many benefits, including timeliness, earlier validation by the auditee, opportunity for immediate corrective action by the auditee, and avoidance of "surprises" on the part of the auditor. Reporting by interim report does not obviate the need or responsibility for reporting the same information in the final report to those arranging for the audit or those with oversight responsibilities for the auditee organization.

Corrective action and change for the better is a key purpose of an audit and its related report on audit results. If advance information can be communicated and the conditions are corrected before a final report is issued, so much the better. That audit is a success, even if the final report is delayed.

Reporting of Performance Audits

Standard No. 3. Auditors should report the audit objectives and the audit scope and methodology.

The objectives, scope, and methodology of a financial statement audit are well known to most persons involved with public and private enterprises, well documented by the AICPA, and often well reported upon by the financial media.

This is not so with respect to a performance audit. In contrast, the objective, scope and methodology of a performance audit is not known and can not be inferred and is seldom reported upon by the media. Each performance audit is unique, specific to the organization, activity, or function to be examined. For this reason each performance audit report must inform the reader of its specific objective, scope, and methodologies applied.

The *objective* section of the report should explain why the audit was made; the *scope* should describe what was done, *i.e.*, the depth and coverage of work conducted to accomplish the audit objective; the *methodology* should explain how the audit was done, *i.e.*, the gathering and analysis techniques used.

To comply with this performance audit reporting standard, GAO requires a performance auditor to report:

● Significant audit findings and, where applicable, audit conclusions;

● Recommendations for corrective action and to improve operations;

● That the audit was made pursuant to generally accepted government auditing standards;

● Significant instances of noncompliance, of abuse, and illegal acts;

● The scope of work on management controls and any significant weaknesses;

● Views of responsible officials relating to the reported findings, conclusions, recommendations, and corrective actions planned or taken;

● Noteworthy accomplishments, particularly management improvements;

● Significant issues needing further audit work should be referred to auditors responsible for planning future audit work; and

● The nature of any information omitted from the performance audit report and the requirement that makes the omission necessary.

With respect to nongovernmental auditors, a careful study should be made of the government auditing standards and legal counsel should be consulted if information is prohibited from general disclosure or when making references to the omitted information in the audit report.

Complete, Accurate, Objective, Convincing Reporting

Standard No. 4. The report should be complete, accurate, objective, and convincing, and as clear and concise as the subject matter permits.

GAO has provided the following interpretation of the key terms of this performance audit standard, for example:

- *Complete*—contains all the information needed to satisfy the audit objectives, promote an adequate and correct understanding of matters reported, and meet the report content requirements;

- *Accurate*—the evidence be true and findings correctly portrayed;

- *Objective*—presentation of the entire report must be balanced in content and tone;

- *Convincing*—the reported results must be responsive to the audit objectives, findings presented persuasively, and conclusions and recommendations follow logically from the facts;

- *Clear*—the report must be easy to read and understand and written in language as clear and simple as the subject permits; and

- *Concise*—the report should be no longer than necessary to convey and support the message.

In earlier editions of its government auditing standards and other publications, GAO has over the years offered suggestions for effective audit reporting, such as:

- Single examples of a single deficiency are insufficient to support broad conclusions and sweeping recommendations;

- One inaccuracy places the entire audit report in doubt and provides opportunity to divert attention from the substance of the audit results;

- If unaudited data is presented in the audit report, the data's limitations should be noted and no unwarranted conclusions or recommendations should be based on this data;

- Avoid any tendency to exaggerate or overemphasize deficient performance; include explanations of unusual difficulties or circumstances;

Financial Related and Performance Audits   145

● The reported information must convince the reader of the validity of the findings, the reasonableness of conclusions and benefits of implementing recommendations;

● Findings should be based on only conditions and circumstances existing at the time the event or transaction took place—avoid "Monday morning quarterbacking;" and

● The auditor's report should describe conditions and circumstances as they now exist or were. The purpose of an audit report is not to "sell," but to inform.

These guidelines apply to more than reporting on performance audits and can be broadly used for any form of exception and evaluative reporting.

Intended Recipients of Performance Audit Reports

Standard No. 5. Written reports are to be submitted by the audit organization to appropriate officials of the auditee and to the appropriate officials of the organizations requiring or arranging for the audits, including external funding organizations unless legal restrictions prevent it. Copies of the reports should also be sent to other officials who have legal oversight authority or who may be responsible for acting on audit findings and recommendations and to others authorized to receive such reports. Unless restricted by law or regulation, copies should be made available for public inspection.

This particular performance reporting standard addresses an important topic—who should get audit reports. The determination of who is entitled to receive the report and who distributes the report is often beyond the control of the auditor, either the independent accountant or governmental internal auditor.

In the case of an independent external auditor, e.g., a public accounting or external consulting firm, the auditor may only forward the audit report in the manner outlined in the audit agreement. The reporting may only be made as outlined in the audit engagement contract and almost always all parties are aware of who will get the report and from whom.

On the other hand, governmental auditors, conducting internal audits of their employing or other organizations or who make external audits of other organizations, must comply with communication policies of their organization.

Under ideal conditions, GAO requires that performance audit reports be distributed to: (1) officials designated in law or regulation to receive such reports; (2) officials responsible for acting on the findings and recommendations; and (3) officials of other levels of government that provided assistance to the audited organization.

But, conditions will not always be ideal. Auditors may be specifically precluded from making certain report distributions or providing report access to all who may have an interest in the report. Alternatively, auditors should refer all requests for copies of performance audit reports to the entity arranging for the performance audit. In government audits, particularly, the entity arranging for the audit may not be the auditee. Further, there may be prohibitions or restrictions imposed on the auditor providing copies of the audit report to the auditee.

As noted earlier in this chapter, laws, statutes, or regulations may preclude the release of certain information except on a designated "need to know" basis. Where such a requirement exists, the pertinent data should be stated in the auditors' report. Auditors external to government, should note that literal compliance with GAO's reporting standard could place the auditor somewhat at odds with past warnings by GAO. In its Exposure Draft that preceded the final issuance of the 1994 revision to the government auditing standards, GAO cautioned:

> "Auditors should be aware that ... reports containing information on fraud or other illegal acts that could result in criminal prosecution, or reports with references that such acts [fraud or other illegal acts] were omitted, could interfere with legal processes or subject the implicated individuals to undue publicity. They also might subject auditors to potential legal action."

AICPA's ATTESTATION STANDARDS

The AICPA attestation standards recognize that independent accountants often perform engagements where the end objective is other than the issuance of the standard audit opinion that accompanies a financial statement. The attestation standards relate to engagements where the auditor issues a written communication expressing a conclusion about the reliability of an assertion that is the responsibility of some party other than the auditor. Considerable care has been taken by the AICPA to describe with precision when, how, and to what engagements attestation standards apply. The AICPA has stated that its attestation standards do not apply to engagements for which reporting is made pursuant to: (1) government auditing standards, (2) the Single Audit Act of 1984, (3) OMB regulations implementing the single audit concept, or (4) to program specific audits performed in accordance with federal audit guides.

Chapter 7

Reporting—Pursuant to the Single Audit Act of 1996

OVERVIEW

Congress passed the Single Audit Act in 1984, and amended the Act in 1996, in an attempt to improve financial management of governments, establish uniform audit requirements for federal monies, and minimize, to the maximum extent, redundant audits by various levels of government and independent auditors. The Act prescribed that one comprehensive audit will be made, once a year, by one auditor of each governmental unit receiving a specified level of federal financial assistance. Congress, in the Single Audit Act, has declared that this audit is to be in lieu of any other financial audit of federal awards which a nonfederal entity is required to undergo.

Until the Single Audit Act, many limited the definition of federal financial assistance to contracts and grants. The Act considerably broadened the definition of federal financial assistance beyond contracts and grants, to include:

> *"... assistance that nonfederal entities receive or administer in the form of grants, loans, loan guarantees, property, cooperative agreements, interest subsidies, insurance, food commodities, direct appropriations, or other assistance, ..."* [1]

The audits of about 20,000 governmental units and another estimated 100,000 non-profit organizations must comply with the requirements of the Single Audit Act. With few exceptions, a single audit must encompass the entirety of the financial operations or entity defined as a covered government or department, agency or establishment or non-profit organization.

---

[1] Pursuant to the 1996 Act and the related implementing federal regulation, OMB Circular A-133, Audits of States, Local Governments, and Non-Profit Organizations, payments or amounts received as reimbursement for services rendered to individuals relating to the federal Medicare and Medicaid assistance programs are specifically excluded from this definition of federal financial assistance.

The Single Audit Act was unprecedented in the level of detailed auditing that Congress prescribed in an attempt to resolve the disparities and inconsistencies in audits of federal programs. This detail extended to the nature, content and format of the audit reports that must be submitted by qualifying governments. In several instances, the reporting is immense in relation to the dollars of federal assistance received by a governmental unit.

A casual reading of the Act and the government auditing standards, as outlined in earlier chapters, might cause one to conclude that these standards and the Single Audit Act are duplicative in the nature of what must be audited and, in some respects, the type of audit reports that must be issued by the auditor. This is not the case. Distinctly different audits must be performed and more and different audit reports are required under the Single Audit Act than under the government auditing standards.

Government auditing standards require auditors of governmental units and other organizations to submit three audit reports: (1) a report on the entity-wide financial statements and mention that the audit complies with government auditing standards, (2) a report on the auditor's audit scope and results of tests of compliance with laws and regulations and (3) a report on the auditor's audit scope and results of tests of compliance with internal controls.

Compliance with the Single Audit Act of 1984 requires that covered governmental units and nonprofit organizations must annually submit three "packages" of audit reports: (1) those audit reports required by the government auditing standards that relate to the entity-wide financial statements, (2) the more detailed audit reports imposed by the Single Audit Act, (3) plus, the additional reports imposed by the OMB Circular A-133, the federal regulation that implements and defines a single audit in great detail. The reporting for the Single Audit Act and Circular A-133 relate to the results of mandated audit testing of individual federal assistance programs.

SIGNIFICANCE OF *MAJOR* FEDERAL ASSISTANCE PROGRAMS

The audit and reporting focus of both the Single Audit Act and Circular A-133 is the individual federal assistance program. The *Catalog of Federal Domestic Assistance* lists, describes and assigns a specific CFDA number to several hundred federal programs. Determination of what constitutes a *major* federal program is important to insure compliance with the Single Audit Act. The significance of a *major* federal program is that special audit procedures and specific audit reporting requirements are attached to all major federal programs.

For example, for each *major* federal program, the Single Audit (§ 7502 of the Act) requires that each single audit shall: (1) cover the operations of the entire nonfederal entity, (2) be conducted in accordance with generally accepted government auditing standards, (3) include specific detailed audit tests, and (4) result in mandated audit opinions and reportings. For example, in conducting a single audit the auditor must:

• Determine whether the financial statements are presented fairly in all material respects in conformity with generally accepted accounting principles;

• Determine whether the schedule of expenditures of federal awards is presented fairly in all material respects in relation to the financial statements taken as a whole;

• With respect to internal controls pertaining to compliance requirements for each major federal program, the auditor shall: (1) obtain an understanding of such internal controls, (2) assess control risk, and (3) perform tests of controls, unless controls are deemed ineffective; and

• Determine whether the nonfederal entity complied with laws, regulations, contracts and grants pertaining to the federal awards that have a direct and material effect on each major program.

A *major* federal assistance program is one with federal awards expended during the audit period exceeding the larger of $300,000 or 3 percent of the total federal awards in the case of an auditee for which total federal awards expended equal or exceed $300,000 but are less than or equal to $100 million. For larger recipients of federal assistance, those exceeding $100 million but less than $10 billion, a *major* federal program is one where $3 million or 3/10th of one percent was expended. For even larger recipients of federal assistance, those exceeding $10 billion, a *major* federal program is one where $30 million or 15/100th of one percent was expended.

These larger federal assistance programs are referred to as Type A programs. Smaller federal assistance programs and low risk Type A programs are referred to in Circular A-133 as Type B.

BASIS OF SINGLE AUDIT ACCOUNTING AND REPORTING

For Entity-Wide Financial Statements

Most governmental units prepare their entity-wide financial statements in accordance with the generally accepted accounting principles promulgated by the Governmental Accounting Standards Board. However, many governmental units are required to prepare financial statements on bases other than generally accepted accounting principles. For example, some states impose a basis of accounting other than generally accepted accounting principles on their subordinate governments. (Entity-wide financial statements are discussed more fully in Chapter 5.)

The most widely used alternative basis of accounting is the cash basis, although other hybrid methods of accounting and reporting might be imposed by law or regulations. Where a basis other than generally accepted accounting principles is used, the auditor must issue the audit opinion on the government's financial statements in accordance with the AICPA's SAS No. 14, *Special Reports*, and identify the basis of presentation actually used for the financial statements, describe how the basis differs from generally accepted accounting principles, and cite the fact that the financial statements are not intended to conform with generally accepted accounting principles.

Neither government auditing standards nor the Single Audit Act prescribe or mandate that generally accepted accounting principles be used in financial statements of federal recipients. Rather the federal government has stated that a federal recipient and its auditor must merely disclose whether generally accepted accounting principles were followed in preparing the financial statements. If a basis of accounting other than generally accepted accounting principles were followed, this fact must be reported by the auditor.

For Schedule of Federal Awards

The Schedule of Expenditures of Federal Awards, another required audited report, details federal assistance programs by their CFDA number and identifies total federal expenditures for each CFDA program for the audited period. The federal government acknowledges that this report could be presented on a basis different than generally accepted accounting and even different from the basis of accounting used by the federal recipient in its entity-wide financial statements.

The federal government does not prescribe a basis of accounting for use on the Schedule of Federal Awards. However, when the basis is other than the basis used for its financial statements, the federal recipient must disclose that basis of accounting and the significant accounting policies used in preparing the Schedule.

For Federal Programs

It is also encumbent on the auditor to note when program information in the Schedule may not fully agree with other federal award reports. A common reason for this disparity might be that program data and reports (1) could be compiled on a different fiscal period or (2) could be based on cumulative-to-date data rather than data for the current year only. This type of reporting may not be at the selection or option of the federal recipient, but could be a request by a federal department or agency.

SINGLE AUDIT REPORTS

Required by Government Auditing Standards

The government auditing standards require that reports of financial audits of qualifying governmental organizations, programs, activities, or functions and nonprofit organizations include the following components:

- A report with an opinion (or disclaimer of opinion) that the financial statements of the audited entity are presented in accordance with generally accepted accounting principles and that an audit was made in accordance with generally accepted government auditing standards.

- A written report on the study and evaluation of the entity's compliance with internal control structure and the results of that study and evaluation made as a part of the audit of the entity's financial statements.

- A written report on tests made of compliance with laws and regulations and the results of those tests made as a part of the audit of the entity's financial statements.

- A separate report, if appropriate, on disclosed or known irregularities or illegal acts, unless clearly inconsequential, must be submitted.

Note that the audit reports on the entity's financial statement submitted to comply with the government auditing standards will satisfy a similar reporting requirement in Section 7502 of the Single Audit Act. The same reporting, pursuant to government auditing standards but described in additional detail, is required by Section 505, *Audit Reporting*, of OMB Circular A-133.

[The reporting required by government auditing standards is described more fully in Chapter 5.]

Required by the Single Audit Act and Circular A-133

Considerable additional audit work is required to comply with the more detailed reporting mandated by the Single Audit Act and the related Circular A-133. The following nine reports are required, in addition to the 3 reports required by the government auditing standards, to comply with all the reporting requirements of the Act and A-133:

(1) A report on whether the audited entity has internal control systems to provide reasonable assurance that federal programs are being managed in compliance with laws and regulations. (§ 500 *Scope of Audit*, and § 505 *Audit Reporting* of OMB Circular A-133.)

(2) A report on whether the audited entity has complied with laws and regulations that may have a direct and material effect upon *each* major federal assistance program. (§ 500 *Scope of Audit*, and § 505 *Audit Reporting* of OMB Circular A-133.)

(3) Schedule of Expenditures of Federal Awards (§ 310 *Financial Statements*, and § 505 *Audit Reporting*, of OMB Circular A-133.)

(4) Schedule of Findings and Questioned Costs (§ 505 *Audit Reporting*, § 510 *Audit findings* of OMB Circular A-133.)

(5) Summary schedule of prior audit findings (§ 315 *Audit findings follow-up* of OMB Circular A-133.)

(6) Audit follow-up report on prior audit findings (§ 315 *Audit findings follow-up*, § 500 *Scope of Audit*, of OMB Circular A-133.)

(7) Corrective action plan (§ 315 *Audit findings follow-up* of OMB Circular A-133.)

(8) Data collection form (§ 320 *Report Submission*, § 500 *Scope of Audit*, 510 *Audit findings* of OMB Circular A-133.)

(9) Known fraud in federal programs. (§ 510 *Audit findings* of OMB Circular A-133.)

1. Report on Controls

A report of a single audit must contain a separate report, prepared by the auditor, on whether the audited entity has internal control systems to provide reasonable assurance that federal programs are being managed in compliance with laws and regulations.

Internal controls are defined by the Act as comprising:

> *"... a process, affected by an entity's management and other personnel, designed to provide reasonable assurance regarding the achievement of objectives in the following categories: Effectiveness and efficiency of operations; Reliability of financial reporting; Compliance with applicable laws and regulations."*

Circular A-133, that implements the Act, embellishes upon this definition of controls, stating that internal control means:

> *"... a process, affected by an entity's management and other personnel, designed to provide reasonable assurance regarding the achievement of the following objectives for federal programs:*
>
> > *Transactions are properly recorded and accounted for to: (1) Permit preparation of reliable financial statements and federal reports; (2) Maintain accountability over assets; and*

(3) Demonstrate compliance with laws and regulations, and other compliance requirements.

Transactions are executed in compliance with: (1) Laws, regulations, and the provisions of contracts or grant agreements that could have a direct and material effect on a federal program; and (2) Any other laws and regulations that are identified in the compliance supplement; and, (3) Funds, property, and other assets are safeguarded against loss from unauthorized use or disposition."

The controls report mandated by the Single Audit Act differs from the internal control report required to satisfy the government auditing standards, mentioned above. The earlier internal control report is a report on controls in relation to the *overall* audited entity. The internal control report, required by the Act, discusses the results of tests of controls in relation to each major federal program.

2. Report on Compliance with Laws and Regulations

A report of a single audit must contain a separate reporting by the auditor, including the auditor's opinion, on whether the audited entity has complied with laws and regulations that may have a direct and material effect upon *each* major federal assistance program. The principal compliance requirements applicable to most federal programs and the compliance requirements of the largest federal programs are included in OMB's *Compliance Supplement*. For this report, the testing must include tests of transactions and application of other auditing procedures necessary to provide the auditor with sufficient evidence to support an audit opinion asserting that for *each* of its major federal programs, the auditee complied in all material respects with legal and regulatory requirements.

This audit report on compliance differs from the compliance report required to satisfy the government auditing standards mentioned above. The earlier compliance report is a report on compliance in relation to the *overall* governmental entity, i.e., entity-wide. This compliance report, required by the Act and Circular A-133, discusses the results of tests for compliance with relation laws and regulations affecting *each* individual federal program.

3. Schedule of Expenditures of Federal Awards

A report of a single audit must contain a separate report, Schedule of Federal Financial Awards, prepared by the auditee but audited and opined upon by the auditor. The Schedule of Federal Financial Awards, is a report that shows the total expenditures for all federal assistance program and details federal assistance programs by each CFDA number, identifying total federal expenditures for each CFDA program for the audited period.

This Schedule, required by the Act and OMB Circular A-133, lists expenditures and other data for all federal assistance agreements, categorized by federal program, that were open or active during the fiscal year audited. While this Schedule is considered to be supplementary information to an auditee's required annual financial statements and reporting, the auditor must state whether this information was subjected to the auditing procedures applied in the audit of the basic financial statements. And, the auditor must state if, in the auditor's opinion, this information is fairly stated in all material respects in relation to the basic financial statements taken as a whole.

4. Schedule of Findings and Questioned Costs

A report of a single audit must contain a separate reporting titled, Schedule of Findings and Questioned Costs. This report or Schedule, prepared by the auditor, will detail several specific types of audit observations, including, but not limited to:

1. All determinations and reportings by the auditor of those deficiencies in internal controls that, in the auditor's determination, are reportable conditions in internal controls over major federal programs. And, the auditor must identify reportable conditions which are individually or cumulatively material weaknesses.

2. All material noncompliance with provisions of laws, regulations, contracts, grant agreements related to a major federal program noted by the auditor. The auditor's determination of whether noncompliance is *material* is in relation to a type of compliance requirement in relation to a major program.

3. All known questioned costs which are greater than $10,000 for a type of compliance requirement for a major federal program. *Known* questioned costs are those specifically identified by the auditor. But, when evaluating the effect of questioned costs on the opinion on compliance, the auditor must consider *likely* questioned costs, i.e., the auditor's best estimate of total questioned costs, not just the known questioned costs.

5. Summary Schedule of Prior Audit Findings

It is the responsibility of an auditee that receives federal financial assistance to follow-up and take corrective action on all audit findings. OMB circular A-133 imposes a responsibility on the auditee to prepare a summary schedule of prior audit findings. This schedule requires the auditee to establish an audit finding reference coding system since the audit findings may have arisen in various or relate to multiple years.

This schedule must indicate the fiscal year in which the finding initially occurred.

As part of the scope of a single audit, the auditor is required to (1) follow-up on prior audit findings, (2) perform procedures and tests to assess the reasonableness of the summary schedule of prior audit findings that was prepared by the auditee, and (3) report, as a finding of the current audit year, when the auditor concludes that the summary schedule of prior audit findings materially misrepresents the status of any prior audit finding. The auditor must perform this follow-up procedure regardless of whether a prior audit finding relates to a major program in the current year.

6. Corrective Action Plan

The auditor's findings must be presented in sufficient detail to permit the auditee to prepare a corrective action plan and take corrective action. Also, the detail must be sufficient to permit federal agencies and pass-through entities to arrive at management decisions related to the reported findings. *Corrective action* is defined, in Circular A-133, to mean action taken by the auditee that (1) corrects identified deficiencies; (2) produces recommended improvements; or (3) demonstrates that audit findings are either invalid or do not warrant auditee action.

Thus, OMB Circular A-133 imposes a responsibility on the auditee to prepare a corrective action plan for current year audit findings. The corrective action plan should be cross referenced to the Summary Schedule of Prior Audit Findings since the audit findings may have arisen in various years or relate to multiple years and require an indication of the fiscal year in which the finding initially occurred.

7. Data Collection Form

In 1997, with the revised Circular A-133, OMB required the auditee to prepare and submit a data collection form that contains an attestation that a single audit was completed in accordance with the Circular and must provide other information about the auditee's federal programs and the results of the audit. A knowledgeable, senior level representative of the auditee (e.g., state controller, director of finance, chief executive officer, chief financial officer) must sign a statement, as part of this form, and assert that: (1) the auditee complied with the requirements of the Circular, (2) the data collection form was prepared in accordance with the Circular, and (3) the information in the form, in its entirety, is accurate and complete.

Specific sections of the data collection form must be completed by the auditor as well. Plus, the auditor must sign a statement, as part of the form, that indicates: (1) the source of information included in this form, (2) the auditor's responsibility for the information, (3) that the form is not a substitute for the single audit reporting package (i.e., the financial statements, schedule of expenditures of federal awards, summary schedule of prior audit findings, auditors report, and corrective action plan) required by Circular A-133, and (4) the content of this form is limited to the data elements prescribed by OMB.

While the preference is that this form be prepared and submitted as part of the annual reporting for a single audit, the Collection Form must be submitted within the earlier of 30 days after receipt of the auditor's report or 9 months after the end of the audit period unless a longer period is permitted by the federal cognizant or oversight agency.

8. Fraud in Federal Programs

Circular A-133 requires that an auditor, conducting a single audit, report known fraud affecting a federal award, unless such fraud is otherwise reported as an audit finding in the schedule of findings and questioned costs for the federal awards. Under the Circular, the auditor does not have to make an additional reporting when the auditor confirms that the fraud was reported outside of the auditor's reports under the direct reporting requirements of the government auditing standards.

For single audits, the auditee is required to report information about irregularities, illegal acts and indications that fraud (a type of illegal act) may have occurred. Under governmental auditing standards, the auditor need not report information about clearly inconsequential irregularities and illegal acts.[2] While the auditee has the primary responsibility for reporting irregularities, illegal acts and indications of fraud to external parties, the auditor also has reporting responsibilities. The auditor must make external reports in two instances, even if the auditor has resigned or been dismissed from the audit:

(1) When the fraud or illegal acts have been reported to the auditee and the auditee fails to make this reporting as soon as possible to external parties, the auditor must communicate their awareness of the failure to report to the auditee's governing body.

(2) When fraud or illegal acts involve federal assistance, the auditor may have a duty to report directly to federal agencies if the auditee management fails to take remedial steps or report the incidences. If the failure causes the auditor to depart from the standard audit report on financial statements or if the auditor resigns, the

---

[2] In its standards, the General Accounting Office issued this caveat to the auditors: "Whether a particular act is, in fact, illegal may have to wait final determination by a court of law. Thus, when auditors disclose matters that have led them to conclude that an illegal act is likely to have occurred, they should take care not to imply that they have made a determination of illegality."

auditor should communicate that conclusion to the auditee's governing body. If this body fails to report the fraud or illegal act as soon as practicable to the governmental body providing financial assistance, the auditor should report directly to that body.

The term *fraud*, an illegal act, is synonymous with irregularities as used in the literature of the generally accepted auditing standards, the government auditing standards, and OMB Circular A-133. Auditors should note that, in contrast to generally accepted auditing standards and government auditing standards, Circular A-133 does not limit the reporting of this information to clearly inconsequential irregularities and illegal acts.

Binding of Single Audit Reports

All of the above reports—those required by the government auditing standards and those required by the Single Audit Act and Circular A-133 may be separately bound or bound as a group into a single document for submission. Further, the two reports on internal controls and the two reports on compliance might also be combined. In past years, some practitioners have found that combining the two internal control and two compliance reports to be cumbersome. Further, some federal reviewers experience difficulty in reviewing and passing on the acceptability of the combined reports.

Optional Reporting

The Single Audit Act provides a reporting option for a single audit of the entire governmental entity receiving the qualifying level of federal financial assistance. This option provides that the audit may consist of a series of audits that cover departments, agencies or other organizations that expended or administered federal awards during the audited year.

Each audit must encompass the financial statements and schedule of expenditures of federal awards for each organization, which is considered as a nonfederal establishment that received, expended, or otherwise administered federal monies. However, when this option is used, the auditee must insure that all subordinate organizations have had the equivalent of a single audit and these auditees have had an audit of their overall general purpose financial statements and that all reports must be submitted at the same time for the same fiscal periods.

Applying the "optional" approach to individual departments or agencies is not recommended for effectiveness, efficiency or economy. When applied, this several-audit approach seems to be dictated more by the political concern with "sharing the wealth" among more than one audit firm. The AICPA (the March 1988, *The CPA Letter*) provided guidance relating to reporting on the optional type audits of subordinate organizations of government entities. When reporting on subordinate organizations, the AICPA required that the auditor's report should clearly describe that the report is for only a portion of the government's overall funds, a particular fund type or a portion of the account groups.

Reporting by Subordinate Organizations

Under this optional reporting, the single audit must still encompass the entirety of the financial operations of the subordinate department, agency or establishment. The auditor must still determine and report (1) whether the financial statements of the subordinate organization are fairly presented in accordance with generally accepted accounting principles; (2) whether the subordinate entity complied with federal laws and regulations that could affect both the financial statements of the subordinate entity as well as the individual federal programs, and (3) whether the internal controls systems provide reasonable assurance that federal programs are being managed in accordance with laws and regulations.

EXAMPLES AND DISCUSSION OF SINGLE AUDIT REPORTS

Under the Single Audit Act of 1984, an annual audit is to be made by an independent auditor and that audit shall encompass the entirety of the financial operations of such government (or by departments, agencies, or establishments if the entity avails itself of the reporting option).

The Single Audit requires that covered governments submit the financial statements and reports required by government auditing standards, which include the audited financial statements, and reports on compliance with laws and regulations and internal controls for the government entity as a whole. (These reports are discussed and illustrated in Chapters 5 and 6.)

Other reports, up to nine depending on who does the counting, must also be submitted to comply with either the Single Audit Act or the OMB Circular A-133, the implementing regulation for the Act. These were defined in the above sections; the following sections illustrate and discuss examples of these reports.

Over the years, a custom has evolved whereby audit practitioners volunteer their knowledge and experience to collaborate with and assist the federal government and task forces and committees of the American Institute of Certified Public Accountants in designing audit and reporting procedures and practices for the guidance of auditors employed by governments or by independent certified public accounting firms. This manner of government and professional cooperation has existed since the 1970s with respect to the single audits. *Exhibit 7-1* through *Exhibit 7-4* are the audit reports that resulted from such collaboration. The illustrated reports are those suggested by practitioners of governmental auditing, in and out of government, and approved by the AICPA. But, these examples are guidance and should be used in circumstances that match the reporting. Auditors must change their reports where the audited facts are otherwise.

COMPLIANCE AND INTERNAL CONTROLS REPORTING

OMB, Circular A-133, requires that there be reports on compliance with laws and regulations and on internal control related to (1) the financial statements and (2) the major programs. In both instances, the reports must describe the scope of testing of internal control and results of tests and, where applicable, refer to a separate schedule of findings and questioned costs.

The government has permitted the reporting on tests for compliance with laws and regulations and on internal controls in a combined manner. In practice, the auditor's reports may be organized in a different manner than those illustrated.

The report's format might appear cumbersome due to the auditor's responsibility to meet several audit reporting requirements in one report, e.g., the government auditing standards, which in turn include all of the generally accepted auditing standards, the Single Audit Act, plus the auditing and reporting requirements in OMB Circular A-133.

Exhibit 7-1 is an example of a combined report to meet the dual requirements of reporting the results of test of compliance and internal controls of federal financial assistance programs in one combined report. The following explanations and discussion have been referenced to specific paragraphs of that report.

● The introductory paragraph for both the *Compliance* and the *Internal Controls over Compliance* confirms that the auditor has complied the audit requirements relating to tests for compliance with laws and regulations and of internal controls in accordance with OMB Circular A-133. This paragraph for both sections also outlines that it is management's responsibility to (1) comply with the requirements of laws, regulations, contracts and grants applicable to *each* of the entity's *major* federal program, and (2) to establish and maintain effective internal control over compliance with requirements of laws, regulations, contracts and grants applicable to the entity's federal program.

● The second or scope paragraph sets forth the auditing criteria used during the audit of *compliance*. For example, with respect to the audit of compliance, the auditor notes that the audit was made in accordance with (1) generally accepted auditing standards (of the

AICPA), standards applicable to financial statement audits in government auditing standards (of the U.S. General Accounting Office), and OMB Circular A-133.

The second and third paragraphs of the *internal control* report define reportable conditions and material weaknesses, both of which are conditions of serious deficiency with respect to an entity's control system. The example report illustrates the reporting of significant deficiency noted during tests of internal controls.

● The third or opinion (or disclaimer of opinion) paragraph in the *compliance* section is required for the auditor's report on compliance. In this example, the auditor expressed a qualified audit opinion and makes specific reference to specific instances of noncompliance as the basis for such a qualification. If the auditor's tests of each major federal program disclosed no exceptions, an unqualified audit opinion would be appropriate and would read as follows: "In our opinion, the Example Entity complied, in all material respects, with the requirements referred to above that are applicable to each of its major federal programs for the year ended June 30, 19X1."

The compliance audit report must include an audit opinion (or disclaimer of an opinion) as to whether the auditee complied with laws, regulations, contracts or grant agreements which could have a direct and material effect on *each major* program. The report must describe the scope of testing and results of tests and, where applicable, refer to a separate schedule of findings and questioned costs. As in the standard audit report on financial statements, the auditor reminds all readers that an audit is performed on a *test* basis, to obtain *reasonable* assurance, concerning *material* matters.

Findings related to noncompliance and the identification of questioned costs in excess of $10,000 must be reported in a schedule of findings and questioned costs that accompanies the auditor's single audit report. This schedule as a minimum should include:

    1. The identification of the program by name, CFDA (the Catalog of Federal Domestic Assistance) number, and specific federal award number, if any.

    2. A description of each finding of noncompliance, addressing all elements of a finding, to the extent possible.

    3. Views of management as well as recommendation of the auditor.

    4. A determination of cost questioned based only on the direct costs. Indirect costs should be allocated to questioned costs in accordance with the approved indirect cost plan and be separately identified.

There is no opinion paragraph required for the auditor's report on tests of *internal control*. For this section of the audit report, the auditor is required to provide specific assurances or conclusions, e.g., "We noted certain matters involving the internal control over compliance and its operation that we consider to be reportable conditions." and, "However, we believe that none of the reportable conditions described above is a material weakness."

It is important to underscore that this reporting provides audit assurances in relation to *each* of the separate major federal assistance programs. This is a considerably lower and more detailed level of audit assurance than the assurance of materiality in relation to the entity-wide financial statements required by generally accepted auditing standards. Auditors must understand that the compliance opinion goes to *each* of the *major* federal assistance programs and not to the aggregate of all federal programs.

The *major* federal programs receive extensive audit coverage during a single audit. Given the definition of a major federal financial assistance program, i.e., the greater of $300,000 or 3 percent total federal expenditures, a government or nonprofit organization could have up to 33 major federal programs. Of course, most recipients of federal awards have much less than this number.

The concluding paragraph is not intended to nor can an auditor restrict the distribution of a single audit report. The objective of the paragraph is to put readers on notice that the audit report was prepared for a specific purpose. An auditor can not be responsible for a use of the audit reports for purposes other than for which the report was prepared.

It is important for auditors to understand that all of these elements must be addressed for *each* of the major federal assistance programs and not just for the aggregate of all federal programs. While a single audit report is submitted for compliance with laws and regulations, a careful reading of the audit report describes that the auditor is, in actuality, rendering an opinion or report on each of the major federal financial assistance programs and not a single overall report for all federal programs as a group.

SCHEDULE OF EXPENDITURES OF FEDERAL AWARDS

OMB, in Circular A-133 Section 310 and 505, requires every recipient of federal financial assistance to prepare a Schedule of Expenditures of Federal Awards for the period covered by the audit. While not required, the entity might provide other information requested by federal awarding agencies and pass-through entities to make the schedule more useful.

Content of Schedule of Expenditures

Similar to financial statements, the Schedule of Expenditures of Federal Awards should be prepared by the auditee. Like the financial statements, the Schedule is a report by the entity's management—not the auditor. As a minimum, OMB's Circular A-133 requires the Schedule of Expenditures of Federal Awards to provide the following information for each federal financial assistance program (§ 310):

● List individual federal programs by federal agency. For programs included in a cluster of programs, in the OMB's *Compliance Supplement*, list individual federal programs within a cluster;

● For federal awards received as a subrecipient, the name of the pass-through entity and identifying number assigned by the pass-through entity shall be included;

● Provide total federal awards expended for each individual federal program and the CFDA number or other identifying number;

● Include notes that describe significant accounting policies used in preparing the schedule;

● To the extent possible, pass-through entities should identify in the schedule the total amount provided to subrecipients from each federal program; and

● Include, in either the schedule or a note to the schedule, the value of federal awards expended in the form of noncash assistance, amounts of insurance in effect during the year, and loans or loan guarantees outstanding at year end.

Other—optional type—information has been suggested by the AICPA and could be meaningful to the federal managers, depending upon the circumstances, such as:

● The amount or value of any matching contributions;

● The total amount of the program awards, i.e., the cumulative totals;

● The receipts or revenues recognized in the reporting period of the governments, since there is a difference in accounting between cash received and recognition of revenues;

● 3 Beginning and ending balances, such as unexpended amounts or accrued or deferred amounts; and

● Subtotals by federal grantor department or agency;

Accounting and Reporting Bases for Schedule

The federal government recognizes that financial information appearing on the Schedule of Expenditures of Federal Awards may not fully agree with or be traceable to other grant reports or to the entity's financial statements. Data in this schedule could be presented on a basis different than generally accepted accounting and even different from the basis of accounting used by the federal recipient in its entity-wide financial statements. It is important that, to the extent practicable, the schedule data be on a basis consistent with the entity's reporting to the federal government. But, differences can exist for several reasons between the financial statements and the Schedule and between the Schedule and the submitted federal financial reports.

The federal government does not prescribe a basis of accounting for use on the Schedule of Federal Awards. However, when the basis is other than the basis used for its financial statements, the federal recipient must disclose that basis of accounting and the significant accounting policies used in preparing the Schedule. These variances between the Schedule, the entity's financial statements and even the federal financial reports could exist due to:

● Different bases of accounting being used;

● Federal programs may be reported in several of the governmental entity's fund types and individual funds;

● Some of the funds for federal programs may have been accounted for as contributions to a funds equity rather that reimbursement for operations;

● Matching contributions may be reported in a fund or fund type that is different than where the federal program is reported;

● Indirect or overhead costs may be reported in a fund type or fund that is different than where the federal program is reported;

● Variances could exist due to differences in reporting bases;

● Federal financial reports may not coincide with the government's fiscal year end; and

● Federal financial reports may provide only cumulative data and not the activity for the current year.

Federal reporting requirements do not require recipients of federal monies to account for the federal funds on the basis of generally accepted accounting principles. From the auditor's viewpoint, the audit report must only state whether the recipient's financial statements are presented in accordance with generally accepted accounting principles and, if not, the auditor must describe the basis used.

Worksheet entries are acceptable to meet the OMB's reporting requirements and may be made to adjust amounts from accounting records to arrive at amount shown in the federal financial reports or on the Schedule, itself. OMB, in another Circular A-102 (the administrative and management guide for funding to state and local governments), states that if a federal agency required accrual information and the government's accounting records are not normally kept on an accrual basis, the recipient government shall not be required to convert its system of accounting. The recipient government is permitted to develop accrual information through analysis of the documentation on hand.

Considered as Supplementary Information

The Schedule of Expenditures of Federal Awards is viewed by the AICPA (in its Statement of Position 98-3, Chapter 10) as supplementary information and is reported as such in the auditor's report on the entity-wide financial statements. In reporting on the Schedule, the auditor should also consult two Statements on Auditing Standards for other relevant guidance by the AICPA:

1. SAS No. 29—*Reporting on Information Accompanying the Basic Financial Statements in Auditor-Submitted Documents*; and

2. SAS No. 42—*Reporting on Condensed Financial Statements and Selected Financial Data.*

Illustrative Schedule of Federal Financial Assistance

The Schedule of Expenditures of Federal Awards is a reporting required by the federal government, but the format or a variation thereof could as well be used to make reportings on state or other governmental assistance. If nonfederal reporting is made, a similar but separate schedule should be prepared and not consolidated with the federal funds.

Exhibits 7-2(a) and 7-2(b) are two illustrations of a Schedule of Expenditures of Federal Awards suggested by the AICPA after consultation with practitioners and the government in its Statement of Position 98-3, *Audits of States, Local Governments, and Not-for-Profit Organizations Receiving Federal Awards,* Chapters 5 and 10, plus the Appendix C.

Exhibit 7-2(a) is an abbreviated schedule that complies with OMB's criteria, but the financial information is limited to only total federal expenditures for the federal programs. As an alternative, **Exhibit 7-2(b)** provides more details and would have greater utility in the management and monitoring of federal awards programs.

The Schedule of Expenditures of Federal Awards is viewed as supplementary information to the entity wide financial statements under the audit profession's guidance, accordingly the following or words similar to the following would appear, if appropriate, in the last paragraph of an auditor's report on the entity-wide financial statements, if this Schedule accompanied those financial statements:

"The accompanying schedule of expenditures of federal awards is presented for purpose of additional analysis as required by the U.S. Office of Management and Budget Circular A-133, Audits of States, Local Governments, and Non-Profit Organizations, and is not a required part of the general purpose financial statements. Such information has been subjected to the procedures applied in the audit of the general purpose financial statements, and in our opinion, is fairly stated in all material respects, in relation to the general purpose financial statements taken as a whole."

SCHEDULE OF FINDINGS AND QUESTIONED COSTS

A report of a single audit must contain a separate reporting titled, Schedule of Findings and Questioned Costs. This report or Schedule, prepared by the auditor must detail several types of audit observations, including: (1) reportable conditions and material weaknesses in internal controls over major federal programs, (2) material noncompliance with provisions of laws, regulations, contracts, grant agreements related to specific major federal programs, and (3) known questioned costs greater than $10,000 for a major federal program.

Questioned costs are those costs that the auditor believes have been incurred, charged, billed, paid, or claimed for a federal program which are: (1) in violation or possible violation of a provision of a law, regulation, contract, grant, cooperative agreement, other agreement or document governing the use of federal funds, including matching funds; (2) are not supported by adequate documentation; or (3) appear unreasonable and do not reflect the actions of a prudent person in the same circumstances.

Exhibits 7-3 illustrates a Schedule of Findings and Questioned Costs, suggested by the AICPA after consultation with practitioners and the government in its Statement of Position 98-3, *Audits of States, Local Governments, and Not-for-Profit Organizations Receiving Federal Awards,* Chapter 6 plus the Appendix E.

This suggested example is comprised of three sections:

● Section I—the *Summary of Auditor's Results* provides readers with summary information concerning the nature or type of auditor's opinion on the overall entity wide financial statements and the results of the auditor's tests of compliance with laws and regulations and internal controls. Plus, the major federal programs are identified by CFDA numbers and the name of the federal program or program cluster. This information, of course, should be in the same sequence as reported in the schedule of expenditures of federal awards.

- Section II—*Financial Statement Findings* provides an identification of reportable conditions and material weaknesses in controls; instances of noncompliance with laws, regulations, contracts, grants and other forms of award assistance that were observed during the audit of the entity-wide financial statements. If there are no findings, the auditor must clearly state this fact.

All findings, to the extent possible should be presented in the prescribed manner and describe, for each finding, the following elements: criteria or specific requirement violated; the condition or circumstances observed by the auditor; the amount of questioned costs; the context or prevalence or consequences of the findings; the effect of the finding; what caused the finding; the auditor's recommendation, and management response.

- Section III *Federal Award Findings and Questioned Costs* provides an identification of reportable conditions and material weaknesses in controls; instances of noncompliance with laws, regulations, contracts, grants and other forms of award assistance that were observed during the audit of each major federal program or award. If there are no findings, the auditor must clearly state this fact.

All findings, to the extent possible, should be presented in the prescribed manner. This section must describe, for each finding, the following several elements: criteria or specific requirement violated; the condition or circumstances observed by the auditor; the amount of questioned costs; the context or prevalence or consequences of the findings; the effect of the finding; what caused the finding; the auditor's recommendation, and management response.

DATA COLLECTION FORM

In 1997, with its revised Circular A-133, OMB first required that a data collection form be submitted at the end of each single audit, with separate sections being completed by both the auditee and the auditor. A knowledgeable, senior level representative of the auditee is to prepare and submit a data collection form that contains an attestation that a single audit was completed in accordance with the Circular and must provide other information about the auditee's federal programs and the results of the audit. The certifying statement must state (1) the auditee complied with the requirements of the Circular, (2) the data collection form was prepared in accordance with the Circular, and (3) the information in the form, in its entirety, are accurate and complete.

Other specific sections of the data collection form must be completed by the auditor. The auditor must sign a statement, as part of the form, that indicates, at a minimum: (1) the source of information included in this form, (2) the auditor's responsibility for the information, (3) that this form is not a substitute for the single audit reporting package (i.e., the financial statements, schedule of expenditures of federal awards, summary schedule of prior audit findings, auditors reports, and corrective action plan) required by Circular A-133, and (4) the content of this form is limited to the data elements prescribed by OMB.

As illustrated by *Exhibit 7-4*, the data collection form for reporting on audits of states, local governments, and non-profit organizations is a detailed summary analysis of almost every aspect of the single audit. Between the auditee and the auditor, this form results in considerably more information being transmitted about the audited entity than has been historically the case for financial type audits.

For example, the data collection form requires specific identification of several facts about the single audit, including but not limited to:

● The type of opinions issued by the auditor (1) on the financial statements, and (2) as a result of the auditor's tests of compliance with laws, regulations, contracts, grants or other agreements related to the major federal programs.

● Citation of reportable conditions and material weaknesses relating to internal controls at both the entity-wide level and at the major program level.

● A statement of whether the audit disclosed any noncompliance with laws, regulations, contracts, grants or other award agreements.

● A statement, Yes or No, as to whether the auditee qualified as a low-risk auditee and the dollar threshold used to distinguish between Type A and Type B federal programs.

● The name, CFDA or other identifying number, amount of expenditures for each federal program.

● Specific statements, Yes or No, as to whether there are audit findings in each of the 14 types of compliance requirements and the amounts of any questioned costs.

While the preference is that this form be prepared and submitted as soon as possible after the annual single audit, the Collection Form must be submitted within the earlier of 30 days after receipt of the auditor's report or 9 months after the end of the audit period unless a long period is permitted by the federal cognizant or oversight agency.

THE OTHER SINGLE AUDIT REPORTS

Corrective Action Plan

The auditor's findings must be presented in sufficient detail to permit the auditee to prepare a corrective action plan and take corrective action. Also, the reported detail must be sufficient to permit federal agencies and pass-through entities to arrive at management decisions related to the reported findings. *Corrective action* is defined, in Circular A-133, to mean action taken by the auditee that (1) corrects identified deficiencies; (2) produces recommended improvements; or (3) demonstrates that audit findings are either invalid or do not warrant auditee action.

In the corrective action plan, the auditee is to address each specific finding in the current year auditor's report. The action plan must, for each finding, also provide names of responsible contact persons, the action planned, and anticipated completion date. If the auditee does not agree with the audit findings or believes corrective action is not required, then the corrective action plan shall include an explanation and the specific reasons.

The corrective action plan should be cross referenced to the Summary Schedule of Prior Audit Findings since audit findings may have arisen in various audits or relate to multiple years and require an indication of the fiscal year in which the finding initially occurred.

Summary Schedule of Prior Audit Findings

An auditee that receives federal financial assistance must followup and take corrective action on all audit findings. Also, the auditee has the responsibility of preparing a summary schedule of prior audit findings. This schedule requires the auditee to establish an audit finding reference coding system since the audit findings may have arisen in various or relate to multiple years. This schedule must indicate the fiscal year in which the finding initially occurred.

OMB outlined, in A-133, circumstances or conditions where auditees may not have to report the status of prior audit findings or that corrective action may no longer be warranted. Some of these include:

● When the audit findings have been fully corrected, this schedule need only list the audit findings and state corrective action was taken.

● When the findings were not or were only partially corrected, this schedule must describe the planned corrective action taken and provide an explanation.

● When corrective action taken is significantly different from corrective action previously reported in an action plan, this schedule must provide an explanation.

● When the auditee believes the audit findings are no longer valid or do not warrant further action, the reason therefore must be described.

OMB identified the following as a basis for considering an audit finding as not warranting further action if *all* of the following have occurred: (1) two years have passed since the audit report was submitted to the federal clearinghouse; (2) the federal agency or pass-through entity is not currently following up with the auditee on the audit finding; and (3) a management decision was not issued.

A management decision, by the federal government, shall clearly state whether or not the audit finding is sustained, the reasons therefore, and the expected auditee action (e.g., repay disallowed costs, make financial adjustment, or other actions). The management decision should describe any appeal process available to the auditee.

Audit Follow-Up Report on Prior Audit Findings

As part of the scope of a single audit, the auditor is required to (1) follow-up on prior audit findings, (2) perform procedures and tests to assess the reasonableness of the summary schedule of prior audit findings that were prepared by the auditee, and (3) report, as a finding of the current audit year, when the auditor concludes that the summary schedule of prior audit findings materially misrepresents the status of any prior audit finding. The auditor must perform this follow-up procedure regardless of whether a prior audit finding relates to a major program in the current year.

* * * * *

The AICPA's audit guide for government and related statements on auditing standards should be consulted for an almost infinite number of illustrative reports displaying numerous reporting conditions and circumstances that might occur as a result of a single audit and could possibly require other than unqualified opinion's from an auditor.

* * * * *

Exhibits 7-1, 7-2(a), 7-2(b), 7-3, and 7-4 follow this page.

EXHIBIT 7-1*

Report on Compliance With Requirements Applicable to Each Major Program and on Internal Control Over Compliance in Accordance With OMB Circular A-133 (*Qualified Opinion on Compliance and Reportable Conditions Identified*)[1]

[*Addressee*]

Compliance

We have audited the compliance of Example Entity with the types of compliance requirements described in the *U.S. Office of Management and Budget (OMB) Circular A-133 Compliance Supplement* that are applicable to each of its major federal programs for the year ended June 30, 19X1. Example Entity's major federal programs are identified in the summary of auditor's results section of the accompanying schedule of findings and questioned costs. Compliance with the requirements of laws, regulations, contracts, and grants applicable to each of its major federal programs is the responsibility of Example Entity's management. Our responsibility is to express an opinion on Example Entity's compliance based on our audit.

We conducted our audit of compliance in accordance with generally accepted auditing standards; the standards applicable to financial audits contained in *Government Auditing Standards*,[2] issued by the Comptroller General of the United States; and OMB Circular A-133, *Audits of States, Local Governments, and Non-Profit Organizations*. Those standards and OMB Circular A-133 require that we plan and perform the audit to obtain reasonable assurance about whether noncompliance with the types of compliance requirements referred to above that could have a direct and material effect on a major federal program occurred. An audit includes examining, on a test basis, evidence about Example Entity's compliance with those requirements and performing such other procedures as we considered necessary in the circumstances. We believe that our audit provides a reasonable basis for our opinion. Our audit does not provide a legal determination of Example Entity's compliance with those requirements.

---

* Reprinted with permission from Auditing Recipients of Federal Awards: Practical Guidance for Applying OMB Circular A-133 and SOP 98-3, Copyright ©1998 by the American Institute of Certified Public Accountants, Inc.

[1] The auditor should use the portions of P/A-22 and this report that apply to a specific auditee situation. For example, if the auditor will be giving an unqualified opinion on compliance but has identified reportable conditions, the compliance section of P/A-22 would be used along with the internal control section of this report. Alternatively, if the auditor will be giving a qualified opinion on compliance but has not identified reportable conditions, the internal control section of P/A-22 would be used along with the compliance section of this report.

[2] The standards applicable to financial audits include the general, fieldwork, and reporting standards described in chapters 3, 4, and 5 of *Government Auditing Standards*.

As described in item [*list the reference numbers of the related findings, for example, 97-10*] in the accompanying schedule of findings and questioned costs, Example Entity did not comply with requirements regarding [*identify the type(s) of compliance requirement*] that are applicable to its [*identify the major federal program*]. Compliance with such requirements is necessary, in our opinion, for Example Entity to comply with the requirements applicable to that program.

In our opinion, except for the noncompliance described in the preceding paragraph, Example Entity complied, in all material respects, with the requirements referred to above that are applicable to each of its major federal programs for the year ended June 30, 19X1.[3]

Internal Control Over Compliance

The management of Example Entity is responsible for establishing and maintaining effective internal control over compliance with the requirements of laws, regulations, contracts, and grants applicable to federal programs. In planning and performing our audit, we considered Example Entity's internal control over compliance with requirements that could have a direct and material effect on a major federal program in order to determine our auditing procedures for the purpose of expressing our opinion on compliance and to test and report on the internal control over compliance in accordance with OMB Circular A-133.

We noted certain matters involving the internal control over compliance and its operation that we consider to be reportable conditions. Reportable conditions involve matters coming to our attention relating to significant deficiencies in the design or operation of the internal control over compliance that, in our judgment, could adversely affect Example Entity's ability to administer a major federal program in accordance with the applicable requirements of laws, regulations, contracts, and grants. Reportable conditions are described in the accompanying schedule of findings and questioned costs as items [*list the reference numbers of the related findings, for example, 97-7, 97-8, and 97-9*].

A material weakness is a condition in which the design or operation of one or more of the internal control components does not reduce to a relatively low level the risk that noncompliance with the applicable requirements of laws, regulations, contracts, and grants that would be material in relation to a major federal program being audited may

---

[3] When other instances of noncompliance are identified in the schedule of findings and questioned costs as required by Circular A-133, the following sentence should be added: "The results of our auditing procedures also disclosed other instances of noncompliance with those requirements, which are required to be reported in accordance with OMB Circular A-133 and which are described in the accompanying schedule of findings and questioned costs as items [*list the reference numbers of the related findings, for example, 97-3 and 97-6*]."

occur and not be detected within a timely period by employees in the normal course of performing their assigned functions. Our consideration of the internal control over compliance would not necessarily disclose all matters in the internal control that might be reportable conditions and, accordingly, would not necessarily disclose all reportable conditions that are also considered to be material weaknesses. However, we believe that none of the reportable conditions described above is a material weakness.[4],[5]

This report is intended for the information of the audit committee, management, [*specify legislative or regulatory body*], and federal awarding agencies and pass-through entities. However, this report is a matter of public record and its distribution is not limited.[6]

[*Signature*]

[*Date*]

---

[4] If conditions believed to be material weaknesses are disclosed, the report should identify the material weaknesses that have come to the auditor's attention. The last sentence of this paragraph should be replaced with language such as the following: "However, of the reportable conditions described above, we consider items [*list the reference numbers of the related findings, for example, 97-1 and 97-8*] to be material weaknesses."

[5] As noted in note 3 of P/A-18 there may be instances in which it would be appropriate to report on the schedule of expenditures of federal awards in this report (that is, a separate single audit package is issued). In such a circumstance, a new section should be added immediately following this paragraph as follows:

Schedule of Expenditures of Federal Awards

We have audited the [*general-purpose or basic*] financial statements of Example Entity as of and for the year ended June 30, 19X1, and have issued our report thereon dated August 15, 19X1. Our audit was performed for the purpose of forming an opinion on the [*general-purpose of basic*] financial statements taken as a whole. The accompanying schedule of expenditures of federal awards is presented for purposes of additional analysis as required by OMB Circular A-133 and is not a required part of the [*general-purpose or basic*] financial statements. Such information has been subjected to the auditing procedures applied in the audit of the [*general-purpose or basic*] financial statements and, in our opinion, is fairly stated, in all material respects, in relation to the [*general-purpose or basic*] financial statements taken as a whole.

Describe any departure from the standard report (for example, a qualified opinion, a modification as to consistency because of a change in accounting principle, or a reference to the report of other auditors). Auditors should also refer to note 5 of P/A-18 for additional guidance.

[6] If the report is not a matter of public record, this sentence should be deleted.

EXHIBIT 7-2(a)*

APPENDIX C

Illustrative Schedules of Expenditures of Federal Awards

Example Entity Schedule of Expenditures of Federal Awards [1] For the Year Ended June 30, 19X1 [2]

Federal Grantor/Pass-Through Grantor/ Program or Cluster Title	Federal CFDA Number [3]	Pass-Through Entity Identifying Number [4]	Federal Expenditures [5]
U.S. Department of Agriculture: Summer Food Service Program for Children—Commodities	10.559		$ 46,000
Total U.S. Department of Agriculture			$ 46,000
U.S. Department of Housing and Urban Development: Community Development Block Grant—Entitlement Grants (note 2) Section 8 Rental Voucher Program	14.218 14.855		$1,235,632 800,534
Total U.S. Department of Housing and Urban Development			$2,036,166
U.S. Department of Education: Impact Aid	84.041		$ 372,555

* Reprinted with Permission from SOP 98-3, *Audits of States, Local Governments, and Not-for-Profit Organizations Receiving Federal Awards*, Copyright ©1998 by the American Institute of Certified Public Accountants, Inc.

[1] To meet state or other requirements, auditees may decide to include certain nonfederal awards (for example, state awards) in this schedule. If such nonfederal data are presented, they should be segregated and clearly designated as nonfederal. The title of the schedule should also be modified to indicate that nonfederal awards are included.

[2] Additional guidance on the schedule is provided in chapter 5 which includes a discussion of the identification of federal awards, the general presentation requirements governing the schedule, pass-through awards, noncash awards, and endowment funds. Chapter 5 also includes a discussion of the auditor's responsibility for reporting on the schedule.

[3] When the CFDA number is not available, the auditee should indicate that the CFDA number is not available and include in the schedule the program's name and, if available, other identifying number.

[4] When awards are received as a subrecipient, the identifying number assigned by the pass-through entity should be included in the schedule.

[5] Circular A-133 requires that the value of federal awards expended in the form of noncash assistance, the amount of insurance in effect during the year, and loans or loan guarantees outstanding at year end be included in either the schedule or a note to the schedule. Although it is not required, Circular A-133 states that it is preferable to present this information in the schedule (versus the notes to the schedule). If the auditec presents noncash assistance in the notes to the schedule, the auditor should be aware that such amounts must still be included in part III of the data collection form.

Bilingual Education	84.288		28,655
Subtotal Direct Programs			$ 401,210
Pass-Through Program From: State Department of Education— Title I Grants to Local Educational Agencies	84.010	23-8345-7612	$1,239,398
Total U.S. Department of Education			$1,640,608
Total Expenditures of Federal Awards			$3,722,774

The accompanying notes are an integral part of this schedule.

Reporting Pursuant to Single Audit Act

Example Entity Notes to the Schedule of Expenditures of Federal Awards
For the Year Ended June 30, 19X1

Note 1. Basis of Presentation [6]

The accompanying schedule of expenditures of federal awards includes the federal grant activity of Example Entity and is presented on the [*identify basis of accounting*]. The information in this schedule is presented in accordance with the requirements of OMB Circular A-133, *Audits of States, Local Governments, and Non-Profit Organizations*. Therefore, some amounts presented in this schedule may differ from amounts presented in, or used in the preparation of, the [*general-purpose or basic*] financial statements.

Note 2. Subrecipients [7]

Of the federal expenditures presented in the schedule, Example Entity provided federal awards to subrecipients as follows:

Program Title	Federal CFDA Number	Amount Provided to Subrecipients
Community Development Block Grant—Entitlement Grants	14.218	$423,965

---

[6] This note is included to meet the Circular A-133 requirement that the schedule include notes that describe the significant accounting policies used in preparing the schedule.

[7] Circular A-133 requires the schedule of expenditures of federal awards to include, to the extent practical, an identification of the total amount provided to subrecipients from each federal program. Although this example includes the required subrecipient information in the notes to the schedule, the information may be included on the face of the schedule as a separate column or section, if that is preferred by the auditee.

EXHIBIT 7-2(b)[*]

Example Entity University Schedule of Expenditures of Federal Awards[8] For the Year Ended June 30, 19X1 [9]

Federal Grantor/Pass-Through Grantor/ Program or Cluster Title	Federal CFDA Number [10]	Pass-Through Entity Identifying Number [11]	Federal Expenditures [12]
Student Financial Aid—Cluster:			
U.S. Department of Education:			
Federal Pell Grant Program	84,063		$ 8,764,943
Federal Supplemental Educational Opportunity Grant	84,007		974,873
Federal Work-Study Program	84,033		575,417
Federal Perkins Loan Program (note 2)	84,038		1,548,343
Total U.S. Department of Education			$11,863,576
U.S. Department of Health and Human Services:			
Nursing Student Loans (note 2)	93,364		$ 823,582
Total U.S. Department of Health and Human Services			$ 823,582
Total Student Financial Aid			$12,687,158
Research and Development— Cluster: [13]			
U.S Department of Defense:			
Department of Army	N.A.		$ 87,403
Office of Naval Research	N.A.		73,107
Subtotal Direct Programs			$ 160,510
Pass-Through Programs From:			
XYZ Labs—Effects of Ice on Radar Images	N.A.	4532	$ 11,987
Total U.S. Department of Defense:			$ 172,497
National Science Foundation:			
National Science Foundation (note 3)	N.A.		$ 432,111
Pass-Through Programs From:			
ABC University—Atmospheric Effects of Volcano Eruptions	N.A.	Abc97-8	$ 25,987
Total National Science Foundation			$ 458,098
U.S. Department of Health and Human Services:			
National Institutes of Health	N.A.		$ 675,321
Administration on Aging (note 3)	N.A.		234,987
Subtotal Direct Programs			$ 910,308
Pass-Through Programs From:			
ABC Hospital—Heart Research	N.A.	5489-5	$ 432,765
State Health Department—Food Safety Research	N.A.	SG673-45	123,987
Subtotal Pass-Through Programs			$ 556,752

---

[*] Reprinted with permission from SOP 98-3, *Audits of States, Local Governments, and Not-for-Profit Organizations Receiving Federal Awards*, Copyright ©1998 by the American Institute of Certified Public Accountants, Inc.

[8] See note 1.

[9] See note 2.

[10] See note 3.

[11] See note 4.

[12] See note 5.

[13] For R&D, Circular A-133 requires that total federal awards expended must be shown either by individual award or by federal agency and major subdivision within the federal agency. This example illustrates the federal agency and major subdivision option.

Reporting Pursuant to Single Audit Act

Total U.S. Department of Health and Human Services			$	1,467,060
Total Research and Development			$	2,097,655
Other Programs:				
U.S. Department of Energy: Educational Exchange—University Lectures and Research	82,002		$	17,823
Total U.S. Department of Energy			$	17,823
U.S. Department of Education: TRIO Talent Search	84,044		$	308,465
Safe and Drug-Free Schools and Communities	84,184			59,723
Subtotal Direct Programs			$	368,188
Pass-Through Programs From:				
State Department of Education—Vocational Education Basic Grant	84,048	874-90-5473	$	3,115
State Department of Education—Tech-Prep Education	84,243	25-8594-2167		176,885
Subtotal Pass-Through Programs			$	180,000
Total U.S. Department of Education			$	548,188
Total Other Programs			$	566,011
Total Expenditures of Federal Awards				$15,350,824

N.A. = Not Available

The accompanying notes are an integral part of this schedule.

178 Government Auditing: Standards and Practices

Example Entity University Notes to the Schedule of Expenditures of Federal Awards For the Year Ended June 30, 19X1

Note 1. Basis of Presentation [14]

The accompanying schedule of expenditures of federal awards includes the federal grant activity of Example Entity University and is presented on the [*identify basis of accounting*]. The information in this schedule is presented in accordance with the requirements of OMB Circular A-133, *Audits of States, Local Governments, and Non-Profit Organizations*. Therefore, some amounts presented in this schedule may differ from amounts presented in, or used in the preparation of, the [*general-purpose or basic*] financial statements.

Note 2. Loans Outstanding [15]

Example Entity University had the following loan balances outstanding at June 30, 19X1. These loan balances outstanding are also included in the federal expenditures presented in the schedule.

Cluster/Program Title	Federal CFDA Number	Amount Outstanding
Federal Perkins Loan Program	84,038	$1,268,236
Nursing Student Loans	93,364	$ 763,127

Note 3. Subrecipients [16]

Of the federal expenditures presented in the schedule, Example Entity University provided federal awards to subrecipients as follows:

Program Title	Federal CFDA Number	Amount Provided to Subrecipients
National Science Foundation	N.A.	$236,403
Administration on Aging	N.A.	$138,095

---

[14] See note 6.
[15] This note is intended to meet the Circular A-133 requirement that loans or loan guarantees outstanding at year end be included in the schedule.
[16] See note 7.

Reporting Pursuant to Single Audit Act 179

EXHIBIT 7-3*

APPENDIX E

Illustrative Schedule of Findings and Questioned Costs

Example Entity
Schedule of Findings and Questioned Costs
For the Year Ended June 30, 19X1

Section I—Summary of Auditor's Results

Financial Statements

Type of auditor's report issued: [*unqualified, qualified, adverse, or disclaimer*]

Internal control over financial reporting:

- Material weakness(es) identified? _____ yes _____ no

- Reportable condition(s) identified that are not considered to be material weaknesses? _____ yes _____ none reported

Noncompliance material to financial statements noted? _____ yes _____ no

Federal Awards

Internal control over major programs:

- Material weakness(es) identified? _____ yes _____ no

- Reportable condition(s) identified that are not considered to be material weakness(es)? _____ yes _____ none reported

Type of auditor's report issued on compliance for major programs: [*unqualified, qualified, adverse, or disclaimer*][1]

Any audit findings disclosed that are required to be reported in accordance with section 510(a) of Circular A-133? _____ yes _____ no

---

* Reprinted with permission from SOP 98-3, *Audits of States, Local Governments, and Not-for-Profit Organizations Receiving Federal Awards*, Copyright ©1998 by the American Institute of Certified Public Accountants, Inc.

[1] If the audit report for one or more major programs is other than unqualified, indicate the type of report issued for each program. For example, if the audit report on major program compliance for an auditee having five major programs includes an unqualified opinion for three of the programs, a qualified opinion for one program, and a disclaimer of opinion for one program, the response to this question could be as follows: "Unqualified for all major programs except for [*name of program*], which was qualified and [*name of program*], which was a disclaimer."

180 Government Auditing: Standards and Practices

Identification of major programs:[2]

CFDA Number(s)[3]   Name of Federal Program or Cluster[4]

_____

_____

_____

Dollar threshold used to distinguish between type A
and type B programs: $ _____

Auditee qualified as low-risk auditee?   _____ yes   _____ no

---

[2] Major programs should generally be identified in the same order as reported on the schedule of expenditures of federal awards.

[3] When the CFDA number is not available, include other identifying number, if applicable.

[4] The name of the federal program or cluster should be the same as that listed in the schedule of expenditures of federal awards. For clusters, auditors are only required to list the name of the cluster and not each individual program within the cluster.

Reporting Pursuant to Single Audit Act 181

Example Entity
Schedule of Findings and Questioned Costs
For the Year Ended June 30, 19X1
(continued)

Section II—Financial Statement Findings

[*This section identifies the reportable conditions, material weaknesses, and instances of noncompliance related to the financial statements that are required to be reported in accordance with paragraphs 5.18 through 5.20 of* Government Auditing Standards. *Auditors should refer to those paragraphs, as well as the reports content section of chapter 7 of* Government Auditing Standards, *for additional guidance on preparing this section of the schedule.*

Identify each finding with a reference number.[5] *If there are no findings, state that no matters were reported. Audit findings that relate to both the financial statements and federal awards should be reported in both section II and section III. However, the reporting in one section may be in summary form with a reference to a detailed reporting in the other section of the schedule. For example, a material weakness in internal control that effects an entity as a whole, including its federal awards, would generally be reported in detail in this section. Section III would then include a summary identification of the finding and a reference back to the specific finding in this section. Each finding should be presented in the following level of detail, as applicable:*

- *Criteria or specific requirement*

- *Condition*

- *Questioned costs*

- *Context*[6]

- *Effect*

- *Cause*

- *Recommendation*

- *Management's response*[7]]

---

[5] A suggested format for assigning reference numbers is to use the last two digits of the fiscal year being audited, followed by a numeric sequence of findings. For example, findings identified and reported in the audit of fiscal year 1997 would be assigned reference numbers of 97-1, 97-2, etc.

[6] Provide sufficient information for judging the prevalence and consequences of the finding, such as the relation to the universe of costs and/or the number of items examined and quantification of audit findings in dollars.

[7] See paragraphs 5.18 through 5.20 and 7.38 through 7.42 of *Government Auditing Standards* for additional guidance on reporting management's response.

182 Government Auditing: Standards and Practices

Example Entity
Schedule of Findings and Questioned Costs
For the Year Ended June 30, 19X1
(continued)

Section III—Federal Award Findings and Questioned Costs

[*This section identifies the audit findings required to be reported by section 510(a) of Circular A-133 (for example, reportable conditions, material weaknesses, and instances of noncompliance, including questioned costs). Where practical, findings should be organized by federal agency or pass-through entity.*

Identify each finding with a reference number.[8] If there are no findings, state that no matters were reported. Audit findings that relate to both the financial statements and federal awards should be reported in both section II and section III. However, the reporting in one section may be in summary form with a reference to a detailed reporting in the other section of the schedule. For example, a finding of noncompliance with a federal program law that is also material to the financial statements would generally be reported in detail in this section. Section II would then include a summary identification of the finding and a reference back to the specific finding in this section. Each finding should be presented in the following level of detail, as applicable:

- *Information on the federal program*[9]

- *Criteria or specific requirement (including statutory, regulatory, or other citation)*

- *Condition*[10]

- *Questioned costs*[11]

- *Context*[12]

- *Effect*

- *Cause*

- *Recommendation*

- *Management's response*[13]]

---

[8] See note 5.

[9] Provide the federal program (CFDA number and title) and agency, the federal award's number and year, and the name of the pass-through entity, if applicable. When this information is not available, the auditor should provide the best information available to describe the federal award.

[10] Include facts that support the deficiency identified in the audit finding.

[11] Identify questioned costs as required by sections 510(a)(3) and 510(a)(4) of Circular A-133.

[12] See note 6.

[13] To the extent practical, indicate when management does not agree with the finding, questioned cost, or both.

EXHIBIT 7-4[*]

```
                                                        OMB No. 0348-0057
FORM SF-SAC              U.S. DEPARTMENT OF COMMERCE - BUREAU OF THE CENSUS
(8-97)                              ACTING AS COLLECTING AGENT FOR
        Data Collection Form for Reporting on    OFFICE OF MANAGEMENT AND BUDGET
   AUDITS OF STATES, LOCAL GOVERNMENTS, AND NON-PROFIT ORGANIZATIONS

▶ Complete this form, as required by OMB Circular A-133, "Audits   RETURN TO   Single Audit Clearinghouse
  of States, Local Governments, and Non-Profit Organizations."                 1201 E. 10th Street
                                                                               Jeffersonville, IN 47132

    PART I      GENERAL INFORMATION (To be completed by auditee, except for Item 7)
1. Fiscal year ending date for this submission          2. Type of Circular A-133 audit
   Month  /  Day  /  Year
                                                          1 ☐ Single audit   2 ☐ Program-specific audit
3. Audit period covered                         FEDERAL        4. Date received by Federal
   1 ☐ Annual      3 ☐ Other –          Months  GOVERNMENT        clearinghouse
   2 ☐ Biennial                                 USE ONLY
5. Employer Identification Number (EIN)

   a. Auditee EIN  [        ]      b. Are multiple EINs covered in this report?   1 ☐ Yes   2 ☐ No

6. AUDITEE INFORMATION                          7. AUDITOR INFORMATION (To be completed by auditor)
   a. Auditee name                                 a. Auditor name

   b. Auditee address (Number and street)          b. Auditor address (Number and street)

   City                                            City

   State                    ZIP Code               State                    ZIP Code

   c. Auditee contact                              c. Auditor contact
      Name                                            Name

      Title                                           Title

   d. Auditee contact telephone                    d. Auditor contact telephone
      (     )     –                                   (     )     –
   e. Auditee contact FAX (Optional)               e. Auditor contact FAX (Optional)
      (     )     –                                   (     )     –
   f. Auditee contact E-mail (Optional)            f. Auditor contact E-mail (Optional)

   g. AUDITEE CERTIFICATION STATEMENT – This is   g. AUDITOR STATEMENT – The data elements and
   to certify that, to the best of my knowledge and   information included in this form are limited to those
   belief, the auditee has: (1) Engaged an auditor to   prescribed by OMB Circular A-133. The information
   perform an audit in accordance with the provisions of   included in Parts II and III of the form, except for Part
   OMB Circular A-133 for the period described in Part I,   III, Items 5 and 6, was transferred from the auditor's
   Items 1 and 3; (2) the auditor has completed such   report(s) for the period described in Part I, Items 1
   audit and presented a signed audit report which   and 3, and is not a substitute for such reports. The
   states that the audit was conducted in accordance   auditor has not performed any auditing procedures
   with the provisions of the Circular; and, (3) the   since the date of the auditor's report(s). A copy of the
   information included in Parts I, II, and III of this data   reporting package required by OMB Circular A-133,
   collection form is accurate and complete. I declare   which includes the complete auditor's report(s), is
   that the foregoing is true and correct.       available in its entirety from the auditee at the
                                                  address provided in Part I of this form. As required by
                                                  OMB Circular A-133, the information in Parts II and
                                                  III of this form was entered in this form by the auditor
                                                  based on information included in the reporting
                                                  package. The auditor has not performed any
                                                  additional auditing procedures in connection with the
   Signature of certifying official    Date       completion of this form.
                                       Month  Day  Year
                                         /     /
   Name/Title of certifying official              Signature of auditor            Date
                                                                                  Month  Day  Year
                                                                                    /    /
```

---

[*] OMB Data Collection Form, Circular A-133, *Audits of States, Local Governments, and Non-Profit Organizations.*

184   Government Auditing: Standards and Practices

EIN: ☐☐☐☐☐☐☐☐☐

PART I   GENERAL INFORMATION – Continued

8. Indicate whether the auditee has either a Federal cognizant or oversight agency for audit. *(Mark (X) one box)*
   1 ☐ Cognizant agency   2 ☐ Oversight agency

9. Name of Federal cognizant or oversight agency for audit *(Mark (X) one box)*

01 ☐ African Development Foundation	83 ☐ Federal Emergency Management Agency	16 ☐ Justice
02 ☐ Agency for International Development	34 ☐ Federal Mediation and Conciliation Service	17 ☐ Labor
10 ☐ Agriculture	39 ☐ General Services Administration	43 ☐ National Aeronautics and Space Administration
11 ☐ Commerce	93 ☐ Health and Human Services	89 ☐ National Archives and Records Administraton
94 ☐ Corporation for National and Community Service	14 ☐ Housing and Urban Development	05 ☐ National Endowment for the Arts
12 ☐ Defense	03 ☐ Institute for Museum Services	06 ☐ National Endowment for the Humanities
84 ☐ Education	04 ☐ Inter-American Foundation	47 ☐ National Science Foundation
81 ☐ Energy	15 ☐ Interior	07 ☐ Office of National Drug Control Policy
66 ☐ Environmental Protection Agency		
08 ☐ Peace Corps		
59 ☐ Small Business Administration		
96 ☐ Social Security Administration		
19 ☐ State		
20 ☐ Transportation		
21 ☐ Treasury		
82 ☐ United States Information Agency		
64 ☐ Veterans Affairs		
☐ Other – *Specify:*		

PART II   FINANCIAL STATEMENTS *(To be completed by auditor)*

1. Type of audit report *(Mark (X) one box)*
   1 ☐ Unqualified opinion   2 ☐ Qualified opinion   3 ☐ Adverse opinion   4 ☐ Disclaimer of opinion

2. Is a "going concern" explanatory paragraph included in the audit report?   1 ☐ Yes   2 ☐ No

3. Is a reportable condition disclosed?   1 ☐ Yes   2 ☐ No – *SKIP to Item 5*

4. Is any reportable condition reported as a material weakness?   1 ☐ Yes   2 ☐ No

5. Is a material noncompliance disclosed?   1 ☐ Yes   2 ☐ No

PART III   FEDERAL PROGRAMS *(To be completed by auditor)*

1. Type of audit report on major program compliance
   1 ☐ Unqualified opinion   2 ☐ Qualified opinion   3 ☐ Adverse opinion   4 ☐ Disclaimer of opinion

2. What is the dollar threshold to distinguish Type A and Type B programs §___ .520(b)?

$ _____

3. Did the auditee qualify as a low-risk auditee (§___ .530)?
   1 ☐ Yes   2 ☐ No

4. Are there any audit findings required to be reported under §___ .510(a)?
   1 ☐ Yes   2 ☐ No

5. Which Federal Agencies are required to receive the reporting package? *(Mark (X) all that apply)*

01 ☐ African Development Foundation	83 ☐ Federal Emergency Management Agency	16 ☐ Justice
02 ☐ Agency for International Development	34 ☐ Federal Mediation and Conciliation Service	17 ☐ Labor
10 ☐ Agriculture	39 ☐ General Services Administration	43 ☐ National Aeronautics and Space Administration
11 ☐ Commerce	93 ☐ Health and Human Services	89 ☐ National Archives and Records Administraton
94 ☐ Corporation for National and Community Service	14 ☐ Housing and Urban Development	05 ☐ National Endowment for the Arts
12 ☐ Defense	03 ☐ Institute for Museum Services	06 ☐ National Endowment for the Humanities
84 ☐ Education	04 ☐ Inter-American Foundation	47 ☐ National Science Foundation
81 ☐ Energy	15 ☐ Interior	07 ☐ Office of National Drug Control Policy
66 ☐ Environmental Protection Agency		
08 ☐ Peace Corps		
59 ☐ Small Business Administration		
96 ☐ Social Security Administration		
19 ☐ State		
20 ☐ Transportation		
21 ☐ Treasury		
82 ☐ United States Information Agency		
64 ☐ Veterans Affairs		
00 ☐ None		
☐ Other – *Specify:*		

PART III FEDERAL PROGRAMS – Continued

6. FEDERAL AWARDS EXPENDED DURING FISCAL YEAR

EIN: _____

CFDA number¹ (a)	Name of Federal program (b)	Amount expended (c)	Major program (a)	Type of compliance requirement² (b)	Amount of questioned costs (c)	Internal control findings³ (d)	Audit finding reference number(s) (e)
		$	1☐Yes 2☐No		$	1☐A 3☐C 2☐B	
		$	1☐Yes 2☐No		$	1☐A 3☐C 2☐B	
		$	1☐Yes 2☐No		$	1☐A 3☐C 2☐B	
		$	1☐Yes 2☐No		$	1☐A 3☐C 2☐B	
		$	1☐Yes 2☐No		$	1☐A 3☐C 2☐B	
		$	1☐Yes 2☐No		$	1☐A 3☐C 2☐B	
		$	1☐Yes 2☐No		$	1☐A 3☐C 2☐B	
		$	1☐Yes 2☐No		$	1☐A 3☐C 2☐B	

TOTAL FEDERAL AWARDS EXPENDED → $ _____

IF ADDITIONAL LINES ARE NEEDED, PLEASE PHOTOCOPY THIS PAGE, ATTACH ADDITIONAL PAGES TO THE FORM, AND SEE INSTRUCTIONS

¹Or other identifying number when the Catalog of Federal Domestic Assistance (CFDA) number is not available.

²Type of compliance requirement *(Enter the letter(s) of all that apply to audit findings and questioned costs reported for each Federal program.)*
- A. Activities allowed or unallowed
- B. Allowable costs/cost principles
- C. Cash management
- D. Davis – Bacon Act
- E. Eligibility
- F. Equipment and real property management
- G. Matching, level of effort, earmarking
- H. Period of availability of funds
- I. Procurement
- J. Program income
- K. Real property acquisition and relocation assistance
- L. Reporting
- M. Subrecipient monitoring
- N. Special tests and provisions
- O. None

³Type of internal control findings *(Mark (X) all that apply)*
- A. Material weaknesses
- B. Reportable conditions
- C. None reported

FORM SF-SAC (8-97)

Part III

CONCERNS/ISSUES OF GOVERNMENTAL AUDITING

"Compliance with laws and regulations is important to governmental organizations, programs, activities, and functions because public officials have a responsibility to comply with the specific laws and regulations which created these organizations and govern their operations. An entity's management is responsible for establishing an internal control structure to reasonably assure compliance with laws and regulations."

United States General Accounting Office

Exposure Draft—Government Auditing Standards

July 26, 1993

Several subjects are of concern when conducting audits pursuant to government auditing standards that may be of minimal or no concern when conducting audits pursuant to generally accepted auditing standards. Of particular importance to audits of public sector entities are the required tests of controls, tests of compliance with laws and regulations, tests of allowable and unallowable costs, stringent audit working paper criteria, auditor quality control practices and audit quality oversight, plus a wide variety of existing auditors and audit relationships:

● The objective and purpose, and mandatory (not optional) testing which must be made of entity-wide and federal program controls of organizations that must conform to federal financial criteria and the reporting that must be made by an auditor of the results of these tests. This level of testing and required reporting is not required by generally accepted auditing standards.

● Mandated tests of compliance with laws and regulations. It is illegal to spend, consume, or otherwise use public funds or properties for a purpose not implicitly or explicitly permitted by law or regulation. Existence of authorizing and appropriation legislation is a condition precedent to every action of government. The extent of testing and reporting upon an auditee's compliance with laws and regulations has no parallel in audits of private sector entities.

● Absent effective competitive pricing constraints, the federal government has long relied on specific criteria for determining those costs deemed allowable and unallowable as charges to or claims under federally financed programs. Adherence to these cost and pricing requirements is an essential characteristic that must be audited and reported upon in almost every audit of governmental programs. Seldom are these tests significant in an audit made pursuant to generally accepted auditing standards.

- Working papers of government audits are reviewed in greater detail, by more parties, relied upon to a greater extent, and used for more intensive independent quality control reviews than working papers in support of audits made pursuant to generally accepted auditing standards.

- In relation to audits of private sector entities, audits of public sector entities are subject to more scrutiny, different quality control criteria, more public and professional, and financially damaging sanctions. To meet government auditing standards and competently perform such audits, special continuing professional education is mandated, in addition to that required for auditors performing audits pursuant to generally accepted auditing standards.

These issues permeate all public sector audits and require extra care in the planning, conducting, and reporting on audits of governments and recipients of government funds. The "rules" related to these issues are continually changing to reflect evolving views of what legislators and citizens deem to be appropriate uses of monies, property, and other resources acquired or supported by their tax dollars.

Chapter 8

Review of Internal Controls— Generally Accepted Standards, Government Standards, Single Audit Requirements

EVOLVING VIEWS ON CONTROLS

Differing Definitions

The auditor's responsibilities for assessing internal controls is greater for audits of governmental entities than is the case when auditing corporate financial statements. These expanded responsibilities for controls are directly related to the differing definitions and importance placed by different parties on controls as well as the purposes of varied scope audits.

The American Institute of Certified Public Accountants, in its Statement on Auditing Standards No. 55 and the amending SAS No. 78: defines three categories of control objectives: the control environment, the control structure, and control procedures. Recognition and advice is provided on each of the five components of an internal control, published by the Committee of Sponsoring Organizations (COSO): control environment, risk assessment, control activities, information and communication, and monitoring.

The Congress and the U.S. Office of Management and Budget define the internal control structure for government purposes even more broadly to encompass non-accounting and non-financial factors as the plan of organization and methods and procedures adopted by management to ensure that resource use is consistent with legal criteria and that resources are safeguarded against waste, loss, and misuse. The U.S. General Accounting Office, in its standards for performance audits, requires auditors to understand management controls that it defines as including the plan of organization, methods, and procedures adopted by management to ensure that its goals are met.

Views on Controls

Over the years, many have had enhanced concerns and have given increased emphasis to the importance to the internal control structures of audited entities. In government, many executives support the thesis that controls are possibly, from a management and oversight perspective, as important as the detailed auditing of financial information. These views have been volunteered by members of the accounting profession, independent commissions, often by Congress and Comptrollers General of the United States.

The concern that internal control structures must be given a higher priority during the course of an audit has been building for years. Some examples would include:

● In April 1988, the AICPA issued 10 SASs, referred to as the "expectation" SASs, with at least four of these SASs outlining new or defining with more specificity the auditor's responsibility for internal controls and for communicating the results of tests of controls under certain adverse conditions.

● An article titled, "*Addressing Early Warning and the Public Interest: Auditor Involvement with Internal Control*," by the former chairman of the AICPA's Auditing Standards Board (*CPA Journal*, 1991) argued that auditors should do more work on internal controls and that such work should provide an early warning of potential problems.

● The Committee of Sponsoring Organizations of the Treadway Commission [1] provided an expanded definition of internal controls that emphasizes increased importance being given to controls. The 1992 COSO report identified five prerequisites of an effective internal control structure to include (1) the control environment, (2) risk assessment, (3) control activities, (4) information and communications and (5) monitoring.

● A former member of the AICPA's Board of Directors, in an article, "*Reinventing the Audit*," discussed the proposition that the public expects assurances that audited entities are well-controlled and that they comply with laws and regulations and auditors should be providing these assurances rather than opining on only whether the historical numbers are in accordance with generally accepted accounting principles at a particular moment in time.

---

[1] The COSO included the following sponsoring organizations: American Institute of CPAs, American Accounting Association, Institute of Management Accountants, and Financial Executives Institute.

- A GAO report on a survey of a number of major bank audit committees asking what they desired from an audit revealed that more reporting on internal controls and compliance with laws and regulations—the financial statement audit, and some "boilerplate" reports on controls, were not meeting the needs of these audit committee members.

- An independent auditor's report on the U.S. General Accounting Office for the year ended September 30, 1992, included both an opinion on the agency's financial statements as well as an opinion on the GAO's system of internal control in effect on September 30, 1992. Later, the independent auditor's report for the AICPA's financial statements for the year ended July 31, 1994, included an audit opinion on the AICPA's financial statements as well as an independent auditor's opinion on management's assertions that the AICPA maintained an effective internal control system. In rendering the control opinions, auditors used the criteria established by the Committee of Sponsoring Organizations of the Treadway Commission.

- A shift in the historic audit "paradigm" was proposed by GAO representatives in 1993. GAO suggested changes in auditing standards to give increased audit coverage to controls and provided evidence to support their thesis that controls were as important, maybe more so, than the auditing and reporting on only historical information. [2] GAO believed that auditing standards should explicitly and implicitly elevate the audit work on internal controls to that now done to substantiate data in financial statements. The desired changes were in several areas: (1) the scope of the controls reviewed should be expanded beyond the internal accounting and administrative controls now envisioned generally accepted auditing standards, (2) the objective of auditing controls should be elevated to a level of emphasis commensurate with the audit of financial data, and (3) there should be a separate reporting—i.e., an opinion on the effectiveness of controls—by the auditor.

Congressional Concerns with Controls

From at least the 1970s, Congress has been concerned that the auditor's examination of internal controls should be given increased priority in audits. There seemed to be a belief that the strength of an organization's controls told much about its performance—financial and otherwise. A feeling persisted that detailed knowledge about internal controls was a predictor of future stewardship. Congress reflected these views in several laws:

- In 1977 the Foreign Corrupt Practices Act placed significant emphasis on internal controls requiring that all publicly held compa-

---

[2] Forum titled, "Standards and Practice: Where Does the Road Lead," Mid-America Intergovernmental Audit Forum, Kansas City, Missouri, May 3-4, 1993.

nies devise and maintain a system of internal controls sufficient to provide reasonable assurance for safeguarding the entity's assets and ensuring that transactions are properly authorized, record and reported.

• In 1982, Congress passed the Federal Managers Financial Integrity Act that required the internal accounting and administrative controls of each federal agency to be established in accordance with standards prescribed by the Comptroller General to insure that obligations and costs comply with law, and that funds, property, and assets are safeguarded against waste, loss, unauthorized use or misappropriation.

• In 1984 and as amended in 1996, the Single Audit Act mandates that auditors were to determine that recipients of federal monies have systems of internal control to provide reasonable assurance that all federally supported programs—not a test of only some—are in compliance with applicable federal laws and regulations.

• In 1991, the Federal Deposit Corporation Improvement Act required that management of certain federally insured financial institutions report on the effectiveness of internal controls over financial reporting and compliance with laws and regulations. Also the 1991 Act required that the institution's independent auditors attest to management's report on the effectiveness of internal controls and to perform certain specified agreed-upon audit procedures related to assessing compliance with laws and regulations.

These initiatives, and others, give growing recognition to the fundamental need for sound internal controls if financial transactions are to be accurately recorded and reliable financial reports are to be prepared. The high transaction volumes and organizational and operational complexities of a modern enterprise—corporate or government—seem to make it mandatory that there be adequate controls to ensure this accuracy and reliability.

No controls or inadequate controls can undermine the bases for decisions and diminish the quality of reports required of creditors and shareholders, regulators and the general public. Increasing volumes of transactions and the invisibility of most transactions and accounting allocations in computer-based financial and managerial systems are creating a significant challenge to the validity of the existing auditing model.

For large organizations—like governments—it is probably not realistic for an auditor to support an audit opinion solely on the basis of substantive tests of transaction. An auditor can not substantively test thousands of transactions and examine the recording and information reporting pyramid sufficient to support a conclusion that the financial statements are fairly presented and ignore the systems of control. Nor is it feasible—cost or volume-wise—to test enough transactions to overcome poor, weak or non-existent controls. Reliance must be placed on controls for all those transactions, accounts and other data not examined directly.

HIERARCHY OF REVIEWS OF CONTROLS

Over the years, the profession's view and context for discussing the auditor's responsibilities for internal controls evolved gradually. But still the role of controls in a financial statement audit may be confusing to many, inside and outside the audited organization, and to those exercising oversight responsibilities. The limited objectives when testing controls as part of a financial statement audit has a significant distinction. To the auditor, because of risks assumed, this distinction is extremely important. There are at least four audit phrases that the auditor is repeatedly called upon to explain with respect to internal controls: (1) a preliminary review, (2) an understanding of controls, (3) test of controls, and (4) an examination of controls.

Preliminary Review of Controls

Historically, auditing literature referred to auditors as making a *preliminary review* of the control environment after which the auditor might conclude that a further study and evaluation was unlikely to permit the auditor to restrict or minimize later tests of the system, categories of transactions, and account balances by placing reliance on the controls. The preliminary review is more in the nature of compiling an inventory of accounting and administrative controls, with extremely limited testing to permit a preliminary assessment of the potential effectiveness of controls, systems, documentation, centralized versus decentralized systems, and extent of automation versus manual accounting. Generally, the objective of a preliminary review is to acquire an accumulation of information to permit commencement of early phases of pre-planning efforts for the audit.

Study and Understanding Controls

The second field standard of generally accepted auditing standards requires the auditor to obtain an *understanding* of the internal control structure, for example the standard states that:

> *"A sufficient understanding of the control structure is to be obtained to plan the audit and determine the nature, timing, and extent of tests to be performed."*

This standard has been further refined by SAS's Nos. 55 and 78 stating that in all audits, the auditor should plan the audit by performing audit procedures to understand (1) the design of policies and procedures relevant to audit planning, and (2) whether they have been placed in operation. This understanding must be documented by the auditor (e.g., flowcharts, checklists, questionnaires, memorandum, decision tables, etc.). The auditor, in this circumstance, does not render a separate report or opinion on the controls as a result of this study and evaluation.

The study and evaluation is the basis for determining the extent to which audit procedures can be restricted because increased reliance can be placed on the functioning controls. This "understanding" of the control structure is important to the overall audit. Based on the "understanding, an auditor will determine the nature (i.e., the type of tests to perform), the timing (i.e., when the tests will be performed), and the extent of testing required (i.e., how much testing is done).

Evaluate Controls

The next requirement is that the auditor *evaluate* the internal controls as part of the financial statement audit. The evaluation of controls is made for purposes of assessing the levels of risk to permit an auditor to reach conclusions on the reliance that can be placed on controls for determining: (1) what areas of transactions and accounts must be tested, (2) when, during the fiscal period, such test should or must be made, and (3) how much or how many tests should be made to support an opinion on the fair presentation of a financial statement.

This phase of tests to comply with generally accepted auditing standards is not sufficient and does not constitute an audit of the underlying systems of controls or accounting. These tests and evaluation activities are intermediate steps in planning and performing the audit and in forming an opinion on the overall fairness of information appearing in the financial statements.

The auditor, in this circumstance, will not render a separate report or audit opinion on controls.

Examination of Controls

There will be instances when an auditor does make an *examination* of the systems of internal controls. In such instances, an examination is an engagement separate and distinct from the financial statement audit. At the conclusion of an examination engagement, the auditor will express an opinion on an entity's system of internal controls. The testing to support an opinion of the internal accounting system is more extensive than the audit tests made of controls to support an opinion on the financial statements, although the audit procedures might appear similar.

AUDITOR RESPONSIBILITY FOR TESTING CONTROLS

Those performing government audits must be cognizant of the differing nature, detail, and purposes of the tests made of internal controls and requirements. These auditors must decide to report or not report on the results of these tests. What is done and what is reported varies depending on the type of audit made, the auditing standards used, and applicable laws and regulations. The differences can be significant.

Minimal Requirements—GAAS

Generally accepted auditing standards require tests be made of the control structure to provide the auditor with an understanding of the controls. Then, additional testing of controls is required if the auditor intends to place reliance on the systems of controls to establish the nature (what is to be tested), timing (when are the tests to be conducted) and extent (how much testing is required) of substantive audit tests to be made of groups of transactions and account balances.

To the AICPA, internal controls means:

"... a process, effected by an entity's board of directors, management, and other personnel, designed to provide reasonable assurance regarding the achievement of objectives in the following categories: effectiveness and efficiency of operations; reliability of financial reporting; and compliance with applicable laws and regulations."

The AICPA's auditing standards do not require that the auditor separately assess each individual element of the internal control structure, these standards do require that the auditor:

1. Obtain a sufficient understanding of each of the elements of the control structure;

2. Conduct tests to determine that control policies and procedures have been placed in operation;

3. Assess control risks for assertions implicit in account balances, transaction classes, and disclosure components of the financial statements.

4. Make additional tests of controls to acquire evidence relating to or supportive of the financial statement assertions to permit the auditor to reduce doubts—or risks—about the audibility of the financial statements.

With respect to reporting, the AICPA's standards require only that "reportable conditions" be communicated to the audit committee and if the audit committee has acknowledged an awareness of the reportable condition, this control deficiency may never be reported to parties external to the auditee. If there is a communication, the AICPA's standards require the auditor to state that the communication is intended solely for information and use of the audit committee, management and others within the audited organization. And, under generally accepted auditing standards, this communication need not be written. An oral communication will suffice, at the option of the auditor.

Increased Requirements—GAGAS

Government auditing standards do not provide for a different definition of internal controls nor do the government standards prescribe audit test standards in addition to the AICPA's.

But, government auditing standards provide extensive "guidance" relating to the evidence an auditor of government financial statements must consider on several specific control subjects, such as: controls environment, safeguarding controls, controls over compliance with laws and regulations; and in making control risk assessments. Through 1994 government standards required auditors to make judgments about audit risk and the evidence needed to support their audit opinion. The 1994 guidance emphasized four specific areas: (1) Control environment; (2) Safeguarding controls; (3) Controls over compliance with laws and regulations, and (4) Control risk assessments.

The government auditing standards also contain a definition of *management controls* that would include:

> "...the plan of organization, methods, and procedures adopted by management to ensure that its goals are met. Management controls include: (1) the processes for planning, organizing, directing, and controlling program operations as well as (2) the systems for measuring, reporting, and monitoring program performance."

And, under government auditing standards, the auditor must submit a separate written report on internal controls describing: (1) the scope of testing performed on controls, (2) the results of those tests, and (3) all reportable conditions. An oral communication between an auditee and auditor will not suffice. Reporting to parties external to the auditee is not a part of the AICPA's generally accepted auditing standards. GAO, in its government standards, acknowledges that these audit responsibilities are in addition to the AICPA's.

More Detailed Requirements—Single Audit Act

The Single Audit Act mandates that the auditor report on whether a recipient of federal financial assistance has internal controls to provide reasonable assurance whether the recipient is managing federal funds in compliance with laws and regulations. Also, the law states federal programs must be tested. Based on these audit responsibilities, Congress defined internal controls in the Act as comprising:

"... a process, effected by an entity's management and other personnel, designed to provide reasonable assurance regarding the achievement of objectives in the following categories: effectiveness and efficiency of operations; reliability of financial reporting; compliance with applicable laws and regulations."

Unlike the controls testing concept implicit in generally accepted auditing standards the tests mandated by the Act must be performed whether or not the auditor intends to rely on the controls as a basis for determining later audit test procedures.

OMB Circular A-133, that implements the Single Audit Act, expands this definition of controls, stating that internal control means:

"... a process, effected by an entity's management and other personnel, designed to provide reasonable assurance regarding the achievement of the following objectives for federal programs:

Transactions are properly recorded and accounted for to: (1) Permit preparation of reliable financial statements and federal reports; (2) Maintain accountability over assets; and (3) Demonstrate compliance with laws and regulations, and other compliance requirements.

Transactions are executed in compliance with: (1) Laws, regulations, and the provisions of contracts or grant agreements that could have a direct and material effect on a federal program; (2) Any other laws and regulations that are identified in the compliance supplement; and (3) Funds, property, and other assets are safeguarded against loss from unauthorized use or disposition."

OMB's Circular A-133, states that to make the review of controls required by the Act, the auditor must study and evaluate the control systems whether or not the auditor intends to place audit reliance on such systems. Additionally, OMB requires that a written report on internal controls specifically identify the following several matters:

1. The audited organization's significant accounting controls;

2. Those controls designed to provide reasonable assurance that all federal programs are managed in compliance with laws and regulations;

3. The controls evaluated by the auditor;

4. The controls not evaluated by the auditor; and

5. The material weaknesses identified as a result of the evaluation.

The Circular directs the auditor to test controls and submit this report for both major and non-major federal financial assistance programs of an entity. This reporting must be made even though the detailed tests of transactions, accounts, reports, other evidence and the financial statements permit the auditor to issue an unqualified or "clean" opinion on the entity's overall financial statements.

Auditors should be aware of the differing contrasting reasons for testing controls. Under generally accepted and government auditing standards, the phases of acquiring the understanding of controls and the later testing of controls are conducted with the view of supporting the opinion on the entity's overall financial statements. These tests of controls are essential only if the auditor intends to place reliance on the controls when determining the detailed audit tests to be made of transactions and account balances. If the auditor elects not to rely on controls, an option exist for performing other corroborating substantive audit procedures.

This option, not to rely on controls, does not exist with respect to Single Audits. In the case of audits made to comply with the Single Audit Act, auditors must test controls and then report on the tests that affect federal programs regardless of whether the auditor intends to place any reliance on the controls.

INTERNAL CONTROL CONSIDERATIONS—GAAS

Generally accepted auditing standards and selected AICPA SASs provide specific guidance on an auditor's responsibilities for studying and evaluating an entity's control structure and conditions under which the systems and structure must be tested. As mentioned in earlier chapters, these SASs are also relevant to government audits because the government auditing standards incorporate all of the SASs of the AICPA as part of the government auditing standards.

The following paragraphs highlight aspects of selected SASs relating to an auditor's responsibility for internal controls when performing an audit of financial statements. These particular SASs include Nos. 53, 54, 55, and 60.

SAS 53—Auditor's Responsibility to Detect and Report Errors and Irregularities

Definitions. SAS 53 defines *errors* as mistakes in gathering or processing accounting data, incorrect accounting estimates, and mistakes in the application of accounting principles. *Irregularities* are intentional misstatements or omissions of amounts or disclosure in financial statements, including fraudulent reporting or management fraud and misappropriation of assets or defalcations and could involve:

● Manipulation, falsification or alteration of accounting records or support documentation;

● Misrepresentation or intentional omission of events, transactions, or other information;

● Intentional misapplication of accounting principles relating to amounts, classification, presentation or disclosure.

Auditor's Responsibility. The auditor must assess the risk that errors and irregularities may cause financial statements to contain a material misstatement. Based on that assessment, SAS 53 states that:

" ... the auditor should design the audit to provide reasonable assurance to detect errors and irregularities that are material to the financial statements."

This assessment of risk should be made during the planning phase, but it is continuing concern throughout the audit. The auditor's understanding of the control structure should either heighten or mitigate concern about risks of material misstatements. Factors considered in assessing risk must be evaluated in combination with all other test results in arriving at an overall judgment. This SAS points out that the presence of some factors in isolation would not necessarily indicate increased risks. The AICPA suggests several factors that should be considered as:

● **Management characteristics**—domination by a single person, unduly aggressive reporting attitude, high turnover, undue emphasis on meeting earnings projections, poor reputation in business community.

● **Operating/Industry characteristics**—profitability of entity relative to industry, sensitivity of operating results to economic factors, rate and/or direction change in industry, decentralized organization with inadequate monitoring, going concern issues.

● **Engagement characteristics**—contentious or difficult accounting issues, difficult-to-audit transactions or account balances, significant or unusual related party transactions not in the ordinary course of business, misstatements in prior audits, new client with no prior audit history or insufficient information available from predecessor auditor.

SAS 53 cautions the profession that audits made in accordance with government auditing standards go beyond the SAS, particularly with respect to notification of parties that may be external to the audited entity.

SAS 54—Illegal Acts by Clients

SAS 54 prescribes the nature and extent of consideration that should be given to the possibility of illegal acts by clients in an audit of financial statements pursuant to generally accepted auditing standards. *Illegal acts* refer to violations of laws or governmental regulations. The AICPA cautions auditors that *illegality* is a determination normally beyond the auditor's professional competence. Thus, such a determination would generally be based on the advice of an informed expert qualified to practice law or a determination by a court of law.

The AICPA states, in SAS 54, that audit made in accordance with generally accepted auditing standards provides no assurance that illegal acts will be detected or that any contingent liabilities that may result will be disclosed. The auditor's responsibility to detect and report misstatements resulting from illegal acts having a direct and material effect on the determination of financial statement amounts is the same as that for errors and irregularities as described in SAS No. 55, *The Auditor's Responsibility to Detect and Report Errors and Irregularities.*

But as stated in SAS 54, normally, an audit in accordance with generally accepted auditing standards *does not* include audit procedures specifically designed to detect illegal acts, although some of the following audit procedures applied to form an opinion on the financial statements may bring possible illegal acts to the auditor's attention:

● Reading minutes;

● Inquiring of client's management and legal counsel concerning litigation, claims, assessments;

● Performing substantive tests of transactions and account balances;

● Inquiries of management relating to controls to prevent illegal acts;

● Reviewing management directives; and

● Reading periodic representations concerning compliance with laws and regulations.

Should the auditor become aware of a possible illegal act, SAS 54 states the auditor should obtain an understanding of the nature of the act, surrounding circumstances, and evaluate the effect on the financial statements. Plus, the auditor should make inquiries of management above the level of those involved, consult with the client's legal counsel and communicate with the audit committee or others having equivalent authority and responsibility.

SAS 55, SAS 78—Consideration of the Internal Control Structure in a Financial Statement Audit

By these SASs, to the AICPA, internal controls means:

"... a process, effected by an entity's board of directors, management, and other personnel, designed to provide reasonable assurance regarding the achievement of objectives in the following categories: effectiveness and efficiency of operations; reliability of financial reporting; and compliance with applicable laws and regulations."

These SASs describe the structure of an entity's internal control system as being comprised of three objectives: (1) the control environment, (2) the accounting system, and (3) control procedures. These SASs state that in all audits, the auditor should obtain a sufficient understanding of each of the three objectives to plan the audit by performing audit procedures to understand: (1) the design of policies and procedures relevant to audit planning; and (2) whether the controls have been placed in operation.

Placed in Operation versus Operating Effectiveness

SAS 55 makes a distinction between an internal control structure policy and procedures actually placed in operation, commenting that it is different from operating effectiveness.

Obtaining a knowledge about controls *placed in operation* means that the auditor must determine what the controls the auditee is using. This understanding is obtained during the pre-planning phase of the audit and must include a review and understanding of the design and operation of policies and procedures.

In contrast, *operating effectiveness* is concerned with how the internal control policies and procedures are applied, the consistency of application and by whom. These SASs do not require the auditor to obtain detailed knowledge about the operating effectiveness of all parts of the control structure to acquire an understanding of the control structure. SAS 78 describes an entity's internal control structure as being comprised of five components outlined in the COSO report.

The AICPA acknowledges that the control structure could include a wide variety of objectives and related policies and procedures. Those identified as relevant to a financial statement audit pertain to an entity's ability to record, process, summarize, and report financial data consistent with the management's assertions regarding financial information.

Components of a Control Structure

SAS 78 describes an entity's internal control structure as comprising five components: the control environment, risk assessment, control activities, information and communication, and monitoring.

Control Environment. This component sets the "tone at the top" for a governmental entity and will directly affect the control consciousness of the public sector executives and employees. The realities of public sector operations dictate that one will not encounter the same control environment. The political and appointive process guarantees that there may never be continuity of leadership and senior management—turnover of leadership and senior management is extremely high at all levels of government. Further, personnel in senior public sector positions need not have any prior qualifying or relevant business or managerial experience.

Risk Assessment. This component is related to the auditee's identification, analysis, and management of risk that affects the organizations financial statement objectives. Some of these risks, in a governmental entity, could relate to the accounting for encumbered financial activities at year end, the failure to fully accrue all costs, the correct accounting for "receipt" of goods and services performed under contract to the government, validity of year-end encumbrances, attainment of legislatively imposed output or outcome measures. Even the compensation policy of a government is a risk—a conservative policy could impinge on personnel competence. Or, wholesale "buyouts" could deplete an entire generation of key personnel.

Control Activities. This component relates to the policies and procedures issued to implement management directives, and ensure that personnel are conforming to the directives. Several types of control activities include periodic personnel and other performance reviews, audited information processing systems and procedures, continual physical check and balance controls, adequate segregation of operational, managerial, and financial duties and functions. Too often legislative and executive branch leadership are reluctant or refuse to provide the necessary financial support for systems improvement, capital equipment acquisition, retention of highly compensated experts, and programs of continuing professional education.

Information and Communication. This component of the control structure consists of the methods and records established to identify, assemble, analyze, classify, record, and report on an entity's transactions and to maintain accountability for related assets and liabilities. Effective controls and accounting systems will give appropriate consideration to methods, records, transaction and account coding, and segregation of functions. Controls should permit one to identify and record all valid transactions; timely describe and properly classify transactions; measure value of transactions for proper authorization and recordation; determine the proper time period for accounting for transactions; and properly present transactions and related disclosures in the financial statements.

Monitoring. This control component relates to the management responsibility of ensuring that the desired and prescribed controls are operating as intended and modified as frequently as changed conditions warrant. This component envisions an on-going process of evaluation and inspections by many—internal auditors, external auditors, outside management evaluators, internal review teams, internal pre- and post-payment reviews. A continuing process or intermittent program of surveys of customer satisfaction would be an integral part of this component. Also to be included are independent checks on performance and valuation of recorded amounts—clerical checks, reconciliation's, comparisons of assets with recorded accountability, computer-programmed controls, management review of reports, and user review of computer-generated reports.

A sufficient understanding of each of the three control objectives and five components of the internal control structure is necessary to plan the audit of an entity's financial statements. In planning it is expected, by the AICPA, that such knowledge should be used to (1) identify types of potential misstatements, (2) consider factors that affect the risk of material misstatement; and (3) to design substantive audit tests.

SASs 55 and 78 provides guidance on the types of evidential matter required to support an assessed level of control risk. These include reliance on the auditor's prior experience with the entity and understanding of the audit entity's classes of transactions plus making inquiries of appropriate entity personnel, and inspection of documents and records (e.g., source documents, journals, ledgers), inspection of systems documentation. All work performed to understand the entity's internal control structure should be documented in the working papers and might include: flowcharts, completed questionnaires and checklists, decision tables, narrative descriptions, and memorandum.

SAS 60—Communication of Internal Control Structure Matters

SAS 60 provides guidance in identifying and reporting conditions that relate to an entity's internal control structure observed during an audit of financial statements. This reporting would generally reside with the audit committee or individuals with equivalent levels of authority and responsibility in the auditee's organization. In this connection, an auditor must be aware of the degrees or seriousness of communicable issues, which SAS defines as either: (1) *reportable conditions*, or (2) *material weaknesses*.

Reportable Condition

The AICPA defines a *reportable condition* as matters coming to the auditor's attention that, in the auditor's judgment, should be communicated to the audit committee because these conditions represent significant deficiencies in the design or operation of the internal control structure which could adversely affect the organization's ability to record, process, summarize, and report financial data consistent with the assertions of management in the financial statements. Such deficiencies may involve any aspect of the internal control structure objectives or components, outlined earlier. SAS 60 recognized that the existence of reportable conditions may already be known to management that has already made a decision—which is known to the audit committee—to accept the degree of risk because of cost or other considerations. In which case, the auditor has the option of not making the communication.

Material Weaknesses

SAS 60 also states that a reportable condition may be of such magnitude as to also be considered a *material weakness*, which is defined as:

> *" ... a reportable condition in which the design or operation of the specific internal control structure elements do not reduce to a relatively low level the risk that errors or irregularities in amounts that would be material in relation to the financial statements being audited may occur and not be detected within a timely period by employees in the normal course of performing their assigned functions."*

GOVERNMENT AUDITING STANDARDS—CONTROL CONSIDERATIONS

The 1994 edition of GAO's government auditing standards added new requirements intended to focus auditor judgment in control areas that are fundamental to the responsibilities of managers and others entrusted with taxpayers money and where audit risks could be significantly increased due to weak controls. These additional requirements relating to internal controls appear in both the government auditing standards relating to the financial audit standards as well as the performance audit standards. These 1994 audit criteria continue to underscore GAO's belief in the importance that adequate controls play in accurate and reliable accounting and reporting and in continually monitoring management and operations.

Internal Controls—Financial Audits

In connection with financial statement audits, GAO, in 1994, required that additional audit work be performed to:

(1) assess whether the control environment contributes to or diminishes the effectiveness of controls, and

(2) assessing audit risk associated with assets that are vulnerable to loss or misappropriation.

In these circumstances, the auditors must report weaknesses in the control environment and in controls over safeguarding assets.

Under government auditing standards, auditors are also required to explain their responsibilities for testing internal controls to audit committees or executives overseeing financial reporting. Auditors must also explain options for expanding tests of internal controls or of compliance beyond that required for a financial statement audit, e.g., by agreed-upon procedures or full scope examinations of internal controls.

When reporting on financial statement audits, auditors are required to state who is responsible for deciding if expanded control and compliance work should be done. This reporting requirement is intended to establish public accountability for decisions about the extent of testing of internal controls and compliance in financial type audits. This, too, is a reporting that is clearly beyond the AICPA's generally accepted auditing standards.

Controls—Performance Audits

The 1994 revision to the government's performance auditing standards required auditors to understand management controls (not just internal controls) and laws and regulations that are relevant to the audit (not only those relevant to financial activities). This understanding would be part of the information the auditor needs to plan a performance audit. The auditors would then be required to test control and compliance issues that are significant to the performance audit objectives. This revision to the performance audit standards places increased emphasis on the management controls and distinguishes tests of controls, laws, and regulations relevant to performance audits from those tests of controls significant to an audit of only financial statements.

Standards Changes—1999

Amendment No. 1, dated May 1999, to the government auditing standards emphasized the documentation requirements for compliance when auditors assess control risks that are significantly dependent upon computerized information systems. This new government auditing standard, states that in planning an audit, auditors should document in working papers:

> *"(1) the basis for assessing control risk at the maximum level for assertions related to material account balances, transaction classes, and disclosure components of financial statements when such assertions are significantly dependent upon computerized information systems, and (2) communication that the planned audit procedures are designed to achieve audit objectives and to reduce audit risk to an acceptable level."*

By this standard, auditors are directed to have documentation that addresses:

- The rationale for determining the nature, timing, and extent of planned audit procedures;
- The kinds and competence of available evidential matter produced outside a computerized information system; and
- The effect on the audit opinion or report if evidential matter to be gathered during the audit does not afford a reasonable basis for the auditor's opinion on the financial statements.

THE SINGLE AUDIT ACT—CONTROL CONSIDERATIONS

As noted, both generally accepted auditing standards and government auditing standards require the auditor to obtain a knowledge and understanding of the internal controls, to conduct tests to insure compliance with these controls as a basis for determining the extent of reliance that might be placed on the systems of controls, and to also reach conclusions on the extent of audit testing that will be required of transactions and accounts. A distinction is made in applying these standards as between the internal accounting controls and the internal administrative controls.

The *internal accounting controls* relate to the methods and procedures concerned with and directly related to safeguarding assets and the reliability of the financial records. *Internal administrative controls* are comprised of the plan of organization and all methods and procedures concerned mainly with operational efficiency and adherence to managerial policies, relating only indirectly to the financial statements.

Under the Single Audit Act, however, controls must be tested for purposes of reporting on the adequacy of such controls for managing federal assistance programs. The objective here is to place audit emphasis on the specific controls established to *manage* the federal programs and to ensure an entity's *compliance* with federal laws and regulations that apply to each of the specific federal programs being operated by the audited entity. Thus, the Single Audit Act imposes a broader definition of internal controls which must be examined by auditors conducting examinations under the Act. Based on these audit responsibilities, Congress defined *internal controls* in the 1996 Act as comprising:

> *"... a process, effected by an entity's management and other personnel, designed to provide reasonable assurance regarding the achievement of objectives in the following categories: effectiveness and efficiency of operations; reliability of financial reporting; compliance with applicable laws and regulations."*

The Single Audit Act mandates that auditors will issue special reports related to the review of accounting and administrative or management controls. In these reports, the auditor must state whether the audited entity's controls provide reasonable assurance that the entity is managing federal financial assistance programs in compliance with applicable laws and regulations.

Thus, to comply with the Single Audit Act and address the increased concern of Congress about controls, the AICPA has issued audit guidance requiring that now auditors must study and evaluate internal control systems—accounting and administrative—used in administering federal programs. The AICPA also states that this study and evaluation should be of the type that the auditor would perform if the auditor intended to rely on the existing controls.

Government auditing standards make reference to the fact that audit compliance that addresses concerns of Congress, in the areas of internal controls and compliance with laws and regulations, exceed the minimum audit requirements of both the government auditing standards and generally accepted auditing standards.

GOVERNMENTAL CONTROLS

The phases of reviews of controls—preliminary review, study and evaluation, tests of controls, examination of controls—and the nature of audit work performed in a government audit has many similarities to the audit procedures applied during an audit of a private entity. Primary differences exists, though, in: (1) the government's definition of controls, (2) a more detailed classification of controls, (3) a different bases of accounting, (4) unique financial statements, and (5) the compliance with controls within audited entities and for individual governmental programs.

Controls Defined

Historically, the AICPA has attempted to define internal *accounting* controls as being within the scope of the study and evaluation of controls contemplated by its generally accepted auditing standards.

Excluded from this definition were the internal *administrative* controls, which in practice were difficult to differentiate in all cases from the accounting controls. Accounting controls comprised the plan of organization and procedures, and records for safeguarding assets and the reliability of financial records. Administrative controls included the plan of organization and procedures and records concerned with decision processes leading to management's authorization of transactions. But, these views of controls have been modified over the years. As noted, the auditor is currently concerned with the entire control structure.

And, from the government's view—the Single Audit Act—internal controls also mean the plan of organization and methods and procedures adopted by management to ensure that: (1) resource use is consistent with laws, regulations, and policies; (2) resources are safeguarded against waste, loss, and misuse; and (3) reliable data is obtained, maintained, and fairly disclosed in reports. This definition encompasses both an organization's internal accounting as well as administrative and management controls.

Classification of Controls

Like audits of private entities, effective audits of governments are performed by dividing the controls, transaction groups, and account balances by the five COSO control components. With governmental audits, these components are particularly important since the auditor must submit a report describing the classification or segmentation used when conducting audit procedures to study and evaluate and later test controls. OMB, in its *Compliance Supplement*, identifies control components of direct concern to an auditor of a public sector subrecipient entity.[3]

By Control Components

Government Control Environment. This objective is concerned with:

● Establishment of the "tone at the top" of management's commitment to monitoring operations and performance.

● Management's intolerance of overriding established monitoring procedures.

---

[3] The OMB *Compliance Supplement*, updated periodically, is a handbook of guidance for auditors conducting Single Audits in which the federal executives and managers have described those items considered important to successful management of federal programs and compliance with legislative intent. Additionally, the Supplement contains numerous audit objectives and suggested audit procedures for conducting a single audit.

- Maintenance of an organizational structure and its ability to provide necessary information flow to monitor operations and performance.

- Provide sufficient resources to monitor operations and performance.

- Ensure personnel have the knowledge, skills, and abilities needed to accomplish monitoring tasks.

- Individuals performing monitoring tasks possess the knowledge, skills, and abilities required.

- The demonstration of a willingness to comply with federal requirements, have information and accounting and operational systems adequate to administer federal assistance programs.

- Take appropriate actions, including imposition of sanctions, for instances of noncompliance.

Risk Assessment. This objective is concerned with:

- Key managers understand the government environment, systems, and controls sufficient to identify the level and methods needed to monitor federal assistance programs.

- Mechanisms exist, are in place, and used to identify risks arising from external sources that could affect the auditee, such as changed economic conditions, new political conditions, modified regulatory environment, generation of unreliable information.

- Mechanisms exist, are in place, and used to identify and react to changes as financial problems that could result in diversion of funds, personnel practices resulting in loss of essential personnel, rapidly expanded program levels, new activities or changed methods of funding, significant organizational restructuring.

Control Activities. This objective is concerned with:

- Continual proper identification of federal awards programs by their CFDA numbers to permit tracking of operational performance, amounts of awards, financing needs, and applicable compliance.

- Design and implement policies and procedures to ensure compliance with federal laws, program regulations, specific contract and grant agreements, particularly the OMB Circular A-133.

- Managers have in place and conform to program monitoring procedures and practices to provide timely exception-based data in a timely manner.

- Where appropriate, the control process include or require site visits to decentralized operations and more remote organizations.

● Manuals and other written policies and procedures describing federal operation and program and financial compliance requirements, the oversight process, and evaluation and audit requirements

Information and Communication. This objective is concerned with:

● Existence of standardized and routine documents used to track and account for operations, activities and finances under federal assistance programs.

● An awareness by senior executives and representatives of responsibilities implicit in executing certification and assertion-type statements similar to the data-collection form required for single audits.

● The need for a controlled records retention program and system of access that is limited or controlled for those with responsibility and authority.

Monitoring. This objective is concerned with:

● Information and financial systems that provide data supportive of critical decisions in a timely manner that is used by management to oversee operations, control properties, and track finances.

● Reviews and briefings of operations are scheduled and attended by senior management on a regular basis and noted problems addressed.

● A system of follow-up be in place to monitor the timely resolution of problems, prior audit findings, and track implementation actions of management decisions.

By Accounting Cycles

Conducting evaluations and tests of controls by the activity cycles or accounting application methodology is generally more efficient than by account balances or trial balance captions. In addition, for government audits, auditors must also tests controls and conduct substantive audit procedures by cycles to ensure that the auditee personnel are complying with laws and regulations. The cycles or applications are similar and the distinction not significant to the actual audit tests, for example:

Activity Cycles	*Accounting Application*
Treasury/financial	Billings/receivables, receipts
Revenue/receipts	
Purchase/disbursements	Payables/accrued liabilities
Payroll	
Property/equipment/inventory	Property/equipment/inventory
External financing/reporting	General ledger/financial statements
Grant management	Grant management

A unique control concern peculiar to governments is existence of controls associated with several assertions associated with expenditures of public monies, such as: eligibility, types of services, matching and level of effort commitments, reporting requirements, allowable costs, indirect or overhead allocations and conditions of specific contracts, grants and other agreements.

1. *Eligibility*—Have controls been established to ensure that distribution of governmental financial assistance is limited only to those persons or organizations who have been identified as being eligible for such assistance by law or regulations?

2. *Types of services*—Have controls been established to ensure that government funds are disbursed or used for only those services permitted by the law or regulation?

3. *Matching, level of effort, or earmarking requirements*—Have controls been established to ensure that the auditee meets commitments made to providers of financial assistance with respect to the nature or kind, amount, or timing of the auditee's contribution to the program?

4. *Reporting requirements*—Have controls been established to ensure that reports and claims for advances and reimbursements are supported by the books and records from which the entity's financial statements were prepared?

5. *Allowable costs*—Have controls been established to ensure that costs proposed, accounted for, reported, and billed are in compliance with public sector criteria related to reasonableness, allocability, and appropriateness?

6. *Indirect or overhead allocations*—Have controls been established to ensure compliance with government regulations relative to allocations of indirect or overhead costs?

7. *Special tests, requirements*—Have controls been established to ensure that conditions, terms, covenants in contracts, grants, special agreements executed by or with the auditee are implemented, complied with or otherwise honored?

Overall, this need to monitor compliance with many laws, statutes, and regulations, ensure mandated segregation of duties and responsibilities, confirm prevalence of advance authorization and approval (i.e., in advance of consummating a transaction), etc., all contribute to a control structure that is reasonably strong and upon which an auditor could place reliance in planning the timing, extent and nature of detailed audit procedures to be performed.

GOVERNMENT CONTROL STRUCTURE CIRCUMSTANCES, CONDITIONS

Checks and Balances

The view of some citizens when they have reason to encounter or deal with their governments is often that of an organization ensnared with detailed procedures, drowning in forms and paperwork, subjected to a never ending authorization and approval process— i.e., "red" tape, bureaucracy, and grid lock. Auditors though might have a more kindly view, seeing these same "impediments" or administrative frustrations as good internal controls and a sound system of internal checks and balances. Each transaction requires multiple authorization, approval and considerable documentation. Perpetrating a fraud requires the cooperation or the acquiescence of several persons.

Many checks and balances and controls exists with respect to the transactions of almost every governmental unit, function, activity or program affecting or maybe impeding the efficiency of transaction processing. This control environment affects the nature, extent and timing of an auditor's substantive detailed audit procedures that should be applied. More often, this control environment provides a basis for placing a high degree of reliance on government controls.

Generally, a detailed system of checks and balances, authorizations and approvals are imposed on all financial activities to meeting rather specific and detailed statutory or legal requirements. The myriad of documentation comprise a rather formidable control structure over how, what, who, when, and where a government's business can be conducted.

Accounts and Financial Statements

The essential components of a government accounting system are no different than the systems of a private enterprise. The financial systems consist of methods, procedures, forms, and processes to, in a routinized and methodical manner, identify, assemble, analyze, classify, accumulate and report the audited entity's financial position and results of financial operations. The objectives of governmental financial systems are no different than those of other sound systems: to identify and record all valid transactions, on a timely basis, in the proper accounts, in the correct fiscal period, and at proper values.

However, there are differences between governmental and private sector bases of accounting and financial reporting. Most distinctly, as noted in an earlier chapter, there are 12 accounting principles that result in different accounting, transaction classification, and financial statements. The prevalent governmental fund accounting and the account group reporting for capital assets and long term debt have no counterpart in the business world. In addition, budgetary and fiscal accounting have a formality and use a terminology (e.g., encumbrances and obligations) that is not practiced by corporate concerns. Further, the financial statements look different, are different and contain different information than is found in a corporate balance sheet or statement of income and expenses.

These differences are readily apparent from even a cursory glance at a governmental financial statement. Unlike the three statements to complete a corporate financial statement—balance sheet, income and expense statement, and cash flow statement—the general purpose financial statements of a government includes up to nine financial statements. The format of a governmental balance sheet might contain 10 to 12 columns of data—corporate statements will contain but two, if a multi-year reporting is made.

Control Procedures and Practices

In some instances a government entity may utilize a single accounting system, i.e., a single cash receipt, cash disbursement and reporting system. Under these centralized system functions, a single study and evaluation of controls by cycles will suffice to meet generally accepted as well as the government auditing standards and, if in enough detail, possibly the Single Audit Act requirements as well but more often this will not be the case.

There will be more than one and possibly several sources or collectors of cash receipts. There may also be a central disbursing office as well as a disbursing activity at one or more of the major departments. Under these circumstances, then, the controls for each of these separate systems must undergo a study and evaluation and the transactions flowing through each of these systems must be tested.

The control procedures to be tested include those pertaining to: the form and content of support documents for transactions; authorization and approval processes and procedures; segregation of approval, accounting, custody and cash receipt and disbursement activities among many persons; safeguarding of assets (e.g., physical control, access, use, security, condition); and independent checks on performance (e.g., clerical checks, reconciliations, validity checks, computer generated exceptions, and management reviews).

Critical and common control procedures often include a post- or pre-disbursement review or audit of checks, controls, and practices as a prerequisite to finally approving vouchers for payment. Additionally, a professional, adequately staffed internal audit function is a most important control procedure from an independent auditor's viewpoint.

Management

While all governments have judicial, legislative, and executive branches or functions, the executive branch is charged with "managing" the government. The executive branch of any government must operate the government in conformance with the legal objectives, fiscal criteria, and program restraints imposed by legislative units. There are instances of legislative entities imposing their will on the executive branch and attempting to micro manage functions of the executive branch. While a legislative unit may be excessive in its oversight, but most legislative units have little desire to manage, implement, or take executive responsibility for operating a public program.

Thus, the executive branch "tone at the top" establishes the control environment in a government. The executive branch is responsible for developing and installing the controls to detect, prevent or minimize vulnerabilities to fraud and misuse of assets and establishing an effective system of internal checks and balances and, preferably, a professional internal audit organization. Clearly the extensiveness of a system of internal controls is a management judgment and, in the private sector the cost of controls is weighed in relation to the benefits.

In corporate settings, minimal controls may be appropriate when management tenure is extensive, knowledge of the business borders on expert, and selected key executives seriously execute their responsibilities relating to authorizing, approving, and monitoring financial and operational performance.

Factors as tenure in office, relevant prior experience and expertise, and possession of necessary authority to accomplish needed improvements or maintenance to systems of accounting and controls are issues of possible greater concern to the public sector manager. For example, at the federal level and the statistics might not vary significantly for other levels of government, the average tenure of senior management (which is usually appointive) is 17 months. Depending upon election cycles, elected executives might serve only two years, possibly four years, and if willing to serve longer there are laws that place an absolute limit on tenure. Since key executives often hold their management position based upon support of the elected executive, managerial expertise or specialty knowledge or technical competence may not be a criteria for appointment to senior governmental positions. Some appointed executives may have minimal insight into the systems, controls, or processes of a government at the time of appointment.

This characteristic is a major weakness in the control structure of government, but one that cannot, under our system of government, be remedied. For this reason, sound systems, control procedures, enforced systems of checks and balances are essential in a public sector operation.

The following sections highlight other aspects of controls, checks, safeguards that are more common to governments than corporate organizations.

Legislative Budgets

Laws or budgets of legislative branches of government for receipts and expenditures cannot be exceeded by executive branch officials without the legislators' formal approval, generally in the form of legally-approved or enacted statutes or budget laws. Once the legal budget is passed by the legislature, the budget then becomes, concurrently, the economic program of the government, the financial plan of the government and, most importantly, the law. The budget and appropriation processes of governments are the most important controls for defining what operations a government may undertake, the size and duration of the operation, and the financial limits of the operation. Few legislators give broad managerial and financial discretion to executive branch management.

At all levels, officials of executive branch governments do not have the authority to establish the nature of taxes to be levied or assessed nor can these executives determine the purposes for which or in what amount governmental funds will be spent. These are all responsibilities of the legislative branch. Until legislators pass revenue and expenditure legislation, the executive branch has no basis for raising or spending public money. Executive branch officials have no authority except that which is conferred by legislative branches.

Receipts

The authority to tax, assess, or otherwise raise funds or receive cash, in whatever form, must be granted by the legislative branch. This authority is specific, being directed to the types of receipts that can be collected, the approved rates of taxation, amounts of fees to be levied, the bases upon which taxes may be assessed or levied, and even upon which constituents of the taxes will be levied and collected. No revenues or receipts may be collected by governments unless such action has prior legislative approval. Legislative bodies commonly exclude, in part or totally, certain constituents from their tax liability, i.e., charitable organizations, relocated companies, the indigent, ill, and low income persons.

Interestingly, a rather effective private sector entity might pride itself on collecting 90 to 95 percent of its accounts receivables, having to write the uncollected portion off as uncollectible. Newcomers to public sector auditing are initially puzzled by the fact that governments routinely collect 99 percent of all taxes receivable. The reason is that penalties, interest costs, and even liens on the property accrue or are assessed when taxes are unpaid. Property with significantly overdue tax bills may ultimately be sold at public auction where the government is a preferred debtor and receives full payment before any proceeds are paid to the delinquent taxpayer. Thus, collectibility of receivables does not have the same risk as in the private sector and influences the extent and manner in which public sector receivables would be confirmed.

Expenditures

The purposes, amounts and even rate or timing of governmental expenditures are determined and authorized by legislative branches. These authorizations are law and contain many caps or limitations mandated in the legislatively approved budgets for executive branches. These caps or limitations on expenditures are detailed and specific, often being directed at budget line items, programs, functions, organizations, projects, even at times to specific classes of expenditures (e.g., payroll, benefits, travel, overtime, fringe benefits, etc.).

In governments—federal, state and local—the over commitment, over obligation or over expenditure of a legislative budget is illegal and a violation punishable, at least at the federal level by personal fines or imprisonment, or both. All financial mangers take these legislative mandates seriously and many controls exist to ensure that there is compliance with budgetary caps and limitations.

The procurement or acquisition process is one example. The authorization, approval, seeking of competition, contracting procedures, monitoring performance, accounting, paying for services, and auditing involves different government officials working in different organizations, each with an assigned responsibility for some part of a procurement action. Almost never is a contract issued without first confirming the availability of unencumbered funds to pay for the intended procurement. Unless initiated by a most senior executive, an illegal or irregular payment will require the involvement and collusion or acquiescence of several persons which significantly increases the probability of disclosure and risk.

The environment relating to personnel and payroll costs is another example where internal checks and balances could exist to the point of impeding operations by delaying hiring decisions for months. Entry onto almost any government payroll is difficult and time consuming. Most government jobs must be first publicly posted and a competitive evaluation is made of all applicants. Interviews and tests will be conducted; offered salaries must be consistent with laws; appointments must be approved by both operating and personnel executives, and often budget and finance executives.

Further, the legislature in approving annual budgets, establish the total dollar amount of authorized payroll; average salary limits; total number of allowed staff; and types and skills of personnel (often by specific salary level). A large part of any government's budget—70 to 75 percent when payroll benefits are included—is closely and continually scrutinized and audited by the government itself. Thus, a material portion of any government's budget is closely controlled both within the executive branch and externally by oversight legislative groups. At times public interest groups and even citizens get concerned and become quite knowledgeable about government's expenditure practices.

Accounting Forms and Records

Forms abound in government. Since many governments have been functioning for decades, even a century or two, the repetitiveness of accounting activities has by now resulted in documents that meet almost every concern of an auditor. For example, generally forms are designed for use by particular programs, functions, activities and types of transactions. These forms are often color coded; pre-numbered, controlled before and after use, and will often be properly voided, filed after use, and be coded by fund, organizations, and budget activity. The authorization and approval processes and procedures implicit or explicit on each form, if followed diligently, provide excellent checks and balances that can be efficiently tested and upon which an auditor can rely in planning the nature, timing and extent of detailed audit procedures.

Signatures

Signatures, authorizing and approving or settling transactions, are required of government officials before transactions are entered into, throughout the life cycle of the transaction, and at the completion and final payment or settlement of transactions. In many instances, because of the tendency of legislative branches to "micro" manage executive branches, these controls and check and balances may have been prescribed by legislative action and are not discretionary on the part of the executive branch. But, from an auditing view, the mandatory nature of these signatory requirements creates an excellent control on fiscal transactions.

Outlay or Fiscal Process

The entire outlay, disbursement or expenditure process of governments is continuously monitored. controls and checks exist at the commencement of a budget, during the life of a budget, and at the conclusion or final accounting to demonstrate compliance with the purposes, amounts, and timing restrictions and limitations appearing in legislatively approved budgets and other spending authority.

At each stage of a fiscal transaction—appropriation, allocation, allotment, commitment, encumbrance or obligation, accruing of expenditures, and disbursing of cash—there are policies, procedures, and prescribed practices performed by many individuals, working in different organizations and functions of the government undergoing the audit. Different functions, different people, different organizations are required to assent to government transactions, which creates a controlled environment in which extensive collusion must exist to perpetrate a fraudulent or illegal act.

Of course this process has two primary objectives: (1) to ensure that expenditures are made for only the purposes permitted in law; and (2) to ensure that actual expenditures do not exceed the legally imposed budget for that government. However, attaining these objectives also results in strong controls.

Treasury Controls, Checks and Balances

The treasury or cash disbursement function of governments is often performed pursuant to an entire set of controls directed to validating, once again, the propriety and appropriateness of contemplated expenditures prior to actual payment. Separate forms, records, and reviews are made of all transactions before treasury personnel (who are often in a function separate from accounting) prepare more forms formally authorizing payment and requesting that a check be written.

These activities are often characterized as the voucher approval or warrant preparation and review process. These activities are often followed by the post-disbursement process (that involves close control and review of unused, canceled, and cleared checks; reviews of bank statements, periodic reconciliations of bank balances to book balances, cash budgeting, etc.). Writing and accounting for government checks takes time, involves a lot of people, but from an auditing view, again, these features of the control process creates an environment of close checks and balances.

Controls for Federal Programs

For the most part, federal financial assistance is often relatively immaterial in relation to a government's overall receipts and expenditures even though the federal expenditures could be in the hundreds of millions of dollars for a large state or city. In the instance of a general government, federal expenditures might not exceed, on the average, 10 percent of total governmental expenditures.

However, the Single Audit Act and the related federal regulations requires that recipients of federal assistance agree to have annual financial statement audits and comprehensive reviews of individual program compliance with laws and regulations and tests of controls to insure that the recipient's policies, procedures, and practices promote an awareness of the federal compliance criteria. The concerns of the federal government with respect to controls to ensure compliance with laws and regulations are not, in substance, vastly different than those of governments with respect to monitoring compliance with their own laws and regulations.

The concern of the federal government, historically, has been with the limited audit coverage that may have been given to compliance with the terms and conditions of federal contracts, grants or other agreements during the audit of a government's overall financial statement. There is the additional belief of federal executives, that comprehensive controls and sound fiscal and management practices have an importance in government that is the same for private organizations.

UNDERSTANDING GOVERNMENTAL CONTROL STRUCTURES

The second field standard of generally accepted auditing standards requires the auditor to obtain an *understanding* of the internal control structure as an initial planning activity of the audit. The AICPA in its SAS No. 55 and 78 details other control considerations that must be included when planning an audit and describes an entity's internal control structure. As noted earlier, the Single Audit Act, by imposing a broader and more detailed definition of internal controls and requires that government audits tests of controls not required by generally accepted auditing standards.

"Understanding" of the control structure has different connotations when auditing governments. This difference has been recognized by the AICPA in the guidance published with respect to public sector auditing. Some of this guidance is the internal control questionnaire in the AICPA's *Audit and Accounting Manual* (AAM § 4600) that addresses the typical control structure of governments. The content of this internal control questionnaire deserves comment and careful consideration by practitioners. The illustrative questions are grouped by elements of the controls structure and a special administrative section is devoted to audit concerns that arise related to the Single Audit Act:

- **Control Environment** (4600.020 through .100)—these questions are directed towards assisting the auditor in obtaining an understanding of the control environment and assessing the control risk. The control environment represents the collective effect of various factors on establishing, enhancing, or mitigating the effectiveness of specific policies and procedures. Such factors include:

  - Management's philosophy and operating style;

- The entity's organizational structure;

- Personnel policies and practices;

- Methods of assigning authority and responsibility;

- Management's control methods for monitoring and following-up on performance, including internal auditing and budgeting; and

- Various external influences that affect an entity's operations and practices.

The control environment reflects the overall attitude, awareness, and actions of the legislative, management, staff, and others concerning the importance of the control and its emphasis in the entity.

- **Accounting System** (4600.110 through .160)—these questions are directed towards assisting the auditor in obtaining an understanding of a government's accounting system and assessing the control risk. The AICPA's manual describes the accounting systems as consisting of the methods and records established to identify, assemble, analyze, classify, record, and report an entity's transactions and to maintain accountability for the related assets and liabilities. The auditor should obtain knowledge of the accounting system to understand:

- The classes of transactions in the entity's operations that are significant to the financial statements.

- How those transactions are initiated.

- The accounting records, supporting documents, computer media, and specific accounts in the financial statements involved in the processing and reporting of transactions.

- The accounting processes involved from the initiation of a transaction to its inclusion in the financial statements, including how the computer is used to process data.

- The financial reporting process used to prepare the entity's financial statements, including significant accounting estimates and disclosures.

- **Control Procedures** (4600.170 through .240)—these questions are directed towards assisting the auditor in obtaining an understanding of the control procedures and assessing the control risk.

The manual describes control procedures as those policies and procedures in addition to the control environment and accounting system that management has established to provide reasonable assurance that specific entity objectives will be achieved. Control procedures have various objectives and are applied at various organizational and data processing levels. They may also be integrated into specific components of the control environment and the accounting system. Generally they may be categorized as procedures that pertain to:

- Proper authorization of transactions and activities.

- Segregation of duties that reduce the opportunities to allow any person to be in a position to both perpetrate and conceal errors or irregularities in the normal course of their duties—assigning different people the responsibilities of authorizing transactions, recording transactions, and maintaining custody of assets.

- Design and use of adequate documents and records to help ensure the proper recording of transactions and events, such as monitoring the use of pre-numbered documents.

- Adequate safeguard over access to and use of assets and records, such as secured facilities and authorization for access to computer programs and data files.

- Independent checks on performance and proper valuation of recorded amounts, such as clerical checks, reconciliation's, comparison of assets with recorded accountability, computer-programmed controls, management review of reports that summarize the detail of account balances and user review of computer-generated reports.

- **Administrative Controls** (4600.250 through .280)—these questions are directed towards assisting the auditor in identifying the required administrative controls that need to be in place to properly administer federal assistance programs. These controls that must be documented and tested to support the auditor's reports on internal controls and compliance with laws and regulations related to (1) the general federal compliance criteria, and (2) the specific program federal compliance criteria. (Both groups of compliance audit criteria are described in a later chapter.)

As structured, this questionnaire provides the necessary inquiries to permit an auditor of a governmental entity to: (a) acquire an understanding of the control structure, (b) conduct detailed tests of controls, and (c) perform substantive audit tests of categories of transactions and account balances while correlating the audit procedures to specific management data assertions.

Chapter 9

Compliance Auditing—Generally Accepted Standards, Government Standards, Single Audit Requirements

COMPLIANCE AUDITING

This chapter describes the substantive audit procedures that must be performed by auditors of governments to determine: (1) if in fact the controls relative to compliance with laws and regulations were implemented, and (2) whether tests of transaction groupings and account balances support the management's assertions that expenditures claimed or charged to programs are made in compliance with applicable laws and regulations.

Recent years have seen increasing emphasis being given to the importance of testing for compliance with laws and regulations and of government oversight entities requiring auditors to report on the results of these tests, in addition to submitting the standard audit opinion. Often these tests for compliance must be made regardless of the relative materiality of expended funds under the rationale that all governments owe an accounting to the providers of financial assistance, i.e., the taxpaying citizens. This compliance accountability report is typically directed to asserting whether governmental funds have been applied to and expended for only those programs and activities set forth in laws and regulations, contracts and grants, or other agreements.

Legal limitations on government operations exist to restrict governmental activities, focus managerial emphasis, limit the amount and rate of governmental spending, and impose caps on new revenues that might be raised or ensure compliance with other concerns of legislators. Monitoring compliance with laws and regulations, to a degree, is a partial surrogate for the absence of the competitive disciplines as the revenue and expenditure and profit factors that motivate executives in the private sector to operate more efficiently.

Changing Views

Until the 1980s, the term *compliance* testing was described in AICPA's literature in relation to tests conducted to assess compliance with an entity's internal accounting control procedures. In those times, tests for compliance with laws and regulations were not ignored by the profession, but such tests were often not conducted because the expenditures for federal programs were not material, in a dollar sense, in relation to the overall receipts and expenditures of the typical general government.

The opinion then required of the auditors addressed only whether the financial statements fairly presented the overall financial position and results of financial operations of the audited governments in all material respects. Such audits were conducted in accordance with generally accepted auditing standards. But, the generally accepted auditing standards were the audit standards of the private sector organizations and did not address issues of public sector entities.

Until implementation of the government auditing standards and passage of the Single Audit Act, Congress and state legislatures received minimal information from the audit process related to the government programs and operations. The Comptroller General of the United States had evidence from years of studies that existing audit standards were not addressing significant risk areas. Throughout the 1960s, 1970s and into the 1980s, there was a growing consensus that the audits of governments required different testing by auditors, different assurances from auditors, and different audit reports.

Changed AICPA Guidance

In 1986 the AICPA, in its guide for audits of state and local governments, noted that tests for compliance with laws and regulations were appropriate in a government environment. Also, the AICPA stated that tests for compliance with laws and regulations were considered to be substantive tests to be accomplished by examining supporting documentation and applying other audit procedures. The auditor, where warranted, could choose to rely on internal controls designed to ensure compliance with laws and regulations in order to reduce the extent of this substantive testing. Or alternatively, the auditor had the option of not relying on the controls, but significantly expanding the detailed audit of transactions and account balances to compensate.

Henceforth, *"compliance testing"* was to include tests performed to determine whether audited governments complied with provisions of laws, regulations, contracts, grants, loans, guarantees, and other financial assistance agreements. The objectives of such tests were two-fold: (1) to determine if there had been events of noncompliance that could have a material effect on the overall financial statements, or (2) to provide a basis for reporting on a government's compliance with laws and regulations to the organizations providing the financing.

The AICPA, in its audit Guide, concluded: "The auditor's role in compliance auditing is one of the most significant environmental differences between governmental and private sector auditing."

Compliance—Government Auditing Standards

Throughout the 1980s, government auditing standards required auditors of governments to test financial transactions of audited organizations, programs, activities, and functions, to determine whether there was noncompliance with laws and regulations that could materially affect the entity's financial statements. In particular, auditors of government had to satisfy themselves that the entity had not incurred significant unallowable expenditures and improper liabilities through the failure to comply with or through violations of laws and regulations. The requirement to test for compliance with laws and regulations encompasses the irregular activities and illegal acts covered by generally accepted auditing standards. But, government auditing standards also included a requirement to test for violations of provisions of contracts, grants, loans, guarantees, and other agreements where such instruments are material to the financial statements.

"Materiality" for Compliance

The level of materiality, which determines what noncompliance the auditor will report for government auditing standards, is no different than under the generally accepted auditing standards of the private sector. In both instances, reportable noncompliance items (e.g., irregularities and illegal acts that are not inconsequential) must be material in relation to the financial statements of the entity taken as a whole.

Testing for compliance with laws and regulations is not the primary objective of the audit. Under government auditing standards the audit of the auditee's financial statements is the primary objective. This is apparent in the compliance report required by government auditing standards. Users of the report should be aware that the auditor is not rendering an opinion on compliance with laws and regulations. This fact is evident from a careful reading of the following audit report that would be rendered under government auditing standards:

"We have audited the financial statements of Example Entity as of and for the year ended ... and have issued our

report thereon dated ... . We conducted our audit in accordance with generally accepted auditing standards and the standards applicable to financial audits contained in government auditing standards.

As part of obtaining a reasonable assurance about whether Example Entity's financial statements are free of material misstatement, we performed tests of its compliance with certain provisions of laws, regulations, contracts, grants, noncompliance with which could have a direct and material effect on the determination of financial statement amounts. However, providing an opinion on compliance with those provisions was not an objective of our audit and accordingly we do not express such an opinion. The results of our tests disclosed no instances of noncompliance that are required to be reported under government auditing standards."

In the 1994 edition of its government auditing standards, GAO mandates that the auditor must design the audit to provide reasonable assurance of detecting material instances of noncompliance with laws and regulations. The standards require that if tests were not performed for compliance, the auditor must report that such tests were not performed. The 1994 standards stated that should specific information come to the attention of the auditor concerning possible noncompliance that could be material to the financial statements, the auditor must apply audit procedures directed to determining whether noncompliance actually occurred. Also, in the 1994 revision, GAO formalized the requirement that the audit must be designed to provide reasonable assurance of detecting material misstatements related to noncompliance with provisions of contracts and grants, as well.

No Audit Opinion on Compliance

The objective of a financial statement audit under both generally accepted and government auditing standards is to determine if the auditee's financial statements are free of material misstatement and to provide an audit opinion on whether those financial statements "present fairly" in all material respects the reported financial information. Under neither of the standards, is providing an opinion on compliance the audit objective. Thus, under government auditing standards, auditors will disclaim an opinion. Alternatively, to meet the reporting criteria of government auditing standards, auditors will issue a positive type assurance on their findings, i.e., "our tests disclosed no instances of noncompliance that are required to be reported under government auditing standards."

The distinguishing feature of government auditing standards is that the scope of compliance tests and results of those tests must be reported, in a separate reporting, to the auditee and to parties external to the auditee. The reporting external to the auditee is not a requirement of the generally accepted auditing standards of the private sector.

Much of this chapter is devoted to the tests that must be performed and audit report that must be made under the Single Audit Act related to compliance with laws, regulations, contracts and grants. The nature of audit responsibilities differs considerably from those under government auditing standards.

PERVASIVENESS OF COMPLIANCE AUDITING

Statements and other promulgations of the Governmental Accounting Standards Board (which establishes the generally accepted accounting principles for governments) demonstrate that government is a different industry requiring different accounting, different financial statements, and different audits. GASB's *Codification* specifically requires that if financial statements in accordance with generally accepted accounting principles do not demonstrate finance-related legal and contractual compliance the audited governments must present additional schedules and explanatory narratives. GASB points out that legal and regulatory compliance are both explicit and implicit in and permeate the fund structure, bases of accounting, financial statements, and other accounting principles and methods of government. Says GASB, "legal and contractual considerations ... are a major factor distinguishing governmental accounting from commercial accounting." [1]

Audit procedures directed towards testing for compliance with laws and regulations must now be applied to a wide variety of audits of governmental units. Both financial statement audits and financial related audits, discussed in earlier chapters, fall within the generally accepted and government auditing standards. And both of these sets of auditing standards require testing to detect material misstatements related to noncompliance.

An auditor might consider the AICPA's generally accepted auditing standards as the basic or "foundation" requirements for financial statement audits. Government auditing standards add to the AICPA's requirements by imposing supplemental auditing standards and reporting standards that exceed those of the AICPA. The Single Audit Act and the related federal regulations mandate that audit procedures be applied to individual federal programs and government operations that

---

[1] *Codification of Governmental Accounting and Financial Reporting Standards*, Governmental Accounting Standards Boards, Norwalk, CT.

might not otherwise be subjected to audit by either the AICPA's or GAO's auditing standards. Further, auditors conducting audits pursuant to the Single Audit Act must submit different and more audit reports and discuss audit findings not considered reportable under either generally accepted or government auditing standards.

Single Audits

Annually tens of thousands of financial audits are made of governments and nonprofit organizations receiving federal financial assistance. These audits are made pursuant to the provisions of the Single Audit Act and implementing federal regulations issued by the Office of Management and Budget. This Act and the related OMB regulations require more detailed audit procedures be applied to detect noncompliance with laws and regulations than the auditing standards of either the AICPA or the GAO.

Materiality for Compliance

The focus of compliance testing and basis for assessed materiality of instances of noncompliance for single audits is an individual federal program. This is a level of materiality considerably below or lower than the financial thresholds of audits made pursuant to either generally accepted or the government auditing standards. For example, the following are excerpts from the type of compliance audit report that would be required by the Single Audit Act:

"We have audited the compliance of Example Entity with the types of compliance requirements described in the U.S. Office of Management and Budget's Circular A-133 Compliance Supplement that are applicable to each of its major federal programs. For the year ended ...."

"We conducted our audit of compliance in accordance with generally accepted auditing standards, the standards applicable to financial audits contained in the government auditing standards, and OMB Circular A-133, Audits of States, Local Governments, and Non-Profit Organizations ...."

"In our opinion, Example Entity complied, in all material respects, with the requirements referred to above that are applicable to each of its major federal programs for the year ended ...."

Under the generally accepted and government auditing standards, the Single Audit findings of noncompliance might not be material, dollarwise, in relation to the overall financial statements. But, under the Single Audit the reference of materiality is not the entitywide financial statements, but the individual or *each* major federal program.

Thus, instances of noncompliance that were inconsequential to the overall financial statements become exceedingly important when compared to the expenditures of a single government program.

Program Audits

Independent auditors will undertake audits of individual governmental programs that mandate even more directed audit procedures to ascertain whether material noncompliance exists. These audits are referred to as *program audits* and are conducted in accordance with specific federal departmental or agency audit guides and programs that require the execution of rather detailed audit procedures to detect noncompliance—of laws and regulations (federal, state and others), regulations (of OMB, federal departments, state and other governments), and conditions and terms (of particular contracts, grants, or agreements) under audit. An audit finding may not be of sufficient importance to be reported in an audit report related to a government's program, but may be extremely significant in relation to contracts and grants of a specific program.

COMPLIANCE AUDITING

In practice, an auditor may design audit test procedures to serve multiple compliance audit objectives. The phases of auditing for compliance with laws and regulations require the auditor to: (1) understand the controls for insuring compliance with federal laws and regulations, and (2) test of these controls to confirm implementation and testing of transactions for each major federal assistance program. Dual testing may be feasible that concurrently achieves audit objectives related to the financial statement audit pursuant to government auditing standards and at the same time complies with the Single Audit Act requirements to test controls over the federal assistance programs and apply audit test procedures for each of major federal assistance program.

Obtaining an Understanding

Obtaining an understanding of the effects of compliance with laws and regulations is an initial, early, requirement in conducting financial statement and financial related audits of governments. As is the case with internal controls, acquiring this understanding of compliance requirements is a necessary prerequisite for an auditor in order to determine the nature, timing and extent of subsequent audit procedures that will form the basis for the required audit opinion on compliance with laws and regulations.

Managers of governments must identify, implicitly or explicitly, those laws and regulations that directly and materially affect their government's financial statements and their major governmental programs. The auditor must proceed to assess this inventory of legal and regulatory compliance criteria and obtain an *understanding* of the effects of noncompliance on the financial statements or individual government programs to be audited.

The AICPA, in its SAS on compliance audit considerations, suggests that auditors perform the following procedures to obtain an understanding of dollar significance, materiality or effect of legal and regulatory criteria:

1. Consider knowledge about such laws and regulations obtained from prior years' audits.

2. Discuss such laws and regulations with the entity's chief financial officer, legal counsel, grant administrators and the responsible government audit organization to determine the sources of revenues received, expenditures permitted and the applicable laws, statutes, regulations and rules.

3. Obtain written representation from management regarding the completeness of management's identification.

4. Review relevant portions of any directly related agreements, such as those related to contracts, grants and loans.

5. Review minutes of the legislative body of the governmental entity being audited for the enactment's of laws and regulations that have a direct and material effect on the determination of amounts in the governmental entity's financial statement.

6. Make an inquiry of the office of the federal, state, or local auditor or other appropriate audit oversight organization about laws and regulations applicable to entities within their jurisdiction, including statutes and uniform reporting requirements.

7. Review information about compliance requirements, such as the information included in OMB's *Compliance Supplement* (which is actually issued by the Government Printing Office).

Noncompliance may exist in a variety of forms. The AICPA's government audit guide suggests a few instances noncompliance would be:

● Expending funds in excess of authorized limits, such as purchases in excess of budgeted amounts regardless of whether the purchases were otherwise properly approved, received, paid for, and used.

● Expending funds for unauthorized purposes, such as expending grant funds for purposes other than permitted by the grantor.

● Failing to file reports required by the state and federal government accurately, completely, and on time, such as monthly reports of grant expenditures required by OMB Circular A-87 containing errors or filed late.

To test compliance with federal-wide administrative requirements for recipients of federal assistance, an auditor must consult two OMB Circulars:

- Circular A-102 (also referred to as A-102 "Common Rule") titled *Uniform Administrative Requirements for Grants and Cooperative Agreements to State and Local Governments*, and

- Circular A-110 titled *Uniform Administrative Requirements for Grants and Agreements with Institutions of Higher Education, Hospitals, and Other Non-Profit Organizations*, and individual agency codification of Circular A-110.

Other instances of noncompliance might be noted by applying the provisions of three specific cost-related OMB Circulars. Each is the federal regulation that defines allowable, unallowable, and indirect costs that may or may not be claimed for specific types of organization:

- Circular A-21 titled *Cost Principles for Educational Institutions*,

- Circular A-87 titled *Cost Principles for State and Local Governments*, and

- Circular A-122 titled *Cost Principles for Non-Profit Organizations*.

COMPLIANCE TESTING

OMB's Compliance Supplement

The *Compliance Supplement* was published by OMB in an effort to halt a proliferation of program-specific audit guides by federal agencies. At the time the *Compliance Supplement* was issued, the number of specific federal audit guides greatly exceeded 100 resulting in innumerable redundant duplicate audits of recipients of federal assistance.

OMB, after requiring an analysis of thousands of pages of federal agency regulations and audit criteria, published the *Compliance Supplement*. As structured, the *Compliance Supplement* provides information on the major compliance features of federal assistance programs, comprising over 90 percent of all federal aid to other levels of government. It is OMB's intent that the *Compliance Supplement* be used in lieu of other federal audit and review guides. The objective of the *Compliance Supplement* was to make possible a "single audit" that could meet the combined needs of many interested in the financial activities of a governmental auditee.

There are varying levels of compliance that require the attention of a government auditor: (1) compliance on a general or organization-wide basis, (2) compliance with specific program requirements, and (3) the compliance related to individual contracts and grants. For financial statement audits, financial related audits and those conducted in accordance with the Single Audit Act criteria, compliance audit test objectives and detailed suggested audit procedures have been developed by federal audit executives in coordination with the AICPA. This is the audit guidance that appears in the *Compliance Supplement*. For governmental programs not included in the *Compliance Supplement*, government auditors must develop an equivalent "compliance audit supplement" to make the necessary substantive tests for compliance with laws and regulations.

Risk Considerations

The Single Audit Act requires the auditor to express an opinion on the auditee's compliance with terms, conditions, and provisions affecting each of its major programs. But, to express that opinion, an auditor must consider risk issues pursuant to several AICPA's Statement on Auditing Standards (e.g., SAS 47 *Audit Risk and Materiality in Conducting an Audit*; SAS 82 *Consideration of Fraud in a Financial Statement Audit*).

The audit risk is a composite of four risks: inherent risks, control risk, fraud risk and detection risk.

● Inherent risk relates to material noncompliance with a major program's compliance criteria for which there exists no compensating controls, such as: program complexity, relative length of program operations, and prior program experience with the compliance criteria.

● Control risk relates to material noncompliance with respect to a major program and would not be prevented or detected in a timely basis by the entity's internal controls.

● Fraud risk relates to intentional material noncompliance with a major program's compliance requirements.

● Detection risk relates to the risk that audit procedures might lead the auditor to conclude that noncompliance does not exist when in fact material instances of noncompliance do exist.

Single Audit

14 Compliance Audit Requirements

The *Compliance Supplement* is based on the requirement of the 1996 amendments to the Single Audit Act and the revised and new OMB Circular A-133.[2] The *Compliance Supplement* (1) describes 14

---

[2] In June 1997, OMB issued the current Circular A-133, titled *Audits of States, Local Governments, and Non-Profit Organizations*, which superseded two earlier Circulars, A-128 titled *Audits of State and Local Governments* and an earlier A-133 titled *Audits of Higher Education and Other Non-Profit Organizations*.

types of compliance matters that must be considered in every Single Audit, and (2) outlines suggested audit procedures for conducting the specific tests for compliance. Compliance audit criteria require the auditor to determine whether the auditee has complied with laws, regulations, and provisions of contracts and grants that can have a material and direct effect on *each* federal program. Therefore, tests for each of these criteria must be made for each federal program.

These compliance requirements that affect all governments receiving federal financial assistance are basically: (1) national policies most often related to laws that would apply to governments as a whole; (2) federal executive orders (issued by the President); (3) governmentwide federal regulations issued by the Office of Management and Budget, the Treasury Department and General Accounting Office, at times, and (4) regulations issued by individual federal departments and agencies that related to programs for which they have legal responsibilities.

In the *Compliance Supplement*, OMB has identified 14 compliance requirements that, if not observed, could have a material effect on an entity's individual federal programs conclusion of the audit, the auditor must prepare a specific audit report which contains the results of tests for compliance with the general compliance requirements.

1. Activities Allowed or Unallowed. Requirements for activities allowed or not allowed are unique to each federal program and exists in the laws, regulations, and other provisions that pertain to the program. The objectives of compliance testing for this category include identifying the types of activities which are either specially allowed or prohibited and then to conduct tests to confirm that all reported activities were allowable and related transactions were properly classified and accumulated into reported totals.

2. Allowable Costs/Costs Principles. The following OMB regulations prescribe the cost accounting policies associated with the administration of federal awards by states, local governments, Indian tribal governments, and non-profit organizations. These cost accounting principles would control amounts accumulated, charged, paid, billed, or reported in relation to a federal contract, grant, cooperative and other agreement. Each is the federal regulation that defines allowable, unallowable, and indirect costs that may or may not be claimed by these specific types of organization:

● Circular A-21 titled *Cost Principles for Educational Institutions,*

● Circular A-87 titled *Cost Principles for State and Local Governments,* and

● Circular A-122 titled *Cost Principles for Non-Profit Organizations.*

These cost principles apply to all federal awards received by a non-federal entity, regardless of whether the awards are received directly from the federal government or indirectly through a pass-through entity.

While the cost principles are substantially identical in the three Circulars, differences do exist due to the nature of the legal and other relationships that have historically existed between the federal government and the specific entities. The *Compliance Supplement* contains two analyses that can assist auditors in distinguishing the differences. The *Supplement* in its *Exhibit 1*, identifies cost items that are not the same among the three Circulars, and in its *Exhibit 2*, identifies cost items that are unallowable under one or more of the costs principle Circulars. (A later chapter discusses this subject in more detail.)

3. **Cash Management**. If an entity is funded on a reimbursement basis, then program costs must be paid by the entity before reimbursement can be requested from the federal government. But for many federal programs, federal financing is provided either in a lump-sum type advance of funds or by a transfer from the U.S. Treasury, whereby the entity makes drawdowns under a letter-of-credit type arrangement. Under the Cash Management Improvement Act, the longest period of time that any drawdown advance may be requested, is three days. These limitations would also apply to subrecipients of the entity. Excessive drawdowns and advances are a reportable item and interest earned on the excess, unless under $100 per year, must be repaid quarterly to the federal government.

4. **Davis-Bacon Act**. Where required by the Davis-Bacon Act, all laborers and mechanics employed by contractors or subcontractors to work on construction contracts in excess of $2,000 financed by federal assistance funds must be paid wages not less than those established for the locality of the project (i.e., the "prevailing wage rates") by the U.S. Department of Labor. This information is available to the auditor by inquiry to DOL's Wage and Hour Division's *Register of Wage Determinations*.

5. **Eligibility**. Eligibility requirements are unique to each federal program, and requires consultation with the laws, regulations, and provisions of contract and grant agreements that pertain to that federal program. The entity must have controls to ensure that only those persons or organizations identified in laws or regulation as being eligible to receive governmental financial assistance are indeed the only recipients of the funds. Only those designated by Congress, state and local legislators may benefit from governmental assistance programs.

6. **Equipment and Real Property Management**. Title to equipment acquired by a non-federal entity with federal monies vests with

the non-federal entity. *Equipment* means tangible nonexpendable property, with a useful life of more than one year and an acquisition cost of $5,000 or more per unit. The auditor must look to the two following OMB Circulars for additional guidance with respect to the federal government's equipment and real property requirements.

- Circular A-102 (also referred to as A-102 "Common Rule") titled *Uniform Administrative Requirements for Grants and Cooperative Agreements to State and Local Governments* (and Indian tribal governments), and

- Circular A-110 titled *Uniform Administrative Requirements for Grants and Agreements with Institutions of Higher Education, Hospitals, and Other Non-Profit Organizations*, and individual agency codification of Circular A-110.

These two OMB Circulars provide additional guidance on the restrictive use, maintenance, bi-annual inventory requirements, property safeguard controls and reporting requirements of this property.

Non-federal entities may, with written approval, use real property for other than the originally authorized program that have purposes consistent with those authorized for support by the federal awarding agency. Acquired property may not be disposed of without prior consent of the federal agency. If such property is sold, the non-federal entity is normally required to remit to the federal agency the federal portion of net sales proceeds. If property is retained after the program is completed, the non-federal entity shall normally compensate the federal agency for the federal portion of the current fair market value.

7. **Matching, level of effort, or earmarking requirements.** Federal laws often prescribe specific matching, level of effort, or earmarking requirements as a condition precedent to receipt of federal funds. This necessitates that the auditor consult the laws, regulations, and provisions of contract and grant agreements that pertain to that federal program. The audit concerns relate to whether controls have been established to ensure that the auditee meets commitments made to providers of financial assistance with respect to the nature or kind, amount, or timing of the auditee's contribution to the program and that there has been compliance in practice. Federal guidance with respect to matching shares and recipient local contributions appear in OMB Circulars A-102 (also known as the "common rule") and A-110 that outlines several administrative and other criteria that must be followed by recipients of federal financial assistance.

8. **Period of Availability of Federal Funds.** All federal awards specify a time period during which the non-federal entity may use the federal funds. When specified, a non-federal entity may charge to the federal award only costs resulting from obligations incurred during the

funding period and any pre-award costs authorized by the federal agency. At times, unobligated or unused balances may be carried over and charged for obligations of the subsequent funding period. Unless a requested extension is granted, non-federal entities must liquidate all obligations incurred under a federal award not later than 90 days after the end of the funding period to coincide with submission of the annual federal *Financial Status Report.*

9. **Procurement and Suspension and Debarment**. With respect to procurement, federal regulations relating to procurements using federal money are contained in OMB Circulars A-102 (also known as the "common rule") and A-110. With respect to suspension and debarment, all non-federal entities are prohibited from contracting with or making subawards under covered transactions to parties that are suspended or debarred, or whose principals are suspended or debarred. A *covered* transaction includes procurement contracts for goods or services equal to or in excess of $100,000 and all subawards to subrecipients.

10. **Program Income**. Program income is gross income received that is directly generated by the federally-funded project during the project period. If authorized by the federal agency, costs incident to the generation of program income may be deducted from gross income to determine net program income. Program income could include fees for services, rental income, sale of commodities or items fabricated under the program, payments of principal and interest on loans made from federal funds, etc. Program income may be used in one of three ways: (1) deducted from program outlays, (2) added to the project budget, or (3) used to meet matching requirements. Unless specified by the federal agency, program income shall be deducted from program outlays.

11. **Real Property Acquisition and Relocation Assistance**. The Uniform Relocation Assistance and Real Property Acquisition Policies Act of 1970 provides for uniform and equitable treatment of persons displaced by federal programs from their homes, businesses, or farms. The Act requires that: (1) property must be appraised by qualified independent appraisers; (2) all appraisals must be examined by a review appraiser to assure acceptability; and (3) review appraisers certify the recommended approved value as just compensation to the owner. This requirement also covers the payment of moving-related expenses and reestablishment expenses incurred by displaced businesses and farm operations.

12. **Reporting**. Recipients of federal financial assistance must use the standard financial reporting forms prescribed by OMB that exist for financial, performance, and special reporting. Recipients must report program outlays and program income on a cash or accrual basis

as prescribed by the federal awarding agency. However, if the federal agency requires accrual data and the recipient is not required to convert its accounting system to the accrual basis, they may develop and submit accrual information as a result of analysis. Among other tests, the auditor must determine that controls have been established to ensure that reports and claims for advances and reimbursements are supported by the books and records from which the entity's financial statements were prepared and to which the data conversion analyses relate.

13. **Subrecipient Monitoring.** Over the years, the federal government has sustained the position that a prime recipient of federal financial assistance has a responsibility for ensuring compliance with federal laws and regulations by all to whom the prime recipient passes along federal funds. The Compliance Supplement requires a pass-through entity, and therefore the subrecipient to which funds are passed-through, to:

● Identify federal award information by federal CFDA number, title, award name, awarding federal agency and applicable compliance requirements.

● Monitor subrecipient activities to provide reasonable assurance that the subrecipient administers the federal awards in compliance with federal requirements.

● Ensure required audits are performed and prompt corrective action taken on any audit findings.

● Evaluate the impact of subrecipient activities on the pass-through entity's ability to comply with federal regulations.

The Single Audit Act defines terms as *recipients, subrecipients, and pass-through* entities. Under the Act, a *"pass-through entity"* means a non-federal entity that provides federal awards to a subrecipient to carry out a federal program. The Act defines a *"subrecipient"* to mean a non-federal entity that receives federal awards through another non-federal entity to carry out a federal program, but does not include an individual who receives financial assistance through such awards. *"Recipient"* means a non-federal entity that receives awards directly from a federal agency to carry out a federal program.

14. **Special tests and provisions**—There will be requirements for special tests and provisions unique to each federal program and are to be found in the laws, regulations, and provisions of contracts and grants pertaining to the program. For federal programs not covered in the *Compliance Supplement*, the auditor must review the program's contract and grant agreement and referenced laws and regulations to identify the compliance requirements. The auditor then must develop the appropriate audit objectives and procedures to test for the special

provisions that could have a direct and material affect on a major program.

Not all compliance requirements apply to all federal financial assistance programs. A federal assistance program may be a single contract or grant or encompass numerous federal contracts, grants, and possibly cooperative agreements under which funds have been received for a common purpose.

Application of the *Compliance Supplement*

Use of OMB's *Compliance Supplement* by an auditor is not mandatory. But, the *Compliance Supplement* is a valuable and time-saving audit tool that will preclude auditors from having to develop their own inventory of all applicable laws and regulations, identify the significant operating procedures for federal programs, structure an audit plan and then design applicable audit procedures.

Further, audits made pursuant to the procedures outlined in the *Compliance Supplement* will constitute a "safe harbor" for an auditor conducting an audit of a governmental unit receiving federal funding. In the initial edition of the *Compliance Supplement*, OMB had even stated that while there may be compliance requirements other than those listed in the *Compliance Supplement*, the auditor was not required to perform tests for compliance with those other requirements. OMB and the federal agencies had determined that generally noncompliance with any other requirements would not materially affect a government's financial statement or financial reports of individual federal programs.

Programs Not in the *Compliance Supplement*

For those federal programs not covered by the *Compliance Supplement* or where the auditor elects not to follow the *Compliance Supplement*, the audit program for selecting and testing transactions and account balances for compliance with laws and regulations or contracts and grants must be based on the auditor's professional judgment. This requires that the auditor examine several sources and publications to identify the appropriate audit coverage. In the past, GAO suggested some sources of information that could form the basis for identifying compliance requirements and developing an audit program when *Compliance Supplement* coverage does not exist or the *Compliance Supplement* is not used.

For example, for federal programs, an auditor would find the following references to be important sources for obtaining compliance criteria when constructing a program for compliance auditing of federal programs:

- **Legal or legislative data**—Including basic legislation, reports, legislative hearings and committee reports, annotated references of related decisions and legal opinions, constitutions, local statutes and resolutions, local charters and ordinances;

- **External administrative requirements**—Including correspondence from federal, state, or local oversight and administrative agencies; federal, state and local government guidelines and regulations about program operations;

- **Contracts, grants, cooperative and other agreements**—Including proposal, approved performance and financial budgets, correspondence between the funding source and audited entity;

- **Federal policies and regulations**—Including the OMB Circulars defining the allowable, unallowable, and appropriate overhead costs (e.g., Circular A-21 for colleges and universities; A-87 for state and local governments; A-122 for non-profit organizations) for federal programs, plus other OMB Circulars that detail managerial and administrative compliance criteria (e.g., the "common rule" or OMB Circular A-102 for state and local governments; A-110 for non-profit organizations) that must be examined by the auditor;

- **U.S. Code of Federal Regulations**—The codification of federal agencies administrative and program regulations and directives, published by the U.S. Government Printing Office;

- **Catalog of Federal Domestic Assistance Programs**—A synopsis of some 1,000 federal aid programs, providing legal and regulatory references, compiled by OMB;

- **Laws and regulations**—Laws specifically for those programs to be audited, including any legislative history for these programs; program regulations possibly issued by the oversight governmental agencies;

- **Executive Orders**—Government-wide policies issued by the President of the United States for the federal government or by governors, mayors or other governmental chief executive officers;

- **Circulars, Bulletins, Pronouncements**—By GAO, OMB, U.S. Treasury or similar centralized departments and agencies for other levels of government; and

- **Special Conditions, Terms**—Appearing in the individual contracts, grants, cooperative or other agreements that were executed by the funding government and the entity under audit.

When developing an audit program to examine an entity's compliance with federal program law and regulation, an essential point is that the research must often extend to an assessment of the compliance criteria of other governments, too. Where such compliance requirements exist they should be included in the designed audit program.

Developing specific compliance audit programs requires resources—time, knowledgeable and experienced personnel, and money. If the resulting program is somewhat deficient or weak, the risk for an audit that does not meet the auditing standards is on the auditor. Some federal inspectors general have recognized the value of having uniform audits of consistent quality and have compiled the equivalent of individual compliance audit programs for many of the government programs not listed in the *Compliance Supplement*. These audit programs, which would be equivalent "safe harbor" audit programs, are available upon request to auditors by communicating with the regional offices of the appropriate federal inspectors general.

Compliance Requirements in the "Common Rule"

The federal government's "Common Rule" establishes the uniform administrative requirements for federal grants and cooperative agreements awarded to state and local governments. Unless required by statute or authorized as a specific exception by OMB, all grants, administration provisions of codified regulations, program manuals, handbooks, and other nonregulatory materials inconsistent with the Common Rule are superseded by the Common Rule. [3]

From an audit perspective, it is important to be aware that several of the Common Rule administrative requirements are explicitly included among the general compliance audit requirements described earlier. But, there are other requirements of the Common Rule that must be assessed by the auditor to acquire "an understanding of the control structure" of a governmental auditee. Additionally, the Common Rule must be considered by the auditor when conducting "tests of controls" to assess the extent of implementation and compliance status.

Several of the Common Rule financial and administration requirements that should be considered in audits made pursuant to either government auditing standards or the Single Audit Act relate to:

● A state must expend and account for federal funds in accordance with state laws and procedures for expending and accounting for its own funds, which should permit preparation of federally required reports; tracing of federal funds to a level of expenditure that will establish that no violations of restrictions or prohibitions occurred.

● Financial management systems of other grantees and subgrantees (non-state) must meet the following standards:

---

[3] The Common Rule—*Uniform Administrative Requirements for Grants and Cooperative Agreements to State and Local Governments*, issued by OMB, March 1988—appears in its entirety in the AICPAs accounting and audit guide for *Audits of State and Local Governments, Appendix F.*

1. Financial reporting and disclosure must be accurate, current and complete and in accordance with the reporting requirements of the grant or subgrant.

2. Accounting records must adequately identify the source and application of funds provided for financially-assisted activities and contain pertinent information, by grant and subgrant—such as awards, authorizations, obligations, unobligated balances, assets, liabilities, outlays or expenditures, and income.

3. Internal controls must be effective and accountability maintained for all grant and subgrant cash, real and personal property, and other assets. Government funds and property must be safeguarded and used solely for authorized purposes.

4. Actual expenditures or outlays as well as budgeted amounts for each grant and subgrant, along with the financial information related to performance or productivity data, including unit cost information when appropriate or required must be compiled and monitored.

5. Applicable OMB cost principles, federal agency program regulations, and the terms of contracts and grants must be followed in determining the reasonableness, allowability, and allocability of cost to federally financed activities.

6. Accounting records must be supported by source documentation such as canceled checks, paid bills, payrolls, time and attendance records, contract and subgrant award documents.

7. Cash management procedures must exist for minimizing the time elapsing between the transfer of funds from the U.S. Treasury and disbursement by the grantee or subgrantee, including compliance with special conditions for cash advances, reimbursements, letters of credit withdrawals, and working capital advances.

8. Except for state recipients, grantees and subgrantees must disburse earned program income, rebates, refunds, contract settlements, audit recoveries, and interest earned on federal monies before requesting additional federal money. Generally, non-state recipients earning interest on advances of federal money must remit the interest earned regularly.

The Common Rule imposes several additional compliance requirements that must be included in an audit of a recipient of federal funds that has been designated as a "high risk grantee" by a federal department or agency. Often these "high risk grantee" requirements relate to restrictions on claims for reimbursements, limits on letter of credit withdrawals, obtaining advance approval before proceeding with subsequent phases of a program, more detailed reporting, or mandates that recipients acquire special training and technical assistance. The Common Rule also imposes certain procedures for closed (completed, terminated, ceased) grants that are unique and arise only at the cessation of the federally financed activity.

Further, since noncompliance with other provisions of the Common Rule might materially affect either the financial statement or individual major federal assistance programs, the AICPA (in its audit guide for government) requires selected requirements of the Common Rule be included when testing controls of federal assistance programs.

Non-Federal Compliance Issues

For many state, and local governmental agencies and nonprofit entities, expenditures made under contracts and grants are significant and relatively material in relation to individual programs or the entity's overall financial statements, in the case of a nonprofit. At times, amounts are of such magnitude that legislators will specifically approve the budgets for such agreements. Special audit tests and separate audit reports may be required in such situations, and at times a special single purpose audit—of one contract or one grant—may be mandated.

Other audit criteria notwithstanding, in its 1994 edition of government standards, GAO formalized a standard that a financial audit must be designed to provide reasonable assurance of detecting material misstatements related to noncompliance with provisions of contracts and grants. Often the audit of compliance of individual contracts or grants or cooperative agreements will require that the auditor:

● Examine the terms and conditions of the agreement and identify the services or performance that is to be rendered and then assess the actual status of performance.

● Compare the approved financial budget and planned expenditure rates to amounts incurred, recorded in the accounting records, and reported and billed to the sponsoring organization.

● Test the costs incurred and charged to the budget categories of the agreements for compliance with terms and conditions and any allowable, unallowable or matching cost prescriptions imposed by the awarding organization.

● Verify that amounts due were properly billed, received, recorded, and deposited and that ending receivables and liabilities reflect the agreement status.

● Test close-out procedures and practices to assess the propriety of settlement in compliance with the agreement terms and conditions.

● Examine the reasonableness, allowability and allocability of indirect or overhead costs charged to the agreement activities.

● Confirm with the awarding organization, the status of the agreement: performance, conditions, amounts billed, payments made, deliveries completed or uncompleted, all changes and modifications, any withholdings and prerequisite conditions for completion or closeout of the agreement.

● Review and confirm that assets and other property furnished by the awarding organization are appropriately accounted for and adequately controlled and properly reported.

The above criteria apply to all federal agreements, but states may have imposed similar conditions on their contractors and grantees. These agreements must be examined and tests made of detailed transactions related to these agreements when auditing the subordinate organizations of governments. In addition to these non-federal externally imposed compliance criteria, the agreement itself may contain specific conditions and terms voluntarily accepted by the audited entity.

Each contract or grant or cooperative agreement is unique: the tests conducted in auditing one contract will provide little information on the extent of compliance or noncompliance that might exist with respect to another contract or grant. For this reason, the terms of each material agreement must be examined and appropriate audit procedures be developed and performed to test an entity's compliance with the agreement.

ASSESSING THE EFFECT OF NONCOMPLIANCE

The AICPA, in its SAS on compliance audit considerations, requires that auditors consider: (1) the *effect* of identified instances of noncompliance on each federal program, and (2) additionally, the effect of identified instances of noncompliance on the financial statements undergoing audit. To make conclusions relating to *effect*, the AICPA requires the auditor to consider:

1. The frequency of noncompliance identified in the audit.

2. The adequacy of a primary recipient's system for monitoring subrecipients and the possible effect on the program of any noncompliance identified by the primary recipient or the subrecipient auditors.

3. Whether any instances of noncompliance identified in the audit resulted in questioned costs, as discussed below, and, if they did, whether the questioned costs are material to the program.

4. To evaluate effect of questioned costs on the auditor's opinion on compliance, the auditor must consider the best estimate (or "likely questioned cost") of total costs questioned for each major federal assistance program and not just the specifically identified (or "known questioned costs").

As a basis of the audit opinion, the auditor must project the amount of known questioned costs identified in the sample to items in major federal programs from which the sample was drawn. However, the AICPA, in its SAS, points out that regardless of the auditor's opinion on compliance, federal regulations require the auditor to report instances of noncompliance that are not inconsequential that were disclosed by the audit. On the other hand for reporting of questioned costs, the auditor is not required to report likely questioned costs, but only the known questioned costs of $10,000 or more.

APPLICATION OF AUDIT JUDGMENT

None—neither Congress, the AICPA, GAO, nor OMB—prescribe the amount of compliance testing that must be performed during an audit of federal programs. Alternatively, reliance is placed on the professional judgment of the auditor in determining the nature, timing, and extent of compliance tests to be made. But, it is clear that the auditor's "judgment" must include considerations other than merely the auditor's personal opinion concerning the extent of compliance audit testing to be made in the circumstances.

Factors to Consider

OMB has required that the auditor evaluate several factors prior to arriving at conclusions relating to the "nature, timing, and extent" of tests to be conducted. The OMB judgment considerations are duplicated in several OMB Circulars, the *Compliance Supplement*, the Single Audit Act criteria, and guidance of GAO. Judgment by government auditors must, therefore, give weight to several factors:

1. Newness of the governmental program or changes in program conditions, size, operations, etc;

2. The amount of program revenues, program expenditures, or government resources at risk;

3. The auditor's prior experience with the program, particularly the assessed adequacy of internal controls and compliance with laws and regulations;

4. Revelations in audits or other evaluations or other form of independent oversight relating to the programs to be audited and the level to which the program is already subject to program reviews or other forms of independent oversight;

5. The extent to which the program is operated or carried-out through subrecipients;

6. The extent to which the programs subcontract for goods and services;

7. Public perceptions and political sensitivity of the areas under audit and the audit report users' expectations;

8. The specific audit standards and scope as well as any agreed-to audit procedures to which the audit must conform; and

9. The potential impact of adverse findings.

Quantitative and Qualitative Issues

Generally accepted auditing standards require an auditor to plan and audit in a manner that cause material errors, irregularities, and instances of noncompliance to have a reasonable likelihood of being detected. Under these auditing criteria, the dollar amount is the key criterion for materiality. But, the government auditing standards have also established that the auditor must consider certain other qualitative and quantitative issues, such as:

- The cumulative effect and impact of numerous immaterial items. Effect and impact must be evaluated both from a dollar effect as well as a frequency impact. Wide spread noncompliance may be considered a fatal program flaw, even though the relative dollars related to the noncompliance is relatively insignificant.

- The objectives for which the audit is undertaken. If the audit is financial in nature, probably dollar criteria would be appropriate. But seldom is a government program subjected to only a financial audit. Audits to assess operating effectiveness, or program achievement or results may not have dollar accountability as the primary audit objective.

- The use to which the audited information is to be put. Audit information that is to form the basis for decisions as future funding, program reduction or expansion, and quality of program performance must provide information relevant to these concerns. Often the standard auditor's opinion on the financial statements will be of minimal utility for these non-financial decisions that must be made by parties external to the auditee.

- The effect that reported information is likely to have on the users. Audit reports describing or providing information on indications of irregularities and illegal acts may not be material from a dollar standpoint. But these reports can still have a significant effect on users and on others receiving the audit report.

COMPLIANCE WITH GOVERNMENT BUDGETS

Much of the forgoing discussion with respect to compliance has been directed at compliance with laws and regulations governing governmental operations and programs, probably most often imposed by organizations external to the government undergoing audit.

An audit program of particular significance in governmental auditing is the program related to the audit of the government's budget. Compliance with a government's legally enacted budget is a paramount audit criteria. In contrast, budgets of a corporation may never be audited and noncompliance with the corporate budget will never be reported upon in the audit of a financial statement.

For public sector entities, the budget is the government's statement of priorities and the government's plan of operations. The operations of many governments are constrained by conformance to some type of balanced budget legislation or requirements. Governmental budgets are legal documents requiring compliance and imposing financial penalties for noncompliance, and in some cases imprisonment for willful or negligent violations.

Once approved by the legislature, the financial budget—the law—is formally recorded in the government's accounting records. Budgetary accounting by governments provide transaction-by-transaction matching of budget to actual revenues and expenditures. Further, generally accepted accounting principles of governments require compliance with budgets. They also require the preparation of a formal financial statement comparing budgeted receipts and expenditures to actual receipts and expenditures.

Again, none of this is true for budgets of a private sector organization.

OTHER RISKS IN GOVERNMENTAL AUDITS

This long-standing primacy of budgets notwithstanding, each generation of elected and appointed government officials, in periods of financial stress, have engaged in a pattern of activities that may in fact be acts of noncompliance or at best be activities not consistent with the reporting practices of past fiscal years.

While described by some as "one-shot accounting," "creative accounting" or "imaginative fiscal practices," other might terms these activities as "chicanery" and "cooking the books." But, when government officials are unable or unwilling to increase taxes or reduce expenditures, such practices might be used to comply with legally enacted budgets, financial securities covenants, and balanced budget statutes. These practices are of particular concern to an auditor of government and must be evaluated to determine if any resulting noncompliance is of sufficient significance that a report must be made by the auditor.

Periodically, the AICPA has published several questionable governmental practices in its *Audit Risk Alert* intended to provide auditors of governments with an overview of current business developments

Compliance Auditing

that may affect the financial statements undergoing audit.[4] Some of the "one-shot" accounting adjustments and other notable practices have included:

- Early retirement programs for employees or delays in pension contributions to reduce cash-based budgets.

- Delaying payment of salaries or benefits to reduce expenditures in budgetary or cash-basis financial statements.

- Backloading of employee benefits to future periods when negotiating new contracts for union employees.

- Delaying payments to internal service funds for insurance or other services.

- Making transfers to the general fund from other funds to decrease the general fund deficit without improving the financial condition of the government.

- Debt restructuring or refinancing to extend the payment period.

- Selling assets or deferring maintenance of buildings or infrastructure, both of which can give the appearance of improving a government's current financial position.

- Special one-time increase in nontax fees.

To this list, one might add "loans" of cash by one fund of a government to another when in reality there is no intention or realistic basis for assuming the funds will be repaid or that the "loan" is other than a routine intragovernmental transfer that should be accounted for in a manner consistent with generally accepted accounting principles. Also, for example, there may be concerns over whether a lease contract is an operating transaction or is, in substance, a capital expenditure which requires recognition of an unrecorded long-term liability to the same extent as in the private sector.

When these and similar practices are encountered, the auditor must also be concerned about the intent to violate laws, statutes, regulations, securities covenants, or contract or grant requirements. If material to the financial statements, to a fund type balance, or to a major federal program, an auditor must insist these irregularities be adequately disclosed in the financial statements and other reports and may even cause the auditor to render a form of qualified audit opinion or a disclaimer.

---

[4] *Audit Risk Alert—State and Local Governmental Developments*—1994, AICPA, New York, NY.

WORKING PAPERS FOR COMPLIANCE AUDITING

Generally accepted auditing standards require that all audit procedures performed in evaluating compliance with laws, regulations and conditions of contracts and grants be documented in working papers. The working papers relating to compliance tests should contain:

(1) The objectives, scope, and methodology, including any sampling criteria used;

(2) Documentation of work performed to support significant conclusions and judgments including descriptions of transactions and records examined that would enable an experienced auditor to examine the same transactions and records; and

(3) Evidence of supervisory reviews and the work performed.

Government auditing standards note that auditors are not required to include in working papers copies of all documents examined, nor must auditors list detailed information from those documents. The 1988 edition of government auditing standards contained more specific guidance that is likely to be used by federal inspectors general in their conduct of quality control reviews of government auditors. This earlier edition of the government auditing standards stated that the working papers should:

● Contain a written audit program, cross-referenced to the working papers;

● Contain the objective, scope, methodology, and results of the audit;

● Contain sufficiency information so that, supplementary oral explanations are not required;

● Be legible with adequate indexing and cross-referencing and include summaries and lead schedules as appropriate;

● Restrict information included to matters that are materially important and relevant to the objectives of the audit; and

● Contain evidence of supervisory reviews of the work conducted.

While these earlier criteria were somewhat controversial in instances when the federal government challenged the quality of audits performed by independent auditors, the criteria if adopted by auditors of government, will mitigate or eliminate questions concerning what audit procedures were applied, when, and with what results. This guidance is more descriptive of the quality of desired working papers than the general criteria appearing in the 1994 revision of the government.

REPORTING ON COMPLIANCE WITH LAWS AND REGULATIONS

Reporting on compliance with laws, regulations and conditions of contract and grant agreements is complex, costly and detailed. However an audit may be the single source that many—legislatures, elected executives, program managers, grantors, creditors and even citizens—rely on to assess whether government executives are "playing by the rules," or otherwise complying with the laws and regulations of those who have provided financial assistance to the government undergoing audit.

Auditors of government must clearly understand that there is a multitude of "clients" for a government audit and the most important of these may not be the entity undergoing the audit or even the party that was required to arrange for the audit. This variety of "clients" have different criteria for assessing or different interests in the nature, timing, purpose, and amounts of activities and expenditures to which the auditor's report must be responsive.

Chapter 10

Auditing for Allowable, Unallowable, Indirect Costs

For decades auditors of governments have had to be knowledgeable of federal policies relating to the allowable, unallowable and indirect costs permitted as charges under or claims to federal contracts, grants and cooperative agreements. The same is true for audits made pursuant to the Single Audit Act. Similarly, auditors of governmental contractors and non-profits in receipt of government grants or cooperative agreements must also be cognizant of the federal cost principles. These federal regulations widely cite generally accepted accounting as the governing reporting criteria, but these same regulations contain so many exceptions and prescriptions that the final reporting by contractors and grants is not consistent with generally accepted accounting.

The government auditing standards point out that *contract audits* and *grant audits* often include both financial and performance objectives. The audits of these agreements are compliance in nature, requiring the auditor to assess compliance with: agreed-to performance; a financial budget; federal regulations concerning allowable and unallowable costs; acceptable indirect cost or overhead allocation procedures; and the agreement for nature and amount of local match and in-kind contribution, if any.

Often noncompliance with these federal allowable and unallowable cost criteria will be significant to the federal funds received and at times even significant to the entity overall. For this reason, these costs must be evaluated for materiality when issuing an audit opinion.

CONTRACT, GRANTS, COOPERATIVE AGREEMENTS

The type of government contracts awarded by the governments programs will depend on the scope of work to be performed and the nature of risk that will be shared between the governmental program and the contractor. Generally, these contracts fall into two groups: cost-reimbursable and fixed-price types of contracts. Cost type contracts are used when the parties are not able to define a scope of work in definite terms or when there is no valid basis for predicting results or determining the ultimate cost. For such contracts the financial risk is predominantly borne by the government desiring the services. Conversely, if the scope of work is definite or performance can be defined and a definite price can be negotiated, a fixed-price contract will be executed.

Over the years, governments and courts have attempted to distinguish grants from contracts with limited success. Grants did differ from contracts through the 1960s when grants where viewed as almost "give aways" or endowments and minimal monitoring, reporting, accounting and almost no auditing was performed of governmental grantees. In the 1990s, grantees are often expected to perform services and accomplish tasks and the terms of grants are almost indistinguishable from those of cost-reimbursable contracts.

When awarding or executing contracts, grants or cooperative agreements, federal law establishes criteria to use in selecting the most appropriate instrument for use. The criteria in the three following sections were established by the Federal Grant and Cooperative Agreement Act of 1977.[1]

Conditions for Use of Contracts

Sec. 4. Each executive agency shall use a type of procurement contract as the legal instrument reflecting a relationship between the federal government and a state or local government or other recipient—

(1) whenever the principal purpose of the instrument is the acquisition, by purchase, lease, or barter, of property or services for the direct benefit or use of the federal government; or

(2) whenever an executive agency determines in a specific instance that the use of a type of procurement contract is appropriate.

Conditions for Use of Grants

Sec. 5. Each executive agency shall use a type of grant agreement as the legal instrument reflecting a relationship between the federal government and a state or local government or other recipient whenever—

(1) the principal purpose of the relationship is the transfer of money, property, services, or anything of value to the state or local government or other recipient in order to accomplish a public purpose or support or stimulation authorized by federal

---

[1] U.S. General Accounting Office, Office of General Counsel, *Principles of Federal Appropriations Law*, Washington, D. C., 1993.

Auditing for Allowable, Unallowable, Indirect Costs

statute, rather than the acquisition, by purchase, lease or barter, of property or services for the direct benefit or use of the federal government, and

(2) no substantial involvement is anticipated between the executive agency, acting for the federal government, and the state or local government or other recipient during performance of the contemplated activity.

Conditions for Use of Cooperative Agreements

Sec. 6. Each executive agency shall use a type of cooperative agreement as the legal instrument reflecting a relationship between the federal government and a state or local government or other recipient whenever—

(1) the principal purpose of the relationship is the transfer of money, property, services, or anything of value to the state or local government or other recipient in order to accomplish a public purpose or support or stimulation authorized by federal statute, rather than the acquisition, by purchase, lease or barter, of property or services for the direct benefit or use of the federal government, and

(2) substantial involvement is anticipated between the executive agency, acting for the federal government, and the state or local government or other recipient during performance of the contemplated activity.

All three instruments are viewed as legally binding instruments. But, GAO points out that grants and cooperative agreements are more closely related than either is to a procurement contract. GAO states that the essential difference between a grant and a cooperative agreement is the degree of federal involvement. [2] But, the single distinction appears to be that grants and cooperative agreements do not have a profit element, while contracts do. Since there is minimal or no distinction between the three instruments, the discussions in this chapter will apply equally to contracts as well as grants.

GAO states that one of the most fundamental principles of "grant law" is that a conditional grant of federal funds is subject to the conditions in that grant. Acceptance of such a grant creates a valid contract between the federal government and the grantee. GAO states that the existence of a grantor-grantee relationship is determined by the same principles that apply to contract law generally, i.e., offer, acceptance, and consideration. The terms of the grant "contract" are contained in the executed agreement, applicable statutes, and refer-

---

[2] GAO, *Principles of Federal Appropriations Law,* 1993.

enced regulations. Once a contract or grant is awarded the parties have certain rights and obligations recognized by law, which can be judicially enforced. The government has a right to expect contractors and grantees will use federal funds for only authorized purposes and only in accordance with the terms and conditions of the contract and grant. If the contractor or grantee complies with the terms and conditions of the grant and incurs "allowable costs," the government is obligated to make payments. [3]

FEDERAL REGULATIONS FOR ALLOWABLE, UNALLOWABLE, INDIRECT COSTS

The field of federal contracts and grants is a specialty in itself. Governments employ tens of thousands of auditors to audit the financial terms, costs claimed or charged to federal agreements and performance of governmental contractors and grantees. Hundreds of independent auditors and attorneys are employed solely for their expertise and knowledge about government policies, court decisions, permissible practices, indirect cost issues, and resolution of government audit disallowances.

Each federal program is characterized by specific legislation, related federal department or agency regulations and the terms and conditions in executed agreements. In addition, there exists several laws and federal-wide regulations related to financial compliance audits that prescribe national policies related to federal contract and grant programs.

Specifically, there has existed for decades, national type policies specifying the types of cost—direct and indirect—that may be claimed and reimbursed under federal programs, federal contracts, federal grants, and cooperative and other agreements. Costs charged to federal contracts and grants that do not meet these national policies are deemed to be unallowable and can not be claimed and, if reimbursed, the amount must be refunded to the federal government, with interest under certain conditions.

These policies or cost regulations have been made law, codified, and as national policy override any regulations of individual federal departmental or agency or terms of specific contracts, grants, and cooperative and other agreements. Auditors will encounter cost regulations in the form of three OMB Circulars that have been tailored to meet specifics of different "industries" or types of recipients of federal assistance. The initial OMB circular prescribing or limiting the costs that can be paid by the federal government under contracts and grants dates back to the 1950s when OMB Circular A-21 was issued.

---

[3] *Id.*

Auditing for Allowable, Unallowable, Indirect Costs 255

Each Circular is a federal regulation that defines allowable, unallowable, and indirect costs that may or may not be claimed by these specific types of organization:

- Circular A-21 titled *Cost Principles for Educational Institutions*;

- Circular A-87 titled *Cost Principles for State and Local Governments* (and Indian tribal governments); and

- Circular A-122 titled *Cost Principles for Non-Profit Organizations*.

The prescriptions of these three Circulars control the nature of costs that may be accumulated, charged, paid, billed, or reported in relation to a federal contract, grant, cooperative and other agreement. These cost principles apply to all federal awards received by a non-federal entity, regardless of whether the awards are received directly from the federal government or indirectly through a pass-through entity.

The OMB allowable and unallowable cost regulations do not establish the level of cost to be reimbursed under a federal assistance program nor do the Circulars describe what costs would be appropriate for funding in a program budget. These are issues decided for departmental or agency programs either nationally by law or individually in a contract or grant between the federal agency and the contractor or grantee.

Under all three cost Circulars, the OMB policy is that no provision for profit or other increment above cost is intended. Thus, claims for "performance fees," "management allowances," "undesignated costs", etc., are not permitted as allowable costs under a grant or cooperative agreement.

The cost principles, promulgated by OMB in its cost Circulars, apply primarily to grants, although the federal departments view grants as similar to cost-reimbursement contracts. The provisions of the cost Circulars are similar in most respects to the cost principles applicable to manufacturing and production contracts of contractors to the Department of Defense and civilian agencies. Quite similar cost principles have been codified in the Defense Acquisition Regulations and the Federal Acquisition Regulations (NASA has its own regulations) for allowable and unallowable cost regulations related to private contractors.

HIERARCHY OF FEDERAL COST REGULATIONS

Auditors of governmental assistance programs, including those auditing contracts and grants, must have working knowledge of the cost regulations, generally how issues on costs have been resolved by administrative laws judges, and occasionally the courts, and the interpretation of these cost regulations in practice.

At times, questions arise about the "hierarchy" of regulations and what regulation, contract or grant condition might prevail in a particular circumstance. All federal departments and agencies must conform to law and government-wide regulations contained in OMB Circulars. Then, in many instances, the departments and agencies negotiate specific terms and conditions into contracts and grants that are more stringent than either law or OMB criteria. Where this is the case, a contractor or grantee is bound by the terms and conditions they accept and are precluded from appealing decisions on the premise that national law or government-wide regulations are more permissive than the specific agreement negotiated between them and the government program.

Conditions of Specific Contracts and Grants

The terms and conditions of individual contracts and grants prevail as between a federal entity and the non-federal entity. If parties to the contract or grant agree to specific cost limitations and cost-sharing conditions, all must comply with these agreements even if the terms and conditions are more stringent than the prescriptions of a federal law, regulation or the OMB Circular. In no event, though, can the terms and conditions of negotiated agreements be more liberal than federal law, department regulations, or OMB government-wide policy.

Department and Agency Regulations

A federal entity may issue regulations that only certain types of costs can be allowable as claims or charges to the entity's programs. A federal entity has the authority, within law and OMB regulations, to determine which costs may be allowed as claims or charges to its programs. Neither the regulations or terms of a federal contract or grant can not abrogate a federal law, OMB Circular, or department or agency-wide regulation.

OMB Regulations

OMB cost circulars are government-wide policy that establish costs that may be allowable as claims or charges to government programs. Costs not permitted by an OMB Circular are deemed unallowable. OMB Circulars are the government-wide implementing regulations for federal law and are consistent with the legislative intent of Congress.

Acts of Congress

Federal law constitutes ultimate government-wide policy and prevail over all of limitations, restrictions, or requirements of the preceding federal promulgation's. The allowability, exclusion, and limitation on costs ultimately payable by federal entities is an example. An otherwise appropriate, necessary and reasonable indirect cost can not be allowed under a federal program or contract or grant if Congress has declared, in law, that the federal program may not reimburse indirect cost.

It is important to note that federal regulations do not attempt to define detailed circumstances or dictate the extent to which individual contractors or grantees can participate in the financing of a federal assistance program. The terms and conditions of individual contracts and grants can and do set forth special requirements and limitations relating to charging and cost-sharing. If contractors and grantees agree to terms and conditions more stringent than those imposed by department or agency regulations, the OMB Circulars, or federal law, the contractors and grantees are bound by the deal they negotiate and cannot later avail themselves of other more liberal federal costing policies.

GOVERNMENT AUDIT REQUIREMENTS

Audit plans and audit programs for the audit of any federal program must contain audit procedures to test for the allowability (or conversely unallowability) of costs claimed or charged to governmental contracts, grants and cooperative agreements. For example, the regulation relating to the conduct of comprehensive single audits (i.e., the OMB Circular A-133) the auditor must determine the amounts charged, reported, claimed, billed or reimbursed in relation to federal assistance programs.

Another OMB regulation, Circular A-102 (also known as the "common rule") and A-110 prescribe administrative and managerial procedures applicable to contracts and grants with states and local governments and non-profit organizations that also require all costs of federal programs comply with the requirements of the three OMB cost regulations. Program audit guides issued by several federal entities contain audit requirements tailored to their specific federal programs and these guides require audit tests be performed to ensure that costs paid by the government are consistent with OMB's cost circulars.

OMB's *Compliance Supplement* prescribes audit requirements that must be applied to the audits of Federal assistance programs with respect to costs. From an auditor's viewpoint, compliance with audit procedures in the *Supplement* constitutes a "safe harbor." If the *Supplement* is not used, the burden is on the auditor to demonstrate the application of more effective audit procedures were used to achieve the audit objectives similar to those outlined in the *Supplement*.

COST ALLOWABILITY FACTORS

When auditing transactions and account balances involving federal funds, an audit objective must be to determine whether the costs meet the OMB general criteria (in OMB's three cost circulars) concerning allowability, unallowability and indirect costs. These criteria, which appear also in the *Compliance Supplement*, have been rather consistent for years and require an auditor to make many decisions related to allowability. These allowability criteria require that auditors determine that:

1. Costs charged to or claimed under contracts and grants are necessary and reasonable for the performance and administration of the federal program and are allocable thereto under the provisions of the three cost circulars.

2. Costs must be allocable to federal awards under the provisions of OMB's cost circulars. A cost would be allocable to a cost objective if the goods or services involved are charged or assigned to the cost objective in accordance with relative benefits received.

3. Cost must be allocable to federal awards under the cost circulars through the application of generally accepted accounting principles appropriate to the circumstances. A direct cost may not be assigned to a federal award if any other cost incurred for the same purpose in similar circumstances was allocated to that federal award as an indirect cost.

4. Costs must conform to any limitations or exclusions set forth in OMB Circulars, federal laws, state or local laws, sponsoring agreements or other governing regulations as to types or amounts of cost items.

5. Costs must be net of applicable credits that result from transactions that reduce or offset direct or indirect costs. For example, costs to federal awards must be reduced for any discounts, rebates, allowances, recoveries, indemnification of losses, insurance refunds, rebates, and adjustments for overpayments or errors.

1. Reasonable and Necessary Costs

Auditors of government programs must conduct sufficient tests of transactions to have a reasonable assurance that only reasonable and necessary costs are being claimed or charged to governmental contracts or grants.

Reasonable costs are defined by OMB as a cost, in its nature and amount, that does not exceed that which would be incurred by a prudent person under the circumstances prevailing at the time the decision was made to incur the cost. When testing transactions for reasonableness, the auditor must consider:

1. Whether the cost is of a type generally recognized as ordinary and necessary for the operation of the organization or the performance of the program or contract or grant award.

2. Restraints or requirements imposed by generally accepted sound business practices, arm's-length bargaining, federal and state laws and regulations, and terms and conditions of contracts, grants or agreements.

3. Whether individuals concerned acted with prudence in the circumstances considering their responsibilities to the organization, its members, employees, and clients, the public at large, and the government.

4. Significant deviations from the established practices of the organization which may unjustifiably increase the costs.

Audit tests for reasonableness are particularly critical when organizations may not be subjected to the normal or effective competitive restraints.

Examples of clearly unreasonable costs under federal awards would include:

1. Purchase of six months of supplies in the last month of the federal program.

2. Purchase of expensive equipment needed for a short period of time when leasing would have been more economical.

3. Costs for which appropriate evidence is not available to show that the program managers employed controls necessary to assure that prices claimed or charged were reasonable.

Necessary costs are defined as those required, implicitly or explicitly, by program regulations or program agreement or negotiated contract, grant, or cooperative or other agreements to achieve agreed-upon objectives or goals. Generally, financial and performance budgets exist to provide an indication of what is *necessary*. Absent specific guides or limitations, certain rules of fiscal prudence—i.e., common sense—would prevail. *Necessary costs* include expenditures for goods or services for the program charged, in quantities that would be considered normal for the nature and activities conducted, and at a price that is competitive.

When testing transactions and account balances, the auditor must assess whether the purpose, timing, amount, authorization and approval for the program charged are all appropriate. An assessment must also be made that each transaction was generally prudent, is relevant to the account or program charged, and the expenditure is necessary to meet the objective or goal of the activity.

2. Allowable Costs

Allowable costs must meet or comply with several criteria in OMB cost circulars. Expenditures or costs that meet these criteria and are not otherwise prohibited by the contract, grant or cooperative agreement conditions are termed "allowable costs." To be an allowable cost, claimed or charged to federal programs and contracts and grants, the charge must meet all of the criteria outlined above.

The allowable costs claimed or charged to federal programs, contracts, grants or other agreements is comprised of (a) the allowable direct cost necessary to the performance of the funded program, plus (b) the program's allocable portion of allowable indirect or overhead costs, less any applicable credits. When defining costs, federal criteria intends that contract and grants costs include total allowable direct and indirect costs.

The federal government has not specified a rule for classifying certain costs as either direct or indirect under every accounting system. It is possible for cost to be direct to some service or function but indirect to the federal program. Thus, consistency of cost accounting practices is essential. The primary concerns of OMB is that federal programs not be charged for cost not permitted under OMB cost circulars or that the government not be double-charged by being billed directly and then indirectly as part of an allocated costs for the same activity.

Direct Costs. OMB defines direct costs as those identified specifically with a particular cost objective. These costs, if not otherwise limited or defined as unallowable, may be charged directly to federal programs, contracts or grants or other programs against which costs are finally lodged. Direct costs may also be charged to cost objectives used for accumulations of cost pending distribution in due course to other ultimate cost objectives.

Indirect Costs. OMB has defined indirect costs as those (a) incurred for a common or joint purpose benefiting more than one cost objective, and (b) not readily assignable to the cost objectives specifically benefited, without effort disproportionate to the results achieved. To facilitate equitable distribution of indirect costs, pools of indirect costs may have to be established. Costs accumulated in these pools must then be distributed to federal and other activities on bases that will produce equitable results relative to the benefits derived.

For indirect costs, there may be limits—in absolute dollars or a percentage or rate—on the indirect costs that may be allowed under a particular federal program. Federal agencies may establish procedures to assure that amount allowed under each program, contract, grant or other agreement do not exceed the maximum allowable under the statutory limitations or amounts otherwise allowable by OMB cost circulars. Properly allocable amounts of indirect costs in excess of the statutory limitation that are not recoverable as indirect cost under the benefiting program and may not be shifted to another federally funded program or activity.

Unallowable Costs. Where a cost is not allowable or, no allowable costs of an equal amount are subsequently incurred and the recipient still has possession of the funds, the recipient must return the amount improperly claimed or charged to the government.

An auditor must consider several factors in questioning or challenging costs—both direct and indirect—claimed or charged to federal supported programs, such as allowability, reasonableness, prior approval, consistency in accounting, etc. But, there are categories of cost that are defined as unallowable that may not be charged to a federal activity regardless of other merits. A partial list of costs considered unallowable under all federal awards include:

Advertising—the promotional use of media (newspapers, radio, television, direct mail, trade papers, etc.) unless done solely for the contract or grant program are unallowable.

Bad Debts—an incurred loss arising from accounts and other claims are unallowable on the premise that the government pays all of its just debts. Further, an accrual of an amount for an estimated bad debt is also unallowable.

Contingencies—estimates for, and contributions to contingency reserves or other similar provision for a future or unforeseen event are unallowable on the premise that the government pays debts when due. An accrual of contingent costs would be unallowable. If the accrual is paid in cash, the federal government may, in certain instances then participate in the loss.

Contributions and Donations—gifts, contributions, and donations of federal monies are unallowable as being contrary to federal policy.

Entertainment—cost of amusements, social activities and related incidental costs (e.g., meals, beverages, lodgings, rentals, transportation, gratuities) are unallowable as being contrary to federal policy.

Fines and Penalties—resulting from violations of or failure to comply with federal, state and local laws and regulations are unallowable on the premise that the government would be paying additional costs for assessing these amounts.

Interest and Other Financial Costs—including the cost of borrowing, bond discounts, cost of financing and re-financing activities, financial campaigns, endowment drives, solicitation of gifts, bequests, and related legal and professional fees in connection therewith are unallowable. The federal government's definition of financially responsible non-federal entities is that such entities should have sufficient funds for operations, without entering into debt.

Underrecovery of Costs Under Grant Agreements—any excess of costs, direct or indirect, over the federal financing under one agreement is an unallowable claim or charge to another agreement either, directly or indirectly. Profits and losses of federal contracts and grants may not be offset nor may profits and losses of federal versus non-federal activities be offset.

First Class Travel Accommodations—the cost differential between first class and coach travel accommodation is unallowable unless such accommodation is necessitated for medical or other reasons.

Cost of pensions and certain post-retirement—accruals for these costs are unallowable. Such costs are allowable only when irrevocably funded in cash.

Additionally, there are several cost categories that are allowable as charges to federal awards but only under certain conditions or circumstances. For example, several costs of educational institutions and non-profit organizations that are allowable, but with federal restrictions, include costs related to: pre-agreement costs, patents, recruiting, relocation, taxes, severance pay, termination costs.

Many unallowable costs are prohibited as claims or charges to federal activities by laws and regulations and must be classified as unallowable as a matter of public policy. That is not to say that such costs are not necessary to the recipient nor that the amounts claimed or charged to the government are unreasonable. OMB, in its cost circulars, is merely stating that the federal government will not reimburse contractors or grantees for these costs. The federal positions, with respect to such cost, often implement Congressional concerns that are directed towards correcting some abuse of the past.

When the cost of an activity is designated as unallowable as a claim or charge to a federal program, the unallowed cost must be accounted for as a direct cost to which a portion of the calculated indirect cost must be allocated. Thus the total unallowed cost would include the unallowed direct cost, plus the indirect cost allocated to the unallowed direct cost. The rationale for including the indirect costs is that the unallowed activity probably includes salaries, space, allocation, support equipment and direction from management.

A cost is *allocable* to a program, contract, grant or other agreement to the extent of benefits received. OMB regulations state that a cost is allocable to a federal program or agreement if: (1) the cost is incurred specifically for the federal program or agreement, (2) the cost benefits

Auditing for Allowable, Unallowable, Indirect Costs

both the federal program or agreement and other work and can be distributed in reasonable proportion to the benefits received, or (3) the cost is necessary to the overall operation of the organization, although a direct relationship to any particular federal program or contract cannot be shown.

Where a cost is determined to be allocable or assignable to a specific federal program or agreement, these same costs cannot be shifted to other federal programs to overcome or meet funding deficiencies, avoid restrictions imposed by law or regulations or for other reasons. A few examples of the latter would include:

1. Cost already claimed as matching costs for another program.

2. An inequitable allocation of indirect costs to a federal program.

3. Costs allocated in total to a federal program when such costs also benefited other programs.

Later sections of this chapter describe the requirements for and concerns about auditing indirect costs in greater detail.

3. Consistent Accounting Treatment

Costs charged to or claimed under contracts and grants must be given consistent accounting treatment within and between accounting periods. Cost may not be allocated to or included as a direct cost of a federal program if the same or similar costs are allocated to the federal program as indirect costs. Costs charged to or claimed under contracts and grants cannot be included as a cost or used to meet cost sharing requirements of other federal-supported activity of the current or prior period. All OMB cost circulars require that costs charged to or claimed under contracts and grants be determine in accordance with generally accepted accounting principles.

Unless specifically permitted or approved by the federal government, recipients managing federally supported programs must insure that the policies, regulations, and procedures are applied consistently and uniformly to all of its activities. Separate policies and procedures are not permitted that would result in different practices being applied to the operation of federal versus non-federal programs. Unless required or approved by the federal government, personnel practices, compensation and related benefits, procurement procedures, to mention a few, must be the same for all programs—federal and non-federal—operated or managed by a state or local government or tribal Indian government.

Recipient governments may not unilaterally alter the accounting treatment subsequent to the approval of a federally supported program and approved budgets. The AICPA's audit guide for government defined *consistent* as "applying the same accounting treatment in a similar manner to similar transactions within a reporting period and from one reporting period to another."

Unless the federal government is notified and approval is provided, recipients of federal assistance are expected to receive, record, expend, account, report, and claim or charge costs in the manner that is implicit or explicitly set forth in the financial budget. The explicit or implicitly approved accounting must prevail for all transactions: (1) in a given fiscal period, (2) between the more than one fiscal period, and (3) between federal and non-federally financed programs. Further, this consistency of accounting criteria applies to the accounting for direct and indirect costs.

The three OMB cost circulars require that costs for federally financed programs be determined in accordance with generally accepted accounting principles, which for governmental entities might be the accounting and financial reporting practices promulgated by one of three standard-setting boards:

● Governmental Accounting Standards Board—is recognized by the AICPA and the GAO as setting the accounting and financial reporting standards for general or primary type state and local governmental units;

● Financial Accounting Standards Board—is recognized by the AICPA and the GAO as setting the accounting and financial reporting standards for business-type state and local governmental units;

● Federal Accounting Standards Advisory Board—is recognized by the AICPA and the GAO as recommending the accounting and financial reporting standards for federal governmental departments and agencies.

But, this requirement is to some degree misleading. Having prescribed generally accepted accounting principles as the basis for cost accounting for federally financed programs, OMB in the details of each of the cost circulars then prohibits the claiming many costs that would appropriately, pursuant to generally accepted accounting principles, be charged to federal programs. Generally accepted accounting principles require that the accounting and reporting comply with an accrual basis of accounting. Yet, OMB's cost circulars state *costs*, as used in the Circular, could mean cost as determined on: (1) a cash basis, (2) accrual basis, or (3) some other basis acceptable to financing federal department or agency as a discharge of the recipient's accountability for federal funds.

Examples of necessary but unallowable accrued costs would include accrued costs for bad debts, interest, advertising, contingencies, post-retirement costs, and certain executive costs as costs that must be compiled, accrued, and reported and are necessary to the operation of

Auditing for Allowable, Unallowable, Indirect Costs 265

any organization. Yet, none of these and some other GAAP-determined costs may be claimed for reimbursement under government contracts and grants even though the accounting is entirely appropriate under generally accepted accounting principles. Several costs may not be charged to federal awards on an accrual accounting basis. But, these same costs are acceptable to federal awards if paid in cash prior to making a claim on the federal government. In these instances, the federal government refers to the costs as allowable "funded" costs.

Thus, from the auditor's view, compliance with generally accepted accounting principles can not be the final determinant for allowability of costs when auditing governmental programs. The criteria for allowable cost is really "GAAP—as modified" by OMB cost circulars.

4. Conform to Law, Circular, Regulations or Agreement

Costs charged to or claimed under contracts and grants must be authorized or not prohibited under federal, state or local laws or regulations. Several costs require specific approval by the federal agency while other costs are not allowable in any circumstances. All costs charged to or claimed under contracts and grants must conform to any limitations or exclusions set forth in the cost Circulars, or limitations in the program agreement or specific requirements in the program regulations.

For certain categories of cost, OMB requires there be specific approval by the federal grantor even though these costs would otherwise meet the tests of reasonableness, necessity and allocability. A separate section in the OMB cost circulars lists categories of allowable costs, unallowable costs and cost for which prior specific federal approval is required. Examples of the latter category include costs associated with space rentals, computers, capital expenditures, insurance, professional services, preagreement costs, proposal costs.

Advance approval or authorization requires that the recipient of federal assistance have documentation evidencing federal consent prior to incurring the specific cost. Many charges to federal awards must, in addition to complying with other criteria, be specifically approved by the federal entity. Further, the federal assistance agreement, itself, must be approved in advance of such costs being claimed or charged to the federal government. Some examples of these types of costs would include:

● Charges to federal awards of costs incurred before the effective date of a federal program.

● Employing consultants and subcontractors whose services or need is not explicit in the approved budget of the federal program.

- The purchase of capital equipment not explicitly described in the approved budget of the federal program.

The contract or grant agreement may exist in the form of federal law and related program regulations. In these circumstances, all governmental units would be required to implement and manage the federally assisted program in a manner consistent with these criteria. Alternatively, the federal program agreement might be specific to a state or local or tribal Indian government. In this instance, the agreement would be the totality of the terms and conditions agreed to between the federal department or agency and the recipient government.

In almost every instance the specific terms and conditions of contracts and grants, will identify or incorporate by reference the compliance criteria for determining what will constitute allowable and unallowable cost claims or charges to the federally-supported program. At times, the federal law, itself, will limit or prohibit certain claims or charges to federally-supported programs.

Auditors of contracts and grants cannot avoid the legal axiom: "When all else fails, read the agreement."

5. Net of Applicable Credits

Costs claimed or charged to federally-financed activities must be *net of applicable credits*, e.g., volume or cash discounts, refunds, rental income, trade-ins, scrap sales, direct billings (in the case of indirect cost), etc.

Under the OMB cost circulars, a federal program may be charged for only the actual cost or the net cost or the actual cash disbursed. This phrase refers to any credit or reduction of expenditure-type transactions which offset or reduce the expense items allocable to a federally-financed activity as either a direct or an indirect cost.

"Net of applicable credits" would require that a federal recipient reduce all charges, billing or claims to the federal government for amounts related to volume or cash discounts, refunds, rental income, trade-ins, scrap sales, purchase discounts, rebates or allowances, recoveries or indemnities on losses, sale of publications or equipment and scrap, income from personal or incidental services, and adjustments of overpayments or erroneous charges.

Additionally, applicable credits may arise when supplemental or additional federal funds are received or are available from sources other than the federal program involved to finance operations. This could include costs charged for depreciation or items donated or financed by the federal government to fulfill matching requirements under another program. These type of credits, too, should be used to offset or reduce related expenditures claimed or charged to a federally financed program.

Documentation

Costs charged to or claimed under contracts and grants must be supported by underlying documentation, e.g., time and attendance payroll records, time and effort records for employees charged to more than one activity, approved purchase orders, receiving reports, vendor invoices, canceled checks, etc., as appropriate. Documentation requirements for salaries and wages, and time and effort distribution are described in the cost circulars. Alternatively, documentation may be acceptable in electronic format. Costs must be also be documented in accordance with OMB Circulars program management administrative guidelines, A-102 and A-110.

AUDIT OF MATCHING, CONTRIBUTED, LEVEL OF EFFORT COSTS

There are specific government criteria for assessing the propriety or type, value, and timing of local contributions or matching share. Such support could be cash or unclaimed direct or allowable indirect costs or in-kind property or services. But, these criteria appear in OMB Circulars A-102 and A-110 regulation, the administrative and management procedures for states and local governments and non-profit organizations.

Cost sharing or matching or in-kind contributions refer to those program costs not shared by the federal government, but which by law, regulations or agreement are to be provided by the recipient of federal funds. Generally the conditions relating to the shared or matched contributions are specific as to: (1) the amount required, (2) the nature or form of the contribution to be made, and (3) the timing or point when the contribution or match must be made available for use or benefit of the federal program or activity. The "common rule" requires that certain exceptions must be examined during audit prior to accepting matching or other forms of cost-shared amounts. Some criteria, exceptions or "unallowable" conditions exist under these circulars that require:

1. Neither contributed costs nor third-party in-kind contributions may satisfy a cost sharing or matching requirement of more than one federal program, contract, grant or other agreement involving federal funds.

2. Costs financed by program income (i.e., income generated by federally-supported activity or earned as a result of a federal agreement) shall not count as satisfying a cost sharing or matching require-

ment unless specifically permitted in the terms of the assistance agreement.

3. No cost of services or property financed by income earned by a recipient of federal assistance may count towards a cost sharing or matching requirement.

4. Volunteer services are to be valued at rates consistent with those ordinarily paid for similar work in other activities of the recipient government. If the skills are not found in the governmental unit, the volunteer's rate should be consistent with those paid for similar work in the labor market in which the government competes for the kind of services involved.

5. Volunteers employed by others shall be valued at the employee's regular rate of pay (exclusive of fringe and overhead costs) provided the services are in the same skill work for which the employee is normally paid. If the services are in a different line of work, the valuation shall be consistent with those paid by other employers in the same labor market.

6. Valuations of donations of expendable personal property and materials, such as equipment, supplies for office, laboratory, workshop or classroom are to be reasonable in amount and not to exceed the fair market value of the property at the time of donation.

7. If the use of equipment or space is donated and the donor retains title, the contribution will be valued at the fair rental valued of the equipment or space.

8. Donations of nonexpendable personal property, buildings, and land or use thereof, will be valued at various rates depending upon the purpose of the federal program receiving the donation, for example:

—The total value of the donation may be charged to the federal program if the purpose of the program is to furnish equipment, building or land to the recipient; or

—Full value, depreciation or use charges may be used depending upon federal approval, if the purpose of the program is to support activities requiring the use of equipment, buildings, or land on a temporary or part-time basis.

Often, special audit procedures must be designed to ensure conformance with these provisions as well as the timing of the contribution. Providing shared or matching contributions later than the promised date or in a different kind could adversely impact program activities.

OMB Circulars A-102 and A-110 require that records supporting or documentation for all shared, matching, or in-kind contributions or donations be the same as that required for other claims and charges

Auditing for Allowable, Unallowable, Indirect Costs

made for any federally-financed program, contract, grant or other agreement. For example, volunteered labor should be documented and supported by the same method and records used to support paid labor costs of the recipient's own employees. Similarly, documentation for contributed or donated materials, equipment, supplies, land, buildings, etc., must be supported by the same documents or evidence used for like items purchased directly for the federally-financed program.

AUDIT REQUIREMENTS FOR INDIRECT COSTS

OMB cost circulars A-21, A-87, and A-122 are the federal regulations that also pertain to the determination of allowable indirect costs. Allocated indirect or overhead costs could be a material portion of the total costs claimed or charged to federally-financed programs, contracts grants or other agreements and must be audited if an audit opinion is to be rendered by the auditor on the accounting for federal program funds.

Documented by Plans

Indirect or overhead cost must meet all of the criteria described in earlier sections with respect to allowability and documentation, but additionally, indirect costs must be compiled, allocated and documented pursuant to the audit requirements outlined by OMB in its cost circulars. To be reimbursed for indirect costs, recipients of federal monies must prepare annually, and retain cost allocation plans and/or indirect cost rate proposals that describe and document the basis for allocating indirect costs to government contracts and grants. OMB has made a distinction in these terms:

Cost allocation plan—Describes the methods used for billing centralized services costs (e.g., cost of computer centers, fringe benefits, motor pools, etc.) to individual user organizations, departments, and activities. It is also a method used for allocating cost of unbilled central services (e.g., accounting, personnel, procurement, etc.) to the individual user organizations, departments or activities.

Indirect cost rate proposal—Combines the billed or allocated costs, if any, appearing in the government-wide cost allocation plan with departmental or local level indirect costs and computes an indirect cost rate that is used in charging indirect costs to direct programs and activities.

States, state departments and major local governmental units and other organizations must submit their cost allocation and indirect cost plans to designated federal agencies for review, analysis and approval. Other governmental and nonprofit organizations are not required to submit their plans annually. But this "other" grouping of organizations must retain the plan for each year, update the plan annually, and submit the plans for audit at the time the federally-financed activity undergoes audit.

Usually these plans are prepared on a prospective basis using actual financial data from the prior year or budgeted data for the current year. When actual costs for the year are determined, the differences between the originally proposed indirect costs and the actual indirect costs are "settled" either by being carried forward to a future indirect cost plan or adjusted on a cash basis with the federal department on a retroactive basis. In instances where a fixed indirect cost rate was determined and approved by the designated federal department, no subsequent adjustment is made to the originally determined indirect cost rate.

Determination of Indirect Costs

Each OMB cost circular describes those indirect cost allocation procedures related to the covered organizations. The form or documentation that the costing methodology must comply with and the process by which the federal government will analyze and accept or reject proposed indirect cost plans is also described in these cost circulars. Auditors of governments must be knowledgeable of these requirements. With respect to indirect costs, audit procedures must be applied to three aspects: (1) the categories or elements of cost, (2) the indirect cost pools in which cost categories or elements are accumulated and which are to be allocated, and (3) the composition and currency of the allocation bases over which the indirect costs will be spread to federal and other programs and activities.

The audit of indirect costs requires that the auditor be familiar with several general terms, definitions, and explanations of which appear in the cost circulars:

Indirect costs. These are costs incurred for common or joint purposes benefiting more than one cost objective that cannot be readily identified with a particular final cost objective without effort disproportionate to the results achieved. Indirect costs include both: (1) the indirect costs originating in each department or agency performing under federal awards, and (2) costs of central governmental services distributed through the central service cost allocation plan and not otherwise treated as direct costs. Indirect costs are normally charged to federally-financed activities by use of an indirect cost rate; generally, a separate indirect cost rate is necessary for each operating department of the recipient government claiming indirect costs.

Indirect cost proposal. This is the required documentation prepared by a state, local or Indian tribal government to substantiate the non-federal entity's claim for reimbursement of indirect costs from the federal government.

Auditing for Allowable, Unallowable, Indirect Costs 271

Indirect cost rate. This is the arithmetic factor used for determining what proportion of indirect cost each federal and all other program or activity should bear. The rate is the ratio, expressed as a percent, of the indirect costs to the direct cost base.

Base. This is the dollar base of accumulated direct costs, normally either (1) total direct salaries and wages, or (2) modified total direct costs. The modified total direct cost basis excludes any extraordinary or distorting expenditures. The direct cost base should result in all programs and activities—federal and non-federal—bearing a fair share of the indirect costs in reasonable relation to the benefits received from the allocated indirect costs.

Types of Indirect Cost Rates

There exists, in the OMB cost circulars, a variety of rates that are used by the federal government for reimbursing indirect costs, each having slightly differing audit implications:

● *Predetermined indirect cost rates*. These rates may apply to a specified current fiscal or future fiscal period and are based on an estimate of costs to be incurred during the designated period. The predetermined rate is generally not subject to later adjustment for the difference between the originally estimated rate and the later actual experienced rate.

● *Fixed indirect cost rates*. Rates that have the same characteristics as the predetermined rate except that the difference between the estimated and actual costs covered by the rate is carried forward as an adjustment to the rate computation of a subsequent period.

● *Provisional indirect cost rates*. Rates that are temporary, indirect cost rates applicable to a specified period used for funding interim reimbursement and reporting indirect costs on contracts, grants and other agreements pending the establishment of a "final" rate for the period.

● *Final indirect cost rates*. Rates that apply to a specified past period which is based on the actual allowable costs of the period. Final rates are not subject to further adjustment.

Methods of Allocating Indirect Costs

The OMB cost circulars describe two methods for allocating and computing indirect cost rates:

Simplified Allocation Base Method. For circumstances where the recipient's major functions benefit from indirect costs to approximately the same degree, the indirect cost allocation may be accomplished by: (1) classifying total costs for the base period as either direct or indirect, and (2) dividing the total allowable indirect costs (net of applicable credits) by an equitable distribution base. The resulting rate is used to distribute indirect costs to individual federally-financed activities. The indirect cost rate is the percentage which the total amount of allowable indirect costs bears to the base selected.

Under this method, the direct and indirect costs should exclude capital and other distortive expenditures and unallowable costs. However, the unallowable costs must be included in the direct cost if they represent activities to which indirect costs would be properly allocable.

Multiple Allocation Base Method. For circumstances where the recipient's indirect costs benefit its major functions in varying degrees, the indirect cost must be accumulated by separate cost groupings. Each grouping is then allocated individually to benefiting functions by means of the base which best measures the relative benefits received by the function.

The distribution base for each function will vary and may be (1) total direct costs (excluding capital expenditures and items as flow-through funds, major subcontracts, etc.), (2) direct salaries and wages, or (3) other base which results in an equitable distribution of costs. Some other common allocation bases include: person hours applied, square feet utilized, hours or dollars of usage or consumption and volume of activities (i.e., documents processed, items handled, populations served, tons moved, miles driven, number of employees served, computer hours, etc.). An indirect cost rate should be developed for each indirect cost pool developed.

SUGGESTED PROCEDURES FOR INDIRECT COST AUDITS

An initial audit determination is required to ascertain whether indirect costs or centralized or administrative services have been allocated or charged to any federally-financed program or activity. If no indirect costs have been allocated or charged, no audit procedures need be applied to test the determination, compilations, and allocation of costs.

But, if indirect costs have been allocated or charged to federally-financed programs or activities, auditors should consider performing the several audit procedures "suggested" in the *Compliance Supplement*. Compliance with the suggested audit procedures will constitute a "safe harbor." If the suggested audit procedures are not used, the burden is on the individual auditor to demonstrate the application of more effective audit procedures to achieve the audit objectives outlined in the *Supplement*.

OMB's *Compliance Supplement* contains the audit guidance for conducting audits of direct and indirect costs of non-federal entities by: (1) requiring that non-federal entities comply with several objectives or

Auditing for Allowable, Unallowable, Indirect Costs 273

cost principles in the OMB cost circulars, and (2) providing specific audit procedures applicable to audits of direct and indirect costs.

Audit of Direct and Indirect Costs

Audit Objectives

The several objectives included in the 1999 Compliance Supplement related to the audit of direct and indirect costs charged by non-federal entities to federal programs state:

● The auditor must determine whether non-federal entities complied with the provisions of applicable OMB cost circulars. The three circulars apply to specific "industries": (1) Circular A-21 to educational institutions; (2) Circular A-87 to state and local governments and Indian tribal governments; and (3) A-122 to non-profit organizations.

● The auditor must determine whether the non-federal entities, charges to cost pools were for only allowable costs, as defined in the three cost circulars. Also, the auditor must determine with respect to non-federal governments and Indian tribal governments that charges to cost pools were made pursuant to properly prepared cost allocation plans.

● The auditor must determine whether the methods of allocating costs comply with OMB cost circulars and produce an equitable distribution of costs. That is, the allocation bases must include all allowable and unallowable base costs to which allowable indirect costs are allocable and the cost allocation methodology complies with the OMB requirements.

● The auditor must determine whether indirect costs were applied in accordance with approved rate agreements and the associated billings to the federal government result from applying the approved rate to the proper base amounts.

● For state and local governments and Indian tribal governments, the auditor must determine whether indirect costs were applied in accordance with cost allocation plans approved by the federal cognizant agency responsible for indirect cost negotiation. Where such plans are not subject to approval, an audit determination must be made that cost allocations were in accordance with the plan on file.

● The auditor must determine whether the cost accounting disclosures required by the Cost Accounting Standards Board represent the actual accounting practices consistently applied.

Audit Procedures

The following audit procedures should be performed to audit indirect costs whenever indirect costs are claimed under, charged to, or reimbursed by a federally-financed activity. These audit procedures, suggested in the *Compliance Supplement*, require that the auditor:

1. Obtain and read the current cost allocation plan and/or indirect cost rate negotiation agreement, and determine the types of indirect cost rates and procedures required.

2. Select a sample of indirect cost claims for reimbursement submitted to a federal department and determine if the amounts charged and rates used are in accordance with the plan and if rates are being properly applied to the appropriate allocation base.

3. Determine if the cost allocation plan or indirect cost plan have been approved by the designated federal department and whether or not the resultant rates or amounts charged are final or are still open to adjustment or revision, either immediately or as a carryover adjustment in a future period. If the rates are approved and final, the results of the audit must be reflected, if appropriate, in recommendations for future procedural improvements.

4. Review, on a test basis, supporting documentation to determine whether:

- The indirect cost pool or centralized service costs contain only items that are consistent with the applicable cost circular and negotiated agreements.

- The methods of allocating the costs are in accordance with OMB cost circulars, other applicable regulations, and the negotiated indirect cost rate agreement.

- Statistical data (e.g., square footage, population, operating time, miles driven, case counts, salaries and wages) in the proposed allocation or rate bases are reasonable, updated as necessary and do not contain any material omissions.

- Time studies or time and effort reports (where and if utilized) are mathematically and statistically accurate, are implemented as approved, and are based on the actual effort devoted to the various functional and programmatic activities to which the salary and wage costs are charged.

- The indirect costs charged to federal programs are supported by amounts recorded in the accounting records from which the most recently issued financial statements were prepared.

- Other adjustments are made to compensate for differences between actual and estimated costs of fiscal years.

5. For state and local government wide plans, the auditor should conduct tests to determine whether:

Auditing for Allowable, Unallowable, Indirect Costs 275

- The indirect cost rate base includes all users and that all users are treated in a consistent manner.

- Fringe benefit allocations, charges or rates deal fairly with differing levels, if any, of benefits provided to different classes of employees.

If the auditor identifies unallowable costs, the auditor should be aware that "directly associated costs" may have also been charged to federal programs. Directly associated costs are costs incurred solely as a result of incurring another cost and would not have been incurred if the other costs had not been incurred (E.g., fringe benefit expenses are directly associated with payroll cost. Under OMB cost circulars both costs are unallowable.).

The AICPA, in its audit guide for governments, provide the following direction with respect to detected errors and the communication of audit findings for indirect cost plans:

- If the auditor detects errors in an indirect cost plan, those errors should be discussed with the appropriate level of management.

- The errors to be discussed may include, but are not limited to, mathematical inaccuracies, improper application of cost accounting practices, other factors affecting the calculated indirect cost rate, or misuse of facts that existed at the time the plan was prepared.

- Also to be discussed are deficient indirect cost plans or errors in the application of indirect cost principles that could materially affect major federal financial assistance programs or federal financial report if such costs are charged to the program.

- Material deficiencies or errors, including the effect on the programs, should be included in the Schedule of Findings and Questioned Costs that must accompany the auditor's report on compliance.

Internal Service Funds—Suggested Audit Procedures

Internal service funds, also known as working capital funds, are established by non-federal entities to provide a common service, and are to be reimbursed for the cost of that service, require particular audit emphasis. Some suggested audit procedures should include:

- When material costs of internal service funds (.e.g., central services, pension funds, computer support units, motor pools, governmentwide risk activities) are charged to federal programs, the auditor must verify that the internal service funds comply with provisions of OMB Circulars. The concern is that the federal programs will be charged for only their fair share of service fund costs and not at a rate considerably in excess of costs.

This is of particular concern when the internal service fund consistently reports significant profits. By definition, internal service funds can not make a profit without charging its customers a price in excess of costs.

● There are several conditions of audit concern with respect to internal service funds. To ensure that all customers are paying a fair and reasonable price for centrally provided and billed services, auditors of these funds must conduct tests to:

—Determine if the fund balance and retained earnings have been computed in accordance with OMB cost circulars. All costs charged to federal awards must be in accord with federal regulations, regardless of whether costs are billed direct to programs or indirect through the guise of an internal service fund.

—Ascertain if the balance of the internal service or working capital fund is excessive in amount. These types of funds, premised on the return of cost, can not consistently earn a profit without charging some customers an amount in excess of cost. Federal policy is that the fund balance should not be greater than 60 days working capital related to cash expenses (not accrued costs) for normal operations, exclusive of depreciation, capital costs, and debt principal costs.

—Tests must be made of refunds to ensure the federal government received its fair share of any amounts transferred or borrowed from the internal service and central service funds for purposes of meeting the operating liabilities of the fund. Transfers of excessive fund balances to finance general government operations, in contrast to refunds to fund customers, would be irregular and explanations required.

—For all customers of the fund:

(1) Billings must be done in a consistent manner. Separate billing practices should not exist for federal versus non-federal programs and entities.

(2) Billed amounts must be for only allowable costs; unallowable costs must be eliminated from charges to federally-financed awards and programs.

(3) Billed rates or charges must be based on actual costs and eliminations made for profits, management allowances, fees or other billings in excess of cost.

(4) When billing rates, costs or charges are actuarially based, the actuarial studies on which billings are based should not be over two years old.

Auditing for Allowable, Unallowable, Indirect Costs 277

QUESTIONED OR UNALLOWED COSTS

Historically some federal agencies required the auditor to determine the allowability or selling of all costs charged or claimed under a government contract or grant based on the audit. In the last decade or so, the auditor's role has shifted slightly to being the agent for "questioning" costs that might not meet federal criteria. The federal agencies have reserved the right for determining whether in fact costs should be classed as unallowable and therefore be refundable to the government.

While the criteria has varied in past years, somewhat by the federal agency, OMB, in Circular A-133, now provides this federal-wide definition:

Questioned costs means a cost that is questioned by the auditor because of an audit finding:

1. Which resulted from a violation or possible violation of a provision of a law, regulation, contract, grant, cooperative agreement, or other agreement or document governing the use of federal funds, including funds used to match federal funds.

2. Where the costs, at the time of audit, are not supported by adequate documentation.

3. Where the costs incurred appear unreasonable and do not reflect the actions that a prudent person would take in the circumstances.

Section 510(a) of Circular A-133 requires that the auditor report, as an audit finding in a schedule of findings and questioned costs, all *known* questioned costs greater than $10,000 for a type of compliance requirement for a major program. Known question costs are those specifically identified by the auditor.

In arriving at the determination of the type of audit opinion on compliance, the auditor must consider the best estimate of total costs questioned (i.e., the *likely* questioned costs) and not just the questioned costs. The auditor must report known questioned costs when likely questioned costs are greater than $10,000 for a type of compliance for a major program. Again, auditor estimate of total questioned costs, i.e., the likely questioned costs, need not be reported.

Questioned costs might include unapproved pre-grant and post-grant costs, costs in excess of approved contract or grant budgets by category or in total, or costs cited as unallowable in the OMB cost circulars. A cost might be "questioned" as *undocumented* if the cost claimed or charged is undocumented, e.g., detailed documentation does not exist, for example, to demonstrate the relationship to the contract or grant or the amounts involved. A cost could be "questioned" as *unapproved* if the cost element claimed or charged is not provided for in the approved contract or grant budget or the costs require the awarding organization's specific approval and no evidence of approval is found. A cost may be "questioned" as *unreasonable* if the cost element claimed or charged does not reflect the actions that a prudent person would take in the circumstances, or reflect assignment of an unreasonably high valuation to in-kind contributions.

ALLOWABLE DETERMINATION BY AUDIT

Selected contracts and grants may contain conditions that require the allowable direct and indirect costs be determined by audit. In these instances, the auditor is the final determinant, i.e., the judge and jury, of the allowability of the nature, level, allocability and reasonableness of indirect cost charged or claimed under the government agreements.

For these contracts and grants, recipients of federal financing must make the necessary effort to resolve all audit questions before the audit is concluded or a final allowability decision could be made by the government solely on the basis of the audit report without further discussion. Once the audit report is issued and the audit findings sustained by the federal department, a claim may be levied on the contractor or grantee for a refund of all questioned and unallowed costs.

Chapter 11

Working Papers and Audit Evidence

STANDARDS FOR GOVERNMENT AUDIT WORKING PAPERS

Working papers and audit evidence are separately postulated standards of generally accepted as well as the government auditing standards. Related to issues of working papers and audit evidence is ownership of the working papers and access to the working papers, regardless of ownership. Government auditing requires a different perspective on these subjects and, often, laws and government regulations dictate practices different than those prevailing in private sector auditing.

As noted in the earlier chapter on government field work standards, the government auditing standards incorporate and build upon the generally accepted auditing standards. Further, the government auditing standards automatically incorporate any new Statement on Auditing Standard unless the U.S. General Accounting Office excludes the standard by formal announcement. No SAS has ever been excluded.

Generally Accepted Standards

Therefore, the government auditing standards on working papers and evidence incorporate the relevant generally accepted auditing working paper standards, revised in 1982 by Statement on Auditing Standard No. 41 that stated:

"The auditor should prepare and maintain working papers, the form and content of which should be designed to meet the circumstances of a particular engagement. The information contained in working papers constitutes the principal record of the work that the auditor has done and the conclusions that he has reached concerning significant matters."

SAS No. 41 describes a two-fold purpose of working papers: (1) working papers are to provide the principal support for the auditor's

280   Government Auditing: Standards and Practices

report, including his representations regarding observance of the standards of field work, and (2) working papers are to aid the auditor in the conduct and supervision of the audit.

Government Auditing Standards

Government auditing standards incorporate the above criteria and add the additional or supplemental standard requiring:

Working papers should contain sufficient information to enable an experienced auditor having no previous connection with the audit to ascertainfrom them the evidence that supports the auditor's significant conclusions and judgements.

And, in 1999, the government auditing standards, relative to working papers, were also amended to require:

In planning the audit, auditors should document in the working papers (1) the basis for assessing control risk at the maximum level for assertions related to material account balances, transaction classes, and disclosure components of financial statements when such assertions are significantly dependent upon computerized information systems, and (2) consideration that the planned audit procedures are designed to achieve audit objectives and to reduce audit risk to an acceptable level.

To the two-fold purpose of working papers noted above, government auditing standard adds a third purpose: working papers allow for the review of audit quality by providing the reviewer written documentation of the evidence supporting the auditors' significant conclusions and judgments.

This additional purpose is occasioned by the fact that the working papers related to audits of public sector entities will be passed-along and reviewed by successions of auditors as governments rotate their audits among various accounting organizations. Plus, the General Accounting Office, as an agent of Congress, along with several federal inspectors general, and possibly state or local government auditors, could also review public sector audit working papers.

CONTENT OF WORKING PAPERS

Generally Accepted Standards

Generally accepted auditing standards require working papers to show that the accounting records agree or reconcile with the financial statements and that applicable audit standards of field work have been observed. While recognizing that the quantity, type, and content of working papers will vary with circumstances, these standards require that the working papers ordinarily include documentation to show:

(1) The work has been adequately planned and supervised—observance of the first standard of field work.

(2) A sufficient understanding of the internal control structure has been obtained to plan the audit and to determine the nature, timing, and extent of tests to be performed—complying with the second standard of field work.

(3) The audit evidence obtained, the auditing procedures applied, and the testing performed have provided sufficient competent evidential matter to afford a reasonable basis for an opinion—indicating observance of the third standard of field work.

The profession's standards recognize that "the form and content of which should be designed to meet the circumstances;" the nature and extent of evidence contained in working papers is dependent upon auditor judgment. But, generally accepted auditing standards note that the auditor's judgment about quantity, type, and content of the working papers should be affected by several factors including: the nature of the engagement; the nature of the auditor's report; the nature of the statements or other information on which the auditor is to report; nature and condition of the auditee's records, assessed level of control risk; and needs in the particular circumstances for supervision and review.

The exercise of judgment notwithstanding, generally accepted standards require the preparation and maintenence of working papers for audit procedures applied, audit tests performed, audit evidence obtained and support for the auditors pertinent conclusions. To achieve this, the generally accepted standards suggest that examples of working papers should include: audit programs, analyses, memoranda, letters of confirmations, management and attorney letters of representations, abstracts of auditee documents, schedules or commentaries prepared or obtained by the auditor, plus tapes, films or other media.

Government Audit Standards

Discussing working paper content, the government auditing standards impose other criteria stating that working papers for government audits should additionally contain:

(1) the objective, scope, and methodology, including any sampling criteria used, and the results of the audit;

(2) evidence of the work performed to support findings, judgments, and conclusions; and

(3) evidence of supervisory reviews of the work conducted.

282   Government Auditing: Standards and Practices

The 1994 GAO revision of its government auditing standards differs from the 1988 edition of the government auditing standards, which contained more detailed guidance. In 1988, there existed a supplemental government field audit standard that working papers for audit of public sector auditees should contain the following data, which seems to still be the expectation of some federal inspectors general:

(a) Contain a written audit program, cross-referenced to the working papers;

(b) Contain the objective, scope, methodology, and results of the audit;

(c) Contain sufficient information so that, supplementary oral explanations are not required;

(d) Be legible with adequate indexing and cross-referencing, and include summaries and lead schedules, as appropriate;

(e) Restrict included information to matters that are materially important and relevant to the objectives of the audit; and

(f) Contain evidence of supervisory reviews of the work conducted.

It is clear that under neither generally accepted nor government auditing standards, will working papers that consist solely of an audit plan, audit programs and checklists, even if annotated or initialed, satisfy these criteria. These are audit tools that must be referenced or indexed to gathered evidence in working papers describing the specific work performed, how exceptions and unusual matters were disclosed, examined, resolved or treated or reported by the auditor and any appropriate comments relating to conclusions and recommendations on significant aspects of the audit. An underlying premise of the government auditing standards for working papers is that well-planned, complete working papers should provide information for several purposes, eliminating the need for successor auditors and reviewers to re-examine the same documents or conduct similar tests to obtain information needed for a variety of reporting purposes.

Working Papers on Tests of Controls

The existence and effective functioning of an auditee's system of controls are critical to the planning of audits, whether of a private sector or public sector entity. One of the basic generally accepted field work audit standards requires auditors to understand the auditee's internal control structure as a prerequisite to planning the audit. For less complex control systems or in the auditor's judgment, an election can be made to not rely on the control structure and conduct increased substantive tests of transactions and accounts. For generally accepted auditing standards communication of reportable conditions and material weakness in the control structure is typically limited to the auditor and the auditee.[1] There exists no standard to make a report on controls external to the auditee organization.

The review of controls in audits of public sector entities, for purposes other than planning the audit, is given greater weight and requires different reporting and more detailed working papers.

Government Standards Relating to Controls

As noted, unless controls of a private sector auditee contain very significant weaknesses, the auditor is not required to make a reporting to management; but in any event, the conditions concerning controls are never reported external to the auditee organization. In contrast, government auditing standards require that tests be made of controls and a public external reporting be made and Single Audits contain more specific audit requirements.

Government auditing standards place different audit and different reporting requirements on auditors of public sector financial statements with respect to controls. The government auditing standards require the auditor's report on the financial statements to describe the scope of the testing of internal controls and present the results of those tests or refer to separate reports containing that information. Also, in making this separate reporting on the tests of controls, auditors must include all reportable conditions relating to the controls. The government standards require auditors to include an introduction summarizing key findings in the audit report of the financial statements and the related controls audit work. This introduction or summary is not a stand-alone report. If an auditor elects to report separately on the audit work related to controls, the audit report for the financial statements must state that these separate additional reports are being issued.

Single Audit Requirements for Control Tests

In the conduct of single audits, the Single Audit Act requires that auditors shall for every major federal program (1) obtain an understanding of internal controls; (2) assess the control risk; and (3) perform tests of controls unless controls are deemed to be ineffective. When reporting on any single audit, the federal regulation, OMB Circular A-133 requires that the single audit report contain a statement as to whether reportable conditions in internal controls over major programs

---

[1] Generally accepted standards define *reportable conditions* as matters, in the auditor's judgment that should be communicated to the audit committee because these matters represent significant deficiencies in the design or operation of the internal control structure which could adversely affect the auditee's ability to record, process, summarize, and report financial data consistent with the management assertions in the financial statements. A *material weakness* is a reportable condition in which the design or operation of one or more of the internal control structure elements does not reduce to a relatively low level the risk that errors or irregularities in amounts that would be material in relation to the financial statements being audited may occur and not be detected within a timely period by employees in the normal course of performing their assigned functions.

by the audit and whether any such conditions were material weaknesses.[2]

Working Papers on Control Tests

Separate folders or sections of the working papers should be established to document in narrative, questionnaires, checklists, and flow charts the various systems applications and controls examined. These working papers might include evidence of:

- Major operating procedures followed by the auditee personnel

- Key accounting documents and forms processed by the systems

- Flows of information from initiation of the transactions to ultimate recordation in the formal accounts of the systems

- Authorization and approval limits for all transactions—receipts, disbursements, procurements, personnel actions, property acquisition and disposition, etc.—often referred to as prevention type controls.

- Descriptions and assessments of validation checks and controls, such as pre-disbursement validation of documents prior to issuing checks or the existence of an effective internal audit function—often referred to as examples of detect type controls.

- Adequacy of fiscal, accounting and management systems to ensure adherence to governmental allowable cost principles and other criteria related to financial execution of a program.

- Policies, procedures and practices relating to controls for ensuring and monitoring compliance with laws and regulations and with terms and conditions of contracts, grants and other agreements.

For audits made pursuant to the Single Audit Act, the federal Office of Management and Budget has established more specific criteria that must be documented with respect to an auditor's test of controls. In the case of single audits, the working papers must contain evidence documenting:

- The significant internal accounting controls of the auditee

- Those controls designed to provide reasonable assurance that federal programs are being managed in compliance with applicable laws and regulations.

- Those specific controls that the auditor tested and evaluated

- Those specific controls that the auditor did not test.

---

[2] The Single Audit Act defines a major federal program as the larger of $300,000 or 3 percent of total federal expenditures for all programs of that auditee, where the total expenditures for all federal programs exceed $300,000 but are less than $100 million. In the case of larger auditees, the dollar criteria rises to $3 million and $30 million for major programs.

Further, the working papers related to the test of controls must fully describe all reportable conditions and any material weaknesses disclosed as a result of the evaluation of the controls.

To simultaneously comply with both generally accepted as well as government auditing standards, working papers in support of tests of specific controls, systems, transaction cycles or groups of transactions should be formatted in a manner that will address or clearly document:

● Transaction test objectives—what controls are intended to be tested and the possible or anticipated errors, issues, or problems

● Universe for tests—including universe sizes, activities included within the universe, anticipated control exceptions

● Sampling—judgmental or statistical sampling—including sampling plan descriptions, size, confidence levels (for statistical procedures), estimated error rates or anticipated issues and methods of sample selection

● Detailed record of all steps applied to test or sample controls by cycles, including transactions, accounts, etc.

● Auditor's conclusions concerning controls and the effect of the test results on other auditing procedures to be used during the balance of the audit.

Working Papers on Tests of Compliance

Government Standards Relating to Compliance.

Government auditing standards give a primacy to testing of compliance with laws and regulations and require that such tests be reported. The Single Audit Act places an even higher responsibility on the auditor requiring an opinion on the auditee's compliance with laws, regulations, and conditions of contracts and grants. The extent of this testing and the reporting to parties external to the auditee is beyond the requirements of generally accepted auditing standards. The American Institute of Certified Public Accountants characterizes the auditor's role in compliance auditing as one of the most significant environmental differences between private sector and governmental auditing.

Generally accepted auditing standards have no requirement specifically related to tests for compliance with laws, regulations, contracts and grants, nor do these standards impose any external reporting requirements on the auditor relating to such compliance tests. However, considerable emphasis and audit responsibilities appear in the government auditing standards. The government's field work standard requires auditors to design audits providing reasonable assurance that financial statements are free of material misstatements resulting from violations of laws and regulations that have a direct and material effect on the determination of financial statement amounts.

Further, government standards require auditors of public sector entities to report on these tests for compliance, stating that the report on the financial statements should describe the scope of the auditors' testing of compliance with laws and regulations, present the results of those tests, and refer to separate reports containing that information. In presenting the results of compliance tests, auditors should report irregularities, illegal acts, other material noncompliance, and reportable conditions in internal controls. In some circumstances, auditors must report irregularities and illegal acts directly to parties external to the audited entity.

In the compliance report, the government standards require the auditors to include an introduction summarizing the key findings in the audit of the financial statements and the related compliance audit work. The government auditing standards state that this introduction should not be issued as a stand-alone report. If an auditor elects to report separately on the audit work related to compliance, the audit report for the financial statements must state that these separate additional reports are being issued.

Single Audit Requirements for Compliance Tests

In conduct of single audits, the Single Audit Act requires that auditors shall determine whether the non-federal entity complied with provisions of laws, regulations, and contracts or grants that have a direct and material effect on each major program. And, when reporting on any single audit, the federal regulation OMB Circular A-133 requires that the single audit report for compliance contain an audit opinion (or disclaimer of opinion) as to whether the auditee complied with laws, regulations, and provisions of contracts or grants which could have a direct and material effect on each major program. This audit opinion does not appear in either the generally accepted or the government auditing standards.

Working Papers on Compliance Tests

It is evident from these field work and audit reporting standards and requirements that audits of public sector entities require greater emphasis on audit procedures employed to examine and also report on auditees' compliance with laws and regulations. As noted in an earlier chapter, there are 14 specific tests that must be made for compliance when conducting a single audit, in addition to the tests made for assuring entity-wide compliance with laws and regulations, contracts and grants.

Since an audit opinion on the results of compliance testing must be provided for each major federal program, many auditors have elected to select and then test samples from each major federal program. Structuring compliance tests by each major program permit the compilation of evidence on tests planned, tests performed and test results for each major program. When audit samples on tests for compliance are selected from the entire universe of major program transactions, demonstration of adequacy of test is more difficult and the sufficiency of audit evidence may not be as apparent with respect to the individual major federal program. In many instances, tests of compliance with laws and regulations for one major program will disclose little or no information about other major federal programs. Most federal programs are authorized by different laws and auditees are required to comply with different federal regulations.

Separate folders or sections of the working papers should be established to document in narrative, questionnaires, and checklists the tests made of a major federal program to conclude the extent of an auditee's compliance with laws, regulations, contracts and grants. These working papers might include evidence of:

- Policies, procedures and practices relating to controls for ensuring and monitoring compliance with laws and regulations and with terms and conditions of contracts, grants and other agreements.

- Major operating procedures followed by the auditee personnel, for the entity as a whole and for each major program, to ensure compliance with applicable with laws, regulations, contracts and grants.

- Authorization and approval and other checks and controls to ensure the auditee's operations, activities and financial expenditures, for the entity as a whole and for each major program, comply with applicable with laws, regulations, contracts and grants.

- Adequacy of fiscal, accounting and management systems to ensure adherence to governmental allowable, unallowable and indirect cost principles and other financial criteria related to financial activities, entity-wide and for each major program.

- Those controls designed to provide reasonable assurance that federal programs are being managed in compliance with applicable laws and regulations.

- Those specific controls, entity-wide and for each major program, that the auditor tested and evaluated, plus an identification of and the reasons therefore of those compliance factors that the auditor did not test.

To simultaneously comply with government auditing standards and single audit requirements for tests of compliance, working papers in support of tests should be formatted in a manner that will address or clearly document:

● Transaction test objectives, entity wide and for each major federal program, outlining testing intentions and the possibility of anticipated errors, issues, or problems.

● Universe for tests, entity wide and for each major federal program, including universe sizes, activities included within the universe, anticipated exceptions.

● Sampling—judgmental or statistical sampling, including sampling plan descriptions, size, confidence levels (for statistical procedures), estimated error rates or anticipated issues and methods of sample selection, entity wide and for each major federal program.

● Detailed record of all steps applied to test or sample cycles, controls, transactions, accounts, etc., compiled for entity wide compliance tests and for compliance tests made of each major federal program.

● Auditor's conclusions and the effect of the compliance test results on other auditing procedures to be used during the balance of the audit related to the auditee's financial statement and each of the major federal programs operated by the auditee.

Working papers evidencing tests of compliance with laws and regulations should be indexed or compiled by specific laws and regulations in relation to the financial statement audit and the audit of individual major programs. If extensive testing for compliance is done, but the evidence of these tests is part of other audit procedures and in several working papers, the auditor should consider establishing specific working paper files to consolidate the evidence related to compliance testing to permit a ready analysis and assessment of the adequacy and totality of audit procedures performed.

WORKING PAPERS STRUCTURE AND PRACTICES

Working Papers by Cycle, Phases, Requirements

Mentioned above was a suggestion to establish separate working paper files, folders, sections, etc., for the major phases of a governmental financial statement audit and the single audit, establishing almost "stand alone" working papers for the statement audit, other working papers for tests of the control structure, and separate working papers for the review of compliance with laws and regulations.

This does not necessarily imply that an audit must be three separate efforts. To the contrary, a well-planned, coordinated audit is most desirable from the view of both the auditee and the auditor. But, subsequent internal and external reviews will be facilitated if the essential evidence to support the two levels of audits and the individual phases of an audit within these levels was aggregated or collected or compiled in separate binder(s).

To insure that accumulated evidence is gathered once, the auditor should consider developing the separate working papers for audit procedures relevant to the tests of controls, auditing procedures relating to compliance with laws and regulations, and evidence supporting audit opinions and reports on financial information. Similarly, if audit work or evidence obtained in other phases of the review is pertinent to areas of the single audit, that information should be cross referenced or reproduced in separate working papers for the single audit.

The compilation of separate sets of working paper files will ensure that the evidence in support of the statement audit, test of controls, or reviews for compliance comes closer to meeting the "stand alone" criteria of the government auditing standards, where such working papers would be understandable without the need for supplementary explanation. Separate working paper files would better permit, as required by the government standard " ... an experienced auditor having no previous connection with the audit subsequently to ascertain from them what work was performed to support the conclusions." Further, if an audit organization must undergo a federal on-site quality control review, separate working paper folders and files documenting the audit work performed by financial reviews, control reviews, and compliance reviews at both the financial statement level and the major federal program level will considerably assist in that exam.

Alternatively, explicit reconciling workpapers should be prepared to show the relationships and considerations of evidence obtained in other phases of the audit.

Types of Working Papers

A common practice for corporate audits is to divide working papers into two general categories—permanent and current working paper files. This same practice exists for governmental audits.

Permanent Working Papers

These files have the more historical and general nature, containing information applicable to recurring audits or audits of more than one year. Permanent working papers have extensive data relating to organization, policies, procedures, controls, systems, forms, and results of earlier research efforts with respect to applicable laws, regulations, contracts and grant agreements.

The term "permanent," however, does not connote unchanging: the information in permanent working papers must be kept current and updated annually for each audit.

Current Working Papers

These working papers contain the evidence of procedures followed, tests performed, conclusions reached, recommendations made, and other information relating to phases of the current audit. With respect to current working papers, auditors will generally use a referencing or annotation scheme for the financial audit that parallels the audit approach. For example, these working papers (supporting the tests of controls, transactions and accounts) might be grouped by "cycles," "accounting applications," "trial balance accounts or financial statement captions," depending upon the preferences of the auditor.

Indexing and Referencing Working Papers

Working papers for audits of only financial statements in accordance with only the generally acceptable auditing standards are more commonly indexed by the accounts—either within a cycle or the sequence of accounts in an entity's trial balance or the phases of the audit. This approach provides for good control over tests planned and performed in examining accounting and financial conditions.

This indexing approach is not as efficient, though, for relating the nonfinancial type data to the work performed, conclusions reached, and findings reported. Much searching, re-analysis, and possibly re-testing can be avoided by, alternatively, indexing working papers by accounting applications or principal phases of a governmental audit, in addition to the financial statement audit phases. Consideration should be given to preparation of summaries of data from various phases of the audit or copying or reconciling workpapers or requiring specific workpapers to show aggregates of data and facts supporting sections in the audit report.

Particularly, for nonfinancial audit aspects, consideration should be given to alternative work paper and report referencing techniques. For example, to support tests performed for compliance or internal controls, separate workpapers can be referenced to the steps in the audit plan, questionnaires, checklists and various audit programs. Reports, or sections or paragraphs of the reports, or specific findings in a report might be referenced to a specific binder that has all of the essential evidence to support that section of the report.

An indexing scheme that relates the audit plan to audit programs to working papers will help insure that no significant test is omitted or reporting responsibility overlooked. Additionally, indexing schemes related to the audit plan or programs will minimize the redundant or duplicate audit efforts that can occur if a source is not referenced and used to both control the work performed as well as assist in evaluating the adequacy of the evidence accumulated for particular phases of a multi-phase audit. The indexing scheme that references sections of the audit report, itself, to the audit plan, programs and supporting working papers would better ensure that reported observations are adequately supported by the acquired evidence.

REVIEWS OF WORKING PAPERS

Audit working papers that support audits made pursuant to government auditing standards and the single audit can and will be scrutinized by many in and out of government, auditors or non auditors:

• All federal laws provide as a condition of acceptance of federal financing, that the Congressional investigators, General Accounting Office and the many federal inspectors general have access and rights to review all records and documents, including working papers of audits paid with government funds, related to programs funded by the federal government.

• Annually the audits for tens of thousands of governmental and non-profit entities are subjected to desk reviews by staffs of federal inspectors general or by accounting firms under contract to the inspectors general. Then, hundreds of these audits also undergo detailed on-site quality control reviews by federal agencies and, in some cases, by designated state auditors. These reviews are in essence "audits of the auditor" and include exhaustive reviews of the auditor's working papers.

• With few exceptions, the tenure of the audit relationship between an audit firm and a governmental entity is considerably shorter than is the case in the private sector. In most instances, audit contracts do not exceed five years, with possibly a permitted renewal for another five years after which the audit firm is required to sever the audit relationship for a specified time. To ensure that all audit knowledge is not lost, some governments make it a requirement of the audit contract that the working papers of the predecessor auditor be made available to the successor auditor.

• The audit contract between audit firms and state and local governments can include a condition that the governmental auditors can access and review working papers related to audits and evaluations of the contracting government.

• Underscoring the government's desire to minimize duplicate audit efforts, the Single Audit Act requires that audits conducted in accordance with its provisions shall be in lieu of any financial audits of federal awards which a non-federal entity is required to undergo under any federal law or regulation. Implicit in this proviso, is the intent that audit information will be shared between government and non-government and by various levels of governments.

● Additionally, the Single Audit Act states that to the extent a single audit meets a federal agency's needs, the agency shall rely upon and use such audits. This law states that any additional audits shall be planned and performed in such a way as to build upon the work performed by other auditors.

OWNERSHIP, ACCESS AND RETENTION OF WORKING PAPERS

Ownership and Custody

Working papers issues—who owns them, who retains them, who has access to them—are important.

Attention must be given to these subjects by any auditor before acceptance of a governmental audit contract. Auditors must closely examine the terms and conditions of each audit contract. There are no standard contracts, nor do audit contracts contain similar "boilerplate" terms. Each is uniquely drafted by the individual contracting government.

Generally, in the absence of conditions to the contrary, working papers belong to the auditor. But, typically, there will be conditions to the contrary. Even without specific reference to working paper ownership or custody, governments under broader conditions may claim that all working papers, reports, and records compiled or related to the audit are property paid for and acquired by the government and, further, that the original copy of all working papers be delivered to the government at the conclusion of the audit. Further, still, there can be instances when, by accepting the terms of a government audit contract, the auditor automatically waives rights to ownership and custody. In these circumstances, the working papers must be transferred in their entirety to the government at the conclusion of the audit.

When a contract for a government audit states that the entity procuring the audit has ownership of the audit working papers, the auditor agrees to perform an audit subject to such conditions and must comply with this condition. In such instances, the auditor should at the outset insist on the right to copy the working papers to ensure retention of a complete record of the work performed. Because of confidentiality or other considerations, a government may not grant the right to copy the working papers. This caution is predicated on the fact that the conditions of an executed contract prevail, and once the working papers are released to the contracting government, the auditor may be precluded thereafter from obtaining a copy.

It is not unreasonable for governments to assume that all property acquired, accumulated, or compiled under a government contract belongs to the government, unless there are specific conditions to the contrary. Also, governments, with some basis, believe that they should have title since many audit contracts are with individual firms for limited time periods and the transition to subsequent auditors will leave the government with no records of the audits made by predecessor auditors.

This is not quite the same issue when auditing private sector entities, where the transitions of auditors are less frequent. In fact, many private corporations have retained the same audit firm for decades, which will never be the case with a governmental entity.

Generally accepted standards make reference to who owns audit working papers, but the reference is brief and may not totally address the circumstances of a government audit. For example, the generally accepted auditing standards state:

"Working papers are the property of the auditor, and some states have statutes that designate the auditor as owner of the working papers. The auditor's rights of ownership, however are subject to ethical limitations relating to the confidential relationship with clients."

The government auditing standards, for financial as well as performance audits, are silent on the subject of ownership of working papers. Reference is made in the field and performance auditing standards for government audits that auditors must ensure that working papers will be made available, upon request, to other government audit staff and individual auditors, and the contractual arrangements should provide for this access.

Working Paper Access

The ownership of the workpapers will often not be in dispute, but access to working papers may be the subject of discussions between government reviewers, the specific government auditee and the auditor. Typically, the right of access will have been unknowingly waived by federal recipients as a conditions precedent to accepting federal assistance, since an access to records clause is a standard condition in almost every law involving federal funding, plus all federal contracts, cooperative agreements, loans, loan guarantees and other forms of federal financial assistance.

Thus, because of laws, regulations, audit contracts, or terms and conditions of federal financial awards, auditees may have agreed as a condition precedent to accepting federal funds, that the funder would have access to all records of the contract, grant or financial assistance, including the auditor's working papers. Under such circumstances, the auditor must acknowledge the rights of these organizations to the working papers.

In July 1994, an interpretation was issued by a task force of the Auditing Standards Board of the AICPA relating to the access of a "regulator" (defined by the AICPA as including federal, state, and local government officials with legal authority over the audited entity).[3] This interpretation states that upon receipt of a request for access to working papers that is made pursuant to law, regulation, or audit contract, auditors should:

(a) Consider advising the client of the request (including photocopies) and the auditor's intent to comply;

(b) Make appropriate arrangements with the regulator for the review;

(c) Maintain control over original working papers; and

(d) Consider submitting the form letter prescribed in this (July 1994) interpretation to the regulator.

When confronted with a request to access working papers, auditors should not grant access without considering the simultaneous transmission of the letter outlined in the July 1994 interpretation. If the regulator engages another party to conduct the working paper review, the auditor must be satisfied that this party is subject to the same confidentiality restrictions as the regulator itself. There may be some instances where a regulator requests access, but that right of access is not otherwise required by law, regulation or audit contract. In these cases, the AICPA cautions the auditor to consider consulting with legal counsel regarding the request.

The AICPA is clear on the fact that providing access to or photocopies of working papers does not constitute transfer of ownership or authorization to the regulator to make the information available to any other party.

Working Paper Retention

The AICPA standards require working papers be retained to meet the needs of the practice and to satisfy any pertinent legal requirements. In practice, the legal requirements will dictate, since this period is often the longer. For example, federal contracts routinely require the retention of all records relating to the audit engagement contract, and this will include retaining working papers, for a period of at least three years after final payment for the audit services. And, this period could

---

[3] Auditing Interpretation, AU Section 339, "Working Papers," Providing Access to or Photocopies of Working Papers to a Regulator, AICPA, New York, Journal of Accountancy, July 1994, pp 108, 110.

be extended if there is litigation or a claim or an audit is in process or if findings have not been resolved.

Under a federal audit contract, the retention period generally starts from the date of submission of the last invoice for the audit services rendered or submission of an invoice for final payment, whichever is later or specified in the audit contract. Auditors must, therefore, adopt reasonable procedures for safe custody of working papers and must retain the working papers for a period sufficient to meet the needs of the practice and to satisfy any pertinent external requirements of records retention.

OMB (in OMB Circular A-133, the implementing regulation for the single audit concept) requires that working papers and audit reports be retained for a minimum of three years from the date of the audit report. And, the cognizant federal agency can extend this retention period by written notification.

Further, a longer retention period might be required by the conditions of the specific federal assistance agreements executed between the federal government and the auditee. While the auditor may not have been a contractual party between the federal and state governments, for instance, the auditor would be bound by these conditions if the audit contract was accepted subject to the federal-state assistance contract or agreement.

AUDIT EVIDENCE

The government auditing standards do not specifically address the level, nature, or sufficiency of evidence that an auditor should observe or otherwise examine, collect and retain when conducting a financial statement or financially-related audit. In this connection, reliance is placed on the generally accepted auditing standards for definition and clarification. This omission in the government auditing standards has not been of concern to practicing auditors who have for years applied the third field standard to their audits of governments:

Sufficient competent, evidential matter is to be obtained through inspection, observation, inquiries, and confirmations to afford a reasonable basis for an opinion regarding the financial statement under audit.

Financial Data Assertions

Evidential matter is compiled by the auditor to support the evaluations and conclusions about the audited financial statements and the assertions made by management with respect to amounts and balances appearing on the audited financial statements. In government, as in audits of corporate entities, these assertions or representations are embodied or implicit in the financial statements proffered by management for audit or examination.

The several assertions of management described in the generally accepted auditing standards relate to: existence or occurrence, completeness, rights and obligations, valuation or allocation, and presentation and disclosure. But, in addition to these assertions, for audits pursuant to government auditing standards, and the more detailed requirements related to audits under the Single Audit Act must be tested, for example:

- With respect to the receipts and expenditure of all public funds, there is an assertion by public sector executives that nature, timing, purpose and amount of expenditure of public monies is in compliance with appropriate laws, statutes, regulations and governmental rules.

- Specific assertions are explicit that public monies be expended:

a. For only allowable services;

b. To only eligible participants or recipients designated by law;

c. Pursuant to agreements by recipients to match, provide a specific level of support effort or resources or earmarking in relation to the expended funds;

d. And reported pursuant to agreed-to conditions;

e. In compliance with all special conditions and provisions related to individual government program criteria.

- With respect to the Single Audit Act, there is an assertion by all recipients of federal financial assistance (and the explicit requirement of Congress) that there are internal control systems to provide reasonable assurance that federal programs are managed in compliance with laws and regulations.

- Governmental programs operated under cost-reimbursement contracts, government grants, and cooperative agreements generally dictate that only certain types or levels of cost—i.e., only allowable costs—are charged and billed to the government program and all unallowable costs have been excluded from claims for reimbursement.

Accounting Data

To audit or test these assertions, the auditor develops audit plans, audit programs, and audit procedures to search for corroborating evidence of compliance with these assertions. Generally accepted auditing standards define some of that supporting evidential matter as consisting of the certain underlying accounting data. But, generally accepted auditing standards note, that by itself, accounting data cannot be considered sufficient support for financial statements. Included within the term, "underlying accounting data" would be:

"... books of original entry, the general and subsidiary ledgers, related accounting manuals, and such informal and memorandum records as work sheets supporting cost allocations, computations, and reconciliation's ...."

Sufficient evidential matter also consists of other corroborating information available to or disclosed by the auditor. Corroborating evidential matter, defined in generally accepted standards, encompass a broad range of knowledge acquired by the auditor through a variety of practices, such as:

● Documentary material such as checks, invoices, contracts, and minutes of meetings;

● Confirmations and other written representations by knowledgeable people;

● Information obtained by the auditor from inquiry, observation, inspection, and physical examination;

● Other information developed by or available to the auditor which permits the auditor to reach conclusions through valid reasoning.

Statement on Auditing Standard No. 48, requires that auditors test this underlying data by analysis and review, retracing certain procedural steps of the accounting and financial statement compilation process, developing work sheets and allocations, by recalculation, and by reconciling types and applications of this information. The generally accepted standards point out that in a soundly conceived and carefully maintained system of accounting records there is an internal consistency discoverable through such audit procedures that will constitute persuasive evidence that financial statements, results of operations, and cash flows are in conformity with generally acceptable accounting principles.

Also, documentary information and corroborating evidence is available to the auditor both: (1) from within the audited entity, and (2) from external sources. Generally, evidence obtained externally that confirms management assertions is considered to have greater weight, having been obtained from sources independent of the audited entity. Auditing standards recognize that the auditor will, at times, have to reach conclusions on less than persuasive evidence. Nonetheless, the evidence that is relied upon must be valid and relevant.

Sufficiency of Audit Evidence

Government auditing standards for *financial statement audits* and *financial related audits* are silent on the subject of evidence, placing reliance on generally accepted auditing standards of the profession. However, the government auditing standards for *performance audits* do address evidence and provide guidance that could be appropriate and of assistance to an auditor examining a government's financial statement, or when performing financial related audits of public entities and single audits. For example, the fifth field work standard for performance audits requires:

> *"Sufficient, competent, and relevant evidence is to be obtained to afford a reasonable basis for the auditors" findings and conclusions. A record of the auditor work is to be retained in the form of working papers. ..."*

This standard categorizes evidence into four groupings: physical, documentary, testimonial and analytical.

Physical Evidence. This evidence is obtained by direct inspection or observation of people, property, or events. The physical evidence may be documented in memoranda summarizing the matters inspected or observed, photographs, charts, maps, or actual samples.

Documentary Evidence. This evidence consists of created information such as letters, contracts, accounting records, invoices, and management information on performance.

Testimonial Evidence. This evidence is obtained from other people through statements received in response to audit inquiries, audit interviews, or response to audit questionnaires. Of course, such evidence must be further evaluated to assess the potential bias of respondents or whether respondents have full or partial knowledge of the subject.

Analytical Evidence. This evidence includes the auditor's computations, comparisons, reasoning, and separation of information into components.

Another performance audit field standard, No. 5, states that audit evidence should be sufficient, competent, and relevant and provides the following definitions of these criteria.

Sufficiency of Evidence. Evidence is sufficient if there is enough of it to support the auditor's findings, meeting a reasonableness test if the following question can be answered: Is there enough evidence to persuade a reasonable person of the validity of the auditor's finding?

In this regard, auditors must use the test of "persuasiveness" as distinguished from a test that the evidence is "conclusive." No audit contract provides the funds, time or other resources to gather all the evidence that might be needed to meet the legal test of "beyond any doubt" or even "beyond a reasonable doubt." As pointed out by the AICPA (AU § 326.21), the auditor must work within economic limits: the audit opinion must be formed within a reasonable length of time, at reasonable costs, within specific time limits, and based on evidence that is persuasive rather than convincing.

Competency of Evidence. Evidence is competent to the extent the data is consistent with fact (i.e., evidence is competent if it is valid). The government auditing standards provide the following assumptions related to competency:

● Evidence from a credible external source is more competent than that obtained from the audited entity.

● Evidence developed under an effective system of controls is more competent than that obtained where such controls are weak or nonexistent.

● Evidence obtained by the auditor's direct physical examination, observation, computation, and inspection is more competent than evidence obtained indirectly.

● Original documents provide more competent evidence than copies.

● Testimonial evidence obtained under conditions where persons can speak freely is more credible than that obtained under compromised conditions.

Relevancy of Evidence. Evidence is relevant if it has a logical, sensible relationship to the audit finding.

Government auditing standards permit obtaining written representations concerning the competency of other evidence obtained. Written representations, under both generally accepted and the government standards, are an audit procedure to assist in confirming oral representations received by the auditor; to indicate and document the continuing appropriateness of such representations; and to reduce the possibility of misunderstanding of subjects cited in the representations.

Other methods of evidence gathering, acceptable under the government's auditing standards, include the use of questionnaires, structured interviews, and direct observations. Auditors can and must use data prepared by the auditee, but the auditing standards require that other evidence be obtained to corroborate this type of information. Similarly, data gathered by third parties must be independently verified. Data from computer-based systems must be tested for validity and reliability to the same extent as data from manual systems or other sources.

AUDIT TESTING

The testing concept, well-established and accepted for audits of private sector entities, applies equally to audits of governments. The scope paragraph of the auditor's opinion for public sector audits states:

> *"An audit includes examining, on a test basis, evidence supporting the amounts and disclosures in the general-purpose financial statements. An audit also includes assessing*

the accounting principles used and significant estimates made by management, as well as evaluating the overall general-purpose financial statement presentation."

Like audits of private entities, the initial phases of a government audit must include reviews, inquiries, tests, observations about the design of relevant policies and procedures and records pertaining to compliance with laws and regulations, and elements of the internal control structure. The objective, ultimately, is to provide a basis for determining the nature (what is to be audited), extent (how much is to be audited) and timing (when audit procedures are to be applied) of the audit procedures to be applied in the examination of transactions and account balances. Such an effort is necessary to plan any audit.

A subsequent phase—testing of compliance and controls—is directed towards the effectiveness of the design or the operational implementation of the policy or procedure. Often "tests of controls" are done concurrently with tests of transactions.

Substantive Audit Tests

The review and testing of controls is followed by the more detailed audit phases, during which an auditor will employ three types of tests, referred to as substantive audit tests:

(1) *Tests of classes of transactions.* The verification of the accuracy of amounts recorded for classes or categories of transactions by the application of more than one audit procedure. Tests of controls and the substantive test of transactions are often done concurrently and can often be done at some interim period before year end, provided that appropriate follow-up tests are conducted at year-end.

(2) *Tests of account balances.* The verification of the accuracy of amounts recorded as balances of accounts by the application of more than one audit procedure, with additional emphasis on the end of period valuation and precision of cut-off procedures for recordation of transactions in the accounts.

(3) *Analytic review procedures.* Analytic procedures are to be used for the following purposes: (a) to assist the auditor in planning the nature, timing, and extent of other auditing procedures; (b) as a substantive test to obtain evidential matter about particular assertions through tests of transactions and end of year tests of account balances; and (c) as an overall assessment of the financial information in the final review stage of the audit. Analytic procedures must be applied to the same extent for government audits as is the case in audits of nongovernment entities. Analytic procedures include comparisons, analyses of data ratios external and internal to the audited entity, of data

Working Papers and Audit Evidence

between fiscal years and other periods; and of nonfinancial as well as financial information.

The acceptance of testing or sampling is based on the reporting premise that the auditor's opinion attests to the fair presentation or reasonableness and not the absolute correctness of balances in the government's financial statements or other reports. As with private sector audits, the auditor is not a guarantor of the reported financial data, nor is detection of fraudulent or illegal acts a primary objective of financial statement audits. This is specifically recognized in the government auditing standard that states:

"An audit made in accordance with generally accepted government auditing standards will not guarantee the discovery of illegal acts or contingent liabilities resulting from them. Nor does the subsequent discovery of illegal acts committed during the audit period necessarily mean that the auditors performance was inadequate, provided the audit was made in accordance with these standards."

Pyramidal Concept

To provide a perspective on the nature of the audit testing, an auditor might view the structure or hierarchy of information as an inverted pyramid.

Financial statements, prepared from a trial balance of the general ledger accounts, are the more general or summarized presentation of data at the top of the inverted pyramid. The detailed transactions comprise the most specific, unaggregated elemental information, which once recorded and accumulated into an account is seldom re-examined unless a specific inquiry requires analysis at this level.

The auditor's opinion relates to the reasonableness of the overall financial statements. The opinion, however, is based on the sum total of all corroborating tests of details to insure the proper classification of accounts and amounts. This in turn reflects the totals of periodic repeated postings of transaction totals from journals and other records of original entry. The transaction totals in journals or other records of original entry (totaled monthly, bi-monthly, or even daily or real-time, if volume warrants) are the summation of a wide variety of transactions, sometimes annually in the millions for large entities, each having an economic consequence to the audited organization. Auditing the proprietary transactions (purchases, disbursements, payroll, capital acquisition, debt issuances) of government is similar to audits of private sector entities.

But, when auditing public sector entities there are other concerns. Governments are required by law and statute to insure compliance with laws and regulations and at all levels of government the budget is a most important law. For this reason, public sector entities, under generally accepted accounting principles, are required to concurrently operate a budgetary as well as proprietary basis of accounting system where actual transactions are, in a single accounting system, matched with available budgetary authority.

The requirement for budgetary accountability means that the life cycle of a governmental transaction begins earlier and involves more entries than would be the case in corporate accounting. The following abbreviated glossary is included to permit a review of the audit test methodology, in the case of a government's:

Appropriation—The specific legislative authorization to obligate or spend governmental resources for authorized governmental activities—a law that is continually monitored for compliance and possible over-obligation and over-expenditure.

Allotment—A subdivision of the legislative appropriation, often made by the chief executive officer, to operating departments or agencies of the government.

Commitment—An early reservation of appropriated funds for a specific purpose, which may or may not be formally recorded in the accounting records.

Encumbrance or obligation—A formal transaction-by-transaction reservation of appropriated funds to meet a legal obligation of the government which should precede the expenditure or disbursement of government funds.

Fund types—A grouping of similar funds (e.g., general, special revenues, capital projects, debt service, enterprise, internal service, and trust and agency) under generally accepted accounting principles for purpose of financial statement presentation.

Object classification of expenditures—The basic or elemental aggregation of financial transactions of a government (e.g., payroll, fringe benefits, equipment, contracts, grants, etc.)

Voucher/voucher schedule—A listing of approved payees submitted by the comptroller or finance office to the treasurer or disbursing agent for the purpose of having a check issued.

Accounting for the life cycle of a governmental transaction requires that a formal accounting entry be made for transactions within each of these several categories. Concerns for compliance with government appropriations laws and regulations require that audits of governments include detailed examination of obligations and expenditures, changes in appropriation balances, and the end-of-period balance of unexpended appropriations.

The testing methodology applicable to governmental entities causes the auditor to initially validate the appropriation or legal authorization approved by the legislative body and then proceed to more detailed records, from the general to the specific, from the highest level to the most detail. In governmental fund accounting this will include the following transaction tests of the following hierarchy or flow:

- The general purpose financial statements of the government, which include the entity-wide statements, the fund-type groupings and could include individual fund balances.

- Subordinate department or agency operating financial reports and at times departmental financial statements.

- Regular reports on the status of appropriations, usually including expenditures to date, unliquidated encumbrances, and the unencumbered balance of each appropriation.

- Continuous, perpetual accounting for commitments and reservations of funds appropriated for specific or contemplated expenditures.

- Periodic accountings for expended funds, confirmed liabilities and accruals that will report encumbered appropriated funds, generally by object classifications.

- Disbursement of funds for specific transactions by the treasury function.

UNIQUENESS OF GOVERNMENT AUDITS

Fund Accounting Audit Issues

A uniqueness of a governmental audit relates to the nature of accounting—fund accounting—that governments employ. Each fund or appropriation could be the accounting entity and be synonymous with an agency. But two or more appropriations might be accumulated into the funding or budget authority for larger operating departments or agencies. The entity-wide financial statements represent a further grouping or aggregation by fund-types for financial statement purposes.

The overall audit strategy should be outlined in a written audit plan that is in turn supported by numerous audit programs for each significant fund, account or account group within a fund. Model audit programs are widely available and used by practitioners to minimize audit costs and ensure comprehensive audits are made. These model audit programs must be tailored or customized for each governmental auditee.

Since most of the audit procedures contained in these programs are similar to those applied in audits of private sector auditees, the follow-

304   Government Auditing: Standards and Practices

ing sections will highlight audit concerns that are uniquely governmental. Audits of governments will be concerned with the existence of and compliance with terms and conditions and amounts appropriated by legislative bodies and spent by executive branches.

Executive branch officials have no authority, absent a legal appropriation, to obligate, encumber, or spend any public monies. A most basic requirement of a government audit is to ensure that legislated revenues are raised pursuant to the revenue appropriation legislation and that expenditures are incurred in strict compliance with expenditure appropriation legislation.

Audit procedures related to appropriated funds, in general, must include:

● A confirmation of a legislative appropriation and an identification of the key characteristics of the appropriation legislation, such as the amount, time period or availability of the appropriation for obligation and expenditure, and the purposes for which each appropriation may be spent.

● A determination of the end-of-period status of the appropriation and fund balances, including amounts expended, encumbered, committed, and otherwise unencumbered or uncommitted.

● An analysis of all changes in appropriated funds, including additions, deletions, transfers in and out of the fund, supplemental appropriation or augmentations, lapsed balances, deficiencies and surpluses and the terms and conditions related to these status.

● The test of transactions might include, among other audit procedure as:

—Confirmation of appropriation numbers, amounts, limitations, expenditure criteria, etc., imposed or detailed by the legislative branch.

—Validating the recordation of the revenue and expenditure appropriations in the accounts and the apportionment or allotment of the appropriation to departments or operating units of the government.

—Verifying the exercise of authority and approvals by executives who obligate and expend the governmental funds.

—Determining of agreement of periodic postings from journals, registers, intermediate records, and documents of support for original entry to the general ledger funds accounts.

—Testing of original documentation in support of specific transactions, including.

a. Examination of support documents and obtaining evidence to demonstrate compliance with law, policy, procedures, and contract and grant terms and conditions affecting the receipt or disbursement of funds.

b. Examination of the accuracy of accounting for tested transactions, including the authenticity of authorization, approval, account coding, recording, processing, posting, accumulating, and reporting of data.

c. Examination of support documentation for individual transactions and related control procedures and practices to ensure that government funds are properly and correctly committed, encumbered, expended and disbursed in strict accord with appropriation conditions and the amounts disbursed are reasonable in amount for the products or services received and amounts do not exceed any total or individual budgetary restriction.

Other Audit Concerns

In other respects, government audits differ from corporate audits, for example:

● The review of minutes of pertinent boards, the legislative function, and senior executive meetings, which are in considerably more detail and much more numerous than the minutes to the quarterly board of directors meetings or the annual stockholders meeting.

● The evaluation of budgetary controls will include identifying the applicable laws and regulations, testing procedures relating to the execution and control over adopted budgets, examining the support documents for the original and all budget amendments, and comparing final budgets to actual expenditures to determine any violations for overexpenditure.

● The legal representation letter(s) should be obtained from government attorneys, all counsel and outside legal firms with respect to pending litigation, contingent liabilities, legal matters, and other items that might materially impact the financial condition of the government. Such letters are more voluminous than encountered in a corporate audit due to the litigious area in which governments operate. Similarly, to be effective, numerous governmental executives should be solicited for end of audit representation letters.

● Assets of governments are subject to verification similar to those made for audits of corporate financial statements. But, the requirements of fund accounting and the accounting sanctity of the individual appropriations and funds complicate somewhat the tests of transactions and certain account balances. Fund accounting requires that the transactions affecting each appropriation or fund be segregated into double entry, self balancing records of proprietary and budgetary transactions and accounts. At the same time all expenditures must be monitored to insure that monies are disbursed for only the purposes and amounts and within the time periods for which the appropriation or fund is available.

Cash balances will often be maintained in several accounts and locations, all of which may have some legal basis, but which complicates the controls over and the counts of cash receipts and disbursements and increased nature of detailed tests that must be made. The failure to record or account for general fixed assets has been the primary reason for many governments receiving qualified audit opinions in past years. Today, most governments are recording these assets, although past practices preclude valuating the total cost of these assets.

• The audit of liabilities will follow closely the audit procedures applied to corporate type entities, except for the impact of the required budgetary accounting procedures. Governments must carefully classify liabilities to specific appropriations and funds. Further, unliquidated or outstanding encumbrances are treated by governments as legal contracts, with liabilities that will mature upon receipt of the ordered products or services.

Since many governments operate on a cash basis of accounting, no controls exist over invoices and monitoring of accounts payable throughout the year. At year end, though, the entity-wide financial statements must reflect expenditures that have been incurred, which requires that tests be made of the adequacy of reported accrued liabilities.

At times, extensive reliance must be placed on confirmations of payables and on specially requested vendors statements and tests of payments, minutes and other data subsequent to the year end to determine the extent of any unrecorded liabilities. Since fund accounting generates many inter-fund transactions, governmental auditors are particularly concerned that all interfund receivables are offset by interfund payables and vice-versa and the cost-accounting employed.

A common practice, and often a covenant of long-term debt contracts and agreements, is that regular cash deposits must be made to sinking funds for maturing debt principal and interest, which must be confirmed during each audit.

• Governmental revenues—taxes, fees, permits, fines, interest on bank accounts and investments, assessments, penalties, etc.—will be collected from a number of sources, although the largest is generally property taxes (in the case of city or municipal governments) and income and sales taxes (in the case of states). No uniformity of administrative function exists for the collection and custody of receipts. In some instances, all payments are received at a single office; other governments permit or are required to have different revenues collected by several officers and often at several locations.

● Receipts and expenditures related to contracts, grants and other agreements under which funds are received from other governments often require detailed audits of each instrument. The specificity of the financial assistance terms precludes overall testing for compliance generally. This is particularly true for those "major" federal financial assistance programs that must be audited pursuant to the Single Audit Act. Under this Act, since audit opinions must be rendered for each major federal program, each major federal program must be audited.

● These transactions, expenditures and purchasing and disbursements and the related support documents, that must be examined on a test basis parallel closely those that are likely to be encountered for similar transactions in a corporate audit. There is a similarity of records—purchase authorizations, purchase orders or contracts, receiving records, vendor invoices, and canceled checks. But, again, the accounting and possible noncompliance is complicated by the accounting precision necessitated by the appropriation or fund accounting practices of governments. Additionally, procurement practices are often codified in statutes, so noncompliance could be a reportable issue.

Among some exceptions will be the extensiveness of withholdings from amounts due to contractors, which if unaccounted for will be among the unrecorded liabilities at year end. Long-term leases for equipment, space, or other property are quite likely to be initially reported as operating leases and treated as current operating expenditures. More appropriate accounting might be to reclassify these transactions as "in-substance" acquisition of fixed assets, for which a corresponding long-term liability should be reflected in the accounts. Vendors invoices could be overlooked in compiling an inventory of year-end payables. Thus cash accounting, year-end accruals and commitments could easily be understated.

Chapter 12

Quality Control and Audit Oversight

In comparison to audits of private sector entities, audits of public sector entities are subject to considerably more scrutiny. In the performance of government audits, the auditor's work, itself, is subjected to different quality control requirements and reporting responsibilities and considerably more direct oversight by the federal government. Evidence of deficient and substandard audits, involving independent accountants are communicated routinely by federal inspectors general and some state audit organizations directly to state boards of accountancy and the American Institute of Certified Public Accountants.

The concerns and requirements applicable to the performance of government audits arise from several sources: the GAO in its government auditing standards, the AICPA through its monitoring of audit quality, and federal inspectors general and state auditors who perform oversight functions with respect to audits of state and local governments and other recipients of federal financial assistance.

QUALITY CONTROL REQUIREMENTS—GOVERNMENT AUDITING STANDARDS

The fourth general standard of the government auditing standard requires that:

> *"Each audit organization conducting audits in accordance with these standards should have an appropriate internal quality control system in place and undergo an external quality control review."*

Thus, by this standard, all audit organizations—government and nongovernment—to comply with government auditing standards must have two quality control systems or review processes in place: (1) an internal quality control system, and (2) an external quality control review program.

Internal Audit Quality Control System

In 1979, the generally accepted auditing procedures, required CPA firms with clients subject to the Securities and Exchange Commission regulations, to have an installed system of quality control, including written quality control policies and procedures and a system for monitoring auditing practices to ensure adherence to their written requirements. Subsequently, similar requirements were imposed on auditors of public sector entities. Since 1988, all audit organizations, in order to comply with government auditing standards, must establish an internal audit quality control system. This system of quality control should provide reasonable assurance:

(1) that applicable auditing *standards* have been adopted and are being followed, and

(2) that adequate audit *policies and procedures* have been established and are being followed.

Generally accepted auditing standards suggest that the nature, formality, extent, and implementation practices of an auditing organization's internal control system will vary depending on several factors: organization size, operating autonomy allowed to audit professionals, the number of offices, organizational structure, the nature of the audits performed and whether the audit organization is part of a governmental unit or is an independent certified public accountant.

The dedication of an audit organization and its senior management—the tone at the top—is essential to a sound system of internal control and the delivery of quality, professional audit services. As noted in the generally accepted auditing standards, the internal audit quality control system of an organization—the control policies, procedures and practices—affect the conduct of individual audit as well as the audit organization as a whole.

An internal quality control system for an audit organization should include written organizational policies and procedures outlining the practices required to meet the generally accepted auditing standards of the AICPA and the government auditing standards of the GAO. Some essential elements of a sound internal quality control system for an audit organization would include audit policies and procedures that result in the following practices:

1. Implementing a personnel development program that mandates required continuing professional education to ensure all professionals currently and continuously meet or exceed the professional auditing standards for their "industries" of interest and involvement, in particular governmental accounting and auditing.

2. Performing all governmental audits pursuant to written, uniquely developed audit plans and programs directed to comply with

audit criteria appearing in law and regulation, and that address the needs of the specific government activities and programs to be audited.

3. Implementing a mandated and enforced process of higher-level professional reviews of audits performed, related working papers prepared, and submitted audit reports that include personal sign-off by the supervising or senior level personnel, audit managers, partners and at least one partner-level person (in the case of a government audit organization) on all governmental audits.

4. Requiring that there be an independent second partner-level review of every audit and of the related audit reports by partner-level management having no other responsibilities for the audit, but who have personal experience with governmental accounting and auditing requirements.

5. Conducting annual quality assurance reviews of governmental audits by review teams comprised of the audit organization's personnel who are independent of the audits reviewed, but are experienced in public sector accounting and auditing requirements.

6. Requiring, for multi-office audit organizations, periodic consultation among senior audit management experts in public sector accounting and auditing requirements.

7. Requiring that multi-office audit organizations undergo periodic, probably annual, quality assurance reviews by review teams whose members are independent of any audits performed by the reviewed office, with a mandate that public sector audits must be included among the audits selected for quality assurance review.

Audit organizations specializing in public sector accounting and auditing, regardless of size, should consider formally documenting their audit planning, performance, review, and report procedures into appropriate manuals, pro-forma or specifically designed questionnaires, checklists, and workpapers. These documents or tools should then be used in all training and professional development programs to promote uniformity of practice among the professionals involved in public sector audits.

External System of Quality Review

In 1979, the generally accepted auditing procedures required CPA firms with clients subject to the Securities and Exchange Commission regulations, and those CPA firms of the AICPA's Division of CPA Firms, to submit to external peer reviews of the firm's accounting and audit practice, at a minimum, every three years. Since the 1988 edition, the government auditing standards have imposed similar requirements on all audit organizations conducting audits pursuant to these standards.

Since then, government auditing standards required audit organizations to have a quality control system that demands that there be an external review at least once every three years. The external reviewers of these audit organizations must examine and confirm that the internal quality control system is in place and is being followed. To meet this standard, external reviewers must be independent of the audit organization being reviewed, its staff, and the auditees whose audits are selected for review.

This governmental audit requirement for periodic external peer reviews is not limited to nongovernmental audit organizations, i.e., independent CPA firms. Governmental audit organizations, too, must have external peer reviews performed by teams that are not part of their government. Independent accounting firms must have external reviews performed by other accounting firms.

Of course, one audit organization can not review another organization that may have conducted its most recent external quality control review. And, members of external review teams must be qualified and have current knowledge of the type of audit work to be reviewed, and have experience with applying governmental accounting principles and auditing standards.

Governmental auditing standards require that the external quality control peer review team follow one of the following approaches in selecting audits for review:

(1) Select audits that provide a reasonable cross section of the audits that the audit organization made in accordance with the government auditing standards, or

(2) Select a reasonable cross-section of the organization's audits, including one or more audits made in accordance with government auditing standards.

Government auditing standards further require that the external quality control review include:

1. Reviews of the audit reports, working papers, and other necessary documents (e.g., correspondence, continuing education documents, etc.).

2. Interviews with the reviewed organization's professional staffs.

3. A written report prepared communicating the results of the external quality control review.

Non-government audit organizations, pursuant to the 1994 revision, seeking to enter into a contract to perform an audit under government auditing standards are required to provide a copy of their most recent external quality control peer review report to the party contracting for the audit. The government standards makes a distinction between the peer review "report" and the separate letter of comment that, at times, accompany the report. Firms must submit only the letter of comment. In Circular A-133, the Office of Management and Budget states that the external peer review report is one factor to be considered when auditees evaluate proposals for single audits of federal assistance programs.

All audit organizations, to comply with government auditing standards, should make their external quality control peer review report available to auditors using their work and to appropriate oversight bodies. The government auditing standards also recommend that auditor organizations make the report available to the public.

All audit organizations should have the required external peer review completed within three years from the date they start their first audit in accordance with government auditing standards. Subsequent external peer reviews should be completed within three years after issuance of the prior peer review report. External peer reviews conducted through or by the following organizations meet the requirements of government auditing standards: the American Institute of Certified Public Accountants, National Association of Local Government Auditors, the President's Council on Integrity and Efficiency (i.e., the common organization of the federal inspectors general), the Institute of Internal Auditors.

DESK REVIEWS AND QCRs BY FEDERAL INSPECTORS GENERAL

Federal agencies, acting through a committee of the President's Council on Integrity and Efficiency (the working organization of federal inspectors general coordinated by OMB) have established and published formal procedures for desk reviews (and for QCRs) to ensure the integrity of audits made of entities receiving federal financial assistance.

In practice, there has evolved a federal quality review system performed and managed by several inspectors general that include two levels of oversight:

(1) *desk reviews* by federal representatives or their agents of submitted government audit reports, and

(2) more detailed, on site, *quality control reviews* of the audit organizations by federal representatives.

OIG Desk Reviews of Single Audits

The desk review is a limited examination, at a central federal location, of public sector audit reports, with some communications transpiring between the federal reviewers and the auditor. The desk review is an off-site examination by federal representatives of the form and content of the audit report. Inspectors general staff conducting the desk reviews will not have, at that time, access to the underlying audit working papers to permit an assessment of the quality of audit work actually performed.

During the 1980s, due to a concern by Congress and the reliance that federal managers desired to place on government audits, most single audit reports underwent a quality control desk review. Almost every independent accounting firm had at least one of their audit reports relating to the Single Audit Act of 1984 reviewed. The desk reviews, made pursuant to a standard questionnaire and checklist, are directed towards establishing the qualification and independence of the auditor and the completeness of the several required components of the audit reports (e.g., the financial statements, compliance report, internal control report, and the auditor's comments on corrective action).

In some instances, the results of the desk reviews are used by the federal government as the basis for identifying those audit organizations that should be subjected to more comprehensive on-site QCRs.

Generally, audit reports of public sector entities undergo a desk review within 30 calendar days from receipt of the audit report by the federal agency, if a desk review is to be made. An audit organization may be notified directly by the federal agency or through the audited governmental entity of any inadequacies or questions relating to the submitted audit report.

For maximum utility, a single audit report should contribute to the management of programs by eliminating or reducing the need for special reviews or additional inquiries or repetitive site visits to the audited entity. Thus, an important objective of a federal desk review is to determine whether the information reported by the auditor is sufficient to facilitate resolution of the audit findings by a federal program executive If the audit findings do not contain sufficient information for resolution, the federal agency will make such a fact known to the audited entity and require that the entity arrange or obtain corrective action from the responsible auditor.

Problems Disclosed in Desk Reviews

By definition, a desk review is a limited evaluation of only the facts appearing in the audit report. No working papers are available to the federal representative at the time of the desk review. Thus, it is not possible for the federal representative to assess the quality of the audit work itself. But even with this limitation, these reviews disclosed problems with a significant percentage of the reports examined.

During the early years of the Single Audit Act, federal representatives would complete more than 15,000 desk reviews annually. In follow-up reports to Congress, the U.S. General Accounting Office reported several categories of problems such as the failure of auditors to: identify instances of noncompliance, identify the controls studied, use due professional care in reporting, or correctly cite the auditing standards followed. The federal inspectors general community, from time to time, has admonished the auditing profession to heed the nature of deficiencies that have been noted during the desk reviews. The auditor problems, mentioned in the following sections, were reported by GAO to the Congress in years past:

Compliance Reporting Problems. Federal desk reviews disclosed many problems in audit reports relating to testing and reporting on compliance with laws and regulations, such as:

● Audit reports did not include a statement of compliance with laws and regulations in the audit report.

● Some audit reports included a general statement, but omitted either the statement of positive assurance that is required by OMB Circular A-133 when reporting on compliance with laws and regulations.

● Numerous report deficiencies were identified where the auditor failed to report or inadequately reported findings of noncompliance with laws and regulations.

Internal Control Reporting Problems. Federal desk reviews disclosed many problems existing in auditors reports relating to the adequacy of the systems of internal controls, such as:

● Audit reports contained no statement on the results of tests of internal controls.

● Other audit reports that included a statement on controls, did not identify the audited entity's significant controls; or

● Having identified the controls, auditors failed to identify the controls that were evaluated.

Due Professional Care Problems. The GAO, in a review of audits relating to the Single Audit Act, found many problems relating to due professional care, such as:

● Audit reports contained financial statements with unexplained inaccuracies—accounts not in balance, reporting of incorrect amounts, reflection of incorrect adjusting entries, improper reporting formats.

● Audit reports with missing schedules and information, and having inadequate descriptions of the scope of audit work performed.

● Other audit reports that omitted the date of the report, did not contain the auditor's signature, or did not properly cite the agency guidance followed in conducting the audit.

Citation of Wrong Standards. Government auditing standards require that audit reports of governments state in the report that the audit was made in accordance with generally accepted *government* auditing standards. GAO's reviews of single audits indicated a general lack of awareness by CPAs of governmental auditing standards and the unique requirements of government audits. The federal desk reviews disclosed that:

● Many submitted audit reports did not cite generally accepted *government* auditing standards.

● Some audit reports did not cite any auditing standards.

● Other audit reports cited specific editions of government auditing standards, but referenced standards that had been superseded.

Over the intervening years, the number of observed audit report deficiencies has decreased significantly, but the areas of audit report deficiencies continue to be similar.

QUALITY CONTROL REVIEWS BY FEDERAL INSPECTORS GENERAL

Regulatory Requirements—"QCRs"

As early as 1984, Congress in the Single Audit Act required that the Office of Management and Budget oversee the implementation of that Act. At that time, OMB, in its implementing regulation for single audits, required that federal agencies:

> "Obtain or make quality control reviews of selected audits made by non-federal audit organizations, and provide the results, when appropriate to other interested organizations."

A federal quality control review, performed on an audit at the audit organization's location, is more extensive and will include many aspects of the audit that were not examined during the desk review. For example, is it common for a QCR to include meetings between federal representatives and all auditors involved in the audit, an examination of all audit working papers supporting the audit reports, a "re-audit" of tests and confirmation of the audit procedures applied and audit practices utilized. In many instances, federal personnel conducting the QCR will meet with the representatives of the auditee organization.

As indicated, the desk reviews provide little information concerning the actual quality of the audit work performed since the desk review checklist criteria is applied to only the form and content of the audit report. To assess the actual audit work performed, federal departments and agencies implemented the process of on-site QCRs. The overall objective of a QCR is to obtain an assurance of the actual quality of audit work performed to comply with government auditing standards and the Single Audit Act criteria. To a degree, a QCR should be viewed as an on-site "audit" of the audit and the auditor.

A QCR will consider the results of any earlier desk reviews. But a QCR will also cover other aspects of audit work performed on the governmental entity with emphasis given to the audit tests made to assess: compliance by auditee with laws and regulations, the effectiveness of auditee controls to manage and monitor federal financial assistance, and the actual accounting and reporting of federal funds submitted by the auditee. QCRs by federal agencies will also inquire into the results of internal quality reviews. QCRs will review external peer reviews made of the audit organization as well as compliance by all audit personnel to the continuing education requirements of auditors of governments. From a documentation viewpoint, it is expected that records relating to the audit and the supporting audit working papers will fully explain the audit work performed without extensive supplementary oral explanations.

Typically, the federal department performing the QCR will have coordinated the scope of review with other federal agencies that provide financing to the audited entity. The guidelines and checklists used for the on-site QCRs are detailed, possibly requiring as much as a week to execute in the case of audits made for the larger governmental units.

QCR Review Guidelines

Quality control review guidelines have been published by the President's Council on Integrity and Efficiency, which outline the following process for a QCR:

1. An entrance conference will be held with the independent auditor's senior management to explain the QCR review process, its purposes, and answer preliminary questions.

2. A review will be made to assess the adequacy of the basis for the independent auditor's opinions and other reporting.

3. A review will be made of the financial statements.

4. A review will be made of the audit working papers.

5. On occasion, working paper evidence could be traced back to the records of the audited entity; discussions might be held between the federal QCR reviewers and the auditee.

The QCR guide and checklist is designed to permit the reviewer to assess whether the working papers include evidence of or demonstrate or show:

a. Sufficient data demonstrating the financial statements or other information upon which the auditor is reporting were in agreement with or reconcilable to the audited organization's records.

b. That the audit had been adequately planned and the audit methodology is supported by detailed written audit programs; that work of assistants has been supervised and reviewed, and evidence exists to show observance to generally accepted government auditing standards.

c. A review was made of the audited organization's system of internal control to assess compliance with laws and regulations.

d. The applied auditing procedures to obtain the supporting evidential matter indicates observance with the standard for field work that working papers should contain sufficient information to enable an experienced auditor with no previous connection with the audit to ascertain from the papers the evidence that supports the auditors significant conclusions and judgments.

e. How exceptions and unusual matters, if any, were disclosed and later resolved or followed up.

f. Appropriate commentary by the auditor indicating conclusions about significant aspects of the audit.

g. Sufficient data to evidence that any guides identified in the audit report were used (e.g., AICPA guide for auditing state and local governments, AICPA checklists and questionnaires for audits of governmental units, OMB *Compliance Supplement,* etc.)

The scope of a QCR will also include inquiries concerning the status of all audit personnel with respect to their current or continuing professional education, the independence of the auditor relative to the audited entity, and identification of any variances from the government auditing standards.

The QCR will conclude with an exit conference with the independent auditor's senior management to discuss the results of the review, advise the auditor of any deficiencies, recommend corrective actions and inform the auditor of the procedure for reconciling or resolving any disagreements relating to the QCR results.

Problems Disclosed in QCRs

Over the years, the federal government has conducted far fewer QCRs than desk reviews. Typically, about five percent or less of audits subjected to desk reviews were subsequently selected for the more detailed QCR examination. Federal inspectors generally acknowledge that audits selected for QCRs were not picked on a random basis, but rather on judgments as to which auditing organizations were more likely to have problems, many of which may have been detected during the federal desk review.

The following listing is a composite aggregation of the problems noted in federal QCRs of audit organizations—either reported by GAO, OMB, inspectors general, or state audit organizations:

● Little or no evidence of the audit being properly planned or supervised, or reviewed.

● Little or no evidence showing the tests for compliance with laws and regulations.

● Insufficient evidence documenting the auditor's study and evaluation of internal controls: evidence was lacking or the work was not performed.

● Insufficient evidence existed to demonstrate the tests made of financial operations, transactions or account balances.

● Material errors existed in major components of the audit report: e.g., failure to include all federal financing programs, large or numerous mathematical errors, editorial mistakes, etc.

● Citation of an inappropriate scope of audit, assuming that the auditor did not misrepresent the scope of audit.

● Unreported, but detected instances of fraud or irregularities and significant findings of noncompliance and material internal control deficiencies.

● The auditor was not qualified by reason of licensing, independence, educational requirements to perform a government audit.

● Failure on the part of the auditor to correct earlier reported instances of substandard audit work on the part of the auditor.

In past years, the GAO study of QCR results reported at least two-thirds of the audits with evidence-related problems: Evidence was lacking in the working papers, or otherwise no testing or inadequate testing for compliance was performed by auditors.

Communication of Observed Audit Deficiencies

Federal guidelines require that the results of QCRs be communicated by the reviewing federal department or agency to the auditee entity and to all federal agencies involved with the auditee entity. Additionally, most federal inspectors general and some state audit organizations simultaneously provide a copy of the audit deficiency report directly to the AICPA and to state boards of accountancy. A copy of the deficiency report may or may not be sent directly to the auditor.

This communication process by the government is of considerable significance to CPA firms even though federal and state auditors have taken the position that their direct communication does not constitute a formal "referral" to the state of a substandard audit. At times, a federal agency may be in error or may have misinterpreted the federal guidance itself. Nonetheless, there may have already been a communication of an alleged deficient audit report to the state accountancy board.

History has shown that both federal agencies and state boards make a record of the communication and are not particularly diligent in "erasing" the file or eliminating the erroneous communication if the auditor's reported position is sustained by a more detailed review of the facts.

Auditors of governments should periodically confirm and authenticate the nature of data residing in files of federal inspector general offices and state boards of accountancy. The organizations will delete erroneous information or correct the record, but only if the CPA takes the initiative.

In instances of major audit inadequacies or repetitive substandard audit work, the auditor will be referred to regulatory and professional bodies for disciplinary action. Initially, a notice of inadequate work will be provided by the federal reviewer to other federal agencies and the audited entity. This notice will generally describe:

- The reasons why the work is deemed inadequate.
- The impact of the inadequacies on the federal programs.
- Recommendations for resolving the inadequacies.
- Sanctions if corrective action is not taken.

If the federal agency concludes that the auditor's reply is not responsive to the initial notification, and, therefore, is not satisfactory, the federal agency will inform all other federal agencies of the facts. Federal audit guidelines provide that the agency performing the review should, as appropriate: (1) recommend that the auditee entity impose penalties and/or sanctions contained in the contract or arrangement under which the audit services were performed, and/or (2) recommend that all other federal funding agencies apply sanctions against the recipient of federal funds.

When the quality of audit work is challenged by a federal organization, the challenge is not, as noted, an issue just between the auditor and the federal organization raising the problems. Audit exceptions will be made known to all federal agencies providing financial assistance to the audited state or local governmental unit and the state boards of accountancy. It can be expected that these governmental organizations and state boards will make closer reviews of the quality of work done by the auditor. It is also likely that a referral will have been made to the Ethics Board of the AICPA for those auditors who are members of that organization.

The Single Audit Act prohibits governments from charging to federal programs the cost of any audit that is not conducted in accordance with the Act. Therefore, federal monies may not be used to pay the fee for an audit alleged to be substandard.

Federal Sanctions for Substandard Audits

Once the audit exception or audit deficiencies have been communicated in writing to the auditor, the auditor should accept the fact that the reported issues can only be resolved formally and in writing. Extensive oral discussions are usually neither particularly helpful to the auditor nor desired by the federal department or agency. Auditors, by failing to provide a complete written response to the audit deficiency report, run a risk that their response will be deemed inadequate by federal inspectors general or, worse, non-responsive to the issues raised.

Further, the absence of reply or reaction by the federal agency to either oral explanations or written rebuttal by the auditor, should never be construed as agreement with the auditor's position. Prudence requires that auditors specifically follow-up with federal agencies and determine, with as much certainty as possible, the final position or resolution by the federal inspector general. There have been instances of federal agencies disagreeing with the auditor's rebuttal, not informing the auditor of the disagreement, and proceeding with formal suspension and disbarment against the audit firm.

In addition to the professional referrals to regulatory agencies and professional organizations, there can be significant financial sanctions imposed on auditors and audit organizations whose audit work is deemed substandard.

Disallowance of the Audit Fee

The federal organization will always communicate the audit deficiencies and recommended disallowances claimed or charged costs to the auditee entity. What is not certain is that any communication will transpire between the federal government and the audit organization. Often the offending audit organizations will receive notice of the initial formal allegation of substandard audit performance from the auditee entity. But, there is a mandated requirement of OMB in its Circular A-133: No audit costs may be charged to a federal award when the audit required by the Circular has not been made, or, has been made but is not in accordance with the Circular.

The failure of the auditor to resolve an allegation of a substandard audit could not only result in disallowance of the audit fee, but could ultimately place the future federal funding of the auditee's programs in jeopardy as well. In cases of continued inability or unwillingness to have an audit that complies with Circular A-133, federal agencies and all pass-through entities must take other sanctions. These could include withholding a percentage of the auditee's federal awards, withholding or disallowing overhead costs, suspending federal awards until the audit is conducted; or terminating the federal award altogether.

Suspension of the Auditor

Depending upon the seriousness of the audit deficiencies, unresolved issues could ultimately result in suspension or debarment of the audit organization from participation in the audit of any federally financed programs.

By federal regulations (Presidential executive order No. 12549 and departmental implementing regulations published in the *Federal Register* October 20, 1987), *suspension* would mean the exclusion of a person or an accounting firm, or an office of a multi-office accounting firm, from receiving payments from any recipient or subrecipient of federal financial assistance for a temporary period, pending completion of an investigation and any legal or debarment proceedings that may emerge.

Debarment of the Auditor

Debarment, by federal regulations (executive order No. 12549 and departmental regulations published in the *Federal Register* October 20, 1987), refer to the governmentwide exclusion of a person or partnership from providing assistance to any recipient or subrecipient of federal financial assistance for a specified period of time.

By OMB regulations, suspension and debarment actions can be instituted by a federal department or agency independent of or in advance of referring the auditor to appropriate professional organizations for disciplinary actions related to the alleged substandard audit performance.

Effect of Suspension and Debarment

Federal agencies or organizations who are recipients of federal assistance may not make awards to, or agree to participate with a suspended or debarred person or organization during the suspension period. The suspension and debarment may be directed toward an owner or partner holding a controlling interest, director or officer. Also, the suspended or debarred party can be the principal investigator, project director or others involved in providing the federally required audit.

Auditees and others receiving federal assistance who continue to do business with a suspended or debarred party, could also face other sanctions such as disallowance of costs, annulment or termination of federal awards, issuance of stop work orders, and suspension or debarment of their programs.

Certified public accountants may experience other repercussions. There exists the likelihood that the involved state board of accountancy, when notified of the suspension or debarment, will institute a formal inquiry into the matter. Also, the AICPA might review the facts, possibly concluding that the deficient audit work constitute "acts discreditable to the profession."

Federal Audit Inventory Control System

All auditees are required to submit the complete audit report and other documents relating to a single audit to a federal clearinghouse for archival purposes, and for each federal awarding agency.

The details vary by federal agency, but all federal inspectors general have established an audit inventory control system to record the results of reviews of audit activity for each state and local governmental unit for which the federal agency has audit cognizance. Pursuant to federal guidelines, federal agencies must establish an audit inventory control register that, as a minimum, contains the following information for each federal assistance recipient:

- Name, address, telephone number of the governmental entity;
- Contact point—name, title, address, telephone number;
- Audit cycle period—fiscal year beginning and ending dates;
- Audit report due dates;
- Information on audit reports received:

—Audit period,

—Date report received,

—Name of audit firm, telephone number, name of person in charge of the audit,

—Results of any or all: (1) federal desk reviews, and (2) QCRs (e.g., "no deficiencies noted," "minor deficiencies noted," "major deficiencies noted."),

—Whether findings were identified for corrective action and which program office is responsible for obtaining corrective action,

—Date audit report is issued to program officials,

—Date desk review results were transmitted to other federal agencies,

324   Government Auditing: Standards and Practices

—Date the audit report was resolved and closed.

● Other information about the audit organization—e.g., referrals to professional and regulatory bodies.

Federal policy directs inspectors general to have all audit reports subjected to a desk review within 30 days of receipt. Any QCRs are also intended to be accomplished within 30 days of receipts of the audit report. If it appears that the review process will be extended to more than 60 days, the reviewing federal agency must notify all other affected federal agencies.

QUALITY CONTROL PRACTICES OF THE AICPA

Compliance with Government Audit Criteria

There is no professional or legal requirement that mandates a certified public accountant must perform government audit engagements. But once such an engagement is accepted by a CPA, the AICPA then believes that the auditor has the obligation to fully comply with the terms of the audit engagement contract.

A CPA is professionally responsible to adhere to generally accepted auditing standards in the conduct of a financial statement audit as well as all other standards and conditions outlined in the scope of work in the audit engagement contract. Mere compliance with generally accepted auditing standards when an engagement contract includes other audit criteria is not sufficient. When the auditor accepts an audit contract to make an audit of a specified scope, such as a single audit, the failure to comply with the contracted criteria must be disclosed in the report and the reasons for noncompliance must be stated. This noncompliance could be deemed an "act discreditable to the profession."

AICPAs Program for Substandard Audits

The AICPA has long-standing procedures with the federal government for monitoring the quality of audits performed by CPAs who are members of the AICPA. Allegedly substandard audit reports may be submitted by the federal government to the Ethics Division of the AICPA for further investigation. Additionally, the AICPA instituted its own program for monitoring the quality of government audits, which includes examination of audit reports of governmental programs by a committee of members of the AICPA.

For those cases submitted by the committee of members to the Ethics Division, the Division can decide among several courses of action, including:

1. Dismissing the case with no further action by the AICPA;

2. Recommending that the CPA be required to attend an educational program;

3. Recommending that the CPA be admonished by the AICPA; and

4. Finding a *prima facie* case against the CPA with a recommendation that the case be referred to the Trial Board of the AICPA.

5. If the Ethics Division's position is sustained the decision of the Trial Board is published to all members of the AICPA.

Considerable resources are devoted by the AICPA to its monitoring role with respect to governmental audits. Regular meetings are held between its members and the federal government to review, discuss, and resolve quality of audit issues.

Act Discreditable to the Profession

The failure to follow government auditing criteria is an "act discreditable to the profession."

The AICPA's Ethic Rule 501, for the auditing profession is broad, but clear: A member shall not commit an act discreditable to the profession.

A subsequent interpretation related to Rule 501-3 found that:

"Engagements for audits of government grants, government units or other recipients of government monies typically require that such audits be in compliance with government audit standards, guides, procedures, statutes, rules, and regulations, in addition to generally accepted auditing standards. If a member has accepted such an engagement and undertakes an obligation to follow such specified government audit standards, guides, procedures, statutes, rules, and regulations, in addition to generally accepted auditing standards, he is obligated to follow such requirements. Failure to do so is an act discreditable to the profession in violation of Rule 501, unless the member discloses in his report the fact that such requirements were not followed and the reasons therefore."

The AICPA's rulings, its program for sanctions, and its monitoring efforts apply only to CPAs that qualify and agree to be bound by the AICPA's standards. When governments elect to contract with licensed public accountants and CPAs that are not members of the AICPA, the government does do not have the same assurance that these nonmember auditors will adhere to professional standards. Thus, nonmember CPAs, non-certified public accountants and unlicensed accountants would be subject to far fewer sanctions in the event of substandard work.

Part IV

ILLUSTRATIVE AUDIT APPROACHES AND METHODOLOGIES

"Investment in planning a government audit mitigates the need for retracing audit steps, changing direction, modifying tests, once the audit has begun. But, even when well planned, audits must be changed to meet conditions that vary from the anticipated.

To undertake a government audit without the benefit of a plan, will assuredly result in duplicate audit efforts, delays in performance, even omission of critical examination steps. Careful planning avoids problems, minimizes risks and, might, avoid budget overruns."

Cornelius E. Tierney

Much has been written about accepted approaches to undertaking a financial statement audit of a corporation, audits which have a singular objective—the issuance of a standard audit opinion on the overall reasonableness of entity-wide financial statements.

Scopes of audits of public sector entities are broader, at times more in depth, and directed to answering different questions. Public sector audits have the objective of providing more assurances to the users of audit reports.

Public entities are audited from several aspects—as a independent, single entity; as an aggregation of departments and agencies; as a conformer to applicable legal and statutory requirements; and as a manager operating with strict budgetary constraints. All this must be done economically, efficiently, and effectively in compliance with laws, and regulations. And, the auditor of a public entity is expected to provide answers and opinions on all of these operations and activities.

A plan for the audit approach must be developed to ensure that the most efficient and effective audit steps, tests, reviews, and applied audit procedures will be performed in a timely manner, in sufficient depth, and in the proper sequence to provide persuasive evidence in support of the opinions, conclusions, and assurances appearing in a governmental audit report. But, one single plan will suffice. Each audit of a public sector entity, designed to address special questions, must be uniquely planned.

Preliminary written audit plans of contemplated audit methodologies and audit programs, in advance of commencing an audit, are essential to setting overall direction and monitoring the execution of a government audit.

Done well, written audit plans, methodologies, and programs serve as invaluable training, orientation, control, management, and review tools while providing assurance that audit goals and objectives will be attained. Absent, all audit work will be viewed as suspect, possibly deficient, and give rise to considerable professional risk, both to the individual auditor and the audit organization.

A hoped-for objective of this part is that the several following chapters will assist the planning and methodology design efforts, possibly highlighting areas, issues, tasks, and sequences that might have otherwise been overlooked in efforts to effectively audit resources to attain all that is desired from a governmental audit.

Chapter 13

Auditor Relationships, Responsibilities and Reliance

AUDITORS OF GOVERNMENT

Tens of thousands of auditors of federal, state and local governments are employed by those governments. Others, most often independent certified public accountants, are retained to perform audits under contract to the governments. Of those employed by a government, many are career civil service personnel, others hold office through political appointment, and still others are elected to their office.

Additionally, the thousands of other auditors of governments are employed by public accounting firms who have contracts to conduct audits of entities of the government that issued the contract. Also, there are instances where contracts are issued by one level of government that require audits of an entity at another level of government. Or, an auditor might receive a contract from a governmental entity to conduct an audit of a non-governmental entity.

Federal Audit Organizations

At the federal level, a distinction exists between types of audit organizations, for example, the General Accounting Office and other auditors employed by the many federal departments and agencies.

GAO, established by the Budget and Accounting Act of 1921, is an audit and investigative organization in the legislative branch of the federal government and is headed by the Comptroller General of the United States. The Comptroller General, once appointed, is subject to removal from office only by a joint resolution of Congress for specified causes or impeachment.

By law, GAO is required to investigate in Washington D.C., and elsewhere, all matters relating to the receipt, disbursement and application of public funds.[1] With few exceptions, the authority of GAO extends to all organizations, programs, activities, and functions, contracts and grants that, directly or indirectly, spend federal monies or have received or use federal resources.

Since 1978, federal agencies have been required to have an inspector general who is appointed to the position, and inspectors general of the larger federal departments and agencies are also confirmed by Congress. In the course of their work, federal inspectors general must concurrently report both to the head of their department or agency and to Congress. All serious and flagrant problems, abuses or deficiencies are reported immediately to the head of the department or agency and then to Congress within seven calendar days.

Some federal departments retain audit organizations that are separate from their offices of inspector general. For example, the Defense Contract Audit Agency, a major and professionally recognized audit organization exists within the Department of Defense, but almost exclusively conducts audits of entities external to the department and federal government. The Department of the Army, with its Army Audit Agency, conducts internal audits of Army operations, but will also audit entities external to the government, as well.

The head and staffs of GAO and the many respective offices of inspectors general, and other audit organizations, with few or no exceptions, are civil servants, appointed to their positions pursuant to government-wide civil service criteria. None of the executives who head these audit and investigative organizations hold their position as a result of winning a general election.

State and Local Government Auditors

Different authorizing legislation and local statute make generalization or categorization of state and local government auditors difficult. And, the titles (e.g., chief or auditor or examiner of public accounts, legislative auditor, auditor general) and responsibilities of these governmental auditors (e.g., comptroller, legislative budget assistant, executive director) are not consistent or, at times, are not indicative of the audit authority they possess.

Many states have prerequisite conditions to holding the auditor position. But, these mainly relate to age, years of U.S. citizenship, residency in the state, and some experience. A few states require that the state auditor be an accountant, have competency in auditing or be a certified public accountant.

---

[1] Budget and Accounting Act of 1921, Washington, D.C.

At city, municipal, and other governmental units, auditors may obtain their positions by political appointment, general election, or a civil service merit-type appointment. These auditors could report to either the legislative or executive governing body, the chief elected official, or another executive in their government.

Independent Public Accountants

The 1980s saw increased retention of certified public accounting firms by all levels of government to perform a wide variety of audits of public sector entities. The method of retaining independent CPA's differ: government entities retain the CPA firm under contract directly, or the CPA will be retained by one level of government and be expected to serve multiple "clients." This latter relationship is the most common with respect to audits made pursuant to the Single Audit Act. For instance, a city appoints an auditor to conduct a single audit and the auditor must audit for compliance with county, state, and federal laws and issue a report that could be used by many external to the city.

GOVERNMENTAL AUDITEES

Over 15 years, the Governmental Accounting Standards Board as well as the American Institute of Certified Public Accountants have expended considerable effort in attempts to define the financial reporting entity in the public sector. Still the definition is evolving. But, there is widespread acceptance of GASB's definition of a primary government as the financial reporting entity as being distinct from component units of a government. This definition is based on the concept of financial accountability.

A Primary Government

GASB defines the *primary government* as any state government or general-purpose local government (e.g., county, city, municipality, town, or township). A primary government might also be a special-purpose government (e.g., a school district or park district), but to do so the special-purpose government must meet *all* of the following criteria:

- The special purpose government must have a separately elected governing body;
- The special purpose government must be legally separate; and
- The special purpose government must be fiscally independent.

The primary government or primary financial reporting entity must consist of all the funds, organizations, institutions, agencies, departments, and offices that make up the legal entity. Therefore, auditors must determine whether the financial statements include all related financial information for all of the governmental entity.

Component Units

GASB provides guidance to assist auditors in determining separate legal standing and fiscal independence of these component units and to determine if many public sector organizations and institutions are, in fact, component units of the primary government.

Component units are legally separate organizations (that will include not-for-profit or for-profit corporations) for which elected officials of the primary government are financially accountable. Such component units would be included as part of the financial reporting entity on the financial accountability concept that these units are fiscally dependent. "Financial accountability" exists if a primary government appoints a voting majority of an organization's governing body, and the primary government is either able to impose its will on that organization or there is a potential for the organization to provide a specific financial benefit to, or impose specific financial burdens on, the primary government.

The determination of the primary government is important since the auditor of a primary government must assume certain audit responsibilities not exercised by other auditors.

Federal Awards

Annually tens of thousands of financial audits, i.e., single audits, are made of governments and nonprofit organizations receiving federal financial assistance. The financial reporting and audit focus, i.e., the reporting entity, under the Single Audit Act is the individual major federal awards. These audits are made pursuant to the provisions of the Single Audit Act. The implementation of federal regulations issued by the Office of Management and Budget requires that a detailed audit be performed to assess compliance with laws and regulations and soundness of controls over state and local government programs managing federal financial assistance. This is a level of auditing considerably more detailed than the financial statement of audits made pursuant to either generally accepted auditing standards or the government auditing standards.

TYPES OF AUDITORS

There exists a designation of auditor that is determined by the entity being audited. For example, the auditors of the primary government, component units, and federal award programs have distinct and different auditing and reporting responsibilities. For the great preponderance of governments, one audit organization will perform the audits of each of these entities. But, for other governments, different auditors may be used or employed to perform audits of these entities. Different auditors, to a degree, complicate the financial reporting for the overall

Auditor Relationships, Responsibilities and Reliance

general or primary governmental unit and require that the principal auditor coordinate and, in some cases, integrate the audit work and reports of other auditors.

Principal Auditors

To serve as the principal auditor of a governmental unit's financial statements, an auditor must meet both of the following criteria:

1. Be engaged by the primary government as the principal auditor of the financial reporting entity, and

2. Be responsible for auditing at least the general fund, or the primary operating fund if no general fund exists for the primary government.

Having met these responsibilities, the auditor of the primary government is required to exercise some additional responsibilities of that position. The additional responsibilities include: confirming the independence of the other auditors, and evaluating any adjustment, combination, or reclassification of component unit financial data to conform to the presentations in the general purpose financial statements of the primary reporting government entity.

As the principal auditor, a decision must be made, in accordance with SAS No. 1, as to whether the principal auditor will make reference in the audit opinion for the primary government to the audit reports of the other auditors. If the part of the audit is done by another auditor and is referred to, the disclosure of the magnitude of audits by others is required. The primary auditor is required to describe that portion of the financial statements audited by other auditors and to include an identification of the fund types and account groups (if blended) or the component unit columns that were audited by others.

Frequently, the audit report of a governmentwide financial statement must include financial statements of component units whose financial statements are audited by auditors other than the auditor engaged by the primary government. The result is the inclusion, in many instances, of the assets, liabilities, revenues, or expenditures for one or more component unit exceeding those of the primary government. These circumstances raise questions about who is the principal auditor of the financial statements of the reporting entity. The Statement on Auditing Standards require a decision as to whether the principal auditor's participation in the audit is sufficient to enable the auditor to serve as the principal auditor and to report as such on the financial statements.

When auditors other than the principal auditor have audited component units or, to a lesser degree, the federal assistance programs, the principal auditor must identify the extent of that audit involvement. The principal auditor may conclude that an unqualified audit opinion is warranted on the general purpose financial statements that contains identified component units that were audited by other than the principal auditor. But the audit report must be modified to include in the introductory or initial paragraph of the auditor's opinion a statement similar to:

> "... Our responsibility is to express an opinion on these financial statements based on our audit. We did not audit the financial statements of the ABC Component Unit, which statements reflect total assets of $100,000,000 as of June 30, 20XX, and the total revenues of $75,000,000 for the year then ended. These financial statements were audited by other auditors whose report has been furnished to us, and our opinion on the financial statements, insofar as it relates to the amounts included for ABC Component Unit in the component unit column, is based on the report of the other auditors."

And, the principal auditors opinion paragraph would have to also be modified to read somewhat as follows:

> "In our opinion, based on our audit and the report of other auditors, the general purpose financial statements referred to above present fairly, in all material respects, ..." "... Also, in our opinion, the combining, individual fund, and account group financial statements referred to above (other than whose financial statements of ABC Component Unit were audited by other auditors whose report espoused an unqualified audit opinion) present fairly, in all material respects. ..."

There are instances where the principal auditor will not have audited some fund types or one or more component units. Under these conditions, an alternative introduction and opinion might read as follows:

> "... Our responsibility is to express an opinion on these financial statements based on our audit. We did not audit the financial statements of the component units and the special revenue funds (identified above) which were audited by other auditors and which represent 25% and 10% of total assets and 20% and 5% of total revenues of the Component Units and the Special Revenue Funds, respectively. These financial statements were audited by other auditors whose reports thereon have been furnished to us, and our opinion on the financial statements, insofar as it relates to the

amounts included for those entities, is based solely on the reports of other auditors."

And, the principal auditors opinion paragraph would have to also be modified to read somewhat as follows:

"In our opinion, based on our audit and the report of other auditors, the general purpose financial statements referred to above present fairly, in all material respects, ..." "... Also, in our opinion, the combining, individual fund, and account group financial statements referred to above (other than the financial statements of the component units and the special revenue funds (identified above) were audited by other auditors whose report espoused an unqualified audit opinion) present fairly, in all material respects. ..."

Multiple auditor-type reports, while not the dominant form of an audit relationship, is common among public sector audits. For example, a survey of the country's 100 largest cities disclosed seven percent of the issued audit reports were by principal auditors that noted a significant part of the audit had been performed by other auditors. This same survey disclosed that for 40 percent of these 100 cities, the single audits were performed by auditors other than or in addition to the principal auditor.[2]

Component Unit Auditor

The auditor of a component unit may not be the same as the auditor of the primary government. In these circumstances, it is important that an appropriate professional relationship be established between the two auditors. The component unit auditor may be required to facilitate the principal auditor's execution of professional responsibilities. The component unit auditor may be expected to participate in presenting financial statements of the component unit on a different basis of accounting or a fiscal year or other reporting period not used by the component unit for its separate reporting.

It is important that principal and component unit auditors and their clients reach an early agreement on reporting responsibilities, including how any additional preparation and audit costs will be borne by the entities.

Auditors for Single Audits

Another common occurrence, in a governmental environment, is the separation of a single audit between the principal auditor of the

---

[2] C. Tierney, A survey, *100 Big City Financials...What's Audited, Reported, When, How and by Whom?*, 1998.

reporting entity and a secondary auditor who may be in addition to the a component unit auditor.

The auditor's report on the financial statements for the reporting entity could be signed by the second auditor or the principal auditor's report could refer to the reporting of the secondary auditor who performed the single audit work. With respect to the single audit, the principal auditor may also need to refer to the programs audited by other auditors in the audit report relating to the schedule of expenditures of federal awards, and in the compliance and internal control reports related to those federal awards.

Joint Audits of Governments

Auditor Roles, Responsibilities

For joint audits, the role and relationship between auditors is different than was the case with the principal and component unit auditors.

Because of federal law, local statutes, or policy of the primary government, certified public accountants must perform audits on a joint venture or subcontract basis with other audit organizations.

Joint audits could entail the conduct of a coordinated, cooperative audit between two public accounting firms or an accounting firm and a government audit organization. Also, a joint audit might be conducted under a prime contract and subcontractor relationship whereby two audit organizations taking equal responsibility.

All auditors participating in joint audits must arrive at a formal understanding of their respective responsibilities, usually through contract or some written agreement. It is imperative that the audit organizations detail certain critical responsibilities to be performed by the respective auditors. As a minimum, the joint auditors must conclude on the following issues as:

- Signing the audit report;

- Determining the compensation of the parties;

- Supervision of the engagement;

- Documenting the engagement in the working papers; and

- Establishing review procedures.

Responsibility for signing the audit report usually dictates the extent of the working paper review and other professional requirements imposed on the participants.

Jointly Signed Audit Reports

Several governments require that the accounting firm provide for involvement of minority or smaller firms in the audit. This type of arrangement might be encountered with respect to the conduct of single audits where federal regulations encourage governmental auditees, whenever possible, to utilize small businesses, minority-owned firms and women's business enterprises.

At times, these requirements have been met by subcontracting a portion of the audit to the smaller firms. Under this audit arrangement, the audit report is signed by only the principal auditor, with no reference being made to the other participating firm. The signatory auditor assumes full responsibility for the performance of the audit and the resultant report.

In other circumstances, the smaller firms participating in the audit desire to jointly sign the audit report in their individual capacities. The profession's standards do not provide for sharing the responsibility of an audit of financial statements of an audited entity by two or more independent auditors. Each individual auditor or firm that signs an audit report is considered to be separately expressing an opinion on the financial statements. Multiple signatures also appear on the audit reports issued for joint audits by a government audit organization and an accounting firm.

Multiple auditor-type reports, while not the dominant form of audit relationship, are common among public sector audits. For example, a survey of the country's 100 largest cities disclosed that while 80 percent of the issued audit reports were by only the principal auditor, other relationships exist.[3]

100 Big-City Analysis
Primary, Joint, and Reliance-type
Audit Opinion

Audit Opinions	No. Cited by Surveyed Cities
Primary auditor, one CPA firm	80
Primary auditor, and government organization	7
Joint opinion with CPA firm(s)	9
Joint opinion, CPA and government audit organizations	2
Not surveyed	2
Total	100 Cities

Signing the report in an individual capacity is appropriate only if the individual or firm has complied with GAAS and is in a position that otherwise justifies being the only signatory of the report. For example, a joint signature audit report for a single audit is appropriate only

---

[3] Id.

when each auditor or firm has complied with generally accepted auditing standards and government auditing standards.

If part of the single audit is performed by government employees, the principal auditor should be satisfied that the government auditors meet the generally accepted auditing standards and government auditing standards. For auditors employed by the government, three standards that pose problems are the independence standard, as well as the continuing professional education standard and the quality control standards applicable to the audit organization.

Joint Ventures

A joint endeavor by two firms to conduct an audit could take the form of a legal entity, just as individuals band together to form a firm. In that situation, the report might be signed with the joint venture name, which is legally the audit organization.

INDEPENDENCE

Not all auditors of government, due to personal relationships, appointive status, and organizational placement, can meet all of the generally accepted auditing standards and the government's auditing standards. Where limitations exist, the limitations should be noted in any audit report issued by the auditor organization.

Generally Accepted Auditing Standards

As noted, auditors employed by governments have, at times difficulty in meeting the independence standards due to employer-employee relationships, organization relationships and the requirement that independent auditors must be independent in fact and independent in appearance. Rule 501 of the Code of Professional Conduct relates to auditor independence and states:

> *"A member in public practice shall be independent in the performance of professional services as required by standards promulgated by bodies designed by the Council."*

Ethics Rulings of the auditing profession prohibit an auditor from having, during the professional engagement or at a time of expressing an opinion, any direct or material indirect financial interest in the examined entity.

Also prohibited is a connection between the cpa (the member) or cpa's (member's) firm with the auditee as promoter, underwriter, voting trustee, director or officer or in any capacity equivalent to that of a member of management or of an employee. Key to these independence rulings is that "member or member firm" includes dependent and nondependent spouses and other dependents, whether or not related to the auditor who might also be independent. The definition of "nondependent spouses and other dependents" include children, parents and grandparents.

Government Auditing Standards

Noted in earlier chapters, was the fact that government auditing standards are additive or in addition to generally accepted auditing standards. Government standards requires auditors consider not only whether they are independent and their attitudes and beliefs permit them to be independent, but also whether the circumstances of the audit might lead others to question the appearance of independence. Thus, the requirement that the auditor be independent in fact as well as appearance.

In this connection the government auditing standard on independence is more specific and exclusionary:

> "**In all matters relating to the audit work, the audit organization and the individual auditors, whether government or public, should be free from personal and external impairments to independence, should be organizationally independent, and should maintain an independent attitude and appearance.**"

To be recognized as independent, all auditors must be free of any obligation or interest in the audited organization.

To comply with this standard, *government* auditors (i.e., those employed by government) and hired consultants and internal experts and specialists of governments must consider the three cited classes of impairments to their independence: (1) personal, (2) external and (3) organizational.

Where an auditor's independence is impaired for any of these or other reasons, the auditor should (1) either decline to perform the audit, or (2) where declination is not possible, the impairment should be reported in the scope section of the audit report. Auditors employed by the audited entity must reflect that fact prominently in the audit report.

Nongovernmental auditors, such as certified public accountants, must consider personal and external impairments to independence that could affect their ability to do the audit and impartially report. Public accountants should follow (1) the profession's code of ethics, (2) the code of professional conduct of the state board with jurisdiction over the accountant and the accounting firm, and (3) comply with the independence and other criteria of the government auditing standards.

Personal Impairments

The profession's ethic rulings require that the auditor be without bias with respect to the auditee, since the auditor would otherwise lack the necessary overall qualifications, however excellent, auditor's technical proficiency. In public accounting, *apparent* independence has also been interpreted as being free of familial, organizational, and financial relationships and other conflicts of interests.

For purposes of governmental audits, public accountants will be viewed as independent if they are independent under the profession's Code of Professional Conduct. Ethical guidance notes that independence does not imply the attitude of a prosecutor, but rather a judicial impartiality that recognizes an obligation for fairness to management, owners, creditors and others who may rely upon the auditor's report.

If auditors are employed by the governments that they audit, the issue of real as well as apparent conflicts requires careful scrutiny. Independence, in both fact and appearance, is necessary to permit the auditor's opinions, conclusions, judgments and recommendations to be impartial and to be viewed as impartial by knowledgeable third parties. Independence, in fact and appearance, is necessary to ensure that the work of the auditor is not later compromised or viewed as less than impartial.

The government auditing standards note that personal impairments to independence may include but not be limited to:

- Official, professional, personal, or financial relationships that might cause an auditor to limit the extent of inquiry, limit disclosure, or weaken or slant audit findings in any way.

- Preconceived ideas toward individuals, groups, organizations, or objectives of a particular program that could bias the audit.

- Previous responsibility for decision-making or managing an entity that would affect current operations of the entity or program being audited.

- Biases, including those induced by political or social convictions, that result from employment in, or loyalty to, a particular group, organization, or level of government.

- Subsequent performance of an audit by the same individual who, for example, had previously approved invoices, payrolls, claims, and other proposed payments of the entity or program being audited.

- Concurrent or subsequent performance of an audit by the same individual who maintained the official accounting records.

- Financial interest that is direct, or is substantial though indirect, in the audited entity or program.

Auditor Relationships, Responsibilities and Reliance 341

- Audits of effectiveness of internal controls after having done consulting services involving the design and implementation of those controls.

When auditing state and local governments, public accountants must be familiar with the profession's ethics interpretation that establish specific rules restricting financial relationships that impair the public accountant's independence. These rulings (Ethics Interpretation 101-10) require:

1. The auditor issuing an audit report on the combined financial or general purpose financial statements of a governmental entity must be independent of the oversight or primary entity as well as each of the component units included in the combined report.

2. The auditor for a material fund type, fund, account group, component unit (but not the primary government) or entity that should be disclosed in the footnotes, must be independent with respect to all of these entities.

3. Auditors of one or more immaterial fund types, funds, account groups, component units or an entity that should be disclosed in the footnotes must be independent of that component unit (but not the primary government) that are immaterial, individually and in the aggregate, in relation to the general purpose financial statements, must be independent with respect to the portion of the entity audited, and the primary government. However, the AICPA considers all component units included in a governmental entity's financial statements to be material unless the auditor can demonstrate otherwise.

In instances where the governmental audit organization acts as the main processor for transactions initiated by the audited entity, the audit organizations must establish policies to reasonably ensure the independence of its auditors and the audited entity has assumed full responsibility for the processed transactions and acknowledges responsibility for the processed transactions and for the financial records and statements.

External Impairments

For auditors, employed by both governments or nongovernment audit organizations, government auditing standards cite several examples of external impairments to independence. External impairments to an auditor's independence will include:

- External interference or influences that improperly or imprudently limits or modifies the scope of an audit.

- External interference with the selection of application of audit procedures or in the selection of transactions to be examined.

- Unreasonable restrictions on the time allowed to complete an audit.

- Interference external to the audit origination in the assignment, appointment, and promotion of audit personnel.

- Restrictions on funds or other resources provided to the audit organization that would adversely affect the audit organization's ability to carry out its responsibilities.

- Authority to overrule or to influence the auditor's judgment as to the appropriate content of an audit report.

- Influences that jeopardize the auditor's continued employment for reasons other than competency or the need for audit services.

Several of the above illustrations probably apply more to government audit organizations than to independent accounting firms.

Organizational Impairments

In the case of *governmental internal auditors*, their independence can be affected by their organization and reporting placement in the governmental structure to which assigned and by whether they audit entities internal or external to their organization. Organizational independence is possible to attain by having the audit organization report and be accountable to the head or deputy of the governmental entity and organizationally be located outside of staff or line management of the unit under audit.

Governmental auditors would be free of organizational impairments to their independence if:

- The audited entity is a level of government other than that to which they are an assigned entity;

- The audited entity is a different branch within that level of government to which the auditors are assigned,

- The head of the audit organization is elected by the citizens, or elected or appointed by a legislative body, and the audit organization reports to that body, or

- The head of the audit organization is appointed by the chief executive but confirmed by, reports to, and are accountable to a legislative body of the level to which they are assigned.

Early in the application of government auditing standards, one federal agency, the Office of Revenue Sharing, had issued criteria relating to independence of auditors employed by governments that were explicit for achieving independence in fact and appearance. This guidance considered two groups of government auditors to be independent:

1. *State auditors* when (a) auditing local governments, or (b) auditing state accounts if the auditor was elected or appointed by and reporting to the state legislature or a committee thereof, or appointed by the governor and confirmed by and reporting to the state legislature.

2. *Local government auditors* when auditing their government's accounts if the auditor is (a) elected by the citizens of the local government, or (b) elected or appointed by and reporting to the governing body of the local government or a committee thereof, or appointed by the chief executive officer and confirmed by and reporting to the governing body.

Generally, auditors employed by state and local governments do not perform financial statement audits, but concentrate more on conducting internal-type audits of these entities, typically voucher audits, procedural or compliance reviews, fiscal post audits, functional and performance audits, and other evaluations of importance to their governments. The financial statement audit is generally done under a government contract by independent CPAs.

As noted earlier in this section, where an auditor's independence is impaired, the auditor should decline to perform the audit or where declination is not possible, the impairment should be clearly reported in the scope section of the audit report. Auditors employed by the audited entity must reflect their lack of independence prominently in the audit report.

Independence for External Auditors

Certified public accountants and other external auditors of government must comply with the independence standards of both generally accepted auditing standards and government auditing standards. Additionally, the federal regulation OMB Circular A-133 that implements the Single Audit Act imposes another independence prohibition on external auditors:

"An auditor who prepares the indirect cost proposal or cost allocation plan may not also be selected to perform the audit required by the Single Audit Act when indirect costs recovered during the prior year by the auditee exceeds $1 million. This restriction applies to the base year used in preparation of the indirect proposal or cost allocation plan and any subsequent years in which the resulting indirect cost agreement or cost allocation plan is used to recover costs."

Chapter 14

Audit Methodology—
Financial Statement Audits

FINANCIAL STATEMENT AUDITS OF PUBLIC ENTITIES

With few exceptions, public sector entities are required to have annual financial statement audits. These audits are required or imposed on governments by their own statutes, federal or state laws or as conditions precedent to the government issuing financial securities to the public or to provide a stewardship accounting under contracts and grant agreements. These audits, historically, have been performed in accordance with the generally accepted auditing standards enunciated by the American Institute of CPAs. The AICPAs accounting and auditing guide for audits of state and local governmental units provides guidance on applying generally accepted auditing standards to the audits of financial statements of public sector entities.

For the most part, the objective of financial statement audits is to provide reasonable assurance that the financial statements present fairly the financial position, results of operations, and cash flows of a governmental entity in accordance with generally accepted accounting principles in a manner that is consistent from one fiscal period to the next. Most public entities conform their financial statements to generally accepted accounting principles recommended by the Governmental Accounting Standards Board. But, many other entities must comply with laws and statutes affecting their financial statements. Where conformance to legal mandates is required, the accounting used for financial statement purposes could be on an accrual basis, a modified accrual basis, a cash basis or a prescribed hybrid basis of accounting.

In this connection, it should be noted that federal audit mandates (e.g., government auditing standards, the federal OMBs accounting and financial reporting regulations, the Single Audit Act, etc.) require an auditor of government to *report* whether the financial statements are presented in accordance with generally accepted accounting principles. Repeatedly, federal executives have stated that federal mandates require only that the auditor *report* whether generally accepted accounting principles were followed. These federal mandates do not require that an entity must comply with generally accepted accounting principles. Where the generally accepted accounting principles are not followed, the auditor must merely submit an audit report on the applied basis of accounting and explain the basis utilized.

To repeat, no federal mandate requires that the financial statements of public entities must be prepared in accordance with generally accepted accounting principles.

Public Sector Audit Reports

In aggregate, generally accepted auditing standards and government auditing standards impose several reporting criteria on auditors of governments. For example, to comply with generally accepted as well as government auditing standards, an audit report on financial statements for public sector entities must conform to several criteria or provide the following information:

● The audit report must state whether the financial statements are presented in accordance with generally accepted accounting principles.

● When such accounting principles have not been applied consistently in the current period in relation to the preceding period, these circumstances must be identified in the audit report.

● Unless otherwise stated in the report, all informative disclosures in the financial statements are to be regarded as being reasonably adequate by the auditor.

● The audit report must contain either an expression of the auditor's opinion regarding the financial statements taken as a whole or an assertion by the auditor to the effect that an opinion cannot be expressed.

● When an auditor's name is associated with financial statements, the audit report must contain a clear-cut indication of the character of the auditor's work and the degree of responsibility the auditor is taking for information in the financial statements.

● Auditors must communicate certain prescribed information related to the conduct and reporting of the audit to the audit committee or those arranging for the audit or those contracting for the audit—and not merely to the management of the entity being audited.

● When the audit on financial statements is submitted to comply with legal, regulatory, or contractual requirements for an audit pursuant to government auditing standards, the audit report must specifi-

Audit Methodology—Financial Statement Audits 347

cally cite government auditing standards. The citation of compliance with only generally accepted auditing standards is unacceptable.

- An audit report on a public entity's financial statements must also contain reports on tests by the auditor of compliance with laws and regulations and internal controls and the results of these tests.

- When encountered, irregularities, fraud and illegal acts are to be reported in a manner that differs from that required by generally accepted auditing standards. Other noncompliance, e.g., with terms and conditions of contracts, grants and other agreements, is to be reported if the noncompliance is material to the financial statements.

- Where selected information relating to a government audit is prohibited from general disclosure, the audit report should state the nature of the information omitted and the requirement that makes the omission necessary.

- The distribution of government audit reports is seldom restricted to only the audited entity or to only the entity arranging for the audit; copies are more often required by others, such as oversight authorities, those with responsibilities for acting on the audit report and, at times, to the general public.

Because of these mandates an audit of a public entity must be conducted and reported in a manner that differs from an audit of a private sector entity. This chapter outlines an audit methodology for conducting financial statement audits of a public sector unit that complies with the prevailing composite audit reporting mandates.

Single Audit Reports

Absent the Single Audit Act, the auditor could limit the audit and reporting concerns to those directly applicable to auditing the comprehensive annual financial report or the general purpose financial statement of a pubic entity. With the Single Audit Act, though, the audit must encompass the entirety of the financial operations of the government and include tests of activities and transactions of operating departments and component units whose programs are financed by funding from the federal government. Thus, to meet the financial reporting criteria and audit requirements imposed by the Single Audit Act, the audit report must include more than a dozen reports.

Over 20,000 governments and an estimated 150,000 non-profit, higher-educational institutions, and Indian tribal governments who annually spend $300,000 in federal financial assistance must comply with the Single Audit Act. For this reason, the prevalent audit practice is to perform, to the extent possible, aspects of the more detailed single audit at the same time as the audit of the overall financial statements.

Planning for audits of these entities often incorporate many procedures and tests to concurrently comply with single audit requirements.

FINANCIAL STATEMENT AUDIT METHODOLOGY

Audits of public sector financial statements presume knowledge of both governmental and non-profit accounting concepts and principles as well as specifically applicable auditing standards. For public sector audits, the list of criteria, legal, regulatory and professional, is imposing and more extensive than the guidance for audits of private sector entities. A partial listing of governmental audit guidance includes:

- *Governmental Accounting Standards Board*—Its codification of standards, statements of governmental accounting standards, interpretations, and technical bulletins. GASB's standards apply to the financial reports of all state and local governmental entities, including general purpose governments, public benefit corporations and authorities, public employee retirement systems, public utilities, hospitals and healthcare providers, and public colleges and universities.

- *Financial Accounting Standards Board*—Its statements of financial accounting standards, interpretations, technical bulletins, and emerging issues task force issuances. FASB statements would apply to some governmental and the business type activities of public entities, unless FASBs pronouncements conflict with or contradict the GASB pronouncements.

- *American Institute of CPAs*—Its generally accepted auditing standards, statements on auditing standards, accounting and audit guide for audits of state and local governmental units, accounting principles board opinions, statement on positions, public sector financial disclosure checklists, illustrative internal control structure questionnaire for public entities, and annual risk alerts relative to public entities.

- *U.S. General Accounting Office*—Its government auditing standards, interpretations, publications series on governmental controls, financial reporting, computer auditing, performance audits, and compliance audits.

An exhaustive, but still partial, listing of specific relevant documents was prepared by, and is updated periodically by, the AICPA's government accounting and audit committee, titled *Compendium of Governmental Accounting and Auditing Pronouncements and Financial Publications.*

Illustrative Plan and Methodology

The selection of detailed audit procedures to comply with generally accepted auditing standards is dependent on auditor judgment. But

Audit Methodology—Financial Statement Audits

compliance with both generally accepted auditing and the government auditing standards is not judgmental.

An illustrative audit methodology that could address both sets of standards and which would minimize duplicate audit efforts if the government was also required to have a Single Audit, must include several specific phases, such as:

- Conducting a Preliminary Survey;
- Obtaining an Understanding of Controls;
- Developing the Audit Plan;
- Testing Controls, Systems, Transactions, and Accounts;
- Conducting Substantive Audit Procedures;
- End of Audit Considerations; and
- Reporting Results.

Sections of this chapter discuss each of these phases and other details in relation to the conduct of a financial statement audit of a governmental unit. *Exhibit 14-2* provides a summary schematic of an audit methodology.

Phase I

Survey Organizations and Operations

The purpose of this initial phase is to conduct a survey a government's organizational structure, operations, systems, policies and procedures. Preliminary identification and familiarity must be acquired with all data processing applications and the extent to which the processes are manual or computerized and centralized or decentralized. Several specific areas must be examined, assessed preliminarily, and data obtained to document evidence acquired or observed by the auditor. The time needed for this phase is directly related to the experience of the auditor in conducting audits of governments and with the specific government undergoing audit. The second and later year's audit will require less effort in this phase. In the later years, the auditor is primarily concerned with changes.

Phase II

Understand Controls

As early as possible during any audit, the auditor must obtain assurances that controls prescribed by policy and procedures have been placed in operation and whether the controls are, in fact, used by entity personnel.

In this stage—understanding the control structure—the audit tasks require the identification of types of significant transactions processed within each accounting application or cycle and knowledge as to how the transactions are processed. This, implicitly, requires an identification of needed controls, the objectives of such controls, noting processing and control points where error and control lapses could occur and if control procedures exist for preventing or detecting potential errors. In a latter stage of the audit, specific tests will be made to confirm the effectiveness of the internal control procedures.

Control Structure Defined

In audits of financial statements, the concern is about the financial controls that have a direct effect on data appearing in the government's financial statements. The AICPA's Statement on Auditing Standards, No. 78, describes an entity's internal control structure as being comprised of five components: the control environment, risk assessment, control activities, information and communication, and monitoring (see *Exhibit 14-1*). This same structure is apropos to audits of public sector entities.

An understanding of each of these five components of the internal control structure is necessary to plan the audit of an entity's financial statements. In planning a single audit, such knowledge should be used to: (1) identify types of potential misstatements, (2) consider factors that affect the risk of material misstatement; and (3) to design substantive audit tests to validate actual control circumstances.

The AICPA's statements on auditing standards provide relevant guidance on the types of evidential matter required to support an assessed level of control risk. These include reliance on the auditor's prior experience with the entity and understanding of the audit entity's classes of transactions, plus making inquiries of appropriate entity personnel, and inspection of documents and records (e.g., source documents, journals, ledgers), inspection of systems documentation.

Work performed to understand the entity's internal control structure should be documented in the working papers and might include: flowcharts, questionnaires, completed checklists, decision tables, narrative descriptions, memorandum.

Audit Evidence

This understanding of controls must be supported by collected evidence. The form and extent of documentation is affected by the size, complexity and nature of controls encountered by the auditor. But, generally the documentation of the understanding of controls will include flowcharts of computer system applications, transaction processing, and data and forms flows. Pro-forma internal control questionnaires, modified to address the uniqueness of public sector audits, and completed decision-tables are invaluable tools to use in acquiring

Audit Methodology—Financial Statement Audits

and understanding of the details of government controls. There is no substitute for "walk-throughs" of data processing facilities, accounting and other key functional areas, as well as program areas to contribute to a more complete understanding of controls.

Discussions with and written inquiries of elected officials, executive policy-makers, attorneys and general counsels, operating managers, and procedural and data processing personnel are also vital to the auditor's understanding. The results of these latter audit procedures should be summarized in narrative memorandum form for review and subsequent validation.

Assessing Controls and Risks

In making judgments about the understanding of internal controls needed to plan the audit, the auditor must consider all knowledge obtained in this phase about possible misstatements, inherent and control risks, concerns about materiality, complexity of the government's operations and systems, degree of data processing sophistication, etc. The understanding phase also extends to and includes an understanding of management's and any governing board's attitude, awareness and actions concerning the control environment. Basically the "tone" for internal controls is set by top management.

This knowledge must then be used to: (1) identify possible or potential misstatements or erroneous data practices, (2) identify and consider factors that increase the risk that there could be material misstatements in the reported financial information, and (3) determine and design the timing, nature and extent of audit procedures that will be applied later to assess the operating effectiveness of controls, and accuracy of accounting transactions, account balances and ultimately the reasonableness of the financial statements.

After obtaining this understanding of controls, the auditor must assess the control risk for the assertions by management which are embodied in the transaction classes, account balances, and disclosure components of the financial statements undergoing audit. These several assertions relate to: (1) existence or occurrence, (2) completeness, (3) rights and obligations, (4) valuation or allocation, (5) presentation, and (6) disclosure. This assessment of the control risks could range from "maximum level" of control risk, to an assessment that the controls are effective and that a much lower level of risk exists.

If control risks are assessed at the maximum level, this is the point where the greatest probability exists that a material misstatement could occur and not be detected by the control structure. An assessment of maximum level of risk requires considerable testing by the auditor and possibly minimal reliance on the efficacy of the control structure.

Phase III

Written Audit Plan

A written audit plan should follow from the audit work performed to acquire an understanding of controls and the judgmental conclusions regarding the assessment of control risk. The overall audit strategy should be reduced to a written audit plan to minimize or preclude performance of costly duplicative audit procedures. A written plan permits independent evaluation of the timing, nature and extent of audit work initially determined as necessary and as the basis for the development of even more detailed audit programs.

All plans should be subjected to regular review and must be continually modified due to observed conditions, unexpected audit results, presence of new information, unanticipated activities of the government and other factors not disclosed during earlier phases.

The AICPA, in its guide for auditing state and local governments (AAA-SLG, § 3.22), recommends that the audit plan include such facts, conclusions, and directions as:

- The objectives of this specific financial statement audit;
- The required staffing levels, skills, and assigned audit responsibilities;
- The manner, timing, and extent in which analytical procedures and other substantive testing are to be applied;
- The assignment of responsibility for and extent of supervision;
- Budgeted hours, preferably by staff and task, and completion dates for each segment of the audit;
- Materiality levels established for planning purposes;
- Preliminary risk assessments flowing from audit work performed to obtain the required understanding of internal control structure elements obtained to permit the planning of the remainder of the audit;
- Guidelines relating to working paper form and content and directions with respect to providing access to or copies of working papers for governmental reviewers; and
- The extent to which outside experts or specialists are required or will be utilized.

The written plan is a blue-print and forms the basis for monitoring and managing the progress of the audit.

Timing of Audit Work

The timing of when the audit work is to be performed is not always within the control of the auditor. Public sector entities frequently

Audit Methodology—Financial Statement Audits

rotate auditors as a matter of policy. As a successor auditor, the new audit contract may not be executed sufficiently in advance of the audit start date to permit the conduct of interim audit tests before the end of the fiscal year to be audited. In other instances, the government may view early or interim audit work as unnecessarily disruptive and might desire to have the audit done it its entirety after the close of the fiscal year. Or, it's possible, that the audit firm may not have sufficient audit resources available to conduct the audit until after the close of the year; thus negating the possibility of performing interim work before year-end.

While the failure to perform interim work is not a fatal audit flaw, there are certain conditions, such as the controls in operation at a particular time, or the practices of specific individuals or other conditions in existence during the year that might not be replicable after the close of the fiscal year. On the other hand, if performed, some of the interim work must be repeated or re-validated after the close of the year to ensure that the conditions observed and tested during the interim phase of the audit still prevail at year end. There are other audit procedures that may only be applied after the end of the year, such as the audit of final account balances, close-out procedures and review of the final financial statements and footnote disclosures.

Determining Transaction Cycles/Applications

Public sector accounting and auditing differs from practices in the private sector. Audits of a government's general purpose financial statements requires a comprehension of the multi-fund accounting structure, the required practice of integrating budgetary and proprietary accounting, the overriding importance of compliance with laws and regulations, multiple and different levels of materiality for audit report purposes, and lead financial statements containing, at times, a dozen columns of financial data.

In many instances, the procedural nature of governments provide increased controls, but the turnover of senior management almost every 18 months, at all levels of government, almost eliminates any top management "corporate memory" and contributes to increased inherent risks.

Auditing governments requires knowledge of the several "bridges" required to reconcile the different systems, data formats, and financial reporting formats. For example, the general purpose financial statements of a government are prepared to display financial data by the fund-type balances and are compiled utilizing a combination of cash, modified accrual and full accrual bases of accounting. But, the "GPFS" formatting is often made only for year-end reporting and for purposes of the GASB prescribed financial statements.

Throughout the year, a public sector's records will probably be maintained on a cash basis or a prescribed hybrid basis of accounting and not on the accrual bases required by generally accepted accounting principles. Alternatively, the departmental operational reports will often be formatted to present current balances and the status of revenue and expenditure appropriations and related encumbrances, but not on a consistently applied cost accounting basis.

Another factor is the organizational structure of a government. The receipt and expenditure of funds and actual accounting operations could be centralized in the office of the chief elected officer or decentralized among several operating departments, agencies, authorities, commissions, and not-for-profits.

For the purpose of acquiring an understanding of the control structure and later testing of controls and auditing transactions and account balances, the audit emphasis of the financial statement audits for government is focused more on the financial functions or financial applications. The testing of each function or application must be related to the subsidiary and general ledger accounts, which are probably structured to provide a continual accounting of departmental operations and appropriation or budgetary tracking. Once data is confirmed in the ledgers, the data must then be "cross-walked or combined to obtain the balances in the general purpose financial statements.

For governmental units particularly, the auditor's opinion refers to the fairness of data in relation to the financial statements taken as a whole. In actuality, though, the auditor must set materiality thresholds and opine on the individual fund type columns in a government's general purpose financial statement.

In most governments, several functions or applications are "cross-cutting," impacting many or all operating departments and the central offices of a government and involving most or all of the financial transactions incurred by any activity. For this reason, the audit tests to understand the control structure and the later tests of controls, and the following tests of transactions, and detailed tests of account balances are directed at these 'cross-cutting" activities. The auditor must test, assess, understand, and evaluate the relevant policies, procedures, practices, authorizations and approvals, transaction processes, forms, data flows and aggregations, financial transaction amounts and values, as well as the balances ultimately appearing in the general ledger accounts for each of the following functions, or activities or applications:

- Budgeting,
- Encumbrances,

Audit Methodology—Financial Statement Audits

- Disbursements,
- Procurement,
- Capital acquisitions,
- Appropriations,
- Receipts,
- Personnel,
- Financing, and
- Contract and grant programs.

Phase IV

Test Controls and Transactions

Tests of controls may also be used simultaneously to test transactions. The objective of the test of controls is to determine whether the internal control structure is operating effectively. These tests require that several audit procedures be performed:

- Determine, by analysis and inquiry, that the controls have been established. Working papers, consisting of preliminary organizational charts, flow charts, and narrative descriptions of observed procedures, should be prepared.

- Perform "walkthroughs" of systems for selected transactions to confirm that the systems are functioning as described and that the controls prescribed for classes of transactions are being applied.

- Document the existing organization, including flowcharts of systems, document routing and information, and preparation of narrative procedural memos for the working papers.

- Determine, through tentative assessment of the systems of controls, the degree of reliance that may be placed on the controls in determining the nature, timing and extent of testing that will be applied to transactions and account balances.

- Re-assess earlier observations, as documented in the working papers, for purposes of confirming, refining, changing or rejecting earlier risk assessments of controls and systems.

- Prepare, on the basis of the study, understanding, and tests, written audit programs for sampling categories of transactions and auditing account balances and compliance with applicable laws and regulations.

With respect to testing controls, it is important to emphasize that controls are specific to a particular function or application. Thus, each function or application must be separately tested. For example, exhaustive tests of controls of budgeting and encumbrance activities provides the auditor with no information on the adequacy or effectiveness of the controls applicable to cash receipts or cash disbursements.

After testing controls, an evaluation must be made to determine whether the initial assessment of the likelihood of errors are still appropriate. Control risk assessment requires evaluating the likelihood of the existence of errors that are sufficiently important to materially affect the accuracy of balances in the financial statements being audited.

With governments, the auditor would expect to encounter two types of control procedures: detect controls and prevent controls. *Detect controls* are designed to detect errors that may have occurred during the transaction initiation and accounting or subsequently; *prevent controls* are designed to prevent errors during processing.

Governments are subjected to more stringent legal and procedural requirements than commercial organizations. Thus, factors are generally present to reduce risks of material errors entering into or remaining undetected in the accounts and account groupings. Some of these factors that would tend to reduce control risks, include:

● Being large entities, the data processing, accounting and financial reporting for most general governments are computerized, often utilizing rather sophisticated coding, data entry, processing, compilation and reporting techniques and operated by personnel who are not involved with authorizing, receiving, storing, or accounting for government resources and property.

● The major functions or applications—cash receipts, cash disbursements, procurement, personnel and payroll, etc.—require extensive coordination among different organizations and executives, specific authorization and approval by selected government executives, detailed documentation and completion of forms, and regular reports in addition to the formal general purpose financial statements. The execution of these roles require many persons employed by different organizations.

● The integrated budgetary control and accounting process that requires close monitoring and management of commitments and obligations of the government minimizes the possibility of large undetected expenditures being incurred or made that might be at variance with laws, regulations, or other policy.

Conduct of these tests require the application of two or more audit procedures such as inquiries of key or knowledgeable personnel, inspection of relevant documentation, observation of operations and practices, reperformance of internal control structure procedures. In this phase of the audit, it is essential that the focus be on testing and assessing the significance of the overall internal control structure

Audit Methodology—Financial Statement Audits

soundness of policies and effectiveness of procedures in achieving the objectives of the controls rather than on specific policies or procedures in isolation. The inadequacy of a specific control policy or procedure may not be a material deficiency if there are other compensating policies or procedures that satisfactorily address the same criterion.

To the extent controls are tested during an interim period, limited reviews of the systems of internal accounting controls, related policies and procedures, and practices should be performed at year end to determine if significant changes occurred that might have to be evaluated anew.

Phase V

Conduct Substantive Audit Procedures

Substantive tests are the detailed tests performed of (1) classes of transactions, and (2) account balances, and (3) analytical review procedures. These terms have the same connotation in governmental auditing as is the case in audits of commercial organizations and as the terms have been defined by the AICPA in its accounting and audit guide.

Test of Transactions

These tests are an examination of relevant support documentation to verify the authenticity of entries appearing in the formal accounting system of an entity. Tests of transactions are made to satisfy several audit objectives such as:

- Whether the recorded transactions, in fact, exist.

- Whether all of the existing transactions have been recorded, i.e., the accounting is complete.

- Whether the transactions are recorded accurately—i.e., the amounts are correct.

- Whether the transactions are properly classified in the journals, and in the accounts of the subsidiary and general ledger accounts, and in the general purpose financial statements.

- Whether the transactions are recorded on the proper date and in the proper fiscal period.

The transactions selected for audit must: (1) include representative transactions whether amounts are estimated or calculated (e.g., depreciation, amortization, write-offs), and (2) encompass the routine versus non-routine transactions.

Test of Account Balances

These tests are an examination of details of accounts to authenticate monetary correctness and other characteristics of general and other ledger balances that appear in the general purpose financial statements. Many of the objectives for testing transactions will apply equally to the test of account balances, but some additional objectives must be considered with respect to auditing the accounts, such as:

- Whether the accounting for transactions entered in the accounts have been properly cut-off at the year end or the balance sheet date.

- Whether the balances in the financial statements tie-in or reconcile to amounts in the general ledger accounts, which are in turn supported by subsidiary ledgers, summarizing journals and other records, which in turn are comprised of transaction entries that have been tested in an earlier phase of the audit.

- Whether the reported financial statement balances reflect the proper valuations, i.e., do asset, investment, debt, and other account balances reflect realizable, market, collectible or settlement amounts.

- Whether the asset and liability amounts represent property or rights owned or are the true obligations and debts owed by the entity.

- Whether the balances in the general purpose financial statements, the statement classifications, and the related footnote disclosures are proper and that there are no misstatements or no material omissions.

Analytic Review Procedures

These are tests made to assess the overall reasonableness of controls, transactions, and account balances utilizing analyses, ratios, comparisons, averages, exception reporting and other techniques to identify unusual, material variances. The objective of analytic review procedures is to highlight significant matters or issues that might require additional or special audit emphasis. Analytic audit procedures would be appropriate and must be used with respect to the audit of fund type data and, particularly, with the individual funds. These procedures would include:

- Comparisons of financial information with prior periods, giving consideration to known changes.

- Evaluating anticipated results (per budgets, forecasts, plans) to actual results, including extrapolations of data.

- Assessing relationships among financial data elements with the period under audit.

- Determining industry-wide information for comparison to the audited entity. i.e., the issues, concerns, trends, problems, of governments generally at the time of audit.

- Developing and assessing relationships between financial and relevant nonfinancial information, i.e., do the recorded costs bear a

Audit Methodology—Financial Statement Audits

reasonable relationship to the level of program activity and accomplishments.

Audit Procedures

These substantive audit tests are seldom accomplished through the performance of a single audit procedure. More commonly, application of several of the following audit procedures is required to obtain evidence to support each of the various financial statement assertions. Procedures that must be used will include several of the following:

- Physical examination by the auditor.

- Confirmation of data with sources external to the government.

- Obtaining and examining documents produced internally and externally to the government.

- Observation or witnessing of activities by the auditor.

- Scanning of records for unusual amounts; performed either manually or in conjunction with computerized audit tools.

- Inquiries by the auditor of senior governmental executives, departmental and agency managers, operating personnel.

- Reperformance or rechecking or reconciling or recalculating of balances, dollar extensions, unit values, etc., by the auditor.

- Vouching amounts recorded in the accounts back to supporting documentation (tests for possible overstatement of amounts) and tracing information recorded in supporting documentation to amounts shown in the account balances (tests for possible understatement of amounts).

- Analytic procedures involving the use of comparisons, ratios, variances and other analytical techniques to identify significant deviations or to corroborate information in the accounts, funds, and fund-type balances.

Of course, these audit procedures are not restricted to use only in audits of public sector entities; similar procedures are applied to audits of financial statements of commercial, not-for-profit and other organizations.

Phase VI

End of Audit Considerations

Several tasks and procedures must be performed after the close of the fiscal period, but before the auditor concludes on the type of opinion to be issued on the financial statements. These audit procedures are similar to those performed when auditing financial statements of commercial organizations. Many accounting firms, government audit organizations and the AICPA have published guidelines and checklists to assist auditors of public entities. This section highlights several tasks, procedures and issues that must be considered at the end of the audit.

Attorneys Representation Letters

Auditors must obtain a letter from the government's general counsel, departmental counsel and all attorneys with whom the government does business for purposes of identifying contingencies, existing and pending or anticipated litigation, and any other information involving legal counsel that is relevant to the financial statements. These letters should be as of a date that is no earlier than the date of the audit report.

Client Representation Letters

Auditors must obtain representation letters from several levels of the government's management (possibly the legislative, executive, departments, program, and operating personnel) to corroborate the more important oral representations made to the auditor during the audit. These letters should be as of a date that is no earlier than the date of the audit report.

The attorney and client representation letters are not adequate audit evidence in themselves. But, the failure of legal counsel and client management to provide this information is likely to constitute a limitation on the audit scope that will preclude rendering an unqualified audit opinion and be a basis for which the auditor must disclaim an audit opinion.

Related Parties

The search for instances of governmental executives doing business with the auditee. i.e., a related party circumstance, is continuous during the audit, and evidence will be re-evaluated at the close out to determine if evidence of such relationships exist. An inquiry, in this regard, should be included among the points requiring management response in the representation letters.

Subsequent Events

Subsequent events are transactions and events that occur after the close of the fiscal year under audit but before the issuance of the audit report that may or may not have an effect on the amounts reported on the general purpose financial statements. Depending on circumstances, a subsequent event could cause the financial statements to be corrected and restated, could require a full explanation of the event in the footnotes, or the event could have no effect on either the statements or the footnotes.

Audit Methodology—Financial Statement Audits

Auditors should consider a request for a management representation letter with respect to any subsequent events.

"Going Concern" Issues

There is minimal risk that a public entity might not continue as a "going concern" in the same sense as a commercial organization. But, there have been instances where taxpayer initiatives have restricted the ability of a government to raise taxes necessary to pay legally incurred debts or other actions that severely restrict a government's ability to meet its debts without disposing of assets, restructuring debt, being forced to drastically revise operations or alter services. Additionally, instances can exist where the revenue stream is insufficient to meet the principal and interest payments of long term debt, and the particular "revenue bonds" are permitted to go into default by the borrowing government.

Where there is doubt about the entity's ability to continue its operations as a "going concern" or where there is doubt as to the willingness of the borrowing government to meet its financial obligations, the effects on the financial statement must be assessed, footnote disclosures must be carefully examined for adequacy, and an evaluation be made on the nature of the audit opinion to be rendered.

Commitment/Contingencies

Commitments and contingencies, once identified, must be examined to determine if amounts must be recorded in the accounts, if footnote disclosures must be made to the financial statements, if the dollar impact is sufficiently material to warrant a qualified audit opinion, or if all of these actions may be appropriate.

Adequacy of Footnotes

The third (AICPA's) generally accepted auditing standard of reporting states:

> *"Informative disclosures in the financial statement are to be regarded as reasonably adequate unless otherwise stated in the report."*

All footnotes must be reviewed and evaluated by the auditor and a conclusion reached as to the adequacy of the disclosures. Further, the auditor must also assess whether there are any material omission. Financial statements and footnote disclosures may be misleading not only because of what is included but also because of what may have been excluded.

The omission of information required by generally accepted accounting principles or which may be material to the financial statements or the inclusion of erroneous information may cause the auditor to express a qualified or an adverse opinion. When such opinions are required, the auditor must provide the reasons therefore in the auditor's report.

Analytic Review Procedures

This substantive audit test must again be applied during the final review stage of the audit for purposes of assessing the audit conclusions reached with respect to the overall financial statements. Once again, analytic review procedures are substantive audit tests made to assess the overall reasonableness of controls, transactions, and account balances utilizing analyses, ratios, comparisons, averages, exception reporting and other techniques to identify unusual, material variances.

Additionally, procedures at this time must include a reading by the auditor of the entire financial statements and all footnote disclosures. The objective is to identify any unusual or unexpected balances or relationships for which additional evidence may be needed.

Phase VII

Audit Reports

Many accounting firms, government audit organizations and the AICPA have published reporting guidelines and financial statement disclosure checklists for use by auditors in preparing reports that meet the broader need of a public sector entity. These assist auditors in evaluating the form and content of the statements and the adequacy of footnote disclosures to ensure compliance with generally accepted auditing standards, the government auditing standards, the Single Audit Act (where applicable), laws and regulations, and contract and grant conditions that are material to the financial statements. *Exhibit 5-5* illustrates an auditor's report on the general purpose financial statements for a governmental unit that resulted from an audit made pursuant to both government as well as generally accepted auditing standards.

Reports on Compliance and Controls

With respect to tests of compliance with laws and regulations and of controls, government auditing standards do not require that an auditor perform additional audit work other than the audit work required as part of a financial statement audit outlined by the generally accepted auditing standards. But, the government standards do require that written reports of these tests be made for distribution to parties external to the auditee. Generally accepted auditing standards do not require that written reports be prepared or issued on tests of either compliance or of internal controls.

Audit Methodology—Financial Statement Audits 363

If separate reports are to be submitted on the results of the auditor's tests of compliance and of internal controls, *Exhibit 5-6* is typical of the report suggested by the government auditing standards.

SEC Reporting and Disclosures

The securities of governments are specifically exempt from the reporting and registration mandates of the Securities and Exchange Commission. But, these same laws (Securities Act of 1933 and Securities and Exchange Act of 1934) have anti-fraud provisions that do apply to public security offerings by governmental units. An auditor has no obligation to perform any procedures to corroborate other information contained in an official offering statement with respect to publicly traded financial securities.

But, to comply with the AICPA SAS No. 8 (Other Information in Documents Containing Audited Financial Statements), the auditor must: (1) read the information in an offering statement, and (2) consider whether such information or the manner of presentation is materially inconsistent with information or the manner of presentation appearing in the financial statements. SAS No. 8 details actions that an auditor must take if there is a material misstatement of fact in this other information.

Auditors having knowledge that the public entity's audited financial statements may be included in an official statement for publicly offered securities should consult the publication titled *Disclosure Guidelines for Offerings of Securities by State and Local Governments* (updated periodically by the Government Finance Officers Association). This document provides guidance to local governments for preparation of official offering statements and suggestions relative to the form and content of information that should be included.

Exhibits 14-1 and 14-2 follow this page.

EXHIBIT 14-1

Elements of Internal Control Structure

- *Control Environment.* The "tone at the top" for a governmental entity will directly affect the control consciousness of the public sector executives and employees.

- *Risk Assessment.* The auditee's identification, analysis, and management of risk that affect the organizations financial statement and major federal program objectives.

- *Control Activities.* The policies and procedures issued to implement management directives and ensure that personnel are conforming to these directives.

- *Information and Communication.* The control structure consisting of the methods and records established to identify, assemble, analyze, classify, record, and report on an entity's transactions and to maintain accountability for related assets and liabilities.

- *Monitoring.* The management responsibility of ensuring desired and prescribed controls are operating as intended and modified as frequently as changed conditions warrant.

EXHIBIT 14-2

Exhibit 14-2

Overview—
- Financial Statements......
- Summary of Audit Phases & Tasks

Phase I
Initiate Audit Survey

Interview Exec., Operating, Financial Personnel

Determine Acctg. Audit Criteria
- States
- GASB
- FASB
- AICPA
- GAO
- OMB
- Single Audit Act
- Other

Review Prior Audits/Issues
- Audit reports
- Single audits
- Financial studies
- Consulting reports
- Government reviews

Review Financial History
- Reports
- Statements

- Accounting Records
- Manuals
- Other
- Budgets
- Cost Accounting
- Internal Reports
- Other

Review Prior Auditor's Workpapers

Legal Issues
- Review Laws
- Financial Statutes, Codes, Regs
- Council Minutes
- Contingencies
- Commitments
- Other

Identify Audit Entity
- GASB Criteria
- Operating Agencies
- Trusts
- Component Units
- "Blended" units
- Joint Ventures
- Separate Investments
- Other

Survey for Single Audit
- Major Programs
- Nonmajor Programs
- Compliance Tests
- Controls Tests
- Sched. Fed Expend

- Laws, regs
- Federal Reports
- Allowable Costs
- Unallowable Costs
- Approved Ind. Costs
- Matching Reqmts
- Other

Prepare Summary Audit Planning Memo

Phase II
Understand Controls Structure

Analyze Accounting, Administration Controls Structure
- Manuals
- Policies
- Procedures
- Practices
- Other

Document Understanding of Controls
- Identify Forms
- Test Authorization
- Trace Approval Process
- Do "Walk Throughs"
- Do Control Questionnaires
- Do Control Checklist
- Flow Chart Controls
- Federal Programs
- Other

Review Financial Cycle Controls
- Receipts, Revenues
- Disbursements, Purchases
- Contracts, Grants
- Fixed Assets
- Inventories

Assess Control Risks
- Transactions
- Indiv. Accounts

366 Government Auditing: Standards and Practices

Phase IV
Test Systems, Controls, Etc.

Evaluate Compliance with
Control Policies, Procedures,
Test Controls in Practice

Conduct
Review of Data Centers

Consolidate Data
on Applications

Document Test
of Controls

Assess
Effectiveness of Controls

Conduct Test
Accounting, Reporting,
Control Risk Areas

Finalize
Financial
Audit Plan

Prepare
Detailed Audit Programs

- FASB Statements
- OMB Circulars
- GAO Standards
- Federal IG Issues
- Other

Draft Preliminary
Single Audit Plan

Highlight Accounting,
Reporting Issues for Followup,
Detailed Audit

Draft Financial Statement
Audit Plan

Phase III
Develop Audit Plan

Review
Controls
Environment
- Accounting Applications
- Accounting Cycles
- Specific Accounts
- Transaction Groups
- Indiv. Trans,
- Financial Sources
- Other

Review Report
and Fund
Structures
- Entitywide Stmts
- Government Funds
- Proprietary Funds
- Major Funds
- Fiduciary Funds
- Assets
- Other

Review Agencies,
Locations to
Visit, Audit

Review for
Single Audit
- Compliance Requirements
- Controls Issues
- Award, Budget
- Financial Plans
- Federal Reports
- Program Evaluations
- Laws, Regs
- AICPA SASs
- GASB Statements

- Account Groups
- Receipt Cycle
- Disb Cycle
- Purchase Cycle
- Contracts Cycle
- Major Programs
- Nonmajor Programs
- Other

Examine Commitments
- Trusts
- Endowments
- Debt
- Debt Guarantees
- Union contracts
- Pensions, etc.
- Gov't Grants
- Gov't Contracts
- Other

Update,
Coordinate
Financial Data
- Past Audits
- Interim Work

Design Detailed
Sample Plans
- Statistical
- Stratified
- Selective
- Judgment
- Other

Develop
Audit
Approaches
- gaas
- gagas
- Single Audit

Audit Methodology—Financial Statement Audits 367

> This overview integrated key tasks required to consider performing an audit required by the Single Audit Act and the OMB Circular A-133 with the audit of financial statements.

Phase V
Perform Substantive Tests

At Interim
or/and
Year End
- Test Transactions
- Confirm Trans.
- Physical Observations
- Test Account Balances
- Analytic Procedures
- Reconcile Stmt Data

Single
Audit
Tests
- Test Program Receipts, Disb.
- Advance Draws
- Test Budgets Conformance
- Program Compliance
- 14 Compliance Criteria
- Allow. Cost
- Unallow. Cost
- Indirect Cost
- Matching Cost
- Representation Letters
- Other

Identify, Inventory
Accounting & Reporting
Issues

Develop Proposed
Adjustments, New or
Revised Notes

Phase VI
Audit Close Out

End of Audit
Tasks
- Tests of Accounts
- Analytic Procedures
- Subsequent Events
- Contingencies
- Related Parties
- Going Concern
- Other
- Audit Checklist
- Stmt Checklist

Review Draft
Financial
Statements,
Reports
- Entity-wide
- Govt. Fund Types
- Proprietary Funds
- Component Units
- Fiduciary Funds
- Sched Fedl Expend.
- Compliance Reports
- Control Reports
- Other
- Notes

Resolve Acctg,
Reporting,
Note Issues

Phase VII
Deliver Audit Reports

Required
Audit Reporting
- Per gaas
- Per gagas
- Per Single Audit Act
- OMB Circular A-133
- Management Letter
- Others

Obtain
Representation Letters
- From Executive Management
- From Counsel,
  Outside Attorneys

Deliver Audit
Reports

Chapter 15

Audit Methodology— Single Audits

Since 1984, Single Audit Act concerns have been a significant component in an audit of governmental units and other entities receiving federal financial assistance. In practice the audit of an auditee's entity-wide financial statements and the audit procedures to conform to the Single Audit Act criteria may and often will be performed concurrently. Whether done in parallel with the financial statement audit or specifically to comply with the Single Audit Act, many special audit procedures are required before an auditor can issue the required audit reports that conform to the Single Audit Act criteria.

BACKGROUND

The Single Audit Act 1984 culminated decades of dissatisfaction on the part of the federal government—Congress and federal departments—with the level of oversight and compliance that recipients of federal assistance were providing over federal monies. At the same time, the Single Audit Act was a partial response by Congress to the pleas of state and local government executives to simplify the managerial and administrative requirements of all federal assistance programs and, in particular, to reduce the excessive number of duplicative audits being made of their governments.

The single audit concept has been imposed by the federal government on those governmental units, non-profit organizations, educational institutions, and Indian tribal governments expending $300,000 or more of federal assistance in a single fiscal year. The Single Audit Act was unprecedented in the level of detailed auditing that Congress prescribed in an attempt to resolve the disparities and inconsistencies in audits of federal programs. This detail extended to the nature, content and format of the audit reports that must be submitted by qualifying governments.

By various estimates, the Act affects tens of thousands of state and local governments and more than 150,000 non-profit organizations, colleges and universities, and Indian tribal governments. The single audit is a comprehensive audit of a public entity's financial statements, internal controls, and compliance with laws and regulations. Since 1997, OMB Circular A-133 is the federal regulation that implements the Single Audit Act. The single audit has been the primary examination obtained by the federal government over most of its financial assistance programs.

The Act forced a significant and beneficial reduction in the number of limited purpose audits made by federal audit staffs of state and local government and not-for-profit entities while increasing the number of governmental assistance programs being audited. At the same time, Congress, by the Single Audit Act, significantly expanded the definition of federal assistance that historically included primarily federal grants and contracts. Under the Single Audit Act, financial assistance provided by the federal government is now defined to include all types of financial assistance in the form of:

> "... assistance that non-federal entities receive or administer in the form of grants, loans, loan guarantees, property, cooperative agreements, interest subsidies, insurance, food commodities, direct appropriations, or other assistance, ..."[1]

OBJECTIVE OF SINGLE AUDITS

The Single Audit Act requires all state and local governmental units, their instrumentality's, non-profit organizations, colleges and universities, and Indian tribal governments spending $300,000 or more within a fiscal year to have such a single audit of their activities annually.

The objectives of the Act and the single audit concept are, in part, to:

(1) Improve the financial management of state and local governments with respect to federal programs;

(2) Establish uniform requirements for audits of federal programs;

(3) Promote efficient and effective use of audit resources; and

(4) Ensure that federal departments and agencies, to the maximum extent practicable, rely on single audits.

Generally, the Act required each recipient of federal financial assistance to have a single audit, for a single fiscal year, made by a single auditor. While welcomed by other levels of government, the

---

[1] Pursuant to the 1996 Act and the related implementing federal regulation, OMB Circular A-133, Audits of States, Local Governments, and Non-Profits Organizations, payments or amounts received as reimbursement for services rendered to individuals relating to the federal Medicare and Medicaid assistance programs are specifically excluded from this definition of federal financial assistance.

single audit concept was still a "mandated" program by the Congress. With "mandated" programs, Congress passes a law, mandates a requirement, but provides no funds to support or implement the legal mandate. Thus, recipient state and local governments, non-profit organizations, colleges and universities, and Indian tribal governments are financially liable for using their own auditors or retaining an independent CPA to make these audits, and, generally, absorbing the cost of the single audits.

In defining the single audit approach, Congress requires that a comprehensive audit and a voluminous set of reports be made available to executives at all levels of government. Compliance with the Single Audit Act requires that covered governmental units, non-profit organizations and educational institutions must annually submit three "packages" of audit reports: (1) audit reports required by the government auditing standards that relate to the entity-wide financial statements; (2) more detailed audit reports imposed by the Single Audit Act; and (3) even more reports imposed by the OMB Circular A-133, the federal regulation that implements and defines the Single Audit Act in great detail.

All single audits must be conducted by an independent auditor in accordance with generally accepted government auditing standards and should encompass the entirety of the financial operations of the audited entity. As an option, the Act also permits a series of audits covering all of the individual departments, agencies, and establishments of the entity for the same fiscal year to be considered as a single audit.

REPORTING FOR A SINGLE AUDIT

The Single Audit Act (§ 7502) requires that each single audit: (1) cover the operations of the entire non-federal entity, (2) be conducted in accordance with generally accepted government auditing standards, (3) include specific detailed audit tests of controls and compliance with laws and regulations, and (4) result in mandated audit opinions and reportings.

Overlooked, at times, by auditors new to governmental auditing, is the fact that there are two distinct levels of audit and other reports imposed by Congress. Congress wants the audit reports: (1) to disclose any instance of noncompliance with federal laws and regulations and internal controls that may have a material effect on the recipient's entity-wide financial statements; and, in addition, (2) to disclose all instances of noncompliance with federal laws and regulations and internal controls that may have a material effect on each individual major federal program.

The General Accounting Office, the President's Council on Integrity and Fitness (the Council of federal inspectors general) and the American Institute of Certified Public Accountants have all studied the single audit reporting condition. By the 1990's many concluded that Congress should, among other suggestions, modify the Single Audit Act to simplify the reporting requirements. The hoped-for simplification did not occur. The 1996 amendments to the Act and the related OMB regulation imposed additional reporting. As separately identified in *Exhibit 15-1*, the list of reports exceeded a dozen if the auditor is to comply with everyone's criteria, Congress, GAO, OMB, and the AICPA criteria.

SINGLE AUDIT REQUIREMENTS

The Single Audit Act is the most detailed prescription of audit reporting, audit procedures and specific audit test requirements passed by Congress. Over the years, for many reasons, all well-intended, the reporting requirements related to a single audit made pursuant to the Single Audit Act of 1984 have expanded, probably beyond comprehension. The Act itself contains several reporting mandates. And, the Office of Management and Budget, by its regulations and Circulars, imposed other audit reports. As noted in *Exhibit 15-2*, the sources, legal or regulatory, that impose these reporting requirements are numerous.

The Single Audit Act [§ 7502] requires that a single audit: (1) cover the operations of the entire non-federal entity, (2) be conducted in accordance with generally accepted government auditing standards, (3) include specific detailed audit tests of every major federal assistance program, and (4) result in mandated audit opinions and reportings.

The audit report responsibilities and specific audit tests directed by the Single Audit Act directs that transactions be selected to evaluate the entity-wide financial statements and to evaluate each/every major federal assistance program. For example, pursuant to the Single Audit Act [§ 7502] and OMB's Circular A-133 [§ 500] which implements the Act, an auditor must:

● Determine whether the financial statements are presented fairly in all material respects in conformity with generally accepted accounting principles.

● Determine whether the schedule of expenditures of federal awards is presented fairly in all materials respects in relation to the financial statements taken as a whole.

● With respect to internal controls pertaining to compliance requirements for *each* major federal program, the auditor shall: (1) obtain an understanding of such internal controls, (2) assess control

Audit Methodology—Single Audits

risk, and (3) perform tests of controls, unless controls are deemed ineffective.

● Determine whether the non-federal entity complied with laws, regulations, and contracts and grants pertaining to the federal awards that have a direct and material effect on *each* major program.

The Single Audit Act requires transactions for every individual major federal assistance program be audited. Determination of *major* federal awards are central to the conduct of a single audit since these larger federal assistance programs are the subject of considerable testing and reporting by the auditor. A *major* federal assistance program is defined as one with federal awards *expended* during the audit period exceeding the larger of $300,000 or three percent of the total federal awards in the case of an auditee for which total federal awards expended in a year equal or exceed $300,000 but are less than or equal to $100 million. [2]

By this definition, the audited entity may have up to 33 major federal programs, although most have only a few major programs, some might have up to a dozen. OMB, in Circular A-133 (§ 520), requires a risk-based approach be used when selecting the major programs to be audited. The intent is to direct the focus of the single audit on the higher-risk programs.

To determine which federal programs are to be audited as major programs, the auditor must first identify programs as either Type A (i.e., the larger federal programs, federal expenditures exceed the larger of $300,000 or three percent of total federal expenditures) or Type B program that do not meet the Type A criteria. (i.e., the smaller federal programs). Generally the programs required to be audited will include all type A programs, except those identified as low risk and the high risk Type B programs. Circular A-133 outlines a procedure for determining risk and risk elements that should be considered.

Percentage of Audit Coverage Rule

Circular A-133 (§ 520) requires the auditor to audit, as major programs, those programs with federal expenditures that equal at least 50 percent of the total federal awards expended. However, if the auditee meets the criteria for a low-risk auditee, the auditor need only audit as major programs those federal programs with federal awards expended that, in the aggregate, include at least 25 percent of the total federal awards expended.

---

[2] For larger recipients of federal assistance, those exceeding $100 million but less than $10 billion in expenditures, a *major* federal program is one where $3 million or 3/10s of one percent was expended. For even larger recipients of federal assistance, those exceeding $10 billion, a *major* federal program is one where $30 million or 15/100s of one percent was expended.

If the total federal awards expended under major programs does not equal 50 percent (or 25 percent if low-risk programs are included) of the total federal awards expended, the auditor must select additional federal programs (either Type A or Type B) to meet the 50 percent criteria. All programs selected to meet the 50 percent criteria must then be audited as if the programs were major programs.

Transaction Testing Objectives

The specific number, selection, and testing of transactions to comply with the Act is based on the professional judgment of the independent auditor. But, the "professional judgment" of the auditor must consider such factors as:

—Amount of expenditures for both the federal programs and individual federal awards;

—Newness of the program or changes in its conditions;

—Prior experience with the program;

—Extent to which the program is carried out by subrecipients;

—Extent of programs contracts for goods and services;

—Level to which the program is already subjected to program reviews and other forms of independent oversight;

—Adequacy of controls for ensuring compliance;

—Expectations of adherence or lack of adherence to applicable laws and regulations; and

—Potential impact of adverse findings.

The Single Audit Act and the *Compliance Supplement* are prescriptive with respect to testing and require that tested transactions be examined to determine whether:

● Amounts reported as expenditures are for allowable services;

● Records show that those receiving services or benefits are the eligible recipients cited in law;

● Legally mandated matching requirements, levels of effort and earmarking limitations are met;

● All federal financial reports and claims for advances and reimbursements are supported by the books and records from which the basic financial statements have been prepared;

● Amounts claimed or billed or used for matching purposes were in accordance with the other OMB cost regulations that define allowable, unallowable, and indirect costs.

Audit Methodology—Single Audits

- Financial and program operations comply with federal laws, statutes, regulations and agreements governing individual federal programs managed by the recipient.

These audit criteria are to be applied to all selected transactions for each major federal assistance program. When transactions related to nonmajor federal programs are selected (possibly in connection with the financial statement examination or the evaluation of the overall system of internal controls), these transactions must also be tested for compliance with federal laws and regulations.

REQUIRED TESTS FOR COMPLIANCE

Over the years, federal agencies catalogued the significant legal and regulatory requirements of most of the major federal assistance programs which must be tested by an auditor when assessing compliance with laws and regulations. These compliance criteria and suggested audit procedures are published in an OMB document, titled *Compliance Supplement*. The *Supplement* highlights the audit requirements for major federal assistance programs comprising about 95 percent of the total federal financial assistance provided to non-federal entities.

There may be special conditions peculiar to individual federal financial assistance agreements with a recipient. These special conditions would have to be considered along with the compliance criteria in the *Supplement*. In addition, there are many federal assistance programs—probably several hundred—whose compliance criteria have not been catalogued in the *Compliance Supplement*. For these programs and those instances where the auditor elects not to use the *Supplement*, the auditor must compile specific audit compliance analyses and audit procedures.

The compliance audit requirements identified in the *Compliance Supplement* are national policies prescribed by federal statute, executive order, or other authoritative regulations that apply to two or more federal programs. OMB and federal agencies have concluded that noncompliance with these policies could materially affect either the recipient's financial statements or its major federal assistance programs.

OMB outlined 14 specific requirements, in the *Compliance Supplement*, as compliance criteria that must be examined as a part of every Single Audit. Chapter 9 earlier described the substantive audit procedures that must be performed by auditors of public sector entities to determine: (1) if in fact the controls relative to compliance with federal laws and regulations were implemented, and (2) whether tests of transactions, groupings of transactions, and account balances support the management's assertions that expenditures claimed or charged to federal programs are in compliance with applicable laws and regulations.

Exhibit 15-3 lists the 14 compliance requirements that auditors must consider in every audit of a non-federal entity conducted pursuant to OMB Circular A-133. In making a determination to not test for one or more of these requirements, the auditor must conclude that the requirement either: (1) does not apply, or (2) that noncompliance could not have a material effect on the major program. At the conclusion of the audit, the auditor must prepare a specific audit report on the results of test for compliance with the requirements in **Exhibit 15-3**.

The *Compliance Supplement* details the specific audit procedures to be applied in testing for types of allowed and unallowed services; eligibility of recipients; matching, level of effort, and earmarking of federal funds; required reporting; and other special provisions.

With few exceptions, federal funds are provided to fully or partially support specific activities or to provide for specific services of state and local governments. As a general rule, the federal funds are not "no strings" grants or entitlement awards. The allowable services and eligible constituents are set forth in the federal law or federal regulation. Also, federal laws will at times contain terms and conditions prohibiting expenditure of federal funds for identified activities. Congress has provided, in greater or lesser detail, the eligibility definitions, generally in terms of social, economic, or other demographics and has often limited the amount of the financial or other benefits to be received. Individuals or organizations that do not possess the qualifying characteristics are not eligible to receive financial assistance or benefits under that particular program.

Understanding the effects of compliance with laws and regulations relating to these 14 subjects is an initial, early, requirement for conducting financial statement, financial related audits, and single audits of non-federal entities that received federal financial assistance. As is the case with internal controls, acquiring this understanding of compliance requirements is a necessary prerequisite for an auditor in order to determine the nature, timing and extent of subsequent audit procedures that will form the basis for the required audit opinions.

It is the responsibility of auditee management to identify, those laws and regulations that directly and materially affect their government's financial statements and their major federal assistance programs. The auditor's responsibility is to assess this inventory of legal and regulatory compliance criteria by, initially, obtaining an *understanding* of the effects of noncompliance on the financial statements or individual government programs to be audited and, then, by testing the systems, controls, transactions and reports that related to the applicable laws and regulations.

Use of the *Compliance Supplement* is a "safe harbor" for the auditor and will satisfy the compliance audit requirements of the Single Audit Act. But, the *Compliance Supplement* covers less than 10 percent of the over one thousand federal assistance programs an auditor is likely to encounter. Some federal inspectors recognized the value of uniform compliance audit criteria and drafted other suggested audit procedures to assist auditors. This guidance may be available upon request and would contain information similar to the data that appears in the *Compliance Supplement*, for the larger federal assistance programs.

Special Program Compliance Provisions

While there may exist a standard program-wide assistance agreements (e.g., grants, contracts, loan agreements) the agreement with individual federal recipients may contain specific limitations, prohibitions, and other conditions that the federal agency and that particular recipient separately negotiated. Review of the special conditions for a federal assistance program could disclose conditions or advance agreements or memorandum of understanding related to such matters as: the use, acquisition or rental or equipment or real property; pre-award costs; insurance, support services, compensation and benefits; health and welfare costs; training and educational costs; relocation; indirect costs; etc. Any of these special conditions, if more restrictive then the program-wide assistance agreement and not in violation of some other law or regulation, would require tests to be made for compliance with the modified conditions.

Two Compliance Audit Reports

Circular A-133 requires that, at the conclusion of the compliance tests, the auditor must submit two compliance audit reports. One is a report on compliance with laws, regulations and provisions of individual contracts or grant agreements, noncompliance with which could have a material effect on the *entity-wide financial statements*. The second report relates to an audit of the major federal programs pursuant to the Single Audit Act. This latter compliance audit report must include an auditor's opinion (or disclaimer of an opinion) as to whether the auditee complied with laws, regulations and provisions of contracts or grant agreements, noncompliance with which could have a material effect on *each* major federal program. Where applicable, the auditor must refer to a separate schedule of findings and questioned costs.

REQUIRED TEST OF CONTROLS

Controls of federal programs must be tested if the auditor is to comply with the requirements of the Single Audit Act and the related OMB Circular A-133. Unlike audits made of private sector entities made pursuant to generally accepted auditing standards, controls of public sector units must be audited whether or not the auditor intends to rely on the controls in determining the extent of tests to be made of transactions and account balances.

Controls Defined

The definition of controls in the Single Audit Act is broader than that used or audited in the private sector. In the Act, Congress defined internal controls as comprising:

> *"... a process, affected by an entity's management and other personnel, designed to provide reasonable assurance regarding the achievement of objectives in the following categories: effectiveness and efficiency of operations; reliability of financial reporting; compliance with applicable laws and regulations."*

OMB Circular A-133, that implements the Single Audit Act, expands this definition of controls, stating that internal control means:

> *"... a process, affected by an entity's management and other personnel, designed to provide reasonable assurance regarding the achievement of the following objectives for federal programs:*
>
> *Transactions are properly recorded and accounted for to: (1) Permit preparation of reliable financial statements and federal reports; (2) Maintain accountability over assets; and (3) Demonstrate compliance with laws and regulations, and other compliance requirements.*
>
> *Transactions are executed in compliance with: (1) Laws, regulations, and the provisions of contracts or grant agreements that could have a direct and material effect on a federal program; (2) Any other laws and regulations that are identified in the compliance supplement; and, (3) Funds, property, and other assets are safeguarded against loss from unauthorized use or disposition."*

Controls Testing Criteria

Many of the internal control test objectives flow directly from several OMB circulars and, to a degree, from the compliance requirements outlined in the OMB *Compliance Supplement*, described earlier.

Those of particular interest in conducting the "single audit" aspect of an audit include:

● *OMB Circulars A-21, A-87, A-122*—The federal government's cost principles relating to allowable costs, unallowable costs, and the indirect costs that may be charged to or claimed against a federal program.

● *OMB Circular A-102, A-110*—The administrative and management guidelines for federal programs that include requirements on several subjects: accounting, management practices, property control and disposition, in-kind and matching and local share contributions, procurement, reporting, contract and grant termination and close out procedures, etc.

● *OMB Circular A-133*—Implements the Single Audit Act of 1996 and includes clarifying language and additional audit requirements not detailed in the Act itself which must be incorporated into a single audit.

● *OMB Compliance Supplement*—Sets forth the major general and program specific compliance requirements, as described in the earlier section of this chapter.

At times the control structure for the auditee's federal programs includes the same systems, policies and procedures as are utilized governmentwide. Where these conditions exist, the study, evaluation and detailed testing of controls for both levels—the federal program level and the governmentwide level—may be done simultaneously. But there are governments where the management, operations, and accounting associated with federal programs may not be integrated with the central systems. Or, the federal programs may be managed by geographically separated or organizationally dispersed entities. These are circumstances that warrant separate testing of controls.

Required Tests of Controls

The varying perspectives between the need for and nature of tests to be made of controls, as set forth in (1) the AICPA's generally accepted auditing standards, (2) GAO's government auditing standards, and (3) those imposed for single audits, are discussed, earlier in Chapter 8. The Single Audit Act significantly expands an auditor's responsibilities for reviewing and reporting on an entity's system of controls. Some examples are:

● The Act requires that internal controls be defined in considerably broader terms to include internal accounting controls, administrative controls and controls relative to complying with laws and regulations;

- The stated purpose of studying controls is not merely for purposes of relying on the controls to possibly reduce the magnitude of audit testing. Rather, the Act requires that tests be made to support a reporting on the adequacy of such controls for managing federal assistance programs in compliance with federal laws and regulations.

- The Act mandates that the controls must be tested, whether or not the auditor intends to rely on the controls in limiting later detailed testing of accounting data.

- The Single Audit Act requires an audit report on the tests of internal controls related to the financial statements as well as the controls related to major federal programs.

There may be instances where controls need not be tested. For example, the 1988 revision to the government auditing standards recognized several reasons why a study and evaluation might not be made of a governmental unit's control structure, including those instances where:

(1) An adequate internal control structure does not exist to permit reliance thereon due to the small size of the entity;

(2) The auditor may conclude that it is inefficient to evaluate the control structure and that it is more efficient to expand the substantive audit tests, thus minimizing the reliance placed on the control structure;

(3) The existing control structure has so many weaknesses that the auditor has no choice but to rely on increased substantive audit tests, ignoring the control structure; or

(4) The objective of a financial-related audit did not require that the auditor must obtain an understanding or make an assessment of the control structure.

Tests Control Structure

The Single Audit Act still requires that a study and evaluation be made of the control structure: (1) for the government as a whole, and (2) to provide reasonable assurance that federally-financed programs are managed and monitored in compliance with laws and regulations.

OMB Circular A-133 is more specific as to the purpose of such mandated tests. The Circular (§ 405) states that in addition to the tests required by the government auditing standards, other tests must be made of controls related to individual federal programs. To comply with this Circular, the auditor must perform audit procedures to *obtain an understanding* of internal controls over federal programs sufficient to plan the audit to support a low assessed level of control risk for each major program. Then, auditors *must plan* the testing of internal controls over major programs to support a low assessed level of control risk for the assertions relevant to the compliance requirements for each major program.

If the controls over some or all of the compliance requirements for a major program are likely to be ineffective in preventing or detecting noncompliance, the planning and performing of tests described are not required for compliance purposes. In this instance, the auditor shall report a reportable condition, assess the control risk at the maximum, and consider whether additional compliance tests are required because of the ineffective internal controls. Where applicable, an auditor's statement that reportable conditions in internal controls were disclosed, and, whether any such conditions were material weaknesses must be reported.[3]

Governmentwide Controls

When an auditee entity utilizes a single, entity-wide system of controls (e.g., a single accounting, cash receipts, and disbursement system), it might be possible that a single study and evaluation of controls could suffice in meeting: (1) generally accepted auditing standards, (2) generally accepted government auditing standards, and (3) the Single Audit Act requirements.

More often, though, this is not the circumstance encountered. There is more than one cash receipts system, or cash disbursement system. Or, operating departments may have autonomous accounting systems or data files that transmit summary inputs to the central accounts of the government. Further, the controls over the federal programs must be specifically tested to ensure that the federally-financed programs are managed in compliance with laws and regulations. This too, requires specific audit tests: the test of controls or compliance for one federal program will provide minimal information about the compliance under another federal program, having different criteria. Under these circumstances, each of these systems impacting the federal programs must be evaluated.

With respect to governments, conditions exist that generally are a basis for placing a high degree of reliance on the structure of controls—i.e., to assess risk at less than the maximum level. For example, almost all activities and actions of a governmental unit must have been earlier authorized by law. Another law, the appropriation law, is required to

---

[3] Generally accepted auditing standards provide the following definitions: *Reportable conditions* are matters coming to the auditor's attention that represent significant deficiencies in the design or operation of the internal control structure that could adversely affect the entity's ability to record, process, summarize, and report financial data consistent with the assertions of management in the financial statements. *Material weakness* is a condition in which the design or operation of one or more of the internal control structure elements does not reduce to a relatively low level the risk that errors or irregularities in amounts that would be material in relation to the financial statements may occur and not be detected within a timely period by employees in the normal course of performing their assigned functions.

financially support the activity or actions annually. The many disclosure requirements and "paper" filings and written affidavits that surround doing business with governments constitute checks and balances or controls over how, what, when, where and who may conduct the government's business. Thus, there is a high probability of discovery and disclosure and lessened risk of nondisclosure of collusive activities.

Additionally, personnel salaries and fringe benefits account for 80 percent or more of all expenditures for many governments. Here, too, laws dictate how many persons will be employed, the pay levels, and the fringe benefits permitted. This also has implications for control testing since salary rates and annual increases are set in law. Entry on a government payroll is an arduous and well documented process. Most government positions are posted for public awareness; competitive applications generally result; many interviews and tests are conducted; aspects of all appointments must be approved by operating, budgeting, personnel, and accounting personnel. And, because payrolls are a large part of a government's budget, this is an area that is closely scrutinized and monitored by the government itself.

While often characterized as "red tape," these processes, procedures, paperwork requirements, authorizations and approvals, and systems of pre-disbursement fiscal reviews (i.e., referred to as "post audits") of public sector entities constitute detailed, documented systems of internal controls and checks and balances.

Federal Program Controls

A major federal assistance program may still be relatively immaterial to the auditor's conclusions on an auditee's overall financial statements. Nonetheless, the federal government requires tests of these controls of each major federal program. The auditor must obtain an understanding of the design of the relevant control structure policies and procedures that affect the federal programs and then determine if these policies and procedures have been placed in operation.

The AICPA's Statement on Auditing Standards, No. 78, describes an entity's internal control structure as being comprised of five components: the control environment, risk assessment, control activities, information and communication, and monitoring (see *Exhibit 15-4)*. This same structure is apropos to audits of public sector entities, too.

An understanding of each of these five components of the internal control structure is necessary to plan the audit of an entity's financial statements. In planning a single audit, such knowledge should be used to: (1) identify types of potential misstatements, (2) consider factors that affect the risk of material misstatements, and (3) to design substantive audit tests to validate actual control circumstances.

Audit Methodology—Single Audits 383

The AICPA's SASs 55 and 78 also provides guidance on the types of evidential matters required to support an assessed level of control risk. These include reliance on the auditor's prior experience with the entity and understanding of the audit entity's classes of transactions, plus making inquiries of appropriate entity personnel, and inspection of documents and records (e.g., source documents, journals, ledgers), inspection of systems documentation.

Work performed to understand the entity's internal control structure should be documented in the working papers and might include: flowcharts, questionnaires, completed checklists, decision tables, narrative descriptions, memorandum. Acquiring this understanding of the control structure also requires that the auditor:

- Identify types of potential material noncompliance.

- Consider matters that affect the risk of material noncompliance.

- Design effective compliance tests to assess compliance with laws and regulations applicable to major federal programs.

- Assess other compliance criteria that may be imposed by a state or other governmental organization on the audited entity for possible impact on federal programs (e.g., debt covenants that could impact on capital assists or construction projects involving federal money.)

In addition to obtaining an understanding of controls, OMB Circular A-133 requires that the auditor conduct tests to determine whether the internal controls are actually functioning and are effective in preventing or detecting instances of material noncompliance.

Two Audit Reports on Controls

Circular A-133 requires that, at the conclusion of a single audit, the auditor must submit two reports on controls. One is a report on internal controls related to the *entity-wide financial statements* of the auditee. The second report is a reporting on the internal controls related to the *major federal programs.*

TESTS OF ALLOWABLE, UNALLOWABLE, INDIRECT COSTS

In addition to uniquely required tests for compliance with laws and regulations and other mandated tests of internal controls, the single audit requires specific audit procedures be applied to determine the allowability of all costs, direct and indirect, recorded against, billed to, or paid for under federal assistance programs.

As described in more detail in Chapter 10, auditors of governments, for decades, have had to be knowledgeable of federal policies relating to the allowable, unallowable and indirect costs permitted as charges under or claims to federal contracts, grants and cooperative agreements. The same is true for audits made pursuant to the Single Audit Act.

Noncompliance with federal allowable and unallowable cost criteria will be significant to the individual major federal programs and at times to the entity overall. For this reason, the audited resolution of these costs must be evaluated for materiality when issuing an audit opinion. National policies—laws, department regulations, OMB circulars—specify types of cost, direct and indirect, that may and may not be claimed or reimbursed under federal programs, federal contracts, federal grants, and cooperative and other agreements.

Costs charged to federal contracts and grants that do not meet these national policies must be "set aside" or questioned and reported in a single audit. If, the questioned costs are later disallowed by the federal agency, the costs cannot be claimed and, if reimbursed, the amount must be refunded to the federal government, with interest under certain conditions.

Federal Cost Policies

These federal cost principles or regulations have been made law, codified, and as national policy, override any individual federal departmental or agency regulations of specific contracts, grants, and cooperative and other agreements. Auditors will encounter cost regulations in the form of three OMB Circulars that have been tailored to meet specifics of different "industries" or types of recipients of federal assistance. Each Circular is the federal regulation that defines allowable, unallowable, and indirect costs that may or may not be claimed by these specific types of organization:

● Circular A-21 titled *Cost Principles for Educational Institutions,*

● Circular A-87 titled *Cost Principles for State and Local Governments* [and Indian tribal governments], and

● Circular A-122 titled *Cost Principles for Non-Profit Organizations.*

The prescriptions of these three Circulars control the nature of costs that may be accumulated, charged, paid, billed, or reported in relation to a federal contract, grant, cooperative and other agreement. These cost principles apply to all federal awards received by a non-federal entity, regardless of whether the awards are received directly from the federal government or indirectly through a pass-through entity.

The OMB allowable, unallowable, and indirect cost regulations do not establish the level of cost to be reimbursed under a federal assistance program nor do the Circulars describe what costs would be appropriate for funding in a program budget. These are issues decided for departmental or agency programs either nationally by law or individually in a contract or grant between the federal department or agency and the auditee.

Under all three cost Circulars, the OMB policy is that no provision for profit or other increment above cost is intended. Thus, claims for "performance fees," "management allowances," "undesignated costs", etc., are not permitted as allowable costs under a grant or cooperative agreement.

Reporting of Unallowed or Questioned Costs

For each federal program where there are audit findings and cost questioned related to unallowable costs and the federal cost principles, the auditor must specifically identify this condition in the data collection form required by Circular A-133. Additionally, identified unallowable costs must be included in the required schedule of findings and questioned costs.

The auditor must report known questioned costs which are greater than $10,000 for a compliance requirement of a major program. Also, the auditor must report known questioned costs when *likely* questioned costs are greater than $10,000 for a type of compliance for a major program. Known questioned costs are those specifically identified by the auditor. When evaluating the effect of questioned costs on the audit opinion related to compliance, the auditor must consider the best estimate of total costs questioned (i.e., the likely questioned costs), not just the questioned costs specifically identified (i.e., known questioned costs).

Questioned Costs for Non-Major Programs

Except for audit follow-up, Circular A-133 notes that the auditor is not required to perform audit procedures for a federal program not audited as a major program. Therefore, the auditor will normally not find questioned costs for a non-major program. However, if the auditor does become aware of questioned costs for an unaudited non-major program and the known questioned costs are greater than $10,000, then the auditor will report this fact as an audit finding.

WORKING PAPERS

With respect to single audits, working papers must contain evidence that the control structure related to: (1) governmentwide operations, and (2) individual federal programs were studied, understood, and tested. The working papers must show evidence as to the nature, number, source, amounts tested in the accounts, reports, and other financial and nonfinancial evidence examined.

Specific formats must vary, but the working papers should include flow charts, checklists, completed questionnaires, memorandum, audit plans, audit programs and other evidence of the controls tested and compliance requirements examined. Additionally a record must be made of the audit procedures applied, expectations noted, commentaries, analyses, and comparative schedules. Also, as is the case with all other working papers, there must be evidence of supervisory review of the audit work performed.

The AICPA's SAS No. 1 requires that the quantity, type, and content of working papers should "fit the circumstances" of the audit engagement. For governmental audits, "fit the circumstances" means that the working papers should also be clear and understandable without extensive supplementary oral explanation. An AICPA Interpretation to SAS No. 22 (*Planning Considerations for an Audit of a Federally Assisted Program*) states that working papers should be in sufficient detail to permit reasonable identification of the work done and conclusions reached. This Interpretation also states that working papers should not consist solely of work programs or checklists on which the auditor has merely indicated the steps that have been performed.

For audits of federal programs, more detailed and different guidance on audit working papers exists. For example, GAO (in its publication *Guidelines for Financial and Compliance Audits of Federally Assisted Programs*) proposed that working papers for audit tests should:

—Describe the transaction test objectives in terms of the criteria that the tests are designed to establish, with respect to the specific controls or compliance examined, the types of possible errors that may be found, and the features to be tested.

—Describe the universe for tests using judgmental or statistical sampling, including the items in the universe, periods over which the items were accumulated, activities, funds or programs covered by the controls or compliance features, similarity or disparity of items in the universe.

—Describe, when statistical sampling is employed, the sampling plan, size, precision, confidence levels or risk levels, and estimated error rates.

—Describe the method of selecting the test sample.

—Describe each of the audit test steps applied to sampled transactions or items by annotating detailed audit programs, which are in turn supported by evidentiary work papers.

—Describe the results of the test, including listing of errors noted and exceptions, follow-up actions required, and test results.

—Describe the conclusions resulting from the test of controls and the impact upon other test and audit procedures to be used throughout the remainder of the audit.

The § 4.35, 1994 edition government auditing standard related to working papers requires that:

"Working papers should contain sufficient information to enable an experienced auditor having no previous connection with the audit to ascertain from them the evidence that supports the auditors' significant conclusions and judgments."

Working papers for the single audit must be retained for a minimum of three years after the date of the audit report or for a longer period if the auditor is notified otherwise by the federal government. All working papers must be made available upon proper request to cognizant federal agencies, their designees, or the GAO.

AN ILLUSTRATIVE AUDIT METHODOLOGY

Since the 1960s, the complexities of federal audits have increased along with the federal funds that increasingly flowed to state and local governments and other public sector entities (e.g., school districts, special districts, authorities, utilities, commissions, boards, universities, public nonprofit organizations, etc.). As noted earlier, the Single Audit Act requires a comprehensive audit of these assistance programs that can result in more than a dozen separate reports.

Illustrative Single Audit

While certain of the audit procedures should, because of standards, requirements or logic, precede others, the development of an audit methodology for the "single audit" is left to the discretion of the auditor.

The following sections outline an illustrative methodology for a single audit that might be performed by either staff of a government agency or an independent CPA firm retained by the government. This example (see *Exhibit 15-5*), while detailed, is a suggested sequential listing of the concerns, issues, procedures, tasks, reports and other factors comprising a "single audit" of a public sector entity. The illustrative tasks have been grouped by several phases. In practice, the phases will be somewhat altered. Audit tasks could be in a different order, but these subjects must be covered by the auditor.

In practice, also, the comprehensive single audit would, in large measure, be performed concurrently with the audit of the governmentwide financial statements. Performance of only the "single audit" portion (i.e., review of only the federal assistance programs) of a governmental audit would be appropriate when a government was availing itself of the option set forth in the Single Audit Act. This option permits the comprehensive single audit to be done in parts—generally by individual departments and for the governmentwide financial statements—and even by two or more auditors. Most commonly, though, the comprehensive single audit is done by one auditor.

Survey Federal Programs

Many of the audit procedures to meet the Single Audit Act will be done concurrent with the audit of the governmentwide financial statements. But, regardless of the excellence of the overall planning efforts, there will be several audit procedures that must be performed to separately meet criteria of only the Single Audit Act.

The scope of an initiating survey depends on the experience of the auditor with performing single audits generally and the auditor's experience with the auditee specifically. In the initial audit year and every succeeding year, the schedule of federal assistance programs must be compiled anew, along with budgets, plans, and reports on actual performance and costs. This is the universe of activity for the single audit. Type A and Type B programs must be identified and major programs selected for audit that encompass at least 50 percent of the total federal expenditures of the auditee for the fiscal year to be audited.

The methods of financing utilized by the auditee is a significant fact to be established early on. Of importance is the amount of activities financed by appropriations, advances from other levels of government, agreements to match or provide in-kind non-federal contributions to support programs, and in some instances public debt, which is generally related to other terms and conditions that must be tested in a single audit.

An inventory of governmental accounting and auditing criteria must be compiled, understood, and incorporated into the audit plan, and later executed pursuant to detailed audit programs. These accounting and auditing criteria are not static, but change frequently in response to new Congressional concerns, federal funding and operating policies, and changes in systems approaches and technologies.

The results of the survey should be tailored to the conditions, circumstances, organization, operations, systems and controls of the auditee.

Develop Audit Plan

The objective of a written, detailed audit plan is to coordinate and control overall aspects of the single audit. The audit plan will outline the audit scope, the overall audit strategy to accomplish the audit scope, personnel budgets and assignments, important auditing and reporting issues, and communication and coordination procedures and may even prescribe selected detailed audit programs that will be applied. A comprehensive audit plan will include discussions, describe general audit applications, and provide guidance on several subjects important to the single audit, such as:

- Historical and statistical information.

- An overview of major controls systems, accounting systems, material legal issues, etc. highlighting weaknesses, strengths, and possible effect on the federal programs under audit.

- Observations about key accounts, transaction groups, risk programs, financing arrangements, completed or terminated federal programs.

- Specific tests for compliance with laws, regulations, and terms and conditions of contract and grant agreements that must be tested for all major programs.

- The scope of the audit consistent with prevailing controls, identifying reviews and tests to be made to comply with GAAS, GAGAS, the Single Audit Act, OMB Circular A-133 and the *Compliance Supplement*.

- Assignment of audit responsibilities to specific personnel, which generally includes responsibilities of both the auditor's staff and the auditee's.

- Detailed staff and time budgets for all tasks; progress report schedules, communication procedures, issue resolution process.

A well done, written, audit plan is an excellent tool for staff orientation, managing and directing the audit, and assessing effectiveness of selected audit strategies and procedures. But even the best plan must be modified and refined as the audit progresses—and this too, should be done in writing. An out-of-date plan that doesn't reflect the conditions or circumstances being encountered in the audit is no plan.

Review and Test of Controls

The federal audit regulations place considerable significance on the controls and systems used by recipients of federal financing to protect the funds, property, and other resources received or acquired for the federal activity. The federal government is concerned that auditors have controls to provide reasonable assurance the recipient is complying with applicable law and regulations. The federal audit regulations direct the auditor to make specific tests of the accounting, financial and managerial systems and controls during the review phase of the audit.

Earlier preliminary tests of the control structure, accounting cycles and administrative practices will provide a basis for acquiring an understanding of the controls, and later aid in determining the nature, timing and extent of detailed audit tests to be conducted. The overall objectives in reviewing controls is to reach conclusions regarding:

- The adequacy of the control structure and all of its major components for managing the federally financed programs, from both a financial and non-financial view;

- The extent of compliance with laws, regulations, terms and conditions of federal programs; and

- The accuracy and reliability of financial and program reports submitted to the federal agencies.

The conclusions about the controls will be an important factor in developing audit programs to direct the detailed tests for compliance and of accounts, account groups, and transactions related to the federal programs. Further, findings from this phase of the audit must be reported in two different reports on controls. One report must be prepared pursuant to the government auditing standards for the audited entity as a whole and the second report is prepared pursuant to the Single Audit Act relating to the controls of major federal programs.

Tests of Compliance

Detailed audit programs must be developed to test a recipient's compliance with such laws and regulations of major programs as: the enabling federal program legislation; the regulations of the sponsoring federal department; OMB's requirements relating to management, operation and administration of federal assistance programs, and the terms and conditions of specific agreements between the audited entity and any sponsoring federal agencies. The audit task is made somewhat easier if the major federal programs appear in the OMB Compliance Supplement, in which case the audit procedures suggested by OMB might be incorporated into the audit programs.

The conclusions about compliance with laws and regulations are an important consideration in developing audit programs to direct the detailed test of accounts, account groups, and transactions related to the federal programs.

These conclusions concerning compliance with laws, regulations and the terms of individual contracts and grants are an important factor in developing audit programs to direct the detailed tests. Further, findings from this phase of the audit must be reported in two different reports on compliance. One report must be prepared pursuant to the government auditing standards for the audited entity as a whole and the second report is prepared pursuant to the Single Audit Act relating to compliance in relation to each major federal program. For this second report on compliance, the auditor must express an audit opinion or a disclaimer of an opinion with respect to compliance with laws and regulations that would apply to *each* major federal program.

Detailed Auditing

The audit programs flowing out of the review of controls and tests of compliance describe the detailed audit procedures required to determine if federal financial reports and claims for advances and reimbursements are supportable by the books and records from which the basic financial statements have been prepared.

Detailed audit tests are required to determine the specific allowability or unallowability of direct and indirect costs incurred, claimed under or charged to, or reimbursement sought by the auditee from the federal government. Additionally, the auditee's procedures for receiving and disbursing cash, obtaining cash advances, making cash draw downs under federal letters of credit and requesting reimbursements must be tested in detail. Audit emphasis is also given to adherence to the program budget and the reasons for unusual, unexpected, or significant variances.

Single Audit Reporting

Reporting pursuant to the Single Audit Act and OMB regulations is an extensive process. Over the years, the single audit has been subjected to a "piling on" of reports to an extent that receivers of single audit reports are perplexed and confused about the message being communicated by the audit. While not all reporting requirements would be appropriate for all single audits, as noted earlier, extensive reporting has been imposed by the federal government and the AICPA on public sector entities receiving federal financing and the auditors conducting single audits of these entities.

Exhibit 15-5 is a suggested sequential listing of the concerns, issues, procedures, tasks, reports and other factors comprising a "single audit" of a public sector entity. The illustrative tasks have been grouped by several phases. In practice, the phases could be altered and tasks could be in a different order. These and other issues must be examined by the auditor. As noted, the comprehensive single audit could, in some measure, be performed concurrently with the audit of the entitywide financial statements. But, in no instance would an audit of the entitywide financial statements meet all of the audit criteria of the Single Audit Act.

Exhibits 15-1, 15-2, 15-3, 15-4, and 15-5 follow this page.

EXHIBIT 15-1

Audit Reports and Opinions Mandated by the Single Audit Act (and OMB Circular A-133)

1. A report with an opinion (or disclaimer of opinion) that the financial statements of the audited entity are presented in accordance with generally accepted accounting principles.

2. A written report on the study and evaluation of the entity's compliance with internal control structure made as a part of the audit of the entity's financial statements.

3. A written report on the tests of compliance with laws and regulations made as a part of the audit of the entity's financial statements.

4. A separate report, if appropriate, on disclosed or known irregularities or illegal acts, unless clearly inconsequential.

5. A report on whether the audited entity has internal control systems to provide reasonable assurance that federal programs are being managed in compliance with laws and regulations.

6. A report on whether the audited entity has complied with laws and regulations that may have a direct and material effect upon *each* major federal assistance program.

7. An audited schedule of expenditures of federal awards.

8. A schedule of findings and questioned costs.

9. A summary schedule of prior audit findings.

10. An audit follow-up report on prior audit findings.

11. A corrective action plan proposed by the auditee.

12. The special OMB data collection form.

13. Management letter of observed conditions and system and control weaknesses.

14. A report on known fraud in federal programs.

EXHIBIT 15-2

Citations of Federal Audit and Reports Requirements

Government Auditing Standards

The U.S. General Accounting Office publishes the federal government's requirements for audits of federal government organizations, programs, activities, and functions providing financial assistance to state and local governments, non-profits, educational institutions, and tribal Indian governments.

The Single Audit Act, as amended in 1996

Congress, through this Act imposed a comprehensive "single audit" on those entities receiving more than $300,000 in any year and the audit must include audited financial statements, a review of controls, and a review of compliance with laws and regulations, with a separate reporting on each of these components of the audit.

OMB Circular A-133

OMB, by this regulation, imposes the detailed audit criteria for federal single audits of: (1) state and local governmental units, (2) non-profit organizations, (3) institutions of higher education, and (4) Indian tribal governments.

OMB Circulars A-21, A-87, and A-122

There has long existed a series of federal regulations published by OMB covering allowable, unallowable and indirect costs that are permissible under federal assistance programs with: (1) institutions of higher education, (2) non-profit organizations, and (3) state and local governmental units, respectively.

OMB Circulars A-102 (the "common rule") and A-110

Two OMB regulations, Circulars A-102 and A-110, constitute the administrative guidelines for federal assistance programs with: (1) state and local governmental units and (2) non-profit organizations and institutions of higher education, respectively.

AICPA's Audit and Accounting Guide and Auditing Standards

The AICPA publishes an audit and accounting guide for audits of state and local governmental units that is periodically revised to meet emerging issues by issuances as its Statements on Auditing Standards.

PCIE Position Statements

Auditing guidance periodically issued by the President's Council on Integrity and Efficiency (the organization of federal inspectors general) related to audit issues involving single audits and other auditing subjects.

EXHIBIT 15-3

Single Audit Compliance Tests

- Allowed or Unallowed Activities
- Allowable, Unallowable and Indirect Costs
- Cash Management of Federal Funds
- Construction Contract Relevant to Davis-Bacon Act
- Program Eligibility Conditions
- Equipment and Real Property Management
- Matching, Level of Effort, or Earmarking
- Availability of Federal Funds.
- Procurement and Suspension and Debarment
- Program Income Determination and Utilization
- Real Property Acquisition and Relocation Assistance
- Reporting of Federal Financial Assistance
- Subrecipient Monitoring
- Special Program Tests and Provisions

EXHIBIT 15-4
Elements of Internal Control Structure

- ***Control Environment.*** The "tone at the top" for a governmental entity will directly affect the control consciousness of the public sector executives and employees.

- ***Risk Assessment.*** The auditee's identification, analysis, and management of risk that affect the organization's financial statement and major federal program objectives.

- ***Control Activities.*** The policies and procedures issued to implement management directives and ensure that personnel are conforming to these directives.

- ***Information and Communication.*** The control structure consisting of the methods and records established to identify, assemble, analyze, classify, record, and report on an entity's transactions and to maintain accountability for related assets and liabilities.

- ***Monitoring.*** The management responsibility of ensuring desired and prescribed controls are operating as intended and modified as frequently as changed conditions warrant.

EXHIBIT 15-5

Exhibit 15-5

Overview—
Single Audit Plan......
Summary of Audit Phases & Tasks

A. Survey Federal Programs

1. Accounting Standards
   - GASB
   - FASB

2. Audit Criteria
   - gaas
   - gagas
   - OMB Circulars
   - Single Audit Act
   - Compliance Supplement

3. Federal Programs
   - Titles
   - CFDA Numbers
   - Budgets
   - Expenditures of Federal awards
   - Programs
   - ...Major "A"
   - Low risk
   - High risk
   - ...Non-Major "B"

4. Funding Methods
   - Appropriations
   - Advances
   - L of C drawdowns
   - Reimbursement
   - "Pass thru's"
   - Matching

5. Single Audit Issues
   - Compliance
   - Controls
   - 50% Coverage
   - Subrecipients
   - Reports

6. Grant, Contracts
   - Conditions
   - Budgets
   - Changes
   - Status

7. Review Reports
   - Past Audit Reports
   - Special Studies
   - Federal IG Reports
   - Other

8. Meet with Auditee

B. Develop Audit Plan

1. Preliminary Survey
   - Financial Policies
   - Systems
   - Controls
   - Accounts
   - Transactions
   - Cost Acctg
   - Computers
   - Forms
   - Authorizations

2. Compliance Tests

3. Program Tests
   - Major, Non-major
   - High, Low Risk
   - Type "A" & "B"

4. 50% Coverage
   - Circular A-133

5. Comp Supp Tests

6. Draft Audit Plan

C. Review, Test Controls

1. Financial
   - Programs
   - Entity wide
   - Systems
   - Computer operations
   - Account Cycles
   - Transactions
   - Data Flow
   - Forms

2. Non-Financial
   - Managerial
   - Property
   - Personnel
   - Programs

3. Compliance Controls
   - Laws
   - Single Audit
   - OMB
   - Federal programs

D. Review, Test Compliance

1. Comp. Supp.
   - Allowed Activities
   - Allowable Costs
   - Indirect Costs
   - Cash Management
   - Davis-Bacon Act
   - Eligibility
   - Property Mgmt
   - Matching Requirements.
   - Availability of Federal Funds
   - Suspension, Debarment
   - Program Income
   - Property Acquisition
   - Relocation Assistance
   - Reports of Assistance
   - Subrecipients
   - Special tests

2. Admin Regs
   - A-102
   - A-110

2. Costs Regs
   - A-21
   - A-87
   - A-122

3. Budgets
   - Plans Actual
   - Variances
   - Revisions

E. Detailed Audit Tests

1. Substantive
   - Accounts
   - Transactions
   - Terms Conditions
   - Comp Supp
   - Reports

2. Analytics
   - Comparisons
   - Ratios
   - Trends
   - Outputs

- Outcomes
- Variances

3. Program Costs
- Allowable
- Unallowable
- Indirect
- Matching
- In-kind

4. Prior Year Followup
- Audit Reports
- Fed Evaluations
- Corrections
- Other Reports

5. Financial A & B Pgms
- Statements
- Schedules
- Reports

6. Non-Financial A & B Pgms
- Property
- Operations
- Close out

7. Rep Letters
- Auditee Mgmt
- Attorneys

8. Close Out Tasks

3. Per A-133--Pgms
- Compliance
- Controls
- Pgm Expend
- Questioned Costs
- Prior Audits
- Corrective Action Plan
- Data Form

4. Others
- Illegal Acts
- Known Fraud
- Mgmt Letter

> As noted in respective chapters, the intent is to conduct, as much as practicable, the Single Audit concurrent with the audit of the entity wide statements. Where this is not possible, specific tests must be conducted to meet the Single Audit Act requirements.

F. Single Audit Reporting

1. Per GAAP, GAGAS
- Entity Stmts

2. Per GAGAS
- Compliance
- Controls

Chapter 16

Audit Methodology—Financial Related Audits

STANDARDS FOR FINANCIAL RELATED AUDITS

Government Auditing Standards

Government auditing standards define financial audits as encompassing two categories of audits: (1) financial statement audits, and (2) financial related audits. The objectives of *financial related* audits appearing in the standards relate to:

1. Determining whether financial information is presented in accordance with established or stated criteria;

2. Determining whether the audited entity has adhered to specific financial compliance requirements; or

3. Determining whether the audited entity's internal control structure over financial reporting and/or safeguarding assets is suitably designed and implemented to achieve the control objectives.

Several examples, of financial related audits are also cited:

● Segments of financial statements—financial information (statements of revenues and expenses, cash receipts and disbursements, fixed assets); budget requests; and variances between estimated and actual financial performance.

● Internal controls over compliance with laws and regulations—such as those related to bidding, accounting for and reporting on contracts and grants proposals, billings, termination claims, etc.

● Internal controls over financial reporting and/or safeguarding assets—including controls using computer-based systems.

● Compliance with laws and regulations and allegations of fraud.

The government auditing standards recognize that, in some instances, it may be more appropriate to apply other guidance by the American Institute of Certified Public Accountants rather than the profession's generally accepted auditing standards to assess the adequacy of audit reports for financial related audits. Therefore for financial related audits, the government auditing standards recommend application of the AICPA's *Statement on Standards for Attestation Engagements*. The SSAE's address a scope of work different than a financial statement audit and provide guidance for:

(1) Reporting on audits requiring the application "agreed upon" (between the client and auditor) procedures and on the nature of reporting required when an audit is made of less than a full financial statement;

(2) Auditing and reporting on compliance-type financial examinations of governmental financial assistance programs;

(3) Reporting on reviews made of computer services organizations, e.g., outside service bureaus, and the reliance that might be placed upon such reports in the appropriate circumstances.

Auditors of public sector entities may, from time to time, conduct audits that do not meet the definitions or examples of financial related audits noted in the government auditing standards. When such audits are performed, auditors must comply with the government's field work and reporting audit standards relating to performance audits.

AICPA's Attestation Standards

The government field auditing standards (§ 5.36) incorporate, as part of the government audit reporting standards for financial related reports, all of the AICPA attestation standards. The attestation standards provide guidance for a variety of engagements where the CPA provides assurances or representations or attestations on financial data or on other than historical financial statements or must report in a format other than the traditional audit opinion report. For this reason, the AICPA's attestation standards specifically omit references to financial statements, opinion-type audit reports and application of generally accepted auditing standards.

GAO incorporates by references all AICPA attestation standards in its field work audit standards (§ 4.39) and in its reporting standards for financial-related audits (§ 5.36). But, the AICPA's attestation standard (SSAE No. 3) excludes the application of the SSAEs to engagements for which the objective is to report in accordance with (1) Government Auditing Standards, (2) the Single Audit Act of 1984, (3) OMB Circulars with respect to audits of federal assistance programs, or (4) program specific audits. These public sector audits are covered by an AICPA Statement on Auditing Standards devoted exclusively to compliance auditing and reporting.

Audit Methodology—Financial Related Audits

Positive and Negative Assurances

In the 1988 edition, government auditing standards provided the following definitions of these terms with respect to compliance and financial related audits of public sector activities:

- *Positive assurance* consists of a statement by the auditor that the tested items were in compliance with applicable laws and regulations.

- *Negative assurance* is a statement that nothing came to the auditor's attention as a result of applying the "agreed upon" or specified procedures that caused the auditor to believe the untested items were not in compliance with applicable laws and regulations.

In a 1994 article, the AICPA's Auditing Standards Board concluded that it was inappropriate to provide negative assurance in engagements related to compliance.

But, if used, a negative audit assurance might contain the following or similar wording:

"With respect to transactions not tested, nothing came to our attention that would lead us to conclude that XX City was not in compliance with laws and regulations for which we noted violations in our testing referred to above."

Engagements to which the AICPA's attestation standards apply closely parallel the financial related engagements performed for many years by the profession for government clients. Thus, the attestation standards provide sound guidance to auditors. This is so, notwithstanding the AICPA's position that excludes the application of the SSAEs to engagements made in accordance with Government Auditing Standards, the Single Audit Act of 1984, and the OMB Circulars with respect to audits of federal assistance and program specific audits.

AUDIT CRITERIA

Financial related audits differ in several aspects from financial statement audits, including: the standards to apply, determination of audit scope, appropriateness of applied audit procedures, and the format and wording of the audit report itself. *Exhibit 16-1* highlights some of the applicable audit criteria for these audits.

Financial Related Audit Scopes

A financial related audit is an audit reporting on selected parts of a public sector entity. For example, the audit might be of only a revenue statement, an expenditures statement, the budget to actual performance, of specified controls, or a reporting on an individual program contract or grant, or a fraud examination. That is, the financial related audit has an audit scope of other than or less than governmentwide financial statements of a primary or oversight government or a component unit of either.

Although financial related audits are limited or specified scope audits, some aspects may be duplicative of parts of other broader audits. When possible, financial related audits should build upon earlier or concurrent relevant audits. Legislatures and governmental managers often require these more focused audits to provide in-depth examinations of individual operations, activities and even specific transactions. Such audits could possibly assess one or more conditions concurrently, e.g., conformance to a budget, compliance to applicable or certain identified laws and regulations, opinions on relative efficiency or economy of operations, appropriateness of benefiting program recipients, or allowability of services being provided, to cite a few.

The scope of each financial related audit is unique. The audit objectives of a financial related audit relate only to a specified audit scope. Seldom will the exact financial related audit be replicated by an audit organization. In practice, government auditors probably perform more financial related audits than independent CPAs. The need for, and the objectives and scope of financial related governmental audits, are almost exclusively identified or determined by the public sector executives—financial, program managers, or auditors then, a decision is reached as to whether the government auditor or a CPA will perform the audit.

Types of Financial Related Audits

The AICPA's standards address certain types of financial related audits—special reports, compliance auditing, audits of computer service organizations, and attestation engagements. These examinations, reviews, audits or other engagements are not financial statement audits and do not come within the clear purview of either generally accepted auditing standards or the government auditing standards. Attestation standards recognize the reality that CPAs have been requested and do provide assurances on other than historical financial statements. They do render reports in forms other than the standard-type audit opinion. Like financial related audits, the objectives and scope of an attestation engagement varies in direct proportion to the number of organizations desiring attestation-type examinations (detailed testing) and reviews (more moderate, less detailed testing).

Objectives of Financial Related Audits

As a matter of practice the objectives and scope, as a minimum, and often the reporting requirements, will be set forth in a formal agreement or memorandum or in an executed contract between the audit organization and the organization arranging for the financial related audit. Objectives of a financial related audit could have their origin in enabling and appropriation legislation, legislative hearings, concerns with implementing program regulations, issues raised by news media or senior executive concerns with the overall management of operations.

The objective of a financial related audit may be established by governmental legislative units, chief elected officials, department heads, financial managers and often the responsible governmental audit office. If the audit is to be performed by the government's auditor, these officials could determine the objectives, scope and other elements of the audit, even specifying the detail audit procedures to be applied in the particular circumstances. A CPA might be retained to actually perform the audit and report on the observed results.

Customized Scope of Financial Related Audits

There is no prescribed, generally accepted, "safe harbor" criteria or guide for financial related audits. Reliance is placed on the knowledge, experience, and application of informed judgment by the auditor to the facts or issues to be addressed and conditions or circumstances to be audited. To a degree, the conduct of financial related audits are more art than science. All aspects of a financial related audit—the objectives, scope, approach, execution, and reporting—must be tailored to the subject areas of concern to those arranging for the audit.

Government auditing standards define an audit *scope* as the depth and coverage of work conducted to accomplish the audit objective. For financial related audits that audit scope must be designed to address the "customer's" or user's audit need. The scope designed for one financial related audit will seldom satisfy the objectives of another financial related audit. This can be demonstrated by just a partial listing of financial related audits performed of governmental operations and activities. For example, the scope of financial related audits could include:

● Reviews of the adequacy of financial systems to support operational decisions.

● Examining and recommending improvements or alternative internal control policies and procedures.

● Conducting a post-audit (or pre disbursement) audit of governmental expenditures.

● Performing audits of controls, expenditures, and compliance of each of the various governmental "functional" activities or organizations, such as personnel and payroll, travel and transportation, property acquisition and control, procurement, grants management.

● Performing program audits of agency management and the constituent program contractors or grantees.

● Auditing end of year obligations, encumbrances and unexpended appropriation balances.

● Settlement or clearance audits of governmental certifying and accountable officers.

This list could be expanded considerably. Certain aspects of any financial related audit could be added to scopes of audits for economy, efficiency, and effectiveness, i.e., performance type audits.

While a preliminary outline of an audit scope responsive to the audit objectives might be developed by the entity arranging for the audit, the auditor is ultimately responsible for ensuring that the audit scope addresses the implicit and explicit issues or objectives of the audit. The auditor should meet with executives of the entity arranging for the audit and the management of the activity, function or operation to be audited. Overview inquiries should be made concerning the existence of applicable laws, regulations, policies, procedures, controls, systems, extent of computerization, decentralization or centralization of operations, organizational structure to be audited, etc. Outlines of audit review protocols, tentative audit programs, anticipated questionnaires, checklists and other audit guidance must be developed by the auditor.

Prior to commencing these audits, the auditor should present a briefing on the auditor's understanding of the scope of the audit, including discussions on the contemplated audit objectives, desired timing, phases, audit procedures to be applied, nature of reporting and specific report distribution desired by the arranger of the audit.

AUDIT METHODOLOGY FOR FINANCIAL RELATED AUDITS

A financial related audit is a special or focused scope audit that includes the application of audit inquiries and procedures agreed to with the party arranging for the audit. Often these audits have several identifiable phases: a survey, a more detailed review, design of an audit plan and programs, execution of a detailed examination, and a reporting of audit findings. *Exhibit 16-2* illustrates the several phases of these type of audits.

Preliminary Survey

At the outset of a financial related audit, someone, some how, some way must conduct a preliminary survey—the background phase of the audit. This is a critical phase and preferably should be done by the auditor. If this survey is not performed by the auditor, the auditor must examine the background data and the results of the survey to ensure that it is sufficiently comprehensive. In this phase the auditor is concerned with researching the history of the program, activity, or function undergoing the audit, for several reasons:

Audit Methodology—Financial Related Audits 405

- A survey of legislative and management guidelines can provide direction for subsequent audit tests.

- An understanding must be gained of program operating characteristics, past and current issues and problems, constituencies (legislative, executive branch, program), nature of services required or provided.

- Policies, procedures, manuals, forms, and other documentation should be inventoried relating to operational and financial systems, internal accounting and administrative controls, budgeting processes and procedures, and other measurement and reporting systems.

- Financial information—management and accounting—should be collected on original and amended budgets, actual costs (cash and accrual bases), budget variances, and financial status of the organization and its component units.

No assessment or validation of the compiled information is attempted during the preliminary survey. The goal is to obtain a cursory, quick overview of what must be audited, against what criteria, the existing controls and systems, and some indication of the existence and quality of supporting documentation. Then, the auditor must tentatively judge whether circumstances, conditions, operations, controls, and systems are sufficiently auditable to permit the performance of an audit scope that addresses the stated objectives of the financial related audit.

Again, not all the surveys must be done by the auditor. In some instances, the entity arranging for the audit or its own the auditee staff can and may have compiled much of this data in advance. The results, though, must be evaluated for sufficiency by the auditor before proceeding with the audit. An inadequate or incomplete preliminary survey will most assuredly result in later duplication of audit efforts, delays in performing the audit, and possibly omission of critical examination procedures. Done well, a preliminary survey will avoid many problems and minimize audit risks.

Preliminary Review

The preliminary review phase of the audit is contrasted with the earlier survey phase by the greater depth and specificity of the inquiries made.

The objectives of this phase are to: (1) identify those areas to be audited in detail, and (2) eliminate or de-emphasize areas that appear to not need a detailed audit.

In the preliminary review phase, primary "target" areas or potential weaknesses are identified. Criteria against which performance will be assessed must be identified and discussed with those arranging for the audit. Less desirable, but often the reality, the auditor must establish the performance criteria to be assessed. Under these circumstances, the auditor should fully discuss and communicate the performance criteria, in writing, to those arranging for the audit for their concurrence.

Work performed during the preliminary review phase will permit a more complete definition of the types of staff skills, experience, and knowledge needed to make competent assessments. The competency and proficiency of the audit team is directly related to the comprehensiveness of the intended financial related audit. Some audits scopes are broader and could entail an examination of an entity's financial operations, management performance, compliance with laws and regulations, soundness of controls, and even responsiveness of financial and operational systems to management and external overseers. Such a scope would demand the audit team, collectively, to have skills other than in accounting and auditing.

Acquired data must be analyzed to permit the determination of specific audit techniques to be applied (analytic review procedures, modeling, interview protocols, site observations programs, survey questionnaires, comparative and other analyses, etc.). Views, impressions and information obtained during the earlier survey must be validated during the review phase. More study and tests must be made of policies, procedures, manuals and documentation, operational and financial systems, internal accounting and administrative controls, budgets and budgeting processes and procedures, and other measurement and reporting systems, depending upon the objectives of the financial related audit.

The concluding effort of this phase should be development of a refined audit scope for the detailed examination to be made. For example, will there be an examination of only a revenue statement or just the expenditures statement, of budget to actual performance, or specified controls and reporting for a program or contract or grant, etc.

As might have been the case with the preliminary survey, the arranger of the audit or its auditor may have performed portions of the preliminary review. Nonetheless, it is the auditor's responsibility to assess the quality of the work of others and to conclude on its adequacy as a basis for developing the detailed audit plan.

Audit Plan

This concluding task of this phase should be the drafting of the audit plan. A written audit plan is necessary to ensure that selected audit procedures and detailed audit strategies and testing approaches are consistent with the audit scope and supportive of the overall objectives of the audit. The plan must describe the nature, timing, and extent of testing—e.g., the inspections, observations, inquiries, confirmations, analyses—to be performed in the audit. The plan must blend the auditor's views, conclusions, beliefs and concerns identified during the survey and review phases into an audit approach and strategies into a single written document, i.e., the audit plan.

An audit plan must be reduced to writing. Because financial related audits are unique to the organization, activity or function to be audited, it follows that the audit plan will be unique. However, all audit plans must contain several component sections: (1) legislative and other history and legal background relevant to the audit; (2) the legal or other authority for the audit; (3) planned audit objectives; (4) proposed scope and methodologies; (5) the audit budget, including staff, funding allocations, audit locations; and (6) the detailed audit programs for each area to be audited.

A written plan will assist in setting the overall direction of the audit, and is invaluable for other reasons, too:

● Written plans can serve as orientation aids for briefing of the organization arranging for the audit, management of the entity to be audited, as well as for the audit team members themselves.

● A written work plan facilitates the drafting of a work plan schematic identifying audit requirements, providing assurance that critical tasks will not be omitted and the sequencing of audit tasks is the most effective.

● A formal written audit plan, kept current, is an important tool of audit management to control the initiation, performance, conclusion and final reporting of the audit.

● Whenever possible, staff responsibilities, financial, and time budgets should be established for each phase, subphase, task, and subtask of the financial related audit. The greater the detail of planning, the greater the likelihood that audit performance and financial estimates will be met.

Uncertainty of problems that might be encountered is not sufficient reason for not drafting a plan. Estimated allocations of always limited audit resources and early identification of requisite skills and disciplines, no matter how uninformed or tentative, still provide benchmarks from which deviations or variances can be assessed, managed and used as a basis for adjusting the plan.

Because financial related audits are not "boiler plate" audits, auditors do not have the security of relying on generally accepted standards and procedures and "packaged" audit plans, a plan reduced to writing is imperative. There will be instances where auditees, and even those arranging for the audit, will challenge the auditor and the audit work performed. For sure, the audit plan will be the first record opposing counsel subpoena should the results of the audit be contested in a court of law.

Detailed Audit

No aspect of the detailed audit should commence without audit programs. Audit *programs* are distinguished from an audit *plan.* There is one plan, modified as conditions require, for a financial related audit. There will be many programs—for phases, areas within phases, accounting cycles, tasks, subtasks of the audit. Programs must be in writing for all the same reasons that the plan was reduced to writing.

The detailed testing phase of the audit is controlled by the timely execution of the several audit work programs. This phase is the confirmation, validation, verification and findings phase of a financial related audit. During this phase the audit team must make tests, evaluations and analysis of the facts and other evidence gathered during the earlier phases of the audit. Then the auditor must accumulate the necessary evidence to make factual, objective, independent assessments and arrive at conclusions relating to the overall objectives of the audit.

Audits of public sector entities could require many audit programs to provide audit guidance and detailed instruction for audit tests and procedures related to: the accounting and information and property systems; the system of controls, checks and balances; object costs such as payroll, travel, encumbrances and obligations, and indirect costs; and the allowability of charged and billed costs.

Audit Report

For reporting on financial related audits, the guidance in the government auditing standards is general, stating that auditors should follow: (1) the AICPA's attestation standards; (2) the governmental financial audit reporting standards, applying or adapting as appropriate; and (3) the government reporting standards for performance audits.

No structured format exists for communicating *findings* or instances of material noncompliance, material weaknesses in internal controls or other results of financial related audits. Generally, though, the report of a financial related audit or those related to noncompliance or internal controls, would consist of (1) a general, and (2) a findings section.

General Section

The general section of the report would identify the scope and objectives of the audit, plus the agreed-upon or applied audit methodologies.

Subjects that might be included in the general section could include:

- The agreed-upon objectives of the audit, including where appropriate, the performance criteria that was established.

- Citation of which of several auditing standards that were applied or used in the audit.

- Significant instances of noncompliance and instances of abuse, and in some circumstances illegal acts.

Findings Section

The findings section would separately discuss each material observation, with each reported observation addressing the several standard elements of a finding.

Subjects that might be included in the findings section could include:

- The scope of the audit made of management controls and significant weaknesses noted.

- The nature of any information omitted and the requirement that makes the omission necessary.

- Views of officials on the reported audit findings, conclusions, recommendations, and identified corrective actions planned or taken.

- Noteworthy accomplishments, management improvements, laudable performance, etc.

- Recommendations for corrective action to improve operations.

Audit Findings and Elements

This section describes the results of financial related audits, generically referred to as "findings." A working definition of the term *finding* (in the 1988 edition of the government auditing standards) has been generally accepted to mean:

> *"The result of information development—a logical pulling together of information to arrive at conclusions (or a response to an audit objective on the basis of the sum of the information) about an organization, program, activity, function, condition, or other matter that was analyzed or evaluated."*

A technique to ensure that sufficient evidence is accumulated for later reporting purposes is to critically examine the evidence in relation to each of the elements of a finding. The elements of an audit finding are several in number: [1]

—*Condition*—The situations, circumstances, or practices that have been identified as contributing to less than desired results.

—*Criteria*—The objectives, goals, standards, laws, regulations, rules, or other guidelines that are not being achieved or with which there are instances of noncompliance.

—*Cause*—The contributory circumstances or practices that have resulted in the less than desired condition or results.

—*Effect*—The relative materiality, damage or cost of impairment or loss resulting from the existence or perpetuation of the less than desired conditions or results.

—*Conclusions*—The auditor's opinion or assessment or attestation of the conditions that have been identified as contributing to less than desired conditions or results.

—*Recommendations*—The auditor's suggested corrective actions or alternative initiatives that will promote more effective, economical, or efficient performance or amelioration of the less than desirable conditions or results.

Common for such audits, is the inclusion of an auditee's views and comments concerning the audit findings and, where appropriate, a description of corrective actions taken or promised.

Reports on financial related audits must, however, be responsive to the objectives of the engagement and provide the results of the audit in an agreed-upon report. Regardless of format, the report must contain:

● All of the information to demonstrate that audit objectives were met.

● The evidence presented must be true, supportable by fact;

● Findings must be correctly portrayed in relation to the audit objectives;

● The report should be balanced in content and tone;

● The reported information should be sufficient to enable readers to assess the validity of the findings, reasonableness of conclusions, and desirability of implementing the recommendations.

The government performance auditing standards point out that the strength of audit conclusions depends on the persuasiveness of

---

[1] The elements of an audit finding are the same as those appearing in the *Standards for the Professional Practice of Internal Auditing*, published by the Institute of Internal Auditors, Altamonte Springs, Florida.

evidence supporting the findings and convincingness of logic to formulate those conclusions. For these types of audits, the auditor's unsupported "opinion," however well-intended or informed, is not acceptable.

Distribution of Financial Related Audit Reports

The government report distribution standard for financial related audits (§ 5.32) and for performance audits (§ 7.66) is the same, requiring that:

"Written audit reports are to be submitted by the audit organization to the appropriate officials of the auditee and to the appropriate officials of the organizations requiring or arranging for the audits, including external funding organizations, unless legal restrictions prevent it. Copies of the reports should also be sent to other officials who have legal oversight authority or who may be responsible for acting on auditing findings and recommendations and to others authorized to receive such reports. Unless restricted by law or regulation, copies should be made available for public inspection."

This standard requires careful reading. When performing financial statements, auditors are accustomed, in fact bound by generally accepted auditing standards, to report to only the auditee, who is typically the client. A reporting to a party other than the auditee, without the auditee's advance permission, would breach ethical standards of client confidentiality.

This is not the prevailing practice nor the reporting standard under the government standards. But, caution must also be exercised when the financial related audit has been commissioned or arranged by an organization other than the auditee. The organization arranging for the audit may not desire that the auditee receive a copy of the audit report, as might be true if an auditor were providing assistance to legal authorities that have reason to believe auditee management may have committed fraudulent acts.

Reports of financial related audits must comply with conditions imposed by the officials arranging for the audits who may not be the auditee. Necessary precautions must be taken to ensure that distribution of the audit report is in strict accord with the objectives and reporting responsibilities defined by those arranging for the financial related audit. With respect to audits in the public sector, there will be instances and reasons when the arranger for the audit will specifically prohibit distribution of the audit report to the auditee. Here, the only responsible compliance by the auditor is to refer all requests for copies of the audit report to the to the officials or organizations that arranged for the audit.

AN AUDIT METHODOLOGY

From the 1970s, federal audit executives attempted to conform to a uniform format that generally followed an audit guide format suggested by the AICPA.[2] This guidance was designed for the audit of specific federal programs and combined audit requirements, required application of specific procedures for rather comprehensive financial related audits of recipients of federal financing, and prescribed specific audit report formats.

Illustrative Financial Related Audit

This section outlines an example of a methodology for a financial related audit that might be performed by either the audit staff of a government agency or a CPA firm retained by contract. This example (see *Exhibit 16-2*) is an adaptation of the detailed methodology developed by the federal Environmental Protection Agency for the audits of state and local governmental entities who received financial assistance under the EPA construction grant program.

Over the years, the audits of many EPA construction grants were performed by auditors employed by government. But, thousands of these audits were also performed by CPAs under contract to EPA. For these audits, the arranger for the audit and the auditee are two distinct organizations.

The illustrative tasks have been grouped by the several audit phases described earlier—the survey, review, execution of the detailed audit and reporting. For these audits, the initial survey and much of the review and the drafting of the audit guide was done by EPA auditors. The actual performance of the detailed audit plan and supporting audit programs was done by federal auditor and CPAs. This audit approach, applied by the EPA, is similar to that used by other federal inspectors general.

Priority of Controls and Systems

The federal audit guides, for audits similar to this illustration, place an importance on testing and evaluating the controls and systems used by auditees to protect the funds, property, and other resources received or acquired for the federal activity. The federal government is concerned that auditees have a system of controls to provide reasonable assurance the recipient is complying with applicable law and regulations.

These auditees (e.g., state and local governmental entities, contractors and nonprofit grantees and educational institutions) must have

---

[2] The AICPA publication was titled, *Suggested Guidelines for the Structure and Content of Audit Guides Prepared by Federal Agencies for Use by CPAs*, New York, NY, 1972.

Audit Methodology—Financial Related Audits

controls to ensure that the federally-financed activities are performed in accordance with program rules, regulations, plans or specifications and that procedures have been placed in operation to periodically monitor this performance.

The federal audit guide directs the auditor to make specific tests of the accounting, financial and managerial systems and controls during the review phase of the audit. The federal government requires the auditor to assess the structure of the financial systems, including components as the adequacy of the account and transaction coding structure, controls over processing and accounting for all transactions, and completeness of supporting documentation, files and underlying records.

The results of these tests serve as a basis for acquiring an understanding of the controls and determining the nature, timing and extent of later audit tests that must be conducted during the detailed audit phase. But, should these review tests disclose material weaknesses, the auditor might be directed to make a full-scope audit of the controls and underlying systems. Instances of deficiencies or other noncompliance or variances from the financial assistance agreement must be identified for later detailed audit.

Some federal programs require more or less sophisticated costing techniques. For both simple or complex federal assistance programs, the federal governments is concerned about the identification of eligible and ineligible costs (e.g., allowable and unallowable costs, pursuant to OMB regulations), direct and indirect costs billed to federal programs (pursuant to the same OMB federal regulations), federal advances received and liquidated, and the correctness of amounts billed and claimed under the federal assistance program. Since an audit is a test, or sampling of transactions, reliance must be placed on controls and accounting systems used by the auditee for assurance that transactions not tested are proper.

Compliance and Legal Examinations

For this federal financial assistance program, detailed audit programs must be developed to assess compliance with laws and regulations such as (in this instance):

- The enabling EPA legislation;
- The EPA regulations for its construction grants program;
- The requirements in OMB's "common rule" relating to managerial, operational and administrative requirements of financial assistance to entities external to the federal government;
- The regulations pertaining to prescribed allowable, unallowable and indirect costs that appear in the OMB cost circulars; and

- The terms and conditions of each specific agreement between EPA and the entity to be audited, since each auditee may have negotiated different detailed terms and conditions.

Federal audit guides have been designed to address experienced problems, known issues, potential risks, and sensitive activities and practices disclosed through past audits and evaluations. Thus, the EPA audit guide, for example, may require that the auditor conduct numerous tests of information and underlying data, many related to nonfinancial management and compliance matters.

Financial or Cost Auditing

Contract and grant accounting is essentially project cost accounting. The federal government requires that specific tests be made to determine the allowability or unallowability of direct and indirect costs actually incurred by, claimed under, charged to, and reimbursed by the federal program. Tests will also be made of required financial reporting made to the federal government.

The cash management practice of all auditees is of concern to federal agencies. An auditee's procedures for receiving cash advances, making cash draw downs under federal letters of credit and requesting reimbursement must be examined in detail. The government prohibits an auditee from drawing down or receiving an excess of federal monies.

Audit emphasis must also be given to adherence to the program budget and the reasons for unusual, unexpected, or significant variances. Depending upon the federal program, there may be other areas for which detailed tests must be performed. For example, under its construction grants program, EPA is continually concerned about the eligibility of those receiving construction grant funds, all unpaid construction bills, the costing and charging of "force labor," billing for engineering services, and "special" cost items charged by auditees are of particular interest to EPA managers.

The overall objective of the audit of costs is to reach a conclusion as to the acceptability of the costs claimed under or charged to the federal program. "Acceptability" must be based on audit tests to determine the allowability, reasonableness, allocability and documentation of costs.

When performing a financial related audit of a federal assistance program, the levels of audit materiality also change. These audits require the auditor to consider materiality of costs incurred by the grantee in relation to the individual federal program and even specific categories or line items of cost (e.g., administrative labor, materials, engineering services, construction costs, etc.). This is a more detailed level of audit materiality than would be applied in the audit of an entity's financial statements. The materiality for the financial statement audit is typically the audited entity as a whole. That is, audit findings are reported if the effect is material to the financial statements of the audited entity taken as a whole.

A common question of financial related audits of contracts or grants is whether the auditor is required to audit and report upon all cost incurred under the federal assistance agreement or only the costs claimed or billed to the federal program. In the case of EPA, but not necessarily other federal agencies, there is a specific answer. EPA audit criteria states:

> *"When the auditee has incurred costs in excess of the amounts claimed, the auditor may not increase the amount of the auditee's claim against EPA. The auditor should, however, disclose by means of footnotes the extent of the unclaimed costs that might otherwise be considered allowable."*

Disclosure requires that the auditor conducts tests of the total incurred costs in the event EPA is required to consider these costs as "acceptable" as a charged to the EPA grant.

Audit of Performance, Output, and Outcomes

At times, an objective of a financial related audit might require an assessment of achievement by the recipient of federal funds. Federal funds are always provided for a budgeted level of performance. Thus, the federal government is interested in monitoring whether the auditee achieved the expected performance for the money spent. Similarly, the auditor might be required to audit non-financial performance or accomplishment indicators, such as outputs and/or outcomes.

OMB has defined *outputs* as a measure of the physical quantity of services provided and *outcomes* as the results or quality or accomplishments of providing those outputs.

Revenues earned by a corporation would be viewed as an indicator of accomplishments, i.e., an accomplishment, an outcome, since profit is its reason for being. But for governments, the important indicators of accomplishments are often nonfinancial.

A government output refers to the quantity of service provided that meets a specific quality criteria, e.g., what was procured for the dollar spent. An accomplished output might be used to assess a defined or measured level of input that produced the achieved output.

Outcomes are different. Some equate outcomes to the impact, effect, or results. Outcome measures would be useful for comparisons to previous years, targets, goals, norms, standards, etc. Outcomes generally presume anticipated performance criteria that may not be defined for federal programs.

Financial Related Audit Reporting

Federal agencies have required the auditor to render the standard short form audit opinion as a result of auditing controls, compliance with specific laws or regulations and related cost reports. More often, or in addition, the federal audit guides often require a narrative report. The structure of the narrative audit report generally requires a description of the audit scope, the auditor's overall opinion or conclusion, the material or reportable findings and related cost questioned or possibly unallowed, and recommendations.

The organization arranging for the audit may require the described audit findings to be presented according to the "finding" definition appearing in the government auditing standards. By that definition, a reporting would be made of the several elements of a finding: i.e., the condition, criteria, cause, effect, recommendation, and possibly conclusion. But, the specific reporting must be developed in response to each of the established audit objectives. Thus, the narrative for a finding would be complete to the extent that the audit objective was satisfied even though the several elements of a finding were not addressed.

The government auditing standards (§ 7.20) require auditors to report conclusions when called for by the audit objectives. The government standards describes conclusions as the logical inferences about the program based on the auditor's findings and that the auditor's conclusions should be specified and not left to be inferred by readers. The strength of the conclusions must depend on the persuasiveness of evidence supporting the finding and of the logic used to formulate the conclusions.

Exhibit 16-3 illustrates a combination of the opinion-type audit report with a detailed reporting of audit findings related to the costs claimed or incurred by the recipient of EPA financing (on Exhibit A). Schedule A-1, of this illustration, compares the cost claimed to the cost audited and accepted by the auditor and amounts of cost questioned by the auditor. Specific footnotes describe the basis for the auditor conclusions relating to the questioned costs. If the recipient of federal assistance had subcontracted or passed along grant funds to a subrecipient, a similar report might be required to reflect the audit of the subrecipient as well (see Schedule A-2 of the illustration).

Exhibits 16-1, 16-2 and 16-3 follow this page.

Audit Methodology—Financial Related Audits 417

EXHIBIT 16-1

Exhibit 16-1

Financial Statement
versus
Financial Related Audits

	Financial Statement Audits	*Financial Related Audits*
Audit Standards	GAAS, SASs, GAGAS	Selective applicability; possibly the SSAEs
Audit Scope	Prescribed, generally accepted	Uniquely designed for individual audit
Audit Procedures	Mandated by GAAS, GAGAS	Developed to meet objectives of specific audit
Audit Report	Prescribed, uniform, standard form and content	Narrative, reporting on results/findings in relation to unique audit objectives

GAAS = generally accepted auditing standards, AICPA

SASs = statements on auditing standards, AICPA

GAGAS = generally accepted government auditing standards, U.S. General Accounting Office

SSAEs = statements on standards for attestation engagements, AICPA

EXHIBIT 16-2
SUMMARY OF AUDIT PHASES AND TASKS OVERVIEW-- FINANCIAL RELATED AUDIT PLAN

A. Conduct Survey	B. Conduct Reviews	C. Detailed Audit
Examine Audit Standards • GAO Standards for Audit • AICPA generally accepted auditing standards • Industry audit guides • EPA audit guide **Review Government Regulations** • OMB circulars • Grant and Contract Cost Principles • Etc. **Survey Other Requirements and Regulations** • Code of Federal Regulations • Applicable Laws • EPA Regulations • Etc. **Obtain Current Relevant Status** • Latest Amendment for Program • Confirmation of Federal Payments • Status of Reporting • Record of Congressional Hearings • Other Areas of Concern • Etc. **Review Program Characteristics** • Level of Funding • Location of Activities • Number of Staff, Organizational Entitites, etc. • Nature of Subgrantees, Subcontractors • Services Rendered • Value of Projects • Status of Projects • Etc. **Prepare Audit Working Papers and Audit Plan**	**Review Accounting System** • Accounting records • Posting procedures • Financial reporting • Cost reconciliations • Cost controls • Allocations of costs • Supporting documentation • Cost accounting projects • Cash **Review Procurement System** • Establish procurement needs • Inventory procedures • Procurement procedures • Competitive bid practices • Contracting procedures **Review Property Management System** • Policies • Records • System of controls • Inventory practices • Use and disposition procedures **Review Other Areas** • Salaries • Travel • Obligations • Indirect costs • Personnel • Other **Update Audit Workpapers and Audit Programs**	**Determine Allowability of Costs** • Necessary and reasonable • Authorized and not prohibited • Consistent with policies, regulations, procedures • Conform to limits in grant/contract • Consistent with GAAP • Net of applicable credits **Review Project Costs** • Properly chargeable to period • Existence of pre-grant cost • Total project costs • Eligible and ineligible cost • Unallowable, unreasonable, unallocable, undocumented, unapproved costs **Evaluate Cost Incurred** • Accepted Costs • Questioned Costs • Disallowed Costs • Matching • Federal Share **Conduct General Audit Steps** • Initial Field Audit Procedures • Verification of Claim • Credits, Rebates and Refunds • Unpaid Bills • Subgrants **Perform Specific Area Audits** • Audit Force Labor Account • Audit Engineering Services • Audit Construction Costs • Audit Special Items of Costs • Audit Other Matters of Interest **Collections** • User Fees • Program Income • Interest Income • Retainages **Program Accomplishments** • Inputs • Outputs • Outcomes

Audit Methodology—Financial Related Audits 419

D. Draft Report

Review Evidence in Work Papers
- Findings
- Conclusions
- Recommendations
- Personnel contacted
- Auditors involved
- Details of discussions
- Summary of comments received from audited organization personnel
- Written comments

Prepare Draft Reports
- Financial exhibits
- Notes
- Questioned, Ineligible costs
- Conclusions, recommendations

Distribute Draft Report
- EPA Area Audit Manager
- EPA Program Personnel
- Audited Organization
- Other interest parties

Conduct Exit Conference
- Notify EPA Area Audit Manager
- Conduct exit conference
- Other Interested parties

Conduct Exit Conference
- Notify EPA Area Manager
- Conduct exit conference
- Obtain written comments

E. Deliver Final Report

Develop Final Audit Report
- Scope paragraph
- Opinion
- Comments on audit of costs
- Comments on audit of compliance, internal controls, performance
- Presentation of findings
  Condition
  Criteria
  Cause
  Effect
  Conclusion
  Recommendation
- Report on subagreement costs

Deliver Final Report
- EPA Area Audit Manager
- Audited organization (if appropriate)
- EPA Program Officials (if appropriate)

Note: For this example, the audit phases and tasks are presented in summary. The EPA Audit Guide contains more detailed requirements and tests to be performed.

EXHIBIT 16-3

EXAMPLE AUDITOR'S REPORTS

Area Audit Manager
Office of Audit
Environmental Protection Agency
Any City, U.S.A.

(Scope) We have examined the statement of costs claimed (Exhibit A) by the City of Anywhere, U.S.A. under EPA Grant No. XXXX for the period (month, day, year) to (month, day, year). Our examination was made in accordance with the "Standards for Audit of Governmental Organizations, Programs, Activities, and Functions" the "Audit Guide for EPA Grants (Other Than Construction Grants)" issued in February 1976 by EPA, and accordingly included such tests of the accounting records and such other auditing procedures as we considered necessary in the circumstances.

As part of our examination, the allowability of costs claimed under the Grant was determined in accordance with the provisions of the Grant and applicable Federal regulations. 3schedule A-I sets forth the costs which we questioned in this regard and includes an explanation of the reason such costs were questioned.

....

(opinion) In our opinion subject to the effects, if any, on Exhibit A of the ultimate resolution by the Environmental Protection Agency of the questionable expenditures referred to in the preceding paragraph, Exhibit A presents fairly the financial information contained therein in accordance with the financial provisions of the Grant and generally accepted accounting principles.

....

(Transition Paragraph) In addition, in connection with our examination of the statement of costs claimed, we have reviewed the Grantee's system of internal control and compliance with provisions of the Grant and applicable Federal regulations. Our report thereon appears as Exhibit B.

This report is intended for use in connection with the grant to which it refers and should not be used for any other purpose.

_____
DATE

_____
SIGNATURE

Audit Methodology—Financial Related Audits

EXHIBIT A

City of Anywhere, USA.
Statement of Costs Claimed Under EPA Grant No. XXXX For the Period (month, day, year) Through (month, day, year)

	Costs Claimed
Personnel	$1,225,373
Indirect Costs	122.537
Equipment	368,848
Subcontracts	94,473
TOTAL COSTS	$1,811,231
FEDERAL SHARE: 44 Percent	$ 796,941

EPA Grant No. XXXX was awarded to the City of Anywhere, USA. on (month, day, year). The grant provided for "........................". Work under the grant began on (month, day, year) and was completed (month, day, year). See Schedule A-I through A-3 for costs accepted and questioned during the audit.

Schedule A-1

City of Anywhere, USA.
EPA Grant No. XXXX
Statement of Costs Claimed, Accepted and Questioned For the Period (month, day,* year) Through (month, day, year)

Description	Costs Claimed	Costs Accepted	Costs Questioned	Reference Notes
Personnel	$1,225,373	$1,225,373	$ -0-	
Indirect Costs	122,537	-0-	122,537	1
Equipment	368,848	291,196	77,652	2
Subcontracts	94,473	86,770	7,703	3
Total Costs	$1,811,231	1603,339	$207,892	
Federal Share—44 Percent	$ 796,941	$ 705,469	$207,892	
Federal Funds Provided		$ 814,000		
Amount due to Government or Grantee		$ 198,531		

Reference Notes

1. The 10 percent indirect cost rate included in the grant was based on an indirect cost rate proposal prepared, audited and negotiated with the Department of Health, Education and Welfare for FY 1969. Since that date, the City had not prepared any indirect cost proposals. The DHEW Guide for Local Government Institutions required local grantees to prepare indirect cost proposals annually. Such proposals should be retained for future audit. Since the City had prepared no such proposals, it has not complied with Federal requirement's and accordingly is not entitled to indirect costs.

Grantee officials indicated that they were unaware of the requirement to prepare indirect cost proposals annually.

2. For an explanation of the amounts questioned, see comments included in property management section of the comments on Compliance, Performance, and Internal Controls. Exhibit B.

3. Amounts accepted and questioned were based on an audit of the subcontractor's records. See Schedule A-2.

Schedule A-2

XYZ Corporation
Subcontract XXXX Under EPA Grant No. XXXX
Statement of Costs Claimed, Accepted, and Questioned For the Period (month, day, year) Through (month, day, year)

		Audit Recommendation		
Description	Costs Claimed	Costs Accepted	Costs Questioned	Reference Notes
Personnel	$ 48,712	$45,797	$2,915	Schedule A-3
Fringe Benefits	13,152	10,067	3,085	1
Indirect Costs	20,859	19,620	1,239	2
Travel	5,000	4,536	464	3
Total Costs	$ 87,723	$80,020	$7,703	
Fee	6,750	6,750	-0-	
Total Costs Plus Fixed Fee	$924,473	$86,770	$7,703	
Funds Provided		$94,473		
Amount Due Grantee		$ 7,703		

Reference Notes

1. The Corporation claimed fringe benefits it a rate of 27 percent of direct payroll costs. This rate covered vacation, sick leave, holidays, and the company's portion of payroll taxes. In analyzing this rate, we noted that the company included the 13 days of sick leave accrued each year. Since Corporation employees are not paid for sick leave unless it is taken, the accrual does not represent an actual cost. Accordingly, we adjusted the hinge benefit rate by removing the accrual and adding in the actual sick leave taken. This reduced the Corporation's fringe benefit rate to 22 percent. We then calculated allowable fringe benefits as follows:

Chapter 17

Audit Methodology—Performance Audits

PERFORMANCE AUDITS

Defined

GAO, in its standards (§ 2.6), defines a performance audit as:

"...an independent assessment of the performance of a government organization, program, activity, or function in order to provide information to improve public accountability and facilitate decision-making by parties with responsibility to oversee or initiate corrective action."

Performance audits have also been described by the General Accounting Office and others, as audits to evaluate the relative economy, efficiency, and effectiveness of an organization's operations. In practice, performance audits are referred to by a variety of terms including operational audits, management audits, and comprehensive audits. But essential to a performance audit is the fact that the audit is an "independent assessment ... to improve public accountability." Other reviews more collaborative in nature, nonjudgmental in conclusions, performed possibly for informational purposes, and maybe more sympathetic to those reviewed would more properly be classified under program evaluations. [1]

Characteristics

Performance audits are unique to the organization being audited. Aside from some transferability of a general audit methodology, each performance audit must be planned anew. Performance audits require the application of skills, disciplines, ethical restraints, independence, and competence in the same manner as financial audits, but these skills often include expertise other than accounting and auditing. And, these

---

[1] Frank L. Greathouse and Mark Funkhouser, "Audit Standards and Performance Auditing in State Government," *Government Accountants Journal*, Association of Government Accountants, Alexandria, VA, Winter 1987-88, pp. 56-60.

other skills are highly dependent upon the organization and its operations that will be audited.

Performance audits require that particular attention be devoted to describing the scope of the performance audit, determining and establishing acceptance of quantifiable performance criteria, developing an audit plan and program unique to the performance audit, and identifying the nature of skills needed to conduct the performance audit. Again, these features will vary and be directly dependent on the organization audited, the nature of it operations, and the objectives of the performance audit.

Limited Audit Guidance

The government's auditing standards for performance audits include general, field work, and reporting standards. The government's *general* standards for performance audits are the same as the government's general standards for financial statement and financial related audits. But, GAO has prescribed additional performance auditing standards with respect to the *field work* and for *reporting* on performance audits. The American Institute of CPAs has no standards for the conduct of performance audits and has not recommended the application of its generally accepted audit guidance to performance audits.

There are no prescribed, generally accepted "safe harbor" audit criteria or guides for performance audits. For performance auditing, considerable reliance is placed on the knowledge, experience, and application of informed judgment by the audit team to the facts or issues to be audited. No audit guides have been published for performance auditing. In fact, a distinguishing feature of performance is the dearth of precedence and guidance. All aspects—objectives, scope, criteria, approach, reporting—of a performance audit must be tailored to the conditions, circumstances and subject areas of concern to those arranging for the performance audit.

TYPES OF PERFORMANCE AUDITS

There is no limit to the types of performance audits one might identify. Because these audits are designed to address the objectives of those arranging for the performance audit, the types or variations of performance audits vary in direct proportion to those desiring such audits. In contrast to financial statement audits, performance audits are not done annually, are not primarily based on validating historical information, are not exclusively concerned with amounts posted in an accounting system, and do not conclude with a standard, single paragraph audit opinion.

Audit Methodology—Performance Audits

Economy and Efficiency Audits

Within the federal government, performance audits have been defined as including audits and evaluations made to assess the relative economy and efficiency of an entities operations. Government auditing standards (§ 2.8) lists several examples that illustrate the variety of economy and efficiency audits that might be made of a governmental entity or activity. [2] The objectives of audits for economy and efficiency audits suggested by the GAO include:

- Whether the entity is following sound procurement practices;

- Whether the entity is acquiring the appropriate type, quality, and amount of resources at an appropriate cost;

- Whether the entity is properly protecting and maintaining its resources;

- Whether the entity is avoiding duplication of effort by employees and work that services little or no purpose;

- Whether the entity is avoiding idleness and overstaffing;

- Whether the entity is using efficient operating procedures;

- Whether the entity is using the optimum amount of resources (staff, equipment, and facilities) in producing or delivering the appropriate quantity and quality of goods or services in a timely manner;

- Whether the entity is complying with requirements of laws and regulations that could significantly affect the acquisition, protection, and use of the entity's resources;

- Whether the entity has an adequate management control system for measuring, reporting, and monitoring a program's economy and efficiency;

- Whether the entity has reported measures of economy and efficiency that are valid and reliable.

Program Reviews or Program Results Audits

The federal government's definition of performance audits also includes those audits or evaluations made to assess an entity's program results and accomplishments, performance attained, and even operational effectiveness. Government auditing standards (§ 2.9) list several illustrative examples. The objectives of these audits might require the auditor to:

---

[2] Unless otherwise noted, the performance auditing standards are those appearing in the June 1994 edition of Government Auditing Standards. Subsequently, the Advisory Council on Government Auditing Standards has been evaluating these standards. Possibly, a revision could be issued in the year 2000, but the effective date would not likely be until 2001 or later.

- Assess whether the objectives of a new, or ongoing program are proper, suitable, or relevant;

- Determine the extent to which a program achieves a desired level of program results;

- Assess the effectiveness of the program and/or of individual program components;

- Identify factors inhibiting satisfactory performance;

- Determine whether alternatives have been considered for carrying out the program that might yield desired results more effectively or at a lower cost;

- Determine whether the program complements, duplicates, overlaps, or conflicts with other related programs;

- Identify ways that will make programs work better;

- Assess compliance with laws and regulations applicable to the programs;

- Assess the adequacy of the management control system for measuring, reporting, and monitoring a program's effectiveness; and

- Determine whether management has reported measures of program effectiveness that are valid and reliable.

The distinction between types of performance audits is clearer in literature than in practice. Generally, aspects of all types of performance audits—economy, efficiency, effectiveness, program results—are included in most performance audits. Some practitioners have suggested that a program results or performance audit actually consist of three components or elements: economy, efficiency, effectiveness. Some have suggested that a fourth, *faithfulness* be added. This latter element, faithfulness, was to assess compliance with laws, regulations, rules, and management assertions. [3]

SOME ESSENTIALS FOR PERFORMANCE AUDITS

The popularity of performance audits, particularly of public sector entities and activities, is directly attributable to legislators, government executives, overseers, and various public constituencies concluding that not all questions about government are answered by financial statement audits or financial related audits. With performance audits, the focus is on whether the audited entity or its activities achieve established objectives, goals or other criteria for which the program exists and for which public funds have been committed, and if that

---

[3] Greathouse and Funkhouser, with references to an initial conceptual definition in Professor Lennis Knighton's book, *The Performance Post-Audit in State Government*, University of Michigan Press, Ann Arbor, 1967.

level of performance could have been achieved at less cost or in a better way.

While accountants are credited with "inventing" performance audits, this method of analysis might be practiced as much by social scientists and those in other disciplines.[4] Over the years, the more successful performance audits appear to be those that included a blending of the scientific methods and rigorous social research tools with the documentation and evidence gathering and discipline of auditing. The result of merging cross or inter-disciplinary practices is a performance audit that would place greater emphasis on current and contemplated practices than historical. This type audit considers equally or more important the nonfinancial decisions and resource allocations than might be the case for the profession's financially focused audit. The conclusions of a performance audit could be clearer and of greater utility than those based on only historical, financial-type evidence.

Certain different or refined prerequisites must exist for performance audits that are not as necessary, critical or, a primary focus of financial statement and financial related audits.

Materiality or Audit Significance

Financial statement audits and many financial related audits are based on audit procedures and testing of the material or significant transactions, groups or categories of transactions, and account balances that comprise the data appearing on the reports. In financial audits, materiality is defined in terms of a dollar threshold or percentage of a dollar base (e.g., total assets, fund balance, excess of revenues over expenditures, variances of actual over budgets, etc.).

Materiality or significance is defined differently for performance audits. Government performance auditing standards (§ 6.7) require that performance audits in the public sector give weight to qualitative as well as quantitative factors in assessing relative materiality and significance. Among qualitative considerations, GAO suggest factors as:

● The visibility and sensitivity of the program under audit. This is often equated to the interest expressed by news media and other interest groups capable of influencing legislative and executive officials.

● Newness of the program or changes in its conditions. Proponents and opponents have an interest in new and changed programs and

---

[4] Frank L. Greathouse and Mark Funkhouser, "Audit Standards and Performance Auditing in State Government," *Government Accountants Journal*, Association of Government Accountants, Alexandria, VA, Winter 1987-88, pp. 56-60.

probably have their own satisfaction in establishing performance or evaluative indicators.

● Role of audit in providing information that can improve public accountability and decision-making. Audits are particularly critical to service institutions (e.g., governments) lacking any market tests that might otherwise put an inefficient, obsolete, unproductive, non-responsive operation out of business.

● Level and extent of review or other forms of independent oversight. Performance audits have value in circumstances where such oversight is non-existent, weak, or at best intermittent.

Observers not known for public sector involvement have, without qualification, concluded that service institutions periodically need an organized audit of objectives and results to identify those institutions no longer serving a purpose or that have proven the objectives are not attainable. [5]

Legislatively Imposed Performance Criteria

Nothing can exist or happen in government unless there exists a prior law. Monies can not be raised by taxes or spent unless the government has legal authority. There must be a preceding law or statute; hence, the relevance of the "faithfulness" criteria mentioned earlier. These enabling laws and legislation play an important role in defining the objectives of a public sector performance audit.

Legislation establishing a governmental department, agency or program may include specific objectives, goals or conditions to be addressed by the initiated program. If so, these actions can be used as criteria for purposes of measuring or assessing performance. To implement legislation and meet specific constituent needs, agency management may have been organized and may have established operating policies and procedures consistent with the enabling legislation. Financial and management information systems and controls may have been designed to monitor and measure progress or achievement in relation to the objectives or goals in the law.

Under these conditions, the audits can be designed, performed and be responsive to those arranging for the performance audit. In these instances, the auditor is concerned with assessing performance in relation to legal and other criteria, testing the validity of financial, operational and other information and data collected, and comparing achievement data and program results with the relevant criteria appearing in the law.

---

[5] Drucker, Peter F., *Management: Tasks, Responsibilities, Practices* (Chapter 14, Managing Service Institutions for Performance), Harper & Row, New York, 1973.

But, these circumstances are ideal and are seldom encountered in practice. In many cases, legislation will contain no statement of objectives, goals or other criteria of expected performance or achievement. Established policies and procedures may not be designed to directly relate to the program audited. Basic financial and managerial data may not be recorded, compiled, or reported by programs and legislative mandates. In short, there might be little or no historical, operating, financial or other data on which to assess performance.

Auditing organizations that do not have a clear legal mandate—financial, operational, constituent base—is difficult and requires more effort on the part of the auditor to design a responsive performance audit. In fact, the initial effort of any performance audit is to conduct a preliminary survey to ascertain the extent to which the lack of sufficient legal criteria and the absence of sound operational, managerial and financial data might limit the desired scope of a performance audit or require substantially more time, staff or other resources.

Structuring the Performance Audit

At different times during the 1970s various committees and tasks forces of the AICPA concerned themselves with the uniqueness and distinctions of performance audits versus the type of audits normally made by CPAs. To assist CPAs to perform these differently focused audits, an AICPA executive committee concluded that evidence, data, information or answers to the following questions would permit auditors to more clearly understand the nature or objective of the performance audit and to structure the performance audit plan: [6]

1. Have agency, program, activity or functional objectives and goals been well defined?

2. Have specific timetables or dates been established for meeting the objectives and goals?

3. Have criteria—in terms of performance levels or costs—been established to permit the evaluation of results or achievement?

4. Have the criteria been quantified to permit objective measurement of results or achievements?

5. Have arrangements been made to insure that this data will be available to the auditor?

6. Has management or someone else prepared a current assessment of the program's results or achievements?

---

[6] American Institute of Certified Public Accountants, Management Advisory Services executive committee, *Guidelines for Participation in Government Audit Engagements to Evaluate Economy, Efficiency, and Programs Results.* New York, NY.

7. Have any previous external evaluations been made of the agency, program, or activities?

8. Have actions been taken by management as a result of these previous evaluations?

Over the years, the AICPA has been reluctant to provide guidance with respect to program results or effectiveness type performance audits. In fact, the AICPA in 1982 concluded that an operational audit was not an audit, but a form of "management advisory services" that may have only some of the characteristics of a financial audit. At that time, the AICPA stated that while distinctions may be drawn between a variety of terms (as operational reviews, performance audits, management audits, comprehensive audits), the most commonly used term is operational audits. [7]

Criteria for Performance Audits

Requests or authorizations for performance audits are often vague and will require definition. Once defined, it is not unusual for the required audit scope to be considerably different than the one initially contemplated. Data gathered to answer the AICPA's questions and inquiries relevant to the specific performance audit will permit clearer definition of a desired scope of audit and mitigate the risk to the auditor of accepting an engagement that is difficult or even impossible to perform within the reality of finite time and cost budgets.

Risks of Auditor Developed Criteria

There will be instances where those arranging for the audit will expect the auditor to establish the objectives, goals, and performance criteria against which performance is to be evaluated. Laws and statutes of the government program may be silent or of little assistance in this regard. This places the auditor at risk. No audit work should commence until those arranging for the audit have examined and commented upon the established performance or achievement factors to be evaluated. If this precaution is not taken, those audited can protest that the criteria are solely those of the auditor and neither relevant nor intended by the founding legislation.

Need for Precedent Data Base

Where there is a dearth of information on the intended purpose of a governmental program, the auditor may be responsible for developing a data base. This data base will often be a precedent condition to planning the performance audit.

---

[7] AICPA, *Operational Audit Engagements*, New York, NY.

When placed in this position, the auditor must test the general acceptance of the developed performance audit criteria. Then a determination is required about the procedures for gathering, collecting and analyzing data relevant to the criteria. Later disagreements over performance criteria or the acquired data may become a critic's basis for invalidating the results of the performance audit. To properly assess the significance of the selected or offered audit objectives, auditors must obtain an understanding of the program. The government performance auditing standards (§ 6.9) requires that the performance audit objectives be determined only after acquiring a familiarity with several factors, including:

1. *Laws and regulations*: Government programs are created by laws and are subject to more specific laws and regulations than the private sector. Laws dictate what can be done, who can do it, the purpose for doing it, for whose purpose it will be done, and the permissible or maximum costs for doing it. Without a law, expending public funds is illegal.

2. *Purpose and goals*: Purpose is the intended or desired result or effect of a governmental program and can exist, explicitly or implicitly. The enabling laws may not expressly or unambiguously set forth the purpose of a program. But, legislated goals could quantify a level of intended or desired performance. The legislature should set the program purpose when enacting enabling laws; management is more often expected to establish goals for program efforts, operations, outputs, and outcomes. Of course, if neither party has documented program expectations, the omission might not be through inadvertence or oversight. Much legislation is deliberately void of this type of specificity.

3. *Efforts*: Efforts are the amount of resources (money, material, personnel, equipment, space, etc.) required to support a program and may come from within or outside the program audited. At times, considerable audit effort must be expended to determine the total cost of a governmental program. Programs will be financed from multiple appropriations. Governmental programs often receive "free support" from governmental support functions. Measures of efforts might be hours, dollars, footage, quality, quantity of output, etc.

4. *Programs operations*: Program operations include the strategies, processes, and activities the auditee uses to convert efforts into outputs and are subject to management control. Performance audits focus legislator and manager attention on accomplishments, or lack thereof and away from the historical fiscal emphasis of spending within one's appropriation limits. An appropriation expenditures underrun of 10 percent should not be applauded as good management if the 90 percent of the appropriated dollars was spent to attain only 45 percent of the desired performance.

5. *Outputs*: Outputs are the quantity of goods and services provided for the input of investment of resources. Examples of output might be tons processed or moved, numbers graduated or serviced, total constituent beneficiaries of a program's products or services. Alternatively, data on outputs can include tabulations, calculations, or recordings of activity or effort that can be expressed in a quantitative or qualitative manner. Output data must have two key characteristics: (1) outputs should be systematically or periodically captured through an accounting or management information system, and (2) there shall be a logical connection between the reported output measures and the program's purposes. [8]

6. *Outcomes*: Outcomes are accomplishments or results that occur, totally or partially, because of the services provided. Outcomes can be controversial or heatedly disputed and are often dependent upon the views of the participants to the anticipated audit. Outcomes may be intended or unintended and may be influenced by cultural, economic, physical or technological factors that could be external to the program. Outcomes must bear a direct relationship to a program's outputs.

The Federal Accounting Standards Advisory Board's more descriptive definition describes outcomes as accomplishments or results that occur because of the service efforts of government entities. FASAB notes that some public entities use terms like "impact," "effect," or "results" to distinguish the change in outcomes specifically caused by the government from the total change in conditions that can be caused by many factors. Also, FASAB suggests that outcomes should be: (1) capable of being described in financial, economic, or quantitative terms; and (2) provide a plausible basis for concluding that the program has had or will have this intended effect. [9]

Establishing Performance Audit Criteria

The absence of existing or predefined objectives or goals or other evaluation factors is often a limiting condition to commencing a performance audit. When legislation does not clearly identify the objective or goals for spending public money, the best those arranging for the audit can do is to infer or conjecture about the program performance criteria that might be used to evaluate relative economy or efficiency or effectiveness or program results. As mentioned, legislators may be reluctant to formally establish and set forth in law the expected performance criteria or desired levels of program achievement. On occasion the law may make reference to the maintenance of performance data or may contain the requirement that periodic evaluations be

---

[8] Federal Accounting Standards Advisory Board, *Consolidated Glossary* of terms presented in Statements of Federal Financial Accounting Standards, Washington, DC.

[9] *Id.*

made and reported to the legislature. Even in these instances, the contents, form and frequency for collecting program statistical and financial data is often left to the discretion of the program officials. At times, the adequacy of the information systems is not evaluated until the need for making an evaluation becomes imminent.

Nonetheless, as noted in the government performance auditing standards (section 6.11), criteria are standards used to determine whether a program meets or exceeds expectations and provide a context for assessing the results of the audit. Possible proxies for criteria or performance factors that could assist in establishing criteria, in the public sector, include:

- Purpose or goals prescribed in law, regulations or set by management.
- Technically developed standards, norms, and levels that might be based on prudence and "common sense".
- Expert opinions within the program area or on subjects relevant to program operations.
- Prior year's performances; comparisons to earlier proposals, budgets, plans, etc.
- Comparative performance to similar government entities, in similar circumstances, and under similar restrictions or conditions.
- Comparative performance to public sector entities, in similar circumstances, and under similar restrictions or conditions.

In the absence of defined objectives, goals, evaluative criteria, the auditor may be charged with the responsibility for describing these factors in qualitative and quantitative terms. There is a general methodology (discussed later in this chapter) that may be applied to this effort. The same methodology might also be used to independently assess the usefulness of previously established performance or achievement criteria.

Staffing Concerns

Staffing for performance audits is different from financial type audits. Whereas generally accepted auditing standards refer to persons having technical training and proficiency as an auditor, a performance audit team, complying with government auditing standards is concerned with the *collective* professional proficiency of the total team to competently undertake the performance audit.

Regardless of competency in other fields, a performance auditor would benefit by having proper education and experience in the field of accounting and auditing. But, to meet this standard auditing where accounting and auditing are only two of several skills that must be blended into a multi-disciplined performance audit team. The need for skills broader than auditing is recognized by GAO in its government auditing standards which requires that the assigned auditors *collectively possess adequate professional proficiency* for the tasks required.

The government's interpretation of this standard requires that the audit team include personnel, consultants, experts and others with acceptable skills in areas in addition to accounting and auditing. Examples of other areas include statistics, law, engineering, actuarial science and related skills. But, each individual member of the team need not themselves possess all of the requisite skills. Staffs involved with planning and conducting performance audits in the governmental environment should, individually or collectively, possess:

● Knowledge of governmental organizations, and their operating programs activities and functions, which must be acquired by education, experience or study.

● Experience with the governmental program or activity to be audited. This could be in such specialized areas as transportation, health, public assistance, crime, education, agriculture, etc., as the case may be.

● Technical skills appropriate for performing the task needed to complete the desired performance audit that requires a diversity of academic and technical background needed to examine the function areas under audit. This may require a team of persons skilled in finance, computer science, statistics, quantitative methods, medicine, law, social sciences as well as accounting and auditing.

● In addition to program experience, it is essential that the team have persons knowledgeable of the specific government department or agency to be audited. This might require the recruiting of personnel with prior knowledge or experience with transit authorities, public hospitals, welfare departments, police departments, school, etc.

● Basic knowledge of accounting and auditing theory and procedures and the education, ability, and experience to apply such knowledge to the type of auditing implicit in the desired performance audit.

The perceived competency of the audit team is particularly critical to the conduct of a successful performance audit and for others to accept the results of the audit. To the maximum extent possible, the objective of personnel assignment to the performance audit is to organize an audit team whose members are viewed by the auditee organization as their professional and technical peers in all ways—knowledge, experience and expertise, education, and overall professionalism.

Unique or Pre-Determined Objectives

Government auditing standards define audit *scope* as the depth and coverage of work conducted to accomplish the audit objective. Like objectives, the audit scope must be designed to address the "customers" or "users" audit needs. Because each performance is unique, the scope designed for one performance audit will not satisfy the objectives of another performance audit with different audit objectives.

The objective of a performance audit may be established by governmental legislative units, chief elected officials, department heads, financial managers and often the responsible governmental audit office. These officials could determine the objectives, scope and other elements down to specifying the detail audit procedures to be applied in the particular circumstances. Once the objectives and, possibly, the scope of the audit has been determined by the government, the audit could be performed by the government's auditor or a CPA might be retained to actually perform the audit and report on the observed results.

As a matter of practice the objectives and scope, as a minimum, and often the reporting requirements will be set forth in a formal agreement or memorandum or executed contract between the audit organization and the organization arranging for the audit. As noted, the objectives of a performance audit might have its origin in enabling and appropriation legislation, legislative hearings, concerns with implementing program regulations, issues raised by news media, or senior government executive concerns with the overall program management.

A PERFORMANCE AUDIT METHODOLOGY

Application of the following methodology will generally assist the auditor in defining the audit objectives, developing an audit scope, designing specific audit work programs and clarifying the nature of the reporting desired for a performance audit.

Structuring a performance audit requires that one proceeds from general objectives and goals to the specific information that must be collected and analyzed to reach conclusions on relative economy, efficiency, effectiveness and results of program activities. This might be done by the following process:

1. General objectives and goals may be obtained or inferred from enabling legislation, records of legislative hearings, polices and procedures issued by the agency management for particular programs, and the nature of information and data collected on program operations.

2. Inquiries concerning program activities and operations can be made or observed to identify and quantify the nature of services provided, constituencies served, frequency and quality of service deliv-

ered, all of which would provide evidence of meeting objectives and goals.

3. Indicators of performance can be obtained by postulating questions to obtain data on levels or quality of performance or activities, such as increases or decreases in service levels, changes in costing and financing needs, decreased backlogs, increased error rates, financial and other budgetary resources and other performance statistics, and activity trend and volume indicators.

4. Methods by which data can be obtained may involve a variety of data collecting techniques and evaluative apparatus, including systems reviews, document examinations, statistical sampling, model development, questionnaires, interview protocols, surveys, data analysis, personal observations, written confirmations, external testimony, etc.

This methodology can be applied in structuring a performance audit of any governmental program or activity. But, the methodology must be implemented by a person's appropriate technical skills and experience, knowledge and training in government, and with an understanding of the functional area to be audited.

Performance Audit Process

Almost 30 years ago, GAO offered its views concerning the conduct of performance audits and reviews, noting at the time that these audits are conducted in an uncertain environment.[10] Numerous variables caused this uncertainty although a process for conducting such examinations has subsequently evolved. At the time, GAO provided an illustration of the flow, interrelationship and purpose of activities comprising a performance audit directed at assessing program results (see *Exhibit 17-1*). This methodology for conducting performance audits has prevailed over the years.

The inquiries made, audit procedures applied, data examined and collected, and the analytic techniques used will necessarily vary and be dependent on the government organization or activity undergoing the performance audit. Nevertheless there is a process that can be applied to ensure that the audit is properly planned, the audit is professionally and objectively performed, and the reporting is fair, complete and reflective of audited conditions. Typically, the phases of a performance audit process will include:

1. Completing certain initial background and orientation activities;

2. Conducting a preliminary survey;

---

[10] U.S. General Accounting Office, *Comprehensive Approach for Planning and Conducting a Program Results Review*, Washington, DC, 1973.

Audit Methodology—Performance Audits 437

3. Conducting a preliminary review;

4. Conducting a detailed audit or examination;

5. Developing and reviewing audit findings; and

6. Preparing draft and final reports.

The descriptors associated with the phases might differ, or an auditor might merge one or more of the phases, but all must be done. There is a general scope of review or work that must be performed. There is an audit methodology or process that should be executed. And, as an objective, a factually based report should be expected by those who arranged for the audit.

Background Orientation

A performance audit should not necessarily be perceived as a critical or negative review. Many such audits have been beneficial to many governments and the management reviewed. In this connection the tone of the initial meetings between the auditor and the organization or activity to be audited will do much to establish relations for the duration of the audit and even afterwards during the critical the implementation period.

An initial, pre-audit meeting with agency management and staff should be held for purposes of introduction and orientation. The auditor should make a full presentation of the contemplated scope, provide copies of review protocols, give a briefing on the various phases of the audit.

Typical subjects that should be discussed at this time are:

1. The audit staff and their qualifications and expertise—from the viewpoint of their education as well as their governmental agency and specific program experience.

2. The scope of the performance audit—in sufficient detail to provide a clear understanding of the nature and scope of the performance audit.

3. The audit guides, protocols, and procedures—to be employed in conducting interviews, making surveys, handling questionnaires, visiting sites, making observations and completing other steps of the audit.

4. The reporting procedures by which observations and findings will be relayed by the auditor to those arranging for the audit and to the auditee's management—in many instances these two parties are not the same.

5. The operational process—to which all should adhere in receiving, coordinating, and evaluating management's comments concerning the audit process and final reporting.

Ensuring a full understanding of the performance audit process has been conveyed to all who will be involved with the audit, the auditor conducting this opening conference should consider providing a written outline of the performance audit phases, the audit procedures to be employed, and a description or bio of the auditors and experts that will be conducting the performance audit.

Preliminary Survey

A preliminary survey must be made at the outset of the performance audit and is particularly needed for audits of governmental activities. In this phase, the auditor is concerned with researching the history of the program. Past legislative and management positions and guidelines that could provide some direction for the audit must be identified, inventoried and reviewed. An understanding must be acquired of the program's operating characteristics. Program or operating issues, problems, accomplishments, constituencies, and services of the program must be identified. Information must be obtained concerning financial and statistical data, agency plans and budgets, and other measurement data and reporting systems relied upon by management for monitoring program performance.

The extent of the work performed in this phase will vary considerably from one performance audit to another. In some instances, agency management and staff will possess an inventory of the needed background materials. In other audits, the auditor will be responsible for identifying background sources, defining objectives and goals, establishing criteria for measurement and performance, obtaining cost and operational information that might be used for assessment purposes.

Generally during the preliminary survey phase, no real attempt is made to assess the veracity of the data and other information obtained. The survey is intended to be a short duration, fast information-gathering process. The emphasis is not on problem exploration or deficiency identification. The primary objective of this phase is to obtain an overview of the agency and the program to be audited and acquire some indications of the specific activities and functions that might require more detailed review later in the audit.

Historical, background, operating, and financial data must be quickly compiled and analyzed. Some of this data must include:

● The laws applicable to the audited activity.

● The history, background, and purpose of the program, activities, and functions undergoing audit.

● The organizational structure of the audited organization: division of duties, responsibilities, delegations of authority, nature or size

Audit Methodology—Performance Audits 439

and location of operations, number of employees by organizational segment, location, hierarchical structure.

● Nature, amount, and location of investments in assets used by the program.

● Performance or operational data: inputs, outputs, outcomes in relation to budgets, plans, standards, other expectations and existence of management information and decision supporting systems.

● Cost and financial data by organization and operations: revenues, expenditures, borrowings, "free" or invisible resources provided to or paid for by other programs.

● Relevant policies, procedures, practices: management, operational, personnel, and administrative manuals, bulletins and pronouncements.

Preliminary Review

The preliminary review phase is contrasted with the survey stage by the greater depth and specificity of inquiries being made. An objective of this phase is the "winnowing" down of possible areas warranting audit and the identification of deficiencies that must be examined in greater detail. There's never enough budget to audit everything; choices must be made. Risk areas and perceived problems that are disclosed during the review phase to be low risks will be eliminated from further audit. Audit resources will be re-focused, redirected to issues, problems, weaknesses that appear to be high risks.

The concluding task of the preliminary review phase is to identify those programs, activities, functions or areas that must be audited further. Unless criteria appears in legislation, regulation, policies or are implicit in published procedures, the auditor must as a result of the review identify the criteria or standards against which performance is to be measured. Once done, a cautionary procedure would be to discuss and obtain agreement on the measurment criteria from the organization arranging for the audit. And, if permissible, the audited organizations should be afforded an opportunity to examine the criteria in an attempt to forestall future rebuttals by auditees on the basis that the "criteria's not objective;" "the criteria's not realistic," "the criteria's the auditor's view, not ours," etc., etc.

The audit emphasis during the review phase is directed towards a more complete definition of the types of skills and experiences needed to make a competent and technical assessment of performance. Specific auditing techniques (statistical sampling, surveys, questionnaires, comparative analyses, modeling, observations, etc.) will be identified and perfected. Another feature of this phase is that the review tests are concurrently assessing the validity of views or impressions and validating evidence obtained during the earlier survey phase. The systems—operational and financial—that management relies upon will be examined more closely to determine the relevancy, currency and accuracy of the data gathered, plus the effectiveness of reporting. The concern at this point is whether the data collected by systems is supportive of the type of decisions made. Also, is the format, content, timeliness, frequency, recipients, etc., appropriate for managing the operations.

The concluding efforts of the preliminary review phase is to revise or refine the earlier performance audit plan and to develop detailed audit programs to guide the work of the next phase in the audit. Ideally, a comprehensive written audit program should be developed for each problem area to be investigated.

Detailed Audit or Examination

Testing Required. The detailed audit phase is the confirmation phase of a performance audit. The currency, completeness, accuracy, relevancy and underlying validity must be determined for all information acquired or data examined. Factual, objective, and independent assessments must be made of the performance and operations by the auditor. The overall objective of this phase is to identify those areas that warrant the attention of management or an overseer group. Throughout this phase, evidence must be obtained to conclude on the relative economy, efficiency, effectiveness and "faithfulness" of performance and attainment of program results.

Evaluations Made. Data to permit such evaluations may be derived from a variety of sources and through a number of techniques. Many include those used in earlier phases, but the focus, detail of inquiry, and nature of evidence sought will be different and more specific. Again, the applied audit procedures could include: use of statistics, mathematical modeling, personal interviews with management and staff, mailed questionnaires, constituency sampling, surveys, comparative analyses, analyzing financial and operational data, written confirmations from third parties, auditor observations, etc. In an overview sense, the detailed audit phase requires the audit team to:

1. Review, appraise, test, and report on the extent and nature of compliance with requirements imposed externally by legislation, statute, regulations, etc.

2. Review, appraise, test, and report on the extent and nature of compliance with requirements imposed internally by policy, regulations, procedures, etc.

3. Review, appraise, test, and report on the adequacy and effectiveness of performance in relation to plans, budgets, policies, procedures and legislative and top management objectives.

4. Review, appraise, test, and report on the effectiveness of accounting, administrative, and managerial controls implemented to plan, budget, organize, direct, monitor and control program operations.

5. Review, appraise, test, and report on the relevance and effectiveness of accounting, administrative, and operational systems and reporting used by management in planning, monitoring, and decision-making.

6. Review, appraise, test, and report on the adequacy and effectiveness of the planning and budgeting, intra- and inter-agency coordination and other required or desired cooperative relationships.

7. Through comparative analyses, assess relative economy, efficiency and effectiveness of the organization's performance and financing of other organizational components in the audited entity and possibly a comparison of the auditee to similar operations outside the audited entity.

Audit Findings

An audit *finding* has been defined (in the 1988 edition of the government auditing standards) as:

"The result of information development—a logical pulling together of information to arrive at conclusions (or a response to an audit objective on the basis of the sum of the information) about an organization, program, activity, function, condition, or other matter that was analyzed or evaluated."

The audit finding or detailed audit phase is primarily related to the compilation, evaluation and analysis of the facts and other evidence gathered during earlier phases of the performance audit in relation to specific findings. Careful evaluation of the identified conditions and circumstances is required to ensure that the audit team does not suffer from or fall victim to the "perfect vision" of hindsight.

A technique to insure that a reportable and significant condition exists is to critically examine audit evidence in support of all elements of a finding, which include:

Condition—The situations, circumstances, or practices that have been identified as contributing to less than desired results.

Criteria—What are the objectives, goals, standards, laws, regulations, rules, or other guidelines that are not being achieved or with which there are instances of noncompliance.

Cause—What are the contributory circumstances or practices that have resulted in the less than desired condition or results.

Effect—What is the relative materiality, damage or cost of impairment or loss resulting from the existence or perpetuation of the less than desired conditions or results.

Conclusions—What is the auditor's opinion or assessment or attestation to the conditions that have been identified as contributing to less than desired conditions or results.

Recommendations—What are the auditor's suggested corrective actions or alternative initiatives that will promote more effective, economical, or efficient performance or amelioration of the less than desirable conditions or results.

Promised Corrective Action—What are the corrective actions taken, promised, or waived, by the auditee, for each of the reported findings.

Findings must be developed with caution. The auditor is responsible for accurately assessing the data acquired and examined during the course of the audit and for obtaining additional facts when a factually based assessment can not be made. Issues and problems must be critically examined to determine whether the condition is an isolated example or if the condition permeates the audited organization. Further, readers must be apprised on whether the reported condition has ceased, has been corrected, or is continuing.

At the conclusion of the detailed audit phase of a performance audit, evidence should have been gathered, consistent with audit objectives, to answer the following evaluative questions, to the extent the questions are relevant to the audit:

—Is the program accomplishing the results intended by the enabling legislation?

—Are objectives and goals being achieved within authorized budgets?

—Is essential and reliable information available on a timely basis and is such information used by management and staff?

—Are program costs reasonably commensurate with the benefits achieved and constituency volume served?

—Does management regularly assess alternative program structures, organization, and delivery systems with the objective of increasing its own economy, efficiency, and effectiveness?

—Is there a continuing need for the program or has the need passed, the original constituency moved or shifted and legislation has not been modified accordingly?

—Are program objectives, however imposed, sufficiently clear to permit managers to accomplish the desired results within the financing provided?

—Are subordinate program activities, functions, component units structured in a manner that is consistent with the overall program objectives?

This list is not all-inclusive. Other questions will be appropriate, depending upon the objectives of the performance audit.

Follow-up, iterative-type audit procedures will frequently be required to more fully respond to these evaluative questions. There will be instances when complete answers are not available and can not be obtained by the auditor without an inordinate expenditure of time, money and other resources. Nonetheless, the evaluative questions can be used to provide a summary assessment of the overall adequacy of the performance audit itself.

Audit Reporting

No structured, standard format exists for communicating *findings* or the results of performance audits. Reports of performance audits must, however, be responsive to the objectives of the audit and provide the results of the audit in an agreed-upon report. Regardless of format, the report must contain: (1) information to satisfy all audit objectives or contain explanations as to why not; (2) the sufficient evidence with the findings correctly portrayed; (3) an organized structure with balance in content and tone; and (4) information sufficient to enable readers objectively to assess the validity of the findings, reasonableness of conclusions, and desirability of implementing the recommendations.

With performance audits, there is no standard scope or audit opinion paragraph in the audit report similar to that required by generally accepted auditing standards for financial statement audits. Alternatively, the number and nature of interviews, observations, tests, independent confirmations, and other audit efforts should be disclosed in the body of the report and the findings be described in a relative context to the universe examined. The fiscal or operating period covered, and financial, statistical, and other information examined should be clearly identified. Then, for each finding, all relevant facts and information on each reported finding must be included in narrative, chart, table, or other graphic form.

Auditors can not ignore the axiom: Facts not reported cannot be evaluated. The reader of a performance audit report should have sufficient information within the report to permit an "audit" of the auditor. For each reported audit finding, all elements of that finding should be clearly and objectively described.

With respect to reporting, the distribution of a performance audit report can be troublesome at times—i.e., Who is entitled to receive a performance audit report? Who is responsible for distributing the report? When is the report to be released, and by whom?

The auditor should, when structuring the performance audit, obtain agreement on addressees and all other recipients of the audit report and who specifically should make the distribution of the report. When the report distribution is made is also, at times, contentious. For example, should the report be distributed before being reviewed with the auditee organization? Should the report be distributed with or without comments of the auditee organization? Is the report important to an imminent public hearing or legislative proceeding or pending court action?

On the other hand, delivery to only the organization that arranged for the audit may not be adequate or satisfactory, either. State and local governmental organizations must agree, in advance, if there is to be a broad release of the audit report, particularly to other levels of government. Federal agencies often make receipt of all such reports as a condition precedent to receiving federal financing. Any later restrictions, by the fund recipient, on report distribution would be a violation of the funding conditions and a reportable condition itself. Even here, an important question for the auditor to resolve as early as possible, is who will physically distribute the audit report?

ILLUSTRATIVE PERFORMANCE AUDIT

The following sections outline a methodology for a performance audit that might be performed by either staff of a government agency or a CPA firm retained under contract to the government. In this instance the methodology discussed earlier is applied to evaluate the effectiveness of a local government's transit operations.

Exhibit 17-2 illustrates, in a general manner, the application of the above methodology to develop some of the initial preliminary audit survey and review inquiries in conducting, for example, a performance audit or review of a governmental transit activity. The listing and suggested analyses is illustrative of the manner in which steps in the survey and how the review phase might proceed and the nature of data, much of it nonfinancial, should be collected.

To achieve objectives and goals, a transit service must perform certain services, which can be evaluated as to relative economy, efficiency, effectiveness and results. Some inquiries to be examined in reaching conclusions on performance indicators might, initially, include:

—What types of transit services are offered? To whom?

Audit Methodology—Performance Audits 445

—When or with what frequency is the service provided? To whom?

—What is the pricing structure? Are prices perceived as reasonable for the services to various constituents?

—Are total costs of operations and services known and periodically reviewed?

—Are fares sufficient to cover operating costs? Capital costs?

—Are other financial sources or subsidies used to support operating cost or capital investments? What is the level of these other financial sources?

—Are the reported costs all inclusive—has any cost (e.g., fringe benefits, retirement costs, maintenance) been under-reported or deferred to future periods?

—Are constituents relatively satisfied with the frequency and type of service provided?

—Should the services be expanded to other constituencies, or, conversely, contracted?

—Are the services provided, constituents served, sources of financial support consistent with state and local laws and statutes and federal legislation and regulations?

To address these and other inquiries, financial, performance, management, and operational information, statistics and other data must be accumulated, studied, analyzed, and concluded upon. In the case of a governmental service, it is often necessary to conduct a survey or census of both the user population as well as of non-users to obtain third-party opinions as to the real or perceived effectiveness of the public service offered. Not infrequently, sufficient or directly relevant documentation does not exist or exists only in part. Often, an audit data base or "system" must be established to collect, compile, array, and report appropriate information. Evidence for performance audits could equally be comprised of financial, statistical, and operational data or judgments, opinions, perceptions held by legislators and public sector officials, and the constituencies being served or who might be served by the public system.

The illustrative tasks have been grouped, on **Exhibit 17-3**, by the several audit phases: preliminary survey, preliminary review, execution of detailed audit programs and reporting. As noted above, what is audited is dependent upon the objectives of a performance audit and the specific organization or its activities undergoing the performance audit.

The initial audit phase is one of *confirming objectives* of the audit to be made, arranging with the auditee for access to make the audit, and gathering background and historical information on the organization and its activities and operations.

During the *survey* phase, while more detailed, there is still no concerted attempt to make final assessments. The purpose of the survey is to obtain an overview of the auditee and an indication of structure, activities, functions, operations or other subjects that might require more detailed examination later in the audit.

The *review* phase is even more detailed than the survey phase and is the phase where critical audit decisions will be made concerning specifically what is and is not to be subjected to detailed audit. By the end of the review phase, the performance audit plan should be refined and specific audit programs developed to provide direction for the detailed audit of specific areas of risk.

The *detailed audit* phase is the confirmation phase of a performance audit. The currency, completeness, accuracy, relevancy and underlying validity of all audit findings must be determined. The overall objective of this phase is to identify those areas that warrant the attention of management or any overseer group. Basically, this is the phase when audit findings will be crystallized and developed for later reporting.

With respect to the *reporting* phase, no structured, standard format exists for communicating *findings* or the results of performance audits. Performance audit reports must be responsive to the specific objectives of the engagement and provide the results of the audit in an agreed-upon report.

And, eventually, the performance report must be distributed to: (1) the party arranging for the audit, (2) officials responsible for taking actions, (3) the audited organizations, (4) federal financing departments and agencies, (5) legislators and others authorized to receive the report, and, eventually if of interest, (6) the general public, news media. Because these groupings may not necessarily be comprised of the same persons, the auditor must exercise caution when submitting the performance audit report and should strictly comply with the reporting objectives established at the outset of the audit.

Exhibits 17-1, 17-2, and 17-3 follow this page.

Audit Methodology—Performance Audits 447

EXHIBIT 17-1

Exhibit 17-1

Program Results Review Process

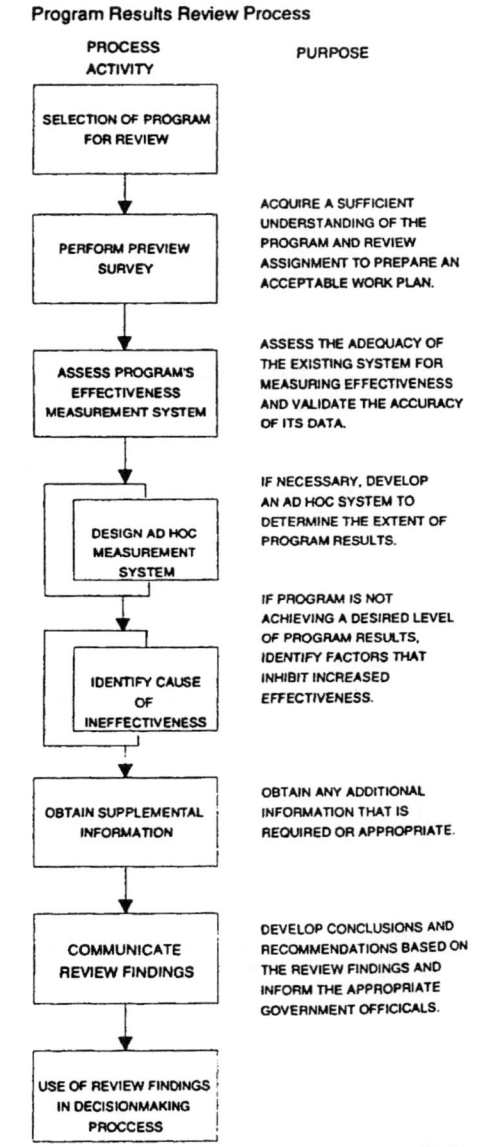

PROCESS ACTIVITY	PURPOSE
SELECTION OF PROGRAM FOR REVIEW	
PERFORM PREVIEW SURVEY	ACQUIRE A SUFFICIENT UNDERSTANDING OF THE PROGRAM AND REVIEW ASSIGNMENT TO PREPARE AN ACCEPTABLE WORK PLAN.
ASSESS PROGRAM'S EFFECTIVENESS MEASUREMENT SYSTEM	ASSESS THE ADEQUACY OF THE EXISTING SYSTEM FOR MEASURING EFFECTIVENESS AND VALIDATE THE ACCURACY OF ITS DATA.
DESIGN AD HOC MEASUREMENT SYSTEM	IF NECESSARY, DEVELOP AN AD HOC SYSTEM TO DETERMINE THE EXTENT OF PROGRAM RESULTS.
IDENTIFY CAUSE OF INEFFECTIVENESS	IF PROGRAM IS NOT ACHIEVING A DESIRED LEVEL OF PROGRAM RESULTS, IDENTIFY FACTORS THAT INHIBIT INCREASED EFFECTIVENESS.
OBTAIN SUPPLEMENTAL INFORMATION	OBTAIN ANY ADDITIONAL INFORMATION THAT IS REQUIRED OR APPROPRIATE.
COMMUNICATE REVIEW FINDINGS	DEVELOP CONCLUSIONS AND RECOMMENDATIONS BASED ON THE REVIEW FINDINGS AND INFORM THE APPROPRIATE GOVERNMENT OFFICICALS.
USE OF REVIEW FINDINGS IN DECISIONMAKING PROCCESS	

Source: *Comprehensive Approach for Planning and Conducting a Program Results Review.* U.S. General Accounting Office, Washington, D.C.

EXHIBIT 17-2

METHODOLOGY FOR PLANNING PERFORMANCE AUDIT OF LOCAL TRANSPORT SYSTEM

A. Goals or Objectives	B. Inquiries to Test Achievement of Goals	C. Data to Indicate Performance or Achievement	D. Data Analyses and Collection Methods
To provide an integrated transit system to serve the population of the county	• Are all areas of county served • Frequency of service in peak and non-peak periods • Traffic logs, passenger counts, surveys of attitudes • Reasonableness of fares—peak, non-peak, group rates, older citizens, school children • Programs for serving commuters, shoppers, aged, handicapped, school children, urban, rural constituencies • Adequacy of route structure; length of runs; need for transfers • Age or condition of trasit equipment, stations, rights-of-way • Financial performance—revenues, operating, capital and administrative costs, projects	• Comparison of route structure to business and residential areas, rural versus urban centers • Records of pre- and post-program initation; comparison to alternative transportation modes, coverage of operating costs • Scheduling of equipment; special parking lots; express buses; curb-to-curb service; dial-a-ridee; shuttle buses • Origin and destination studies; analysis of transfer usage • Acquisition, maintenance and repair records • Other data reflective of levels or volume of service, comparative costs and statisitical data; surveys, complaints, legislative concerns, voter preferences, etc.	• Document reviews • Interviews • Questionnaires • Comparisons to other governments and services • Trend and comparative analyses • Statistical sampling • Personal observations • Independent confirmations • Survey and polls of public, customers, legislatures • Accounting and information systems

EXHIBIT 17-3

Exhibit 17-3

Overview—Performance Audit Plan......
Summary of Audit Phases & Tasks

A. Initiate Audit

1. **Organizing Conference**
   - Arrangers of audit
   - Oversight entities
   - Sponsors
2. **Conference/Auditee** Management, Staffs
   - Orientation
   - Arrangements
3. **Entrance Conference**
   Discuss audit:
   ...Objectives
   ...Protocols
   ...Process
   ...Personnel
   ...Report process
   ...Timing
   ...Cooperation
   ...Coordination
4. **Outline Audit Plan/Program**

B. Preliminary Survey

1. **Review Program History**
   - Audit reports
   - Consultants
   - External reviews
   - Surveys
   - Financial reports
   - Operational
2. **Review Legal History**
   - Federal, state laws
   - Local statutes
   - Legislative history
   - Policies, procedures
   - Regulations, rules
   - Court rulings
   - Other
3. **Inquire of Performance**
   Issues
   - Accomplishments
   - Problems
   - Deficiencies
   - Outcomes
   - Outputs
   - Other
4. **Program Status** Services/Activities
   - Variety, types
   - Constituencies
   - Service levels
   - Frequencies
   - Locations
   - Plant, equipment
   - Staffing, skills
   - Technology factors
5. **Identify Financing**
   - Appropriations
   - Fees, billings
   - Debt
   - Donations
   - In-kind
   - Other
6. **Budgets/Plans**
   - Financial
   - Operations
   - Budgets
   - Personnel
   - Capital equipment
   - Legislative
7. **Financial/Info Systems**
   - Types
   ...Financial
   ...Operational
   ...Management
   ...Personnel
   ...Measurement
   ...Property
   ...Procurement
   ...Other
   - Automation
   ...Computerization
   ...Documentation
   ...Equipment
   Locations
   Volume
   Currency
   ...Personnel
8. **Summarize Survey**
   - Survey observations
   - Refine audit plan, programs

C. Preliminary Review

1. **Confirm Audit Scope**
   - Organization
   - Program
   - Function
   - Activity
   - Financial systems
   - Info systems
   - Operational
   - Other
2. **Determine Performance Indicators**
   - For service levels
   - Frequency, usage
   - Constituencies
   - Service criteria
   - Costs
   - Backlogs
   - Complaints
   - Other
3. **Evidence Techniques**
   - Sampling
   - Survey
   - Data analysis
   - Audit observations
   - Comparative studies
   - Analyses
   - Interviews
   - Other
4. **Summarize Review**
   - Review observations
   - Refine audit plan, programs

D. Detailed Audit

1. **Sampling Methods**
   - Stat/Judgment
   - Methodology
   - Samples
   ...Stratification
   ...Sizes
   ...Timing
   ...Reliabilities
   ...Results
   ...Projections
   - Analyses
2. **Questionnaires**
   - Nature
   - Guide

- Audiences
- Breadth
- Results
- Analyses
3. Interviews
- Subjects
- Appointments
- Interviewees
- Results
4. Observations
- Site visits
- Personal inspections
- Confirmations
- Physical tests
5. Financial, Statistical
- Systems
- Controls
- Data
  ...Sources
  ...Utility
  ...Timeliness
  ...Relevance
  ...Completeness
  ...Documentation
6. Data Analyses
- Pre & post periods
- Trends
- Variances
- Comparisons
- Ranges
- Limitations
- Forecasts
- Plans to actual
- Models
7. Summarize Audit
- Workpapers
- Observations

E. Compile Audit Findings

1. Develop Findings
- Condition
- Criteria
- Cause
- Effect
- Conclusions
- Recommendations
- Corrective action
2. Review Findings
- Written presentation
- Oral review
- Comment period
- Corrective actions
- Review comments
3. Draft Audit Report
- Present draft report
- Discuss report
- Comments
- Review comments
- Revise report

F. Final Reporting on Audit Findings

1. Complete Audit Report
- Scope of audit
- Objectives of audit
- Methodology
- Period of audit
- Executives contacted
- Audit findings
  ...Condition
  ...Criteria
  ...Cause
  ...Effect
  ...Conclusions
  ...Recommendations
  ...Corrective action
2. Distribute Report
- Arrangers of audit
- Auditee
- Oversight officials
- Oversight entities
- Authorized others
- General public

Note: Additional discussion on these phases and tasks appear in the chapter text.

Chapter 18

Audit Methodology— Contracts and Grants

With their own auditors or utilizing CPAs under contract, public sector entities have for decades made audits of government contracts and grants awarded to a variety of recipients—corporations, educational institutions, nonprofit organizations, as well as state and local governments.

At times, federal law dictates the overall and often specific contract and grant agreement requirements and form the basis for a standard, national type contract or grant agreement. In other instances, the enabling federal legislation plus federal Office of Management and Budget and departmental or agency regulations constitute the general terms for contract and grant agreements. But, the standard terms and conditions of these agreements may be altered in negotiations with individual recipients of this federal assistance.

The terms of all federal contracts and grants require that costs charged to projects and claims for reimbursement be only for allowable and properly allocable costs and that the control and accounting systems of recipients clearly identify costs that by regulation are allowable and unallowable. Compliance with negotiated budgets—performance and financial—will also be monitored by the governmental departments and agencies. Decades before government auditing standards introduced terms such as "financial related" audits or "compliance" audits, these types of audits were being made of federal contracts and grants.

AUTHORITY FOR CONTRACT AND GRANT AUDITS

The authority for auditing contracts and grants awarded to other governments is implicit in the stewardship responsibilities of a federal department or agency. The requirement for these audits are explicit in most authorizing and appropriation laws of Congress and in the terms and conditions of government contracts and grants. Generally, the head of a federal agency is charged by law to establish and maintain a system of internal controls and accounting to properly discharge specific stewardship responsibilities. A program for auditing the agency's contracts and grants is viewed as an important and integral part that agency's system of internal controls. Further, field audits are, in many instances, an agency's only on-site review of contractors and grantees performance during the period of the agreements.

Since the 1960s, as federal funding increased and partnerships were formed with state and local governments to support numerous governmental programs, federal laws became more specific with respect to requirements for contract and grant audits. Now, federal laws dictate when such audits will be made, the frequency of these audits, the general scope of such audits and even detailed audit procedures that must be applied by the auditor when examining contracts or grants. Many state and local governments "piggyback" or duplicate and pass-through the federal contract and grant requirements to their own contractors and grantees.

In the 1990s, several inspectors general designed programs for auditing the contracts and grants related to specific federal programs. Also, OMB in its *Compliance Supplement* describes the compliance criteria that must be examined in an audit of federal contract, grant and other programs and outlines detailed audit procedures by individual programs, in some instances. OMB Circulars for many years have required that administrative and managerial practices of contractors and grantees be reviewed and that costs claimed or charged to federal contracts and grants be tested for reasonableness, allowability and allocability. Thus, the authority to audit emanates from several sources: Congress, the OMB, federal operating departments, and state and local governments, rules and regulations of various governmental levels, and negotiated terms and conditions of contracts and grants.

AUDITORS OF CONTRACTS AND GRANTS

Audits of federal contracts and grants are performed by auditors who might be employed by the federal department. State or local governmental auditors might also conduct audits of the federal and other contracts and grants awarded to units of their employing governments. Then, at all levels of governments, independent under contract, auditors are employed to assist with these types of audits.

At times, the independence of the auditor requires particular scrutiny and may cause more difficulty for an auditor employed by a government than a CPA. Governmental auditors auditing contracts and grants of another government are independent. Internal auditors of a state government, for example, are viewed as independent and external to the audited entity if, organizationally, the auditee reports to a secretariat or chief executive who is different from those to whom

Audit Methodology—Contracts and Grants

the auditors report. Auditors employed by the legislative branch that conduct audits of executive branch activity are also independent of executive branch programs. Still, auditors within each of these categories must continuously examine their relationship to the contract or grant program, the governmental organization that issued the instrument, and their financing and reporting relationships.

While the independence of CPAs is not a question when retained by governments to audit government contracts and grants, there is concern by governments and the CPAs with respect to the scope of audits and financial budgets for these audits. At times and for specific audits, governments retain CPAs under contracts that outline scopes of audit procedures that will be applied and the format of the audit report. The audit engagement contract will include the financial budget within which the audit must be performed or which limits the amount the government will pay for the audit. But there is a risk since neither the contracting government nor the CPA know in advance what the audit will ultimately cost.

Audit contracts with CPAs are of two general types—cost type or fixed price type—that differ in the nature of the scope of audit to be performed and the financing risk to be borne by either the government or the CPA.

Cost Type Audit Contracts

Under federal procurement regulations, cost reimbursement type contracts are generally used when the scope of the audit cannot be defined with specificity. Under such contracts, the CPA is required to make a "best effort" to perform the contracted scope of audit for the estimated contract amount and within a described time period. Should the estimated contract amount or the estimated time period be insufficient to complete the contracted audit scope, the government must provide additional funds or time or the CPA firm is not required to continue to render audit services.

This "best effort" requires the CPA firm to staff the audit in the manner proposed, perform the audit as proposed or as desired by the government, and make a diligent attempt to complete the contracted audit scope within the proposed time period. If, unexpected or unusual events are observed or uncovered during the audit, the auditor does not have the unilateral authority to expand or alter the contracted audit scope to examine these conditions in greater detail. The observed conditions must be reported to the entity arranging for the audit. If the contracted audit scope is not modified by the arranging entity, the CPA is not authorized to deviate from the original audit scope, dollar budget, or time limitations. In essence, for cost type contracts, when the funds or time run out, the contract is over.

There are a variety of federal cost reimbursement type contracts including: cost-plus-fixed-fee contracts, labor hour contracts, time and material contracts. Under these contracts the CPA is permitted to recover the negotiated costs and fee, plus any negotiated out-of-pocket expenses. Again, cost type contracts are "best efforts" contracts: the CPA is responsible for making its best effort within the time budget and financial budget to perform the contracted scope of work.

Fixed Price Audit Contracts

In contrast to cost type contracts, firm fixed price contracts place maximum performance and financial risk on the CPA. Under fixed price contracts, CPAs agree to perform the scope of the contracted audit regardless of the cost or time required. The CPA is entitled to all savings resulting from cost or budget underruns, but conversely must assume risk for all cost overruns required to complete the contracted audit scope.

With fixed price contracts, it is imperative that the CPA clearly understand the negotiated audit scope, the nature of the audit to be performed, all particulars concerning special audit procedures to be applied, and any special contract conditions that must be observed. Additionally, if the CPA is unwilling or unable to complete a fixed price audit contract, the CPA could then be liable for all cost incurred by the government to retain a successor CPA firm to complete the audit.

Fixed price contracts make the CPA liable for performance of the contracted audit scope for the contracted fixed price regardless of the price initially proposed by the CPA or the actual cost later incurred by the CPA to complete the audit.

Audit Contracts

There is no universal manner by which audit contracts are issued by governments or whom the governmental client might be. But, two types of arrangements seem to prevail.

By Federal Agencies

A federal agency can award a contract to a CPA to audit other contracts and grants awarded to governments and non-federal entities. These audit contracts might be issued either by a central procurement office or from a regional office of the federal agency. In these circumstances, no dispute arises with these contracts as to who is the audit client. The performance of the audit must be in accordance with the federal audit guidance as detailed or referenced in the audit contract.

By Other Governments

Federal assistance programs require the recipients of financial assistance to retain a CPA to make an independent audit of the recipient's contract or grant. Under these circumstances, one level of government (i.e., a state, county or city) will hire and pay a CPA, but the audit scope used by the CPA is mandated by another level of government, in this case the federal government. Alternatively, a government arranging and paying for the audit might select the CPA, but, may have to give notice or seek approval from the federal government for the retained CPA. Under these contracts, the CPA has multiple clients—the government that issued the audit contract, and each of the several federal agencies who awarded federal assistance grants. Even the U.S. General Accounting Office and the federal Office of Management and Budget might have audit concerns and have to be viewed as clients or parties whose needs must be met.

CONTRACT AND GRANT AUDITING

Within governments, auditing contract and grant programs are viewed from two perspectives:

(1) Audits are made of the procurement or grants function or managing activity within a government. In this instance, the audit scope might include an evaluation of contract or grant negotiations, the award process, the administration or monitoring of performance, and settlement or closeout practices. These audits, more often conducted by a government's own internal auditors, may be more in the nature of performance audits, as defined in government auditing standards.

(2) External audits or reviews are also made of individual contracts and grants awarded to non-federal entities. These examinations have varying descriptors primarily related to the depth or breadth of the examination. Some include such efforts as: contract or grant pricing reviews, pre-award surveys, post-award surveys, and cost incurred audits. These examinations fall within the government auditing standards definition of financial related audits and are often contracted out to CPA firms, but can and are done by auditors employed by governments.

Surveys, Reviews, Audits of Contracts and Grants

The type and nature of reporting made for contract and grant audits conform closely to the requirements set forth in government auditing standards for financial related audits and performance audits. These examinations, while, primarily financial, must assure that there is compliance with non-financial conditions. This is particularly true of audits made pursuant to the Single Audit Act, witness OMB's *Compliance Supplement* which details financial and non-financial audit procedures to be applied.

To obtain assurance that prospective contractors and grantees have competent management to accept and perform federal assistance programs, the government may require these recipients to undergo a variety of special scope audits or reviews, such as: a pre-award survey; post-award survey; periodic audit; pricing or cost review, cost audit, as well as a close-out audit.

Pre-Award Survey

The objective of a pre-award survey is to determine the adequacy of the prospective contractor's or grantee's systems of accounting, administration, management, and internal controls. The survey is part of the government's process for determining if the recipient organization is or can be a financially responsive recipient of governmental financial assistance. In some instances, systems and controls are weak or non-existent and must be re-designed or designed and implemented as a condition to full funding of the contract or grant. Many of the "high risk" contractors or grantees have these deficiencies.

A pre-award survey may be required by a government agency in those instances where the contractor or grantee has not previously received a federal contract or grant or the recipient entity was previously funded and failed in some respect to comply with federal laws or regulations. It would not be unusual for a federal government agency to request performance information about prospective contractors or grantees and even state and local governments.

Post-Award Surveys

A post-award or follow-up survey is made of a grantee between 60 to 90 days after a contract or grant award. The objective of this examination is to determine, early in the performance period, whether the recipient has, or is in process of installing effective management and financial controls. The governmental agency is particularly concerned with progress made to eliminate, fix, or minimize deficiencies highlighted in the pre-award survey. Selected tests are made of performance and financial management activities to assess compliance with contract or grant conditions and as a condition precedent to full funding or authorizing maximum program operations.

Periodic Financial Audits

Periodic, usually annual, financial audits and compliance examinations are made of federal governmental contractors and grantees to determine the program performance and the allowability, reasonableness, and allocability of costs charged to or claimed under federal contracts and grants. Audits conducted pursuant to the Single Audit Act must include tests for compliance with laws and regulations of other governments and not just the federal government's.

The scope of these financial audits will include tests of controls, audits of transactions, observations of practices, inquiries of management, and detailed examination of supporting documentation. The charged or claimed costs will be compared to negotiated or approved budgets, and any ceilings or limitations or other restrictions will be examined for compliance. Local match or other cost-sharing or contributed amounts will be audited to determine their appropriateness and value. The compliance aspect of the audit will be directed towards evaluating adherence to the special and general conditions of the formal agreements, which may often relate to non-financial or performance matters of significance to the government agency.

Reports of audits of contractor or grantee management will generally be in narrative form. The audit findings or observations will be set forth, along with any conclusions, the effects of observed conditions, and recommendations. Federal agencies will often require the preparation of financial exhibits comparing costs charged or claimed to the approved contract or grant financial budget. Exceptions are highlighted in the report, generally with a description of the conditions or circumstances relating to the exception and comments from management of the audited entity.

In 1984, with the Single Audit Act, the federal government moved to make these audits more regular, uniform, consistent and comprehensive in scope. Single audits are now made of tens of thousands of state and local government and nonprofit contractors and grantees.

Pricing Reviews

A pricing or cost review is a limited-purpose audit, generally of a prospective federal contractor or grantee. The objective of this type review is to examine the reasonableness of the price or cost proposal submitted to the federal government in anticipation of a contract or grant award. The scope of this type of audit includes an assessment of the factual bases and underlying documents and circumstances from which the contractor or grantee developed its estimate of proposed direct costs. An examination is also made of the level of proposed indirect cost and the reasonableness of allocations in relation to past and projected sales, cost bases, volume, and nature of business or program operations. Cost estimates for subcontractors or subgrantees and other costs (e.g., travel, supplies, utilities, space, etc.) will be reviewed to determine the reasonableness and appropriateness of such estimates in relation to the work to be performed or services to be rendered.

The primary audit criteria for assessing pricing or cost data are the allowable, unallowable and indirect cost principles set forth in the federal governments procurement or acquisition regulations and the OMB Circulars relating to the determination of allowable, unallowable and indirect costs (i.e., Circulars A-87—for state and local governments; A-122—for nonprofit organizations; and A-21—for institutions of higher education).

Additionally, the Cost Accounting Standards Board, a federal entity, has issued separate regulations that must be considered during these reviews. CASB's regulations, among other subjects, establish criteria for proposing, accounting, allocating, and billing cost to the federal government. Proposing, charging, or claiming costs in contravention to CASB regulations could result in the federal government instituting a defective pricing action against a recipient of federal funds.

Costs Incurred Audits

An audit of incurred costs could be made during or at the completion of a contract or grant. These are limited scope audits of the costs incurred and charged to the federal contract or grant, including a comparison of actual costs to approved budgets. A comparison or estimate of percentage of completion is made to cost incurred to assess relative performance. Tests will be made of contractor or grantee accounting and control systems and management processes. Supporting documentation is examined for various costs and a determination or conclusion is reached as to the allowability, allocability, and reasonableness of the costs in relation to federal program and procurement regulations, OMB criteria and the conditions and terms of the specific contracts and grants undergoing audit.

Reports of these audits seldom have a prescribed format. The findings and observations are described in a narrative form and the report will include the auditor's conclusions and recommendations and highlight any cost that the auditor concludes are questioned or are clearly unallowable for the contract or grant. These audits may also require the preparation of financial exhibits comparing cost charged to negotiated budgets, with exceptions highlighted along with any comments from the management of the audited activity.

Close-Out Audits

There are special "close-out" audit concerns or emphases that must be addressed for inactive or completed or terminated contracts and grants. "Completed" generically includes contracts and grants where: (1) performance is inactive, (2) performance has been completed in accordance with the terms and conditions, or (3) where the performance is terminated earlier than planned by the government or the recipient.

The overall objectives of close-out audits are to evaluate compliance with any government end-of-contract or grant termination procedures and confirm the accuracy of reported receivables, payables, amounts withheld, unexpended advances and other amounts claimed from or to be refunded to the federal agency. Contracts and grants will have specific terms and conditions relating to conducting a final inventory of government furnished or procured property, equipment and other resources.

OMB regulations—the common rule or OMB Circular A-102 and OMB Circular A-110—mandate specific management, financial and administrative type contract and grant closeout procedures that must be performed within definite times upon completion or earlier termination of a federal program. Some of these close-out procedures will require tests to determine amounts and property due to or from the federal government, inventory and property disposal requirements, assessment of performance, etc. Under these OMB circulars, final performance or progress reports, a financial status report, reports on any federally-owned property and requests for final payment, if appropriate, must be completed within 90 days after completion, expiration or termination of the contract or grant.

GENERAL AUDIT CONSIDERATIONS

There exists comprehensive audit checklists, control questionnaires and detailed audit programs for the audit of government contracts and grant, prepared by the AICPA and many of the federal inspectors general. Selected controls, checks and balances, and practices may be unique to government or may have increased importance in public sector audits because public monies are at issue. Generally, contractors and grantees would be expected to employ the following practices:

1. Forms related to the contracting and granting process should be prenumbered, controlled, properly voided, and filed. These supporting documents should be coded by the individual contract and grant, applicable fund, organization, functions, budget activity, type of expense and the object classification.

2. Signatures on authorizing or approval forms and other documents should be prescribed by policy or procedures or even legislation, in some instances.

3. All contract or grant modifications, changes, budget adjustments, fund transfers, line item changes, or altered performance should be monitored under prescribed sound managerial and accounting control.

4. Commitments, obligations and encumbrances, expenditures and disbursements for awarded contracts and grants should be continually monitored to avoid exceeding legal limits, contract ceilings, or fiscal or other requirements of the contract or grant.

5. The reported end-of-period balances of receivables and payables for contracts, represent valid commitments or obligations and encumbrances; tests must be made to determine the extent of unprocessed, unrecorded or unreported transactions receivables and payables related to contracts and grants.

6. All contract and grant disbursements are for only legal, authorized purposes, made during the appropriate fiscal period, to obtain goods or services or other performance permitted by law and regulations.

7. Internal controls and checks exist to ensure that only costs permissible in the OMB cost principles circulars (i.e., those regulations for allowable, unallowable, and indirect costs) are charged, reported, and billed to the federal award programs.

8. All supporting documentation for contracts and grants exist, must be properly completed and processed (e.g., procurement requests, procurement authorizations, contract and grant agreements, progress or performance reports, invoices, vouchers, request for advances, payments, reimbursements, letters of credit withdrawals, receiving reports, property records, etc.), and:

—Are marked or otherwise mutilated to avoid reuse, are properly coded, and the content of such records are reconcilable with the ledgers, books of original entry, and posted transactions.

—Contain evidence that these records were properly prepared, expenditures were for authorized purposes; documents are annotated for receipt of goods, services, or performance; all amounts are arithmetically correct, cited accounts are charged properly, and approvals are obtained and noted before disbursement of funds.

—Are reconcilable to journal entries, amounts in books of original entry, and the formal accounts of the government.

9. Plans and budgets for contracts and grants are regularly compared to actual financial results. Performance, deliveries, and all significant variances analyzed for changed practices or required corrective action.

10. All refunds, reimbursements, error corrections, write-offs and other adjustments of earlier expenditures and disbursements are properly approved and correctly coded and processed for management and financial purposes.

For many federal, state and local governmental agencies, contract expenditures are significant. At times, contract values may be of such magnitude that legislatures will specifically approve the amounts budgeted for such expenditures. Special reporting may be required in such situations and, at time, special and frequent audits may be mandated.

CONTRACT AND GRANT PROCESS

Contracts Definitions

All levels of government enter into contracts and issue purchase orders for equipment, supplies, materials, and services. The terminology for contracts and purchase orders, while not uniform, is rather consistent between the governmental levels. For example, some basic terms include:

Contracts—Agreement, commitment or obligation resulting from acceptance of an offer, issuance of notice of award, job orders, letter contracts, letters of intent, and purchase orders calling for the construction or delivery of items, such as: buildings, roads, equipment, supplies, materials, or provision of services.

Purchase order—A small contract (the dollar amount varies by government but could be as high as $25,000 for some federal agencies) for services, supplies, or materials that often simultaneously authorize delivery, make delivery and provide authority to bill the government.

Cost type contracts—Entered into when the precise scope of services to be performed are not definable; contractors are reimbursed for cost incurred plus a prenegotiated profit; maximum risk for performance or financing the contract is assumed by the contracting government.

Fixed price contracts or lump sum contracts—Issued for services and products that are definable; contractors must perform the contracted scope regardless of actual costs incurred; maximum risk for performance and financing are assumed by the contractor who benefits if performance is accomplished at less than the fixed or lump sum price. (Purchase orders are viewed as fixed-price contracts.)

Contract Process

There have been efforts among the states to develop procurement regulations similar to the federal governments; however, no uniform codification of contracting regulations exists countrywide. But, the process for acquiring supplies, property, and services is quite similar, for example:

1. Operating or program officials generally will be responsible for deciding that the desired services or goods cannot be performed by governmental personnel and must be obtained from a contractor or vendor. Or, laws and regulations might mandate the use of contracts.

2. The initial official record of such a decision is the completion of a procurement request or authorization. This form will most often

include fiscal, descriptive, as well as approval and authorizing data, and is the record that often supports the accounting entries for dollar commitments.

3. The actual obligation or encumbrance of a governmental unit is represented by the execution and award of a formal contract, for which another accounting entry is required. As services are performed or goods received, other accounting entries are made to liquidate or reduce the dollars committed related to the procurement authorization and record outstanding obligation or encumbrance appearing in the awarded contract.

4. Payments, and accounting entries for cash disbursements, to contractors are made after proper acceptance of contract deliverables and submission of expenditures and other periodic reportings.

5. Receiving reports for goods and services received and other approvals of completed deliveries are generally required and constitute the supporting documents for accounting entries for property, equipment and other tangible assets.

Exhibit 18-1 illustrates a general overview of the several offices or governmental functions that could be involved with a contracted procurement and the activities performed by each in acquiring goods or services and the accounting over the life cycle of a procurement or contracting transaction.

Definitions of Grants

Over the years, the purposes, terms, conditions, and compliance requirements for federal grants have become increasingly stringent to the point that, in the 1990s, it became difficult to distinguish between a federal contract and a federal grant. In fact, some federal agencies use the terms "contracts" and "grants" interchangeably. Almost identical programs are operated by one federal agency through agreements it declares to be contracts; another agency refers to its operating agreements as grants. In the 1990s, performance was demanded and compliance required with detailed terms and conditions of grant agreements that contain the same terms and conditions of contract agreements of another federal agency.

The definition of a "grant" has evolved since the 1960s to the point where considerably more responsibilities are assumed by and expected of grantees by federal grantors. Through the 1960s, federal grants were viewed almost as endowments and in some instances almost "give aways"—the period of performance may have been rather indefinite, minimal accounting was required, possibly no progress reporting was demanded, and few audits were made. [1]

In the 1970s, OMB refined and made more specific the federal government's concept of grants, which were now viewed as "money or property in lieu of money, paid or furnished by the federal government to a grantee under programs that provide financial assistance through grant or contractual arrangements." Excluded from this definition were technical assistance, revenue sharing, loans, loan guarantees, and insurance programs. Generally, federal grants are now viewed as providing assistance for specified purposes, ranging from studies and research to program operations.

By the 1990s, OMB (in the "common rule") refined the definition of **grants** to now mean:

> *". . . an award of financial assistance, including cooperative agreements, in the form of money, or property in lieu of money, by the federal government to an eligible grantee."*

OMB specifically excludes from this definition of "grants," technical assistance which provides services instead of money, or other assistance in the form of revenue sharing, loans, loan guarantees, interest subsidies, insurance, or direct appropriations or other lump sum award, for which the grantee is not required to account. The "common rule" that prescribes the administrative requirements for grants to state and local governments also defines "grantees" and "local government:"

> *"Grantees mean the government to which a grant is awarded and which is accountable for the use of funds provided. The grantee is the entire legal entity, even if only a particular component of the entity, as designated in the grant award document."*

These federal definitions parallel closely those used by the Governmental Accounting Standards Board in prescribing the generally accepted accounting and reporting standards for grants, entitlements, and shared revenues. GASB defines a grant as a contribution or gift of cash or other assets from another government to be used or expended for a specified purpose, activity, or facility, and including two types: operating grants and capital grants. *Operating grants* are intended to finance operations or might be used for both operations and capital outlays; *capital grants* are restricted for the acquisition or construction of fixed, capital assets.

---

[1] Cornelius E. Tierney, *Federal Grants-in-Aid: Accounting and Auditing Practices*, American Institute of CPAs, New York, N.Y., 1977.

Additionally, terms like formula grants, block grants, and project grants have also been used in practice:

- *Formula grants*—Issued pursuant to law, with entitlement or amount being determined by Congress; minimal discretion is exercised by the federal grantor agency or OMB.
- *Block grants*—Issued for broad program purposes, such as education, transit, housing, employment programs.
- *Project grants*—Issued by grantors for specific services or performance, with conditions similar to contracts for purposes such as research, pilot projects, training or planning programs.

As is evident from the above, grant titles are more descriptive in nature but not necessarily mutually exclusive; some grants might fit within one or more definitions. Aside from the absence of a profit element, which is involved in contracts, grants may not materially differ from contracts. From an accounting and audit perspective, the federal government and the GASB treat grants as being the equivalent of cost-type contracts.

Grant Process

In instances where a state or local governmental unit might be the grantee, the execution of an agreement to accept the federal funds and make expenditures might also have to be approved by the state or local government legislative branch. Then, all expenditures, even those under a federal grant, must conform to all laws (federal, state, and local) and be in compliance with specific terms and conditions of the grant agreement.

Exhibit 18-2 illustrates the activities and documentation often required by a federal grantor when issuing and accounting for its grants. In many ways, the award, monitoring and accounting for a grant closely parallels the process used for federal contracts. This exhibit highlights the federal letter-of-credit process, another grant practice that is equally applicable to the financing of federal contracts issued to governmental units.

Letters of Credit

Inter-governmental grants, as well as contracts, often provide for a system of advanced funding under the federal letters-of-credit procedures. The letter-of-credit is a negotiable instrument, certified by a federal executive, that permits authorized grantees to draw funds when needed, direct from the U.S. Treasury. A letter of credit is a form of advanced funding, for which a later accounting and reconciliation must be made between funds withdrawn and cost incurred. Letters-of-credit are used when there is a continuing relationship between grantees and a federal grantor agency and total advances are within a prescribed amount. (Under the Cash Management Improvement Act, the advance drawdowns of federal funds may not exceed 3 days.)

AUDITS OF CONTRACT AND GRANT FUNCTIONS

An audit of a government agency's contract or grant management function might closely parallel performance auditing since such an audit is an examination of government personnel and their administrative and management practices. These audits are primarily legal and financial compliance audits, possibly with ancillary objectives of assessing the relative efficiency and economy or effectiveness of the contract or grant management function.

These audits often include assessments of procedures and practices by which government personnel:

- Determine eligible constituents or select contractors or grantees;

- Prepare internal cost and program financial estimates;

- Conduct outreach efforts or methods of soliciting interest from prospective contractors or grantees;

- Methods by which proposals are requested, reviewed and negotiated, and successful contractors and grantees announced, with particular attention being given to repeat awardees or "permanent" awardees;

- Practices that might be used to thwart legal, policy and other limitation criteria (e.g., several smaller awards are made to the same awardee to circumvent higher level and more review than would be required for awards made above the ceiling);

- Degree to which contractors and grantees are monitored;

- Application of procedures to administer contract and grants, particularly in ensuring compliance with constituent eligibility, match or level of effort requirements, allowable and unallowable cost conditions, allocability of indirect costs;

- The adequacy of procedures and practices for managing any government property and other resources provided to contractors or grantees (e.g., advance funding, letters of credit withdrawal privileges, government furnished property, equipment, and materials);

- The management of any terminations (for convenience of the government or for default of the contractor or grantee) including final cost determinations, property inventory and disposal, critique of actual versus negotiated performance or delivery terms; and

- The appropriateness of and compliance with contract or grant closeout procedures.

In many government departments, the procurement or contracting function and the grants administration function are major activities with responsibilities for disbursing and overseeing the expenditure of significant sums of government funds. Many of the more significant fraud and embezzlement crimes in the public sector are perpetrated in the procurement and grant functions. Common examples of such irregularities might be: an internal government employee collaborating with parties external to the government; payment of vouchers for which no services are performed; disbursing cash as refund payments to parties but for which government properties were not returned prior to payment; personal service or other agreements awarded to parties not competent to perform or from whom the government will not receive performance.

At the federal level, these departments and agencies are typically grantors, responsible for the award, monitoring and audit of performance and funds disbursed to grantees. Whereas, at state and local government levels, these departments and agencies may simultaneously be grantees under a federal program and grantors or sub-grantor issuing grants to other subordinate organizations. Under these conditions, the audit procedures must consider the appropriate tests to be made of both the grantor and grantee roles in arriving at conclusions relating to the reasonableness of operations and financial performance.

The designation of the governmental department or the appropriate fund in which the contract or grant is to be accounted for is the responsibility of the recipient government. The decision is dependent on the nature and conditions of the contract or grant and the organizational structure of the grantee. Seldom does the federal government dictate the specific accounting that must be used by recipient governments. Rather, the federal government is concerned with the accuracy of reporting and monitoring of performance.

A basic concern is that controls and accounting procedures are established and that the contract or grant is monitored to ensure that all costs charge or claimed are in accord with the terms and conditions of the agreements and in compliance with applicable laws and regulations. Noncompliance by a federal recipient could jeopardize the current contracts and grants, subsequent reimbursement, or lead to actual disallowance of claims. Any of these actions can affect payments received and any outstanding receivables—important concerns to the auditor.

Knowledge of the manner in which contracts and grants are awarded and of the existence of governing policy and procedures must be acquired early in the audit of a contract or grant program to ensure that appropriate modifications will be made to internal control questionnaires and checklists to adequately address the particular aspects of financial and management processes unique to that auditee. A

Audit Methodology—Contracts and Grants 467

system of controls for contract and grant activities should, minimally, provide for:

1. Clearly written and widely disseminated policies and procedures relating to the award, acceptance, performance, monitoring, reporting, accounting and closing of these agreements.

2. Consistency between these contract and grant policies and procedures with legal and administrative requirements—federal, state, and local government.

3. Controls—related to authorization, approval, accounting, payments, audit—to ensure that payments under these agreements are made only for goods or services in compliance with the language of the enabling, authorizing, and funding legislation and the terms and conditions of the individual agreements.

4. Whether a contract or grant function, controls should include a description of procedures and practices relating to the solicitation of offers, evaluation of offers, selection of the most advantageous offer, awards to only responsible organizations, monitoring of performance, and the orderly close-out of completed or terminated contracts and grants.

5. Mandated management, administrative, financial and monitoring procedures exist in writing, that implement and comply with these procurement policies and procedures.

6. Written procedures for the awards to subcontractors and subgrantees and the requirements defining performance by these organizations, as well as a program for monitoring actual performance.

7. For both types of agreements, procedures should exist for the efficient award of small awards and be monitored to ensure that actual practices do not circumvent the more formal contracting processes, limits and controls.

8. A system of prepayment audits is in place to verify information on invoices, letter of credit drawdowns, claims, and other requests for payment under contracts and grants and assess compliance with the agreement terms and conditions before money is expended.

9. Appropriate controls and checks to prevent or at least minimize erroneous, duplicate, improper, and unallowable payments to be made and charged to or claimed under the contract or grant.

10. An orderly, and documented system exists for marking, mutilating, coding, and filing supporting documents related to specific contracts and grants and government programs to prevent re-use and submission for multiple or repeated payment requests.

11. A formal accounting is made in the records of the governmental contractor or grantee for all events in the transaction life cycle—from the initial authorization, evaluation of competing solicitations (if required), obligation or encumbrance, advances, disbursements, and withheld amounts to ultimate close-out of the project.

12. Procedures for the end-of-period audit and review to establish the accuracy or status of receivables, payable and unliquidated advances—in compliance with contract or grant terms and conditions.

13. Procedures for inventorying contract or grant property and providing periodic accounting of variances from procurement and controls records.

14. Monitoring or determining the existence of any unallowable, inappropriate, direct or indirect costs charged to, claimed or billed in violation or noncompliance with the contract or grant terms and conditions.

End-of-period audit tests for transaction cutoffs have the same significance with respect to audit of government as is the case with corporate entities. It is possible for unreported, unrecorded, end-of-period contract withholdings and contract and grant payables to exist.

Also, audit cognizance must be given to the fact that contract and grant receivables may also exist. A government agency may have advanced funds to contractors and grantees. These advances should have, at the time of disbursement, been formally recorded by a contractor or grantee as an accounts payable or amounts due to the government.

Circumstances will exist where a recipient has in place an adequate system of controls, but these controls may not be in strict accord with federal program requirements. Under these circumstances, the recipient government should obtain a formal waiver, in writing, of such requirements from the awarding federal entity. This waiver or special condition is necessary to avoid subsequent, never-ending discussions and repetitive federal audit reportings of noncompliance about the adequacy of controls.

Under certain conditions, the recipient government agency may, in turn, issue contracts to another level of government or be in the role of a grantor. This would arise in instances where a non-federal entity provides a federal award to a subrecipient to carry out a federal program (i.e., a "pass-through" entity under the Single Audit Act). Under these conditions, additional controls must exist to:

1. Ensure that any contractual liability of the government is properly reflected in the formal accounting records in a timely manner.

2. Monitor the governmental unit to determine that the desired service or performance is delivered consistent with contract or grant conditions, including obtaining and reviewing periodic audit reports of subrecipient activities.

3. Determine if procedures exist to ensure that cash advances and payments for contract or grant performance are consistent with contract and grant conditions, that properly deferred credits has been recorded, and that end-of-period receivables and liabilities are appropriately valued.

4. Ensure that billings and request for advances or letters of credit drawdowns are made currently, collections are monitored, and receipts properly recorded.

5. Provide that contract close-out procedures are adhered to and contract and grant settlements—receivables/payables, cash, property, inventory, buildings, leases, etc.—are made or settled in a timely manner.

Discussions of other chapters are relevant to audits of contracts and grants. **Chapter 8** describes other audit concerns with governmental controls, which impact contract and grant activity; **Chapter 9** summarizes the federal government's concerns with compliance by entities receiving contracts and grants; **Chapter 10** discusses the federal regulations relating to allowable, unallowable and indirect costs related to federal contracts and grants.

AUDIT METHODOLOGY—CONTRACTS AND GRANTS

Certain audit procedures or tests that should be considered in auditing an individual government contract or grant, assessing the reasonableness of the costs charged to or claimed under a single contract or grant, and tests for compliance with laws, regulations, and a contract's or grant's terms and conditions.

Circumstances exist where governments will require an audit of a single contract or grant, often referred to as a cost audit, cost incurred audit, direct cost audit, project management audit, performance audit, or other descriptors. Those desiring the audit and the auditor must acknowledge that there will be difficulties when audits are restricted to a single agreement. With a restricted audit scope, tests for compliance with federal regulations concerned with allowable, unallowable and indirect costs as well as the consistency of accounting are not always possible, for example:

- Test of the allowability of costs in a common cost pool will require an audit scope broader than a single contract or grant. These common costs are generally entity-wide and not related to a specific contract or grant.

470   Government Auditing: Standards and Practices

● Test of the allocability of costs will require the audit scope broader than a single contract or grant. Allocability is a relative compliance test requiring the auditor to assess the cost allocation practice used for activities under all contracts or grants in order to conclude on the appropriateness of allocability of accounting and costs applied to the contract or grant under audit.

● Tests for consistency in accounting and costing of federal versus non-federal activities requires that the audit scope be broader than the single contract or grant. Consistency is a relative compliance test requiring the auditor to assess the accounting used for activities other than the contract or grant in order to conclude on the consistency of accounting and costing applied to the contract or grant under audit.

● Tests to assess the auditee's compliance with applying generally accepted accounting principles requires that the audit scope be broader than the single contract or grant. Consistency with generally accepted accounting is a relative compliance test requiring an assessment of activities other than the audited contract or grant.

● Tests to ensure that an auditee has not double-billed or made duplicate charges of costs must, of necessity, require an examination of the auditee's practices employed for non-federal activities as well as other federal activities not within the scope of an audit for a single contract or grant. An audit scope limited to a single contract or grant will not provide sufficient perspective as to payments made elsewhere by the audited entity.

Because of these and other compliance factors, a contract or grant audit might be limited to an assessment of only direct costs. But this would, at best, be a partial audit. Under these circumstances, prudence dictates that the auditor carefully describe the scope of audit performed and the necessity of issuing a qualified audit opinion.

This section and *Exhibit 18-3* outline a more comprehensive contract or grant audit methodology that might be performed by auditors employed by governments or CPAs under contract to government where the scope extends to financial, compliance and performance factors.

Need for an Audit Survey

In contrast to private sector audits, the party arranging for a contract or grant audit may not always be the auditee. A government's legislative branch may authorize or arrange for an audit of an executive branch activity. Also, a federal department could authorize a CPA to make an audit of a contract or grant awarded to a state or local government or a non-profit entity. Under the Single Audit Act, auditees must arrange for their audit, but the scope of the audit, in large part, is mandated by federal departments who provided financial assistance to the auditee. So, a meeting is necessary between the party arranging for the audit as well as the auditee, particularly when the arranger and the auditee are not the same.

Seldom will the auditor be able to use OMB's *Compliance Supplement* as more than a general guide when auditing a single contract or grant. The guidance will have to be modified, tailored or even expanded to develop a program to audit an individual agreement. Where the auditor cannot follow the *Compliance Supplement*, the audit program for selecting and testing transactions and account balances and tests for compliance must be based on auditor judgment. The auditor must develop an audit program that attains the mandated audit objectives, examines many of the items, sources and publications noted in *Exhibit 18-3*.

Developing specific compliance audit programs requires resources—time, knowledgeable and experienced personnel, and money. And if the resulting program is somewhat deficient or weak, the risk of a substandard audit is on the auditor. Some federal inspectors general have compiled the equivalent of individual compliance audit programs for many of the government programs, which would be "safe harbor" audit guidance. These audit programs, which must still be modified to meet the circumstances of a single contract or grant audit, are available by communicating with the regional offices of the appropriate federal inspectors general.

Unless required by statute or authorized as a specific exception by OMB, all federal contracts and grants must be in compliance with provisions of its circulars, federal law, regulations and rules. Several OMB Common Rule requirements must be considered in the audit of any federal contract and grant. Additionally, the Common Rule imposes special audit requirements for the audit of "high risk" contractors and grantees. The Common Rule also mandates certain procedures for closed (completed, terminated, ceased) contracts and grants that are unique and arise only at the cessation of the federally-financed activity.

While a survey of an individual contract or grant may not be as extensive as that outlined in *Exhibit 18-3*, auditors who cannot or do not make these inquiries or obtain the suggested information may be handicapped in doing the audit or reporting on the audit findings.

Conference with Auditees

The auditor, at the conclusion of the survey, should draft an initial, tentative audit plan—possibly preliminary is the better descriptor. No final audit plan can be developed until the auditor has met with the auditee, examined the specific terms and conditions of the individual contract or grant, and made inquiries and tests of the auditee's systems, controls, and management process.

This caution should be heeded because the auditee, for reasons known only to it or the federal department, may have accepted terms and conditions that vary considerably or are more restricted or could include more compliance requirements than exist in laws, program regulations and OMB circulars. Additionally, the auditor at the entrance conference will often encounter circumstances relating to systems, controls, practices and even personnel competence that differ considerably from those disclosed during the earlier survey. And, the audit program will have to be modified to reflect reality. *Exhibit 18-3* lists many facts and factors that must, to some degree, be considered in an audit of a federal contract or grant.

Detailed Audit of a Contract or Grant

Earlier paragraphs outlined certain scope limitations implicit in any audit directed at examining an individual contract or grant. Many of the federal concerns related to the equitable, reasonable and consistent treatment of an individual federal contract or grant in relation to other federal activity and non-federal activity that may be managed by the auditee. If the audit scope is restricted to a single contract or grant, significant and material instances of weak controls, deficiency systems processes, unallowable and ineligible costs, misallocated or inappropriately charged overhead could go undetected.

Exhibit 18-3 lists many factors, issues, requirements, and practices that should be considered in the audit of a federal contract or grant. And, this is a partial list. To the extent the audit does not or can not address these and others, the auditor must carefully weigh the nature of the audit opinion desired by the arranger of the audit or the auditee, or both.

Reporting on Contract and Grant Audits

The standard opinion-type audit report will often not be sufficient to fully convey the results of a contract or grant audit. While an audit opinion, of sorts, might be required of the auditor, audit reports for these audits will generally be in narrative form. The report format and supporting financial schedules could be prescribed by the entity arranging for the audits. Where an explicit report format is not mandated, auditors will find the reporting guidance in the government auditing standards relative to performance audits of assistance.

The government performance auditing standards provide that, for audits of this type, auditors should report the audit objectives, scope and methodology applied. Additionally, for each finding, the audit report should address each element of each finding. There are several

Audit Methodology—Contracts and Grants

elements to a finding: (1) the auditor's observed condition, (2) identification of the audit or compliance criteria used in the audit, (3) documentation and description of the cause of the reported condition, (4) identification of the dollar consequence or other effect or damage relative to the reported finding, (5) the auditor's conclusion, (6) auditor recommendations to correct, alleviate, or mitigate the resultant problem or condition, and (7) corrective action, if any, promised by the auditee.

Reports for contract and grant audits will generally require preparation of financial exhibits with annotated footnotes that compare and discuss costs charged to or claimed under the contract or grant in relation to the originally or formally approved amended budgets. Exceptions are highlighted in the report, generally accompanied with comments from the auditee along with the auditor's evaluation of the auditee's comments.

Exhibits 18-1, 18-2, and 18-3 follow this page.

474 Government Auditing: Standards and Practices

EXHIBIT 18-1

Exhibit 18-1

Overview of Government Procurement Process...
Functions, Offices, Documents & Accounting

A. Program Office

1. Responsibilities
...Determine need for contractor
...Prepare cost estimate
...Identifies sources of supply
...Prepare procurement request
...Monitor performance
...Accept delivery
...Recommend payment

2. Purchase Authorization
...Goods/services needed
...Needed delivery
...Budget estimate
...Possible sources
...Fund availability
...Authorizing official
...Approving official

3. Purchase Request
...Goods/services requested
...Needed delivery
...Budget estimate
...Possible sources
...Fund availability
...Authorizing official

4. Route Purchase Request
...To Procurement: for contract award

...To Accounting: for commitment accounting

5. Receiving Report
...Acknowledge receipt of goods/services
...Complete receiving report
...Distribute report:
 ...To Procurement: close contract file
 ...To Accounting: liquidate obligation

B. Procurement Office

1. Responsibilities
...Solicits possible contractors
...Issues request for bids
...Receives bids from vendors
...Evaluates bids, negotiates
...Awards contract
...Administers contracts
...Closes out contract

2. Awards Contract
...Goods/services
...Delivery dates
...Contract price
...Contract terms

3. Distribute Contract
...To Procurement: for info and monitoring
...To Accounting: for encumbrance entry

C. Contractor Vendor

1. Responsibilities
...Submits bid, quote
...Negotiate contract terms, schedule, price
...Accepts contract
...Submits invoice for payment

D. Accounting Office

1. Responsibilities
...Confirms funds available for contract
...Commit funds
...Encumbers/Obligates funds
...Examines invoice
...Conduct pre-payment audit
...Records payment
...Completes internal/external financial reports
...Schedules payment by Treasury
...Performs accounting for contract

2. Accounting for Contract
...Purchase Authorization: no entry
...Purchase Request: commitment entry
...Contract award: encumbrance entry
...Receiving Report: liquidation entry
...Vendor Invoice: expense/payable entry
...Voucher: payment entry

E. Treasury Office

1. Responsibilities
...Review disbursement voucher data
...Make payment on recommendation of other functional offices
...Issue check for payment

Comparison: Documents and Accounting
1. Purchase Authorization: no entry
2. Purchase Request: commitment entry
3. Contract award: encumbrance entry
4. Receiving Report: encumbrance liquidation entry
5. Vendor Invoice: expense/payable entry
6. Voucher: payment entry

Audit Methodology—Contracts and Grants 475

EXHIBIT 18-2

Exhibit 18-2

Overview of Government Grant Process...
Functional Offices, Documents & Accounting

A. Program Office

1. <u>Functions/Responsibilities</u>
   a. Identify eligible constituents
   b. Informs public of available monies
   c. Award grants
   d. Advance funds
   e. Review progress
   f. Monitor performance
   g. Recommend payments

2. <u>Grant Process</u>
   a. Prepare public notice:
      ...Media announcement
      ...Mailings
      ...Public bulletins
   b. Award process:
      Perform due diligence
      ...Eligibility
      ...Responsibility
      ...Administrative
      ...Legal
      ...Select grantees
      ...Execute grant agreement
      ...Authorize advance funding
      ...End of grant closeout
   c. Execute Formal Grant Agreement:
      ...Goods/services
      ...Delivery dates
      ...Grant $ amount
      ...Conditions for advances

3. Distribute Grant Agreement
   a. To Accounting for: oblig or encumb entry

4. Monitor Performance:
   a. Review program performance
   b. Analyze cost reports
   c. Distribute cost report:
      ...To Accounting: for oblig liq entry

B. Accounting Office

1. <u>Functions/Respon</u>
   a. Confirms funds available for grant
   b. Commit funds
   c. Encumbers/Obligates funds
   d. Establish advance or letters of credit account
   e. Monitors drawdown of advance
   f. Pre-payment audit cost reports
   g. Completes internal/external financial reports
   h. Schedules for payment by Treasury

2. <u>Performs Accounting</u>
   a. Grant award:
      encumbrance entry
   b. Receive Cost Report:
      liquidation entry
      and
      expense/payable entry
   c. Voucher file: reduce advance; make payment entry
   a. Reviews disbursement voucher data
   b. Make payment on recommendation of other functional officesc.
   c. Issues check for payment

D. Grantee

a. Prepare, Submit Grant Proposal
b. Negotiate terms
c. Executes grant
d. Performs grant
e. Submits reports
f. Closes out grant
g. Final settlement with govt.

<u>Comparison of Documents and Accounting</u>
1. Grant award:
   encumbrance entry
2. Cost Report:
   encumbrance liquidation entry
   and
   expense/payable entry
3. Voucher: payment entry

EXHIBIT 18-3

Exhibit 18-3
Overview—Contract, Grant Audit Plan
Summary of Phases & Tasks

A. Conduct Survey

1. Audit Conference
   a. Arrangers of audit
   b. Oversight entities
   c. Sponsors
2. Inquire about Auditee
   a. Issues
   b. Accomplishments
   c. Problems
   d. Deficiencies
   e. Outcomes
   f. Outputs
   g. Other
3. Review Auditee History
   a. Audit reports
   b. Consultant reports
   c. External reviews
   d. Other Surveys
   e. Financial reports
   f. Operational reports
4. Inventory Legal Criteria
   a. Federal, state laws
   b. Local statutes
   c. Legislative history
   d. Policies, procedures
   e. Regulations, rules
   f. Court rulings
   g. OMB Circulars
       ...A-21 Education
       ...A-87 Governments
       ...A-122 Nonprofits
       ...A-102 Admin regs
       ...A-110 Admin regs
   h. Contract, grant terms, conditions
   i. Other requirements
5. Contract, Grant Status
   a. Services/Activities
   b. Constituencies
   c. Service levels
   d. Locations
   e. Furnished property
   f. Staffing levels
   g. Technology factors
6. Financing Sources
   a. Appropriations
   b. Allowed fees
   c. Billings
   d. Debt, borrowings
   e. Donations
   f. In-kind contributions
   g. Other
7. Obtain Perform. Factors
   a. Service levels
   b. Frequency, usage
   c. Constituencies
   d. Costs
   e. Backlog
   f. Complaints
   g. Other
8. Sampling Options
   a. Methodology
   b. Sampling issues
       ...Stratification
       ...Sizes
       ...Timing
       ...Reliability
       ...Results
       ...Projections
       ...Analyses
9. Audit Techniques
   a. Survey
   b. Data analysis
   c. Audit observations
   d. Comparative studies
   e. Documents
   f. Confirmations
   g. Analyses
   h. Interviews
   i. Other
10. Confirm Audit Scope
    a. Organization
    b. Program
    c. Function
    d. Activity
    e. Financial
    f. Management
    g. Operational
    h. Other
11. Audit Plan Draft

B. Meet with Auditee

1. Entrance Conference
   a. Discuss
       ...Audit objectives
       ...Audit protocols
       ...Audit processes
       ...Audit team
       ...Review report
       ...Timing of audit
       ...Auditee contacts
2. Examine Contract, Grant Conditions
   a. Financial
   b. Operations
   c. Personnel
   d. Capital equipment
   e. Legislative
3. Confirm Contract, Grant Status
   a. Underruns
   b. Overruns
   c. Excess over draws
   d. Met delivery dates
   e. Met performance goals
   f. Expiration dates
   g. Cost issues
4. Inventory Systems
   a. Types
       ...Financial
       ...Operational
       ...Management
       ...Personnel
       ...Measurement
       ...Property
       ...Procurement
       ...Other
   b. Automation
       ...Computerization
       ...Documentation
       ...Equipment
           Locations
           Volume
           Currency
       ...Personnel

Audit Methodology—Contracts and Grants

5. Confirm Review Scope
   a. Organization
   b. Program
   c. Function
   d. Activity
   e. Operations
   f. Other

6. Develop Programs
   a. Test controls
   b. Test compliance laws, regs
   c. Audit costs
   d. Audit compliance

C. Audit Contract, Grant

1. Test Sys/Controls
   a. Accounts structure
   b. Transaction codes
   c. Cost codes
   d. Ledgers
   e. Registers
   f. Support documents
   g. Project reporting
   h. Financial reporting
      ...Utility
      ...Timeliness
      ...Relevance
      ...Completeness

2. Audit Costs
   a. Budget vs actual
   b. Cost allowability
      ...Eligible, ineligible
      ...Allowable, unallow.
      ...Direct, indirect
   c. Cost tests
      ...Necessary
      ...Reasonable
      ...Authorized
      ...Per agreement
      ...Consistency
      ...Per gaap
      ...Net of credits
   d. Ineligible costs
      ...Comply with law
      ...Comply with regs
      ...Comply with OMB
      ...Comply with program regs
      ...Contract, grant
      ...Authorized recipients
      ...Authorized purposes
   e. Unallocable cost tests
      ...No cause/benefit
      ...No indirect cost plan
      ...Cost pools
      ...Cost allocation bases
      ...Currency of allocation factor
      ...Currency of indirect cost plan
   f. Cost reporting
      ...Internal
      ...External
      ...Program
      ...Financial statements

3. Test compliance
   a. Exceeded any $ limits
   b. Comply with regs
   c. Comply with OMB
   d. Comply with program regs
   f. Authorized recipients
   g. Authorized purposes

4. Test Management Compliance
   a. Cost, Schedule Controls
      ...Financial
      ...Performance
      ...Technical
      ...Laws, regs
      ...Property management
          Receiving
          Custody
          Inventory
          Use, disposal
   b. Contract, grant reporting

5. Analyze Data
   a. Variances
   b. Comparisons
   c. Ranges
   d. Trends
   e. Limitations
   f. Forecasts
   g. Plans to actual
   h. Exceptions
   i. Noncompliance

D. Compile Audit Findings

1. Complete work papers
   a. Review
   b. Index
   c. Review
   d. Reference
      To plan
      To programs
      To report findings

2. Develop Findings
   a. Condition
   b. Criteria
   c. Cause
   d. Effect
   e. Conclusions
   f. Recommendation

3. Auditee Conference
   a. Finding presentation
   b. Oral review
   c. Comment period
   d. Corrective actions
   e. Review comments

4. Draft Audit Report
   a. Present draft report
   b. Discuss draft
   c. Receive comments
   d. Review comments
   e. Revise report

F. Final Reporting

1. Complete Audit Report
   a. Scope of audit
   b. Audit objective
   c. Audit period
   d. Execs contacted
   e. Present findings
   f. Conclusions
   g. Recommendations
   h. Auditee comments

2. Distribute Report
   a. Arrangers of audit
   b. Auditee
   c. Responsible officials
   d. Oversight entities
   e. Authorized others
   f. General public

Note: Additional discussion on these phases and tasks appear in the chapter text.

Chapter 19

Audit Methodology— Special Focus Government Audits

Auditors of the federal government, some states and local governments, conduct special focus audits that are exclusive to governments. Two such audits include: (1) accountability or "turnover" audits of public sector accountable officers, and (2) audits of year-end obligations or encumbrance and appropriation fund balance status.

Other audits, primarily performed by governmental internal auditors, are directed towards monitoring adherence by governmental executives and personnel to public policies and desired operating procedures. These internal audits, at times referred to as "functional" or "cross-cutting," may concentrate on a particular activity of government, e.g., an audit of the procurement, grants management, personnel, maintenance, etc. These audits may involve an audit that cuts across organizations, e.g., an audit of payroll, travel, transportation, property controls, compliance with some governmentwide policy, etc.

Other reviews, pre-audits and post-audits, are described in this chapter. These are not audits of the type that are defined by either generally accepted auditing standards or government auditing standards.

ACCOUNTABILITY OR TURNOVER AUDITS

One special focus audit of government has been referred to as a settlement or "turnover" audit. Public sector executives responsible for collecting and disbursing funds, certifying or executing contracts, or authenticating a proposed commitment or validating the availability of unencumbered funds are often referred to as *accountable officers*. Many governments require that the "accounts" (i.e., the records transactions transpired during the tenure of accountable officer) of these accountable officers be settled or audited when one accountable officer relieves another. These audits are generally not performed to conform to a specific fiscal year, but are more often dictated by the tenure in office of the official whose activities must be audited.

Accountable Officers in Government

Public sector executives responsible for collecting and disbursing funds, certifying or executing contracts on behalf of the government, or certifying to the authenticity of a proposed commitment or the availability of funds, are often referred to as *accountable* officers.

For some governments, laws or statutes require that the "accounts" (i.e., the financial transactions that transpired during the tenure of the accountable officer) of these accountable officers must be settled or audited. This accountability, settlement or turnover audit must generally be made at least upon the death, resignation, removal, retirement or termination of an accountable officer.

In the federal government, accountable officers would include collecting and disbursing officers, contracting officers, finance managers, and designated program executives having an official warrant to financially commit their departments or agencies. At the state or local government levels, accountable officers would encompass executives as treasurers and directors of finance and other officials performing the duties of these executives.

Settlement or Turnover Audits

Audit Procedures

These settlement or turnover audits could be made on an interim basis if the officer has been in office for a long time period, but such audits are generally required when one accountable officer relieves another or will "turnover" their accounts to another. Exceptions or variances between the "account" and factual conditions, as determined by audit, must be "settled" financially by the departing official.

Personal liability may, in some cases, result from the exceptions noted in the settlement or turnover audit. Within the federal government, the knowing or willful violation by over obligating an appropriation is subject to administrative discipline and, when warranted, suspension without pay and if convicted, a personal fine of not more than $5,000 or imprisonment for not more than two years. [1] Within the federal government, accountability audits are made by the U.S. General Accounting Office to settle the larger accounts.

Similarly, at state and local government levels, an official may be legally designated to conduct such audits. This would be so with respect

---

[1] Antideficiency Act of 1870, as amended.

Audit Methodology—Special Focus Audits 481

to the Commonwealth of Virginia.[2] Often it is the government auditor that will conduct the turnover audit, but an independent CPA could be retained, under contract, to make the audit.

The objective of a settlement or turnover audit is to provide an accounting of the stewardship of an accountable officer. An audit determination is required as to the reasonableness of the balances that are to be transferred from one accountable officer to the successor. Typically, the accountable officer renders or prepares a specially prescribed financial statement of his or her "account," which is not intended to be a complete presentation in complete conformity with generally accepted accounting principles.

Generally, the scope of the settlement or turnover audit is fiscally oriented, with audit tests consisting of examining the documents in support of transactions and account balances. The support documentation for transactions relating to receipts, disbursements, unliquidated obligations or encumbrances and all unexpended assets and outstanding liabilities during and at the time of leaving office would be the subject of a settlement or turnover audit.

While the audit tests will vary to meet the circumstances and the specific account to be settled, a settlement or discharge, or accountability or turnover audit might consist of audit procedures such as:

● There may be a requirement for the audit to conform to generally accepted auditing standards or the government auditing standards as well as specific terms and conditions related to the accountable officer undergoing audit. In these circumstances, the auditor must be aware that not all of the profession's or government's auditing standards would apply. The auditor would be responsible for ensuring that the selected audit procedures complied with the legal and other professional requirements as deemed necessary by the circumstances.

● Similarly, there may be references that the financial statements and reports of an accountable officer be compiled in accordance with generally accepted accounting principles. Again, the auditor must recognize the special nature of an accountable officer's statement of account. More often the ending balances and results of operations are not intended to reflect a reporting in accordance with generally accepted accounting principles.

● Given the volume of transactions that might be involved, the auditor should plan the audit, including acquiring an understanding of controls (e.g., the environment, accounting systems, and policies and

---

[2] Auditor of Public Accounts, Commonwealth of Virginia, *Specifications for Audits of Counties, Cities, and Towns*, Chapter 10—Treasurer's Turnover Audits," revised 1993.

procedures) and then test the effectiveness of these controls since reliance will in most cases be placed on some aspects of the system of controls.

The turnover audit often does not require a comprehensive review of internal controls, but the volume of transactions might necessarily require that controls be tested to determine the extent the controls can be relied upon to possibly limit the number of actual transactions that might otherwise have to be examined.

● Accountability or settlement audits place a premium on the precision of a proper cut-off or "turnover" date for receipts, expenditures or disbursements and transferred properties. To ensure the accuracy of the cut-off, a government might require that an accountable officer's office be closed several days prior to or following the turnover date to facilitate the cut-off of transactions and posting to accounts.

● Consistent with the primacy given to the cut-off determinations, audit procedures relating counts of cash and securities, deposits of receipts, warrants for and actual disbursements of cash, determination of receivables due the government, inventorying assets and property, and validation of liabilities, check signing, to mention a few procedures, must be done with care. In many instances, the accountable officer might be required to be present during the audit and personally sign attestation statements certifying to the accuracy of audited and verified amounts.

● External confirmations will often be required from all banks, debtors and creditors, amounts due to and due from the accountable office being audited and reconciliations of bank accounts and ledger accounts will be necessary.

● A mandated task of a turnover audit could be that the auditor ensure all accounting adjustments and changes in procedures necessary for a proper accounting to have been implemented, the books are in balance, and necessary guidance has been prepared for the successor.

● Selected audit procedures will have to address compliance with legal requirements and details, such as having the auditor:

—Obtain signatures of the incoming and outgoing accountable officers on financial statements, the audit report, statements of transferred assets, etc.

—Have signatures of accountable officers and the auditor witnessed by a notary public.

—Make a specific, but limited, distribution of the settlement or turnover audit report, and possibly an oral presentation to an oversight body.

—Provide a physical copy of final account balances.

Audit Methodology—Special Focus Audits

Report Format

The report for a settlement or turnover audit could consist of an auditor's opinion on the overall fairness of balances and amounts presented on the accountable officer's statement of account and contain a narrative explanation of any exceptions or variances for which an accounting or resolution must be made.

The reporting requirements might mandate that the auditor disclose weaknesses in internal controls, particularly should the weakness be of a magnitude to meet the AICPA's definition of a reportable condition. Quite often, the auditor must report on any errors, irregularities, illegal acts, indication of fraudulent actions, or shortages of assets and other property.

Limitation for Audits

There are legal statutes of limitation governing the currency of accountability or settlement audits. Governments, by law, must commence these audits within a designated time period of an accountable officer leaving the position.

Failure to conform to the imposed statute of limitation will preclude the government from later bringing a charge against the accountable officer. At the federal level, the accounts of accountable officers must be "settled" by government agencies within three years from the date of receipt of substantially complete accounts unless fraud or criminality is involved. For some state or local governments, legal limitations require accountable officers to submit their reports to the executive branch or courts and that settlement must be completed within a specified time period.

Responsibility to Discharge and Settle Accounts

The responsibility to formally settle with or discharge an accountable officer from further liability to the government is a legal role that is not performed, per se, by the auditor. The settlement or turnover audit is generally viewed as "advice" and the basis used by the discharging official for settling the accounts of the outgoing accountable officer.

Historically the General Accounting Office, at the conclusion of a settlement audit, was required to notify the accountable officer, the Department of Treasury and the Congress on the results of these audits. Any exceptions were brought directly, by letter, to the attention of Congress, the President of the United States, and the Office of Management and Budget. [3]

---

[3] U.S. General Accounting Office, *Comprehensive Audit Manual*, Basic Audit Objectives and Policies, Washington, D.C.

At the state and local levels, the accountable officer may be required to submit the financial statement of account to a designated court. Then following the settlement or turnover audit, a formal notice is published by the court to discharge the outgoing accountable officer from all liability. [4]

Audits of the accounts of accountable officers and settling or discharging accounts through audits has a legal precedence dating back to the early 1600s and the Massachusetts Bay Colony operating under charter from King James I of England. Records exist of a court order accepting an audit committee's report on an Andrew Belcher, Esquire, who in 1709 was an accountable officer in the Bay Colony, the Colony's "Commissary General." In this instance, auditors rendered to the court what might be the auditing profession's earliest unqualified opinion stating that:

> "We attended the Said Service & Examined his Accompts from March 30th 1706 to January 23rd 1706/7 and find them right Cast and well Avouch'd."

The reference to having "attended the Said Service" goes to the then current audit practice of holding a hearing where a committee "audited" or listened while a bookkeeper or clerk read the account. The committee was responsible for "auditing" or hearing and concluding on the reasonableness of the data presented. (Generally, the word "auditor" is derived from "audire," a Latin verb meaning to hear.) [5]

OBLIGATION OR ENCUMBRANCE AUDITS

A year-end obligation or encumbrance audit will asses the fairness of the year-end outstanding obligations or encumbrances. These are amounts that if in error affect both the past and current years financial accounts. Within the federal government, over obligation can, if willful and negligent, result in the violator being personally liable and subject to imprisonment.

The definition of **obligations** versus **encumbrances** vary slightly between federal, state and local governments, but the substance of the transactions is similar and the concerns with accounting and reporting obligations or encumbrances at year end is identical at all levels of government.

At fiscal year-end, special or limited scope audits are made by governments to examine obligations and encumbrances. Generally,

---

[4] Auditor of Public Accounts, Commonwealth of Virginia, *Specifications for Audits of Counties, Cities, and Towns*, Chapter 10—Treasurer's Turnover Audits," revised 1993.

[5] While intended as a history of accountancy in Massachusetts, this example and several other examples of auditing appear in *Three Centuries of Accounting in Massachusetts*, by William Holmes, Linda H. Kistler and Louis S. Corsini, by Arno Press, New York, 1978

these audits are made by government auditors rather than independent CPAs since the effectiveness of these audits is more dependent on detailed knowledge of the internal transaction processing, authorization and approval procedures, and actual practices that a government might use to affect what amounts are included in the year-end obligations or encumbrances.

The concept of obligating or encumbering governmental funds is central to appropriation law and statutes. It is fundamental to appropriation laws that an obligation or encumbrance may be charged only against the relevant appropriation, in accordance with the legislatively mandated rules and regulations that govern the purpose, timing, and amounts of governmental spending. Further, all appropriations expire after which no further obligations or encumbrances may be incurred or charged against the expired appropriation.

Obligations

The federal Office of Management and Budget defines an ***obligation*** as the amount of orders placed, contracts and grants awarded, services received, and similar transactions entered into during a given fiscal period that will require payments during the same period or a future fiscal period. At the federal level, the term obligation refers to the incurrence of a commitment of federal funds and a liability that the government may ultimately pay. To the accountants of government, an obligation is an economic and financial event that must be formally recorded in the official records of an agency. [6]

Encumbrances

State and local governments use the term ***encumbrance*** in lieu of obligations. GASB has defined an encumbrance as a commitment by a government related to unperformed (or "executory") contracts for goods and services. Historically some governments have treated year-end encumbrances as a part of the year-end expenditures or liabilities, a practice that is no longer in accordance with generally accepted accounting principles. Encumbrances represent the estimated amount of a future expenditure that will result if the unperformed contracts in process are completed. [7]

Objectives of Obligation and Encumbrance Audits

The objective of the year-end audit of obligations or encumbrances is to authenticate, on a test basis, the overall reasonableness of these reported amounts. Valid obligations or encumbrances represent com-

---

[6] Office of Management and Budget, Circular A-34, Instructions on Budget Execution, Washington, D.C., 1995.

[7] Government Finance Officers Association, *Governmental Accounting, Auditing, and Financial Reporting*, Chicago Illinois, Appendix B, Terminology.

mitments against either the current year's appropriated funds or which will be reflected as valid claims against the next year's appropriation.

Excess Appropriation Balances. The focus or concern of the audit of obligated or encumbered balances is dependent upon the end-of-year status of appropriated balances. If year-end finds the government with an excess of uncommitted appropriated funds, there could be an inclination to report anticipated obligations and encumbrances. Also, government executives, at times with consent of the legislative branch, may attempt to "use up" the balance of an existing appropriation prior to year-end. This tactic is referred to as "year end buying." For the most part, legislative appropriations are one-year funds. That is, the authority to obligate funds or encumber appropriated funds expires on midnight on the last day of the fiscal year.

There is considerable incentive on the part of program executives to report the smallest unobligated or unencumbered appropriation balance at year-end. With some basis, an expired appropriation amount is "lost" money to a government executive. As noted, this creates an incentive to engage in year-end "shopping sprees" by governments in an attempt to use up appropriation balances that might otherwise expire. Under these circumstances, the emphasis of the audit would be to test whether amounts reported as outstanding obligations or encumbrances fully meet the legal or statutory definitions for such commitments.

At times the fiscal year may end and certain amounts are reported as if the amounts were valid obligations or encumbrances. But, audits often disclose that the necessary authorizations, approvals, legal procedures, or formalities were not completed for these transactions before the fiscal year end or before the expiration date of the appropriation, which may not always be the year end.

Inflated appropriated amounts, unsupported amounts for obligations and encumbrances and types of year-end spending would be questioned and may be reviewed and disallowed. Such an action could make the accountable officer personally liable. If the questioned transactions are found, upon audit, to not be appropriate charges against expiring appropriations, these amounts cannot be reported as year-end obligations or encumbrances. The obligated and encumbered amounts may have to be reversed in the financial records. Worse, the restored amounts may then be lost to the operating unit since the appropriation balance will have expired.

Limited Appropriation Balances. Contingent liabilities are a common type of unreported and unrecorded obligations or encumbrances. The audit program must include tests to detect possible unreported contingency or commitments. In many instances, these contingencies qualify and should be reported as legal obligations and encumbrances of a government. The under-reporting is often related to a concern that formal recordation of all legal obligations or encumbrances would result in the government being over-obligated or over-encumbered, in excess of a legislatively approved appropriation.

As noted, at the federal level and at many local governments, over obligation or over encumbrance of an appropriation is illegal—a violation of specific law and statute.

Correctness of Appropriations Charged. Timely and proper accounting for expenditures and obligations or encumbrances against the correct appropriation is another emphasis of an audit of obligations and encumbrances. To the extent that the incorrect appropriation is charged, the unobligated or unencumbered balance of two appropriations are misstated. Charging obligations or encumbrances to the wrong appropriation unintentionally is erroneous; charging of obligations or encumbrances to an incorrect appropriation intentionally is considered an irregularity or an illegality, depending on the jurisdiction.

Obligations and encumbrances, by law or statute, are to be charged to only appropriations designed by the governing legislatures. In no jurisdiction does executive branch management have the option of selecting the appropriation to be charged depending on whether or not there is a remaining balance of an appropriation.

LEGALITY OF OBLIGATIONS AND ENCUMBRANCES

Federal Requirements

At the federal level, legislation (initially the Anti-Deficiency Act of 1870 and then other laws over the years) contain specific prohibitions relating to obligations and expenditures that would form the basis for audit tests to examine these transactions. By law, no federal officer or employee of the United States shall make or authorize an expenditure or create or authorize an obligation under an appropriation in excess of the amount available in that appropriation, which is a law of Congress. Violations, when warranted, could result in disciplinary action, suspension without pay, removal from office, restitution of the amount of the irregularity, personal fine, and even imprisonment.

Other laws (initially the Supplemental Appropriation Act of 1955 and then others) define the legal form for an obligation to be a legal claim against the United States. To be a valid obligation of the federal government and be appropriately recorded, one of the following documents must exist for every obligated amount:

- A binding agreement in writing between the parties,
- A valid loan agreement in writing between the parties,

- An order required by law,
- An order issued pursuant to law to meet a public exigency or for perishable subsistence supplies,
- A grant or subsidy,
- A liability arising from pending litigation,
- Employment or services of persons or expenses of travel and services by public utilities, and
- Other legal liabilities of the United States government.

Any commitment or transaction not supported by one of the above eight forms of documentation (properly authorized, approved, and processed) is not a legal obligation of the United States government and should not be reported as a charge against an available appropriation balance.

State and Local Governments

There is no universal legislation governing all local governments with respect to accounting and reporting of encumbrances. But, generally accepted accounting principles applicable to state and local governments require that all encumbrances (i.e., commitments related to unperformed executory contracts) be recorded, especially in the general fund and special revenues funds of these governments. Proper accounting and reporting of encumbrances require: [8]

- Encumbrance accounting be used to assure effective budgetary control and accountability, and cash planning and control.
- Encumbrances outstanding at year-end represent estimated amounts of expenditures that will ultimately result if unperformed contracts in process at year-end are completed.
- Encumbrances at year-end will not constitute expenditures or liabilities and should not be reported as such.
- If performance of an executory contract is complete or virtually complete, the expenditure or liability must be recognized rather than reflecting the transaction as an encumbrance.
- If by law or statute, appropriation balances lapse at year-end, but the government intends to honor encumbered commitments, then (1) the outstanding encumbrances must be disclosed in footnotes to the financial statements or as reservations to reported fund balances, and (2) the subsequent year's appropriations must provide authority to honor or complete these encumbrance transactions.

---

[8] Governmental Accounting Standards Board, *Codification of Governmental Accounting and Financial Reporting Standards*, Norwalk, Connecticut, as of June 1993. Section 1700.129.

- Where appropriations do not lapse at year-end or only the unencumbered amount lapses. The outstanding encumbrances should be reported as reservations of fund balances available for subsequent year expenditures based on the encumbered appropriation authority carried over to the following year.

Consideration of outstanding encumbrances at the beginning and end of a year is necessary to reconcile the amounts on the statement of revenues and expenditures with the budgetary reports. The method by which encumbrances are accounted and reported must be consistently applied, fully disclosed in the significant accounting policies footnote.

Controls over Obligations and Encumbrances

The obligation or encumbrance process is a control that monitors transactions to prohibit or guard against appropriations of legislative bodies from being over committed or overspent. All obligations or encumbrances charged to a specific appropriation must be consistent with the conditions of that appropriation, must be made with the appropriate time period, and must be for only purposes authorized by the legislation. Almost always, an obligating or encumbering action is required in advance of the receipt of goods or services and before the recognition of a liability or the disbursement of government funds.

While not uniformly mandated for all governments, generally the following practices and controls prevail for all levels of government, consisting of:

- *Formal authorization followed by approval*—Action by separate government executives stating intents to commit appropriated funds of a government.

- *Prevalidation of obligations or encumbrances*—Procedures requiring formal acknowledgment by a designated executive that the remaining free balance of the appropriation is sufficient or equal to the intended obligation or encumbrance.

- *Commitment of funds*—A control preceding (if used) the actual obligation or encumbrance of funds. It may require formal recording of an amount. Commitment accounting is used when there is expected to be a significant delay between an earlier prevalidation and later actual obligation or encumbrance. Generally, the commitment actions do not involve parties external to the government.

Amounts accounted for as commitments must be adjusted to the amounts ultimately obligated or encumbered. Funds earlier committed that are in excess of amounts ultimately obligated or encumbered revert to an uncommitted status provided the appropriation has not expired in the interim.

● *Obligation or encumbrance of funds*—The formal recognition (i.e., legal and accounting) of a potential liability that could result in the expenditure of appropriated funds. For most governments this economic and accounting event must be preceded and supported by completion of several documents that when properly executed become valid and legally binding upon a government. Obligations or encumbrances will involve parties external to the government. As noted above, obligations and encumbrances must meet certain documentary requirements and must be charged against only the correct appropriation, within the proper time period, for the proper purpose, and in the proper amount.

● *Liquidation of Obligations or Encumbrances*—This refers to the procedures or practices for reducing or adjusting amounts previously obligated or encumbered for goods or services that have been received. The formal accounting requires dual entries: (1) one entry reverses or adjusts the earlier obligation or encumbrance entry for the actual cost of services or goods received (i.e., budgetary accounting), (2) the second entry records the amount of goods or services received and the corresponding liability for which a payment must legally be made (i.e., proprietary accounting).

Examples of actions that would require liquidation, reduction or reversal of earlier obligations or encumbrances include:

—Receipts of the contracted goods or services;

—Receipt of an expenditure report for payment under a long-term contract or grant;

—Receipt of an invoice for goods received or services rendered;

—Completion of a receiving report supporting possession of ordered goods or services;

—The formal termination of and earlier obligation or encumbrance prior to delivery of goods or services;

—Transfers of goods or assistance performed by another agency for which payment is due, and;

—Recording of payroll and legal incurrence of other employee-related expenses.

Nature of Obligation or Encumbrance Audits

As noted, the incurrence of obligations or encumbrances in excess of legislatively approved appropriations is illegal for many governmental units. And, in no jurisdiction do executives have the option of selecting the appropriation to be charged depending on whether or not there is a remaining balance of an appropriation.

Internal controls, accounting systems, and reporting procedures and audits must be directed towards ensuring that appropriation limitations are observed and reported amounts are correct. If the rate of obligation or encumbrance is controlled, no improper prospective or contingent liabilities can exist and generally no violations of appropriations will result.

The audit of obligations or encumbrances takes on special significance at year-end. Governmental executives should know, with a high degree of certainty, the amount of future liabilities, the amount of unobligated or unencumbered appropriation balances, and the amount of potential liabilities that could affect the next year's appropriated funds. Some governmental audit organizations annually make year-end audit of the unliquidated balances of obligations and encumbrances.

At year-end, amounts reported as unliquidated obligations and encumbrances must constitute legally valid claims against an appropriation for which the government may later have to make payment. If in error, the misstatement of year-end obligations or encumbrances precludes an accurate accounting of either the current or following years, appropriations. Thus, a primary, but not the exclusive objective, of an audit of year-end obligations or encumbrances is to provide management, legislators, overseers, and others with a report on the reasonableness of appropriation balances reported by operating agencies. Inaccurate reports could result in erroneous payments, force governments to provide for unplanned liabilities, or disguise a violation of appropriation laws and statutes.

The report for this type of audit may contain an opinion by the auditor as to the overall fairness or reasonableness of year-end obligations and encumbrances. Additionally, audit reports may set forth, in a narrative section, an explanation of audit exceptions taken in relation to reported balances and the reasons therefor.

FUNCTIONAL OR CROSS-CUTTING AUDITS

Examples

Much of the professional auditing literature is about financial statement audits, the generally accepted auditing standards and after, 1972, the government auditing standards. The Single Audit Act imposed a comprehensive financial and compliance type audit on tens of thousands of governments and over 100,000 nonprofit organizations. But, these types of audits are not the principal professional occupation of tens of thousands of auditors employed by governments. Governmental auditors are predominantly occupied conducting other types of audits—generically referred to as internal audits, more closely related to performance audits.

Functional or cross-cutting audits are concerned with improving the efficiency and economy of operations, assessing compliance with internal checks and balances and other controls, and assessing how governmental executives are discharging managerial and political responsibilities. Most of these audits are a blend of financial and nonfinancial examinations and evaluations.

Contrasts to Financial Audits

For these audits, governmental auditors would more often consult the publications and literature of the Institute of Internal Auditors which provides guidance relating to planning, conducting and reporting on audits for which there often are no clearly defined management assertions that can be tested by the auditor.

Criteria to assess operations, performance and compliance may not exist. Laws and regulations may deliberately be drafted with a vagueness relative to setting standards of expected program achievement, operations, or accomplishment In many instances, for these audits, the governmental auditors are "on their own" and must design audit plans and programs for the unique conditions or circumstances of their particular governmental unit, activity, and function. The differences between these audits and those made pursuant to either or both generally accepted auditing standards or government auditing standards demonstrate the "one of a kind" audits with which most government auditors are concerned: [9]

• In a financial audit management, assertions are explicit, implicit and imbedded in the audited financial statements. In performance or internal type audits, there are few or no specific management assertions—explicit or implicit. It is a function of the internal auditor to examine management's performance and measure the results against relative criteria such as economy, efficiency, and effectiveness—for which there is no "generally accepted" auditing standard. It is the responsibility of the governmental auditor to establish audit criteria that is persuasive and convincing to recipients of the audit report who judge the value of these audits.

• The auditor of financial statements has limited control over the annual financial statements. The auditor can not change the statements and the auditor's reporting options are somewhat limited—the choices being unqualified or "clean opinion," a qualified opinion, an adverse opinion, or a disclaimer. Quite often, financial statements are not the focus of performance and internal audits.

---

[9] Government Finance Officers Association, *Governmental Accounting, Auditing, and Financial Reporting* (i.e., the "GAAFR"), Chapter 16, *Auditing Government Entities*, Chicago, Illinois.

Audit Methodology—Special Focus Audits

- These government audits differ in scope from financial type audits. The scope of a financial statement audit is that tests have been proscribed in advance and the audit effort has one objective: assessing the reasonableness of financial data. Performance and internal audits, in contrast, focus on a specific or single operation, activity, function, issue, problem, law or regulation for which there is minimal literature addressing the focus of the audit. Standardized checklists, prepared questionnaires, generalized audit guides, and all the literature associated with financial audits do not exist for these governmental audits.

- The manner of execution is another distinction. The detailed tests required by generally accepted and government auditing standards must be performed in a financial statement audit. It is expected that the auditor will faithfully conform to all of these standards and related interpretations. If these standards are not followed, the audit will be substandard, and this fact must be acknowledged in the auditor's opinion.

Somewhat in contrast, the audit plan and audit programs for government performance and internal audits are being continually refined, honed and focused. There is no standard guidance or prescribed methodology. If areas of initial audit concern are found to have no or minimal risk or limited opportunity for significant efficiencies or economies, those parts of the audit can be terminated. Further testing in these areas will stop and audit resources will be re-directed towards other areas that appear to have greater problems.

Other chapters provided background and other relative to program audits, financial related audits and performance auditing. All of these are specially focused audits that will or may include auditing of financial and nonfinancial information or may include the audit of an activity or operation.

Special Focus Audits

The following sections provide discussion on types of audits often made by governmental auditors: audits of systems and controls, operational reports and performance data; personnel and payrolls; travel and property, to mention a few.

Audits of Accounting Systems and Controls

Periodically audits are made of a government's financial systems (as distinguished from the financial statement audits) and related internal controls. Some objectives of such audits might be to: (1) obtain an indication of the accuracy of information being reported to management, (2) to test compliance with the controls designed to maintain the continued integrity of the data, (3) assess the extent of compliance, or noncompliance, with governing laws and regulations, management policies, procedures and prescribed practices.

Controls will be observed during systems audits and test-checked to assess observance in practice. Financial policy statements, procedural manuals will be analyzed and compared to current practices. Internal controls and checks and balance tasks will be examined to assure that:

● Responsibility for receipts and disbursements, accounting, computer processing, property custody and disposal functions is segregated to the extent practicable.

● There has been compliance with all prescribed authorization and approval (including any delegations thereof), pre- and post-audit and internal audit requirements.

● Policies exists with respect to applicable or governing laws, regulations, rules, and operating procedures and that responsible personnel manage and monitor systems in compliance with these criteria.

● Forms, support documents, routing procedures, validation and other formal checks continue to serve as a deterrent to fraudulent or irregular actions on the part of involved management or employees and reflect current, accurate, and complete data for the transactions.

● Practices relating to coding, entry, recording, processing (manual or automated) summarizing and reporting of financial data are sound and continually observed.

● There is a continued usefulness and timeliness of information and that all representations in the accounts, records, financial reports and statements are supported by properly completed documentation.

The following are suggestions of audit inquiries that might be made when auditing systems and controls of government agencies: [10]

● Do effective controls exist over revenues and receipts, disbursements and expenditures, purchases, assets, and liabilities?

● Does proper accounting exist for all liquid assets, property, liabilities, and operations?

● Is there compliance with all applicable laws, regulations, rules, and are these guidance consistent with one another?

● Are the management policies, operational procedures, and controls of financial operations, data processing, and accounting and reporting adequate and are these criteria and guidance followed?

---

[10] U.S. General Accounting Office, *Internal Auditing in Federal Agencies—Basic Principles, Standards, and Concepts*, Washington, D.C.

Audit Methodology—Special Focus Audits 495

● Are all revenues and receipts collected and accounted for; are all expenditures made for only authorized and approved purposes?

● Do recorded financial transactions reflect prices, rates, fees and amounts allowed by laws and regulations?

● Are the financial data used by management for internal and external reporting reliable? Does this data serve a purpose? Is the data presented in a format or media that is of maximum utility?

● Is there uniformity of definition of recorded cost and other data between the several organizations of a government? Is reported data consistent from one period to another?

● Are all assets, property, funds, etc., protected from loss, misuse, or deterioration?

● Are there any indications of possible fraud, dishonesty or other questionable practices that could lead to losses, damages, or theft of government resources?

These type audits require an auditor to critically examine the adequacy of an agency's financial and information accumulation and reporting policies. Then the desired criteria must be compared to the actual procedures and practices being applied. Systems and other support documentation must be examined to verify that operating practices conform.

Selected observations must be made of activities such as: coding, recording, processing, accumulating, and reporting of data. Tests are required to ensure that the prescribed controls contribute to the continual integrity of the information reported to and used by management. The uniformity of data among organizations and consistency of data between two or more fiscal periods must be confirmed. Audit visits and personal observations must be made of geographically dispersed locations, operations, and activities to assess the quality of data received, from these sources.

While many of these concerns are similar to those tested in a financial statement audit, special emphasis will be required to provide more detailed coverage of financial and statistical accounts, controls, computer applications, data flows, and participating personnel.

The resultant audit report could be addressed to the auditee, the chief elected official, the legislature, senior management, or operating personnel who may not be part of the auditee organization. Rather than an opinion, the audit report would be in narrative form and outline the specific audit scope applied, summarize the audit observations or findings, and contain audit conclusions and recommendations for change.

Selected Expenditure Audits

Governments are particularly concerned with disbursements of public funds for certain classifications of expenditures, such as personnel and payroll, travel and transportation, and property and equipment. The concern is focused towards those expenditures that offer an opportunity for abuse or personal gain. The controls, checks and audit processes related to such expenditures are detailed and quite restrictive. To provide management, legislators and needed assurances, government auditors perform periodic audits of expenditures for payroll, travel, property, etc.

The following selected audit areas are merely illustrative of some special focus audits. Other types special focus audits, that combine aspects of financial, performance compliance, and internal auditing include directed audits of taxes, royalties, communications and utility costs, transportation costs, investments and portfolio management, printing and graphics, computer acquisition and utilization, personal training and professional development, etc.

Personnel and Payrolls. Personnel and payroll is a major cost of any government and, therefore, a function that is rather micro-managed and possibly excessively documented. A periodic audit of this function often has the objective of assessing the extent of compliance with personnel laws, civil service regulations, departmental and agency rules and a host of other compensations and compliance criteria that affect the conditions of employment, competence, compensation, size of staffs, and other factors related to public sector employment.

Governments can only hire for positions authorized by the legislature or other governing body. Levels and rates of compensation, annual increases, bonuses, severance payments, and fringe benefits must be set forth in law, statute, ordinance, or union contracts. The government's budget also establishes the level and numbers of personnel that may be retained. Special focus audits for these functions might be divided into audits of the personnel practices and a separate audit of payroll practices.

If the audit was focused on a review of an entity's personnel policies, procedures and implemented practices, tests would be made to:

- Assess the application of policies and procedures and related practices for persons to be appointed to a governmental position, including the: determination of personnel need, legal and budgetary authorization, approval to solicit applications from current employees and formal advertising to the public, and the competitive selection of appointees.

Audit Methodology—Special Focus Audits 497

● Examine the methods and types of personnel appointments, giving special emphasis to: executive-level and support personnel appointments; compliance with the letter and intent of legislation governing public sector positions; the grade or salary level of appointment and whether there has been compliance with applicable personnel criteria.

● Review the appropriateness of decisions (1) related to employment from advertised and appointive positions, the educational and technical requirements of the job in comparison to the qualifications of appointees, and the correctness of salary levels in relation to personnel laws and regulations, qualifications, budget authorizations, available funding resources; and (2) related to changes in pay status due to promotions, performance, transfers, termination's, retirements.

● Authenticate the payrolls and time keeping procedures, check cost and labor distribution and recording and accounting processes, witness payroll distributions, and perform other checks to assure payments are made to only authorized, appropriate and eligible persons at the rate set by law or personnel policy.

Meeting payrolls of government is generally quite systematized: checks are issued on a routine basis; exception payment bases are used (employees are issued a check for the normal work period unless notice is received to the contrary); exception payments (less than the normal hours, overtime, etc.,) are met by processing special payrolls.

The primary difficulty is the volume of records that must be continuously updated, the detailed compliance criteria that must be met. Non-payroll, but personnel related, transactions such as awards, bonuses, and special allowances are often processed by the payroll function, but require special documentation and are subject to exceptional type authorizations and approvals.

Exhibit 19-1 illustrates, in overview form, the nature of a payroll process that would exist in most governmental agencies.

If the audit was focused on a review of payroll policies, procedures and an examination of implemented practices, tests would be made to confirm payments, appropriateness of disbursements and cost allocations, and compliance with legal and governmentwide civil service requirements. The payroll audit would include audit procedures to:

● Verify the fundamental arithmetic accuracy of payroll by examining support records as time and attendance sheets, time clock cards, other records of employment and work performed, and posting of vacations and sick leave taken and accrued.

- Reconciliation of all payroll imprest fund accounts to the master payroll register and general ledger payroll disbursement, expense, and liability accounts for each fund having payroll costs.

- Determine that payroll disbursements and related personal services comply with federal, state, and local laws, statutes, regulations and civil service requirements and budget limits, including the levels of pay, rates of pay, persons paid, total amounts paid.

- Reconcile and tie-in the essential payroll forms, records, and documents, such as attendance records, period payroll listings, journal and labor cost allocation entries, subsidiary and general ledger postings and account balances, and legislative appropriations or funding sources.

- If warranted, conduct attendance or "floor checks" and witness a "payoff" or check distribution on an unannounced or surprise basis, controlling time cards and unclaimed checks, canceled checks, and validating the liability recorded to identified as well as unidentified employees.

- Verify payments to the authorizing documentation for all special type payrolls to terminated employees, vacation and sick leave, overtime, hazardous duty, etc.

Travel. The costs related to travel are seldom material in relation to any government's total expenditures. Nonetheless, extremely close monitoring is defended because of the opportunity that travel presents for personal abuse or private gain. At all levels of government, a prospective traveler is subjected to a gauntlet of authorizations and approvals and often pre- and post-payment audit reviews.

Government agencies will typically require an executive to assent to an advance authorization for an anticipated trip; then funds will often be approved, budgeted or encumbered by another executive; next the travel must be performed in strict accord with applicable travel regulations or the traveler risks disallowances of reimbursement claims; after the trip a voucher detailing all specifics surrounding all travel costs is submitted, certified, and later audited prior to reimbursement of the traveler.

An objective of the travel function and related costs is to determine that there is an operating system of controls and a functioning process that requires full compliance with laws, regulations, and rules relating to executive and employee travel. The scope for such periodic special focus audits will vary, but could include an assessment of compliance (by responsible executives and personnel as well as the traveler) with laws, regulations, policies and practices relating to:

- Cost limitations (e.g., mileage, taxis, public transportation, etc.);

Audit Methodology—Special Focus Audits 499

● Per diem costs (e.g., lodging, meals, other costs incidental to travel, over-weekend accommodations, etc.);

● Relocation costs (common carrier rates, permitted tonnage moved at government cost, permitted distances moved, elapsed time periods, etc.);

● Use of public conveyers (e.g., selection of common carriers, class of travel accommodations used, direct versus indirect routings, etc.,);

● Travel funds advanced (e.g., procedures for requesting, authorizing, approving, advancing, liquidating, and settling); and

● Accounting procedures and practices (e.g., the process for inputting, posting, recording, accumulating, distributing, and reporting of travel costs).

Exhibit 19-2 illustrates, in overview form, the nature of a travel function process that would exist in most governmental agencies.

If the audit of travel were to focus on an examination of implemented practices, tests would be made to confirm payments, appropriateness of accounting for disbursements, cost allocations, and compliance with legal and governmentwide limitations. This focus might require that an audit of travel would include audit procedures to:

● Determine the validity of obligated and encumbered amounts for travel in relation to amounts formally budgeted in appropriations and later authorized and approved by management; then validate that unliquidated amounts are still committed for only valid or authorized unperformed travel obligations.

● Determine compliance with governmentwide and agency policy, regulations, and procedures through a comparison of the amount, purpose, timing, etc., of travel expense vouchers paid to these criteria.

● Determine the required management authorizations were obtained in advance of travel performance, that budgeted funds were available for travel, and approval was obtained for all claims of payment.

● Examine the practices related to awarding, accounting, advancing, liquidating, and settling travel advances.

● Confirm the age of outstanding travel advances; consider whether aged advances are being used by employees as interest-free personal loans; and assess the possibility of recommending periodic settlements of all travel advances.

● Reconcile outstanding travel authorizations to amounts obligated or encumbered; confirm that unliquidated amounts and outstanding amounts are proper; and verify that authenticity of amounts actually disbursed for travel reimbursements.

● Verify the manner and appropriateness of computing and claiming reimbursement for travel costs as per diem; mileage for use of personal vehicles, rentals, public transportation, charters or other group arrangements and contracts issued for transportation.

● Trace original authorizations to claims for payments, to payment support documents, to various journals, and to ledger accounts, including those used for appropriation, fund and cost accounting purposes.

● Assure, that for the transportation of things, bills of lading are properly completed, filed, matched with receiving documents and that all discounts and other payment terms are honored.

● Test for duplicate payments, particularly (1) when payments have been delayed for extended periods and duplicate copies of billings and vouchers were submitted as follow-up claims; (2) when carrier invoices have been submitted to more than one government location for payment; and (3) when adjusted claims are received after payment has been made.

● Determine that reviews (pre- or post-payment "audits") are made of all documents and records in support of requests or claims for payments

Property and Equipment. Historically the failure to account, both physically and financially, for the properties of a government has been the most frequent basis for auditors rendering qualified opinions on a government's financial statements. Many governments do not have or require compliance with policies and procedures to continually account for, adequately document, periodically validate, and report on nonexpendable property.

Governments hold title to considerable inventories of property (including buildings, equipment, supplies, furniture, fixtures, etc.) directly and also provide considerable amounts of property to contractors and grantees (referred to as GFM or GFE—government furnished materials or equipment). And, in other cases, government provided monies for their contractors and grantees to purchase property. Title to this property also vests with the government and must be audited.

However acquired and whom ever has possession, regular special focused audits are conducted of government property to evaluate compliance with laws, regulations, and policies related to procuring, storing, recording, accounting, using, maintaining, inventorying, protecting, preserving, and properly disposing of these properties. These audits also require evaluating the adequacy of controls: validating

Audit Methodology—Special Focus Audits 501

procurement and inventory records location, condition, and existence; inventories counts are confirmed to property records; procuring, receiving, counting, storing, and protecting procedures and practices are also tested.

In most instances, the accounting and controls used by private sector entities would be equally applicable to governments. But, there are some aspects of a special focus audit of property that might be more appropriate to governments and warrant specific attention, for example:

● Acquisition of buildings, equipment, fixtures and construction of infrastructure assets are generally approved in a capital budget appropriation. The acquisitions then require specific approval of legislative and executive management at the time of procurement or construction, with the purchase of property or construction made under competitively awarded contracts.

● Nonexpendable property, acquired or constructed under contracts and grants received from other governments generally require adherence to specific conditions relating to purchase, use, control, accounting, preservation, inventory and disposal.

● Separate accounting, reporting, and controls are often implemented for all assets furnished by a government to others or purchased by a government for use and possession by others (GFM or GFE—government furnished materials or equipment).

● Donated or contributed assets should be controlled, accounted for in the same manner as purchased or constructed assets, and valued pursuant to accepted pubic sector accounting.

● General fixed assets of governments should not be recorded as operating expenditures, but rather as capital transactions, in the general fixed asset account group, or in the appropriate enterprise or working capital type fund.

● Depreciation accounting may or may not be applied or consistently applied among various asset types, from one accounting period to another, or in the same manner between two units of the same governmental entity.

● Many governments do not account and report on the financial and physical status of "infrastructure assets" (streets, bridges, sewers, sidewalks, etc., and on occasion, buildings).

● Quite often, governments do not provide or purchase insurance on all properties, preferring to be self-insured, which is more often a euphemism for no insurance.

PRE-AUDITS AND FISCAL POST-AUDITS

Pre-Audits

Many governments have established an internal control or check procedure referred to as a "voucher pre-audit." Pre-audits are not audits in the sense of audits made pursuant to professional standards by an independent auditor.

A pre-audit is an internal control feature that generally consists of the clerical examination by government employees of vouchers and supporting documentation for completeness prior to formalizing an encumbrance or preparing a disbursement voucher and disbursing cash to pay a debt of the government. The objective of the pre-audit is to determine, in advance of consummating a transaction, the accuracy of the contemplated transaction; whether the contemplated obligation or encumbrance is legal; if the money has been appropriated and funds are available to pay the claim.

The scope of pre-audit will often include:

● A review of the purpose of the contemplated encumbrance or expenditure for appropriateness and consistency with the appropriating and other enabling legislation.

● The timing of the encumbrance or disbursement, certification of an amount required to insure the sufficiency of unexpended appropriation balances, avoiding any over disbursement of an appropriation.

● The examination of the form, content, authorizing and approval signatures and the presence or existence of all completed and required records supporting the correctness of accounting and reporting.

While pre-audits are prevalent in government, government auditors must be cognizant of the various phases or events in the life cycle of a government transaction. These audits have a limited deterrent effect and are often too late in the transaction cycle to be a preventative type internal control. Typically, such reviews would be considered as a "detect" type control feature.

A voucher pre-audit, while of value to an accountable officer, has limited value to the government as a whole. If the government had earlier entered into a legally binding obligation or encumbrance, and if the contracted goods or services have been delivered and accepted by government executives, and an accurate vendor invoice rendered, the accountable officer has no choice but to pay the invoice, regardless of the results of the voucher pre-audit. The accountable officer may have a finding or a procedural or compliance exception with respects to adherence to controls or practices of other government officials, but a payment must nonetheless be made.

Audit Methodology—Special Focus Audits 503

As an accountability control or internal check, the pre-audit might occur too late in the transaction cycle to be a significant factor in any decisions relating to the economy, efficiency, or effectiveness regarding a government's expenditures. Nonetheless, where performed, this procedure is an excellent detection control feature that should be considered and evaluated by an independent auditor.

Fiscal Post-Audits

Fiscal post-audits, like pre-audits, are not "audits" in the professional sense of the term. Post-audits are not audits made pursuant to professional standards by an independent auditor. Fiscal pre-audits are clerical checks or reviews made by government personnel after the life cycle of a transaction has been completed.

Fiscal post-audits generally consist of:

● Reviews of the completeness and adequacy of accounts, records, forms and other support documenting the disbursement made.

● Samples of transactions may consist of all or a large portion of expenditures or disbursements made during the year or a sample fiscal period.

● Post (after disbursement has been made) reviews or examinations of data performed at a central location with all support documentation being transferred to the central audit site or performed at dispersed agency sites where the support documentation originated and is retained.

● Objectives of determining whether the disbursements were consistent with governing legislation applicable policies and regulations and operating procedures; whether the amount is proper and supported by the proper and completed documentation; and whether accounting for the disbursement is correct and was made in the proper fiscal period.

As was the case with pre-audits, post-audits might occur too late in the transaction cycle to be a significant factor in any decisions relating to the efficacy of amounts obligated or disbursed from a government's fund. Where performed, fiscal post-audits are generally in response to state or local laws or statutes and often performed by the comptrollers function and not the governmental audit function. Nonetheless, where performed, this procedure is an excellent control feature that should be considered and evaluated by an independent auditor.

Exhibits 19-1 and 19-2 follow this page.

EXHIBIT 19-1

Exhibit 19-1 Overview of Government Personnel and Payroll Process... Functions, Documents, Accounting

A. Individual Employee
1. Makes application
2. Request deductions
3. Submits approved attendance records:
   ...time worked
   ...vacation
   ...sick
   ...compensatory time

B. Human Resources Personnel Function
1. List vacancies
2. Monitor staffing levels
3. Advertise, screen, recommend new hires
4. Issues notices:
   ...appoint,
   ...initiate payroll process
5. Issue forms to change pay status:
   ...promotion,
   ...demotion,
   ...retirements,
   ...dismissals,
   ...transfers,
   ...terminations

C. Payroll Unit
1. Enter employee into system
2. Monitor pay rolls, master and individual employee accounts:
   ...gross pay
   ...deductions
   ...changes
   ...contributions
   ...net pay
3. Maintain documents of support for historical and current periods
4. Process authorized changes to payroll
5. Account for payroll related transactions:
   ...withholdings,
   ...deductions,
   ...changes,
   ...check requests
6. Prepares voucher for total and individual payroll amounts for Treasury function

D. Accounting Function*
1. Confirm funds available for payroll
2. Record obligation for estimated payroll
3. Record payroll:
   ...gross,
   ...withholdings,
   ...deductions,
   ...net pay
4. Account for costs:
   ...appropriation,
   ...apportionment,
   ...encumbrance,
   ...obligation,
   ...cost accounting
5. Make cash payment entries
6. Make cost allocations:
   ...appropriation,
   ...program,
   ...organization,
   ...activity, etc.
7. Perform accounting and reporting:
   ...fund
   ...budgetary
   ...proprietary accounting
8. Prepares internal and external financial reports
9. Financial analysis

E. Treasury Function
1. Pay payrolls:
   ...check,
   ...direct deposit to accounts
2. Report payment to department and agency

*****Accounting Process**
- Record, monitor encumbrance of funds
- Record gross to net payroll
- Distribute labor costs by organization, location, activity, object class, etc.
- Account for payroll expenses: withholdings and deductions from employees; employer tax and other match; required deposits, etc.
- Record actual disbursement of cash by appropriation
- Maintain document files

EXHIBIT 19-2

Exhibit 19-2

Overview of Government Travel Process...
Functions, Documents, Accounting

A. Individual Employee

1. Submit travel request
   ...time period
   ...destination
   ...mode of travel
   ...cost estimate
2. Request travel advance
   ...amount
   ...purpose
3. Perform travel
4. Submit travel voucher:
   ...Cost of travel, meals, lodging, other
   ...itinerary
   ...time period
5. Settle travel advance
6. Custody of public carrier payment forms

B. Authorizing Officer

1. Approve travel request
2. Approve travel advance
3. Review, approve travel expense voucher

C. Common Carrier

1. Honors transportation payment form
2. Provide transportation
3. Honors payment form
4. Submits payment form to agency for payment

D. Accounting Function*

1. Confirm funds available for commitment
2. Record obligation for approved travel cost
3. Account for advances due from traveler
4. Review cost claimed on travel expense voucher
5. Prepare schedule of vouchers for issuance of checks by Treasury function
6. Settle advance balance
7. Record payment
8. Perform fund and cost accounting
9. Prepare internal and external financial reports
10. Financial analyses

E. Treasury Function

1. Issue travel advance check
2. Issue check for due net travel expenses

E. *Accounting Process

- Record, monitor obligation or encumbrance of funds for estimate of travel costs
- Establish advances receivable account due from traveler
- Account for liquidation of advances, obligation, record expenditures and travel cost liability.
- Authorize payment of net travel cost to traveler
- Record actual disbursement of cash by appropriation, organization, activity, object class, etc.
- Maintain document files

Appendices to

Government Auditing:

Standards and Practices

APPENDIX A

Text of Single Audit Act (31 U.S.C. § § 7501-7507), as amended by the

Single Audit Act Amendments of 1996 (P.L. 104-156)

AN ACT

To streamline and improve the effectiveness of chapter 75 of title 31, United States Code (commonly referred to as the "Single Audit Act").

Be it enacted by the Senate and House of Representatives of the United States of America in Congress assembled,

SECTION 1. SHORT TITLE; PURPOSES.

(a) Short Title.—This Act may be cited as the "Single Audit Act Amendments of 1996".

(b) Purposes.—The purposes of this Act are to—

(1) promote sound financial management, including effective internal controls, with respect to Federal awards administered by non-Federal entities;

(2) establish uniform requirements for audits of Federal awards administered by non-Federal entities;

(3) promote the efficient and effective use of audit resources;

(4) reduce burdens on State and local governments, Indian tribes, and nonprofit organizations; and

(5) ensure that Federal departments and agencies, to the maximum extent practicable, rely upon and use audit work done pursuant to chapter 75 of title 31, United States Code (as amended by this Act).

SEC. 2. AMENDMENT TO TITLE 31, UNITED STATES CODE.

Chapter 75 of title 31, United States Code, is amended to read as follows:

CHAPTER 75—REQUIREMENTS FOR SINGLE AUDITS

Sec. 7501. Definitions. (a) As used in this chapter, the term—

(1) "Comptroller General" means the Comptroller General of the United States;

(2) "Director" means the Director of the Office of Management and Budget;

(3) "Federal agency" has the same meaning as the term "agency" in section 551(1) of title 5;

(4) "Federal awards" means Federal financial assistance and Federal cost-reimbursement contracts that non-Federal entities receive directly from Federal awarding agencies or indirectly from pass-through entities;

(5) "Federal financial assistance" means assistance that nonFederal entities receive or administer in the form of grants, loans, loan guarantees, property, cooperative agreements, interest subsidies, insurance, food commodities, direct appropriations, or other assistance, but does not include amounts received as reimbursement for services rendered to individuals in accordance with guidance issued by the Director;

(6) "Federal program" means all Federal awards to a nonFederal entity assigned a single number in the Catalog of Federal Domestic Assistance or encompassed in a group of numbers or other category as defined by the Director;

(7) "generally accepted government auditing standards" means the government auditing standards issued by the Comptroller General;

(8) "independent auditor" means—

(A) an external State or local government auditor who meets the independence standards included in generally accepted government auditing standards; or

(B) a public accountant who meets such independence standards;

(9) "Indian tribe" means any Indian tribe, band, nation, or other organized group or community, including any Alaskan Native village or regional or village corporation (as defined in, or established under, the Alaskan Native Claims Settlement Act) that is recognized by the United States as eligible for the special programs and services provided by the United States to Indians because of their status as Indians;

(10) "internal controls" means a process, effected by an entity's management and other personnel, designed to provide reasonable assurance regarding the achievement of objectives in the following categories:

(A) Effectiveness and efficiency of operations.

(B) Reliability of financial reporting.

(C) Compliance with applicable laws and regulations;

(11) "local government" means any unit of local government within a State, including a county, borough, municipality, city, town, township, parish, local public authority, special district, school district, intrastate district, council of governments, any other instrumentality of local government and, in accordance with guidelines issued by the Director, a group of local governments;

(12) "major program" means a Federal program identified in accordance with risk-based criteria prescribed by the Director under this chapter, subject to the limitations described under subsection (b);

(13) "non-Federal entity" means a State, local government, or nonprofit organization;

(14) "nonprofit organization" means any corporation, trust, association, cooperative, or other organization that—

(A) is operated primarily for scientific, educational, service, charitable, or similar purposes in the public interest;

(B) is not organized primarily for profit; and

(C) uses net proceeds to maintain, improve, or expand the operations of the organization;

(15) "pass-through entity" means a non-Federal entity that provides Federal awards to a subrecipient to carry out a Federal program;

(16) "program-specific audit" means an audit of one Federal program;

(17) "recipient" means a non-Federal entity that receives awards directly from a Federal agency to carry out a Federal program;

(18) "single audit" means an audit, as described under section 7502(d), of a non-Federal entity that includes the entity's financial statements and Federal awards;

(19) "State" means any State of the United States, the District of Columbia, the Commonwealth of Puerto Rico, the Virgin Islands, Guam, American Samoa, the Commonwealth of the Northern Mariana Islands, and the Trust Territory of the Pacific Islands, any instrumentality thereof, any multi-State, regional, or interstate entity which has governmental functions, and any Indian tribe; and

(20) "subrecipient" means a non-Federal entity that receives Federal awards through another non-Federal entity to carry out a Federal program, but does not include an individual who receives financial assistance through such awards.

(b) In prescribing risk-based program selection criteria for major programs, the Director shall not require more programs to be identified as major for a particular non-Federal entity, except as prescribed under subsection (c) or as provided under subsection (d), than would be identified if the major programs were defined as any program for which total expenditures of Federal awards by the nonFederal entity during the applicable year exceed—

(1) the larger of $30,000,000 or 0.15 percent of the nonFederal entity's total Federal expenditures, in the case of a nonFederal entity

for which such total expenditures for all programs exceed $10,000,000,000;

(2) the larger of $3,000,000, or 0.30 percent of the nonFederal entity's total Federal expenditures, in the case of a nonFederal entity for which such total expenditures for all programs exceed $100,000,000 but are less than or equal to $10,000,000,000;

or

(3) the larger of $300,000, or 3 percent of such total Federal expenditures for all programs, in the case of a non-Federal entity for which such total expenditures for all programs equal or exceed $300,000 but are less than or equal to $100,000,000.

(c) When the total expenditures of a non-Federal entity's major programs are less than 50 percent of the non-Federal entity's total expenditures of all Federal awards (or such lower percentage as specified by the Director), the auditor shall select and test additional programs as major programs as necessary to achieve audit coverage of at least 50 percent of Federal expenditures by the nonFederal entity (or such lower percentage as specified by the Director), in accordance with guidance issued by the Director.

(d) Loan or loan guarantee programs, as specified by the Director, shall not be subject to the application of subsection (b).

Sec. 7502. Audit requirements; exemptions. (a)(1)(A) Each non-Federal entity that expends a total amount of Federal awards equal to or in excess of $300,000 or such other amount specified by the Director under subsection (a)(3) in any fiscal year of such non-Federal entity shall have either a single audit or a programspecific audit made for such fiscal year in accordance with the requirements of this chapter.

(B) Each such non-Federal entity that expends Federal awards under more than one Federal program shall undergo a single audit in accordance with the requirements of subsections (b) through (i) of this section and guidance issued by the Director under section 7505.

(C) Each such non-Federal entity that expends awards under only one Federal program and is not subject to laws, regulations, or Federal award agreements that require a financial statement audit of the nonFederal entity, may elect to have a program-specific audit conducted in accordance with applicable provisions of this section and guidance issued by the Director under section 7505.

(2)(A) Each non-Federal entity that expends a total amount of Federal awards of less than $300,000 or such other amount specified by the Director under subsection (a)(3) in any fiscal year of such entity, shall be exempt for such fiscal year from compliance with—

(i) the audit requirements of this chapter; and

(ii) any applicable requirements concerning financial audits contained in Federal statutes and regulations governing programs under which such Federal awards are provided to that non-Federal entity.

(B) The provisions of subparagraph (A)(ii) of this paragraph shall not exempt a non-Federal entity from compliance with any provision of a Federal statute or regulation that requires such nonFederal entity to maintain records concerning Federal awards provided to such non-Federal entity or that permits a Federal agency, passthrough entity, or the Comptroller General access to such records.

(3) Every 2 years, the Director shall review the amount for requiring audits prescribed under paragraph (1)(A) and may adjust such dollar amount consistent with the purposes of this chapter, provided the Director does not make such adjustments below $300,000.

(b)(1) Except as provided in paragraphs (2) and (3), audits conducted pursuant to this chapter shall be conducted annually.

(2) A State or local government that is required by constitution or statute, in effect on January 1, 1987, to undergo its audits less frequently than annually, is permitted to undergo its audits pursuant to this chapter biennially. Audits conducted biennially under the provisions of this paragraph shall cover both years within the biennial period.

(3) Any nonprofit organization that had biennial audits for all biennial periods ending between July 1, 1992, and January 1, 1995, is permitted to undergo its audits pursuant to this chapter biennially. Audits conducted biennially under the provisions of this paragraph shall cover both years within the biennial period.

(c) Each audit conducted pursuant to subsection (a) shall be conducted by an independent auditor in accordance with generally accepted government auditing standards, except that, for the purposes of this chapter, performance audits shall not be required except as authorized by the Director.

(d) Each single audit conducted pursuant to subsection (a) for any fiscal year shall—

(1) cover the operations of the entire non-Federal entity; or

(2) at the option of such non-Federal entity such audit shall include a series of audits that cover departments, agencies, and other organizational units which expended or otherwise administered Federal awards during such fiscal year provided that each such audit shall encompass the financial statements and schedule of expenditures of Federal awards for each such department, agency, and organizational unit, which shall be considered to be a nonFederal entity.

(e) The auditor shall—

(1) determine whether the financial statements are presented fairly in all material respects in conformity with generally accepted accounting principles;

(2) determine whether the schedule of expenditures of Federal awards is presented fairly in all material respects in relation to the financial statements taken as a whole;

(3) with respect to internal controls pertaining to the compliance requirements for each major program—

(A) obtain an understanding of such internal controls;

(B) assess control risk; and

(C) perform tests of controls unless the controls are deemed to be ineffective; and

(4) determine whether the non-Federal entity has complied with the provisions of laws, regulations, and contracts or grants pertaining to Federal awards that have a direct and material effect on each major program.

(f)(1) Each Federal agency which provides Federal awards to a recipient shall—

(A) provide such recipient the program names (and any identifying numbers) from which such awards are derived, and the Federal requirements which govern the use of such awards and the requirements of this chapter; and

(B) review the audit of a recipient as necessary to determine whether prompt and appropriate corrective action has been taken with respect to audit findings, as defined by the Director, pertaining to Federal awards provided to the recipient by the Federal agency.

(2) Each pass-through entity shall—

(A) provide such subrecipient the program names (and any identifying numbers) from which such assistance is derived, and the Federal requirements which govern the use of such awards and the requirements of this chapter;

(B) monitor the subrecipient's use of Federal awards through site visits, limited scope audits, or other means;

(C) review the audit of a subrecipient as necessary to determine whether prompt and appropriate corrective action has been taken with respect to audit findings, as defined by the Director, pertaining to Federal awards provided to the subrecipient by the pass-through entity; and

(D) require each of its subrecipients of Federal awards to permit, as a condition of receiving Federal awards, the independent auditor of the pass-through entity to have such access to the subrecipient's records and financial statements as may be necessary for the pass-through entity to comply with this chapter.

(g)(1) The auditor shall report on the results of any audit conducted pursuant to this section, in accordance with guidance issued by the Director.

(2) When reporting on any single audit, the auditor shall include a summary of the auditor's results regarding the non-Federal entity's financial statements, internal controls, and compliance with laws and regulations.

(h) The non-Federal entity shall transmit the reporting package, which shall include the non-Federal entity's financial statements, schedule of expenditures of Federal awards, corrective action plan defined under subsection (i), and auditor's reports developed pursuant to this section, to a Federal clearinghouse designated by the Director, and make it available for public inspection within the earlier of—

(1) 30 days after receipt of the auditor's report; or

(2)(A) for a transition period of at least 2 years after the effective date of the Single Audit Act Amendments of 1996, as established by the Director, 13 months after the end of the period audited; or

(B) for fiscal years beginning after the period specified in subparagraph (A), 9 months after the end of the period audited, or within a longer timeframe authorized by the Federal agency, determined under criteria issued under section 7504, when the 9month timeframe would place an undue burden on the non-Federal entity.

(i) If an audit conducted pursuant to this section discloses any audit findings, as defined by the Director, including material noncompliance with individual compliance requirements for a major program by, or reportable conditions in the internal controls of, the non-Federal entity with respect to the matters described in subsection (e), the non-Federal entity shall submit to Federal officials designated by the Director, a plan for corrective action to eliminate such audit findings or reportable conditions or a statement describing the reasons that corrective action is not necessary. Such plan shall be consistent with the audit resolution standard promulgated by the Comptroller General (as part of the standards for internal controls in the Federal Government) pursuant to section 3512(c).

(j) The Director may authorize pilot projects to test alternative methods of achieving the purposes of this chapter. Such pilot projects may begin only after consultation with the Chair and Ranking Minority Member of the Committee on Governmental Affairs of the Senate and the Chair and Ranking Minority Member of the Committee on Government Reform and Oversight of the House of Representatives.

Sec. 7503. Relation to other audit requirements. (a) An audit conducted in accordance with this chapter shall be in lieu of any financial audit of Federal awards which a non-Federal entity is required to undergo under any other Federal law or regulation. To the extent that such audit provides a Federal agency with the information it requires to carry out its responsibilities under Federal law or regulation, a Federal agency shall rely upon and use that information.

(b) Notwithstanding subsection (a), a Federal agency may conduct or arrange for additional audits which are necessary to carry out its responsibilities under Federal law or regulation. The provisions of this chapter do not authorize any non-Federal entity (or subrecipient thereof) to constrain, in any manner, such agency from carrying out or arranging for such additional audits, except that the Federal agency shall plan such audits to not be duplicative of other audits of Federal awards.

(c) The provisions of this chapter do not limit the authority of Federal agencies to conduct, or arrange for the conduct of, audits and evaluations of Federal awards, nor limit the authority of any Federal agency Inspector General or other Federal official.

(d) Subsection (a) shall apply to a non-Federal entity which undergoes an audit in accordance with this chapter even though it is not required by section 7502(a) to have such an audit.

(e) A Federal agency that provides Federal awards and conducts or arranges for audits of non-Federal entities receiving such awards that are in addition to the audits of non-Federal entities conducted pursuant to this chapter shall, consistent with other applicable law, arrange for funding the full cost of such additional audits. Any such additional audits shall be coordinated with the Federal agency determined under criteria issued under section 7504 to preclude duplication of the audits conducted pursuant to this chapter or other additional audits.

(f) Upon request by a Federal agency or the Comptroller General, any independent auditor conducting an audit pursuant to this chapter shall make the auditor's working papers available to the Federal agency or the Comptroller General as part of a quality review, to resolve audit findings, or to carry out oversight responsibilities consistent with the purposes of this chapter. Such access to auditor's working papers shall include the right to obtain copies.

Sec. 7504. Federal agency responsibilities and relations with nonFederal entities. (a) Each Federal agency shall, in accordance with guidance issued by the Director under section 7505, with regard to Federal awards provided by the agency—

(1) monitor non-Federal entity use of Federal awards, and

(2) assess the quality of audits conducted under this chapter for audits of entities for which the agency is the single Federal agency determined under subsection (b).

(b) Each non-Federal entity shall have a single Federal agency, determined in accordance with criteria established by the Director, to provide the non-Federal entity with technical assistance and assist with implementation of this chapter.

(c) The Director shall designate a Federal clearinghouse to—

(1) receive copies of all reporting packages developed in accordance with this chapter;

(2) identify recipients that expend $300,000 or more in Federal awards or such other amount specified by the Director under section 7502(a)(3) during the recipient's fiscal year but did not undergo an audit in accordance with this chapter; and

(3) perform analyses to assist the Director in carrying out responsibilities under this chapter.

Sec. 7505. Regulations. (a) The Director, after consultation with the Comptroller General, and appropriate officials from Federal, State, and local governments and nonprofit organizations shall prescribe guidance to implement this chapter. Each Federal agency shall promulgate such amendments to its regulations as may be necessary to conform such regulations to the requirements of this chapter and of such guidance.

(b)(1) The guidance prescribed pursuant to subsection (a) shall include criteria for determining the appropriate charges to Federal awards for the cost of audits. Such criteria shall prohibit a nonFederal entity from charging to any Federal awards—

(A) the cost of any audit which is—

(i) not conducted in accordance with this chapter; or

(ii) conducted in accordance with this chapter when expenditures of Federal awards are less than amounts cited in section 7502(a)(1)(A) or specified by the Director under section 7502(a)(3), except that the Director may allow the cost of limited scope audits to monitor subrecipients in accordance with section 7502(f)(2)(B); and

(B) more than a reasonably proportionate share of the cost of any such audit that is conducted in accordance with this chapter.

(2) The criteria prescribed pursuant to paragraph (1) shall not, in the absence of documentation demonstrating a higher actual cost, permit the percentage of the cost of audits performed pursuant to this chapter charged to Federal awards, to exceed the ratio of total Federal

awards expended by such non-Federal entity during the applicable fiscal year or years, to such non-Federal entity's total expenditures during such fiscal year or years.

(c) Such guidance shall include such provisions as may be necessary to ensure that small business concerns and business concerns owned and controlled by socially and economically disadvantaged individuals will have the opportunity to participate in the performance of contracts awarded to fulfill the audit requirements of this chapter.

Sec. 7506. Monitoring responsibilities of the Comptroller General. (a) The Comptroller General shall review provisions requiring financial audits of non-Federal entities that receive Federal awards that are contained in bills and resolutions reported by the committees of the Senate and the House of Representatives.

(b) If the Comptroller General determines that a bill or resolution contains provisions that are inconsistent with the requirements of this chapter, the Comptroller General shall, at the earliest practicable date, notify in writing—

(1) the committee that reported such bill or resolution; and

(2)(A) the Committee on Governmental Affairs of the Senate (in the case of a bill or resolution reported by a committee of the Senate); or

(B) the Committee on Government Reform and Oversight of the House of Representatives (in the case of a bill or resolution reported by a committee of the House of Representatives).

Sec. 7507. Effective date. This chapter shall apply to any non-Federal entity with respect to any of its fiscal years which begin after June 30, 1996.

SEC. 3. TRANSITIONAL APPLICATION.

Subject to section 7507 of title 31, United States Code (as amended by section 2 of this Act) the provisions of chapter 75 of such title (before amendment by section 2 of this Act) shall continue to apply to any State or local government with respect to any of its fiscal years beginning before July 1, 1996.

APPENDIX B

Chief Financial Officers Act of 1990

An Act

To amend title 31, United States Code, to improve the general and financial management of the Federal Government

Be it enacted by the Senate and House of Representatives of the United States of America in Congress assembled.

TITLE I—GENERAL PROVISIONS

Sec. 101. SHORT TITLE.

This Act may be cited as the "Chief Financial Officers Act of 1990".

SEC. 102. FINDINGS AND PURPOSES

(a) FINDINGS—The Congress finds the following:

(1) General management functions of the Office of Management and Budget need to be significantly enhanced to improve the efficiency and effectiveness of the Federal Government.

(2) Financial management functions of the Office of Management and Budget need to be significantly enhanced to provide overall direction and leadership in the development of a modern Federal financial management structure and associated systems.

(3) Billions of dollars are lost each year through fraud, waste, abuse and mismanagement among the hundreds of programs in the Federal Government.

(4) These losses could be significantly decreased by improved management, including improved central coordination of internal controls and financial accounting.

(5) The Federal Government is in great need of fundamental reform in financial management requirements and practices as financial management systems are obsolete and inefficient, and do not provide complete, consistent, reliable, and timely information.

(6) Current financial reporting practices of the Federal Government do not accurately disclose the current and probable future cost of operating and investment decisions, including the future need for cash or other resources, do not permit adequate comparison of actual costs among executive agencies, and do not provide the timely information required for efficient management of programs.

(b) PURPOSES.—The purposes of this Act are the following:

(1) Bring more effective general and financial management practices to the Federal Government through statutory provisions which would establish in the Office of Management and Budget a Deputy Director for Management, establish an Office of Federal Financial Management headed by a Controller, and designate a Chief Financial Officer in each executive department and in each major executive agency in the Federal Government.

(2) Provide for improvement, in each agency of the Federal Government, of systems of accounting, financial management, and internal controls to assure the issuance of reliable financial information and to deter fraud, waste, and abuse of Government resources.

(3) Provide for the production of complete, reliable, timely, and consistent financial information for use by the executive branch of the Government and the Congress in the financing, management, and evaluation of Federal programs.

TITLE II—ESTABLISHMENT OF CHIEF FINANCIAL OFFICERS

SEC. 201. DEPUTY DIRECTOR FOR MANAGEMENT.

Section 502 of title 31, United States Code, as amended by this Act, is amended—

(1) by redesignating subsections (c), (d), and (e), as amended by this section, as subsections (d), (e), and (f); and

(2) by inserting after subsection (b) the following:

"(c) The Office has a Deputy Director for Management appointed by the President, by and with the advice and consent of the Senate. The Deputy Director for Management shall be the chief official responsible for financial management in the United States Government."

SEC. 202. FUNCTIONS OF DEPUTY DIRECTOR FOR MANAGEMENT.

(a) CLERICAL AMENDMENTS.—Sections 503 and 504 of title 31, United States Code, are redesignated in order as sections 505 and 506, respectively.

(b) FUNCTIONS OF DEPUTY DIRECTOR FOR MANAGEMENT.—Subchapter I of chapter 5 of title 31, United States Code, is amended by inserting after section 502 the following:

"§ 503. Functions of Deputy Director for Management

"(a) Subject to the direction and approval of the Director, the Deputy Director for Management shall establish governmentwide financial management policies for executive agencies and shall perform the following financial management functions:

"(1) Perform all functions of the Director, including all functions delegated by the President to the Director, relating to financial management.

"(2) Provide overall direction and leadership to the executive branch on financial management matters by establishing financial management policies and requirements, and by monitoring the establishment and operation of Federal Government financial management systems.

"(3) Review agency budget requests for financial management systems and operations, and advise the Director on the resources required to develop and effectively operate and maintain Federal Government financial management systems and to correct major deficiencies in such systems.

"(4) Review and, where appropriate, recommend to the Director changes to the budget and legislative proposals of agencies to ensure that they are in accordance with financial management plans of the Office of Management and Budget.

"(5) Monitor the financial execution of the budget in relation to actual expenditures, including timely performance reports.

"(6) Oversee, periodically review, and make recommendations to heads of agencies on the administrative structure of agencies with respect to their financial management activities.

"(7) Develop and maintain qualification standards for agency Chief Financial Officers and for agency Deputy Chief Financial Officers appointed under sections 901 and 903, respectively.

"(8) Provide advice to agency heads with respect to the selection of agency Chief Financial Officers and Deputy Chief Financial Officers.

"(9) Provide advice to agencies regarding the qualifications, recruitment, performance, and retention of other financial management personnel.

"(10) Assess the overall adequacy of the professional qualifications and capabilities of financial management staffs throughout the Government and make recommendations on ways to correct problems which impair the capacity of those staffs

"(11) Settle differences that arise among agencies regarding the implementation of financial management policies.

"(12) Chair the Chief Financial Officers Council established by section 302 of the Chief Financial Officers Act of 1990.

"(13) Communicate with the financial officers of State and local governments, and foster the exchange with those officers of information concerning financial management standards, techniques, and processes.

"(14) Issue such other policies and directives as may be necessary to carry out this section, and perform any other function prescribed by the Director.

"(b) Subject to the direction and approval of the Director, the Deputy Director for Management shall establish general management policies for executive agencies and perform the following general management functions:

"(1) Coordinate and supervise the general management functions of the Office of Management and Budget.

"(2) Perform all functions of the Director, including all functions delegated by the President to the Director, relating to—

"(A) managerial systems, including the systematic measurement of performance;

"(B) procurement policy;

"(C) grant, cooperative agreement, and assistance management;

"(D) information and statistical policy;

"(E) property management;

"(F) human resources management;

"(G) regulatory affairs; and

"(H) other management functions, including organizational studies, long-range planning, program evaluation, productivity improvement, and experimentation and demonstration programs.

"(3) Provide complete, reliable, and timely information to the President, the Congress, and the public regarding the management activities of the executive branch.

"(4) Facilitate actions by the Congress and the executive branch to improve the management of Federal Government operations and to remove impediments to effective administration.

"(5) Provide leadership in management innovation, through—

"(A) experimentation, testing, and demonstration programs; and

"(B) the adoption of modern management concepts and technologies.

"(6) Work with State and local governments to improve and strengthen intergovernmental relations, and provide assistance to such governments with respect to intergovernmental programs and cooperative arrangements.

"(7) Review and, where appropriate, recommend to the Director changes to the budget and legislative proposals of agencies to ensure that they respond to program evaluations by, and are in accordance with general management plans of, the Office of Management and Budget.

"(8) Provide advice to agencies on the qualification, recruitment, performance, and retention of managerial personnel.

"(9) perform any other functions prescribed by the Director.".

SEC. 203. OFFICE OF FEDERAL FINANCIAL MANAGEMENT.

(a) ESTABLISHMENT.—Subchapter I of chapter 5 of title 31, United States Code, as amended by this Act, is amended by inserting after section 503 (as added by section 202 of this Act) the following:

"§ 504. Office of Federal Financial Management

"(a) There is established in the Office of Management and Budget an office to be known as the 'Office of Federal Financial Management'. The Office of Federal Financial Management, under the direction and control of the Deputy Director for Management of the Office of Management and Budget, shall carry out the financial management functions listed in section 503(a) of this title.

"(b) There shall be at the head of the Office of Federal Financial Management a Controller, who shall be appointed by the President, by and with the advice and consent of the Senate. The Controller shall be appointed from among individuals who possess—

"(1) demonstrated ability and practical experience in accounting, financial management, and financial systems; and

(2) extensive practical experience in financial management in large governmental or business entities.

"(c) The Controller of the Office of Federal Financial Management shall be the deputy and principal advisor to the Deputy Director for Management in the performance by the Deputy Director for Management of functions described in section 503(a).".

(b) STATEMENT OF APPROPRIATIONS IN BUDGET.—Section 1105(a) of title 31, United States Code, is amended by adding at the end the following:

"(28) a separate statement of the amount of appropriations requested for the Office of Federal Financial Management.".

(c) CLERICAL AMENDMENT.—The table of contents at the beginning of chapter 5 of title 31, United States Code, is amended by striking the items relating to sections 503 and 504 and inserting the following:

"503. Functions of Deputy Director for Management.

"504. Office of Federal Financial Management.

"505. Office of Information and Regulatory Affairs.

"506. Office of Federal Procurement Policy.".

SEC. 204. DUTIES AND FUNCTIONS OF THE DEPARTMENT OF THE TREASURY.

Nothing in this Act shall be construed to interfere with the exercise of the functions, duties, and responsibilities of the Department of the Treasury, as in effect immediately before the enactment of this Act.

SEC. 205. AGENCY CHIEF FINANCIAL OFFICERS.

(a) IN GENERAL.—Subtitle I of title 31, United States Code, is amended by adding at the end the following new chapter:

"CHAPTER 9—AGENCY CHIEF FINANCIAL OFFICERS

"Sec.

"901. Establishment of agency Chief Financial Officers.

"902. Authority and functions of agency Chief Financial Officers.

"903. Establishment of agency Deputy Chief Financial Officers.

"§ 901. Establishment of agency Chief Financial Officers

"(a) There shall be within each agency described in subsection (b) an agency Chief Financial Officer. Each agency Chief Financial Officer shall—

"(1) for those agencies described in subsection (b)(1)—

"(A) be appointed by the President, by and with the advice and consent of the Senate; or

"(B) be designated by the President, in consultation with the head of the agency, from among officials of the agent who are required by law to be so appointed;

"(2) for those agencies described in subsection (b)(2)—

"(A) be appointed by the head of the agency;

"(B) be in the competitive service or the senior executive service; and

"(C) be career appointees; and

"(3) be appointed or designated, as applicable, from among individuals who possess demonstrated ability in general management of, and knowledge of and extensive practical experience in financial management practices in large governmental or business entities.

Chief Financial Officers Act

"(b)(1) The agencies referred to in subsection (a)(1) are the following:

"(A) The Department of Agriculture.

"(B) The Department of Commerce.

"(C) The Department of Defense.

"(D) The Department of Education.

"(E) The Department of Energy.

"(F) The Department of Health and Human Services.

"(G) The Department of Housing and Urban Development.

"(H) The Department of the Interior.

"(I) The Department of Justice.

"(J) The Department of Labor.

"(K) The Department of State.

"(L) The Department of Transportation.

"(M) The Department of the Treasury.

"(N) The Department of Veterans Affairs.

"(O) The Environmental Protection Agency.

"(P) The National Aeronautics and Space Administration

"(2) The agencies referred to in subsection (a)(2) are the following:

"(A) The Agency for International Development.

"(B) The Federal Emergency Management Agency.

"(C) The General Services Administration.

"(D) The National Science Foundation.

"(E) The Nuclear Regulatory Commission.

"(F) The Office of Personnel Management.

"(G) The Small Business Administration.

"§ 902. Authority and functions of agency Chief Financial Officers

"(a) An agency Chief Financial Officer shall—

"(1) report directly to the head of the agency regarding financial management matters;

"(2) oversee all financial management activities relating to the programs and operations of the agency;

"(3) develop and maintain an integrated agency accounting and financial management system, including financial reporting and internal controls, which—

"(A) complies with applicable accounting principles standards and requirements, and internal control standards;

"(B) complies with such policies and requirements as may be prescribed by the Director of the Office of Management and Budget;

"(C) complies with any other requirements applicable to such systems; and

"(D) provides for—

"(i) complete, reliable, consistent, and timely information which is prepared on a uniform basis and which is responsive to the financial information needs of agency management;

"(ii) the development and reporting of cost information;

"(iii) the integration of accounting and budgeting information; and

"(iv) the systematic measurement of performance;

"(4) make recommendations to the head of the agency regarding the selection of the Deputy Chief Financial Officer of the agency;

"(5) direct, manage, and provide policy guidance and oversight of agency financial management personnel, activities, and operations, including—

"(A) the preparation and annual revision of an agency plan to—

"(i) implement the 5-year financial management plan prepared by the Director of the Office of Management and Budget under section 3512(a)(3) of this title; and

"(ii) comply with the requirements established under sections 3515 and subsections (e) and (f) of section 3521 of this title;

"(B) the development of agency financial management budgets;

"(C) the recruitment, selection, and training of personnel to carry out agency financial management functions;

"(D) the approval and management of agency financial management systems design or enhancement projects;

"(E) the implementation of agency asset management systems, including systems for cash management, credit management, debt collection, and property and inventor management and control;

"(6) prepare and transmit, by not later than 60 days after the submission of the audit report required by section 3521(f) of this title. an annual report to the agency head and the Director of the Office of Management and Budget, which

"(A) a description and analysis of the status of financial management of the agency;

"(B) the annual financial statements prepared under section 3515 of this title;

"(C) the audit report transmitted to the head of the agency under section 3521(f) of this title;

"(D) a summary of the reports on internal accounting and administrative control systems submitted to the President and the Congress under the amendments made by the Federal Managers' Financial Integrity Act of 1982 (Public Law 97-255);

"(E) other information the head of the agency considers appropriate to fully inform the President and the Congress concerning the financial management of the agency;

"(7) monitor the financial execution of the budget of the agency in relation to actual expenditures, and prepare and submit to the head of the agency timely performance reports; and

"(8) review, on a biennial basis, the fees, royalties, rents, and other charges imposed by the agency for services and things of value it provides, and make recommendations on revising the charges to reflect costs incurred by it in providing those services and things of value.

"(b)(1) In addition to the authority otherwise provided by this section, each agency Chief Financial Officer—

"(A) subject to paragraph (2), shall have access to all records, reports, audits, reviews, documents, papers, recommendations, or other material which are the property of the agency or which are available to the agency, and which relate to programs and operations with respect to which that agency Chief Financial Officer has responsibilities under this section;

"(B) may request such information or assistance as may be necessary for carrying out the duties and responsibilities provided by this section from any Federal, State, or local governmental entity; and

"(C) to the extent and in such amounts as may be provided in advance by appropriations Acts, may—

"(i) enter into contracts and other arrangements with public agencies and with private persons for the preparation of financial statements, studies, analyses, and other services; and

"(ii) make such payments as may be necessary to carry out the provisions of this section.

"(2) Except as provided in paragraph (1)(B), this subsection does not provide to an agency Chief Financial Officer any access greater than permitted under any other law to records, reports, audits, reviews, documents, papers, recommendations, or other material any Office of Inspector General established under the Inspect General Act of 2978 (5 U.S.C. App.).

"§ 903. Establishment of agency Deputy Chief Financial Officers

"(a) There shall be within each agency described in section 901(b) an agency Deputy Chief Financial Officer, who shall report directly to the agency Chief Financial Officer on financial management matters. The position of agency Deputy Chief Financial Officer shall be a career reserved position in the Senior Executive Service.

"(b) Consistent with qualification standards developed by, and in consultation with, the agency Chief Financial Officer and the Director of the Office of Management and Budget, the head of each agency shall appoint as Deputy Chief Financial Officer an individual with demonstrated ability and experience in accounting, budget execution, financial and management analysis, and systems development, and not less than 6 years practical experience in financial management at large governmental entities.".

(b) CLERICAL AMENDMENT.—The table of chapters at the beginning of subtitle I of title 31, United States Code, is amended by adding at the end the following:

"9. Agency Chief Financial Officers 901.".

(c) CHIEF FINANCIAL OFFICERS OF DEPARTMENT OF VETERANS AFFAIRS FAIRS AND DEPARTMENT OF HOUSING AND URBAN DEVELOPMENT.—

(1) DESIGNATION.—The Secretary of Veterans Affairs and the Secretary of Housing and Urban Development may each designate as the agency Chief Financial Officer of that department for purposes of section 901 of title 31, United States Code, as amended by this section, the officer designated, respectively, under section 4(c) of the Department of Veterans Affairs Act (38 U.S.C. 201 note) and section 4(e) of the Department of Housing and Urban Development Act (42 U.S.C. 35233(e)), as added by section 121 of Public Law 101-235, are repealed.

(2) CONFORMING AMENDMENT.—Section 4(c) of the Department of Veterans Affairs Act (38 U.S.C. 201 note) and section 4(e) of the Department of Housing and Urban Development Act (42 U.S.C. 3533(e)), as added by section 121 of Public Law 101-235, are repealed.

SEC. 206. TRANSFER OF FUNCTIONS AND PERSONNEL OF AGENCY CHIEF FINANCIAL OFFICERS.

(a) AGENCY REVIEWS OF FINANCIAL MANAGEMENT ACTIVITIES.—Not later than 120 days after the date of the enactment of this Act, the Director of the Office of Management and Budget shall require each agency listed in subsection (b) of section 901 of title 31, United States Code, as amended by this Act, to conduct a review of its financial management activities for the purpose of consolidating its accounting, budgeting, and oher financial management activities under the agency Chief Financial Officer appointed under subsection (a) of that section for the agency.

(b) REORGANIZATION PROPOSAL.—Not later than 120 days after the issuance of requirements under subsection (a) and subject to all laws vesting functions in particular officers and employees of the United States, the head of each agency shall submit to the Director of the Office of Management and Budget a proposal for reorganizing the agency for the purposes of this Act. Such proposal shall include—

(1) a description of all functions, powers, duties, personnel, property, or records which the agency Chief Financial Officer is proposed to have authority over, including those relating to functions that are not related to financial management activities; and

(2) a detailed outline of the administrative structure of the office of the agency Chief Financial Officer, including a description of the responsibility and authority of financial management personnel and resources in agencies or other subdivisions as appropriate to that agency.

(c) REVIEW AND APPROVAL OF PROPOSAL.—Not later than 60 days after receiving a proposal from the head of an agency under subsection (b), the Director of the Office of Management and Budget shall approve or disapprove the proposal and notify the head of the agency of that approval or disapproval. The Director shall approve each proposal which establishes an agency Chief Financial Officer in conformance with section 901 of title 31, United States Code, as added by this Act, and which establishes a financial management structure reasonably tailored to the functions of the agency. Upon approving or disapproving a proposal of an agency under this section, the Director shall transmit to the head of the agency a written notice of that approval or disapproval.

(d) IMPLEMENTATION OF PROPOSAL.—Upon. receiving written notice of approval of a proposal under this section from the Director of the Office of Management and Budget, the head of an agency shall implement that proposal.

SEC. 207. COMPENSATION.

(a) COMPENSATION, LEVEL II.—Section 5313 of title 5, United States Code, is amended by adding at the end the following:

"Deputy Director for Management, Office of Management and Budget.".

(b) COMPENSATION, LEVEL III.—Section 5314 of title 5, United States Code, is amended by adding at the end the following:

"Controller, Office of Federal Financial Management, Office of Management and Budget.".

(c) COMPENSATION, LEVEL IV.—Section 5315 of title 5, United States Code, is amended by adding at the end the following:

"Chief Financial Officer, Department of Agriculture.

"Chief Financial Officer, Department of Commerce.

"Chief Financial Officer, Department of Defense.

"Chief Financial Officer, Department of Education.

"Chief Financial Officer, Department of Energy.

"Chief Financial Officer, Department of Health and Human Services.

"Chief Financial Officer, Department of Housing and Urban Development.

"Chief Financial Officer, Department of the Interior.

"Chief Financial Officer, Department of Justice.

"Chief Financial Officer, Department of Labor.

"Chief Financial Officer, Department of State.

"Chief Financial Officer, Department of Transportation.

"Chief Financial Officer, Department of the Treasury.

"Chief Financial Officer, Department of Veterans Affairs.

"Chief Financial Officer, Environmental Protection Agency.

"Chief Financial Officer, National Aeronautics and Space Administration."

TITLE III—ENHANCEMENT OF FEDERAL FINANCIAL MANAGEMENT ACTIVITIES

SEC. 301. FINANCIAL MANAGEMENT STATUS REPORT; 5-YEAR PLAN OF DIRECTOR OF OFFICE OF MANAGEMENT AND BUDGET.

(a) IN GENERAL.—Section. 3512 of title 31, United States Code, is amended by striking the heading thereof, redesignating subsections (a) through (f) in order as subsections (b) through (g), and by inserting before such subsection (b), as so redesignated, the following:

"§ 3512. Executive agency accounting and other financial management reports and plans

"(a)(1) The Director of the Office of Management and Budget shall prepare and submit to the appropriate committees of the Congress a financial management status report and a governmentwide 5-year financial management plan.

"(2) A financial management status report under this subsection shall include—

"(A) a description and analysis of the status of financial management in the executive branch;

"(B) a summary of the most recently completed financial, statements—

"(i) of Federal agencies under section 3515 of this title; and

"(ii) of Government corporations;

"(C) a summary of the most recently completed financial statement audits and reports—

"(i) of Federal agencies under section 3521(e) and (f) of this title; and

"(ii) of Government corporations;

"(D) a summary of reports on internal accounting and administrative control systems submitted to the President and the Congress under the amendments made by the Federal Managers' Financial Integrity Act of 1982 (Public Law 97-255); and

"(E) any other information the Director considers appropriate to fully inform the Congress regarding the financial management of the Federal Government.

"(3)(A) A governmentwide 5-year financial management plan under this subsection shall describe the activities the Director, the Deputy Director for Management, the Controller of the Office of Federal Financial Management, and agency Chief Financial Officers shall conduct over the next 5 fiscal years to improve the financial management of the Federal Government.

"(B) Each governmentwide 5-year financial management plan prepared under this subsection shall—

"(i) describe the existing financial management structure and any changes needed to establish an integrated financial management system;

"(ii) be consistent with applicable accounting principles, standards, and requirements;

"(iii) provide a strategy for developing and integrating individual agency accounting, financial information, and other financial management systems to ensure adequacy, consistency, and timeliness of financial information;

"(iv) identify and make proposals to eliminate duplicative and unnecessary systems, including encouraging agencies to share systems which have sufficient capacity to perform the functions needed;

"(v) identify projects to bring existing systems into compliance with the applicable standards and requirements;

"(vi) contain milestones for equipment acquisitions and other actions necessary to implement the 5-year plan consistent with the requirements of this section;

"(vii) identify financial management personnel needs and actions to ensure those needs are met;

"(viii) include a plan for ensuring the annual audit of financial statements of executive agencies pursuant to section 3521(h) of this title; and

"(ix) estimate the costs of implementing the governmentwide 5-year plan.

"(4)(A) Not later than 15 months after the date of the enactment of this subsection, the Director of the Office of Management and Budget shall submit the first financial management status report and governmentwide 5-year financial managagement plan under this subsection to the appropriate committees of the Congress.

"(B)(i) Not later than January 31 of each year thereafter, the Director of the Office of Management and Budget shall submit to the appropriate committees of the Congress a financial management status report and a revised governmentwide 5-year financial management plan to cover the succeeding 5 fiscal years, including a report on the accomplishments of the executive branch in implementing the plan during the preceding fiscal year.

"(ii) The Director shall include with each revised governmentwide 5-year financial management plan a description of any substantive changes in the financial statement audit plan required by paragraph (3)(B)(viii), progress made by executive agencies in implementing the audit plan, and any improvements in federal Government financial management related to preparation and audit of financial statements of executive agencies.

"(5) Not later than 30 days after receiving each annual report under section 902(a)(6) of this title, the Director shall transmit to the Chairman of the Committee on Government Operations of the House of Representatives and the Chairman of the Committee on Governmental

Affairs of the Senate a final copy of that report and any comments on the report by the Director.".

(b) CLERICAL AMENDMENT.—The table of contents at the beginning of chapter 35 of title 31, United States Code, is amended by striking the item relating to section 3512 and inserting the following:

"3512. Executive agency accounting and other financial management reports and plans.".

SEC. 302. CHIEF FINANCIAL OFFICERS COUNCIL.

(a) ESTABLISHMENT.—There is established a Chief Financial Officers Council, consisting of—

(1) the Deputy Director for Management of the Office of Management and Budget, who shall act as chairperson of the council;

(2) the Controller of the Office of Federal Financial Management of the Office of Management and Budget;

(3) the Fiscal Assistant Secretary of Treasury; and

(4) each of the agency Chief Financial Officers appointed under section 901 of title 31, United States Code, as amended by this Act.

(b) FUNCTIONS.—The Chief Financial Officers Council shall meet periodically to advise and coordinate the activities of the agencies of its members on such matters as consolidation and modernization of financial systems, improved quality of financial information, financial data and information standards, internal controls, legislation affecting financial operations and organizations, and any other financial management matter.

SEC. 303. FINANCIAL STATEMENTS OF AGENCIES.

(a) PREPARATION OF FINANCIAL STATEMENTS.—

(1) IN GENERAL.—Subchapter II of chapter 35 of title 31, United States Code, is amended by adding at the end the following:

"§ 3515. Financial statements of agencies

"(a) Not later than March 31 of 1992 and each year thereafter, the head of each executive agency identified in section 901(b) of this title shall prepare and submit to the Director of the Office of Management and Budget a financial statement for the preceding fiscal year, covering—

"(1) each revolving fund and trust fund of the agency; and

"(2) to the extent practicable, the accounts of each office, bureau, and activity of the agency which performed substantial commercial functions during the preceding fiscal year.

"(b) Each financial statement of an executive agency under this section shall reflect—

"(1) the overall financial position of the revolving funds, trust funds, offices, bureaus, and activities covered by the statement, including assets and liabilities thereof;

"(2) results of operations of those revolving funds, trust funds, offices, bureaus, and activities;

"(3) cash flows or changes in financial position of those revolving funds, trust funds, offices, bureaus, and activities; and

"(4) a reconciliation to budget reports of the executive agency for those revolving funds, trust funds, offices, bureaus, and activities.

"(c) The Director of the Office of Management and Budget shall prescribe the form and content of the financial statements of executive agencies under this section, consistent with applicable accounting principles, standards, and requirements.

"(d) For purposes of this section, the term commercial functions includes buying and leasing of real estate, providing insurance, making loans and loan guarantees, and other credit programs and any activity involving the provision of a service or thing of value for which a fee, royalty, rent, or other charge is imposed by an agency for services and things of value it provides.

"(e) Not later than March 31 of each year, the head of each executive agency designated by the President may prepare and submit to the Director of the Office of Management and Budget a financial statement for the preceding fiscal year,

(2) EFFECTIVE DATE OF SUBSECTION.—Subsection (e) of section 3515 of title 31, United States Code, as added by paragraph (1), shall take effect on the date on which a resolution described in subsection (b)(1) of this section is passed by the Congress and approved by the President.

(3) WAIVER OF REQUIREMENT.—The Director of the Office of Management and Budget may, for fiscal year 1991, waive the application of section 3515(a) of title 31, United States Code, as amended by this subsection, with respect to any revolving fund, trust fund, or account of an executive agency.

(b) RESOLUTION APPROVING DESIGNATION OF AGENCIES.—

(1) RESOLUTION DESCRIBED.—A resolution referred to in subsection (a)(2) is a joint resolution the matter after the resolving clause of which is as follows: "That the Congress approves the executive

agencies designated by the President pursuant to section 3515(e) of title 31, United States Code.".

(2) INTRODUCTION OF RESOLUTION.—No later than the first day of session following the day on which the President submits to the Congress a designation of executive agencies authorized to submit financial statements under section 3515(e) of title 31, United States Code, as added by subsection (a), a resolution as described in paragraph (1) shall be introduced (by request) in the House by the chairman of the Committee on Government Operations of the House of Representatives, or by a Member or Members of the House designated by such chairman; and shall be introduced (by request) in the Senate by the chairman of the Committee on Governmental Affairs of the Senate, or by a Member or Members of the Senate designated by such chairman.

(3) REFERRAL.—A resolution described in paragraph (1) shall be referred to the Committee on Governmental Affairs of the Senate and the Committee on Government Operations of the House (and all resolutions with respect to the same designation of executive agencies shall be referred to the same committee) by the President of the Senate or the Speaker of the House of Representatives, as the case may be. The committee shall make its recomendations to the House of Representatives or the Senate, respectively, within 60 calendar days of continuous session of the Congress following the date of such resolution's introduction.

(4) DISCHARGE OF COMMITTEE.—If the committee to which is referred a resolution introduced pursuant to paragraph (2) (or, in the absence of such a resolution, the first resolution introduced with respect to the same designation of executive agencies) has not reported such resolution or identical resolution at the end of 60 calendar days of continuous session of the Congress sfter its introduction, such committee shall be deemed to be discharged from further consideration of such resolution and such resolution shall be placed on the appropriate calendar of the House involved.

(5) PROCEDURE AFTER REPORT OR DISCHARGE OF COMMITTEE; VOTE ON FINAL PASSAGE.—(A) When the committee has reported, or has been deemed to be discharged (under paragraph (4)) from further consideration of, a resolution described in paragraph (1), it is at any time thereafter in order (even though a previous motion to the same effect has been disagreed to) for any Member of the respective House to move to proceed to the considerationof the resolution. The motion is highly priviliged and is not debatable. The motion shall not be subject to adjournment, or to a motion to postpone, or a motion to proceed to the consideration of other business. A motion to reconsider the vote by which the motion is agreed to or disagreed to

shall not be in order. If a motion to proceed to the consideration of the resolution is agreed to, the resolution shall remain the unfinished business of the respective House until disposed of.

(B) Debate on the resolution, and on all debatable motions and appeals in connection therewith, shall be limited to not more than 10 hours, which shall be divided equally between individuals favoring and individuals opposing the resolution. A motion further to limit debate is in order and not dabatable. An amendment to, or a motion to postpone, or a motion to proceed to the consideration of other business, or a motion to recommit the resolution is not in order. A motion to reconsider the vote by which the resolution is passed or rejected shall not be in order.

(C) Immediately following the conclusion of the debate on the resolution and a single quorum call at the conclusion of the debate if requested in accordance with the rules of the appropriate House, the vote on final passage of the resolution shall occur.

(D) Appeals from the decisions of the Chair relating to the application of the rules of the Senate or the House of Representatives, as the case may be, to the procedure relating to a resolution described in paragraph (1), shall be decided without debate.

(E) If, prior to the passage by one House of a resolution of that House, that House receives a resolution with respect to the same designation of executive agencies from the other House, then—

(i) the procedure in that House shall be the same as if no resolution had been received from the other House; but

(ii) the vote on final passage shall be on the resolution of the other House.

(F) It shall not be in order in either the House of Representatives or the Senate to consider a resolution described in paragraph (1), or to consider any conference report on such a resolution, unless the Director of the Office of Management and Budget submits to the Congress a report under subsection (e).

(c) REPORT ON SUBSTANTIAL COMMERCIAL FUNCTIONS.—Not later than 180 days after the date of the enactment of this Act, the Director of the Office of Management and Budget shall determine and report to the Congress on which executive agencies or parts thereof perform substantial commercial functions for which financial statements can be prepared practicably under section 3515 of title 31, United States Code, as added by this section.

(d) PILOT PROJECT.—(1) Not later than March 31 of each of 1991, 1992, and 1993, the head of the Departments of Agriculture, Labor, and Veterans Affairs, the General Services Administration, and the Social Security Administration shall each prepare and submit to the Director of the Office of Management and Budget financial statements for the preceding fiscal year for the accounts of all of the offices, bureaus, and activities of that department or administration.

(2) Not later than March 31 of each of 1992 and 1993, the head of the Departments of Housing and Urban Development and the Army shall prepare and submit to the Director of the Office of Management and Budget financial statements for the preceding fiscal year for the accounts of all of the offices, bureaus, and activities of the department.

(3) Not later than March 31, 1993, the head of the Department of the Air Force, the Internal Revenue Service, and the United States Customs Service, shall each prepare and submit to the Director of the Office of Management and Budget financial statements for the preceding fiscal year for the accounts of all of the offices, bureaus, and activities of that department or service.

(4) Each financial statement prepared under this subsection shall be audited in accordance with section 3521(e), (f), (g), and (h) of title 31, United States Code.

(e) REPORT ON INITIAL FINANCIAL STATEMENTS.—Not later than June 30, 1993, the Director of the Office of Management and Budget shall report to the Congress on the financial statements prepared for fiscal years 1990, 1991, and 1992 under subsection (a) of section 3515 of title 31, United States Code (as added by subsection (a) of this section) and under subsection (d) of this section. The report shall include analysis of—

(1) the accuracy of the data included in the financial statements;

(2) the difficulties each department and agency encountered in preparing the data included in the financial statements;

(3) the benefits derived from the preparation of the financial statements; and

(4) the cost associated with preparing and auditing the financial statements, including a description of any activities that were foregone as a result of that preparation and auditing.

(f) CLERICAL AMENDMENT.—The table of sections at the beginning of chapter 35 of title 31, United States Code, is amended by inserting after the item relating to section 3514 the following:

"3515. Financial statements of agencies.".

SEC. 304. FINANCIAL AUDITS OF AGENCIES.

(a) IN GENERAL.—Section 3521 of title 31, United States Code, is amended by adding at the end the following new subsections:

"(e) Each financial statement prepared under section 3515 by an agency shall be audited in accordance with applicable generally accepted government auditing standards—

"(1) in the case of an agency having an Inspector General appointed under the Inspector General Act of 1978 (5 U.S.C. App.), by the Inspector General or by an independent external auditor, as determined by the Inspector General of the agency; and

"(2) in any other case, by an independent external auditor, as determined by the head of the agency.

"(f) Not later than June 30 following the fiscal year for which a financial statement is submitted under section 3515 of this title by an agency, the person who audits the statement for purpose of subsection (e) shall submit a report on the audit to the head of the agency. A report under this subsection shall be prepared in accordance with generally accepted government auditing standards.

"(g) The Comptroller General of the United States—

"(1) may review any audit of a financial statement conducted under this subsection by an Inspector General or an external auditor;

"(2) shall report to the Congress, the Director of the Office of Management and Budget, and the head of the agency which prepared the statement, regarding the results of the review and make any recommendation the Comptroller General considers appropriate; and

"(3) may audit a financial statement prepared under section 3515 of this title at the discretion of the Comptroller General or at the request of a committee of the Congress.

An audit the Comptroller General performs under this subsection shall be in lieu of the audit otherwise required by subsection (e) of this section. Prior to performing such audit, the Comptroller General shall consult with the Inspector General of the agency which prepared the statement.

"(h) Each financial statement prepared by an executive agency for a fiscal year after fiscal year 1991 shall be audited in accordance with this section and the plan required by section 3512(a)(3)(B)(viii) of this title.".

(b) WAIVER OF REQUIREMENTS.—The Director of the Office of Management and Budget may waive application of subsections (e) and (f) of section 3521 of title 31, United States Code, as amended by this section, to a financial statement submitted by an agency for fiscal years 1990 and 1991.

SEC. 305. FINANCIAL AUDITS OF GOVERNMENT CORPORATIONS.

Section 9105 of title 31, United States Code, is amended to read as follows:

§ 9105. Audits

"(1) The financial statements of Government corporations shall be audited by the Inspector General of the corporation appointed under the Inspector General Act of 1978 (5 U.S.C. App.) or by an independent external auditor, as determined by the Inspector General or, if there is no Inspector General, by the head of the corporation.

"(2) Audits under this section shall be conducted in accordance with applicable generally accepted government auditing standards.

"(3) Upon completion of the audit required by this subsection, the person who audits the statement shall submit a report on the audit to the head of the Government corporation, to the Chairman of the Committee on Government Operations of the House of Representatives, and to the Chairman of the Committee on Governmental Affairs of the Senate.

"(4) The Comptroller General of the United States—

"(A) may review any audit of a financial statement conducted under this subsection by an Inspector General or an external auditor;

"(B) shall report to the Congress, the Director of the Office of Management and Budget, and the head of the Government corporation which prepared the statement, regarding the results of the review and make any recommendation the Comptroller General of the United States considers appropriate; and

"(C) may audit a financial statement of a Government corporation at the discretion of the Comptroller General or at the request of a committee of the Congress.

An audit the Comptroller General performs under this paragraph shall be in lieu of the audit otherwise required by paragraph (1) of this subsection. Prior to performing such audit, the Comptroller General shall consult with the Inspector General of the xxx which prepared the statement.

"(5) A Government corporation shall reimburse the Comptroller General of the United States for the full cost of any audit conducted by the Comptroller General under this subsection, as determined by the Comptroller General. All reimbursements received under this paragraph by the Comptroller General of the United States shall be deposited in the Treasury as miscellaneous receipts.

"(b) Upon request of the Comptroller General of the United States, a Government corporation shall provide to the Comptroller General of the United States all books, accounts, financial records, reports, files, workpapers, and property belongings to or in use by the Government corporation and its auditor that the Comptroller General of the United States considers necessary to the performance of any audit or review under this section.

"(c) Activities of the Comptroller General of the United States under this section are in lieu of any audit of the financial transactions of a Government corporation that the Comptroller General is required to make under any other law."

SEC. 306. MANAGEMENT REPORTS OF GOVERNMENT CORPORATIONS.

(a) IN GENERAL.—Section 9106 of title 31, United States Code, is amended to read as follows:

§ 9106. Management reports

"(a)(1) A Government corporation shall submit an annual management report to the Congress not later than 180 days after the end of the Government corporation's fiscal year.

"(2) A management report under this subsection shall include—

"(A) a statement of financial position;

"(B) a statement of operations;

"(C) a statement of cash flows;

"(D) a reconciliation to the budget report of the Government corporation. if applicable;

"(E) a statement on internal accounting and administrative control systems by the head of the management of the corporation, consistent with the requirements for agency statements on internal accounting and administrative control systems under the amendments made by the Federal Managers' Financial Integrity Act of 1982 (Public Law 97-255);

"(F) the report resulting from an audit of the financial statements of the corporation conducted under section 9105 of this title; and

"(G) any other comments and information necessary to inform the Congress about the operations and financial condition of the corporation.

"(b) A Government corporation shall provide the President, the Director of the Office of Management and Budget, and the Comptroller General of the United States a copy of the management report when it is submitted to Congress.".

(b) CLERICAL AMENDMENT.—The table of sections for chapter 91 of title 31, United States Code, is amended by striking the item relating to section 9106 and inserting the following:

"9106. Management reports.".

SEC. 307. ADOPTION OF CAPITAL ACCOUNTING STANDARDS.

No capital accounting standard or principle, including any human capital standard or principle, shall be adopted for use in an executive department or agency until such standard has been reported to the Congress and a period of 45 days of continuous session of the Congress has expired.

Approved November 15, 1990.

543

APPENDIX C

Office of Management and Budget

Circular No. A-133

62 FR 35278, June 30, 1997

Subject: Audits of States, Local Governments, and Non-Profit Organizations

Subpart A—General

1. Purpose. This part sets forth standards for obtaining consistency and uniformity among Federal agencies for the audit of non-Federal entities expending Federal awards.

2. Definitions. *Auditee* means any non-Federal entity that expends Federal awards which must be audited under this part.

Auditor means an auditor, that is a public accountant or a Federal, State or local government audit organization, which meets the general standards specified in generally accepted government auditing standards (GAGAS). The term *auditor* does not include internal auditors of non-profit organizations.

Audit finding means deficiencies which the auditor is required by §—.510(a) to report in the schedule of findings and questioned costs.

CFDA number means the number assigned to a Federal program in the *Catalog of Federal Domestic Assistance* (CFDA).

Cluster of programs means a grouping of closely related programs that share common compliance requirements. The types of clusters of programs are research and development (R&D), student financial aid (SFA), and other clusters. "Other clusters" are as defined by the Office of Management and Budget (OMB) in the compliance supplement or as designated by a State for Federal awards the State provides to its subrecipients that meet the definition of a cluster of programs. When designating an "other cluster," a State shall identify the Federal awards included in the cluster and advise the subrecipients of compliance requirements applicable to the cluster, consistent with §—.400(d)(1) and §—.400(d)(2), respectively. A cluster of programs shall be considered as one program for determining major programs, as described in §—.520, and, with the exception of R&D as described in §—.200(c), whether a program-specific audit may be elected.

Cognizant agency for audit means the Federal agency designated to carry out the responsibilities described in §—.400(a).

544   Government Auditing: Standards and Practices

Compliance supplement refers to the *Circular A-133 Compliance Supplement*, included as Appendix B to Circular A-133, or such documents as OMB or its designee may issue to replace it.

This document is available from the Government Printing Office, Superintendent of Documents, Washington, DC 20402-9325.

Corrective action means action taken by the auditee that:

(1) Corrects identified deficiencies;

(2) Produces recommended improvements; or

(3) Demonstrates that audit findings are either invalid or do not warrant auditee action.

Federal agency has the same meaning as the term *agency* in Section 551(1) of title 5, United States Code.

Federal award means Federal financial assistance and Federal cost-reimbursement contracts that non-Federal entities receive directly from Federal awarding agencies or indirectly from pass-through entities. It does not include procurement contracts, under grants or contracts, used to buy goods or services from vendors. Any audits of such vendors shall be covered by the terms and conditions of the contract. Contracts to operate Federal Government owned, contractor operated facilities (GOCOs) are excluded from the requirements of this part.

Federal awarding agency means the Federal agency that provides an award directly to the recipient.

Federal financial assistance means assistance that non-Federal entities receive or administer in the form of grants, loans, loan guarantees, property (including donated surplus property), cooperative agreements, interest subsidies, insurance, food commodities, direct appropriations, and other assistance, but does not include amounts received as reimbursement for services rendered to individuals as described in § __.205(h) and § __.205(i).

Federal program means:

(1) All Federal awards to a non-Federal entity assigned a single number in the CFDA.

(2) When no CFDA number is assigned, all Federal awards from the same agency made for the same purpose should be combined and considered one program.

(3) Notwithstanding paragraphs **(1)** and **(2)** of this definition, a cluster of programs. The types of clusters of programs are:

(i) Research and development (R&D);

(ii) Student financial aid (SFA); and

(iii) "Other clusters," as described in the definition of cluster of programs in this section.

GAGAS means generally accepted government auditing standards issued by the Comptroller General of the United States, which are applicable to financial audits.

Generally accepted accounting principles has the meaning specified in generally accepted auditing standards issued by the American Institute of Certified Public Accountants (AICPA).

Indian tribe means any Indian tribe, band, nation, or other organized group or community, including any Alaskan Native village or regional or village corporation (as defined in, or established under, the Alaskan Native Claims Settlement Act) that is recognized by the United States as eligible for the special programs and services provided by the United States to Indians because of their status as Indians.

Internal control means a process, effected by an entity's management and other personnel, designed to provide reasonable assurance regarding the achievement of objectives in the following categories:

(1) Effectiveness and efficiency of operations;

(2) Reliability of financial reporting; and

(3) Compliance with applicable laws and regulations.

Internal control pertaining to the compliance requirements for Federal programs (Internal control over Federal programs) means a process—effected by an entity's management and other personnel—designed to provide reasonable assurance regarding the achievement of the following objectives for Federal programs:

(1) Transactions are properly recorded and accounted for to:

(i) Permit the preparation of reliable financial statements and Federal reports;

(ii) Maintain accountability over assets; and

(iii) Demonstrate compliance with laws, regulations, and other compliance requirements;

(2) Transactions are executed in compliance with:

(i) Laws, regulations, and the provisions of contracts or grant agreements that could have a direct and material effect on a Federal program; and

(ii) Any other laws and regulations that are identified in the compliance supplement; and

(3) Funds, property, and other assets are safeguarded against loss from unauthorized use or disposition.

Loan means a Federal loan or loan guarantee received or administered by a non-Federal entity.

Local government means any unit of local government within a State, including a county, borough, municipality, city, town, township, parish, local public authority, special district, school district, intrastate district, council of governments, and any other instrumentality of local government.

Major program means a Federal program determined by the auditor to be a major program in accordance with § __.520 or a program identified as a major program by a Federal agency or pass-through entity in accordance with § __.215(c).

Management decision means the evaluation by the Federal awarding agency or pass-through entity of the audit findings and corrective action plan and the issuance of a written decision as to what corrective action is necessary.

Non-Federal entity means a State, local government, or non-profit organization.

Non-profit organization means:

(1) any corporation, trust, association, cooperative, or other organization that:

(i) Is operated primarily for scientific, educational, service, charitable, or similar purposes in the public interest;

(ii) Is not organized primarily for profit; and

(iii) Uses its net proceeds to maintain, improve, or expand its operations; and

(2) The term *non-profit organization* includes non-profit institutions of higher education and hospitals.

OMB means the Executive Office of the President, Office of Management and Budget.

Oversight agency for audit means the Federal awarding agency that provides the predominant amount of direct funding to a recipient not assigned a cognizant agency for audit. When there is no direct funding, the Federal agency with the predominant indirect funding shall assume the oversight responsibilities. The duties of the oversight agency for audit are described in § __.400(b).

Pass-through entity means a non-Federal entity that provides a Federal award to a subrecipient to carry out a Federal program.

Program-specific audit means an audit of one Federal program as provided for in § __.200(c) and § __.235.

Questioned cost means a cost that is questioned by the auditor because of an audit finding:

(1) Which resulted from a violation or possible violation of a provision of a law, regulation, contract, grant, cooperative agreement, or other agreement or document governing the use of Federal funds, including funds used to match Federal funds;

(2) Where the costs, at the time of the audit, are not supported by adequate documentation; or

(3) Where the costs incurred appear unreasonable and do not reflect the actions a prudent person would take in the circumstances.

Recipient means a non-Federal entity that expends Federal awards received directly from a Federal awarding agency to carry out a Federal program.

Research and development (R&D) means all research activities, both basic and applied, and all development activities that are performed by a non-Federal entity. *Research* is defined as a systematic study directed toward fuller scientific knowledge or understanding of the subject studied. The term research also includes activities involving the training of individuals in research techniques where such activities utilize the same facilities as other research and development activities and where such activities are not included in the instruction function. *Development* is the systematic use of knowledge and understanding gained from research directed toward the production of useful materials, devices, systems, or methods, including design and development of prototypes and processes.

Single audit means an audit which includes both the entity's financial statements and the Federal awards as described in § __.500.

State means any State of the United States, the District of Columbia, the Commonwealth of Puerto Rico, the Virgin Islands, Guam, American Samoa, the Commonwealth of the Northern Mariana Islands, and the Trust Territory of the Pacific Islands, any instrumentality thereof, any multi-State, regional, or interstate entity which has governmental functions, and any Indian tribe as defined in this section.

Student Financial Aid (SFA) includes those programs of general student assistance, such as those authorized by Title IV of the Higher Education Act of 1965, as amended, (20 U.S.C. 1070 *et seq.*) which is administered by the U.S. Department of Education, and similar programs provided by other Federal agencies. It does not include programs which provide fellowships or similar Federal awards to students on a competitive basis, or for specified studies or research.

Subrecipient means a non-Federal entity that expends Federal awards received from a pass-through entity to carry out a Federal program, but does not include an individual that is a beneficiary of such a program. A subrecipient may also be a recipient of other Federal awards directly from a Federal awarding agency. Guidance on distinguishing between a subrecipient and a vendor is provided in § __.210.

Types of compliance requirements refers to the types of compliance requirements listed in the compliance supplement. Examples include: activities allowed or unallowed; allowable costs/cost principles; cash management; eligibility; matching, level of effort, earmarking; and, reporting.

Vendor means a dealer, distributor, merchant, or other seller providing goods or services that are required for the conduct of a Federal program. These goods or services may be for an organization's own use or for the use of beneficiaries of the Federal program. Additional guidance on distinguishing between a subrecipient and a vendor is provided in § __.210.

Subpart B—Audits

3. Audit requirements.

(a) *Audit required.* Non-Federal entities that expend $300,000 or more in a year in Federal awards shall have a single or program-specific audit conducted for that year in accordance with the provisions of this part. Guidance on determining Federal awards expended is provided in § __.205.

(b) *Single audit.* Non-Federal entities that expend $300,000 or more in a year in Federal awards shall have a single audit conducted in accordance with § __.500 except when they elect to have a program-specific audit conducted in accordance with paragraph **(c)** of this section.

(c) *Program-specific audit election.* When an auditee expends Federal awards under only one Federal program (excluding R&D) and the Federal program's laws, regulations, or grant agreements do not require a financial statement audit of the auditee, the auditee may elect to have a program-specific audit conducted in accordance with § __.235. A program-specific audit may not be elected for R&D unless all of the Federal awards expended were received from the same Federal agency, or the same Federal agency and the same pass-through entity, and that Federal agency, or pass-through entity in the case of a subrecipient, approves in advance a program-specific audit.

(d) *Exemption when Federal awards expended are less than $300,000.* Non-Federal entities that expend less than $300,000 a year in Federal awards are exempt from Federal audit requirements for that year, except as noted in § __.215(a), but records must be available for review or audit by appropriate officials of the Federal agency, pass-through entity, and General Accounting Office (GAO).

(e) *Federally Funded Research and Development Centers (FFRDC)*. Management of an auditee that owns or operates a FFRDC may elect to treat the FFRDC as a separate entity for purposes of this part.

4. Basis for determining Federal awards expended.

(a) *Determining Federal awards expended.* The determination of when an award is expended should be based on when the activity related to the award occurs. Generally, the activity pertains to events that require the non-Federal entity to comply with laws, regulations, and the provisions of contracts or grant agreements, such as: expenditure/expense transactions associated with grants, cost-reimbursement contracts, cooperative agreements, and direct appropriations; the disbursement of funds passed through to subrecipients; the use of loan proceeds under loan and loan guarantee programs; the receipt of property; the receipt of surplus property; the receipt or use of program income; the distribution or consumption of food commodities; the disbursement of amounts entitling the non-Federal entity to an interest subsidy; and, the period when insurance is in force.

(b) *Loan and loan guarantees (loans)*. Since the Federal Government is at risk for loans until the debt is repaid, the following guidelines shall be used to calculate the value of Federal awards expended under loan programs, except as noted in paragraphs **(c)** and **(d)** of this section:

(1) Value of new loans made or received during the fiscal year; plus

(2) Balance of loans from previous years for which the Federal Government imposes continuing compliance requirements; plus

(3) Any interest subsidy, cash, or administrative cost allowance received.

(c) *Loan and loan guarantees (loans) at institutions of higher education.* When loans are made to students of an institution of higher education but the institution does not make the loans, then only the value of loans made during the year shall be considered Federal awards expended in that year. The balance of loans for previous years is not included as Federal awards expended because the lender accounts for the prior balances.

(d) *Prior loan and loan guarantees (loans)*. Loans, the proceeds of which were received and expended in prior-years, are not considered Federal awards expended under this part when the laws, regulations, and the provisions of contracts or grant agreements pertaining to such loans impose no continuing compliance requirements other than to repay the loans.

(e) *Endowment funds.* The cumulative balance of Federal awards for endowment funds which are federally restricted are considered awards expended in each year in which the funds are still restricted.

(f) *Free rent.* Free rent received by itself is not considered a Federal award expended under this part. However, free rent received as part of an award to carry out a Federal program shall be included in determining Federal awards expended and subject to audit under this part.

(g) *Valuing non-cash assistance.* Federal non-cash assistance, such as free rent, food stamps, food commodities, donated property, or donated surplus property, shall be valued at fair market value at the time of receipt or the assessed value provided by the Federal agency.

(h) *Medicare.* Medicare payments to a non-Federal entity for providing patient care services to Medicare eligible individuals are not considered Federal awards expended under this part.

(i) *Medicaid.* Medicaid payments to a subrecipient for providing patient care services to Medicaid eligible individuals are not considered Federal awards expended under this part unless a State requires the funds to be treated as Federal awards expended because reimbursement is on a cost-reimbursement basis.

(j) *Certain loans provided by the National Credit Union Administration.* For purposes of this part, loans made from the National Credit Union Share Insurance Fund and the Central Liquidity Facility that are funded by contributions from insured institutions are not considered Federal awards expended.

5. Subrecipient and vendor determinations.

(a) *General.* An auditee may be a recipient, a subrecipient, and a vendor. Federal awards expended as a recipient or a subrecipient would be subject to audit under this part. The payments received for goods or services provided as a vendor would not be considered Federal awards. The guidance in paragraphs **(b)** and **(c)** of this section should be considered in determining whether payments constitute a Federal award or a payment for goods and services.

(b) *Federal award.* Characteristics indicative of a Federal award received by a subrecipient are when the organization:

(1) Determines who is eligible to receive what Federal financial assistance;

(2) Has its performance measured against whether the objectives of the Federal program are met;

(3) Has responsibility for programmatic decision making;

(4) Has responsibility for adherence to applicable Federal program compliance requirements; and

(5) Uses the Federal funds to carry out a program of the organization as compared to providing goods or services for a program of the pass-through entity.

(c) *Payment for goods and services.* Characteristics indicative of a payment for goods and services received by a vendor are when the organization:

(1) Provides the goods and services within normal business operations;

(2) Provides similar goods or services to many different purchasers;

(3) Operates in a competitive environment;

(4) Provides goods or services that are ancillary to the operation of the Federal program; and

(5) Is not subject to compliance requirements of the Federal program.

(d) *Use of judgment in making determination.* There may be unusual circumstances or exceptions to the listed characteristics. In making the determination of whether a subrecipient or vendor relationship exists, the substance of the relationship is more important than the form of the agreement. It is not expected that all of the characteristics will be present and judgment should be used in determining whether an entity is a subrecipient or vendor.

(e) *For-profit subrecipient.* Since this part does not apply to for-profit subrecipients, the pass-through entity is responsible for establishing requirements, as necessary, to ensure compliance by for-profit subrecipients. The contract with the for-profit subrecipient should describe applicable compliance requirements and the for-profit subrecipient's compliance responsibility. Methods to ensure compliance for Federal awards made to for-profit subrecipients may include pre-award audits, monitoring during the contract, and post-award audits.

(f) *Compliance responsibility for vendors.* In most cases, the auditee's compliance responsibility for vendors is only to ensure that the procurement, receipt, and payment for goods and services comply with laws, regulations, and the provisions of contracts or grant agreements. Program compliance requirements normally do not pass through to vendors. However, the auditee is responsible for ensuring compliance for vendor transactions which are structured such that the vendor is responsible for program compliance or the vendor's records must be reviewed to determine program compliance. Also, when these vendor transactions relate to a major program, the scope of the audit shall include determining whether these transactions are in compliance with laws, regulations, and the provisions of contracts or grant agreements.

6. Relation to other audit requirements.

(a) *Audit under this part in lieu of other audits.* An audit made in accordance with this part shall be in lieu of any financial audit required under individual Federal awards. To the extent this audit meets a Federal agency's needs, it shall rely upon and use such audits. The provisions of this part neither limit the authority of Federal agencies, including their Inspectors General, or GAO to conduct or arrange for additional audits (e.g., financial audits, performance audits, evaluations, inspections, or reviews) nor authorize any auditee to constrain Federal agencies from carrying out additional audits. Any additional audits shall be planned and performed in such a way as to build upon work performed by other auditors.

(b) *Federal agency to pay for additional audits.* A Federal agency that conducts or contracts for additional audits shall, consistent with other applicable laws and regulations, arrange for funding the full cost of such additional audits.

(c) *Request for a program to be audited as a major program.* A Federal agency may request an auditee to have a particular Federal program audited as a major program in lieu of the Federal agency conducting or arranging for the additional audits. To allow for planning, such requests should be made at least 180 days prior to the end of the fiscal year to be audited. The auditee, after consultation with its auditor, should promptly respond to such request by informing the Federal agency whether the program would otherwise be audited as a major program using the risk-based audit approach described in § __.520 and, if not, the estimated incremental cost. The Federal agency shall then promptly confirm to the auditee whether it wants the program audited as a major program. If the program is to be audited as a major program based upon this Federal agency request, and the Federal agency agrees to pay the full incremental costs, then the auditee shall have the program audited as a major program. A pass-through entity may use the provisions of this paragraph for a subrecipient.

7. Frequency of audits. Except for the provisions for biennial audits provided in paragraphs **(a)** and **(b)** of this section, audits required by this part shall be performed annually. Any biennial audit shall cover both years within the biennial period.

(a) A State or local government that is required by constitution or statute, in effect on January 1, 1987, to undergo its audits less frequently than annually, is permitted to undergo its audits pursuant to this part biennially. This requirement must still be in effect for the biennial period under audit.

(b) Any non-profit organization that had biennial audits for all biennial periods ending between July 1, 1992, and January 1, 1995, is permitted to undergo its audits pursuant to this part biennially.

8. Sanctions. No audit costs may be charged to Federal awards when audits required by this part have not been made or have been made but not in accordance with this part. In cases of continued inability or unwillingness to have an audit conducted in accordance with this part, Federal agencies and pass-through entities shall take appropriate action using sanctions such as:

(a) Withholding a percentage of Federal awards until the audit is completed satisfactorily;

(b) Withholding or disallowing overhead costs;

(c) Suspending Federal awards until the audit is conducted; or

(d) Terminating the Federal award.

9. Audit costs.

(a) *Allowable costs.* Unless prohibited by law, the cost of audits made in accordance with the provisions of this part are allowable charges to Federal awards. The charges may be considered a direct cost or an allocated indirect cost, as determined in accordance with the provisions of applicable OMB cost principles circulars, the Federal Acquisition Regulation (FAR) (48 CFR parts 30 and 31), or other applicable cost principles or regulations.

(b) *Unallowable costs.* A non-Federal entity shall not charge the following to a Federal award:

(1) The cost of any audit under the Single Audit Act Amendments of 1996 (31 U.S.C. 7501 *et seq.*) not conducted in accordance with this part.

(2) The cost of auditing a non-Federal entity which has Federal awards expended of less than $300,000 per year and is thereby exempted under §___.200(d) from having an audit conducted under this part. However, this does not prohibit a pass-through entity from charging Federal awards for the cost of limited scope audits to monitor its subrecipients in accordance with §___.400(d)(3), provided the subrecipient does not have a single audit. For purposes of this part, limited scope audits only include agreed-upon procedures engagements conducted in accordance with either the AICPA's generally accepted auditing standards or attestation standards, that are paid for and arranged by a pass-through entity and address only one or more of the following types of compliance requirements: activities allowed or unal-

lowed; allowable costs/cost principles; eligibility; matching, level of effort, earmarking; and, reporting.

10. Program-specific audits.

(a) *Program-specific audit guide available.* In many cases, a program-specific audit guide will be available to provide specific guidance to the auditor with respect to internal control, compliance requirements, suggested audit procedures, and audit reporting requirements. The auditor should contact the Office of Inspector General of the Federal agency to determine whether such a guide is available. When a current program-specific audit guide is available, the auditor shall follow GAGAS and the guide when performing a program-specific audit.

(b) *Program-specific audit guide not available.* (1) When a program-specific audit guide is not available, the auditee and auditor shall have basically the same responsibilities for the Federal program as they would have for an audit of a major program in a single audit.

(2) The auditee shall prepare the financial statement(s) for the Federal program that includes, at a minimum, a schedule of expenditures of Federal awards for the program and notes that describe the significant accounting policies used in preparing the schedule, a summary schedule of prior audit findings consistent with the requirements of § ___.315(b), and a corrective action plan consistent with the requirements of § ___.315(c).

(3) The auditor shall:

(i) Perform an audit of the financial statement(s) for the Federal program in accordance with GAGAS;

(ii) Obtain an understanding of internal control and perform tests of internal control over the Federal program consistent with the requirements of § ___.500(c) for a major program;

(iii) Perform procedures to determine whether the auditee has complied with laws, regulations, and the provisions of contracts or grant agreements that could have a direct and material effect on the Federal program consistent with the requirements of § ___.500(d) for a major program; and

(iv) Follow up on prior audit findings, perform procedures to assess the reasonableness of the summary schedule of prior audit findings prepared by the auditee, and report, as a current year audit finding, when the auditor concludes that the summary schedule of prior audit findings materially misrepresents the status of any prior audit finding in accordance with the requirements of § ___.500(e).

(4) The auditor's report(s) may be in the form of either combined or separate reports and may be organized differently from the manner

presented in this section. The auditor's report(s) shall state that the audit was conducted in accordance with this part and include the following:

(i) An opinion (or disclaimer of opinion) as to whether the financial statement(s) of the Federal program is presented fairly in all material respects in conformity with the stated accounting policies;

(ii) A report on internal control related to the Federal program, which shall describe the scope of testing of internal control and the results of the tests;

(iii) A report on compliance which includes an opinion (or disclaimer of opinion) as to whether the auditee complied with laws, regulations, and the provisions of contracts or grant agreements which could have a direct and material effect on the Federal program; and

(iv) A schedule of findings and questioned costs for the Federal program that includes a summary of the auditor's results relative to the Federal program in a format consistent with § __.505(d)(1) and findings and questioned costs consistent with the requirements of § __.505(d)(3).

(c) *Report submission for program-specific audits.* (1) The audit shall be completed and the reporting required by paragraph **(c)(2)** or **(c)(3)** of this section submitted within the earlier of 30 days after receipt of the auditor's report(s), or nine months after the end of the audit period, unless a longer period is agreed to in advance by the Federal agency that provided the funding or a different period is specified in a program-specific audit guide. (However, for fiscal years beginning on or before June 30, 1998, the audit shall be completed and the required reporting shall be submitted within the earlier of 30 days after receipt of the auditor's report(s), or 13 months after the end of the audit period, unless a different period is specified in a program-specific audit guide.) Unless restricted by law or regulation, the auditee shall make report copies available for public inspection.

(2) When a program-specific audit guide is available, the auditee shall submit to the Federal clearinghouse designated by OMB the data collection form prepared in accordance with § __.320(b), as applicable to a program-specific audit, and the reporting required by the program-specific audit guide to be retained as an archival copy. Also, the auditee shall submit to the Federal awarding agency or pass-through entity the reporting required by the program-specific audit guide.

(3) When a program-specific audit guide is not available, the reporting package for a program-specific audit shall consist of the financial statement(s) of the Federal program, a summary schedule of prior audit findings, and a corrective action plan as described in paragraph **(b)(2)** of this section, and the auditor's report(s) described

in paragraph **(b)(4)** of this section. The data collection form prepared in accordance with § __.320(b), as applicable to a program-specific audit, and one copy of this reporting package shall be submitted to the Federal clearinghouse designated by OMB to be retained as an archival copy. Also, when the schedule of findings and questioned costs disclosed audit findings or the summary schedule of prior audit findings reported the status of any audit findings, the auditee shall submit one copy of the reporting package to the Federal clearinghouse on behalf of the Federal awarding agency, or directly to the pass-through entity in the case of a subrecipient. Instead of submitting the reporting package to the pass-through entity, when a subrecipient is not required to submit a reporting package to the pass-through entity, the subrecipient shall provide written notification to the pass-through entity, consistent with the requirements of § __.320(e)(2). A subrecipient may submit a copy of the reporting package to the pass-through entity to comply with this notification requirement.

(d) *Other sections of this part may apply.* Program-specific audits are subject to § __.100 through § __.215(b), § __.220 through § __.230, § __.300 through § __.305, § __.315, § __.320(f) through § __.320(j), § __.400 through § __.405, § __.510 through § __.515, and other referenced provisions of this part unless contrary to the provisions of this section, a program-specific audit guide, or program laws and regulations.

Subpart C—Auditees

11. Auditee responsibilities. The auditee shall:

(a) Identify, in its accounts, all Federal awards received and expended and the Federal programs under which they were received. Federal program and award identification shall include, as applicable, the CFDA title and number, award number and year, name of the Federal agency, and name of the pass-through entity.

(b) Maintain internal control over Federal programs that provides reasonable assurance that the auditee is managing Federal awards in compliance with laws, regulations, and the provisions of contracts or grant agreements that could have a material effect on each of its Federal programs.

(c) Comply with laws, regulations, and the provisions of contracts or grant agreements related to each of its Federal programs.

(d) Prepare appropriate financial statements, including the schedule of expenditures of Federal awards in accordance with § __.310.

(e) Ensure that the audits required by this part are properly performed and submitted when due. When extensions to the report submission due date required by § __.320(a) are granted by the cognizant or oversight agency for audit, promptly notify the Federal clearinghouse designated by OMB and each pass-through entity providing Federal awards of the extension.

(f) Follow up and take corrective action on audit findings, including preparation of a summary schedule of prior audit findings and a corrective action plan in accordance with § ___.315(b) and § ___.315(c), respectively.

12. Auditor selection.

(a) *Auditor procurement.* In procuring audit services, auditees shall follow the procurement standards prescribed by the Grants Management Common Rule (hereinafter referred to as the "A-102 Common Rule") published March 11, 1988 and amended April 19, 1995 [insert appropriate CFR citation], Circular A-110, "Uniform Administrative Requirements for Grants and Agreements with Institutions of Higher Education, Hospitals and Other Non-Profit Organizations," or the FAR (48 CFR part 42), as applicable (OMB Circulars are available from the Office of Administration, Publications Office, room 2200, New Executive Office Building, Washington, DC 20503). Whenever possible, auditees shall make positive efforts to utilize small businesses, minority-owned firms, and women's business enterprises, in procuring audit services as stated in the A-102 Common Rule, OMB Circular A-110, or the FAR (48 CFR part 42), as applicable. In requesting proposals for audit services, the objectives and scope of the audit should be made clear. Factors to be considered in evaluating each proposal for audit services include the responsiveness to the request for proposal, relevant experience, availability of staff with professional qualifications and technical abilities, the results of external quality control reviews, and price.

(b) *Restriction on auditor preparing indirect cost proposals.* An auditor who prepares the indirect cost proposal or cost allocation plan may not also be selected to perform the audit required by this part when the indirect costs recovered by the auditee during the prior year exceeded $1 million. This restriction applies to the base year used in the preparation of the indirect cost proposal or cost allocation plan and any subsequent years in which the resulting indirect cost agreement or cost allocation plan is used to recover costs. To minimize any disruption in existing contracts for audit services, this paragraph applies to audits of fiscal years beginning after June 30, 1998.

(c) *Use of Federal auditors.* Federal auditors may perform all or part of the work required under this part if they comply fully with the requirements of this part.

558   Government Auditing: Standards and Practices

13. Financial statements.

(a) *Financial statements.* The auditee shall prepare financial statements that reflect its financial position, results of operations or changes in net assets, and, where appropriate, cash flows for the fiscal year audited. The financial statements shall be for the same organizational unit and fiscal year that is chosen to meet the requirements of this part. However, organization-wide financial statements may also include departments, agencies, and other organizational units that have separate audits in accordance with § __.500(a) and prepare separate financial statements.

(b) *Schedule of expenditures of Federal awards.* The auditee shall also prepare a schedule of expenditures of Federal awards for the period covered by the auditee's financial statements. While not required, the auditee may choose to provide information requested by Federal awarding agencies and pass-through entities to make the schedule easier to use. For example, when a Federal program has multiple award years, the auditee may list the amount of Federal awards expended for each award year separately. At a minimum, the schedule shall:

(1) List individual Federal programs by Federal agency. For Federal programs included in a cluster of programs, list individual Federal programs within a cluster of programs. For R&D, total Federal awards expended shall be shown either by individual award or by Federal agency and major subdivision within the Federal agency. For example, the National Institutes of Health is a major subdivision in the Department of Health and Human Services.

(2) For Federal awards received as a subrecipient, the name of the pass-through entity and identifying number assigned by the pass-through entity shall be included.

(3) Provide total Federal awards expended for each individual Federal program and the CFDA number or other identifying number when the CFDA information is not available.

(4) Include notes that describe the significant accounting policies used in preparing the schedule.

(5) To the extent practical, pass-through entities should identify in the schedule the total amount provided to subrecipients from each Federal program.

(6) Include, in either the schedule or a note to the schedule, the value of the Federal awards expended in the form of non-cash assistance, the amount of insurance in effect during the year, and loans or loan guarantees outstanding at year end. While not required, it is preferable to present this information in the schedule.

14. Audit findings follow-up.

(a) *General.* The auditee is responsible for follow-up and corrective action on all audit findings. As part of this responsibility, the auditee shall prepare a summary schedule of prior audit findings. The auditee shall also prepare a corrective action plan for current year audit findings. The summary schedule of prior audit findings and the corrective action plan shall include the reference numbers the auditor assigns to audit findings under § __.510(c). Since the summary schedule may include audit findings from multiple years, it shall include the fiscal year in which the finding initially occurred.

(b) *Summary schedule of prior audit findings.* The summary schedule of prior audit findings shall report the status of all audit findings included in the prior audit's schedule of findings and questioned costs relative to Federal awards. The summary schedule shall also include audit findings reported in the prior audit's summary schedule of prior audit findings except audit findings listed as corrected in accordance with paragraph **(b)(1)** of this section, or no longer valid or not warranting further action in accordance with paragraph **(b)(4)** of this section.

(1) When audit findings were fully corrected, the summary schedule need only list the audit findings and state that corrective action was taken.

(2) When audit findings were not corrected or were only partially corrected, the summary schedule shall describe the planned corrective action as well as any partial corrective action taken.

(3) When corrective action taken is significantly different from corrective action previously reported in a corrective action plan or in the Federal agency's or pass-through entity's management decision, the summary schedule shall provide an explanation.

(4) When the auditee believes the audit findings are no longer valid or do not warrant further action, the reasons for this position shall be described in the summary schedule. A valid reason for considering an audit finding as not warranting further action is that all of the following have occurred:

(i) Two years have passed since the audit report in which the finding occurred was submitted to the Federal clearinghouse;

(ii) The Federal agency or pass-through entity is not currently following up with the auditee on the audit finding; and

(iii) A management decision was not issued.

(c) *Corrective action plan.* At the completion of the audit, the auditee shall prepare a corrective action plan to address each audit finding included in the current year auditor's reports. The corrective action plan shall provide the name(s) of the contact person(s) responsible for corrective action, the corrective action planned, and the anticipated completion date. If the auditee does not agree with the audit findings or believes corrective action is not required, then the corrective action plan shall include an explanation and specific reasons.

15. Report submission.

(a) *General.* The audit shall be completed and the data collection form described in paragraph **(b)** of this section and reporting package described in paragraph **(c)** of this section shall be submitted within the earlier of 30 days after receipt of the auditor's report(s), or nine months after the end of the audit period, unless a longer period is agreed to in advance by the cognizant or oversight agency for audit. (However, for fiscal years beginning on or before June 30, 1998, the audit shall be completed and the data collection form and reporting package shall be submitted within the earlier of 30 days after receipt of the auditor's report(s), or 13 months after the end of the audit period.) Unless restricted by law or regulation, the auditee shall make copies available for public inspection.

(b) *Data Collection.* (1) The auditee shall submit a data collection form which states whether the audit was completed in accordance with this part and provides information about the auditee, its Federal programs, and the results of the audit. The form shall be approved by OMB, available from the Federal clearinghouse designated by OMB, and include data elements similar to those presented in this paragraph. A senior level representative of the auditee (e.g., State controller, director of finance, chief executive officer, or chief financial officer) shall sign a statement to be included as part of the form certifying that: the auditee complied with the requirements of this part, the form was prepared in accordance with this part (and the instructions accompanying the form), and the information included in the form, in its entirety, are accurate and complete.

(2) The data collection form shall include the following data elements:

(i) The type of report the auditor issued on the financial statements of the auditee (i.e., unqualified opinion, qualified opinion, adverse opinion, or disclaimer of opinion).

(ii) Where applicable, a statement that reportable conditions in internal control were disclosed by the audit of the financial statements and whether any such conditions were material weaknesses.

(iii) A statement as to whether the audit disclosed any noncompliance which is material to the financial statements of the auditee.

(iv) Where applicable, a statement that reportable conditions in internal control over major programs were disclosed by the audit and whether any such conditions were material weaknesses.

(v) The type of report the auditor issued on compliance for major programs (i.e., unqualified opinion, qualified opinion, adverse opinion, or disclaimer of opinion).

(vi) A list of the Federal awarding agencies which will receive a copy of the reporting package pursuant to § __.320(d)(2) of OMB Circular A-133.

(vii) A yes or no statement as to whether the auditee qualified as a low-risk auditee under § __.530 of OMB Circular A-133.

(viii) The dollar threshold used to distinguish between Type A and Type B programs as defined in § __.520(b) of OMB Circular A-133.

(ix) The *Catalog of Federal Domestic Assistance* (CFDA) number for each Federal program, as applicable.

(x) The name of each Federal program and identification of each major program. Individual programs within a cluster of programs should be listed in the same level of detail as they are listed in the schedule of expenditures of Federal awards.

(xi) The amount of expenditures in the schedule of expenditures of Federal awards associated with each Federal program.

(xii) For each Federal program, a yes or no statement as to whether there are audit findings in each of the following types of compliance requirements and the total amount of any questioned costs:

(A) Activities allowed or unallowed.

(B) Allowable costs/cost principles.

(C) Cash management.

(D) Davis-Bacon Act.

(E) Eligibility.

(F) Equipment and real property management.

(G) Matching, level of effort, earmarking.

(H) Period of availability of Federal funds.

(I) Procurement and suspension and debarment.

(J) Program income.

(K) Real property acquisition and relocation assistance.

(L) Reporting.

(M) Subrecipient monitoring.

(N) Special tests and provisions.

(xiii) Auditee Name, Employer Identification Number(s), Name and Title of Certifying Official, Telephone Number, Signature, and Date.

(xiv) Auditor Name, Name and Title of Contact Person, Auditor Address, Auditor Telephone Number, Signature, and Date.

(xv) Whether the auditee has either a cognizant or oversight agency for audit.

(xvi) The name of the cognizant or oversight agency for audit determined in accordance with § __.400(a) and § __.400(b), respectively.

(3) Using the information included in the reporting package described in paragraph (c) of this section, the auditor shall complete the applicable sections of the form. The auditor shall sign a statement to be included as part of the data collection form that indicates, at a minimum, the source of the information included in the form, the auditor's responsibility for the information, that the form is not a substitute for the reporting package described in paragraph (c) of this section, and that the content of the form is limited to the data elements prescribed by OMB.

(c) *Reporting package.* The reporting package shall include the:

(1) Financial statements and schedule of expenditures of Federal awards discussed in § __.310(a) and § __.310(b), respectively;

(2) Summary schedule of prior audit findings discussed in § __.315(b);

(3) Auditor's report(s) discussed in § __.505; and

(4) Corrective action plan discussed in § __.315(c).

(d) *Submission to clearinghouse.* All auditees shall submit to the Federal clearinghouse designated by OMB the data collection form described in paragraph (b) of this section and one copy of the reporting package described in paragraph (c) of this section for:

(1) The Federal clearinghouse to retain as an archival copy; and

(2) Each Federal awarding agency when the schedule of findings and questioned costs disclosed audit findings relating to Federal awards that the Federal awarding agency provided directly or the summary schedule of prior audit findings reported the status of any audit findings relating to Federal awards that the Federal awarding agency provided directly.

(e) *Additional submission by subrecipients.* (1) In addition to the requirements discussed in paragraph (d) of this section, auditees that are also subrecipients shall submit to each pass-through entity one copy of the reporting package described in paragraph (c) of this section for each pass-through entity when the schedule of findings and questioned costs disclosed audit findings relating to Federal awards that the pass-through entity provided or the summary schedule of prior audit findings reported the status of any audit findings relating to Federal awards that the pass-through entity provided.

(2) Instead of submitting the reporting package to a pass-through entity, when a subrecipient is not required to submit a reporting package to a pass-through entity pursuant to paragraph **(e)(1)** of this section, the subrecipient shall provide written notification to the pass-through entity that: an audit of the subrecipient was conducted in accordance with this part (including the period covered by the audit and the name, amount, and CFDA number of the Federal award(s) provided by the pass-through entity); the schedule of findings and questioned costs disclosed no audit findings relating to the Federal award(s) that the pass-through entity provided; and, the summary schedule of prior audit findings did not report on the status of any audit findings relating to the Federal award(s) that the pass-through entity provided. A subrecipient may submit a copy of the reporting package described in paragraph **(c)** of this section to a pass-through entity to comply with this notification requirement.

(f) *Requests for report copies.* In response to requests by a Federal agency or pass-through entity, auditees shall submit the appropriate copies of the reporting package described in paragraph **(c)** of this section and, if requested, a copy of any management letters issued by the auditor.

(g) *Report retention requirements.* Auditees shall keep one copy of the data collection form described in paragraph **(b)** of this section and one copy of the reporting package described in paragraph **(c)** of this section on file for three years from the date of submission to the Federal clearinghouse designated by OMB. Pass-through entities shall keep subrecipients' submissions on file for three years from date of receipt.

(h) *Clearinghouse responsibilities.* The Federal clearinghouse designated by OMB shall distribute the reporting packages received in accordance with paragraph **(d)(2)** of this section and §__.235(c)(3) to applicable Federal awarding agencies, maintain a data base of completed audits, provide appropriate information to Federal agencies, and follow up with known auditees which have not submitted the required data collection forms and reporting packages.

(i) *Clearinghouse address.* The address of the Federal clearinghouse currently designated by OMB is Federal Audit Clearinghouse, Bureau of the Census, 1201 E. 10th Street, Jeffersonville, IN 47132.

(j) *Electronic filing.* Nothing in this part shall preclude electronic submissions to the Federal clearinghouse in such manner as may be approved by OMB. With OMB approval, the Federal clearinghouse may pilot test methods of electronic submissions.

Subpart D—Federal Agencies and Pass-Through Entities

16. Responsibilities.

(a) *Cognizant agency for audit responsibilities.* Recipients expending more than $25 million a year in Federal awards shall have a cognizant agency for audit. The designated cognizant agency for audit shall be the Federal awarding agency that provides the predominant amount of direct funding to a recipient unless OMB makes a specific cognizant agency for audit assignment. To provide for continuity of cognizance, the determination of the predominant amount of direct funding shall be based upon direct Federal awards expended in the recipient's fiscal years ending in 1995, 2000, 2005, and every fifth year thereafter. For example, audit cognizance for periods ending in 1997 through 2000 will be determined based on Federal awards expended in 1995. (However, for States and local governments that expend more than $25 million a year in Federal awards and have previously assigned cognizant agencies for audit, the requirements of this paragraph are not effective until fiscal years beginning after June 30, 2000.) Notwithstanding the manner in which audit cognizance is determined, a Federal awarding agency with cognizance for an auditee may reassign cognizance to another Federal awarding agency which provides substantial direct funding and agrees to be the cognizant agency for audit. Within 30 days after any reassignment, both the old and the new cognizant agency for audit shall notify the auditee, and, if known, the auditor of the reassignment. The cognizant agency for audit shall:

(1) Provide technical audit advice and liaison to auditees and auditors.

(2) Consider auditee requests for extensions to the report submission due date required by §__.320(a). The cognizant agency for audit may grant extensions for good cause.

(3) Obtain or conduct quality control reviews of selected audits made by non-Federal auditors, and provide the results, when appropriate, to other interested organizations.

(4) Promptly inform other affected Federal agencies and appropriate Federal law enforcement officials of any direct reporting by the auditee or its auditor of irregularities or illegal acts, as required by GAGAS or laws and regulations.

(5) Advise the auditor and, where appropriate, the auditee of any deficiencies found in the audits when the deficiencies require corrective action by the auditor. When advised of deficiencies, the auditee shall work with the auditor to take corrective action. If corrective action is not taken, the cognizant agency for audit shall notify the auditor, the auditee, and applicable Federal awarding agencies and pass-through

entities of the facts and make recommendations for follow-up action. Major inadequacies or repetitive substandard performance by auditors shall be referred to appropriate State licensing agencies and professional bodies for disciplinary action.

(6) Coordinate, to the extent practical, audits or reviews made by or for Federal agencies that are in addition to the audits made pursuant to this part, so that the additional audits or reviews build upon audits performed in accordance with this part.

(7) Coordinate a management decision for audit findings that affect the Federal programs of more than one agency.

(8) Coordinate the audit work and reporting responsibilities among auditors to achieve the most cost-effective audit.

(9) For biennial audits permitted under § __.220, consider auditee requests to qualify as a low-risk auditee under § __.530(a).

(b) *Oversight agency for audit responsibilities.* An auditee which does not have a designated cognizant agency for audit will be under the general oversight of the Federal agency determined in accordance with § __.105. The oversight agency for audit:

(1) Shall provide technical advice to auditees and auditors as requested.

(2) May assume all or some of the responsibilities normally performed by a cognizant agency for audit.

(c) *Federal awarding agency responsibilities.* The Federal awarding agency shall perform the following for the Federal awards it makes:

(1) Identify Federal awards made by informing each recipient of the CFDA title and number, award name and number, award year, and if the award is for R&D. When some of this information is not available, the Federal agency shall provide information necessary to clearly describe the Federal award.

(2) Advise recipients of requirements imposed on them by Federal laws, regulations, and the provisions of contracts or grant agreements.

(3) Ensure that audits are completed and reports are received in a timely manner and in accordance with the requirements of this part.

(4) Provide technical advice and counsel to auditees and auditors as requested.

(5) Issue a management decision on audit findings within six months after receipt of the audit report and ensure that the recipient takes appropriate and timely corrective action.

(6) Assign a person responsible for providing annual updates of the compliance supplement to OMB.

(d) *Pass-through entity responsibilities.* A pass-through entity shall perform the following for the Federal awards it makes:

(1) Identify Federal awards made by informing each subrecipient of CFDA title and number, award name and number, award year, if the award is R&D, and name of Federal agency. When some of this information is not available, the pass-through entity shall provide the best information available to describe the Federal award.

(2) Advise subrecipients of requirements imposed on them by Federal laws, regulations, and the provisions of contracts or grant agreements as well as any supplemental requirements imposed by the pass-through entity.

(3) Monitor the activities of subrecipients as necessary to ensure that Federal awards are used for authorized purposes in compliance with laws, regulations, and the provisions of contracts or grant agreements and that performance goals are achieved.

(4) Ensure that subrecipients expending $300,000 or more in Federal awards during the subrecipient's fiscal year have met the audit requirements of this part for that fiscal year.

(5) Issue a management decision on audit findings within six months after receipt of the subrecipient's audit report and ensure that the subrecipient takes appropriate and timely corrective action.

(6) Consider whether subrecipient audits necessitate adjustment of the pass-through entity's own records.

(7) Require each subrecipient to permit the pass-through entity and auditors to have access to the records and financial statements as necessary for the pass-through entity to comply with this part.

17. Management decision.

(a) *General.* The management decision shall clearly state whether or not the audit finding is sustained, the reasons for the decision, and the expected auditee action to repay disallowed costs, make financial adjustments, or take other action. If the auditee has not completed corrective action, a timetable for follow-up should be given. Prior to issuing the management decision, the Federal agency or pass-through entity may request additional information or documentation from the auditee, including a request for auditor assurance related to the documentation, as a way of mitigating disallowed costs. The management decision should describe any appeal process available to the auditee.

(b) *Federal agency.* As provided in § __.400(a)(7), the cognizant agency for audit shall be responsible for coordinating a management decision for audit findings that affect the programs of more than one Federal agency. As provided in § __.400(c)(5), a Federal awarding agency is responsible for issuing a management decision for findings that relate to Federal awards it makes to recipients. Alternate arrangements may be made on a case-by-case basis by agreement among the Federal agencies concerned.

(c) *Pass-through entity.* As provided in § __.400(d)(5), the pass-through entity shall be responsible for making the management decision for audit findings that relate to Federal awards it makes to subrecipients.

(d) *Time requirements.* The entity responsible for making the management decision shall do so within six months of receipt of the audit report. Corrective action should be initiated within six months after receipt of the audit report and proceed as rapidly as possible.

(e) *Reference numbers.* Management decisions shall include the reference numbers the auditor assigned to each audit finding in accordance with § __.510(c).

Subpart E—Auditors

18. Scope of audit.

(a) *General.* The audit shall be conducted in accordance with GAGAS. The audit shall cover the entire operations of the auditee; or, at the option of the auditee, such audit shall include a series of audits that cover departments, agencies, and other organizational units which expended or otherwise administered Federal awards during such fiscal year, provided that each such audit shall encompass the financial statements and schedule of expenditures of Federal awards for each such department, agency, and other organizational unit, which shall be considered to be a non-Federal entity. The financial statements and schedule of expenditures of Federal awards shall be for the same fiscal year.

(b) *Financial statements.* The auditor shall determine whether the financial statements of the auditee are presented fairly in all material respects in conformity with generally accepted accounting principles. The auditor shall also determine whether the schedule of expenditures of Federal awards is presented fairly in all material respects in relation to the auditee's financial statements taken as a whole.

(c) *Internal control.* (1) In addition to the requirements of GAGAS, the auditor shall perform procedures to obtain an understanding of internal control over Federal programs sufficient to plan the audit to support a low assessed level of control risk for major programs.

(2) Except as provided in paragraph **(c)(3)** of this section, the auditor shall:

(i) Plan the testing of internal control over major programs to support a low assessed level of control risk for the assertions relevant to the compliance requirements for each major program; and

(ii) Perform testing of internal control as planned in paragraph (c)(2)(i) of this section.

(3) When internal control over some or all of the compliance requirements for a major program are likely to be ineffective in preventing or detecting noncompliance, the planning and performing of testing described in paragraph (c)(2) of this section are not required for those compliance requirements. However, the auditor shall report a reportable condition (including whether any such condition is a material weakness) in accordance with §__.510, assess the related control risk at the maximum, and consider whether additional compliance tests are required because of ineffective internal control.

(d) *Compliance.* (1) In addition to the requirements of GAGAS, the auditor shall determine whether the auditee has complied with laws, regulations, and the provisions of contracts or grant agreements that may have a direct and material effect on each of its major programs.

(2) The principal compliance requirements applicable to most Federal programs and the compliance requirements of the largest Federal programs are included in the compliance supplement.

(3) For the compliance requirements related to Federal programs contained in the compliance supplement, an audit of these compliance requirements will meet the requirements of this part. Where there have been changes to the compliance requirements and the changes are not reflected in the compliance supplement, the auditor shall determine the current compliance requirements and modify the audit procedures accordingly. For those Federal programs not covered in the compliance supplement, the auditor should use the types of compliance requirements contained in the compliance supplement as guidance for identifying the types of compliance requirements to test, and determine the requirements governing the Federal program by reviewing the provisions of contracts and grant agreements and the laws and regulations referred to in such contracts and grant agreements.

(4) The compliance testing shall include tests of transactions and such other auditing procedures necessary to provide the auditor sufficient evidence to support an opinion on compliance.

(e) *Audit follow-up.* The auditor shall follow-up on prior audit findings, perform procedures to assess the reasonableness of the summary schedule of prior audit findings prepared by the auditee in accordance with §__.315(b), and report, as a current year audit finding, when the auditor concludes that the summary schedule of prior audit findings materially misrepresents the status of any prior audit finding. The auditor shall perform audit follow-up procedures regardless of whether a prior audit finding relates to a major program in the current year.

(f) *Data Collection Form.* As required in § __.320(b)(3), the auditor shall complete and sign specified sections of the data collection form.

19. Audit reporting. The auditor's report(s) may be in the form of either combined or separate reports and may be organized differently from the manner presented in this section. The auditor's report(s) shall state that the audit was conducted in accordance with this part and include the following:

(a) An opinion (or disclaimer of opinion) as to whether the financial statements are presented fairly in all material respects in conformity with generally accepted accounting principles and an opinion (or disclaimer of opinion) as to whether the schedule of expenditures of Federal awards is presented fairly in all material respects in relation to the financial statements taken as a whole.

(b) A report on internal control related to the financial statements and major programs. This report shall describe the scope of testing of internal control and the results of the tests, and, where applicable, refer to the separate schedule of findings and questioned costs described in paragraph **(d)** of this section.

(c) A report on compliance with laws, regulations, and the provisions of contracts or grant agreements, noncompliance with which could have a material effect on the financial statements. This report shall also include an opinion (or disclaimer of opinion) as to whether the auditee complied with laws, regulations, and the provisions of contracts or grant agreements which could have a direct and material effect on each major program, and, where applicable, refer to the separate schedule of findings and questioned costs described in paragraph **(d)** of this section.

(d) A schedule of findings and questioned costs which shall include the following three components:

(1) A summary of the auditor's results which shall include:

(i) The type of report the auditor issued on the financial statements of the auditee (i.e., unqualified opinion, qualified opinion, adverse opinion, or disclaimer of opinion);

(ii) Where applicable, a statement that reportable conditions in internal control were disclosed by the audit of the financial statements and whether any such conditions were material weaknesses;

(iii) A statement as to whether the audit disclosed any noncompliance which is material to the financial statements of the auditee;

570   Government Auditing: Standards and Practices

(iv) Where applicable, a statement that reportable conditions in internal control over major programs were disclosed by the audit and whether any such conditions were material weaknesses;

(v) The type of report the auditor issued on compliance for major programs (i.e., unqualified opinion, qualified opinion, adverse opinion, or disclaimer of opinion);

(vi) A statement as to whether the audit disclosed any audit findings which the auditor is required to report under § __.510(a);

(vii) An identification of major programs;

(viii) The dollar threshold used to distinguish between Type A and Type B programs, as described in § __.520(b); and

(ix) A statement as to whether the auditee qualified as a low-risk auditee under § __.530.

(2) Findings relating to the financial statements which are required to be reported in accordance with GAGAS.

(3) Findings and questioned costs for Federal awards which shall include audit findings as defined in § __.510(a).

(i) Audit findings (e.g., internal control findings, compliance findings, questioned costs, or fraud) which relate to the same issue should be presented as a single audit finding. Where practical, audit findings should be organized by Federal agency or pass-through entity.

(ii) Audit findings which relate to both the financial statements and Federal awards, as reported under paragraphs **(d)(2)** and **(d)(3)** of this section, respectively, should be reported in both sections of the schedule. However, the reporting in one section of the schedule may be in summary form with a reference to a detailed reporting in the other section of the schedule.

20. Audit findings.

(a) *Audit findings reported.* The auditor shall report the following as audit findings in a schedule of findings and questioned costs:

(1) Reportable conditions in internal control over major programs. The auditor's determination of whether a deficiency in internal control is a reportable condition for the purpose of reporting an audit finding is in relation to a type of compliance requirement for a major program or an audit objective identified in the compliance supplement. The auditor shall identify reportable conditions which are individually or cumulatively material weaknesses.

(2) Material noncompliance with the provisions of laws, regulations, contracts, or grant agreements related to a major program. The auditor's determination of whether a noncompliance with the provisions of laws, regulations, contracts, or grant agreements is material for

the purpose of reporting an audit finding is in relation to a type of compliance requirement for a major program or an audit objective identified in the compliance supplement.

(3) Known questioned costs which are greater than $10,000 for a type of compliance requirement for a major program. Known questioned costs are those specifically identified by the auditor. In evaluating the effect of questioned costs on the opinion on compliance, the auditor considers the best estimate of total costs questioned (likely questioned costs), not just the questioned costs specifically identified (known questioned costs). The auditor shall also report known questioned costs when likely questioned costs are greater than $10,000 for a type of compliance requirement for a major program. In reporting questioned costs, the auditor shall include information to provide proper perspective for judging the prevalence and consequences of the questioned costs.

(4) Known questioned costs which are greater than $10,000 for a Federal program which is not audited as a major program. Except for audit follow-up, the auditor is not required under this part to perform audit procedures for such a Federal program; therefore, the auditor will normally not find questioned costs for a program which is not audited as a major program. However, if the auditor does become aware of questioned costs for a Federal program which is not audited as a major program (e.g., as part of audit follow-up or other audit procedures) and the known questioned costs are greater than $10,000, then the auditor shall report this as an audit finding.

(5) The circumstances concerning why the auditor's report on compliance for major programs is other than an unqualified opinion, unless such circumstances are otherwise reported as audit findings in the schedule of findings and questioned costs for Federal awards.

(6) Known fraud affecting a Federal award, unless such fraud is otherwise reported as an audit finding in the schedule of findings and questioned costs for Federal awards. This paragraph does not require the auditor to make an additional reporting when the auditor confirms that the fraud was reported outside of the auditor's reports under the direct reporting requirements of GAGAS.

(7) Instances where the results of audit follow-up procedures disclosed that the summary schedule of prior audit findings prepared by the auditee in accordance with § __.315(b) materially misrepresents the status of any prior audit finding.

(b) *Audit finding detail.* Audit findings shall be presented in sufficient detail for the auditee to prepare a corrective action plan and take corrective action and for Federal agencies and pass-through entities to arrive at a management decision. The following specific information shall be included, as applicable, in audit findings:

(1) Federal program and specific Federal award identification including the CFDA title and number, Federal award number and year, name of Federal agency, and name of the applicable pass-through entity. When information, such as the CFDA title and number or Federal award number, is not available, the auditor shall provide the best information available to describe the Federal award.

(2) The criteria or specific requirement upon which the audit finding is based, including statutory, regulatory, or other citation.

(3) The condition found, including facts that support the deficiency identified in the audit finding.

(4) Identification of questioned costs and how they were computed.

(5) Information to provide proper perspective for judging the prevalence and consequences of the audit findings, such as whether the audit findings represent an isolated instance or a systemic problem. Where appropriate, instances identified shall be related to the universe and the number of cases examined and be quantified in terms of dollar value.

(6) The possible asserted effect to provide sufficient information to the auditee and Federal agency, or pass-through entity in the case of a subrecipient, to permit them to determine the cause and effect to facilitate prompt and proper corrective action.

(7) Recommendations to prevent future occurrences of the deficiency identified in the audit finding.

(8) Views of responsible officials of the auditee when there is disagreement with the audit findings, to the extent practical.

(c) *Reference numbers*. Each audit finding in the schedule of findings and questioned costs shall include a reference number to allow for easy referencing of the audit findings during follow-up.

21. Audit working papers.

(a) *Retention of working papers*. The auditor shall retain working papers and reports for a minimum of three years after the date of issuance of the auditor's report(s) to the auditee, unless the auditor is notified in writing by the cognizant agency for audit, oversight agency for audit, or pass-through entity to extend the retention period. When the auditor is aware that the Federal awarding agency, pass-through entity, or auditee is contesting an audit finding, the auditor shall contact the parties contesting the audit finding for guidance prior to destruction of the working papers and reports.

(b) *Access to working papers.* Audit working papers shall be made available upon request to the cognizant or oversight agency for audit or its designee, a Federal agency providing direct or indirect funding, or GAO at the completion of the audit, as part of a quality review, to resolve audit findings, or to carry out oversight responsibilities consistent with the purposes of this part. Access to working papers includes the right of Federal agencies to obtain copies of working papers, as is reasonable and necessary.

22. Major program determination.

(a) *General.* The auditor shall use a risk-based approach to determine which Federal programs are major programs. This risk-based approach shall include consideration of: Current and prior audit experience, oversight by Federal agencies and pass-through entities, and the inherent risk of the Federal program. The process in paragraphs **(b)** through **(i)** of this section shall be followed.

(b) *Step 1.* (1) The auditor shall identify the larger Federal programs, which shall be labeled Type A programs. Type A programs are defined as Federal programs with Federal awards expended during the audit period exceeding the larger of:

(i) $300,000 or three percent (.03) of total Federal awards expended in the case of an auditee for which total Federal awards expended equal or exceed $300,000 but are less than or equal to $100 million.

(ii) $3 million or three-tenths of one percent (.003) of total Federal awards expended in the case of an auditee for which total Federal awards expended exceed $100 million but are less than or equal to $10 billion.

(iii) $30 million or 15 hundredths of one percent (.0015) of total Federal awards expended in the case of an auditee for which total Federal awards expended exceed $10 billion.

(2) Federal programs not labeled Type A under paragraph **(b)(1)** of this section shall be labeled Type B programs.

(3) The inclusion of large loan and loan guarantees (loans) should not result in the exclusion of other programs as Type A programs. When a Federal program providing loans significantly affects the number or size of Type A programs, the auditor shall consider this Federal program as a Type A program and exclude its values in determining other Type A programs.

(4) For biennial audits permitted under § __.220, the determination of Type A and Type B programs shall be based upon the Federal awards expended during the two-year period.

(c) *Step 2.* (1) The auditor shall identify Type A programs which are low-risk. For a Type A program to be considered low-risk, it shall have been audited as a major program in at least one of the two most recent audit periods (in the most recent audit period in the case of a biennial audit), and, in the most recent audit period, it shall have had no audit findings under §__.510(a). However, the auditor may use judgment and consider that audit findings from questioned costs under §__.510(a)(3) and §__.510(a)(4), fraud under §__.510(a)(6), and audit follow-up for the summary schedule of prior audit findings under §__.510(a)(7) do not preclude the Type A program from being low-risk. The auditor shall consider: the criteria in §__.525(c), §__.525(d)(1), §__.525(d)(2), and §__.525(d)(3); the results of audit follow-up; whether any changes in personnel or systems affecting a Type A program have significantly increased risk; and apply professional judgment in determining whether a Type A program is low-risk.

(2) Notwithstanding paragraph **(c)(1)** of this section, OMB may approve a Federal awarding agency's request that a Type A program at certain recipients may not be considered low-risk. For example, it may be necessary for a large Type A program to be audited as major each year at particular recipients to allow the Federal agency to comply with the Government Management Reform Act of 1994 (31 U.S.C. 3515). The Federal agency shall notify the recipient and, if known, the auditor at least 180 days prior to the end of the fiscal year to be audited of OMB's approval.

(d) *Step 3.* (1) The auditor shall identify Type B programs which are high-risk using professional judgment and the criteria in §__.525. However, should the auditor select Option 2 under Step 4 (paragraph **(e)(2)(i)(B)** of this section), the auditor is not required to identify more high-risk Type B programs than the number of low-risk Type A programs. Except for known reportable conditions in internal control or compliance problems as discussed in §__.525(b)(1), §__.525(b)(2), and §__.525(c)(1), a single criteria in §__.525 would seldom cause a Type B program to be considered high-risk.

(2) The auditor is not expected to perform risk assessments on relatively small Federal programs. Therefore, the auditor is only required to perform risk assessments on Type B programs that exceed the larger of:

(i) $100,000 or three-tenths of one percent (.003) of total Federal awards expended when the auditee has less than or equal to $100 million in total Federal awards expended.

(ii) $300,000 or three-hundredths of one percent (.0003) of total Federal awards expended when the auditee has more than $100 million in total Federal awards expended.

(e) *Step 4.* At a minimum, the auditor shall audit all of the following as major programs:

(1) All Type A programs, except the auditor may exclude any Type A programs identified as low-risk under Step 2 (paragraph **(c)(1)** of this section).

(2) (i) High-risk Type B programs as identified under either of the following two options:

(A) *Option 1.* At least one half of the Type B programs identified as high-risk under Step 3 (paragraph **(d)** of this section), except this paragraph **(e)(2)(i)(A)** does not require the auditor to audit more high-risk Type B programs than the number of low-risk Type A programs identified as low-risk under Step 2.

(B) *Option 2.* One high-risk Type B program for each Type A program identified as low-risk under Step 2.

(ii) When identifying which high-risk Type B programs to audit as major under either Option 1 or 2 in paragraph **(e)(2)(i)(A)** or **(B)**, the auditor is encouraged to use an approach which provides an opportunity for different high-risk Type B programs to be audited as major over a period of time.

(3) Such additional programs as may be necessary to comply with the percentage of coverage rule discussed in paragraph **(f)** of this section. This paragraph **(e)(3)** may require the auditor to audit more programs as major than the number of Type A programs.

(f) *Percentage of coverage rule.* The auditor shall audit as major programs Federal programs with Federal awards expended that, in the aggregate, encompass at least 50 percent of total Federal awards expended. If the auditee meets the criteria in §__.530 for a low-risk auditee, the auditor need only audit as major programs Federal programs with Federal awards expended that, in the aggregate, encompass at least 25 percent of total Federal awards expended.

(g) *Documentation of risk.* The auditor shall document in the working papers the risk analysis process used in determining major programs.

(h) *Auditor's judgment.* When the major program determination was performed and documented in accordance with this part, the auditor's judgment in applying the risk-based approach to determine major programs shall be presumed correct. Challenges by Federal agencies and pass-through entities shall only be for clearly improper use of the guidance in this part. However, Federal agencies and pass-through entities may provide auditors guidance about the risk of a particular Federal program and the auditor shall consider this guidance in determining major programs in audits not yet completed.

(i) *Deviation from use of risk criteria.* For first-year audits, the auditor may elect to determine major programs as all Type A programs plus any Type B programs as necessary to meet the percentage of coverage rule discussed in paragraph (f) of this section. Under this option, the auditor would not be required to perform the procedures discussed in paragraphs (c), (d), and (e) of this section.

(1) A first-year audit is the first year the entity is audited under this part or the first year of a change of auditors.

(2) To ensure that a frequent change of auditors would not preclude audit of high-risk Type B programs, this election for first-year audits may not be used by an auditee more than once in every three years.

23. Criteria for Federal program risk.

(a) *General.* The auditor's determination should be based on an overall evaluation of the risk of noncompliance occurring which could be material to the Federal program. The auditor shall use auditor judgment and consider criteria, such as described in paragraphs (b), (c), and (d) of this section, to identify risk in Federal programs. Also, as part of the risk analysis, the auditor may wish to discuss a particular Federal program with auditee management and the Federal agency or pass-through entity.

(b) *Current and prior audit experience.* (1) Weaknesses in internal control over Federal programs would indicate higher risk. Consideration should be given to the control environment over Federal programs and such factors as the expectation of management's adherence to applicable laws and regulations and the provisions of contracts and grant agreements and the competence and experience of personnel who administer the Federal programs.

(i) A Federal program administered under multiple internal control structures may have higher risk. When assessing risk in a large single audit, the auditor shall consider whether weaknesses are isolated in a single operating unit (e.g., one college campus) or pervasive throughout the entity.

(ii) When significant parts of a Federal program are passed through to subrecipients, a weak system for monitoring subrecipients would indicate higher risk.

(iii) The extent to which computer processing is used to administer Federal programs, as well as the complexity of that processing, should be considered by the auditor in assessing risk. New and recently modified computer systems may also indicate risk.

(2) Prior audit findings would indicate higher risk, particularly when the situations identified in the audit findings could have a significant impact on a Federal program or have not been corrected.

(3) Federal programs not recently audited as major programs may be of higher risk than Federal programs recently audited as major programs without audit findings.

(c) *Oversight exercised by Federal agencies and pass-through entities.* (1) Oversight exercised by Federal agencies or pass-through entities could indicate risk. For example, recent monitoring or other reviews performed by an oversight entity which disclosed no significant problems would indicate lower risk. However, monitoring which disclosed significant problems would indicate higher risk.

(2) Federal agencies, with the concurrence of OMB, may identify Federal programs which are higher risk. OMB plans to provide this identification in the compliance supplement.

(d) *Inherent risk of the Federal program.* (1) The nature of a Federal program may indicate risk. Consideration should be given to the complexity of the program and the extent to which the Federal program contracts for goods and services. For example, Federal programs that disburse funds through third party contracts or have eligibility criteria may be of higher risk. Federal programs primarily involving staff payroll costs may have a high-risk for time and effort reporting, but otherwise be at low-risk.

(2) The phase of a Federal program in its life cycle at the Federal agency may indicate risk. For example, a new Federal program with new or interim regulations may have higher risk than an established program with time-tested regulations. Also, significant changes in Federal programs, laws, regulations, or the provisions of contracts or grant agreements may increase risk.

(3) The phase of a Federal program in its life cycle at the auditee may indicate risk. For example, during the first and last years that an auditee participates in a Federal program, the risk may be higher due to start-up or closeout of program activities and staff.

(4) Type B programs with larger Federal awards expended would be of higher risk than programs with substantially smaller Federal awards expended.

24. Criteria for a low-risk auditee. An auditee which meets all of the following conditions for each of the preceding two years (or, in the case of biennial audits, preceding two audit periods) shall qualify as a low-risk auditee and be eligible for reduced audit coverage in accordance with § __.520:

(a) Single audits were performed on an annual basis in accordance with the provisions of this part. A non-Federal entity that has biennial audits does not qualify as a low-risk auditee, unless agreed to in advance by the cognizant or oversight agency for audit.

(b) The auditor's opinions on the financial statements and the schedule of expenditures of Federal awards were unqualified. However, the cognizant or oversight agency for audit may judge that an opinion qualification does not affect the management of Federal awards and provide a waiver.

(c) There were no deficiencies in internal control which were identified as material weaknesses under the requirements of GAGAS. However, the cognizant or oversight agency for audit may judge that any identified material weaknesses do not affect the management of Federal awards and provide a waiver.

(d) None of the Federal programs had audit findings from any of the following in either of the preceding two years (or, in the case of biennial audits, preceding two audit periods) in which they were classified as Type A programs:

(1) Internal control deficiencies which were identified as material weaknesses;

(2) Noncompliance with the provisions of laws, regulations, contracts, or grant agreements which have a material effect on the Type A program; or

(3) Known or likely questioned costs that exceed five percent of the total Federal awards expended for a Type A program during the year.

Index

A

Accounting and Auditing...33
Accounting for Federal Government...40-42
Auditing in America...14-15
Auditing Standards
. AICPA's generally accepted auditing standards...45-47
. expanded auditing standards...60-61
. GAO's government auditing standards...50-54
. government auditing standards
.. application of...61-62
.. financial audits...62-63
.. general standards...59-60
.. performance audits...63-64
.. scope...62

Auditor Communication...81-82
Auditor Relationships
. governmental
.. component units...332
.. federal audit organizations...329-330
.. federal awards...332
.. independent public accountants...331
.. primary government defined...331
.. state and local government auditors...330-331
. independence
.. generally accepted auditing standards...338-339
.. government auditing standards...339-343
. types of auditors
.. component unit...335
.. joint...336-338
.. principal...333-335
.. single audits...335-336

C

Changing Emphasis of Audits...15-16
Chief Financial Officers Act of 1990...519-541
Compliance Auditing
. application of judgment
.. factors to consider...244-245
.. quantitative and qualitative issues...245
. assessing the effect...243-244
. audit opinion...226-227
. changing views and guidance...224-225
. compliance testing
.. non-federal issues...242-243
.. OMB's compliance supplement...231-232; 238-242
.. risk considerations...232
.. single audit...232-238
. government auditing standards...225
. government budgets...245-246
. materiality for...225-226
. obtaining an understanding...229-231
. other risks...246-247
. overview...223
. pervasiveness
.. materiality for compliance...228-229
.. program audits...229
.. single audits...228
. reporting with laws and regulations...249
. working papers...248

Contracts and Grants
. audit methodology...469-473
.. auditors of...452-455
.. authority for...451-452

Contracts and Grants—continued
. audit methodology—continued
.. functions...465-469
.. general considerations...459-461
.. government grant process...475
.. government procurement process...474
.. process...461-465
.. reviews...455-45
.. summary of phases and tasks...476-477
.. surveys455-459

Coordination of Audits
. coordination with other governments...30-31
. cross-servicing of federal audits...30

D

Data Collection Form...183-185
. explanation of...166-167
Due Professional Care...74-76

E

Evidence and Working Papers
. supplemental standard no. 5...95-97

F

Federal Audit Responsibilities
. GAO...44
. inspectors general...44
. OMB...43

Field Work Audit
. AICPA's standards...79
. auditor communication...81-82
. design audit to detect noncompliance
.. material non-compliance...83-89
. evidence and working papers...95-97
. financial related audits...97-98; 119-146
. follow-up on prior audits...82
. government auditing standards...80-81
. internal control and risk...89-90
. risk and materiality
.. control risk assessments...93-95
.. controls over compliance with laws and regulations...92-93
.. safeguarding controls...92

Financial Related Audits
. AICPA's attestation standards...400
. audit methodology...404-416
.. costs...421-422
.. criteria...401-404
.. example auditor's reports...420
.. financial related...417
.. financial statement...417
.. standards...399-401
.. summary of audit phases and tasks...418-419
. defined...119
. field audit standards...97-98
. report content
.. criteria for...125
.. findings definition...125-126
.. structure of...126
. reporting on
.. audit methodologies...128
.. audit objectives...127
.. audit scope...127-128
.. distribution...130-131
.. elements of a finding...128-130
.. findings section...128

FIN

Financial Statement Audits
. applicable auditing standards
. . generally acceptable auditing standards
. . . 99
. . generally accepted government auditing standards . . . 99
. audit methodology . . . 348-363
. . elements of internal control structure . . . 364
. . financial statement audits of public entities . . . 345-348
. . summary of audit phases and tasks . . . 365-367
. differences, public versus private sector
. . accompanying information . . . 103
. . balance sheets . . . 102
. . financial information . . . 102-103
. . financial statements . . . 100-101
. . materiality thresholds . . . 101-102
. . reporting responsibilities . . . 100
. government auditing standards
. . conditions limiting tests of controls . . . 107-108
. . distribution of audit reports . . . 109-110
. . reference to . . . 103-104
. . reporting on tests of compliance, controls . . . 105-107
. . reporting sensitive data . . . 108-109

G

Governmental Auditing
. standards and practices . . . 31-32

I

Independence
. impairments
. . external . . . 72
. . organizational . . . 72-73
. . personal . . . 70-72

Indirect Costs
. allowable and unallowable . . . 251-278
. audit methodology
. . single audits . . . 383-385
. audit requirements
. . CAP defined . . . 269
. . determination of indirect costs . . . 270-271
. . ICRP defined . . . 269
. . rates . . . 271-272
. contracts . . . 251-254
. cooperative agreements . . . 251-254
. cost allowability
. . application credits . . . 266-267
. . consistent accounting treatment . . . 263-265
. . definition of . . . 260-263
. . documentation . . . 267
. . reasonable and necessary . . . 258-259
. . requirements . . . 265-266
. federal regulations for . . . 254-257
. government audit requirements . . . 257
. grants . . . 251-254
. questioned costs . . . 277-278
. suggested procedures . . . 272-276
. unallowable costs . . . 277-278

Internal Controls
. auditor responsibility
. . requirements . . . 195-198
. evolving views
. . congressional concerns with controls . . . 191-193
. . differing definitions . . . 189-190
. . views on controls . . . 190-191
. GAAS
. . SAS 53 . . . 198-199
. . SAS 54 . . . 200

Internal Controls—continued
. GAAS—continued
. . SAS 55 . . . 201-203
. . SAS 60 . . . 203-204
. . SAS 78 . . . 201-203
. government auditing standard-control consideration
. . controls-performance audits . . . 205
. . internal controls-financial audits . . . 205
. . standards changes-1999 . . . 205-206
. government control structure circumstances, conditions
. . accounting forms and records . . . 217
. . accounts and financial statements . . . 212-213
. . checks and balances . . . 212
. . control procedures and practices . . . 213
. . controls for federal programs . . . 218-219
. . expenditures . . . 216-217
. . legislative budgets . . . 215
. . management . . . 214-215
. . outlay or fiscal process . . . 217-218
. . receipts . . . 215-216
. . signatures . . . 217
. . treasury controls, checks and balances . . . 218
. governmental controls
. . accounting cycles . . . 210-211
. . classification of . . . 208
. . components . . . 208-210
. . controls defined . . . 207-208
. hierarchy of control reviews
. . evaluate controls . . . 194
. . examination of controls . . . 194
. . preliminary review of controls . . . 193
. . study of understanding . . . 193-194
. Single Audit Act of 1996 . . . 206-207

O

Office of Management and Budget
. Circular A-133 . . . 543-578

P

Performance Audits
. audit methodology
. . essentials . . . 426-435
. . illustrative performance audit . . . 444-446
. . local transport system audits . . . 448
. . performance audit methodology . . . 435-444
. . program results review process . . . 447
. . summary of audit phases and tasks . . . 449-450
. . types . . . 424-426
. characteristics . . . 423-424
. defined . . . 423
. . economy and efficiency audits . . . 121
. . examples of economy and efficiency audits . . . 121-122
. . examples of program audits . . . 123-124
. . performance audits by other names . . . 124
. . program audits . . . 122
. report content
. . criteria for . . . 125
. . findings definition . . . 125-126
. . structure of . . . 126
. reporting
. . audit methodologies . . . 128
. . audit objectives . . . 127
. . audit scope . . . 127-128
. . distribution . . . 130-131
. . elements of a finding . . . 128-130
. . findings section . . . 128
. standards
. . evidence . . . 138-140
. . field work . . . 132
. . general . . . 131-132

Index

Performance Audits—continued
. standards—continued
. . planning...133-135
. . reporting...141-146
. . staffing...135
. . testing for non-compliance...135-137
. . understand management controls...137-138
. . working papers...140-141

Q

Quality Control
. AICPA practices
. . compliance with gov't audit criteria...324
. . ethical ruling 501...325
. . substandard audits program...324-325
. desk reviews
. . OIG desk reviews...313-314
. . problems disclosed...314-316
. federal focus and oversight
. . auditor debarment and suspension...322-323
. . communication of observed deficiencies...319-321
. . disallowance of the audit fee...321-322
. . inventory control...323-324
. . problems disclosed...318-319
. . regulatory requirements...316-317
. . reviews guidelines...317-318
. . sanctions for substandard audits...321
. internal and external...76-78; 310-313
. quality control requirements
. . external system...311-313
. . internal audit quality...310-311

S

Single Audit Act of 1996
. amendments...509-518
. basis of single audit accounting and reporting
. . entity-wide financial statements...149-150
. . federal programs...150
. . schedule of federal awards...150
. compliance and internal controls reporting...159-161
. data collection form...166-167
. major federal assistance programs...148-149
. other reports
. . audit follow-up...169
. . corrective action plan...167-168
. . summary schedule of prior audit findings...168-169
. schedule of expenditures of federal awards
. . accounting and reporting...162-164
. . content of...162
. . illustrative schedule...164-165
. . supplementary information...164
. schedule of findings and questioned costs...165-166
. single audit reports
. . binding of...157-158
. . examples and discussion...158-159
. . required by government auditing standards...151
. . required by the single audit act and A-133...151-157

Single Audits
. amendments of 1996...509-518
. audit methodology
. . background...369-370
. . citations of federal audit and report requirements...393-394
. . compliance...375-377; 395
. . controls...378-383; 396
. . illustrative...387-391
. . indirect costs...383-385

Single Audits—continued
. audit methodology—continued
. . objectives...370-371
. . reporting for a single audit...371-372
. . reports and opinions...392
. . requirements...372-375
. . summary of audit phases and tasks...397-398
. . working papers...385-387
. auditor relationships...335-336
. compliance...228
. governmental...26-27
. indirect costs...383-385
. reports
. . binding of...157-158
. . examples and discussion...158-159
. . required by government auditing standards...151
. . required by the single audit act and A-133...151-157
. requirements...509-518

Special Focus Government Audits
. cross-cutting audits...491-501
. encumbrances audits...484-491
. fiscal post-audits...502-503
. functional audits...491-501
. government personnel and payroll process...504
. government travel process...505
. obligation audits...484-491
. pre-audits...502-503
. turnover audits...479-484

State and Local Governmental Accounting
. governmental accounting standards board (GASB)...38-39
. National Council on Governmental Accounting...34-37

T

Types of Government Auditors
. federal auditors...27-28
. independent public accountants...29-30
. state and local auditors...28-29

Types of Government Audits
. functional audits...24-26
. performance audits...26
. single audits of governments...26-27
. systems audits...23

W

Working Papers and Evidence
. access...292-295
. audit testing
. . pyramidal testing concept...301-303
. . substantive...300-301
. content
. . compliance...285-288
. . controls...282-285
. . generally accepted standards...280-281
. . government audit standards...281-282
. evidence
. . accounting data...296-297
. . financial data assertions...295-296
. . sufficiency of evidence...297-299
. government audits
. . fund accounting issues...303-305
. . other audit concerns...305-307
. ownership...292-295
. retention...292-295
. reviews...291-292
. standards...279-280
. structure and practice of working papers
. . current working papers...290
. . cycle, phases, requirements...288-289
. . indexing working papers...290-291
. . permanent working papers...289-290
. . types of working papers...289